Authored by three accomplished scholars, this tex  diverse features of contemporary corrections. The book's foundation rests on its concep-tual and research rigor that provide essential details on correctional trends, populations, and system components. Most innovative, it is designed to engage students in the learn-ing enterprise by offering real-world examples and challenging them to think critically. At once accessible and scholarly, *Contemporary Corrections* is ideal for classroom use.

Francis T. Cullen, Distinguished Research Professor Emeritus,
University of Cincinnati

Contemporary Corrections: A Critical Thinking Approach represents a needed addition to the extant stock of corrections texts, particularly those with an essentials or foundations orientation. It is concise enough to be thoroughly covered in a semester or abbreviated term and strikes the right balance between conveying the scope of the field and the depth of issues. It is written by seasoned authors who understand the complexities and challenges facing the field and know how to teach others to begin doing the same.

Kevin I. Minor, Foundation Professor of Justice Studies,
Eastern Kentucky University

I recommend the revised edition of *Contemporary Corrections* by Ruddell, Mays, and Win-free. Not only does the text provide an in-depth look into the essentials in corrections, the authors also contextualize the topics using examples from actual case studies. This approach provides an opportunity to launch class discussions and engage students in problem-solving activities. As a scholar in gender and justice, I appreciate the authors' coverage of the ways in which race, class, and gender intersect to impact justice.

Dawn Beichner, Professor, Women's and Gender Studies and
Criminal Justice Sciences, Illinois State University

Contemporary Corrections

Contemporary Corrections: A Critical Thinking Approach introduces readers to the essential elements of the US corrections system without drowning students in a sea of nonessential information. Unbiased and accessible, the text includes coverage of the history of corrections, alternatives to incarceration, probation/parole, race/ethnicity/gender issues in corrections, re-entry into the community, and more. The authors' unparalleled practical approach, reinforced by contemporary examples, illuminates the role corrections plays in our society.

The authors have reinvigorated earlier work with additional content on international comparative data to increase our understanding of how prison officials in other nations have developed different types of responses to the problems that challenge every US correctional administrator, a new chapter on correctional personnel, and an integration of race and ethnicity issues throughout the book.

Unrivalled in scope, this book offers undergraduates a concise but comprehensive introduction to corrections with textual materials and assignments designed to encourage students' critical thinking skills.

Rick Ruddell is Professor and Law Foundation of Saskatchewan Chair in Police Studies at the University of Regina. Prior to this appointment, he served as Director of Operational Research with the Correctional Service of Canada and held faculty positions at Eastern Kentucky University and the California State University, Chico. In addition to publishing over 130 articles and technical reports, his recently published books include *Oil, Gas, and Crime: The Dark Side of the Boomtown* (2017), *Policing Rural Canada* (2017), *Exploring Criminal Justice in Canada* (2020), and *Making Sense of Criminal Justice* (2019).

G. Larry Mays is Regents Professor Emeritus at New Mexico State University. He has published more than 100 journal articles, practitioner texts, book chapters, and encyclopedia entries. Among the books he has coauthored are *America's Courts and the Judicial Process* (2017), *Introduction to Criminal Justice* (2019), and *Making Sense of Criminal*

Justice (2019). Mays has received numerous awards, including the Carnegie Foundation's Professor of the Year for the State of New Mexico, and he is a life member of the Academy of Criminal Justice Sciences.

L. Thomas Winfree, Jr. is Professor Emeritus in the Department of Criminal Justice at New Mexico State University. Besides teaching literally tens of thousands of students over his 40-year academic career, Winfree authored or coauthored over 130 refereed articles and book chapters. Moreover, he is the coauthor of two anthologies and eight textbooks, most recently *Essentials of Criminological Theory* (2017); *Mental Illness and Criminal Justice* (2019); and *Introduction to Criminal Justice: The Essentials* (2019).

Contemporary Corrections

A Critical Thinking Approach

Rick Ruddell, G. Larry Mays, and L. Thomas Winfree, Jr.

Routledge
Taylor & Francis Group

NEW YORK AND LONDON

First published 2021
by Routledge
52 Vanderbilt Avenue, New York, NY 10017

and by Routledge
2 Park Square, Milton Park, Abingdon, Oxon, OX14 4RN

Routledge is an imprint of the Taylor & Francis Group, an informa business

Library of Congress Cataloging-in-Publication Data
A catalog record for this title has been requested

ISBN: 978-0-367-02865-7 (hbk)
ISBN: 978-0-367-02867-1 (pbk)
ISBN: 978-0-429-01920-3 (ebk)

Typeset in Stone Serif
by codeMantra

Visit the eResources: www.routledge.com/9780367028671

To all the people who took a chance on me; especially my wife Renu.

Rick Ruddell

For Brenda, Greg, Lisa, Mina, Robert, and Knox; Gelaine, Gabe, Lucy, Cooper, Oliver, and Maggie.

G. Larry Mays

To my wife, Eileen, whose courage in the face of adversity is matched only by her love of her extended family.

L. Thomas Winfree, Jr.

Contents

Preface

A variety of television shows and movies explores various aspects of law enforcement, some fictional and some real. However, the corrections component of the criminal justice system does not garner the same attention as programs related to policing or the courts. Even when corrections is a topic of the media, they often get it wrong, confusing jails with prisons, reporting that a convicted felon was sentenced to ten years in jail rather than a ten-year prison term. Equally galling for those with even the most basic knowledge of correction is the conflating of probation and parole. Granted they are similar in associated policies and practices, but quite different in who authorizes them.

This lack of attention to corrections is surprising given that there are over 6.6 million adults in the United States under some form of correctional supervision. Moreover, every year over 275,000 new youth probation cases are added to officer caseloads and on any given day there are over 40,000 youths residing in juvenile facilities. By any measure, correctional agencies and operations in the United States are a big industry that employs over 800,000 persons and local, state, and federal expenditures on corrections exceed $80 billion each year. Nevertheless, for many people much of the corrections component of the criminal justice system remains out-of-sight and out-of-mind.

The three authors of this book have found the world of corrections to be both fascinating and frustrating. Collectively, we have spent more than 90 years working around or within correctional facilities, researching, and teaching about corrections. In some ways, the three of us feel like we know less now than when we began our respective journeys into the field of corrections. Why is that? Several reasons are apparent.

The field of corrections involves a complex and often interrelated array of people, places, institutions, and agencies. The successes of the people who work in this field seldom are publicized. In fact, most correctional officers measure success if nothing bad happened during their shifts. The failures, by contrast, make local, state, national, and even international news. When we talk to our former students and colleagues who are working in corrections, they express optimism that they are doing something really worthwhile for their communities and the larger society. By the same token, they are often disappointed that legislators, the general public, and the news media do not understand the difficulties of their work and thanks are seldom conveyed to them for a job well done. They also feel that the large correctional populations, along with insufficient resources to manage those populations, further disadvantage them. Like many employees of the criminal justice system, of which corrections is a big part, these workers, but especially those who have daily contact with the clients of the system, point to the role that politics play in administering punishment.

In addition, the field of corrections is an ever-changing enterprise, and it is much different today than it was even ten years ago. Correctional agencies have been affected by changing laws at the state and federal levels, and the influence of prisoner litigation is an ever-present reality. Finally, movements to improve the quality of correctional employees, their work environment, professionalization, and a heightened sense of ethics all play major parts in contemporary corrections. One of the ongoing challenges, however, is that correctional personnel at all levels are seldom given the resources, let alone the community support, they need to do a proper job.

THE GOALS OF THIS BOOK

There are already more than a dozen corrections texts, and we had some important reasons for writing a brand-new book. Most of the textbooks we have used to teach corrections throughout the years provide a good description of the field of corrections. Our goal for this book was to provide such an overview, but also frame that description within the challenges of mass probation and imprisonment and question who benefits from America's high incarceration policies. Thus, we introduce readers to a critical perspective on corrections, and draw their attention to some of the emerging controversies, such as practices that benefit the corporations, business owners, and some very well-paid stakeholders at the expense of the poor. Our perspective is not controversial. After reviewing this book, most readers will come to the same conclusion as the authors. Having stated that position, let's take a closer look at how we meet those goals.

First, although we recognize that instructors must teach from the book, we want our work to be accessible to students from a variety of backgrounds and degrees of preparation. If readers cannot grasp the material we have presented, then our efforts have been in vain. Comprehension is an essential step in mastery. We view students as our target audience.

Second, we have made every effort to present the material in a logical format. We want the material to flow from one chapter to the next and for the book to "tell a story." In this regard, we have attempted to minimize our separate voices in the writing process, and to present the material as if it were written by a single person. That was not much of a chore as the three of us have collaborated on various books and research studies for decades.

Third, we want to present the broad sweep of the corrections component to students who may or may not end up working in the field. Although the aim was to make this an essential book, we have been as thorough as possible without drowning readers in a sea of interesting but nonessential information. We recognize that some colleges and universities may require this course, whereas others offer it as an elective. Whichever is the case, we want the students who read this book to complete the course to feel relatively secure in the breadth if not depth of their knowledge of corrections in the United States and the world beyond.

Fourth, we continue to include some materials that we consider classics in the field of corrections while focusing on the most recent material available. The newer material is taken from scholarly monographs, research articles, or federal government documents prepared by the Bureau of Justice Statistics, National Institute of Corrections, or otherwise available through the National Criminal Justice Reference Service. We also make careful use of information retrieved from newspapers and different government and non-government organizations to present the most recent information about corrections.

CONTEMPORARY CORRECTIONS: A CRITICAL THINKING APPROACH

Before considering the individual chapters, it is useful to outline some of the features of this book. All 14 chapters have boxed materials dealing with current issues and controversies in corrections. Each chapter starts with a short account of an issue in corrections by describing actual incidents, or profile individuals involved in the system that we call a case study. Examples include the challenges of responding to natural disasters when they hit a prison, who wins (and loses) when legislators are considering bail reforms that are intended to decrease jail populations, the challenges of prison reform, and the question of whether jails have become a new type of debtor's prison that holds non-criminal inmates such as people who cannot pay their traffic tickets. These materials are followed by a number of critical questions intended to increase student engagement.

We also build on international examples and these comparative boxes include issues related to using volunteers to provide supports to high-risk sexual offenders released to Canadian communities, what we can learn from Norway's focus on prison rehabilitation, and various cross-national comparisons of imprisonment, capital punishment and access to the courts. The purpose of these sections is to increase the reader's understanding of how prison officials in other nations have developed different types of responses to the problems that challenge every US correctional administrator such as responding to special needs inmates or confronting problems such as correctional overcrowding or personnel shortages.

We also address issues of gender, race, and class in corrections throughout each of the book's chapters rather than in a single chapter. These boxed examples related to corrections are used to explore how and why one's race and ethnicity matter when it comes to issues such as opportunities for treatment in community corrections, placement in jails or prisons, and the use of the death penalty. Other examples include identifying recent trends such as the rapid growth of rural Whites being admitted to prison. Our intent in addressing these issues in each chapter is to enhance student learning by giving readers an opportunity to review these issues every week rather than addressing them only once in their course.

Each chapter also includes short text boxes, what could be called a closer look, which highlights controversies in corrections. These specific boxes include why many books are banned in correctional facilities, and how our understanding of adolescent brain development is changing the way we treat juveniles. Again, these contributions are intended to stimulate discussion and critical thinking about issues corrections professionals confront on a daily basis.

At the end of each chapter, we have provided three different devices that support student efforts to develop a mastery of the material. First, we provide a list of key terms. These terms are emphasized and are defined for the students in the book's glossary. Second, we include a series of critical review questions. Rather than asking students simply to repeat information discussed in the text, our intent was for them to use these questions to test themselves on the degree to which they really grasp the material presented in the chapter. However, we believe that the questions can be used in quite a few different ways. For example, students can be assigned to answer the questions in small groups. The questions could also be used for essay exams. Third, we believe very strongly in developing students' abilities to write, so in addition to the critical review questions, we have provided a list of writing assignments. Each of these writing assignments is designed to have students create one to two-page essays that make them think critically and then express their answers in written form. We believe that both students and instructors will find these writing assignments useful and thought provoking.

CHAPTER FEATURES

Every chapter features the following:

1. Outline.
2. Objectives.
3. Case Study.
   Each chapter starts with an example of a current controversy in corrections and a set of critical questions. These case studies describe a contemporary issue or event in US corrections and are intended to stimulate classroom discussions. Examples include: What happens when a natural disaster hits a prison? And the jail suicide of Jeffrey Epstein.

4. Comparative Issues in Corrections. These boxed examples are intended to draw attention to innovative or unusual practices from other nations and are written in a way that engages students. Examples include: What can we learn from Norway's prisons?

5. Race, Class, and Gender in Corrections. These boxed examples are somewhat longer and are used to explore how and why one's race and ethnicity matter when it comes to corrections. Both historical and contemporary examples are used and include topics such as Native Americans and the justice system and the rapid growth in rural White imprisonment. Adding this content to each chapter allows us to eliminate a separate chapter on issues related to race and ethnicity.

6. A Closer Look. These examples provide a brief introduction to a controversial or emerging issue in corrections, and are intended to spotlight specific issues and stimulate classroom discussion. Examples of these controversies include: "Banning books in prison," and "Even a prisoner's last meal can be controversial."

7. Writing Assignments. Thinking About Correctional Policies and Practices. Each chapter ends with five essay-type questions intended to stimulate critical thinking.

8. Critical Review Questions. Each chapter ends with ten questions that are intended to reinforce student learning.

9. Key Terms. These terms are intended to increase the student's mastery of the materials, and are emphasized in the text, listed at the end of each chapter, and defined for students in the book's extensive glossary.

COMPREHENSIVE ONLINE ANCILLARY RESOURCES

Unlike the case of many textbook ancillaries, the Instructor's Section been prepared by the authors of the text. We consider this to be a value-added feature, as the ancillaries for many textbooks are written by third parties who might not fully grasp the goals and intent of the authors. In addition, the Instructor's Section includes new materials we did not have space for in the text itself. We provide numerous suggestions for classroom exercises (such as discussions and group work), films, other books, and the types of guest speakers that might be appropriate at various points in the course.

We used the American Psychological Association (APA) style throughout this book, and their sixth edition of their publication manual specifies that all racial and ethnic groups be capitalized. We did not, however, change the capitalization of any work that is quoted from another source. In accordance with the APA guidelines we use the term Latinx to write about people who identify as Hispanic, Latino, or Chicano.

CLOSING REMARKS

In a series of work experiences that ranged from supervising probationers in the community to serving as a Director of Research for the Correctional Service of Canada, Rick

Ruddell was always motivated to find the most effective ways of helping people to make the most of their lives. Larry Mays's initial contact with the correctional system likewise left an indelible mark, as he worked in and around local jails for five years as a municipal police officer. Tom Winfree, a tower guard at Berlin's Spandau Prison, which housed a single criminal, Nazi Rudolf Hess, clearly remembers the feeling of isolation he felt as a guard and wondered how Hess, who had been imprisoned for over 30 years by that point, got up in the morning. Corrections is intrinsically an interesting, complex, and sometimes impenetrable part of the nation's criminal justice system. We cannot seem to divest ourselves of it, after all these years. We also hope that you find it as compelling.

Rick Ruddell
G. Larry Mays
Tom Winfree

Acknowledgments

While the reader only sees the names of the authors on a book's cover, this work involved a team of workers who supported us throughout the planning, writing, and editing of this book. First, all three of us would like to thank the help and support we received from Ellen Boyne and Kate Taylor and the production team at Routledge, including Emma Harder. We also very much appreciate the efforts of Jeanine Furino and her team at codeMantra, including copyeditors Joy and Erin who worked on this book. We also thank our former and current students and colleagues who commented on our previous books. Their insights and suggestions have helped us make a stronger contribution.

Chapter 1
Introduction to Corrections

OUTLINE

- Introduction
- Overview of American Correctional Systems
- Philosophies of Punishment
- Direct and Indirect Costs of Imprisonment
- Five Trends Affecting Corrections Today
- Summary

OBJECTIVES

After reading this chapter you will able to:

- Describe the extent of correctional populations

- Explain how six philosophies of punishment underlie the operations of community and institutional corrections

- Describe how vested interests influence the operations of correctional systems

- Describe the differences between the direct and indirect costs of correctional interventions

- Describe five key trends shaping corrections today

CASE STUDY

Incarcerating Deadbeat Dads

On any given day there are tens of thousands of jail inmates being held for not paying their fines, fees, or failing to make their court-ordered payments, including child support. We lack a national estimate of those numbers but the National Conference of State Legislatures (2019, para. 5) cites one study showing that 13% of South Carolina's jail population "were behind bars for civil contempt related to nonpayment of child support." Most of these inmates are poor and unemployed, and unable to make their court-ordered payments. Writing about deadbeat dads in Philadelphia jails, Melamed (2017, para. 11) cites a lawyer who says that "it was routine for parents found in contempt to be incarcerated 30, 60, or 90 days. Even six months is not unheard of."

Wesley Bell, a reformist prosecutor, took over the role of district attorney for St. Louis County, Missouri in January 2019 and one of the first policy changes he introduced was stopping the prosecutions of individuals who were not paying their court-ordered child support because they have no money. Prior to Bell's appointment, about 500 St. Louis parents were prosecuted every year for this offense, and some were incarcerated or ended up with **felony** convictions. He says that situation is like the English **debtors' prisons** from hundreds of years ago where individuals were imprisoned until their debts were paid. Bell questions the wisdom of incarcerating these people as they are unable to earn any income and being saddled with a felony conviction for failing to pay child support creates a barrier to their lifetime employment prospects.

Bell's policy change has been controversial as many women are fearful that they will not receive their court-ordered payments. The St. Louis County Police Association has waged a public war with the prosecutor over this issue, and it has argued that "The decriminalization of failure to pay child support puts livelihoods of hardworking single parents in jeopardy" (as cited in Byers, 2019). Nonpayment of child support is also a significant national issue, and there are over $100 billion in unpaid court-ordered support payments.

This issue of incarcerating individuals unable to pay fines, fees, or court-ordered payments is drawing more attention as many believe that is an inappropriate use of custody, and some say it is an example of a war on the poor. Awareness of these cases has resulted in Missouri's Republican Attorney General introducing legislation making it difficult to hold an individual in jail for debts, and he said that "De facto debtors' prisons have no place in Missouri, and I am proud to stand up against a system that seeks to treat its poorer citizens as ATMs" (Erickson, 2019, para. 3).

Critical Questions

1. Are there other alternatives, both within and outside the justice system, to ensure single parents receive their court-ordered support?
2. What is the benefit to taxpayers, to hold a deadbeat dad for six months because he cannot pay his court-ordered payments?
3. Why would prosecutors and police officers oppose the introduction of policies intended to reduce incarceration?

INTRODUCTION

What comes to mind when you hear the word corrections? Do you think about prisons with massive stone walls and the inmates portrayed in movies and television series such as *Orange Is the New Black*? Perhaps you think about inmates in orange jumpsuits picking up litter alongside a highway or prisoners in white uniforms working in a field. Do those images accurately reflect contemporary corrections?

The answer is yes, to a degree. But today corrections encompasses more than the custody supervision of convicted offenders inside or outside the fences of a secure facility. According to the U.S. Department of Justice, there were 6.8 million individuals, or about one in every 36 adults, under some type of correctional supervision in 2017. Most of them were serving probationary sentences in the community (3.7 million) while another 875,000 were on parole (Kaeble, 2018). Almost 1.5 million inmates were held in federal or state prison systems (Bronson & Carson, 2019), and almost 750,000 were in local jails (Zeng, 2019). Others were held in immigration detention, military confinement facilities, and a growing number of ex-prisoners are civilly confined, which means they are held past their release dates because of their potential risk to the public. Tens of thousands of youths were also held in detention and custody facilities throughout the country. Figure 1.1 shows the entire US correctional population from 1980 to 2017.

Probation. Parole. Prisons. Jails. These are critical components of corrections in the twenty-first century and every nation holds individuals accused of committing crimes or have been convicted and sentenced to a community or custody sentence. What differentiates the United States from other nations is the sheer number of people under correctional

PHOTO 1.1
The drawing captures a common moment in the life of a nineteenth-century debtor in London, England, who, without the personal resources to maintain himself in debtor's prison, must rely on the charity of others, in this case a small boy. Credit: Pictorial Press Ltd/ Alamy Stock Photo.

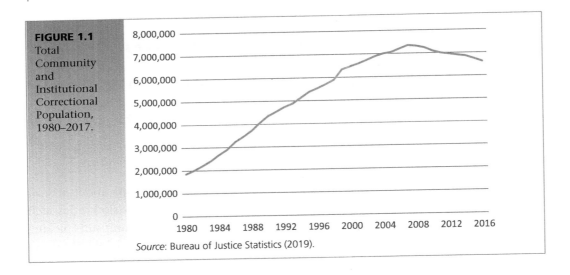

FIGURE 1.1 Total Community and Institutional Correctional Population, 1980–2017.

Source: Bureau of Justice Statistics (2019).

supervision, and we lead the world in the number of persons living behind bars. While the world's average incarceration rate is about 150 persons per 100,000 residents, the United States incarcerates 655 per 100,000 residents (Walmsley, 2018, p. 2). The extensive use of custody has been called **mass incarceration**, and a growing number of scholars are now using the term **mass probation** to describe how America has the highest rates of probation in the world as well (see Phelps, 2017). Probationers and parolees who violate the conditions of their probation orders or releases contribute to these high jail and prison populations.

Being a world leader in the use of punishment has implications for American society. Throughout this book we describe the costs and benefits of an approach to crime control based on mass imprisonment and mass probation. We point out who loses and who benefits when various crime control strategies are carried out. Ultimately, these practices shape the operations of the entire justice system. Regardless of whether high imprisonment practices are an effective crime reduction approach or not, we all pay for these policy choices in higher taxes. There are also indirect costs to incarcerating so many individuals, including losses to individuals, families, and communities.

In this chapter we explore the philosophical and practical underpinnings of contemporary corrections. In order to gain a better understanding of our nation's formal response to criminals, we provide a brief overview of US corrections and examine the philosophies that provide the foundation for "correcting" people convicted of committing crimes. We find that the approaches we have developed to control crime are very costly and we introduce the topics of the direct and indirect costs of corrections, and that section is followed by a brief overview of five trends affecting corrections today.

OVERVIEW OF AMERICAN CORRECTIONAL SYSTEMS

The following section contains an overview of correctional systems that provide a foundation to better understand some of the issues presented in the next three chapters. When considering the different correctional interventions used in the United States, we must remember they are delivered by a range of federal, state, and local governments, and in some cases private corporations are paid to supervise probationers or parolees living in the community or in correctional facilities. As a result, there are hundreds of different approaches to delivering correctional interventions and they are administered by tens of thousands of officials in thousands of community and institutional settings. That diversity in programming and delivery mechanisms makes it difficult to make any broad statements about American corrections, but those differences are one of the things that make it so interesting to learn about how we use correctional systems to respond to crime.

Community-Based Programs

Most people under correctional supervision are on **probation** and these individuals are typically supervised by probation officers working for local or county-run agencies, although these operations are also provided by state employees. A smaller number are serving probationary sentences supervised by federal probation officers working for the US courts. Regardless of who operates these agencies probationary programs treat offenders in the community under supervision and they are required to abide by conditions imposed by a judge. Kaeble (2018) notes that 60% of all probationary sentences are for felony offenses and while the average felony probationer serves sentences of about three years (Rosenmerkel, Durose, & Farole, 2009) judges in some states impose very lengthy probationary sentences. In 2017, for example, Georgia lawmakers made it possible for probationers to apply to end their sentences after three years as some individuals were required to serve the rest of their lives on probation and the average probationary sentence was about seven years, which was more than twice the national average (Georgia Legislature, 2011; Wiltz, 2017).

Prisoners released prior to the expiration of their state or federal prison terms are placed on **parole** although the federal prison system labels this a **supervised release** (for those sentenced after 1987) and all these individuals had been convicted of committing a felony. In slightly more than one-half of cases decisions about releasing them are made by parole boards while the remaining offenders are released to the community because their sentences ended or they had earned good time credits (for their good behavior in prison) resulting in their early releases (Kaeble, 2018).

Individuals serving probationary sentences or placed on parole are subject to many court-imposed conditions and some are placed in **intermediate-sanction programs** that may require them to live in a community-based half-way house or other structured living arrangement. Some of these individuals are on house arrest, where they are required to live at home and are supervised by **electronic monitoring (EM)**. EM transmits information about the offender's whereabouts using devices strapped to their ankles that are monitored and reported to the probation officers. There is a broad range of programs that probationers and parolees can be ordered to attend, and they are delivered by private operators as well as government employees. In the chapters that follow we describe approaches to offender supervision that are intended to reduce their likelihood of reoffending.

Institutional Programs

The area most closely associated with our notion of corrections is secure institutional confinement and this option falls into two broad categories: jails and prisons. There are over 3,000 jails in the United States and most of them are operated by local governments and hold individuals awaiting their court dates or transfers to other components of the justice system (such as immigration hearings or transfers to prisons) or are serving sentences of less than one year. Like the probation examples reported earlier there is considerable diversity in these arrangements and some smaller states and Alaska have integrated jail-prison systems, the federal government holds inmates in several large cities such as New York, and there are several dozen small jails on tribal lands (Zeng, 2019). Hundreds of US jails have fewer than 25 beds, while jails in Chicago and Los Angeles each hold over 5,500 inmates. Unlike prisons, most American jails hold men and women. Another factor differentiating jails and prisons is that few jails offer any sort of rehabilitative programs as most inmates have not been convicted of committing an offense; and most sentenced inmates serve very short sentences. Despite those short terms, however, most jails are high-security facilities, as they provide a safe and secure environment to inmates who pose little threat to other inmates or staff to those who represent considerable threats to both. Finally, except for big city jails (and integrated jail-prison systems in some states) most of these institutions are stand-alone facilities as they are not part of a larger network of facilities, whereas state or federal prisons are part of a larger system.

Prisons in the United States are operated by state governments and the federal government holds about 175,000 individuals in facilities throughout the nation (Bureau of

Prisons, 2020). About 8% of these inmates are held in privately operated prisons where the federal or state government pays corporations such as CoreCivic to hold their prisoners (Bronson & Carson, 2019). Correctional institutions typically fall into three security classifications: *minimum security* (inmates are relatively free to move around the facility and some have no fences surrounding the facility); *medium security*, where the inmates have some freedom of movement within the institution; and *maximum security*, where the prisoners have few opportunities for movement. Supermax facilities extend levels of control and allow inmates almost no movement and some remain in their cells for 23 hours or more each day and have very little human contact. Unless they pose a threat to security or escape, most individuals are placed in medium security prisons and then earn their way into less restrictive settings through their positive behaviors, while the most secure settings are reserved for individuals who have committed serious offenses or have histories of escape or misconduct.

Like jails, there is a broad range of prison facilities and they defy an easy description in terms of their size or the programs they offer. Some smaller prison systems have facilities designed to offer several security levels and while most prisons only hold men or women, there are several dozen coed facilities throughout the nation. Some institutions offer inmates the opportunity to participate in a variety of rehabilitative activities such as finishing their high school education, engaging in vocational programs, or participating in individual or group counseling for substance abuse and other problems. Other prisons offer few rehabilitative opportunities, but all prisons require inmates to engage in work programs to clean and maintain the facilities, prepare meals, and do the laundry. A key question that comes from that observation is why such differences between facilities exist, and in the following section we describe how different ideas about punishment shape the programs delivered and the living conditions in correctional facilities.

When you add all these correctional populations together, we find that 2,045 of every 100,000 Americans is under some form of correctional supervision in the community or in an institution (Jones, 2018). But, as we note throughout the book, averages include places where the use of correctional punishments is very high and those with far less use. As shown in Figure 1.2, in which Jones (2018) represented the total use of corrections state-by-state, Georgia (5,143 per 100,000 state residents) has almost six times the rate of persons under correctional supervision than New Hampshire (864 per 100,000 state residents) and is more than twice the national average. What factors explain these differences? Is there six times more crime in Georgia than New Hampshire, or are Georgians more likely to support the harsh punishments of offenders? These are easy questions to ask, but difficult ones to answer.

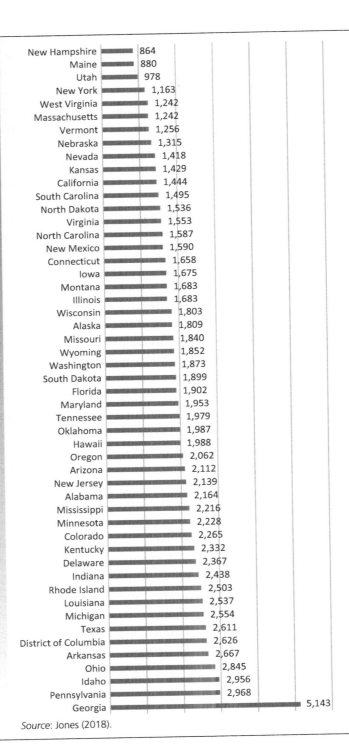

FIGURE 1.2
State Population under Community and Institutional Control per 100,000 State Residents.

New Hampshire	864
Maine	880
Utah	978
New York	1,163
West Virginia	1,242
Massachusetts	1,242
Vermont	1,256
Nebraska	1,315
Nevada	1,418
Kansas	1,429
California	1,444
South Carolina	1,495
North Dakota	1,536
Virginia	1,553
North Carolina	1,587
New Mexico	1,590
Connecticut	1,658
Iowa	1,675
Montana	1,683
Illinois	1,683
Wisconsin	1,803
Alaska	1,809
Missouri	1,840
Wyoming	1,852
Washington	1,873
South Dakota	1,899
Florida	1,902
Maryland	1,953
Tennessee	1,979
Oklahoma	1,987
Hawaii	1,988
Oregon	2,062
Arizona	2,112
New Jersey	2,139
Alabama	2,164
Mississippi	2,216
Minnesota	2,228
Colorado	2,265
Kentucky	2,332
Delaware	2,367
Indiana	2,438
Rhode Island	2,503
Louisiana	2,537
Michigan	2,554
Texas	2,611
District of Columbia	2,626
Arkansas	2,667
Ohio	2,845
Idaho	2,956
Pennsylvania	2,968
Georgia	5,143

Source: Jones (2018).

Cross-National Imprisonment Rates: A Comparison

There is a significant difference in the use of incarceration around the globe. Walmsley (2018) has gathered information about incarceration rates for the *World Prison Population List* since 1999. Since that time the United States has been the world's leader in the use of incarceration and the 2.1 million individuals held in jails and prisons is far more than China with 1.65 million prisoners—although China's population is three times larger. When converted into rates per 100,000 residents the United States has an incarceration rate that is about four times the international average. Figure 1.3 shows the rates for the G7 nations, which are the most economically advanced nations, and the median incarceration rate for the entire world: half of all countries would be lower (the median is the value separating the higher half from the lower half of all imprisonment rates). When making international comparisons it is often best to compare countries with similar levels of development, as poor nations are less able to afford to place individuals in jail or prison.

After reviewing Figure 1.3 we ask why does the United States hold so many people in jail or prison? Although a good answer might be related to crime rates, researchers have found that crime rates in wealthy nations, such as the G7 countries, are generally similar, although the homicide rates in the United States tend to be higher than in other developed nations. It is possible that Americans favor more punitive solutions to crime, a topic we consider in the section examining the philosophies of punishment.

Walmsley (2018) observes that the number of incarcerated persons in the entire world increased by about 24% between 2000 and 2018. Although some of this is

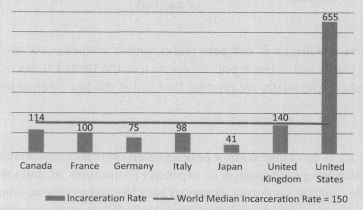

FIGURE 1.3
Incarceration Rates in the G7 Nations per 100,000 Residents.
Source: Walmsley (2018).

due to an increase in the global population, in Africa the prison population went up by 57.5%, while in Europe only 4.4% more people were incarcerated. Scholars have tried to explain this increased use of incarceration as a result of economic, political, and legal factors combined with the histories in the use of punishment. In addition, other factors such as a nation's legal system and the composition of the national population (including places with more diverse populations) all seem to influence the use of punishments such as prison or the death penalty (Ruddell & Jones, 2017).

How to Calculate the Imprisonment Rate per 100,000 Residents

Throughout this book we use the term imprisonment rates, and it is helpful to understand how they are calculated as we use this method of comparison in all the chapters. The imprisonment rate for every 100,000 persons in a population is a standard comparison and these rates are calculated by multiplying the total number of prisoners (or persons on probation or parole) by 100,000 and then dividing that total by the population. Rates can be calculated for a city, county, state, or an entire nation. For example, the following formula and calculations were used to determine the imprisonment rates for two of the G7 countries shown in Figure 1.3.

$$\text{Formula:} \quad \frac{\text{Number of prisoners} \times 100,000}{\text{National population}}$$

$$\text{United States:} \quad \frac{2,121,600 \text{ prisoners} \times 100,000}{323,900,000} = 655$$

$$\text{Canada:} \quad \frac{41,145 \text{ prisoners} \times 100,000}{35,940,000} = 114$$

Using rates enables us to compare places with a smaller population (such as Canada) to places with a larger population such as the United States. For those of us who struggle with math, we promise that this is the last formula presented in the book.

The United States has crime control policies based on mass incarceration and we observe that incarcerating individuals is an expensive proposition. In states with high government salaries, such as California, taxpayers paid $81,203 to keep an inmate in a state prison for one year (Legislative Analyst's Office, 2019). When making comparisons about crime control strategies it is important to note that policymakers make choices based on factors including changes in crime rates, as well as their nation's history and their legal and economic development. Policymakers in other nations have chosen to spend tax-payer dollars in other ways that might lead to less crime such as delivering better social programs to their citizens.

PHILOSOPHIES OF PUNISHMENT

In the chapters that follow we describe different correctional programs, agencies, and institutions. Each one is guided by a set of beliefs that define both the potential and the limitations of corrections treatment, what are called philosophies of punishment. Throughout history different philosophies have dominated the corrections field, and most correctional systems or facilities have experienced crises and periods of reform as the priorities and goals of correctional systems change. These periods of change are some-what predictable and Goodman, Page, and Phelps (2017) point out that reformers are continually at work to achieve the next change: whether that change is to get tough on crime and criminals, or to provide offenders with supports to aid in their rehabilitation.

There are six main crime control philosophies and they fall into two broad catego-ries. The first three philosophies focus on the crimes that were committed and the pun-ishments that offenders ought to receive: typically, those punishments are harsh. The second set of philosophies focuses on offenders and considers the support they need to live crime-free. Being able to describe these broad philosophies is important because they shape the operations of correctional systems, and ultimately how the individuals in those jurisdictions are treated. Lilly, Cullen, and Ball (2019, p. 5) say that ideas have consequences, which means that our ideas about crime and offenders shape the crime control solutions criminal justice systems develop and they observed the following:

> If offenders are viewed as genetically deranged and untrainable—much like wild animals—then caging them would seem to be the only option available. But if of-fenders are thought to be mentally ill, then the solution to the problem would be to treat them with psychotherapy. Or if one believes that people are moved to crime by the strains of economic deprivation, then providing job training and access to employment opportunities would seem to hold the promise of diminishing their waywardness.

For example, local politicians who believe in deterring impaired drivers may ask the county sheriff to deliver jail-based interventions to reduce drunk driving. Those inter-ventions might include imposing fees to administer a breathalyzer test, requiring sus-pected drunk drivers to pay jail booking fees, and requiring drunk drivers to serve short jail sentences. Politicians in communities with a more rehabilitative orientation, by con-trast, may provide the sheriff or probation department with funding to place convicted impaired drivers in alcohol treatment programs. All jurisdictions blend a number of these approaches in response to the crime problem, and most political leaders consider the public's opinions about priorities for reducing crime.

"Tough on Crime" Practices: Retribution, Deterrence, and Incapacitation

Individuals supporting the approach of getting tough on offenders typically focus on the crimes they committed and the harm they caused. These approaches generally assume that the individual weighed out the costs and benefits of committing a crime and acted on those impulses. The three philosophies that are closely tied to that focus on the offense that occurred are retribution, deterrence, and incapacitation.

PHOTO 1.2
Nemesis, the Greek goddess of divine retribution and revenge, was a relentless seeker of justice against those who exhibited foolish pride or arrogance, and was later called the avenger of crime. Interestingly for corrections, she had a shrine in Attica, an isolated area of Greece, and the name of an upstate New York prison that saw one of the nation's worst prison riots in 1971. Credit: Charles Walker Collection/Alamy Stock Photo.

Retribution

One of the oldest correctional philosophies is retribution. In simplest terms, retribution is the belief that punishment avenges for a harm done to another. Archaeologists have unearthed written codes dating back more than 3,500 years that clearly are based on retribution. For example, the Code of Hammurabi states that:

If a man destroy the eye of another man, they shall destroy his eye. If he break a man's bone, they shall break his bone. If a man knock out a tooth of a man of his own rank, they shall knock out his tooth.

Likewise the Law of Moses found in the King James Version of the Bible stipulates that "thou shalt give life for life, eye for eye, tooth for tooth, hand for hand, foot for foot, burning for burning, wound for wound, stripe for stripe" (Exodus 21:23–25). From such harsh rules has come the *lex talionis*, the law of retaliation or revenge. Lengthy prison terms and capital punishment are often associated with retribution.

Although the concept of *lex talionis* has been around for thousands of years this philosophy became more popular by the 1980s as the nation was experiencing increasing crime rates and the public lost faith that the justice system could successfully reduce crime or reform offenders. New ideas about retribution emerged including the expressions **just deserts** and **retributive justice**, which suggests that wrongdoers get "what's coming to them" and the punishments they receive should be proportional to the seriousness of the crimes they committed (von Hirsch, 1994). By the 1990s critics of the corrections system suggested that the retributive justice philosophy had evolved into a philosophy of **penal harm**—the belief that punishments such as incarceration should be uncomfortable and go beyond just the deprivation of liberty.

Deterrence

The deterrence philosophy is based on the idea that people weigh the costs and benefits of engaging in a crime and then decide whether they should commit that crime. Although most of us think that the rewards for crime are financial, Nagin (2013, p. 205) points out that other benefits include "defending one's honor, expressing outrage, demonstrating dominance, cementing a reputation, or seeking a thrill." The costs of crime range from informal sanctions such as the disapproval of our friends and relatives and they can also involve the formal interventions of the justice system. Offenders are also at some risk from the public and there is no shortage of media accounts of criminals being shot by armed citizens.

When it comes to the formal operations of the criminal justice system, there are two important dimensions. The first is specific deterrence, the assumption that punishments discourage the individual from repeating the same offense or committing a new one. The ultimate form of specific deterrence is the death penalty: we know with certainty that people who are executed will not commit any further crimes. Although specific deterrence may be very important in contemporary corrections, the second dimension—general deterrence—seems equally important. General deterrence is based on the proposition that punishing an individual prevents other community members from committing the same or similar crimes. This philosophy assumes that people can learn through the experiences of others and that punishments meted out to other people serve as a lesson for the rest of us.

Incapacitation

This approach to crime control is based on the notion that if offenders are held apart from society (incapacitated), they are not able to commit further crimes in the community. Social scientists long ago observed that a relatively small number of individuals were responsible for many crimes (Wolfgang, Figlio, & Sellin, 1972). Since that time many researchers have confirmed those results (Sullivan & Piquero, 2016). Policymakers have based some sentencing schemes on repeat offenders (career criminals) and one practice is called **selective incapacitation**. At the heart of selective incapacitation lies the assumption that offenders can be identified early in their criminal careers. Once they are identified the criminal justice system can be used to manage their behavior. Policy-makers have used this strategy to ensure that career criminals are caught, convicted, and sentenced to lengthy prison terms. Their goal is to reduce the crime rate by removing these persistent offenders from the street during their most crime-prone years. These are not new ideas. Although we call these individuals persistent offenders or career criminals today, they were known as habitual offenders dating back to the 1890s, and criminal codes a century ago enabled these recidivists to be sentenced to lengthy prison terms.

One example of applying a sentencing policy to selective incapacitation is **three-strikes sentencing**, where individuals who have committed three felony offenses are sentenced to decades of imprisonment. Although the idea of selective incapacitation has a common-sense appeal it has proven difficult to identify the people who become involved in crime and later become persistent offenders. Many young people who are involved in crime never commit any further offenses and sentencing them to lengthy prison terms is an expensive proposition for taxpayers, and ruins the life of the individual who would not go on to commit any more crimes.

Selective incapacitation assumes there is a finite number of these persistent offenders, and that if we catch and imprison the most active offenders, then nobody will take their place. Both national and state governments have pursued this strategy despite research showing these policies only have modest crime reduction benefits. Why? One answer may be that the image of the career criminal frightens the public, which creates an opportunity for savvy politicians—from local prosecutors to presidential candidates—to express their intention to get tough on criminals. Pratt (2007) calls this practice **penal populism**, where politicians argue for getting tough on criminals and supporting crime victims. As the public generally has little compassion for criminals these strategies have helped politicians win elections dating back to the 1970s.

Focusing on the Offender: Rehabilitation, Reintegration, and Restorative Justice

Whereas some policymakers focus on the crimes a person committed and the harm they caused, others focus on the offender and try to understand why they committed a crime and try to help them make changes in their attitudes, skills, and knowledge so they can live crime-free. There are three philosophies that are closely tied to that focus on the offender: rehabilitation, restitution, and restoration.

Rehabilitation

The most prominent correctional philosophy in this country for many years was rehabilitation, the belief that responding to an offender's unmet needs could reduce the likelihood of future recidivism. Rehabilitation is based on the notion that people—whatever their age or their crime—can change. The key to change is treatment such as individual and group counseling, drug and alcohol treatment, remedial and vocational education.

Between the 1950s and 1970s rehabilitation was the philosophy most frequently promoted by penologists; scholars who study punishment. After an assessment of correctional programs in the mid-1970s, the effectiveness of these interventions came into question (Lipton, Martinson, & Wilks, 1975). Some critics wondered whether rehabilitation worked and Martinson (1974) went even further by arguing that "nothing works." The message that nothing works struck a chord with the public, who were increasingly intolerant of the rising crime rates of the era.

Much has changed since the 1970s. When we look back at the correctional rehabilitation programs offered during that time, we find they were seldom based on sound ideas about what motivates us to commit crime and were instead based on misguided or incorrect ideas about crime and offenders. Sometimes these correctional programs were based on customs and traditions that might have little application to the real world but continued because "that is the way we have always done things." Latessa, Cullen, and Gendreau (2002) say the programs that were introduced were often **correctional quackery** and pointed out that correctional systems would introduce programs that were supposed to change offenders by providing them with acupuncture, a more wholesome diet, engaging in drama therapy, placing them in healing lodges, or giving them a pet while in prison. While none of these strategies were harmful, they did little to give them the skills they needed to live crime-free.

Our knowledge of why individuals commit crime and how we can help them to reduce their likelihood of recidivism has been informed by research. As a result, correctional treatment today often focuses on changing an individual's attitudes and beliefs. In the chapters that follow we describe interventions based on an individual's **Risk-Needs-Responsivity (RNR)**, where the risks to reoffend are based on challenging their criminal thinking and addressing their unmet needs. Evaluations of correctional interventions based on the RNR model in various countries have shown they result in significant decreases in recidivism (Bonta & Andrews, 2017). As this is becoming a leading model of correctional rehabilitation, we will refer to the RNR model in most of the chapters.

Restitution

One of the oldest approaches to reforming offenders and repairing some of the harm they caused is **restitution**, which is when a wrongdoer compensates victims, their families, or the community for their losses. Restitution dates back centuries and offenders and their families made reparations to the families of murder victims. As there were no social programs during those times, making restitution was a significant step to ensure that the victim's family could survive. Giving the victim's family some payment also reduced the likelihood they would take revenge on the offender. Much has changed in how restitution works today.

Some individuals are required to make restitution as part of their sentence, and it can be a condition of probation. Restitution can be made for the losses that victims experience such as damaged or lost property after someone breaks into their home or medical bills and lost wages due to an assault (National Center for Victims of Crime, 2012). Rosenmerkel et al. (2009, p. 8) observed that about one in five felony offenders is required to make restitution, and this increased to 27% of all property offenders. Although judges can order that an offender must make restitution, if they are in jail or prison they are seldom able to make payments, and even when they are living in the community they may be too poor to make restitution. A U.S. Government Accountability Office (2018, p. 25) report found that less than 10% of restitution was collected from federal offenders.

Restoration

The most recent philosophy that is influencing corrections is restoration, which is typically called **restorative justice (RJ)**. RJ practices focus on repairing the harm that was done to the victim(s) and community when a criminal act occurs. Supporters of the RJ model believe that the traditional or mainstream approaches to justice focus on the offense, assigning blame, and imposing punishments. They claim this approach does not fully recognize the harms the victim(s) experienced, nor does it make sense to many offenders as punishments are based on abstract notions such as harms committed against the state. Zehr (2014) contends that seeking justice using the criminal justice system can increase harm and conflict because victims often feel frustrated and excluded about decisions made about their cases and the persons that harmed them.

Most RJ approaches involve bringing offenders and crime victims together in a safe setting that is facilitated by probation staff. In some cases, other people who have a stake in the proceedings, such as a victim's supporters or the police, can also participate in these meetings. Victims are encouraged to describe the impact of the offense(s) on their lives and offenders are encouraged to find ways to repair the harms they caused. Most of these meetings end with the offender promising to pay restitution to the victim. Research shows that RJ approaches are successful in reducing recidivism (Sherman, Strang, Mayo-Wilson, Woods, & Ariel, 2015), although some are critical of these positive findings given the range of different programs that are offered and the different ways they were examined (Piggott & Wood, 2019). Some nations, such as New Zealand, have based their entire justice system on RJ approaches, and some of these ideas are built into diversion and mediation programs in the United States. While we do not know about the future of this approach Ruddell (2017, p. 66) observes that "Despite the fact that restorative justice has a popular appeal and research shows that it is an effective crime control strategy, it is unlikely to reduce jail or prison populations."

These six philosophies of punishment guide the practice of contemporary corrections in one form or another. Does one of them dominate? The answer is probably no, but each of these philosophies will continue to have an influence on correctional operations and some of them will become more popular while others fade away. It is important to acknowledge, however, that programs are continually shifting as a result of the actions of reformers and policymakers (Goodman, Page, & Phelps, 2017). Our hope is that the future of corrections is guided by scientific evidence that is the product of research rather than correctional quackery.

Native Americans: A Forgotten Population?

When it comes to research on issues related to race and ethnicity in corrections most of the commentary focuses upon African Americans and Latinx as members of these two groups account for over 30% of the US population (U.S. Census Bureau, 2018). One group often absent from discussions about their over-involvement in the criminal justice system is American Indians and Alaskan Natives (AIAN). These peoples account for 1.3% of the US population (U.S. Census Bureau, 2018) but are overrepresented in state (1.5%—see Bronson & Carson, 2019) and federal prison populations (2.3%—see Bureau of Prisons, 2020). Those national averages, however, mask the fact these individuals are very overrepresented in states with higher numbers of Native Americans in their population such as Arizona, Montana, North Dakota, Oklahoma, and South Dakota.

In terms of placements in local jails, a study by the Bureau of Justice Statistics shows the number of AIAN individuals incarcerated increased by an average of 4.3% per year between 1999 and 2014 while members of all other races increased by only 1.4% (Minton, Brumbaugh, & Rohloff, 2017). Minton and Cowhig (2017, p. 5) say this results in a jail incarceration rate for AIAN almost twice the national average (398 and 237 residents per 100,000 residents, respectively). There are also 80 jails on tribal lands (what the US government calls Indian Country) and the population in those facilities increased by 41% between 2000 and 2016 (Minton & Cowhig, 2017).

Altogether, an analysis carried out by the Prison Population Initiative (2017) shows the Native American incarceration rate for 2010—for all forms of incarceration—from jails to prisons is about twice the rate for Whites and this is shown in Figure 1.4.

AIAN youths are also overrepresented in detention and custody facilities. Sickmund, Sladky, Kang, and Puzzanchera (2019) found that these youths represented 1.7% of all

RACE, CLASS, AND GENDER

incarcerated youths. The Sentencing Project (2017) reports that the national incarceration rate for American Indians was three times that of White youths (86 and 261 per 100,000 residents), and this disparity has been getting worse since 2001. Moreover, the rate for Native American girls is much higher than for boys (Wiltz, 2016).

Because the national population of Native Americans and Alaska Natives is so small and many of them live in out-of-the-way places in rural America they tend to be out-of-sight and out-of-mind when it comes to their interactions with the justice system.

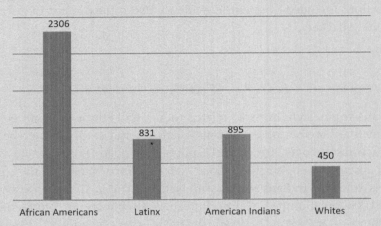

FIGURE 1.4
US Incarceration Rates per 100,000 Residents by Racial and Ethnic Groups.
Source: Prison Policy Initiative (2017).

Throughout this book we describe different choices that politicians and policymakers can make about correctional spending and it has been suggested that we can lock up fewer inmates but provide the ones that are left with more opportunities to make positive changes, or we can **warehouse** prisoners. Warehousing means delivering only the basic care and hoping for the best when these people are released. Before you dismiss these views as the ramblings of do-gooders, consider this: if you treat human beings as wild animals, abusing them at every turn, they tend to respond as wild animals (Lilly, Cullen, & Ball, 2019). Now consider that more than 90% of inmates are released into the community and we interact with them daily. The person sitting next to you in class, the cook who made your meal at the fast food restaurant, the technician who changed the oil on your car, or your Uber driver could have been on probation, been admitted to jail, or served time in prison. Humane treatment is not just a moral issue; it is a practical matter too.

DIRECT AND INDIRECT COSTS OF IMPRISONMENT

Locking people up is an expensive business, and politicians are questioning whether our current levels of imprisonment represent the most effective crime reduction strategy. As the economic recovery from the 2008 recession has been slow, and after the impact of the 2020 downturn, there is increased awareness about whether the costs of punishing offenders make good economic sense and whether there are alternatives that might have a better crime reduction benefit. For example, if we only imprisoned a million individuals in state and federal prisons (rather than 1.5 million inmates), could we instead use those funds for improving the opportunities for at-risk young people by providing better physical and psychological health care, or placing them in pre-school programs, improved educational programs, or pre-employment training and support? This is the idea that underlies the concept of **justice reinvestment** where the funds used for corrections could be used for programs intended to prevent further crime. Other nations, for example, tend to invest more taxpayer dollars into different social programs and this approach has reduced their use of incarceration. Many of us question whether that would be possible in the United States, with our strong values of self-reliance. Moreover, what would happen if we did decide to release one-third of our prison population: Who would we release early? Clearly these are very difficult questions to answer and we address them throughout this book. As a first step, we provide a brief description of the direct and indirect costs of mass imprisonment policies.

The **direct costs** of institutional and community corrections are relatively easy to calculate as that total includes all the salaries, food, health care, and institutional costs (e.g. electricity) needed to run a jail or prison. The costs in delivering probation and parole programs are lower as these community-based programs do not house offenders (exceptions include half-way houses). Every year each state provides information to the **Bureau of Justice Statistics** about the number of workers employed in the justice system and the total expenditures on corrections. In 2017, state, and local governments spent about $79 billion for correctional programs, or about $242 for every person in the United States, and that does not count federal prison spending (Urban Institute, 2020). However, there are fewer taxpayers than people in the population (about 141.2 million—see York, 2018) and that works out to about $559 for every taxpayer. If we asked whether that amount was a good investment in public safety, we probably wouldn't get much agreement and some of us would say we are spending too much while others would say we should be spending more to keep more offenders locked up, or to keep them behind bars longer. But there is also a limit to criminal justice spending and some argue that increasing police spending has a better crime control benefit than locking up more individuals (Pfaff, 2017).

The average cost to imprison a person in a federal Bureau of Prisons facility was $37,449 in the 2018 fiscal year (Federal Register, 2019). This amount is quite close to the national average as some states have much higher or lower costs. Some people are upset that it costs as much to incarcerate an inmate as it does to enroll a student in a private college, but those correctional costs have been similar to private school tuition for decades. Most of the imprisonment costs are paid in the salaries of the correctional personnel, from the officers supervising inmates to the administrative support staff who are responsible for ensuring these operations run efficiently.

So, what does it cost to imprison someone? Very few states provide a breakdown of the costs of imprisonment, but California publishes the annual costs to house an inmate in their state prison system, and those amounts are presented in Table 1.1. When

TABLE 1.1 Costs of Imprisonment, California, 2018–2019

Security	**35,425**
Inmate health care	**26,665**
Medical care	16,100
Psychiatric services	6,051
Pharmaceuticals	3,124
Dental care	1,389
Facility operations and records	**7,687**
Facility operations (maintenance, utilities, etc.)	4,610
Classification services	2,109
Maintenance of inmate records	794
Reception, testing, assignment	150
Transportation	24
Administration	**4,840**
Inmate food and activities	**3,733**
Food	2,119
Inmate employment and canteen	997
Clothing	362
Religious activities	135
Inmate activities	120
Rehabilitation programs	**2,478**
Academic education	1,277
Cognitive behavioral therapy	742
Vocational training	459
Miscellaneous	**375**
Total	**$81,203**

Legislative Analyst's Office (2019).

considering this amount, we acknowledge that costs in California are very high due to the high government salaries, and costs would be less for states with lower living costs. Moreover, jail incarceration tends to be cheaper than imprisonment as inmates held in jails tend to have very little access to any sort of rehabilitative programming and long-term health care costs are much lower as few jail inmates stay longer than a month.

While talking about these costs in our classes we are often asked about the high costs of health care, but in the chapters that follow we discuss that jail and prison inmates tend to have very poor psychological and physical health and providing correctional health care is required due to Supreme Court decisions ruling that the agencies holding these individuals are responsible for these costs.

Before ending our discussion of direct costs, it is important to note that whenever we use national or state averages, we are including cases that may have very high or low costs. Thus, some special needs populations may cost two or three times the state average. Elderly inmates, for example, often require health care costs that are several times greater than their younger counterparts (Psick, Simon, Brown, & Ahalt, 2017). In addition, persons with mental illness typically require expensive care, and offenders posing a greater risk to prison safety are often placed in maximum security or supermax facilities and the costs of housing these individuals are much higher than those for an average inmate.

There are also indirect or hidden costs of correctional systems that are borne by the taxpayers, as well as offenders, their families, and communities. These costs are rarely considered by policymakers, but organizations that oppose mass imprisonment policies are developing estimates and publicizing these costs. For example, McLaughlin et al. (2016, p. 1) calculate that for every dollar spent on corrections, there are ten dollars in indirect costs. Pfaff (2017, p. 119) says that ex-prisoners impose costs on society that are rarely considered, including health care and unemployment. With respect to health care, some inmates contract infections while incarcerated that are spread to the community after their release. Moreover, there are long-term costs when we return inmates to the community more damaged than before they were incarcerated because of psychological or physical health problems they developed or because they were victimized while incarcerated.

While we expect that former prisoners will find work there are few decent employment opportunities for these people and few business owners want to hire them.

Pfaff (2017) observes that many former prisoners find it difficult to find a job and "unemployed and underemployed former prisoners pay less in taxes…and need more government support." Not only is work important to maintain a living, but employment is a constructive use of an individual's time and enables them to build their social capital through their relationships with co-workers and employers.

The greatest indirect costs of imprisonment, however, fall upon the offender's family members and they include the expense of visiting their loved ones in jail or prison, the damage to families when a parent is no longer able to provide supervision and support. Bear in mind, too, that some critics, including Turanovic, Rodriguez, and Pratt (2012), contend that crime-involved parents are poor role models. In terms of parental supervision, some researchers nonetheless argue that when one parent is removed from the household the remaining parent is less effective in supervising the children. Wakefield and Wildeman (2011) report that when a parent is incarcerated, the children have a higher likelihood of mental health and behavioral problems. This is a significant problem, especially considering the large number of mothers who are imprisoned: Sawyer (2017) reports that half of state prisoners and 80% of jail inmates are mothers. When women are incarcerated their parents typically provide childcare, but if their family members are unable to care for them, these children end up in foster care, which further increases the indirect imprisonment costs.

Some scholars take a more controversial position by saying that the use of imprisonment causes a direct harm to communities (Clear & Frost, 2014). They contend that many prisoners from America's largest cities come from a relatively small number of neighborhoods. As a result, being placed in jail or prison is seen as commonplace or routine, and when that happens, these sanctions are not effective deterrents to criminal behavior (Piehl, Useem, & DiIulio, 1999). High incarceration rates also disrupt community life in these places. Lynch and Sabol (2004, p. 267) say that "Mass incarceration disrupts patterns of social interaction, weakens community social organization, and decreases the stigma of imprisonment; its longer-run effects may be to reduce its effectiveness." Although this brings us back to our earlier description of deterrence theory, some might also argue that increasing the certainty of being punished contributes to lower crime rates (Nagin, Cullen, & Jonson, 2018).

Most of us would agree that there are indirect costs of imprisonment, but is it really ten times greater than the direct costs, as McLaughlin, Pettus-Davis, Brown, Veeh, and Renn (2016) have reported? While not everyone would agree on those estimates, when considering the total costs of mass imprisonment Mays and Ruddell (2019, p. 228) say that it is important to recognize "(1) the human costs in terms of lost opportunities; (2) the indirect economic costs of high imprisonment policies; and (3) the risk that mass imprisonment may erode trust in and legitimacy of criminal justice systems." Thus, imprisonment has a social benefit in reduced crime, but it also has costs, and both figures are difficult to estimate.

Our brief review of correctional programs, philosophies of punishment, and how we use ideas about offender motivation to reduce their involvement in crime shows the complexity of these issues. Unfortunately, we have raised more questions than we can answer. Throughout the following chapters, however, we examine issues related to these different strategies more closely. Before setting out on that undertaking, however, we take a brief look at five key trends affecting contemporary corrections. We include this section to set the stage for the chapters that follow. As you read through the rest of this book, we encourage you to think about these trends and how they might create opportunities for working in community and institutional corrections.

Power and Crime: Do the Rich Really Get Richer, and the Poor get Prison?

In the late 1960s and early 1970s a growing number of criminologists attacked the dominant social structural, biological, and psychological theories that identified individuals as being solely responsible for crime and how society fails to consider how social forces influence criminal behavior. **Critical Criminologists** such as Reiman and Leighton (2017, p. 9) argue that the justice system was set up to maintain the status of the rich and powerful and we fail to protect people from the crimes they fear by refusing to reduce the conditions of poverty that are breeding grounds for crime. Most research confirms the assessment that as inequality and poverty increase, so does crime (Kang, 2016). Reiman and Leighton also argue that the justice system focuses on the crimes of the poor but fails to treat crimes committed by the rich very seriously, even when they have dire outcomes. One example is the deaths of at least 124 persons and the injuries of 275 more due to ignition switches that General Motors engineers and managers knew were faulty (Daalder, 2018). Even after 124 people died due to crashes because these switches failed nobody was ever charged or convicted of a crime, although General Motors paid a $900 million dollar fine to the federal government.

Contrast the harm to society made by General Motors against the example that started this chapter where about 500 deadbeat dads are incarcerated in St. Louis jails every year because they did not pay their court-ordered support. Making these comparisons leads us to question whether our ideas about crime and justice are correct. Reiman and Leighton (2017, p. 9) contend that the rich and powerful create the image of crime as being associated with the poor, people we consider "the outsider" or "the other." Those images divert our attention from the crimes of the powerful. Reiman originally made these claims in the 1970s and he has a sizable following of scholars who believe these arguments are correct.

In their analysis of criminal justice policies, Mays and Ruddell (2019) raised the issue of **vested interests** and how many individuals are enriched for the crime control activities and the supervision and management of offenders they undertake. We return to this point throughout this book, but briefly consider that corrections is extremely profitable for private corrections firms such as CoreCivic (formerly the Corrections Corporation of America), a corporation that contracts with state and federal governments to hold their prisoners and immigration detainees. In addition, bail bondsmen operate businesses that rake in billions of dollars every year. In Los Angeles County in 2017, for example, bail companies made a $41 million profit (Bryan, Allen, & Lytle-Hernandez, 2018), and most of those funds came from poor neighborhoods.

Furthermore, hundreds of thousands of correctional staff members earn their living working in community corrections, jails, and prisons, and few want their jobs to disappear. Some of these officials are very well-paid, and in 2019 there were 13 correctional sergeants who worked for the California Department of Corrections and Rehabilitation who earned more than $225,000 that year, and the highest paid received $337, 422 (see Transparent California, 2020). Our guess is that very few of them would support policies that would reduce the state prison population. Altogether, there is very little incentive for any of these businesses or workers to advocate for changes that would harm their livelihood and this attitude is shared by most workers in the criminal justice system. One might even say that is true for the authors of textbooks on corrections and if mass imprisonment did not exist, there would be less demand for our books.

FIVE TRENDS AFFECTING CORRECTIONS TODAY

This section briefly describes five trends affecting corrections. One of the challenges developing a "top five" or "top ten" list is there is seldom agreement about our choices, as other researchers, policymakers, or advocacy groups might argue for a different set of issues such as the one published by the Sentencing Project (2018). Our choices were based on the most far-reaching topics impacting the greatest number of jurisdictions and throughout the chapters that follow we address these issues in much greater detail.

Correctional Populations Are Slowly Decreasing

Between the early 1980s and 1999 the United States underwent an enormous increase in the number of adults under correctional supervision: going from about two million in 1980 to almost seven million today. As Figure 1.5 shows, the imprisonment rate for federal and state prisoners rose fourfold between 1950 and 2017, with their numbers peaking in 2007 and slowly decreasing since that time. When discussing this decrease in correctional populations we acknowledge that not all state and local populations are

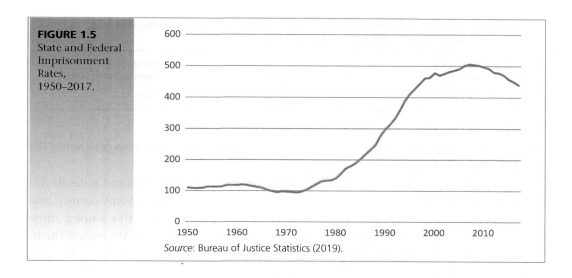

FIGURE 1.5
State and Federal Imprisonment Rates, 1950–2017.

Source: Bureau of Justice Statistics (2019).

dropping at the same time and the imprisonment of women has been increasing, as are Whites from rural counties.

While critics of mass imprisonment policies are pleased with any decrease, the Sentencing Project estimates that at the current decline it will take 75 years before our incarceration rate will drop by one-half (Ghandnoosh, 2018). The only way to decrease that total is to send fewer individuals to prison or keep them in custody for shorter periods of time and neither of those choices is politically popular.

The Overrepresentation of Individuals from Minority Groups Is Slowly Decreasing

One of the most controversial issues in corrections is the overrepresentation of African Americans and Latinx under correctional supervision. A review of U.S. Census Bureau (2018) statistics shows that African Americans represented 13.4% of the population and Latinx accounted for 18.1% of the national population in 2017, but these two groups are overrepresented in federal and state prison populations (Bronson & Carson, 2019, p. 6). While those statistics are discouraging the federal and state imprisonment rates of African American and Latinx populations decreased between 2007 and 2017 (Bronson & Carson, 2019, p. 9) and this is shown in

PHOTO 1.3
African Americans and Latinx are overrepresented among persons under correctional supervision, including jails and prisons. Credit: Marjorie Kamys Cotera/Bob Daemmrich Photography/Alamy Stock Photo.

TABLE 1.2 Changes in Imprisonment Rates per 100,000 Residents by Racial Group, December 31, 2007 to December 31, 2017

African American Imprisonment Rate	Latinx Imprisonment Rate	White Imprisonment Rate
−31%	−25%	−14%

Source: Bronson and Carson (2019).

Table 1.2. Interestingly, rural Whites seem to be the population that is experiencing the highest growth in imprisonment (Oliver, 2017).

The unequal representation of African Americans and Latinx in adult and juvenile justice systems is called **disproportionate minority contact** (DMC). Many correctional experts consider the overrepresentation of racial and ethnic minorities among those convicted and sentenced in the United States to be a national tragedy. We review the issues of race and ethnicity in terms of community and institutional corrections throughout this book. Once we examine the issue more closely, however, we find that there is no easy answer or quick solution to this practice.

There Is a National Movement for the More Humane Treatment of Prisoners

A series of reforms throughout the country are resulting in the more humane treatment of people who are incarcerated (Vera Institute of Justice, 2018). For example, there is a growing concern over the use of long-term solitary confinement given the evidence of the harmful psychological effects of this practice (Haney, 2018). Some states are limiting the number of days individuals can be placed in solitary confinement. Other states are offering inmates better access to higher education, which is intended to provide better opportunities once they are released.

There also seems to be a movement to protect the most vulnerable inmates. A first step in helping to protect prisoners was the enactment of the **Prison Rape Elimination Act** in 2003, and this legislation was intended to deter the sexual abuse of prisoners. Since that time there has been increasing awareness that some prisoners are more vulnerable to physical and sexual assaults, including members of sexual minorities (e.g. LGBT inmates) as well as persons with mental illnesses (Beck, Berzofsky, Caspar, & Krebs, 2013; Rantala, 2018). Pregnant prisoners and jail inmates are also a vulnerable population, and many states, local jails, and the federal prison system have banned the practice of placing shackles on these women giving birth (King, 2018).

Many of the reforms taking place in jails and prisons throughout the country are modest but have a significant impact on prison life. A greater number of correctional facilities are now providing feminine hygiene and other personal care products free of charge rather than making women buy these items with their own funds. Other correctional systems are providing more privacy to inmates or are attempting to keep inmates closer to their homes so they can increase family visits, which increases their morale and reduces misconduct. Some facilities have improved the quality of their meals or let some inmates wear their street clothes rather than uniforms. Furthermore, the federal government and some states are allowing more elderly or dying prisoners to return to the community using **compassionate release** policies. Although most of these reforms result in very modest changes, they can increase their quality of life, well-being, and dignity.

Decisions about Corrections Will Be Increasingly Made Using Cost-Benefit Analysis and Based on Evidence

There is increasing interest across all levels of government in introducing interventions that are evidence-based, which means that research has demonstrated their effectiveness. Originally developed for the practice of medicine dating back to the 1980s, the movement toward **evidence-based practice** is affecting every aspect of the criminal justice system as policymakers attempt to get the best return on the money they invest in correctional programs. The ultimate motivation for introducing evidence-based practices is that organizations use of these initiatives will reduce recidivism. With respect to corrections, these efforts include introducing interventions that reduce technical violations of probation, decrease jail and prison misconduct, and result in lower recidivism of ex-prisoners. An increasing number of correctional practices are also based on **cost-benefit analysis**, which is when researchers estimate the benefits of a correctional practice and compare that with the intervention costs. Washington State was one of the first jurisdictions requiring all their government social programs, including the operations of the justice system, be based on analyses of the costs and benefits of different programs.

Public Attitudes toward Tough on Crime Strategies Are Softening

After five decades of getting tough on crime there are indicators that the public's attitude toward offenders is softening. While ideas such as prison rehabilitation were popular until the 1970s, the get tough on crime movement become a dominant strategy and sentencing schemes such as three-strikes policies, mandatory minimum sentences, and truth-in-sentencing guidelines that imposed harsh sentences were adopted by most states during the 1980s and 1990s. Several decades after these practices were introduced, however, we are finding that some of these policies had only a modest crime control benefit. As a result, policymakers and criminal justice reformers advocated for changes to the system. Goodman, Page, and Phelps (2017) say that current reforms are the end result of an ongoing struggle by stakeholders including the family members of offenders,

PHOTO 1.4

Matthew Charles, a former prison inmate and the first person released under the *First Step Act*, is acknowledged during President Donald Trump's 2019 State of the Union Address to a joint session of Congress. Charles, convicted of selling 216 grams of cocaine to an informant and for illegal possession of a firearm, was sentenced to 35 years and served 25 before being released. Credit: White House Photo/Alamy Stock Photo.

well-regarded and non-partisan organizations dedicated to criminal justice reform (such as the Vera Institute of Justice, or the Sentencing Project), academic researchers, and politicians.

When it comes to corrections, actions are more important than words and one of the most significant changes is the reduction in correctional populations highlighted previously. Another symbolic change was the December 2018 enactment of prison reform legislation called the *First Step Act*. This Act gives federal judges the ability to impose less severe sentences on some drug offenders, improves their access to rehabilitation, increases the number of days of good time credits for federal prisoners, and reduces the life sentences for some federal drug offenders to 25 years (Associated Press, 2018). There are also a growing number of reforms occurring throughout the country. Voters in California, for example, authorized legislation making it more difficult to sentence offenders to a third strike and now allows some non-violent third strike inmates to apply for an early parole. Other indicators of change include the lower number of youths being held in custody facilities and the reduction in individuals sentenced to death or executions taking place (Death Penalty Information Center, 2020).

But change and reform often occur slowly. Throughout 2017 and 2018 the issue of eliminating cash bail was popular throughout the country and California passed legislation in 2018 to restrict the practice. While controversial in the United States, this would make California's practices like most nations, where bail is rarely used. Elias (2019, para. 5), however, notes that:

> This law…appears doomed by the new referendum sponsored by the state's more than 3,000 bondsmen. They of course, have a vested interest in keeping the present system: If cash bail goes, they would lose established businesses, jobs and income amounting to about $2 billion a year.

This issue of vested interests returns us to our point about considering who wins and who loses when changes are proposed to the system. While Elias notes that California bail bondsman would lose their income, the $2 billion in lost profits would stay in poor neighborhoods and reduce jail incarceration as more people accused of crimes would be **released on their own recognizance**. An important question emerging from this example is whether our public safety would increase or decrease due to this change.

"A Storm Is Coming": The COVID-19 Pandemic and Corrections

A combination of crowding, unsanitary conditions, and holding a large number of elderly and unhealthy inmates enables communicable diseases to quickly spread through jails and prisons. As of May 2020 tens of thousands of inmates tested positive for the COVID-19 virus and the rate of confirmed cases was almost three times greater in prisons than in the community population (COVID Prison Data, 2020; Park et al., 2020). In some prisons over 90% of the inmates tested positive for COVID-19 and a growing number of them became very sick or died. Viruses do not distinguish between inmates and correctional personnel, and for every three state inmates testing positive for COVID-19 there was one correctional officer who tested positive (COVID Prison Data, 2020). In juvenile facilities, about two staff members tested positive for every youth who had the virus (Rovner, 2020). These personnel are returning the virus into the community, which shows the relationship between correctional and community health. Media accounts report that a growing number of these officers are dying.

In order to reduce the possibility of contracting the illness judges sent less people to jail. Moreover, fewer individuals who had violated the conditions of their probation or parole were incarcerated. As the crisis progressed local and state governments took steps to release low-risk inmates prior to the end of their sentences. The passage of the CARES Act in March 2020 also allowed federal prisoners with less than a year remaining in their sentences to be home confined, but only a small proportion of them were released (Neff & Blakinger, 2020).

Although releasing inmates and diverting people from incarceration have only dented the correctional population, relaxing these rules has been called a "big social experiment" (Schwartzapfel, 2020, para. 6). This is because releasing them may have reduced their exposure to the virus, but many returned to locked-down communities where levels of unemployment were higher than in the great depression. We know that the transition from incarceration to the community is tough at the best of times and the conditions created by the pandemic make that change more challenging.

For those remaining in custody, the conditions were often grim. As the numbers of infected inmates grew—and their feelings of powerlessness to escape the virus rose—the tensions in correctional facilities increased. Media reports described an increasing number of inmate protests, uprisings, riots, and escapes (Elison & Gurman, 2020). In hundreds of institutions neither correctional officers nor the inmates had access to personal protective equipment, such as masks, gloves, or sanitizer. Inmates were further frustrated because family visits in most facilities were stopped to reduce the spread of the virus. Family members expressed fear that their loved ones would die alone in a youth or adult facility.

While we cannot predict the long-term impacts of COVID-19 on American corrections, we know that society's responses to the pandemic will stimulate discussions about the treatment of the people we incarcerate, the relationships between correctional and community health, and how to balance prison and public safety for years to come.

SUMMARY

We expect corrections to achieve many goals in contemporary society. As a part of the American justice system, it touches on the lives of millions of people every year. The key points to note from this chapter are the following:

- No universal agreement exists about what the word corrections means, and what exactly we are trying to correct.
- In some ways, it is easiest to think of the corrections component of the criminal justice system as comprising thousands of loosely connected agencies that fit within community responses, intermediate sanctions, and institutional placements.
- Generally speaking, there was an explosive growth in the number of people under some form of correctional supervision during the past three decades, although that number started a slow decrease in 2008, and minority populations have experienced the largest decrease.
- There are six punishment philosophies (retribution, deterrence, rehabilitation, incapacitation, restitution, and restoration) and these ideas have shaped our crime reduction strategies for centuries.
- There has been a gradual softening of punitive attitudes toward offenders and there have been modest improvements in the living conditions for some jail and prison inmates.
- When considering changes in criminal justice policies it is important to consider who wins and who loses.

One of the constant factors when it comes to corrections is that community and institutional correctional interventions have always been used to respond to long-term social problems such as addictions, individuals with mental illnesses, poverty, and homelessness. Throughout this book we question whether using the justice system is the best means to solving these problems.

KEY TERMS

- compassionate release
- correctional quackery
- cost-benefit analysis
- debtors' prisons
- deterrence
- direct costs
- electronic monitoring
- evidence-based practice
- felony
- free will
- incapacitation
- intermediate-sanction programs
- justice reinvestment
- *lex talionis*
- mass incarceration
- mass probation
- penal harm
- penal populism
- Prison Rape Elimination Act
- probation
- rehabilitation
- reintegration
- released on their own recognizance
- restitution
- restoration
- retribution
- risk-needs-responsivity
- selective incapacitation
- three-strikes sentencing
- vested interest
- warehousing

THINKING ABOUT CORRECTIONAL PRACTICES AND POLICIES: WRITING ASSIGNMENTS

1. Examine the trends in correctional populations presented in Figure 1.1. Although numbers have decreased somewhat from their peak in 2007, what is the best way to describe this chart? How does this trend compare against levels of crimes reported to the police as reported by the Federal Bureau of Investigation in their *Crime in the United States* reports?

2. Think about the ways retribution may appear in modern correctional practices. Write two or three paragraphs describing why (or why not) retribution is a legitimate correctional philosophy today.

3. Rehabilitation fell out of favor with the public throughout the 1970s and 1980s, but interest in reforming offenders seems to have increased in the past decade. Prepare a summary about whether correctional rehabilitation is a viable goal. What programs today (delivered in prisons or the community) still exemplify rehabilitation?

4. Search for the term restorative justice using Google Trends. In a short paper, describe whether mentions of this concept have increased or decreased over the long-term? Are there regions in the country that seem to have more interest in this topic? Explain why interest in restorative justice would be higher in certain parts of the country?

5. Go online and find the figures for your state's current prison population and the costs associated with housing these inmates. Are these figures easy to obtain? Contrast the costs of incarceration with the costs to attend your college or university.

CRITICAL REVIEW QUESTIONS

1. What is being corrected in corrections, or is the term itself being misapplied?
2. How do you feel about having a murder victim's next-of-kin asking to view an execution?
3. Restitution orders do not typically include compensation for pain and suffering: describe why that is a good/bad practice.
4. Describe the concept of vested interests and "who wins" and "who loses" when a nation has very high imprisonment rates.
5. What does the term mass imprisonment mean to you? What factors might have led to this practice?
6. Why is it important to explain both the total direct and indirect costs of imprisonment when we are debating different crime control policies?
7. Why is it important to understand the forces that shape our ideas about crime, justice, and corrections? What factors influenced your ideas about these concepts?
8. If levels of crime are relatively similar between wealthy industrialized countries, such as the G7 nations, why are US imprisonment rates so much higher?
9. Native Americans tend to be overrepresented in correctional systems: Can you link this overrepresentation with any political or historical factors that affected those peoples?
10. After reviewing this chapter can you provide some reasons why the public attitudes toward crime and criminals seem to be softening?

REFERENCES

Associated Press. (2018, Dec. 18). U.S. Senate passes criminal justice reform bill in bipartisan = win for Trump. *CBC News*. Retrieved from https://www.cbc.ca/news/world/criminal-justice-reform-1.4951888

Beck, A. J., Berzofsky, M., Caspar, R., & Krebs, C. (2013). *Sexual victimization in prisons and jails reported by inmates, 2011–2012*. Washington, DC: Bureau of Justice Statistics.

Bonta, J., & Andrews, D. A. (2017). *The psychology of criminal conduct*. New York: Routledge.

Bronson, J., & Carson, E. A. (2019). *Prisoners in 2017*. Washington, DC: Bureau of Justice Statistics.

Bryan, I., Allen, T., & Lytle-Hernandez, K. (2018). *The price of freedom: Bail in the city of Los Angeles*. Retrieved from http://milliondollarhoods.org/wp-content/uploads/2018/05/The-Price-of-Freedom-May-2018.pdf

Bureau of Justice Statistics. (2019). *Total correctional population*. Retrieved from https://www.bjs.gov/index.cfm?ty=kfdetail&iid=487

Byers (2019, Jan. 7). St. Louis County prosecutor says change in child support policy will not help parents get and keep jobs. *St. Louis Post Dispatch*. Retrieved from https://www.stltoday.com/news/local/crime-and-courts/st-louis-county-prosecutor-says-change-in-child-support-policy/article_4a1ac9c2-9e8d-50dd-802f-5857d834f8a1.html

Clear, T. R., & Frost, N. A. (2014). *The punishment imperative: The rise and failure of mass incarceration in America*. New York: New York University Press.

COVID prison data. (2020). Reported positive COVID-19 tests. Retrieved from https://covidprison-data.com/

Daalder, M. (2018, Sept. 20). GM fulfills ignition switch scandal terms, feds dismiss case. *Detroit Free Press*, Retrieved from https://www.freep.com/story/money/cars/general-motors/2018/09/20/general-motors-ignition-switches/1365941002/

Death Penalty Information Center. (2020). *Facts about the death penalty (March 12, 2020)*. Washington, DC: Author.

Elias, T. (2019, April 20). Opinion: California's cash bail system likely will stay. *The Madera Tribune*. Retrieved from http://www.maderatribune.com/single-post/2019/04/20/Opinion-California%E2%80%99s-cash-bail-system-likely-will-stay

Elinson, Z., & Gurman, S. (2020). Prisoners riot as Coronavirus tensions rise. *The Wall Street Journal*. Retrieved from https://www.wsj.com/articles/prisoners-riot-as-coronavirus-tensions-rise-11586469284

Erickson, K. (2019, Jan. 8). New Missouri attorney general lends legal hand in fight over debtors' prisons. *St. Louis Post Dispatch*. Retrieved from https://www.stltoday.com/news/local/crime-and-courts/new-missouri-attorney-general-lends-legal-hand-in-fight-over/article_204d3e4b-fc54-51e0-ac47-c851fb186b60.html

Federal Register. (2019, November 19). *Annual determination of average cost of incarceration*. Retrieved from https://www.federalregister.gov/documents/2019/11/19/2019-24942/annual-determination-of-average-cost-of-incarceration-fee-coif

Georgia Legislature. (2011). *Report of the special council on criminal justice reform for Georgians*. Retrieved from http://www.legis.ga.gov/Documents/GACouncilReport-FINALDRAFT.pdf

Ghandnoosh, N. (2018). Can we wait 75 years to cut the prison population in half? *The Sentencing Project*. Retrieved from https://www.sentencingproject.org/publications/can-wait-75-years-cut-prison-population-half/

Goodman, P., Page, J., & Phelps, M. (2017). *Breaking the pendulum: The long struggle over criminal justice.* New York: Oxford University Press.

Haney, C. (2018). The psychological effects of solitary confinement: A systematic critique. *Crime and Justice, 47*(1), 365–416.

Jones, A. (2018). Correctional control 2018: Incarceration and supervision by state. *Prison Policy Initiative.* Retrieved from https://www.prisonpolicy.org/reports/correctionalcontrol2018. html

Kaeble, D. (2018). *Probation and parole in the United States, 2016.* Washington, DC: Bureau of Justice Statistics.

Kang, S. (2016). Inequality and crime revisited: effects of local inequality and economic segregation on crime. *Journal of Population Economics, 29*(2), 593–626.

King, L. (2018). Labor in chains: The shackling of pregnant inmates. *Policy Perspectives, 25*(1), 55–68.

Latessa, E. J., Cullen, F. T., & Gendreau, P. (2002). Beyond correctional quackery: Professionalism and the possibility of effective treatment. *Federal Probation, 66*(2), 43–49.

Legislative Analyst's Office. (2019). *California's annual costs to incarcerate an inmate in prison.* Retrieved from https://lao.ca.gov/policyareas/cj/6_cj_inmatecost

Lilly, J. R., Cullen, F. T., & Ball, R. A. (2019). *Criminological theory: Context and consequences, 7th edition.* Los Angeles: Sage.

Lipton, D. S., Martinson, R., & Wilks J. (1975). *The effectiveness of correctional treatment: A survey of evaluation studies.* New York: Praeger Publishers.

Lynch, J. P., & Sabol, W. (2004). The effects of mass incarceration on informal social control in communities. *Criminology & Public Policy, 3*(2), 267–294.

Martinson, R. (1974). What works? Questions and answers about prison reform. *The Public Interest, 35*(1), 22–54.

Mays, G. L., & Ruddell, R. (2019). *Making sense of criminal justice, 3rd edition.* New York: Oxford University Press.

McLaughlin, M., Pettus-Davis, C., Brown, D., Veeh, C., & Renn, T. (2016). *The economic burden of incarceration in the U.S.* St. Louis, MO: Concordance Institute for Advancing Social Justice, Washington University in St. Louis.

Melamed, S. (2017, Oct. 27). How Philly fathers are winding up in debtors' prison. *The Inquirer.* Retrieved from https://www.philly.com/philly/living/child-support-debt-incarceration-fathers-philly-wheres-daddy-20171027.html?arc404=true

Minton, T. D., Brumbaugh, S., & Rohloff, H. (2017). *American Indian and Alaska Natives in local jails, 1999–2014.* Washington, DC: Bureau of Justice Statistics.

Minton, T. D., & Cowhig, M. (2017). *Jails in Indian country.* Washington, DC: Bureau of Justice Statistics.

Nagin, D. S. (2013). Deterrence in the twenty-first century. *Crime and Justice, 42*(1), 199–263.

Nagin, D. S., Cullen, F. T., & Jonson, C. L. (2018). *Deterrence, choice, and crime: Contemporary perspectives.* New York: Routledge.

National Center for Victims of Crime. (2012). *Restitution.* Retrieved from http://victimsofcrime.org/ help-for-crime-victims/get-help-bulletins-for-crime-victims/restitution

National Conference of State Legislatures. (2019). *Child support and incarceration.* Retrieved from http://www.ncsl.org/research/human-services/child-support-and-incarceration.aspx

Neff, J., & Blakinger, K. (2020). Few federal prisons released under COVID-19 emergency policies. *The Marshall Project*. Retrieved from https://www.themarshallproject.org/

Oliver, P. (2017). *Rural white imprisonment rates*. Retrieved from https://www.ssc.wisc.edu/soc/racepoliticsjustice/2017/07/07/white-rural-imprisonment-rates/

Park, K., Meagher, T., & Li, W. (2020). Tracking the spread of coronavirus in prisons. *The Marshall Project*. Retrieved from https://www.themarshallproject.org

Pfaff, J. F. (2017). *Locked in: The true causes of mass incarceration and how to achieve real reform*. New York: Basic Books.

Phelps, M. S. (2017). Mass probation: Toward a more robust theory of state variation in punishment. *Punishment & Society, 19*(1), 53–73.

Piehl, A. M., Useem, B., & DiIulio, J. J. Jr. (1999). *Right-sizing justice: A cost benefit analysis in three states*. New York: Manhattan Institute.

Piggott, E., & Wood, W. (2019). Does restorative justice reduce recidivism? Assessing evidence and claims about restorative justice and reoffending In E. W. Wood & T. Gavrielides (Eds.), *Routledge handbook of restorative justice* (pp. 359–376). New York: Routledge.

Pratt, J. (2007). *Penal populism*. London, UK: Routledge.

Prison Policy Initiative (2017). *United States profile (Incarceration rates)*. Retrieved from https://www.prisonpolicy.org/graphs/2010rates/US.html

Psick, Z., Simon, J., Brown, R., & Ahalt, C. (2017). Older and incarcerated: policy implications of again prison populations. *International Journal of Prisoner Health, 13*(1), 57–63.

Rantala, R. R. (2018). *Sexual victimization reported by adult correctional authorities, 2012–2015*. Washington, DC: Bureau of Justice Statistics.

Reiman, J., & Leighton, P. (2017). *The rich get rich and the poor get poorer*. New York: Routledge.

Rosenmerkel, S., Durose, M., & Farole, D. (2009). *Felony sentences in state courts 2006 statistical tables*. Washington, DC: Bureau of Justice Statistics.

Rovner, J. (2020). COVID-19 in juvenile facilities. *The Sentencing Project*. Retrieved from https://www.sentencingproject.org

Ruddell, R. (2017). *Exploring criminal justice in Canada*. Toronto, ON: Oxford University Press.

Ruddell, R., & Jones, N. A. (2017). Cross-national imprisonment. In K. R. Kerley, H. Copes, J. Li, & S. Sharpe (Eds.), *The encyclopedia of corrections* (pp. 169–176). New York: Wiley Blackwell.

Sawyer, W. (2017). Bailing moms out for mother's day. *Prison Policy Initiative*. Retrieved from https://www.prisonpolicy.org/blog/2017/05/08/mothers-day/

Schwartzapfel, B. (2020). Probation and parole officers are rethinking their rules as Coronavirus spreads. *The Marshall Project*. Retrieved from https://www.themarshallproject.org/

Sentencing Project. (2017). *Native disparities in youth incarceration*. Retrieved from file:///C:/Users/R&R/Downloads/Native-Disparities-in-Youth-Incarceration.pdf

Sentencing Project. (2018). *Trends in U.S. corrections*. Retrieved from https://www.sentencingproject.org/wp-content/uploads/2016/01/Trends-in-US-Corrections.pdf

Sherman, L. W., Strang, H., Mayo-Wilson, E., Woods, D. J., & Ariel, B. (2015). Are restorative justice conferences effective in reducing repeat offending? Findings from a Campbell systematic review. *Journal of Quantitative Criminology, 31*(1), 1–24.

Sickmund, M., Sladky, T. J., Kang, W., & Puzzanchera, C. (2019). *Easy access to the census of juveniles in residential placement*. Retrieved from http://www.ojjdp.gov/ojstatbb/ezacjrp/

Sullivan, C. J., & Piquero, A. R. (2016). The criminal career concept: Past, present, and future. *Journal of Research in Crime and Delinquency, 53*(3), 420–442.

Transparent California. (2020). *Public salary database.* Retrieved from https://transparentcalifornia.com

Turanovic, J. J., Rodriguez, N., & Pratt, T. C. (2012). The collateral consequences of incarceration revisited: A qualitative analysis of the effects on caregivers of children of incarcerated parents. *Criminology, 50*(4), 913–959.

Urban Institute. (2020). *Police and corrections expenditures.* Retrieved from https://www.urban.org/policy-centers/cross-center-initiatives/state-and-local-finance-initiative/state-and-local-backgrounders/police-and-corrections-expenditures

U.S. Bureau of Prisons. (2020). *Inmate race (March 7, 2020).* Retrieved from https://www.bop.gov/about/statistics/statistics_inmate_race.jsp

U.S. Census Bureau. (2018). *Quick facts.* Retrieved from https://www.census.gov/quickfacts/fact/table/US/IPE120217

U.S. Government Accountability Office. (2018). *Federal criminal restitution.* Washington, DC: Author.

Vera Institute of Justice. (2018). *The state of justice reform, 2017.* Retrieved from https://www.vera.org/state-of-justice-reform/2017

von Hirsch, A. (1994). Proportionality in the philosophy of punishment. *Crime and Justice, 16,* 55–98.

Wakefield, S., & Wildeman, C. (2011). Mass imprisonment and racial disparities in childhood behavioral problems. *Criminology & Public Policy, 10*(3), 793–817.

Walmsley, R. (2018). *World prison population list, 12th edition.* London, UK: Institute for Criminal Policy Research.

Wiltz, T. (2016). American Indian girls often fall through the cracks. *Pew Charitable Trusts.* Retrieved from https://www.pewtrusts.org/en/research-and-analysis/blogs/stateline/2016/03/04/american-indian-girls-often-fall-through-the-cracks

Wiltz, T. (2017). Doing less time: Some states cut back on probation. *Pew Charitable Trusts.* Retrieved from https://www.pewtrusts.org/en/research-and-analysis/blogs/stateline/2017/04/26/doing-less-time-some-states-cut-back-on-probation

Wolfgang, M. E., Figlio, R. M., & Sellin, T. (1972). *Delinquency in a birth cohort.* Chicago: University of Chicago Press.

York, E. (2018). *Summary of the latest federal income tax data, 2017 update.* Tax Foundation. Retrieved from https://taxfoundation.org/summary-federal-income-tax-data-2017/

Zehr, H. (2014). *The little book of restorative justice.* New York: Good Books.

Zeng, Z. (2019). *Jail inmates in 2017.* Washington, DC: Bureau of Justice Statistics.

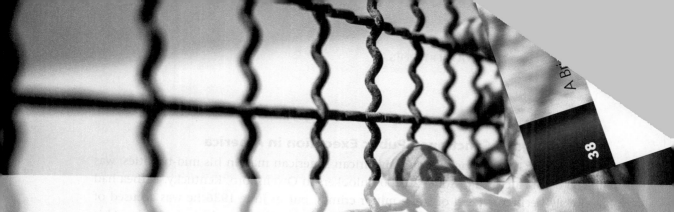

Chapter 2
A Brief History of Punishments and Corrections

OUTLINE

- Introduction
- A History of Punishments
- The Origins and Evolution of American Jails
- The Development of the Penitentiary
- Prison Reform
- Summary

OBJECTIVES

After reading this chapter you will able to:

- Explain how the nature of formal punishments has evolved throughout history

- Describe the evolution of American jails and prisons

- Explain why the early jail and prison arrangements and operations still influence today's correctional operations

- Explain why there was a move from rehabilitation to the justice model

CASE STUDY

The Last Legally Sanctioned Public Execution in America

On 14 August 1936, Rainey Bethea, an African American man in his mid-twenties, was hanged before a crowd of some 20,000 onlookers in Owensboro, Kentucky. Bethea had previously been convicted of some minor crimes, but in June 1936 he was accused of having raped and murdered a 70-year-old White woman. There was little doubt about his guilt, and he was convicted of committing rape by a jury after a short deliberation. After that finding the judge imposed the maximum penalty, which was death by hanging.

As Bethea had only been prosecuted and convicted of the rape offense, any punishment would take place in the county where the offense occurred, rather than in a Kentucky penitentiary, which would have been the case if he had been convicted of murder *and* sentenced to death. At that time all executions at the penitentiary were carried out by electrocution, which "was widely considered 'progress' because it removed execution from community view, placed it in the hands of professionals, and utilized the modern technology of electricity" (Pitzulo, 2017, p. 378). By the 1900s public executions were rare and Kentucky was the last state allowing these events.

This case drew national attention because the Owensboro sheriff was a 44-year-old woman named Florence Thomas, who had been appointed sheriff by the governor after her husband, who had been sheriff, died unexpectedly three months before the murder of the elderly woman. Although Sheriff Thomas expressed some reluctance at being required to execute Bethea, she undertook her duty and organized the construction of the gallows and presided at the hanging

The execution occurred at dawn amid a carnival-like atmosphere. Vendors sold lemonade and hot dogs to the onlookers as alcohol sales ended at midnight to reduce the possibility that drunken behavior would lead to trouble. The number of witnesses to the execution was roughly the size of Owensboro's population, which was about 20,000 residents in 1936. It was estimated that two-thirds of the witnesses were from out-of-town, including dozens of reporters who had been sent by their newspapers to cover the story (Pitzulo, 2017).

The execution occurred without any problems, and while some reporters claimed that crowd members stripped the executioner's

PHOTO 2.1

Rainey Bethea was the last person to be publically executed in 1936. The execution was a public spectacle that involved thousands of onlookers, many of whom travelled from around the country to attend the hanging. Credit: Everett Collection Historical/Alamy Stock Photo.

hood from Bethea's body, there is no agreement that this act occurred. Reporters wrote extensively about the hanging and some of these accounts horrified the public, and especially the sheriff's role in arranging the execution. This outcry resulted in Kentucky banning public executions. Most developed nations had eliminated public executions prior to 1900s, but there were exceptions. The French carried out the last execution in Western Europe in 1977, although they stopped public executions in 1939. Public executions are still occurring in China and Iran (Amnesty International, 2018a). Moreover, in April 2019, 37 Saudi Arabians were executed at sites throughout the country: some occurred in public and at least one body was left on display to deter potential offenders (Hubbard, 2019).

Critical Questions

1. This case raises issues of gender (requiring a widow only three months into her law enforcement career to preside over an execution), modernizing execution methods, and banning executions from becoming public spectacles. Which of these issues is most interesting to you; Why?
2. Why would attending a public execution deter you from committing a crime? Do you think watching an execution on television would have the same deterrent effect as attending a public execution in person?
3. Family members of victims can witness the execution of offenders in many states. Why should this practice occur?

INTRODUCTION

The key to understanding contemporary correctional systems is having an awareness of the historical and philosophical roots of punishments. How have societies through the ages dealt with people who committed crimes? The answer depends on the era, but generally punishments throughout recorded history needed to make wrongdoers suffer for their acts, protect those in power, and exploit the labor of lawbreakers. It is also important to better understand how arrangements to detain or punish inmates that were established centuries ago, such as the use of locally funded jails or placing prisons in rural areas, are still carried out today.

Looking back throughout history we find that our punishments have become more humane, although incarcerating people is a relatively new form of punishment and the first penitentiaries were only introduced several centuries ago. Prior to that time almost every sanction inflicted physical pain on the wrongdoer using corporal punishments such as flogging (whipping) or executing them. As human lives began to have more value the forms of punishments became somewhat less severe, although every society at different points through time experimented with various ways of punishing individuals, and most of those methods are considered barbaric today.

The ancient Greeks, for example, favored stoning and disemboweling offenders, but they also crucified, garroted (strangled with a cord or wire), and drowned criminals when they thought it was appropriate. In the centuries that followed other civilizations developed their own forms of physical and capital punishments and most were cruel. In ancient Rome, for example, enemies of the Republic were beheaded, although prisoners of war often served the rest of their lives as galley slaves who were forced to do the rowing on large ships. Life was short and brutal for these galley slaves and they often died chained to their oars in battle or from illness, old age, or injuries suffered from their masters. Ordinary criminals in the Roman era were often stoned or buried alive. Others were treated as slaves and were worked to death in mines or quarries (where rocks were mined for use in construction).

While the physical punishments inflicted on wrongdoers were only limited by the imagination of the authorities of the day, there was also a high degree of ceremony attached to these events. Executions, like the example beginning this chapter, were public events and viewing corporal or capital punishments was one way the authorities could communicate that an individual's misdeeds could have horrible consequences. As most people were illiterate and had no access to any form of mass communication, these public events were thought to be a sure way of deterring potential criminals.

The way punishments are carried out has also evolved over time. Before an individual can be punished in the United States, a prosecutor must prove guilt beyond a reasonable doubt, and a judge imposes a sentence from a range of punishments that are specified in formally defined legal codes. In death penalty cases, the jury also has a say in the punishment that is inflicted. In the past, there were few due process protections and punishments were imposed by the royalty and ruling classes in the hundreds of kingdoms in Europe that existed in the Middle Ages. Religious, political, and military authorities were also responsible for imposing punishments. Prior to the development of formal societies with written laws, groups of roving hunter-gathers and other tribal groups or clans also imposed sanctions on group members and individuals from other groups, tribes, or clans. Thus, there was very little consistency in the manner individuals were punished.

This chapter explores how the practice of corrections has developed over time and how our methods of punishing wrongdoers evolved from brutal public spectacles of corporal or capital punishment to placing offenders on probation or incarcerating them. While reading through the sections that follow, however, we acknowledge that there is no clear path to this evolution given the number of societies and the various punishments that were imposed over the past few thousand years. Moreover, we focus primarily on how punishments were imposed in England and Europe, and how those ideas about punishment were imported by the colonists to the lands that became America.

A HISTORY OF PUNISHMENTS

A comprehensive history of punishments is beyond the scope of a single chapter, but certain benchmark events, laws, and penal systems shaped our responses to crime and criminals. Most of these developments have occurred fairly recently in human history, and the evolution from capital or corporal punishments to placing individuals under community supervision or behind bars has only been carried out for the past 200 years. Still, it is important to understand how our efforts to deter and reform wrongdoers have changed, and in the following pages we describe crime and punishment from the prehistorical context to the end of the Middle Ages in Europe.

At this point it is important to note that these early justice systems evolved differently across the globe and there is no distinct timeline when formal laws and punishments were developed. For example, Middle Eastern and Asian countries had written laws centuries before Europeans were literate. Moreover, while South Americans had built great monuments and were living in cities, most Indigenous peoples in North America were nomadic when the first Europeans were exploring these lands in the late 1400s. Explorers, military officials, and traders from the more powerful and technologically sophisticated civilizations took the desirable resources from these lands and they introduced their religious and legal systems to these peoples, along with their methods of punishing wrongdoers. The English, for example, introduced their common-law system to the lands they colonized, including Australia, the Caribbean, India, and North America. The French, Portuguese, and Spanish, by contrast, introduced their civil law system to their colonies in Africa and South America. Many of these colonial arrangements have persisted and continue to shape the operations of today's justice systems, including the ways we punish offenders (Ruddell & Jones, 2017).

Crime and Punishment in the Prehistoric Context

Prior to the development of formal legal systems or writing most people lived in the countryside and there were few large cities. Before growing food became commonplace, these individuals lived in clans or tribal arrangements and many were nomadic, roaming the countryside to hunt and gather food. Individuals violating the community's **norms** (the rules that governed everyday life) were subject to rituals based on reconciliation or exclusion. These rules were passed down from generation to generation and they defined which acts were inappropriate and how to punish wrongdoers. Most community members, whether they were nomadic or lived in settlements, were well-known to each other and conformed with these rules as they did not want to disappoint their families or neighbors; this is what we call **informal social control**. As a result, most rule violations were minor and sanctions, which were also mild and informal, were quickly imposed. For example, people who failed to do their chores might be teased by the group. In effect the tribe members used humor to regain their authority and remind individuals that they must comply with the rules. If the rule violations were more serious, such as theft or an assault, the wrongdoers were judged by the group's elders who imposed sanctions that were proportional to the seriousness of the rule violation.

The purpose of imposing harsher sanctions for individuals who committed more serious rule violations was based on ending strife in communities where everybody shared similar backgrounds and values. As a result, reconciliation was the goal where the community would attempt to restore the relationships between the victim, perpetrator, and the larger group by repairing the harm that had been done. Restitution was a common ritual and the wrongdoer and his kin were often required to repay the victim's losses. These notions have existed for centuries and are the foundation of restorative justice (see Chapter 1).

Given the strong relationships in most tribes one of the worst sanctions that could be inflicted was banishment or exclusion. These punishments were reserved for the most serious offenses such as the unprovoked killing of another group member. Banning the perpetrator from any future contacts with tribal members, including their relatives, was often equivalent to a death sentence. If the person who was banished couldn't find acceptance in another group their life expectancy declined dramatically because of the difficulty in obtaining shelter and food on their own. Anthropologists tell us that when faced with banishment, some individuals would kill themselves rather than leave their community (Edgerton, 1976).

It was rare that blood revenge would take place between members of these groups given the importance of every person in the group's survival. However, when an individual's rule violation involved a serious injury or death, both parties and their families usually agreed to some type of restitution. Some transgressors might be forced to take the place of the injured or killed individual, becoming a member of the victim's family or serving as a slave (Pfohl, 1981). Ultimately these punishments were imposed to preserve and solidify the community relationships and conformity by responding to wrongdoing and sending a message to the rest of the group members.

Imposing Punishments Based on Written Laws

As the populations of small towns and villages increased the informal norms that had served for thousands of years gave way to more formal justice systems that were based on written rules and laws. Stearns (1936, p. 221) says that several different cultures started to develop these written laws at about the same time, including the Egyptians, Babylonians, Hebrews, Muslims, Indians, and Chinese. The underlying goals of these early legal systems were similar as they all had a religious component in that punishments were intended to purify the wrongdoer and the state would step in to reduce the likelihood of bloodshed from disputes between individuals and families.

The most well-known codification of laws emerged about 4,000 years ago when a Babylonian king named Hammurabi defined his kingdom's rules in 282 clauses that specified penalties or punishments for various crimes and is known as the **Code of Hammurabi**. This code outlines a range of punishments from fines to executions and is based on *lex talionis*, the principle of an eye for an eye and a tooth for a tooth (from Chapter 1). One factor that makes this code distinct is that punishments were carried out on behalf of the state, rather than by victims or the victim's relatives.

The concept of *lex talionis* appears again in Judaic views of punishment and that is not surprising given that Judaism was evolving as a religion, culture, and legal system in the same region and about the same time as the Babylonians. These ideas about justice were transmitted by trade and commerce and ideas about correctional and criminal justice practices are similarly transmitted today. Punishments for Jewish wrongdoers were similar to the Babylonians as they were harsh and are exemplified by the **Law of Moses**, which states "Your eye shall not pity: it shall be life for life, eye for eye, tooth for tooth, hand for hand, foot for foot." Penalties for other misdeeds were equally harsh. For example, the punishment for practicing idolatry—the worship of an idol other than God—was death by the sword, and that fate could be extended to an entire city if all its residents had been led astray. Minors were not spared from these harsh punishments and death by public stoning was the fate of a son who was "stubborn and unruly" (as highlighted in the Old Testament's Book of Deuteronomy Chapters 13 and 21). Although Mosaic penalties were severe, underlying these laws was a fundamental respect for human dignity and Chapter 21 in Deuteronomy proclaims that "If a man guilty of a capital offense is put to death and his corpse hung on a tree, it shall not remain on the tree overnight. You shall bury it the same day."

In many respects, these early laws represented the codification and ritualization of earlier crime control practices. They also served another purpose. Specifically, rules of this nature, once written down and passed down from one generation to the next, became the bedrock upon which city-states and later nations would be built. Often there was little distinction between the rules of the kings and the rules of the gods. The one set of rules served the interests of the other. The movement toward less religious views on laws and punishments began to emerge in ancient Rome and Greece nearly 3,000 years ago.

Greek and Roman Laws

Although the Greeks established city-states around 1000 BCE, individuals continued to settle their disagreements by reverting to the prelegal tribal practices including engaging in feuds and consulting with oracles. Most disputes in ancient Greece, including those arising from murders, were considered private matters and they were resolved by the injured person's family members and the state played no significant role. Like other emerging civilizations of the era, punishments were severe and were advocated by members of the ruling class such as Draco, a seventh century BCE politician from Athens who sought capital punishment for most offenses, which led to the term **draconian**. Although some individuals went into exile to avoid punishment, those who would not accept banishment were harshly treated. Common punishments for the era were being starved to death (or dying from exposure) after being staked in public places (a form of crucifixion), while more fortunate offenders were tossed from tall buildings, cliffs or poisoned. People committing less serious crimes were punished by fines, the confiscation or destruction of their property, forbidding anybody from communicating with them, or other forms of public denunciation.

Several hundred years later the harshness of these punishments was mitigated by reformers such as Solon, who was an Athenian politician and poet. Among these new punishments were fines, public humiliation, and banishment. Convicted thieves, for instance, could be ordered to return the property they stole or make restitution for its value and pay a fine. Solon distinguished between two kinds of lawsuits: private suits, brought only by injured parties, and public suits, which anyone could launch. Philosophers of the era considered these public lawsuits a very democratic reform as they enabled members of the lower classes to seek justice.

For the first five centuries of Rome's history the citizens abided by laws based on customs enforced by members of the ruling classes. But justice was rare, and especially for the poor. The introduction of the **twelve tables** placed these customs, along with property matters and contracts, into a legal code and historians regard this act as one of Rome's finest achievements (Gibbon, 1932). Like the legal codes established by the Babylonians and the Greeks, the twelve tables authorized the death penalty for various crimes, including bribery, libel, and participating in meetings at night. A range of less serious punishments could also be imposed and if a person was assaulted, the victim could retaliate or expect compensation from the offender. The twelve tables of Rome was also one of the first to mention incarceration as a punishment for not paying one's debts, but sentences were limited to 60 days.

Execution methods in the Roman era were also harsh and included scourging (when an individual was whipped until their flesh was laid bare and then crucified), burying offenders alive, while the *culleus* was reserved for those who killed a family member. These murderers were bound, placed in a leather sack with wild animals (e.g. an ape, dog, rooster, and snake were a preferred combination) and thrown into the sea. Although these are considered horrible punishments, Caesar argued that executions were not punishments at all, and questioned "Is an execution any punishment at all? I deny it. To kill is not to punish, but it simply puts him out of the way and beyond all human punishment" (Green, 1929, p. 272).

Long-term imprisonments were also imposed and (a) minor offenders could serve up to two years in public buildings located near marketplaces, (b) more serious offenders were held for up to five years, and (c) incorrigibles were housed in prisons located near wilderness areas until they died (Peters, 1998, pp. 6–7). Thus, almost 2,000 years ago these individuals were placed in different custody arrangements based on the seriousness of their crimes and their criminal histories. While much has changed in respect to corrections, these factors are still considered in sentencing and correctional placement.

Roman laws evolved over the centuries that followed and were adopted and adapted by other empires and kingdoms. These early laws formed the basis of **canon law** (the law governing churches) which later evolved into the **civil law**, which became the dominant justice system throughout Europe. The civil law system deals with matters on a case-by-case basis rather than interpreting laws based on prior legal decisions, or precedence, which is the foundation of the **common law**. Most nations colonized by the British, including Australia, India, New Zealand, and the United States, use the common law.

Crimes and Punishments in the Middle Ages

By the end of the Middle Ages, a period that lasted from about 500 to 1500 BCE, the colonists were starting to settle the lands that would become America and they imported their views of crime and punishment to the new world. These ideas had been evolving for over a thousand years since the fall of the Roman Empire. One of our limitations in describing how forms of punishment changed over time is that few scholars of that era ever wrote about why punishments were imposed, or what approaches failed or were effective in reducing crime. Moreover, while we know that harsh punishments were imposed, we don't know how often these sanctions were mitigated, and how decisions to lessen these punishments were made. A second limitation in our understanding of controlling crime is the diversity of societies during that era as there were over 1,000 kingdoms throughout Europe in the Middle Ages and we don't know whether there was much uniformity in how punishments were imposed.

Several different legal customs evolved throughout the Middle Ages including the *lex salica*, which placed a priority on compensating victims and/or their families. This compensation was called **botes** and one example is **wergild**, where the family of a murder victim received compensation. The notion behind making restitution was to avoid blood feuds, but getting this compensation was also the only way that families could survive given there were no social programs. Offenders were expected to make restitution, and these amounts were sometimes very high and represented a considerable loss to them.

Toward the end of the Middle Ages the feudal system was established and a system of punishments, called *wites*, allowed the local lord or king to collect and keep the *botes*. This change was significant and for certain crimes the victim was now the state. In murder cases, the amount of the *wites* collected varied with the victim's status: slaves were worth one amount, freemen another, lesser nobility still more, and at the top was the king. Violations of the king's peace—crimes committed in the king's presence or against one of his officers—often resulted in fines ten times the normal amount or even in the offender's death.

During the Middle Ages most people who were incarcerated were held in makeshift places such as the cellars of fortresses or castles until they could appear before a court or a member of the nobility who decided their fate. Charlemagne, the King of the Franks (and later Emperor of the Romans), ordered that each county in his empire has a prison and maintains a gallows (the structure used to hang people) nearby. Hence the ancient custom of using prisons to confine people, and not punish them, continued throughout this era.

Between the fifth and fifteenth centuries, most corporal and capital punishments were reserved for those who threatened the king's peace and religious offenders. Medieval punishments, like those in ancient Greece and Rome, often served a religious function. For example, crucifixion, breaking on the wheel, and disembowelment combined torture and an agonizing death which gave individuals the opportunity to confess before dying. Following feudal principles, medieval codes reserved many of the cruelest forms of capital punishment—for example, drawing and quartering (where the individual was hanged, disemboweled, and then cut into quarters), disembowelment, and beheading—for important political criminals threatening the political status quo. Common criminals, by contrast, were hanged or impaled on a stake.

By the twelfth century, nobles were building larger and more-fortified castles to defend their lands against foreign and domestic enemies. Henry II of England (1133–1189) ordered each sheriff to build a prison within his county or shire. An alternative site for local prisons was near or in the gatehouse that protected the town walls. However, with a few notable exceptions (such as the Tower of London)—royal buildings were seldom used for incarceration, and when they were, the prisoners generally were awaiting the "pleasure of the monarch" or were being confined because they were too politically dangerous to run free and too well connected to be executed. Living conditions in the royal prisons ranged from foul to reasonably comfortable, although commoners rarely saw conditions approaching the latter. In London's royal prison, inmates paid jailers fees for food, fuel, and bedding; these fees were regulated by public law (Peters, 1998). The practice of charging fees continued in English jails and was brought to the American colonies. Jail inmates today still may be charged for their incarceration, and in Michigan, for example, the state authorizes jails to charge $12 to be booked into a county jail and $60 per night to cover the costs of an inmate's stay, although Riley (2018) says that most individuals booked into jails are poor and seldom pay these charges.

A Two-Tiered System of Punishments: Yesterday and Today

When we look back at the punishments that individuals from different classes received throughout history it is not surprising that the poor are almost always disadvantaged in their treatment by justice systems. Advocacy organizations, such as the Sentencing Project (2013, p. 1), contend these tiers still exist and observe that "The United States in effect operates two distinct criminal justice systems: one for wealthy people and another for poor people and minorities." While our justice system promotes the notion of equality before the law, some are more equal than others. For example, the French novelist and journalist Anatole France (1894, p. 91) observes the law "forbids the rich as well as the poor to sleep under bridges, to beg in the streets, and to steal bread." Looking back at the historical accounts of life in jails and prisons, we find that it is always better to be rich than poor.

There is evidence dating back to the Greek and Roman eras that punishments for the rich were mitigated and that crimes punished by incarceration for the ruling classes, such as senators, would result in execution for commoners. Moreover, harsher punishments were meted out to non-citizens than citizens (Garnsey, 1968). Yet, even when punishments were the same for the rich and the poor, the poor can be at a disadvantage, especially when it comes to paying fines. Fines have been used for thousands of years to sanction wrongdoing but those unable to pay were often physically punished or executed. Spierenberg (1998) notes that in the Middle Ages the poor seldom had the ability to pay their fines, so they were whipped.

From the earliest days of detention, individuals awaiting their court appearances were responsible for paying for their basic needs such as food and amenities. Poor inmates placed in these jails depended on the support of their friends and families and were often forced to beg to the people passing by the gaol (the original term for jail) for food. McConville (1998, p. 275) observes that "starvation, intimidation, disease, and desperation were the lot of the poor prisoner." The rich, by contrast, could pay to sleep in warmer, safer, or less crowded surroundings. Some were able to afford residing in the jailer's quarters and ate at their table, rather than living in a common area that held every class of prisoner in crowded and unhealthy conditions. The most luxurious conditions of confinement were reserved for members of royal families and some received temporary releases to go shopping or hunting. Receiving the fees enabled jailers to earn a living and reduced the burdens on governments to pay for corrections. These fees could add up, and even though a court might order their release, some individuals stayed in the gaol until their fees were paid.

So, what are the similarities today? Inmates who have funds in their accounts are able to purchase items for their basic needs such as food, toothpaste, or toiletries from the facility's commissary. There are also businesses that will mail various amenities directly to an inmate, including electronic devices (such as televisions), reading materials, or clothing and footwear that are approved for correctional facilities. Like the jails and prisons of the past, some facilities also allow inmates to purchase special meals, such as pizza, using money from their inmate accounts, and these meals are brought to the individual's cell.

Individuals in some states can arrange to serve their entire pretrial incarceration or jail sentences in privately operated facilities that offer upscale custody conditions (like flying business class instead of coach). Santo, Kim, and Flagg (2017) describe the conditions in a Southern California jail housing a sex offender serving a one-year jail term:

> For $100 a night, he was permitted by the court to avoid county jail entirely. He did his time in Seal Beach's small city jail, with amenities that included flat-screen TVs, a computer room and new beds. He served six months, at a cost of $18,250, according to jail records.

While privately operated jails are not luxurious, they tend to be much safer than county-operated facilities and most inmates are older, middle-class men serving sentences for driving while intoxicated and other traffic offenses (Santo et al., 2017). Some of these facilities also have work-release programs that enable inmates to go to work each day, which allows them to keep their jobs or remain in school and avoid their confinement for a few hours.

European Punishments at the End of the Middle Ages

At the close of the fifteenth century, nearly all felonies—some 200 different crimes—were punishable by death, and corporal punishments were used to punish minor offenders. The following describes a range of non-capital punishments used in England and Europe:

- **Stocks** are wooden planks with holes cut for the individual's feet and hands. The person in the stocks was seated on the ground (or on a stool). While stocks were initially used to hold individuals awaiting their day in court, they were also used to punish public drunkenness and other minor crimes.

- **Pillories** are constructed of a wood timber with spaces cut for the individual's head and hands. Pillories were used to shame offenders and the townspeople sometimes threw waste at the individual, although if they were guilty of serious crimes they might throw rocks, which could kill them. Eaton (1916, p. 896) describes how an attorney in conflict with religious officials in the 1630s lost both his ears in the pillory and was disbarred, fined, imprisoned, and branded on both cheeks.

- **Branding** was a punishment in which thieves and other minor offenders were sometimes branded with a red-hot iron. Some cities used a brand of their coat of arms so that other people could tell where the individual had been punished. The French, by contrast, would use initials in their brands to communicate the type of sanction the person had served such as forced labor.

- **Amputations and mutilations** was a common punishment in which some individuals had their fingers, hands, limbs amputated, or their ears cut off (Spierenburg, 1998). Castration and cutting holes in the person's tongue (boring) were also used as punishments; others were blinded.

- **Running the gauntlet** was a military punishment and required the offender to run between two lines of soldiers who beat him with clubs.

- **Dunking stools** involved strapping the offender to a chair that was immersed in water and many drowned.

- **Whipping** is one of the oldest forms of corporal punishments and the outcome for the person being whipped (also called flogging, lashing, or caning) could be death if the strikes were excessively harsh or they were in poor health. Whips, rods, and even the branches of trees were used to carry out this punishment. This practice was imported to the Americas and was used as a correctional punishment until the 1960s in some states. Individuals are still being whipped in Iran, Saudi Arabia, Singapore, and other nations (Amnesty International, 2018a).

PHOTO 2.2
Living conditions in transportation ships were often horrible and the convicts were placed in cells below decks and few had access to fresh air during their travel to Australia. Credit: Colin Watrs/Alamy Stock Photo.

- **Pressing** was a form of punishment in which individuals were placed on a hard surface and their chests covered with a board, upon which weights were placed, suffocating them. This practice was used as a method of obtaining confessions from suspects as well as a punishment.

- **Galley slavery** was a punishment used as an alternative to execution although the severe physical demands placed on these individuals, and the possibility of being killed in combat (if rowing on a military ship), made these sentences into virtual death penalties.

- **Transportation** was a practice that various countries were transporting criminals to other lands and it was authorized in England by the *Vagrancy Act* of 1597. Most of these people were shipped to penal colonies such as Australia and New Zealand, although some were also transported to Georgia and Virginia. Most individuals who were transported were required to work in the **penal colony** to earn their freedom, although a very small proportion of them ever returned to their homelands. Transportation served a variety of purposes including reducing the use of capital punishment, banishing offenders from society, exploiting convict labor, and reforming them (Langbein, 2006).

Individuals sentenced to capital punishment could either be put to death quickly or suffer prolonged executions. Spierenburg (1998, p. 49) says that beheading, garroting, hanging, and being buried alive were considered merciful deaths. There was a variety of prolonged deaths, and these methods were only limited by the imagination of the executioners, and include:

PHOTO 2.3
Being burned at the stake was commonly used in England and Europe but was not used in legal executions in America. This drawing shows Katherine Cawches and her two daughters who were executed in 1556 for promoting their Protestant beliefs. One of the women gave birth during the execution and the male child was thrown back into the flames. Credit: Chronicle/Alamy Stock Photo.

- **Breaking at the wheel**, which involved binding the victim to a scaffold and using a large wooden wheel from a cart to break the individual's bones—starting with the legs and working upward. After their bones were broken the individuals were left to suffer and some did not die for days. Afterward their bodies were placed on display and the remains were often eaten by birds and animals. Used throughout Europe, the practice was also carried out in Asia.

- **Burning alive** involves tying individuals to a large wooden post and a fire set at their feet. If the wood pile was small, the individual would suffer for a longer period whereas if the fire was larger, they would often die from carbon monoxide poisoning. Executioners sometimes granted mercy by strangling the individual prior to lighting the fire. There were several variations of burning alive, and some executions involved pouring molten liquids (such as lead) into the individual's mouth or ears.

- **Stoning** starts with burying an individual up to their chest in the ground and then a group gathers and throws rocks at them until they die; these executions can last from 10 to 20 minutes. Although this method of execution dates back thousands of years, it is still practiced today in some Muslim countries (Amnesty International, 2018b).

Most of these punishments were imposed soon after the individual was found guilty of an offense and the sentences were carried out in the courtyards of the local gaol. While these places of temporary detention existed for centuries, the following section describes how they evolved in England and how ideas about local corrections were imported to the Americas by the colonists.

From Palaces to Prisons

Looking back several centuries, there was a blurred relationship between royal palaces and places of punishment. For example, today the Tower of London is a much sought-after tourist destination, an arsenal, a museum, and the repository of the queen's jewels. For most of its history, however, the Tower was a fortress and a royal residence. It was also the place where enemies of the Crown awaited their fate—for most, execution on the grounds of nearby Tower Hill. The Tower was built by a Norman lord in the late eleventh century. Over the next several hundred years, many people met their fate there, including Sir Thomas More (1478–1535), who was a statesman, author, and martyr for the Roman Catholic Church. When England's Henry VIII (1491–1547) ordered More to disavow the Pope's authority in favor of the king's, More refused. In short order, More was imprisoned in the Tower and beheaded. A similar fate—albeit for different reasons—awaited Anne Boleyn, Henry's second queen consort. Elizabeth I, Henry's daughter by Boleyn, also imprisoned a number of prominent individuals at the Tower, many of whom were later executed, including Sir Walter Raleigh, an explorer who helped colonize North America.

In Paris, on the Ile de la Cite near Notre Dame, is the Palais de la Cite. It was built in the eleventh century by Robert II (972–1031) to consolidate his family's holdings in France. The Palais was enlarged over the centuries, and during the reign of Philip IV (1268–1314) parts of the complex took on a judicial function. In time, French rulers moved their residence from the Ile de la Cite, and the structure functioned solely as a court of law and prison.

The Conciergerie, the prison attached to the court at the Palais, was first used in the fourteenth century to detain suspects before trial; by the fifteenth century, it was

COMPARATIVE ISSUES IN CORRECTIONS

one of the largest prisons in Paris. Its location was convenient: prisoners could be tortured to confess and then taken immediately to the court for sentencing. On their way to the Place de Greve for their execution, the condemned were allowed a brief detour to the Notre Dame Cathedral to make amends for their sins.

Some of the people held in these early French facilities were political prisoners who posed a threat to the king. During the French Revolution (1789–1794) and the Reign of Terror (1793–1794), the tables had turned and the nobility had lost most of their power, and some of them resided temporarily within the Conciergerie's walls. The opening salvos of the revolution were fired at the Bastille, another famous fortress and prison in Paris. It too was used as a place of arbitrary and secret imprisonment at the whim of the Crown. On 14 July 1789, a Parisian mob stormed the Bastille and set free its inmates. In the coming years, individuals were taken from the Conciergerie and executed, among them Marie Antoinette (1755–1793), who was the Austrian born wife of Louis XVI (1754–1792), and Maximilien Robespierre (1758–1794), who was one of the major leaders of the revolution and one of the architects of the Reign of Terror.

After the French Revolution, the Conciergerie was no long royal property. It continued to function as a state prison until 1934. Today, the southeast corner of the Palais, the Quai des Orfevres, is a courthouse. Defendants here, however, need no longer fear the torture chambers of the Conciergerie.

THE ORIGINS AND EVOLUTION OF AMERICAN JAILS

English Gaols: The Foundation for American Jails

Like other elements of America's criminal justice systems, the development of jails in the United States closely resembles those established in twelfth century England. As a result, today's local corrections systems have been shaped, in large part, by decisions and arrangements made centuries ago. Unlike nations with national, state (provincial), or regional funding that are overseen using national-level standards, modern American jails are defined by the local character of these facilities: most are dependent upon county funding and operated by local politicians. In order to better understand the challenges presented by these arrangements in America, it is necessary to take a brief look at the early history of English gaols.

Conditions in early English gaols were defined by the **keepers** (another name for warden) indifference toward inmates, the brutal conditions of confinement, and chronic under-funding. Families of the detainees were often forced to pay for their loved one's confinement and wealthy defendants could purchase better accommodations. Some poor families, by contrast, moved into the gaol with the inmate if they had nowhere else to live. Like current jail populations most of these inmates were poor, suffered from physical or mental illnesses, or had substance abuse problems. As a result, jails were violent places. Defendants often waited months prior to their trials, and some starved to death or died of exposure, illnesses, or jail fever (which was another name for typhus) before they had their day in court.

As prisons had not yet been established, most defendants found guilty of an offense were corporally punished, transported to another continent, or executed. The time between sentencing and the imposition of punishments was typically very short. Executions frequently took place at the jail or in the jail's courtyard and these acts were shocking spectacles attended by large crowds of drunken onlookers. Their corpses were sometimes displayed for days or even months after execution to serve as a deterrent. After the pirate Captain William Kidd was executed in 1701, for instance, his body was covered in tar, placed in an iron cage, and hanged alongside the Thames River in London for several years (Kearney, 2006).

The first English gaols were established in the twelfth century, about the same time that the common law was emerging. As informal methods of maintaining order were becoming less effective as individuals became more anonymous in the cities there was an increased need for more formal methods of controlling those who violated social norms or the formal laws. In 1166, King Henry II ordered that the sheriff of each county establish a jail to detain lawbreakers, although the development of these places did not emerge uniformly throughout England. Smaller communities established gaols in courthouse cellars, stables, castle dungeons, or some other place not originally intended to detain wrongdoers.

These local houses of confinement were often used temporarily and then abandoned when more appropriate places were constructed. Pugh (1968, p. 101) notes how lockups or "some kind of prison seems likely to have been tucked away in the cellar or attic of every fifteenth-century guildhall." Reliance upon these make-do structures resulted in several problems, which increased along with the individual's time in detention. The longer people were held the more likely they would starve or become sick. While no formal standards existed in those days, officials in some places were concerned about the quality of the detention facilities. Pugh (1968, p. 79) reports that the sheriff of one early English gaol was ordered five times up to the year 1233 to repair the facility. Local politicians, even 800 years ago, were reluctant to spend much on incarcerating people accused of committing crimes and the sheriffs managing London's infamous Newgate prison were under constant pressure to repair and rebuild this facility. First established in the 1200s, this facility finally closed in 1902, although it had been transformed into a prison for sentenced offenders.

Three institutions originated during the medieval era to control individuals threatening to the social order:

- Gaols served as places of temporary detention to house the accused until they appeared in court.
- Workhouses were established to control beggars, vagrants, orphaned children, and debtors.
- Houses of correction, also called **bridewells**, were intended to provide long-term confinement, although sentences seldom lasted longer than a year. Moynahan and Stewart (1980, p. 18) say these institutions acted as "training schools for youths, a place of refuge for the old and infirm, a place for the poor who could not find work elsewhere, and an institution that served to punish and correct the vagrant."

Gaols in smaller communities served many purposes although as they evolved these make-do facilities were gradually replaced with more formal structures. Inmates in these places were fortunate if they received their basic needs, and Hanawalt (1974, p. 291) notes that, "In the summer of 1316 twenty-three people died in Northampton Castle gaol from a lack of food and drink...All of these people had been imprisoned for thefts."

One of the oddest jail arrangements was the use of decommissioned naval vessels called **hulks** to hold prisoners when all other structures were overcrowded. Conditions on these ships were miserable and inmates were chained to the hulls. Although intended as a temporary measure they were moored on the Thames River in London from 1776 to 1850. Oftentimes offenders would be held in these ships until their transportation to Australia or some other colony. Jail reformers such as John Howard (1726–1790) were successful in ending the practice of using these ships as floating jails.

PHOTO 2.4
English prisoners were held on floating jails called hulks until the 1850s, and New York City's Department of Corrections copied this idea and have been placing their jail inmates on a floating jail barge called the Vernon C. Bain Correctional Center since 1992 (see Chapter 5). Credit: Robert K. Chin/Alamy Stock Photo.

Like American jails today, medieval English gaols housed a variety of inmates and not all were criminals. In addition to individuals awaiting trial, debtors were also detained. The mentally ill were also held in gaols for very long periods of time because no alternative placements existed. Further, these operations also held persons who had run afoul of the Crown, clergy who had violated religious decrees, and landless serfs. Finally, some Jews living in England in the thirteenth and fourteenth centuries were confined because of their faith. College students were also held in local jails and they could be held by the order of a University's chancellor, most often because they engaged in disorderly or drunken behavior. Altogether, jails have always held groups of difficult-to-manage people by default (as no alternative exists) and have been called a "catchall" (Casey, 1954). Holding these difficult-to-manage populations when no other alternative exists was a long-term pattern a century or longer ago and remains a challenge for today's jail operations.

Early American Jails

Even though America's early correctional systems started with a clean slate, they were quick to import the worst of British gaol systems into the new colony. The forms and functions of American jails, however, evolved in several distinctive ways and there was a significant regional flavor to these institutions. The first American jails were established in the 1600s, and like their British counterparts, a wide variety of temporary or make-do structures were used. In 1642, for example, a New Amsterdam tavern held inmates until funds were provided by the city of Portsmouth to construct a proper jail. While a patchwork of jails appeared throughout the colonies, in 1676 the Duke of York ordered that jails be constructed in each colony in a system parallel to that of England:

> Every town shall at their charge provide a pair of stocks for offenders, and a pound for the impounding of cattle; and prisons and pillories are likewise to be provided in these towns.
>
> (Charter and Laws of Pennsylvania, 1682–1700)

The first American jails, like those in rural England, were typically small and built close to the courthouse or occupied the same structure. In many cases sheriffs and their families would live in the jail annex and operate these facilities and these "mom and pop" jail arrangements were common until the 1970s (Kerle, 1998). American jailers were no more professional than their English counterparts, and Greenberg (1975, p. 181) describes the jailor Thomas Shreeve as, "An idiot, a glutton, a drunk, a frog, a fool, and an ignoramus." Jailers were often corrupt, and they collected bribes to release prisoners or fix juries, and they often took money from inmates in return for preferential treatment (Greenberg, 1975).

American criminal justice systems, including local corrections, developed as the population grew. The Northeastern states experienced rapid population growth and a strong tax base enabled them to establish more formal structures and operations. Patterns of incarceration in the South, by contrast, reflected the region's rural and agricultural nature. These states were large and sparsely populated. As a result, county-level incarceration was slower to evolve than in the Northeast. The development of local jails in Mississippi, for example, lagged their Pennsylvania examples by almost a century. As formal justice systems evolved in the West, rudimentary jails were constructed and jails in early frontier settlements were originally businesses or homes modified for use as correctional facilities. Consequently, it was often easy for individuals to escape from these structures. In order to reduce the possibility of escape San Francisco converted a merchant ship into a floating municipal jail. Instead of chaining inmates to the hull, like the inmates in the British hulks, a heavy ball and chain were fixed to their ankles and attempts to swim for the shore ended in drowning.

One of the most important descriptions of the conditions within American jails in the early 1900s comes from Joseph Fishman's book entitled *Crucibles of Crime*. Fishman (1923, p. 13), a jail inspector who worked for the federal government, labeled jails as "human dumping grounds" and places of debauchery, dirt, disease, and dependency. Fishman inspected hundreds of jails that held federal inmates and he was concerned that most jail inmates lived in inhumane conditions. These places were typically filthy, and Fishman notes that one sheriff saved money by never washing inmate bedding.

Most US jails of this time were operated by elected sheriffs and newly elected sheriffs regularly fired all the jail employees and hired their friends, political cronies, and relatives to replace these officers. Consequently, the deputies operating these jails were often untrained and had little interest in correctional careers. As a result, these places were often characterized by brutality and indifference, conditions that still exist in some jails. Kinsella (1933) reports the findings from inspections of 2,200 jails where federal inmates were held and over 90% failed to meet the minimum standards. Many of these facilities, he notes, suffered from corrupt jail staff, unsafe living conditions, and a lack of professional correctional practices.

A key factor contributing to the squalid conditions in county jails was the **fee system**. Sheriffs collected a set fee per day for each inmate held in the facility and they kept any funds that remained after their basic needs were met. Greedy sheriffs spent very little on inmate care, and Fishman (1923, p. 70) observes these people were :

> Thrown into jail in the most demoralizing surroundings, every incentive to cleanliness, decency, and self-respect is taken away from him, and then, as a crowning injury, his keeper is paid for feeding him in proportion to the amount of food he succeeds in forcing him to do without.

Inmates serving long detention periods with an inadequate diet increased the likelihood of a physical breakdown, and their morale also suffers. Some sheriffs, however, still receive fees and an Alabama sheriff was criticized after diverting $750,000 in funds meant to feed inmates for his personal spending. Although his actions were well documented in the media, they were not illegal as this practice has been occurring for almost a century (Domonoske, 2018).

The dismal conditions in American jails persisted throughout most of the twentieth century although they have gradually become more professional. One of the ongoing challenges for these facilities, however, is that most jails are operated by local politicians, including sheriffs. These elected officials are reluctant to spend scarce taxpayer dollars on providing decent living conditions for people who had committed crimes or were awaiting their day in court. Most developed nations have solved that problem by making their detention facilities part of larger networks that are funded by national or provincial/state governments. This approach also enables them to reduce the number of jails within a jurisdiction and staff their facilities with more highly paid, better trained, and professional jail officers. This change is unlikely to happen anytime soon in the United States, as most jails are operated by sheriffs—who are elected officials in most counties—and few would willingly agree to merge jail operations with surrounding counties or the state. While consolidating jail operations makes good economic sense for the taxpayers, this approach reduces sheriffs' political power and influence. Again, we see how these vested interests (and who wins or loses) can hinder correctional reforms. This issue is addressed in more detail in Chapter 5.

THE DEVELOPMENT OF THE PENITENTIARY

By the 1600s scholars such as Isaac Newton, Francis Bacon, John Locke, Rene Descartes, and Baruch Spinoza were making enormous scientific and intellectual advances. Their work set the stage for the emergence of a group of philosophers and social critics who shared a belief in **natural law**—a system of rules and principles growing out of and conforming to human nature. Science, they claimed, held the answers to all of society's social, political, economic, and moral challenges and the state could use that scientific knowledge to advance human progress. This group of philosophers formed a rationalist, humanitarian, and scientific movement known as the **Age of Enlightenment**. Their thinking had an important impact on law and punishment. Several concepts, such as proportionality (that individuals should be punished in proportion to the harm they caused), and that punishments only be used to prevent crime rather than to terrorize the people emerged from their work. During this time Cesare Beccaria (1738–1794) came up with the notion of deterrence: that individuals could be prevented from committing crimes if punishments were certain, swift, and severe (see Chapter 1), a theory that is still popular. Beccaria also introduced ideas considered radical at the time such as segregating inmates by age (e.g. juveniles and adults), gender, and offense seriousness. Some of these ideas were so radical that they were published using an alias as promoting the just and humane treatment for prisoners—whether they had been convicted of a crime or not—was just as unpopular in the 1700s as it is today.

Although the notion of correctional rehabilitation was not formally established until the 1800s there was considerable criticism about jail operations and reformers such as John Howard (1726–1790), a member of the British ruling class, and Benjamin Rush (1743–1813), an American, sought to improve the conditions in these places. Howard participated in jail inspections in England and Europe and he found that fewer of these facilities were defined by their squalor or exploitation of inmates. Howard's efforts at jail reform led to the **Penitentiary Act of 1779**, legislation requiring the humane treatment of inmates, sanitary living conditions, and providing inmates with opportunities to engage in productive labor. However, Howard soon learned that passing a law did not guarantee jailers would comply with the legislation and some jailers did not change their operations or improve the conditions of confinement.

Later generations of jail and prison inspectors also met with resistance from the politicians funding these operations and improving the conditions of confinement came slowly. The criticisms of those opposed to higher spending for prison inmates in the late 1700s and early 1800s were not all that different from those voiced today: operating a humane correctional facility costs too much money and prisoners deserve the lowest standard of living capable of sustaining life.

Benjamin Rush, a prominent American physician who became a jail reformer, encountered a similar set of obstacles as John Howard. Like Howard, Rush was highly regarded and was a signer of the Declaration of Independence. He counted among his friends such notables as Thomas Jefferson and John Adams. In 1786 Rush spoke out against a series of changes in Pennsylvania's penal laws. He voiced two concerns: that punishment should not be public, and that an individual's reformation could be achieved through punishment that encouraged apology and making amends. The next year the Friends' Society, or Quakers, of Pennsylvania formed the Philadelphia Society for Alleviating the Miseries of Public Prisons. Although Rush was a Presbyterian, he became associated with the Quakers and became the organization's spokesperson. His first success in correctional reform was convincing the Pennsylvania General Assembly that conditions in Philadelphia's Walnut Street Jail be improved. A year later, a special cell block was constructed so that prisoners could be placed in solitary confinement to meditate on their crimes and ask for repentance. In time, the former jail became a model of prison reform. Among its most impressive achievements were that prisoners were paid for their work, men and women inmates were separated, corporal punishment was forbidden, and religious instruction was required.

The Pennsylvania and Auburn Penitentiary Systems

The establishment of American penitentiaries in the 1820s captured the attention of the world's penologists, policymakers, and social critics. Pittsburgh's Western State Penitentiary (WSP), which opened in 1826, and Philadelphia's Eastern State Penitentiary (ESP), which admitted its first inmates in 1829, became the world's most prominent penitentiaries. These new prisons were built from the ground up as state-run penitentiaries and were guided by a penal philosophy other than prison-as-punishment. These facilities are examples of what penologists call the **Pennsylvania system**, an imprisonment approach in which individuals were kept in solitary confinement. The design of the new facilities reflected that method. The massive structures resembled gigantic stone wheels laid on their side, and the cells lined corridors that extended like spokes from a central rotunda (see Figure 2.1). The cells at ESP measured about 8 by 12 feet and each had two locked doors: one leading into the corridor, the other to a small walled-in yard where the inmates engaged in solitary exercise. The prison's philosophy was based on the reformation of prisoners, who were expected to reflect on their crimes and their efforts to make positive changes in their lives. To help them make those changes every individual was given a Bible, but as rates of illiteracy were very high in the early 1800s, it is likely that few learned much from these books.

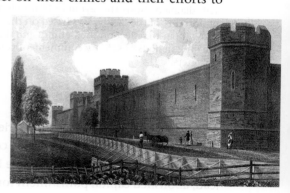

Correctional officers took measures to ensure inmates didn't communicate with each other, including placing covers over prisoners' heads when they were escorted within the facility. The combination of long-term confinement and a lack of communication is said to have increased mental illnesses in these people (Gibbons, 1996). Although basing crime control on isolating prisoners was innovative, few other states adopted the approach, and Pennsylvania discontinued the practice by 1913. In a sense, the Pennsylvania system contained the seeds of its own demise in its basic philosophical element: solitary confinement. First, building and supervising hundreds of individual cells was a very costly undertaking. Second, separation and isolation did not allow for the profitable exploitation of inmate labor. New York's Auburn system addressed these shortcomings.

PHOTO 2.5
When it opened in 1829, the Eastern State Penitentiary was one of the largest public buildings in the United States and the castle-like structure was intended to send a powerful message to the public that wrongdoing would not be tolerated. Credit: Everett Collection Historical—Classic Stock/Alamy Stock Photo.

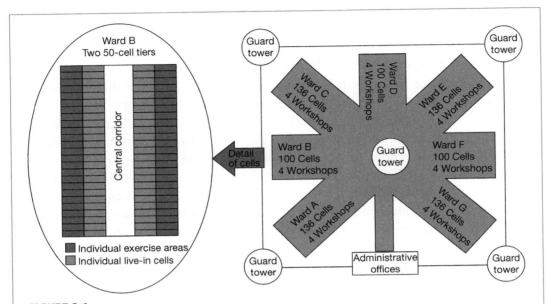

FIGURE 2.1
Layout of Philadelphia's Eastern Penitentiary.
This diagram shows the layout of Philadelphia's Eastern Penitentiary. Opened in 1829, the philosophy of the facility was based on the notion that the solitary confinement of prisoners would allow them to reflect on their crimes and that would contribute to their rehabilitation. Instead, the long periods of solitary confinement contributed to breakdowns in the mental health of these prisoners.

The Auburn System

After the American Revolution, a series of events in New York State led to the creation of the **Auburn system**, which would compete with and eventually replace Pennsylvania's approach to corrections. In 1796, the New York State legislature, following Pennsylvania's lead, abolished capital punishment for all offenses except first-degree murder and treason. As a result, the state experienced an immediate need for space to house convicted felons. The legislature authorized the construction of a prison within New York City. Newgate Prison, once a tin mine, opened in 1797. The prison housed adults and juveniles, men and women, and many of them had been convicted of relatively minor offenses. By 1800, Newgate had nearly twice the number of inmates called for in its original design and had experienced two large-scale riots. Newgate Prison was ruled a failure by the state legislation and closed in the early 1820s, after a new prison had opened in upstate New York.

In 1816, the state legislature authorized construction of a prison in the town of Auburn. The initial design of the Auburn Prison, as shown in Figure 2.2, included two main cell wings: the prison's south cell wing had both two-person cells and congregate cells

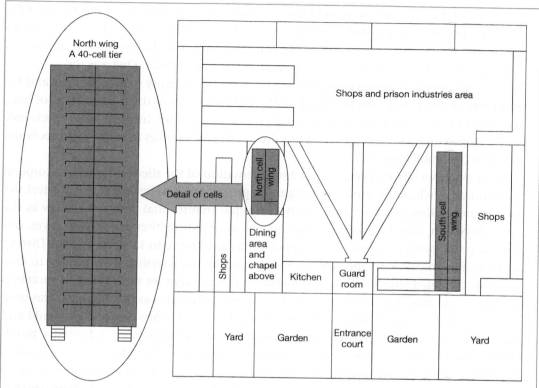

FIGURE 2.2
Layout of New York State's Auburn Prison. New York's Auburn Prison was opened in 1818 and its rehabilitative approach was based on inmates working together in groups that were overseen by guards who enforced a "silent system" where they were not permitted to speak with each other. Despite some problems with this approach this rehabilitative model proved to be more successful than the Pennsylvania system.

housing large groups of inmates whereas prisoners in the north cell wing were placed in single-person cells. After a riot in 1821, inmates followed a strict regimen of both physical and social isolation that was intended to subdue their "depraved hearts and stubborn spirits." Auburn had three classes of inmates: the first was the prison's most dangerous and difficult-to-manage inmates who were kept in solitude. Less-dangerous prisoners, by contrast, lived in solitude three days a week and worked in groups the other four. The third group, considered the "least guilty and depraved," worked together in prison workshops six days a week. By 1825, the three-class system at Auburn Prison was abandoned and all were required to work together in workshops and eat in dining halls. When they were not working or eating, though, all inmates were confined to their cells to reflect on their crimes. Even reading—except the Bible—was strongly discouraged.

Regimentation was central to maintaining discipline at Auburn, but it was not the only tool used by the custodial staff. Guards strictly enforced a rigid silent system, and inmates marched, worked, and ate in complete silence. Prison officials instituted a number of other innovations, many of which were used well into the 1900s. One was the **lockstep shuffle** where each inmate stood in line, his right foot slightly behind the left and his right arm outstretched with the hand on the right shoulder of the man in front of him. These columns of men moved forward together in a shuffle. Inmates wore black-and-white striped uniforms and caps, and this dress code still survives in some US correctional facilities (see BobBarker, 2020).

Hard work, social isolation, the strict regimentation of the silent system, and corporal punishments (whipping inmates engaging in prison misconduct) are the characteristics of a prison philosophy that along with its unique architectural design we know as the Auburn system. Was it a success? If success means imitation, then the answer is yes. Auburn was the most copied prison system of its day and spread to 11 states and the District of Columbia in just a decade, and an additional New York facility was founded in Ossining (nicknamed Sing Sing) using the Auburn model. Another measure of its success is longevity and here, too, the Auburn system scores high marks as the approach was used in some US prisons well into the 1900s. Although they were less expensive to build and operate than Pennsylvania-style prisons, Auburn-type prisons rarely returned a profit, despite the fact that the prisoners were required to engage in hard labor. Prison contractors often found the labor unreliable and the goods manufactured by the inmates were considered shoddy. Looking for cheap workers, contractors often got what they paid for.

The legacy of the Auburn system is hard to deny. First, modern prisons continue to rely on strict regimentation by security staff to maintain control. Another legacy is the big house layout: one- and two-person cells stacked in tiers and a facility enclosed by high stone walls and guard towers, and this style of prison was used until the 1970s in most states. And yet another element introduced in the Auburn model is inmate classification by security levels, a topic to which we return in later chapters.

Chain Gangs and Convict Leasing: Southern Alternatives to the Penitentiary

The sparsely populated Southern states and their dependence on agriculture created economic conditions that were in sharp contrast to the more populated and wealthier Northeastern states where the population was becoming increasingly urban and industrialized throughout the 1800s. These economic and social differences influenced the ways that punishments were carried out, as there was considerable opposition to prison construction in the South from political and religious groups. Despite that opposition Ayers (1984, p. 35) reports that prisons were established in Virginia (1796), Maryland (1829), Tennessee

(1831), Georgia (1832), Louisiana (1834), Mississippi (1837), and Alabama (1842), but no prisons were built in Florida or the Carolinas until after the Civil War. Southern prison facilities were often small, and the Kentucky prison established in 1800 only held 100 individuals.

Several decades prior to the Civil War a model of incarceration called **convict leasing** emerged to reduce the costs of confining inmates. Convict leasing allowed private individuals to lease sentenced prisoners who worked in farming, logging, and other industries until their sentences expired. Contractors paid the state a set amount for each prisoner per month and were responsible for providing the inmate's basic care. This was an economically sound scheme for cash-strapped governments by reducing their costs of imprisonment. This approach was used in Kentucky in 1825 when one individual leased the entire Kentucky prison population and in 1858 Virginia leased all their prisoners to canal construction and railroad companies (Banks, 2005, p. 55).

PHOTO 2.6
This picture shows guards and their prisoners on a Georgia chain gang prior to 1900. These prisoners often received very little care and most died within a few years of being placed on a chain gang. Many of them were leased to farmers and businessmen and there was a common saying that "If one dies, get another." Credit: FAY 2018/Alamy Stock Photo.

The outbreak of the Civil War in 1861 shifted the focus from the confinement of criminals to prisoners of war. Conditions of confinement were deplorable, and many individuals died due to malnutrition, poor health care, and substandard living conditions. Although Southern military prisons such as Andersonville are often singled out as being places of harsh treatment, there is some commentary suggesting that some Northern prisoner of war camps were not much better. For instance, Allen (2018) calculates that one-in-four Confederate prisoners died at the Elmira prison camp (see also Gillispie, 2008). The treatment of these soldiers between 1861 and 1865 speaks volumes about the nature of punishment and the disregard for humane conditions.

After the Civil War, the impoverished Southern states fully embraced the practice of convict leasing. As many of these inmates worked on farms, these arrangements are sometimes called **plantation style prisons**. While convict leasing was a win-win arrangement for the private operators and state governments, conditions were harsh for prisoners and the convict leasing system was called worse than slavery (Oshinsky, 1996). That was because slave owners had higher profits if the people they enslaved had long and productive lives. A businessperson leasing a convict, by contrast, had no financial interest in the inmate's long-term well-being and Oshinsky (2004, p. 2) reports that "between 1877 and 1879 the G&A [Greenwood and August] Railroad lost 128 of their

285 prisoners to gunshots, accidents, and disease (a death rate of 45%) and another 39 to escapes." When an inmate died—often due to illnesses caused by malnutrition, overwork, and exposure, or some combination of these factors—the contractor simply arranged for a replacement (Mancini, 1996).

One of the worst aspects of Southern corrections was the **chain gang**, which used chains to bind groups of inmates together. These inmates were required to work during the day on various agricultural and construction projects and they were chained 24 hours a day. In the evenings these inmates slept in trailers that were covered with steel cages to prevent escapes. These people were fed the bare minimum to enable them to continue working and received almost no medical care. Being overworked combined with insufficient food and exposure to the elements contributed to their physical breakdown, illness, and death (Mancini, 1996). Sellin (1933) notes that the conditions in some of these camps were horrible in the 1930s and flogging was common. Although chain gangs were condemned for their brutality—inmates rarely lived longer than five years in these camps—they were widely used, and only discontinued in the late 1930s. In addition to being part of the convict lease system they were also widely used in local corrections, and these inmates built many roads throughout the South.

One way that Southern prison systems could further reduce costs was to use inmates as guards called **trustees** and inmates also carried out most of the support jobs in the prisons. When the prison reformer Tom Murton was appointed warden of an Arkansas prison farm in 1967, for instance, the prison's doctor was the only other paid employee: all the other jobs were done by the prisoners. These inmate-guards went by different names throughout the nation, and in Texas they were known as building tenders and were responsible for maintaining control in the cellblocks and living units until the 1970s. The use of inmate trustees and building tenders is seen as a low point in American corrections because of their use of violence in maintaining order.

In return for controlling the other inmates, building tenders and trustees were granted privileges such as separate bathing and recreational periods, higher quality and better laundered uniforms, they lived in unlocked cells, and could carry clubs or knives. Aggressive inmates were often appointed as building tenders, and some prison officials placed murderers who had killed family members in these roles as most of them had not been in trouble prior to their first offense. By the 1980s the practice of using inmates to supervise and control other prisoners had ended, in part due to of lawsuits launched by prisoners (such as *Ruiz v. Estelle*), and because reformers had drawn attention to the abuses carried out by these individuals. While the days of surrendering control of correctional institutions to the prisoners have passed, inmates still perform most of the daily chores such as cleaning, preparing and serving meals, repairing the facility, and working on the grounds.

The chain gang and convict leasing schemes are considered a low point in corrections. Yet, sanctions based on being tough on offenders have a popular appeal with the public and they briefly re-emerged in the 1980s and 1990s. In some respects, American corrections has been driven by fads, such as the introduction of boot camps, as well as various internal and external crises. Many of these crises have led to prison reform, which is addressed in the next section.

PRISON REFORM

Penal Tourism and the American Penitentiary

Long before the term **penal tourism** was introduced, visitors were drawn to Eastern State Penitentiary. Wilson, Hodgkinson, Piche, and Walby (2017, p. 3) observe that:

> The moment it opened, visitors began flocking by the thousands from all corners of the Earth to tour the facility, to marvel at its architectural boldness and to gaze at its prisoners. Such spectatorship of the incarcerated was not, it must be noted, an especially novel pastime; sightseeing within operational total institutions had been commonplace since the seventeenth century...But the key difference in the case of Eastern State, and what made it a watershed in the "modern" prison, was that a large percentage of its visitors were dignitaries, policy-makers, penal reformers, and prison architects, who noted the institution's apparent success and returned to their respective cities and homelands afire with a vision of the ideal prison and determined to emulate it.

Some of the most prominent of these dignitaries included Gustave de Beaumont (1802–1866) and Alexis de Tocqueville (1805–1859), who were lawyers and social critics who traveled widely to learn how punishments were carried out across the globe. Upon his return to France in 1832, de Tocqueville wrote a book entitled *On the Penitentiary System in the United States and its Applications to France*. de Tocqueville's analysis of US prisons led to plans to build similar facilities in France, but by 1853 France increased its transportation of inmates to penal colonies, including Devil's Island (that colony was popularized by a 1969 book entitled *Papillon*, which was later made into movies in 1973 and 2017).

Another famous visitor was William Crawford (1788–1847), a London philanthropist who was sent by the British Home Office in the early 1830s to investigate whether US prisons were suitable to be introduced in Britain. Crawford traveled extensively, visiting penitentiaries in 14 states and the District of Columbia; he also toured a number of jails along the way. In a massive document entitled *Report on the Penitentiaries of the United States* (1834), he included detailed descriptions and assessments of the facilities he visited. By the late 1830s, the Home Office had approved plans for prisons based on Pennsylvania's Eastern Penitentiary and two started admitting prisoners in 1842 and 1844.

The Pennsylvania model did not fare well in Britain and by 1857 every inmate was assigned to a nine-month period of Pennsylvania-type solitary confinement followed by an Auburn-type placement.

A fourth prominent visitor to the US prisons was less complimentary than other English reformers. Charles Dickens (1812–1870) made several trips to the United States and although famous for writing five novels, he was no stranger to law, justice, and punishment, having served as a court stenographer and parliamentary reporter. Dickens generally disliked American ways, but he reserved his most biting comments for the American penal system. Describing his visit to Eastern Penitentiary, Dickens (1842, p. 91) wrote:

> In the outskirts, stands a great prison, called the Eastern Penitentiary; conduced on a plan peculiar to the state of Pennsylvania. The system here is rigid, strict, and hopeless solitary confinement. I believe it, in its effects, to be cruel and wrong...I believe that very few men are capable of estimating the immense amount of torture and agony that this dreadful punishment, prolonged for many years, inflicts upon the sufferer...I hold this slow and daily tampering with the mysteries of the brain, to be immeasurably worse than any torture of the body.

One wonders what Dickens would think of today's use of long-term segregation in super-max prisons. While there was some debate about the outcomes of long-term placements of individuals in solitary confinement in the 1800s, current research shows these placements have adverse effects on their mental health (Haney, 2018).

Eras of Correctional Reform

Since the emergence of formal correctional systems in the late 1700s, jails and prisons have been almost continuously involved in cycles of crisis and reforms. These crises have emerged due to external factors, such as legal decisions and economic downturns, and internal factors such as corruption, misconduct, and the abuse and exploitation of prisoners. Arguably, one the most overarching long-term challenges since the 1800s is the underfunding of correctional systems. While politicians since the mid-1970s generally have been enthusiastic about imprisoning more offenders, they are equally reluctant to provide more than their basic care, what we called warehousing in the previous chapter. As a result, seldom is there much funding for any type of meaningful rehabilitative programs, and California, for example, spends less than 3% of their correctional funding on rehabilitative efforts (see Legislative Analyst's Office, 2019).

Reforms to correctional operations also have occurred, and they are often in response to crises as well as the long-term efforts of reformers who work tirelessly to make correctional operations more humane and rehabilitative (Goodman, Page, & Phelps, 2017). These reformers include Americans such as Benjamin Rush and the individuals highlighted in the Pioneers in American Corrections box (below). The interests of these reformers, however, are pitted against an equally committed group of activists, policymakers, and legislators who believe that few offenders can be reformed and we should "lock them up and throw away the key." Many of these beliefs are related to philosophies of punishment outlined in Chapter 1. In this section, we identify three distinct eras of change and reform occurring since the late 1800s.

The late 1800s were exciting times in the emerging fields of criminology and penology. A key question asked by reformers and the public was how criminals should be treated: should we just incapacitate them or allow them to work toward their reform? Ideas about rehabilitation were becoming popular as philosophers of the era proposed that individuals could make positive changes in their lives. By the late 1800s reformation held sway in penological theory and practice. Many American penologists of this era believed that science held the key to understanding the disease—crime—and that medicine provided the model for its cure.

From Medical Model to Rehabilitation

The 1870 conference of the National Prison Association resulted in a number of recommendations about rehabilitating offenders. The most popular approach was to develop an individualized treatment plan for inmates that would serve as a roadmap for their rehabilitation. Steeped in nineteenth-century progressive beliefs, treatment equated crime with illness, and rehabilitation with cure. A careful reading of Rush's writings reveals that diet and physical well-being were part of the good doctor's overall plan for a successful prison. Increasingly in the late nineteenth and early twentieth centuries, prison officials turned to the emerging social and behavioral sciences for answers to a vexing question: How can we change the criminal?

The **medical model** of corrections became the dominant approach to prisoner management in the early twentieth century. The specific treatments emerged alongside new findings in social and behavioral science research; in time, most prison therapists settled on group therapy and behavior modification as their treatments of choice. Prison administrators would add educational and vocational training in the hopes of giving prisoners skills that would be useful in free society.

A turning point in correctional treatment came in 1929 with the adoption of a scientific treatment regimen by the U.S. Bureau of Prisons. Within a decade, nearly every state had expressed its commitment to rehabilitation. Rehabilitation, the process of returning offenders to orderly or acceptable behaviors, became a primary goal of the nation's correctional systems. Between the 1870s and the 1950s, the locus of the rehabilitation process moved from the prison and reformatory to the community. Reintegration, a popular concept in the 1970s, provided a bridge between institutions and community. Advocates of this position understood the importance of minimizing the problems inmates encountered as they moved from a restrictive lifestyle to a free one. But a series of events in the mid-1970s cast doubts on rehabilitation's future in the US penal system.

Just Deserts and the Justice Model of Punishment

During the 20-year period following World War II, US prisons experienced a rash of inmate uprisings and riots. By the late 1960s, prison officials began to question the efficacy of prison-based rehabilitation. Also, after a decade of legal and social liberalism that started in the 1960s, a wave of conservatism flooded the nation, cresting with Ronald Reagan's election as president in 1980. One factor in the nation's move to the right was Robert Martinson's (1974) very negative report on corrections and adjudication programs, in which he questioned whether rehabilitation was possible within the current corrections system.

Other critics also questioned the system's ability to get the job done. For example, as the American Friends Service Committee (1971, p. 20) notes in its report on punishment in the United States that "Retribution and revenge necessarily imply punishment, but it does not necessarily follow that punishment is eliminated under rehabilitative regimes." In the early 1970s, the organization called for a moratorium on new prison construction.

Law professor and criminologist Norval Morris (1974), concerned about the rights of all citizens, including prison inmates, responded to calls to abandon the prison system in the *Future of Imprisonment*. Prisons, he speculated, would outlive him and all of his contemporaries. The challenge was to eliminate what Morris saw as a destructive conflict between the sentences meted out by judges and the treatment goals set by prison administrators. Indeed, he expressed little faith in the ability of the 1970s prison system to rehabilitate inmates. Prison, Morris (1974, p. xi) wrote, is necessary to control the dangerous; moreover, it is the criminal's "just deserts." He called for new prisons solely for repeat violent offenders. Treatment, he insisted, should be provided only for inmates who want to change: if criminals do not want to change, the government should not expend its resources to make them change, even if it could.

As the attacks on prison rehabilitation raged, David Fogel (1975) articulated a "new" model of justice. Fogel proposed a punishment model in which people who committed crimes take responsibility for their own actions. The **justice model** rests on the assumption that individuals have free wills: they choose to violate laws and deserve to be punished. Within this model, rehabilitation and other forms of treatment should not be primary goals of correctional systems.

Just deserts and the justice model are mixtures of liberal thinking on crime and criminals (the concern for due process, monitoring the excesses of an all-powerful criminal justice system, and reining in an insulated correctional system) and conservative thinking (an emphasis on punishment for its own sake and retribution as embodied in the *lex talionis*). Also, the justice perspective seems to be a recasting of the classical views of humanity and crime: all rational human beings should be accountable for their own actions. Andrew von Hirsch (1976, p. 49) characterizes this behavior as follows: "Someone who infringes on the rights of others does wrong and deserves blame for his conduct. It is because he deserves blame that the sanctioning authority is entitled to choose a response that expresses moral disapproval; namely punishment." But advocates of this model left a key question unanswered: What effect will a justice model of punishment have on corrections systems in the United States?

Looking Forward

This section shows that corrections practice is dynamic and evolving over time in response to various social forces. In some respects, the field of American corrections seems to be looking for the "next big thing." As we noted in the previous chapter, there has been a gradual softening in the "get-tough-on-crime" practices as between 2007 and 2018, and 35 states amended their sentencing and corrections policies to reduce correctional populations and some of them have invested those savings in community-based programs (Pew Charitable Trusts, 2018). The passage of the *First Step Act* in December 2018, described in Chapter 1, also serves as an indicator of federal prison reform. There has also been a growing interest in using evidence-based practices (programs that have been validated by research to reduce recidivism) to increase correctional intervention effectiveness. Altogether, these changes have resulted in a slow decrease in imprisonment rates since their peak in 2007 (Bronson & Carson, 2019).

Five Pioneers in American Corrections

A CLOSER LOOK

Benjamin Rush and John Howard were not the only corrections pioneers and some of the first US wardens along with social activists, reformers, religious officials, and scholars of the era made important contributions when penitentiaries were first being established throughout the nation. For the most part these individuals maintained that the penitentiaries were failing to provide humane care for prisoners and had difficulty in rehabilitating them. The following briefly highlights the contributions of five of these reformers:

- Zebulon Brockway (1827–1920) started his correctional career at age 21 as a prison guard and for the next 50 years he worked in facilities in three states, but his best-known role was the superintendent of the Elmira, NY reformatory, a 500-bed facility that specialized in reforming first-time offenders. During his time at Elmira he developed a system where inmates could earn early releases based on receiving positive "marks" for participating in rehabilitative or work programs. This reformatory model was adopted by nearly half of the states by the 1930s.

- Dorothea Dix (1802–1887) became an advocate for prisoners after witnessing conditions in a Massachusetts prison where she worked as an educator. After visiting jails and prisons throughout the country she authored reports criticizing the poor care and the violent conditions in these places. Dix was especially concerned with the plight of persons with mental illnesses in correctional facilities and she advocated for the establishment of separate asylums for them.

- Theodore Dwight (1822–1892) had an early interest in prison reform and published annual reports about the state of prisons as a college student. Dwight eventually became a law professor, and he accompanied Enoch Wines on a tour of North American prison facilities and co-authored the 1867 report entitled *A Report on Prisons in the United States and Canada*. This report highlighted the administrative corruption and prisoner abuse occurring in these facilities. The report called for educational, religious, and work programs that would lead to a prisoner's rehabilitation.

- Abigail Hopper Gibbons (1801–1893) was a social activist who opposed slavery and advocated for women's rights although she is best known for founding the Women's Prison Association (WPA) of New York City in 1845. This Association also established the world's first half way house for women prisoners returning to the community. In her work with the WPA, she toured New York correctional facilities and used her insight from these experiences to lobby the state government to hire matrons to work with women prisoners and establish women-only prisons.

- Enoch Wines (1806–1879) was an educator and a Christian minister who became a prison reformer. Wines opposed the harsh treatment of prisoners and believed in the power of religious training and hard work as keys to an individual's success. He advocated for rewarding an inmate's positive steps toward rehabilitation and restricting the use of harsh punishments for those who failed. Wines helped organized the Cincinnati meeting of the National Prison Association in 1870, a conference that introduced the modern penal reform movement in America.

These reformers approached the problems confronting 1800s era prisons by pointing out the shortcomings of these institutions and lobbying legislators to make improvements. Meskell (1999, p. 864) observes that many prison reformers are successful in instituting some positive changes, but it is very difficult to maintain reforms over the long-term as institutions revert to their familiar operations, much like someone who finds it hard to keep a new year's resolution.

SUMMARY

The idea that those who break community rules must pay a debt to society is as old as civilization. In some ways the community's responses have changed dramatically over the past 3,000 years; in other ways, we have not progressed very far in the search for appropriate penalties for lawbreakers. Some of the key points presented in this chapter include the following:

- The punishment philosophies that exist in the United States today have been influenced by practices that date back to the Code of Hammurabi and the Law of Moses.
- The Greeks and Romans laid the groundwork for what can be considered contemporary attitudes and practices toward corrections.
- The political and social philosophers from the Age of Enlightenment advocated that punishments should be swift, certain, and proportionate.
- The nation's focus on punitive measures for criminals regardless of type of crime or history of the offender has generated new laws and changes in sentencing policies that have resulted in unprecedented crowding in both jails and prisons—called mass imprisonment.
- Local jails in America closely resembled the English gaols as ideas of corrections were imported from England by the colonists.
- While the Auburn and **Pennsylvania** systems competed for dominance in penitentiary operations, the Southern states embraced the convict leasing system to reduce costs.
- American prison reformers advocated for better living conditions for inmates and increasing their access to rehabilitative opportunities.

- There was a significant movement away from rehabilitation and the medical model of corrections in the 1970s. While incapacitation has been the dominant correctional philosophy since the 1970s there seems to be more optimism for correctional rehabilitation and evidence-based practices.

Throughout history there was a gradual softening of using harsh physical punishments that were replaced by incarceration. Even when it comes to imprisonment sentences in most nations have become shorter and more rehabilitative. Although the United States still uses harsh sentences for non-violent offenses, there seems to be a move to reduce the severity of those punishments.

KEY TERMS

- Age of Enlightenment
- Amputations (mutilations)
- Auburn system
- botes
- branding
- breaking at the wheel
- bridewells
- building tenders
- burning alive
- canon law
- chain gang
- civil law
- Code of Hammurabi
- common law
- convict leasing
- draconian
- dunking stools
- fee system
- galley slavery
- gaol
- hulks
- informal social control
- just deserts
- justice model
- keeper
- Law of Moses
- *lex salica*
- lockstep shuffle
- medical model
- natural law
- norms
- penal tourism
- Penitentiary Act of 1779
- Pennsylvania system
- pillories
- plantation style prisons
- pressing
- rehabilitative ideal
- running the gauntlet
- stocks
- stoning
- transportation
- trustees
- twelve tables
- wergild
- whipping (flogging)
- wites

THINKING ABOUT CORRECTIONAL PRACTICES AND POLICIES: WRITING ASSIGNMENTS

1. "Law and punishment were far fairer before the invention of written laws." Attack or defend this statement.
2. Summarize the contributions of the Age of Enlightenment to modern theories of crime and punishment.
3. Develop a chart comparing the Pennsylvania and Auburn prison systems. What are the strengths and weaknesses of each approach? Was the Pennsylvania system doomed from the start? Why or why not?
4. Write a brief essay on the differences between the medical and just deserts models.
5. Briefly review punishment history in Europe and the United States. What themes can you identify from the various sanctions that were used? Look to the future. What do you think lies ahead given this brief history of punishments and corrections?

CRITICAL REVIEW QUESTIONS

1. The goal of early punishments was to restore balance in the community. To that end, social groups relied primarily on reconciliation rituals and restitution. To what extent was this goal similar to or different from the goals of restorative justice? Would these rituals work today: Why or why not?
2. The Code of Hammurabi and the Law of Moses have both been described as examples of *lex talionis*. How are they similar? How do they differ?
3. Did the ancient Greeks and Romans place a value on human life? In this sense, how were the laws in these societies different from the laws in earlier societies?
4. "Feudal law favored the rich and powerful." Is this statement accurate? Explain your answer.
5. Who are the voices of prison reform today?
6. While corporal punishments were eliminated in prisons school children are still subject to corporal punishment in 19 states, and over 100,000 youths received these punishments in 2013–2014 (U.S. Department of Education Civil Rights Data Collection, 2017). Discuss why corporal punishments are suitable for children but not adults?

7. Provide some reasons why punishment in Southern states evolved differently than what occurred in the Northeastern states.
8. Why did the colonists import approaches such as jails that were already recognized as failing institutions from England?
9. Can you think of some economic, social, and political reasons that led to the creation of prisons?
10. What do history's lessons tell us about our current and future approaches to "correcting" the behaviors of criminals?

CASE

Ruiz v. Estelle, 503 F. Supp. 1265 (S.D. Tex. 1980)

REFERENCES

Allen, J. R. (2018). Elmira prisoner of war camp. *The Civil War*. Retrieved from http://www.nella-ware.com/blog/elmira-prisoner-of-war-camp.html

American Friends Service Committee. (1971). *Struggle for justice*. New York: Hill & Wang.

Amnesty International. (2018a). *Death sentences and executions, 2017*. London, UK: Author.

Amnesty International. (2018b). *The state of the world's human rights*. London, UK: Author.

Ayers, E. L. (1984). *Vengeance and justice: Crime and punishment in the 19th-century American south*. New York: Oxford University Press.

Banks, C. (2005). *Punishment in America: A reference handbook*. Santa Barbara, CA: ABC-CLIO.

BobBarker. (2020). *Prison Uniforms*. Retrieved from https://www.bobbarker.com/products/uniforms/jumpsuits.html

Bronson, J., & Carson, E. A. (2019). *Prisoners in 2017*. Washington, DC: Bureau of Justice Statistics.

Casey, R. (1954). Catchall jails. *Annals of the American Academy of Political and Social Political and Social Science, 193*, 28–34.

Dickens, C. (1842). *American notes*. London, UK: Chapman and Hall.

Domonoske, C. (2018, Mar. 14). Alabama sheriff legally took $750,000 meant to feed inmates, bought beach house. *National Public Radio*. Retrieved from https://www.npr.org/sections/thetwo-way/2018/03/14/593204274/alabama-sheriff-legally-took-750-000-meant-to-feed-inmates-bought-beach-house

Eaton, M. (1916). Punitive pain and humiliation. *Journal of Criminal Law and Criminology, 6*(6) 894–907.

Edgerton, R. (1976). *Deviance: A cross-cultural perspective*. Menlo Park, CA: Cummings.

Fishman, J. F. (1923). *Crucibles of crime: The shocking story of the American jail*. Montclair, NJ: Patterson Smith.

Fogel, D. (1975). *We are the living proof: The justice model for corrections*. Cincinnati, OH: Anderson.

France, A. (1894). *The red lily*. New York: The Macauley Company

Garnsey, P. (1968). Why penalties become harsher: The Roman case, late republic to fourth century empire; Note. *Natural Law Forum, 13,*141–162. Gibbons, D. C. (1996). Pennsylvania system. In M. D. McShane & F. P. Williams (Eds.), *Encyclopedia of American prisons* (pp. 351–352). New York: Garland.

Gibbon, E. (1932). *The decline and fall of the Roman Empire.* New York: Modern Library.

Gillispie, J. M. (2008). *Andersonvilles of the North: The myths and realities of Northern treatment of civil war confederate prisoners.* Denton: University of North Texas Press.

Goodman, P., Page, J., & Phelps, M. (2017). *Breaking the pendulum: The long struggle over criminal justice.* New York: Oxford University Press.

Green, W. M. (1929). An ancient debate on capital punishment. *The Classical Journal, 24*(4), 267–275.

Greenberg, D. (1975). The effectiveness of law enforcement in eighteenth-century New York. *The American Journal of Legal History, 19*(3), 173–207. Hanawalt, B. A. (1974). Economic influences on the pattern of crime in England, 1300–1348. *The American Journal of Legal History, 18*(4), 281–297.

Haney, C. (2018). The psychological effects of solitary confinement: A systematic critique. *Crime and Justice, 47*(1), 365–416.

Hubbard, B. (2019, April 19). Saudi Arabia executes 37 in one day for terrorism. *The New York Times.* Retrieved from https://www.nytimes.com/2019/04/23/world/middleeast/saudi-arabia-executions.html

Kearney, G. (2006). Shock factor is an effective learning tool, despite being gruesome. *Australian Nursing Journal, 14*(2), 40–45.

Kerle, K. (1998). *American jails: Looking to the future.* Woburn, MA: Butterworth-Heinemann.

Kinsella, N. (1933). County jails and the federal government. *Journal of Criminal Law and Criminology, 24*(Summer), 428–439.

Langbein, J. H. (2006). *Torture and the law of proof.* Chicago: University of Chicago Press.

Legislative Analyst's Office. (2018). *California's annual costs to incarcerate an inmate in prison.* Retrieved from https://lao.ca.gov/policyareas/cj/6_cj_inmatecost

Mancini, M.J. (1996). *One dies, get another: Convict leasing in the American south, 1866–1928.* Columbia: University of South Carolina.

Martinson, R. (1974). What works? Questions and answers about prison reform. *Public Interest, 35*(1), 22–54.

McConville, S. (1998). Local justice. In N. Morris & D. J. Rothman (Eds.), *The Oxford history of the prison* (pp. 44–70). New York: Oxford University Press.

Meskell, M. W. (1999). An American resolution: The history of prisons in the United States from 1777 to 1877. *Stanford Law Review, 51*(4), 839–865.

Morris, N. (1974). *The future of imprisonment.* Chicago: University of Chicago Press.

Moynahan, J. M., & Stewart, E. K. (1980). *The American jail, its development and growth.* Chicago, IL: Nelson-Hall.

Oshinsky, D. M. (1996). *Worse than slavery: Parchman farm and the ordeal of Jim Crow justice.* New York: Free Press.

Oshinsky, D. M. (2004, Oct. 23). *Forced labor in the 19th century South: The story of the Parchman farm: From chattel bondage to state servitude.* Presentation made at the Gilder Lehrman Center for the Study of Slavery, Resistance, and Abolition Slavery in the 20th century meetings. New Haven, CT: Yale University.

Peters, E. M. (1998). Prison before the prison. In N. Morris & D. J. Rothman (Eds.) *The Oxford history of the prison* (pp. 3–43). New York: Oxford University Press.

Pew Charitable Trusts. (2018). *35 states reform criminal justice policies through justice reinvestment.* Retrieved from https://www.pewtrusts.org/-/media/assets/2018/07/pspp_reform_matrix.pdf

Pfohl, S. J. (1981). Labeling criminals. In H. L. Ross (Ed.), *Law and deviance* (pp. 65– 97). Beverly Hills, CA: Sage.

Pitzulo, C. (2017). The skirted sheriff: Florence Thompson and the nation's last public execution. *Register of the Kentucky Historical Society, 115*(3), 377–410.

Pugh, R. B. (1968). *Imprisonment in medieval England.* Cambridge, MA: Cambridge University Press.

Riley, K. (2018, June 15). Neither inmates nor counties get out of jail free. *Mackinac Center for Public Policy.* Retrieved from https://www.mackinac.org/neither-inmates-nor-counties-get-out-of-jail-free

Ruddell, R., & Jones, N. A. (2017). Cross-national imprisonment. In K. R. Kerley, H. Copes, S. Li, J. Lane, & Sharpe, S. (Eds.), *The encyclopedia of corrections* (pp. 169–176). New York: Wiley Blackwell.

Santo, Y., Kim, V., & Flagg, A. (2017, March 9). Upgrade your jail cell – For a price. *Los Angeles Times.* Retrieved from https://www.latimes.com/projects/la-me-pay-to-stay-jails/

Sellin, T. (1933). A quarter century's progress in penal institutions for adults in the United States. *Journal of the American Institute of Criminal Law and Criminology, 24*(1), 140–160.

Sentencing Project. (2013). *Report of the Sentencing Project to the United Nations Human Rights Committee regarding racial disparities in the United States criminal justice system.* Washington, DC: Author.

Spierenburg, P. (1998). The body and the state. In N. Morris & D. J. Rothman (Eds.), *The Oxford history of the prison* (pp. 44–70). New York: Oxford University Press.

Stearns, A. W. (1936). The evolution of punishment. *Journal of Criminal Law and Criminology, 27*(2), 219–230.

U.S. Department of Education Civil Rights Data Collection. (2017). *Corporal punishment, national estimates 2013–2014.* Retrieved from https://ocrdata.ed.gov/StateNationalEstimations/Estimations_2013_14

von Hirsch, A. (1976). *Doing justice.* New York: Hill & Wang.

Wilson, J. Z., Hodgkinson, S., Piche, J., & Walby, K. (2017). Introduction: Penal tourism in context. In J. Z. Wilson, S. Hodgkinson, J. Piche, & K. Walby (Eds.), *The Palgrave handbook of prison tourism* (pp. 1–12). New York: Palgrave Macmillan.

Chapter 3
Sentencing and Criminal Sanctions

OUTLINE

OBJECTIVES

After reading this chapter you will able to:

- Describe how the criminal law affects corrections

- Explain the people, agencies, and organizations involved in sentencing

- Describe the range of sentencing options

- Explain the differences between felony and misdemeanor sanctions

- Explain why mass imprisonment has occurred

CASE STUDY

A Pennsylvania Judge Is Sentenced to 28 Years behind Bars

In August 2011, former juvenile court Judge Mark Ciavarella was sentenced in a Pennsylvania court to a 28-year federal imprisonment term after he and another judge were convicted of taking several million dollars in bribes to place juveniles appearing before their courts in privately operated detention facilities. The operators of these facilities, who paid the bribes, earned greater profits when they housed more youths. Many of the youths who were incarcerated had committed relatively minor acts, such as vandalism, and their placement in custody was seldom proportionate to their misdeeds. In his book entitled *Kids for Cash*, Ecenbarger (2012, p. 11) describes the case of Charlie, a 15-year-old whose parents bought him a used motorcycle for $50. Several weeks after the purchase police officers told the family the motorcycle was stolen and arrested all three; the charges were eventually dropped for the parents. Charlie, by contrast, was required to appear before the juvenile court for the felony charge of receiving stolen merchandise. At his court appearance he was given an **indeterminate sentence** and he served several months before his first release, although after that experience he had difficulty getting his life on-track, and he served a total of almost three years in juvenile facilities.

Charlie's case was not unusual, as noted by the Juvenile Law Center (2018, para. 5):

> From 2003 to 2008, the Luzerne County judicial corruption scandal altered the lives of more than 2500 children and involved more than 6000 cases. Over 50 percent of the children who appeared before Ciavarella lacked legal representation; 60 percent of these children were removed from their homes. Many of them were sent to one or both of the two facilities at the center of the corruption scandal.

Incarcerating these youths had a range of negative impacts on their lives including labeling them as delinquent, removing them from their families, interrupting their progress in school, and exposing them to the abuse that often occurs in juvenile facilities. Placement in custody, whether warranted or not, also harms future employment and educational opportunities. Some of these youths are alleged to have committed suicide after their release from custody.

One of the factors that is difficult to understand about this case is that the court workers, probation staff, defense attorneys, and law enforcement agencies knew that the treatment of these youths was wildly out of proportion to the acts they were committing. In Ciavarella's courtroom, incarceration was the first option for youths, rather than the last resort, which is the norm in most juvenile courts. While these officials were aware of the treatment of these youths, nobody spoke up, and lawyers from the Juvenile Law Center became involved in the case after receiving calls from worried parents.

Ultimately, four adults were sentenced to prison for their roles in this corruption. The families of the youths involved in this case launched a class-action lawsuit and almost $18 million was paid to 3,000 youths. With respect to their status in the legal system, Schuppe (2015) reports that several thousand convictions were tossed out. Like many other high-profile cases reported throughout this book, this case continues to make the news and in 2018 a federal court overturned several of Ciavarella's convictions, and in 2020 federal prosecutors announced that they would not retry his case, which might result in his early release (Halpin, 2020).

Critical Questions

1. Why did the court staff or members of the local legal community fail to report or publicize the unjust treatment of these youths?
2. Discuss why we expect juveniles who are less mature and have fewer options than adults to be deterred from engaging in crime by the prospect of harsh punishments, but the prospect of prison did not deter these well-educated juvenile court judges?
3. How would a one-month placement in a juvenile facility, when you were 14 or 15 years old, have affected your family life, relationships with friends, education, and work prospects?

INTRODUCTION

The sentencing process embodies several social goals. These goals correspond in large measure to the punishment philosophies described in the opening chapter: deterrence, incapacitation, rehabilitation, reintegration, restitution, and retribution. In some states, we can find those specific terms in the criminal codes. Sentencing also reflects other factors that judges, legislators, and the general public consider important. For example, many people may believe in proportionality—where the punishment reflects the seriousness of the crime—and equity, when offenders with similar histories and current offenses should be treated more or less equally (Tonry, 2020). Phrased another way, most of us believe that individuals who are sentenced for committing a crime, and who have similar criminal records should receive about the same sentence no matter where they live in a state, and regardless of their age, class, race, or gender. While this goal sounds simple on paper, it is difficult to achieve in the real world.

The statement that a person is innocent until proven guilty means that the state must prove guilt and that the defendant need not prove innocence. This **presumption of innocence** is the foundation of the common law justice system and it requires that juries only consider the evidence in their deliberations. In an adversarial system, the prosecution bears the burden of proof in criminal cases and must demonstrate a level of evidence sufficient to result in a conviction. In civil cases in the United States, juries are instructed to base their verdicts on the preponderance of the evidence. Although this term does not have a precise meaning, it is generally understood to mean that a verdict should be based on the amount of evidence necessary to "tip" the case in favor of one party over the other.

In criminal cases, by contrast, a verdict must be based on evidence sufficient to prove the defendant's guilt beyond a reasonable doubt. Again, one of the problems is this term does not have a precise definition (Pi, Parisi, & Luppi, 2018). The U.S. Department of Justice (2019a) provides us with a working definition, which is "The idea that the evidence in a criminal trial must show that the defendant is guilty to the point that the jury is convinced and morally certain that the defendant did commit the crime." Yet, despite what we watch on television, jury trials in the United States are relatively rare, and about 98% of the guilty outcomes in felony cases and 99% of misdemeanor cases in the nation's 75 largest counties were the result of plea bargains (Reaves, 2013, p. 24). Conrad and Clements (2018) say that the decreasing numbers of trials has been occurring since the early 2000s and they are rare in the federal courts.

Sentencing is a key factor in understanding what happens to individuals as they flow through the criminal justice system, and why the United States became so reliant on using imprisonment as a crime-reduction strategy. Throughout this chapter we take a closer look at who wins and who loses when sentences are imposed. Last, we also consider the use of the death penalty, a punishment that is popular with the public but is rarely imposed today.

SENTENCING

Explaining the mechanics behind mass imprisonment is relatively simple: we increased incarceration rates by placing more people in jail or prison, and are holding them for longer periods of time. Policymakers supported this practice because they wanted to get tough on crime, and they didn't have much faith in correctional systems to rehabilitate offenders. As a result, there was a shift to practices based on incapacitation, retribution, and deterrence. The public generally supported this approach as the messages they received from politicians and the media were that crime was rising and drastic steps had to be taken. The result of these practices was that the United States now has the highest rates of incarceration and probation in the world and is one of the few wealthy nations still using capital punishment.

As we observe throughout this book, correctional officials generally have very little say in these policy discussions. Local jailers, state prison officials, and federal administrators are often reacting to the activities of law enforcement and courts. As a result, when national politicians decide to declare a "war on drugs" by incarcerating a larger number of low-level drug offenders, correctional officials must respond to a growing number of new admissions to community corrections, jails, and prisons. That challenge can become overwhelming when there is not a corresponding increase in funding for these agencies. America's imprisonment binge has led to under-staffed, overcrowded, and under-funded jails and prisons. The stress on probation and parole agencies, and the health, educational, and social service agencies that support their operations has also occurred because of these increasing demands.

In the following section, we describe who has the power when it comes to making sentencing decisions. When reading through this section, it is useful to remember that most sentencing decisions are made by local politicians (prosecutors) who advocate for punishments that are paid for by all the state's taxpayers. There are both positive and negative impacts about this arrangement. For instance, it is important that local justice systems can respond to specific offenses that might be threatening to their community; an example might be armed robberies resulting in violence. As a result, punishments for people engaging in these crimes might be more severe in one city than the rest of the state. Consequently, there will always be some variation in sentencing within a state. By contrast, there are significant implications when prosecutors, who are local politicians, can wage wars on crime at no cost to the local taxpayers as the state pays for all the prison costs.

Sentencing: Who Decides?

Most people are not familiar with the sentencing process for those convicted of a crime. Even if a trial has been well-publicized, sentencing often takes place after the adjudication is completed and the public's fascination with the trial has faded. Once the press reports that an individual has been convicted, media attention typically focuses elsewhere. Three elements of the sentencing process are a key to understanding that process: the decision-makers, the decisions available to them, and the decision-making process itself. In this section, we consider the first of these elements and they are the individuals who decide. There are four sets of decision-makers who influence sentencing outcomes: Lawmakers define crimes, and in the process, appropriate penalties; prosecutors determine whether cases will proceed, the charges an individual will face, and will plea bargain over 95% of cases; juries or (in some cases called bench trials) judges, will decide a defendant's guilt; and judges impose sentences.

The Role of Lawmakers

Congress and each of the 50 state legislatures have the power to make **substantive law**, to define those behaviors that constitute crimes in the jurisdiction under their control. Legislatures also determine by statute, and courts add by case law, the laws of criminal procedure. Unlike substantive law, which defines criminal behavior, **procedural law** governs the arrest, prosecution, and trial of criminal offenders.

All crimes are not equal: some are more serious than others. At the most basic level we divide offenses into misdemeanors and felonies. States do not define crimes in the same way, but **misdemeanors** are always the least serious and felonies the more serious offenses. The U.S. Department of Justice (2019b) defines the former as "usually a petty offense, a less serious crime than a felony, punishable by less than a year of confinement." Felonies, by contrast, may prescribe sentences of one year or more, including life in prison or the death penalty. Substantial fines also may be imposed. Although there are some exceptions, individuals incarcerated for committing felonies serve their sentences in state or federal prisons, while those incarcerated for misdemeanors typically serve their sentences in county jails.

States can further differentiate degrees of seriousness within the misdemeanor and felony categories. For instance, some jurisdictions have a classification for infractions or violations. These offenses are often labeled **petty misdemeanors**, the least-serious crimes. The usual penalty for petty misdemeanors is a fine. Most states also distinguish among degrees (first, second, third) or classes of felonies (A or B, or I or II). A first-class felony or a Class A or I felony is more serious than the other degrees or classes.

Beginning in the 1980s, federal and state legislators introduced a series of legislative changes to get tough on crime with the intention of imposing harsher sanctions and imprisoning offenders for longer periods of time, and they include:

- *Mandatory minimum sentences*: Impose a sentence that specifies a minimum penalty for a crime; for example, there is a five-year mandatory prison sentence for individuals guilty of using a firearm in a federal crime of violence or drug trafficking crime (U.S. Sentencing Commission, 2018, p. 8). State and federal legislators developed these laws to minimize the discretion that judges had when imposing a sentence.
- *Three-strike laws*: Impose a lengthy sentence, such as 25 years to life in prison, for offenders convicted of serious and repeat offending. Although it was possible to impose severe sentences for habitual offenders a century ago, these laws became very popular in the 1990s, but have fallen out of favor.
- *Truth in sentencing*: Ensure that inmates serve a significant portion of their prison term prior to their release, typically 85% of their sentence. The federal government created a financial incentive for states adopting these practices for violent offenders in the 1994 *Violent Crime Control and Law Enforcement Act*, and over one-half of the states adopted these policies.

States adopted other practices to get tough on crime including making it more difficult for prisoners to earn their parole. In summary, lawmakers are responsible for defining criminal conduct, defining substantive law, and defining the procedural rules that govern the criminal trial process. One component of that task is deciding the nature and the severity of sentences. Another is deciding whether sentences are indeterminate or determinate.

The Role of Prosecutors

Prosecutors are the most powerful individuals in the criminal justice system and their role in determining the number and severity of charges a defendant faces in court has been identified as a key driver in high US imprisonment rates. According to the Brennan Center for Justice (2018, p. 3):

> Prosecutors wield enormous influence at every stage of the criminal process, from initial charging decision to the sentences sought and imposed. Along the way, they often control decisions about plea bargains and whether mandatory minimum sentences will be triggered, and thus greatly impact whether (and for how long) defendants remain in jail or prison.

Only a very small proportion of defendants proceed to trial and over 95% of cases result from plea agreements. There are several features about the role of prosecutors that deserve a brief review.

First, there are about 2,400 US counties where prosecutors are the key law enforcement official and the district attorney is an elected politician. For the most part, these prosecutors are only accountable to the electorate and most of the time when they stand for election, they often run unopposed. When there are opponents, a key issue in these races is that each candidate frequently campaigns on being tough on crime and once elected, they must maintain that tough on crime image or they will lose their job. We saw a change in this practice in 2018 and 2019 as reformist prosecutors throughout the country were elected in large cities such as Chicago, Houston, Orlando, and St. Louis—as well as smaller communities throughout the nation—after promising to eliminate or ease prosecutions for some drug and non-violent offenders, making it easier for some non-violent individuals to obtain bail, or reducing incarceration rates by sending fewer individuals to jail or prison (Lavoie, 2018). These reformist district attorneys are attracting attention as they are now introducing

PHOTO 3.1
Bail is a pre-trial option for some but not all defendants. From right, Charles Archuleta, a bail bondsman, sits with Nicholas Miramontes, a defendant, as they talk with attorney Mike Jones in First District Court in Santa Fe, NM. At left, Jon Fisher, a probation officer, is the lead officer in the First District's Pre-Trial Services. Credit: Eddie Moor/Albuquerque Journal via ZUMA/Alamy Stock Photo.

these policies. While some of these changes are supported by the public, police asso-ciations and the prosecutors already working in these offices are generally opposed to such reforms. Some assistant prosecutors have quit their jobs to show their opposition to these changes.

Second, prosecutors can act with very little transparency and most of their decisions to proceed with an indictment, on how a defendant is charged, or how they will proceed with a plea negotiation are largely hidden from the public. Pfaff (2017) contends that these factors make it easy for prosecutors to wage their own wars on crime with very little oversight, as highlighted in the following box.

Prosecutors and Imprisonment

In a high-profile story in the *New York Times*, Keller and Pearce (2016) describe how Dearborn County, Indiana—with a population of about 50,000 residents—sends more individuals to prison than San Francisco, California and Durham, North Car-olina and those cities have a combined population of almost 1.2 million people. They find that sentences for relatively minor offenses in this county such as drug possession are punished as harshly as murder sentences in larger cities. Table 3.1 shows examples of the sentences meted out to three Dearborn county offenders. We do have to interpret these three sentences carefully as they do not report their prior criminal histories or any aggravating factors (Eagle Country, 2016).

TABLE 3.1 Sentence Comparisons from Dearborn County Indiana and Selected Cities

Individual (Age)	Scott H. (36 years)	Dakota F. (22 years)	Donnie G. (41 years)
Offense	Sold 6.8 grams of heroin	Admitted to 10 burglaries	Sold 15 oxycodone pills
Likely sentence in Brooklyn	0–3 years	4–7 years	Drug treatment
Likely sentence in Cincinnati	2–5 years	4–5 years	Up to 6 months
Likely sentence in San Francisco	0–3 years	2–4 years	Drug treatment
Actual sentence in Dearborn County	35 years	31.5 years	12 years

Source: Keller and Pearce (2016).

These reporters contend that the local prosecutor's war on crimes has created an imprisonment binge and quote Aaron Negangard, the former Dearborn-Ohio County prosecutor, as saying:

> I am proud of the fact that we send more people to jail than other counties. That's how we keep it safe here....My constituents are the people who decide whether I keep doing my job. The governor can't make me. The legislature can't make me.

Negangard's comments tell us a lot about the political independence of local prosecutors and when they decide to get tough on crime, there are few limits on their powers. When considering the actions of these prosecutors, however, we must consider that state taxpayers are left with the bill for the high imprisonment rates in Dearborn-Ohio County. As for Mr. Negangard: he was the District Attorney for Dearborn-Ohio County from 2006 to 2016 and then was appointed as Chief Deputy for the Indiana Attorney General. Figure 3.1 shows the changes in new prison admissions from that county between 2005 and 2018, and this figure reveals that after Negangard departed there was a substantial decrease in prison admissions (Indiana Department of Corrections, 2019). This example shows how one prosecutor can have a significant impact on an entire correctional system.

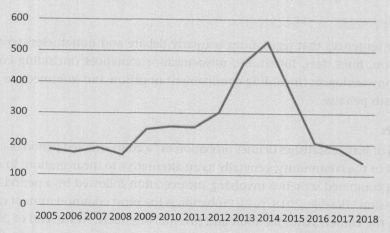

FIGURE 3.1
Dearborn County New Prison Admissions, 2005–2018.
Source: Indiana Department of Corrections (2019).

The Role of Juries

As noted earlier, jury trials have become rare events, although the cases they hear tend to be the most serious felonies such as homicides. As the "trier of facts" the jury is responsible for deciding who is telling the truth, what evidence means, and eventually, whether the defendant is guilty. Given the presumption of innocence, the jury decides whether the state has produced enough evidence to prove guilt beyond a reasonable doubt. In most criminal cases, the jury's responsibilities have been discharged once it decides that the defendant is innocent or guilty. However, under certain circumstances—particularly in death penalty cases—the jury, rather than the judge, decides the sentence.

The Role of Judges

The jury is the trier of facts and the judge is the "trier of the law." The judge rules on trial procedures and evidence and decides what instructions will be given to the jury. In bench trials, the judge serves as both trier of fact and trier of law.

In most criminal cases, once a verdict is reached the judge requests a presentence investigation report and sets a date for sentencing. The judge is also responsible for imposing a sentence on the convicted offender. There is an important distinction here: lawmakers define crimes and, in the process, appropriate penalties: judges impose sentences, but lawmakers decide what sentences can be imposed. Ultimately, however, the prosecutor determines the charges for the individual, and in the case of mandatory minimum sentencing, the judge's hands are tied when it comes to imposing a minimum sentence.

SENTENCING OPTIONS

Among the sentences that legislatures regularly debate and nonetheless write into law are probation, fines, fees, forfeitures, misdemeanor sentences (including confinement in jail), felony sentences (including confinement in prison and intermediate sanctions), and the death penalty.

Probation

The Bureau of Justice Statistics defines probation as "a court-ordered period of correctional supervision in the community, generally as an alternative to incarceration. In some cases, it may be a combined sentence involving incarceration followed by a period of community supervision" (Kaeble, 2018, p. 2). Probation is the most common form of criminal disposition in the United States for adult and juvenile offenders. At the end of 2016, almost 3.8 of the 6.7 million people under correctional supervision (55.5%) were on probation (Kaeble & Cowhig, 2018, p. 2). Several facts about probation are important to remember:

- *Probation is a sentence.* Although probation, in some rare instances and with the accused's written consent, can be imposed on alleged violators, virtually everyone who is sentenced to probation has pleaded or been found guilty. The fact that probation is a sentence means that the court has continuing jurisdiction over probationers.

- *Probation is a judicial function.* It is imposed and supervised by a judge.
- The probation department, including the officers who work directly with probationers, can be a part of the local court or executive agency at the state level. In either case, probation officers must work closely with the sentencing judges. This is especially true in the preparation and presentation of presentence investigation reports.
- *Probation is imposed in lieu of incarceration.* It offers offenders a chance to remain in the community instead of serving a custody sentence.
- *Probation is conditional.* This means that the probationer's continued freedom depends on his or her meeting the terms of probation.

That so many individuals today are on probation is a by-product of the get-tough-on-crime agenda that dates back to the late 1970s and early 1980s. We are sending more people to jails and prisons and despite a building boom in prison facilities we simply do not have enough bed space for all the country's convicted offenders. The result? There are more people on probation and more of them have committed serious offenses: on 31 December 2016, almost three in five had been convicted of a felony and one in five (20%) had committed a violent offense (Kaeble, 2018, p. 9).

With the changing makeup of the probationer population have come new, tougher probation conditions. For instance, a growing number of states use house arrest and electronic monitoring devices to track probationers' movements (Pew Charitable Trusts, 2016). House arrest, with or without electronic monitoring, is designed to keep probationers off the street. The idea behind house arrest is that by confining individuals to their homes, they will be less tempted and will have fewer opportunities to commit new crimes. Although effectiveness of house arrest continues to be debated, researchers have found that the benefits are likely to exceed the costs in more than nine out of ten cases (Washington State Institute of Public Policy, 2019) and recidivism rates for adult offenders decrease when used after a release from custody (Bouchard & Wong, 2018).

Given the generally favorable results of electronic monitoring and house arrest programs, some judges have turned to these interventions with increased frequency, and the Pew Charitable Trusts (2016) estimates about 125,000 individuals are being monitored. For many, house arrest has become more an add-on to probation than an alternative to incarceration. Although these programs can be successful, they are controversial in that adult probationers are often required to pay for the monitoring costs and about one-third of these devices require a telephone with a landline: costs range from $5 to $25 per day which puts this out of reach for many of the poor (Kilgore & Sanders, 2018) (Chapter 4 provides a more in-depth discussion of this issue). More controversial is the practice of requiring probationers to pay for their supervision and Human Rights Watch (2018) calls this practice a war on the poor.

Another condition imposed on probationers is restitution, the court-ordered payment of money or services to the victim. In 2006, restitution was ordered for 18% of the felons convicted in state courts and most of them had committed property crimes (Rosenmerkel, Durose, & Farole, 2009). Forcing probationers to make monetary payments to their victims creates several problems:

- It is easy for a judge to order that restitution be paid as part of a probated sentence, but the mechanics of collecting the money are another matter. In most jurisdictions, responsibility for collecting restitution falls largely to overburdened probation officers.
- A restitution order presumes some ability to pay. Probationers are often unemployed or underemployed and simply do not have the money to meet the restitution conditions.
- Finally, some still question the purpose of restitution. Although advocates believe the practice increases offenders' accountability and victims' satisfaction, cause and effect are not always obvious. This has led critics to argue that restitution is simply another probation add-on.

Restitution can also take the form of court-ordered community service. Judges ordered 11% of the felons convicted in state courts to perform community service in addition to any other sentence they received (Rosenmerkel et al., 2009). Supervision is a problem here also, and the effectiveness of the practice is questionable.

Fines

Fines have been used as sanctions for over 2,000 years, and they have been rediscovered as governments at all levels are increasingly cash-strapped and require new forms of revenue to maintain their operations. The most common form of fines today is for traffic offenses. In most states, people charged with motor vehicle violations are subject to a fine and court costs. But the use of fines has been expanding, and in some places the revenue from these tickets is used to fund local governments. After the shooting of Michael Brown in Ferguson, Missouri in 2014, a U.S. Department of Justice (2015, p. 2) report found that the police department was organized around issuing tickets and collecting fines; moreover:

> This emphasis on revenue has compromised the institutional character of Ferguson's police department, contributing to a pattern of unconstitutional policing, and has also shaped its municipal court, leading to procedures that raise due process concerns and inflict unnecessary harm on members of the Ferguson community.

What happened in Ferguson is not an isolated incident and continues as many local governments throughout the country rely on revenue from fines. This practice is hardest on the poor, and when they fail to pay their fines, they are sometimes incarcerated. Jackson City, Tennessee reporters found that over one-third (35%) of fines cases resulted in an arrest warrant when the individual failed to appear in court (Stephenson, 2018). This impacts local corrections as some of these individuals are eventually jailed.

Some individuals are placed on **pay only probation**, which means that their only condition of probation is paying their fines or court costs, and if they were able to pay their fines, they would not be on probation. Judges place these individuals on probation as the likelihood of getting this revenue is increased. The poor are disadvantaged in these arrangements and Human Rights Watch (2014, p. 28) provides a hypothetical example of three persons ordered to pay a $1,200 fine:

- The first person pays the $1,200 fine on the day of the hearing and she goes home without any further obligations and she is not placed on probation.
- The second person can afford to make monthly payments of $335. She will pay off her fines and leave probation after four months, having paid $140 in supervision fees and $1,340 in total.
- The third person can only afford to pay $85 per month. She will leave probation after 24 months, having paid $840 in supervision fees and $2,040 in total.

As the third person does not have the money to pay the fine outright and must pay over time, she pays 70% more than the first individual. Of course, one of the challenges for the third person is by failing to pay her fine or supervision fees, she could be arrested and placed in jail, and this would require her to pay additional fees and may also add to her period of supervision. Last, anytime people are placed on probation for several years, there is the chance they will violate the terms of their probation—such as failing to notify their probation officer of a change of circumstances or failing to pass a drug test—which places them in jeopardy of further punishments.

One way that justice systems can treat individuals more fairly is to impose a **day fine** (also called a structured fine). Day fines have been around for a long time in other nations, but they were only introduced to the United States in the late 1980s and they haven't caught on. The idea behind day fines is that the amount of the fine is based on the severity of the offense and then the individual's ability to pay is considered when determining the amount of the fine the individual pays. By using this approach, Kantorowicz-Reznichenko (2015, p. 481) says that:

> criminals with different socioeconomic status committing the same crime would pay the same portion of their wealth but not the same absolute amount of money. Using this structure, the day-fine has a potential to deter equally both the rich and the poor and to avoid the costly sanction of imprisonment.

PHOTO 3.2
US Attorney for the Southern District of New York David Kelley (left) and US Attorney General Alberto Gonzales (right) participate in a news conference to discuss a settlement with accounting firm KPMG regarding tax fraud at the Justice Department on 9 August 2005. The firm avoided criminal prosecution by paying $456 million in fines, restitution, and penalties. Credit: UPI/Alamy Stock Photo.

For example, if the President of your university or college and you violated the same traffic regulation—such as speeding 10 miles per hour over the limit, the amount of the fine is the same for both persons, say $250. That amount probably wouldn't be much of a deterrent to the President given his or her income, but it might create a significant hardship for you. By contrast, if that fine was indexed to income, then the President might have to pay $1,000 while you would pay $50. Is that a fair approach? While this idea has been slow to catch on in the United States, fines based on an individual's income are used for all manner of regulations in the United Kingdom, Europe, and some Latin American nations. One example of tying traffic fines to income has resulted in very steep fines for the very wealthy, and Schierenbeck (2018) reports the case of a businessman in Finland who received a $67,000 ticket for driving 14 miles an hour over the speed limit. England introduced these income-based fines for different traffic offenses in 2017 and speeding fines, for example, range from $130 to $1300 and are based on the individual's income (Smith, 2018).

Fines are also used to sanction individuals and organizations involved in major criminal offenses, and the federal **Racketeer Influenced and Corrupt Organizations** (RICO) statute has been used for this purpose since 1970. The law was originally designed to deal with organized crime, but since the 1980s it has been applied to a variety of criminal activities. Those convicted of RICO violations, or their state-level equivalents, can find themselves facing hefty fines, ranging from hundreds of thousands to several million dollars. They may also forfeit the assets accumulated through their crimes. There has been a significant increase in the number of civil suits carried out by the federal government that have resulted in fines. Most of these actions are directed against individuals or businesses. Civil matters, however, do not result in imprisonment and Pavlo (2018, para. 9) observes that "maybe we are returning to payment for misdeeds rather than incarceration."

Fees and Surcharges

In order to reduce the burden on taxpayers, the police, courts, and corrections are imposing fees and surcharges on individuals in their interactions with the justice system. Like the fines described earlier, these fees often pose a burden on the poor. For example,

Johnson and Waldman (2019) report that everybody convicted of a minor non-criminal violation in New York State, such as disorderly conduct, is required to pay a $120 surcharge in addition to any other fines or punishments imposed by a judge. If convicted of a misdemeanor, such as possession of marijuana, the individual must pay a $250 surcharge.

Although the police impose fewer fees than courts, the Criminal Justice Policy Program at Harvard Law School (2019) lists various fees individuals can be billed for police services, including being transported to court. Being admitted to jail can also be expensive, and Maher (2018, p. 1) describes how Wisconsin jails "may include fees for booking, daily room and board, work release, physicals, medication, hospital visits, and dental visits." The average booking fee for Wisconsin county jails is about $28, and Maher (2018, p. 2) estimates that an average jail stay of 25 days will cost the inmate about $450. Policy analysts have described cases where people released from jail are sometimes given invoices for over $10,000 (Riley, 2018; Roelof, 2016). Only a small percentage of these fees and surcharges are ever recovered as the reason why many people are kept in jail awaiting their court dates is because they are too poor to make bail.

What happens to the individuals unable to pay their fees or surcharges? Johnson and Waldman (2019) report that civil judgments can be levied against them and their driving privileges can be suspended in 40 states, they may become ineligible for public housing, and their voting rights suspended in seven states. Having unpaid fines can also affect one's ability to visit family members in prison, and 64-year-old Joyce Davis explains that she cannot visit her two sons, who are in a Michigan prison, because she has $1,485 in unpaid tickets for parking and having an expired registration (as cited in Hager, 2017). As Davis is on a fixed income, it is unlikely she will ever pay her debt. Moreover, some states levy interest charges on these unpaid fees, so the debt continues to grow. Although all these fees and surcharges apply equally to everybody in society the middle-class or rich individuals are able to pay their debts and move forward with their lives, while the debt from fees and surcharges may follow a poor person for years.

So, how does the imposition of fines, fees, and surcharges influence corrections? Natapoff (2018) estimates that between 20% and 25% of jail admissions are for nonpayment of fines, and Blanks (2019) says that 18% of all jail admissions in Rhode Island are for debt. Zeng (2019) reports that there are about 750,000 jail inmates in US jails. If we were to apply the one in five statistic to the entire jail population, it suggests that there are 150,000 people in jail today because they are too poor to pay their fines.

Forfeiture

Law enforcement organizations can seize cash or property that was obtained from the proceeds of criminal activity. Like other forms of punishment, forfeiture has been around for centuries and is intended to deter potential offenders by removing their rewards for engaging in crime. Ruback (2018, p. 65) says there are four reasons for asset forfeiture, and they include: (a) the item is an illegal object, such as drugs, (b) the property was obtained illegally, (c) the resources were obtained through illegal activities, and (d) the property was used in conjunction with illegal activities. Ruback notes that regulations in most states enable the police to seize assets using civil or criminal methods, but they proceed civilly in most cases as the standard of proof to seize assets (a preponderance of the evidence) is less than the criminal standard, which is beyond a reasonable doubt. As a result, the police do not have to conclusively prove the assets they seized were involved in criminal activity.

Seizing assets related to criminal activities has become increasingly controversial as the use of civil forfeiture has been growing and the U.S. Department of Justice (2017, p. i) says that in the past ten years, law enforcement agencies seized almost $3 billion in assets a year. As the assets seized in these operations flow to law enforcement organizations in most states there is a clear incentive for officers to engage in these practices. Pursuing funds through forfeiture can also distort law enforcement priorities by motivating officers to investigate and prioritize crimes that provide the largest economic return (Pimentel, 2018). There seems to be growing opposition to civil forfeiture and Nebraska, New Mexico, and North Carolina have banned the practice, and reforms to restrict asset forfeiture have been instituted in over one-half the states.

Abuses of forfeiture statutes were recognized by the Supreme Court in February 2019 when they issued a rare unanimous ruling that local and state governments were prohibited from seizing assets that were disproportionate to the proceeds of the crimes alleged to have been committed (Liptak & Dewan, 2019). The case leading to this decision involved the seizure of a $40,000 vehicle from an individual who had been arrested for selling less than $400 worth of heroin. While law enforcement agencies can still seize assets officials believe came from criminal activities, the individual can take the matter to court if he or she believes the forfeiture was excessive.

Misdemeanor Sentences

Legislative bodies decide which offenses are misdemeanors and which are felonies. The distinction is important because how a crime is classified determines how harshly a person can be punished. Misdemeanor sentences can take several forms and most cases are managed in the community through fines and probationary sentences. But when most people think about misdemeanor sentences, they think about the county jail. County jails do play a significant role in the sanctioning of misdemeanants, as do county workhouses, penal farms, and other local detention facilities (see Chapter 5).

Because misdemeanor offenses are not considered very important by most social scientists, there had been very little research or attention paid to this issue. However, there has been a growing interest in misdemeanor justice and several influential books have been published on the topic (Kohler-Hausmann, 2018; Natapoff, 2018). Stevenson and Mayson (2018, pp. 771–772) say that the "misdemeanor justice system is vast" and courts process about 13.2 million of these cases every year, about three times as many cases as felonies. Natapoff (2018, p. 3) observes that misdemeanor offenses range from relatively minor acts (speeding, loitering, spitting, disorderly conduct, and jaywalking) to more serious crimes such as impaired driving and domestic violence. While many of us see these acts as fairly benign and the punishments relatively minor, arrest and conviction under the "misdemeanor process commonly strips the people who go through it of their liberty, money, health, jobs, housing, credit, immigration status, and government benefits" (Natapoff, 2018, p. 3).

More than a half-century ago, Packer (1968, p. 159) recognized that the justice system operated like an assembly-line, where minor cases were handled informally and brought to a quick and final close. Little has changed today, as individuals who are jeopardy of jail sentences of less than six months are not eligible for a jury trial, nor are most misdemeanants eligible for a public defender if they are not in jeopardy of incarceration. As a result, many cases are handled quickly. For example, Schultz (2019, para. 1) observes how a Cook County judge processed 88 misdemeanor cases in two hours, which works out to about one and a half minutes per case. Blanks (2019) observes that misdemeanant defendants are often given a "take it or leave it offer" by the prosecutors and most take the deal, and plead guilty in order to put these offenses behind them and move on with their lives. If unable to make bail, for example, they might sit in jail for months to get their day in court, even if they are innocent of the offense. The long-term consequences of a criminal conviction, however, can limit their employment options, licensure for various professions, immigration, and the person has to live with the stigma of a criminal conviction.

Felony Sentences

For decades felony sentences meant prison, but this is no longer true. Today, fines are increasingly being used and, as noted earlier, over one-half (59%) of the individuals serving probationary sentences had been convicted of a felony (Kaeble, 2018). This means that probation is no longer the sentence of choice just for first-time and property offenders; it is becoming a common sentence for serious and repeat offenders—a fact that could lead to significant differences in the way probation services are structured and delivered (see Chapter 4).

Short of prison, convicted felons are subject to a variety of **intermediate sanctions**—punishments that are more severe than standard probation but less harsh than imprisonment (see Chapter 4). Intermediate sanctions include day reporting centers, electronic monitoring or house arrest, and intensive supervised probation. Each of these approaches is intended to make individuals more accountable by increasing the intensity of community supervision (e.g. more face-to-face contact with probation officers, more frequent drug testing, or mandatory participation in treatment). Some jurisdictions have developed community-based alternatives for serious or repeat offenders who would otherwise go to jail or prison, but for the most part these intermediate sanctions have increased the stakes for these people without providing them with much additional support.

Of the defendants convicted in the nation's largest state courts, Figure 3.2 shows that almost three-quarters (73%) were incarcerated (36% were sent to prison while 37% were jailed), while one-quarter were placed on probation, and 3% were fined or sentenced to some other court-ordered condition such as making restitution or engaging in community service (Reaves, 2013, p. 29). Patterns of sentencing in federal courts were somewhat similar, and Motivans (2019, p. 10) reports that in 2015 over three-quarters (78%) were incarcerated, while 10% were placed on probation, 9% were given a suspended sentence, and 2% received a fine (Figure 3.3).

With respect to sentence severity, the average prison sentence in state and federal courts is almost the same, with a median sentence length of 30 months. When it comes to probation, by contrast, the sentences imposed in the federal courts are somewhat longer than their state counterparts (36 and 30 months, respectively). One difference in these results is that state courts also place offenders in local jails and their median sentence length was four months. These results are shown in Table 3.2. We must use some caution when comparing these results as the information from the federal government

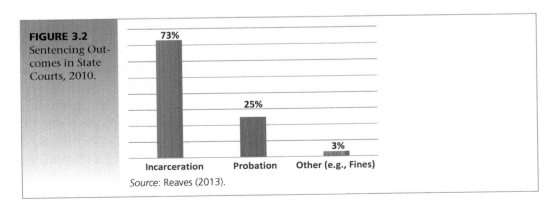

FIGURE 3.2 Sentencing Outcomes in State Courts, 2010.

73% — Incarceration
25% — Probation
3% — Other (e.g., Fines)

Source: Reaves (2013).

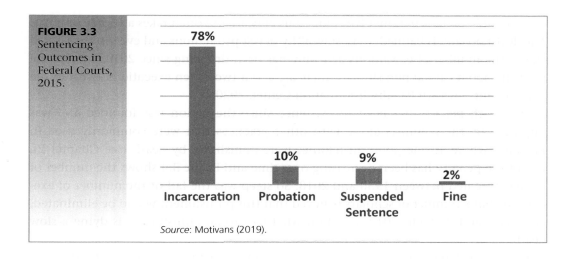

FIGURE 3.3
Sentencing Outcomes in Federal Courts, 2015.

Source: Motivans (2019).

TABLE 3.2 Median Sentence Length in State Courts (2009) and Federal Courts (2015)

	• Median Probation Sentence	• Median Jail Sentence	• Median Prison Sentence
• State Courts	30 months	4 months	30 months
• Federal Courts	36 months	Not applicable	30 months

Median: The midpoint for all sentences, and, for example, of the probationary sentences imposed in state courts, one-half are 30 months or less, while one-half are greater than 30 months.

Sources: Motivans (2019); Reaves (2013).

is newer and includes all sentences imposed. The information from the state courts, by contrast, is older (but is the most current available) and only includes information from the largest urban courts and does not include cases from rural areas.

The Death Penalty

Kaeble's (2018) research shows that one-fifth of homicide offenders serve less than five years and about 30 to 40 offenders a year are sentenced to death (Death Penalty Information Center, 2020). In some respects, a discussion of the death penalty does not belong in a book about corrections as the death penalty has nothing to do with correcting criminal behavior but is more closely related to the philosophy of retribution and death is the ultimate form of incapacitation. But our topic here is sentencing and the death penalty is a sentence that states, and the federal government can impose in certain circumstances. Furthermore, corrections officials must carry out this sanction, including holding the condemned inmate on death row (or its equivalent) until the sentence is carried out, a process that involves numerous appeals and often takes a decade or more. The death penalty is banned in most wealthy developed nations and even in the United States, the number of executions generally has been dropping since 2010. Despite the publicity about capital punishment, there are about two dozen executions a year in the entire country (Death Penalty Information Center, 2020).

The death penalty has been in existence since the nation was founded and was imported by the colonists along with other practices that were commonly used in England, where at one point all felonies were punishable by death (see Chapter 2). Use of the penalty has been decreasing over time and Figure 3.4 shows the number of people executed between 1930 and 2018. So steep was the fall of the number of executions that a number of scholars believed that this punishment would be eliminated, and Mays and Ruddell (2019) question whether capital punishment is dying a slow death.

The death penalty places several demands on corrections, including holding individuals on death row, which numbered 2,620 at the end of 2019 (Death Penalty Information Center, 2020). Even carrying out an execution today has become complicated as few firms making the three-drug cocktail required for lethal injections will sell them to correctional systems as they want to distance themselves from these executions. The following box explores the issue of executions from a cross-national perspective.

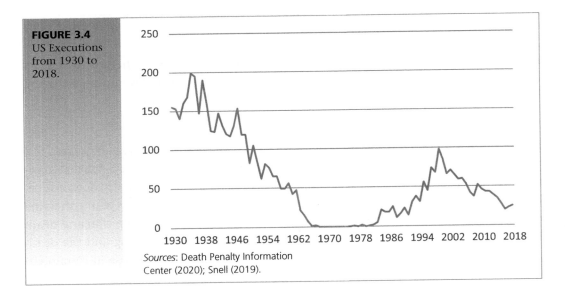

FIGURE 3.4 US Executions from 1930 to 2018.

Sources: Death Penalty Information Center (2020); Snell (2019).

Cross-National Use of the Death Penalty

Amnesty International reports that 20 nations carried out executions in 2018 and altogether 690 persons were executed, which was down almost one-third from the previous year. One of the challenges of estimating the global use of the death penalty is that the total in China is unknown as it is considered a state secret but could number in the thousands. Amnesty International reports that almost all executions took place in five nations: China, Egypt, Iran, Saudi Arabia, and Vietnam.

There are significant differences in the way the death penalty is applied throughout the world, and some nations still execute individuals for non-homicide crimes such as drug-related offenses in 15 nations. Unlike in the United States, individuals who committed crimes as juveniles are still executed in some nations, and persons with mental health problems or disabilities were executed in 2018. With respect to the methods of execution, lethal injection, hanging, and deaths by firing squads are the most common, although beheading is still used and while most executions are conducted in correctional facilities, Iran and Saudi Arabia still carry out public executions.

Source: Amnesty International (2019).

DECISION-MAKING AND SENTENCING

You might think that it would be fairly simple to figure out how much time an offender should get and then how much time that person does actually serve. But in practice, sentencing often is complicated by several factors. Some of those factors are related to judicial decision-making while others relate to prosecutorial decision-making in the form of plea bargaining.

Judicial Decision-Making

Again, legislatures make laws that define criminal behaviors and punishments, and judges impose those punishments on persons who have been convicted of a crime in the form of sentences. In the sentencing role, judges traditionally had a great deal of discretion. Although lawmakers defined sentences, they tended to define them in broad terms—a sentence range of two to five years, for example. As we have observed previously that practice changed in the late 1970s, as legislators began to set determinate and later mandatory sentences for certain types of crimes or offenders. Here, we examine an area where judges continue to have almost total discretion: the decision to impose concurrent or consecutive sentences.

The question of **concurrent** or **consecutive sentences** arises when a defendant is convicted of multiple offenses. Concurrent sentences are two or more sentences imposed and then served at the same time. The sentences do not have to be for the same term—all ten years for example. If they are different, the prisoner's release usually is calculated on the basis of the longest term. So, an individual sentenced to terms of 10 and 15 years to be served concurrently would not be released before the parole eligibility date for the 15-year sentence. Consecutive sentences are two or more sentences imposed at the same time but served in sequence. Thus, consecutive sentences increase the maximum time an offender can be confined or under correctional supervision.

How do judges decide between concurrent and consecutive sentences? Some suggest that concurrent sentences are one way in which judges protect defendants they believe have had too many charges brought against them—a plea bargaining tactic used by prosecutors we discuss later. Concurrent sentences have the effect of limiting time served to a single sentence, regardless of how many charges a defendant was facing. With consecutive sentences, judges have the power to maximize punishment. They are more likely to impose these sentences on repeat offenders or people who have committed crimes that are unusually cruel. It also has been suggested that some judges use consecutive sentences to retaliate against defendants who refuse to plea bargain, insisting on their right to a trial. This "jury trial penalty" in effect says to the defendant, "You took up my time, now I'm going to take up some of yours." Neily (2018, para. 14) says that:

> we should be deeply suspicious of a criminal justice system in which people almost never choose to exercise their constitutional right to a jury trial. The fewer trials there are, the less opportunity there is for citizens to participate in the process and the less transparent—and accountable—our criminal justice system becomes.

As noted earlier, the person who decides on what charges will be brought and how a case will proceed, including engaging in plea negotiations, is the prosecutor.

Prosecutorial Decision-Making: Plea Bargaining

Plea bargaining is the negotiation that goes on between the defense attorney and the prosecutor regarding sentences, counts, and charges. In effect, it is the attempt to exchange a guilty plea for some form of leniency. Plea bargaining has long been a component of the criminal justice system in the United States. Guilty pleas were entered in the first courts established in this country, and the bargaining process has been referred to in court proceedings as far back as the 1800s. Today, more than 95% of the felony cases in the United States each year are negotiated to disposition.

The average person believes that plea bargaining is all about the sentence and nothing else. Although the sentence is important, it is not the only focus of the negotiations. For example, a defendant may plea bargain, not to reduce the time served—with concurrent sentencing, the time served for one count or five counts could be the same—but to reduce the number of counts. In some states, the number of counts is one basis for the decision to charge a defendant as a habitual offender, a classification that can increase the term of incarceration and eliminate the possibility of parole.

PHOTO 3.3
Defendant, prosecuting attorney, and defense attorney stand before judge in Jackson County (MO) Circuit Court. Credit: Mikael Karlsson/Alamy Stock Photo.

The particular charge can be of concern too. The charge determines the length of the sentence and the form of the sentence. Consider homicide, for example. In most states, a conviction for first-degree murder carries a death sentence or a sentence of life in prison without parole. By contrast, a person who pleads guilty to second-degree murder may spend many years in prison, but he or she cannot be sentenced to die behind bars.

Accepting a plea has several advantages and disadvantages for the criminal justice system and the defendant, and they are shown in Table 3.3. Trials, for example, are expensive undertakings and a prosecuting attorney might not have enough evidence to ensure a conviction. Even if the prosecutor does have a "solid case" juries may be reluctant to convict some defendants. For instance, it might be difficult to get a conviction

TABLE 3.3 Advantages and Disadvantages of Plea Bargaining

Advantages	Disadvantages
• Contributes to the efficiency of the justice system	• Can lead to sloppy investigations
• Reduces the costs and workloads of prosecutors and defense attorneys	• Encourages abuses of power by prosecutors and judges
• Provides certainty for all parties	• Creates a situation where defense attorneys may put their interests over those of their client.
• Reduces demands and stress on witnesses	• Results in some individuals receiving lenient sentences
• Allows prosecutors to gain convictions on weak cases	• Increases the risk of wrongful convictions

Source: Adapted from Ruddell (2020).

PHOTO 3.4
A criminal defendant's most gut-retching moments are often spent awaiting a judge's decision. Credit: Wavebreak Media ltd/ Alamy Stock Photo.

for possession of marijuana in a college town, as many potential jurors might be sympathetic to the accused. As a result, prosecutors might be very willing to plea bargain those types of cases.

Some specific criticisms of plea bargaining are also shown in Table 3.3, and legal scholars—and everybody interested in justice—are concerned about increasing unjust outcomes for defendants. Dervan and Edkins (2013), for example, observe that some innocent defendants plead guilty to avoid an expensive trial or harsh sentences if convicted. Prosecutors can pressure defendants to plead guilty by charging them with a more serious charge than is warranted such as attempted murder rather than assault or by charging them with several offenses and then agreeing to drop all but one charge in return for a guilty plea. Some defendants may have an advantage in negotiating these plea agreements, and a defendant who can afford a skilled lawyer who has the time and resources to investigate the prosecutor's case may receive a less severe sentence than a defendant with an overworked public defender who does not have the resources to fully engage in fact-finding. Lucas (2018) summarizes the barriers that public defenders must overcome to achieve just outcomes for their indigent clients, but they all boil down to a lack of funding.

RACE, CLASS, AND GENDER

Crack and Powder Cocaine: Similar Drugs, Vastly Different Sentencing Outcomes

Almost one-half the inmates in the U.S. Bureau of Prisons were sentenced to violations of drug laws and almost all of them were convicted of trafficking offenses. To deter potential crack users and sellers as part of the war on drugs, the federal government imposed a sentence differential for regular powder cocaine versus crack cocaine of 100:1. This means that a person apprehended with one gram of crack cocaine would receive a sentence equal to having 100 grams of powder cocaine. The United States Sentencing Commission (USSC), a body that oversees sentencing on federal crimes, found these policies were discriminatory as crack cocaine was overwhelmingly used by African Americans. The problem with this sentencing differential is that crack cocaine and powder cocaine are chemically indistinguishable; they are essentially the same drug, but crack cocaine is cheaper and better suited to smoking, which makes it faster acting.

The law was changed in 2010 to reduce the differential from 100:1 to 18:1 and the *First Step Act*, which was signed into law in 2018, enables federal prisoners sentenced under the old 100:1 guidelines to petition for release before a judge, which has the potential to shorten the sentences of over 2,500 federal inmates, and over 500 of them were released early by April 2019.

Sentencing Strategies

The United States has an adversarial legal system and defendants have a right to a vigorous defense. Given that right, we ask, why are most misdemeanor and felony cases processed so quickly, and why are there so few trials? In response to those questions, two concepts are introduced. The first is the presence of a group of court professionals who have been called the **courtroom work group**. These individuals have a long-term working relationship within a court and are comprised of the judges, prosecutors, defense attorneys, and other players including court personnel. This group has a stake in getting along by ensuring that most minor cases move quickly through the system. In order to achieve that goal, they informally develop a **going rate**, which is a shared understanding of the typical sentencing outcomes for a crime given the individual's current offense and prior criminal record (Walker, 2015). Once these going rates or sentencing norms are adopted by the group, there may be resistance to change.

As a result of this long-term working relationship and going rate, some defendants may believe that their public defenders are not very effective lawyers. Those defendants, however, often represent a one-time appearance before the court and the vested interests of the work group may be more important to the members than providing a vigorous defense for a one-time client. So, does the presence of a courtroom work group mean that a defendant cannot receive a vigorous defense? Our observations pertain to minor criminal matters, and as the potential range of punishments increases, there is a similar increase in adversarial lawyering.

Determinate Sentences

For most of our nation's recent history, state laws have used indeterminate sentences—ranges of time rather than specific periods—to define prison terms. A statute might require a minimum of two years and a maximum of five years for a given offense. In most states, judges must impose the statutory range, although some states allow the judge to choose a specific term within the statutory range. The actual time served, however, is determined by the parole board.

In most of the states using indeterminate sentences, individuals become eligible for parole after they have served some fraction—say one-third or one-half—of their minimum sentence. For example, an individual is sentenced to serve one to five years in a state requiring that one-half of the minimum sentence be served before parole can be granted. This inmate would be eligible for parole (although not guaranteed to receive it) after serving just six months in prison. The discrepancies between sentences imposed and the amount of time a prisoner actually serves led to truth-in-sentencing laws that were described earlier.

Starting in the 1970s, jurisdictions throughout the country began to introduce **determinate sentences**—specific periods of confinement. Arazan, Bales, and Blomberg (2018) describe this change as a significant shift in sentencing practices. Most of the states that have changed from indeterminate to determinate sentencing also have limited or eliminated parole. In its place, these states use some form of good-time credits: time deducted from a prison sentence for good behavior. This discount rate for good-time credits differs, and, in some states, it is as high as 50%, which is a day's credit for each day served. Several states also offer earned time credits, which gives a further sentence reduction for completing rehabilitative programs. Steiner and Cain (2018, p. 71) report that "inmates can earn good time credits in 32 states, while 37 states have laws that afford inmates earned time credits." In 1987, Congress set the maximum amount of good-time credits for federal prisoners at 54 days a year, or a 15% discount rate (if they were serving more than one year in prison), although the *First Step Act* now allows for a slightly greater reduction to 54 days for every day of their imposed sentence rather than the inmate's sentenced served.

Traditionally, reform in the criminal justice system has the support of one or the other political camp: right (conservatives) or left (liberals). The shift to determinate sentencing, however, was supported by both groups. Conservatives desired truth-in-sentencing as they wanted sentences that reflect the time an inmate would actually serve. They also felt that judges had too much discretion. Liberals, by contrast, argued that parole boards had too much discretion, and they often based their decisions on factors unrelated to an individual's likely success on parole. Ultimately, determinate sentencing was designed to place limits on both judges and parole boards.

Sentencing Guidelines

Sentencing guidelines prescribe the sentences judges must impose based on the seriousness of the particular offense and the individual's criminal history. The goal of these guidelines is to limit the sentencing disparities that can occur from one individual to another and from one judge to the next. Nineteen states and the federal government have **sentencing guidelines** to make certain that sentences are more uniform and

TABLE 3.4 States with Sentencing Guidelines

	Indeterminate (Parole) States	Determinate (Fixed Term) States
Sentencing Guidelines	AL, AR, MD, MA, MI, PA, TN, UT	DE, FL, KS, MN, NC, OH, OR, US, VA, WA
No Sentencing Guidelines	AK, CO, CT, GA, HI, IA, ID, KY, LA, MS, MT, ND, NE, NH, NJ, NV, NY, OK, RI, SC, SD, TX, VT, WV, WY	AZ, CA, IL, IN, ME, NM, WI

Source: Sentencing Guideline Resource Center (2018).

reduce differences based on gender, race, and class, and to ensure that sentences are proportional to the severity of the offense. Table 3.4 shows the use of sentencing guidelines for the states and is divided into states that have parole (indeterminate jurisdictions) and those where the prisoner cannot access parole, which are called determinate jurisdictions. In addition to these states, the District of Columbia (which is an indeterminate jurisdiction), and the federal government, which abolished discretionary parole, also have sentencing guidelines.

Judges in states with sentencing guidelines still have some discretion as these guidelines typically enable them to impose a range of sanctions. As a result, judges can consider aggravating or mitigating factors when imposing a sentence. **Aggravating factors** are circumstances that warrant a harsher sentence such as using a firearm in the commission of a crime or belonging to a gang. **Mitigating factors**, by contrast, include information about the individual or offense that might warrant a reduced sentence, including cooperating with the police during the investigation, making restitution to a victim prior to sentencing, or evidence of their good character (such as involvement in voluntary activities) or being a veteran.

AFTER THE VERDICT

Once a defendant has been found guilty, the judge typically delays sentencing until a presentence investigation can be completed. The investigation, which is carried out by a probation department (or through the courts in some jurisdictions), entails a thorough examination of the defendant's life history, including family, employment, personal, and legal status (see also Chapter 4).

For every defendant placed on probation, a probation officer must develop a plan that sets out the conditions the probationer must meet. If the person is sentenced to prison, a different set of actors comes into play. In most states, these individuals are first sent to a correctional reception and diagnostic center. At this facility, staff members determine where each offender will be sent initially. In some states, judges have the authority to sentence individuals to specific facilities, but in most jurisdictions, this authority is reserved for the corrections department. Once this assessment has been completed, new inmates are transported to the designated institution. There, they typically face more screening to determine whether assignment to the general population is appropriate and which housing unit seems best suited to their individual needs. One component of this process is a risk assessment to determine the threat each inmate poses to the general population and the inmate's likelihood of attempting to escape. An individual's housing assignments may change as their circumstances change and new assessments are made.

Appeal

Prison inmates are stripped of many of their rights and practically all their possessions, but they have an abundance of time. Some of them spend their time scheming some type of misconduct, such as escaping, disturbing those around them, arranging to have **contraband** smuggled into the institution, or carrying on with their criminal enterprises. Others spend their time in more positive pursuits: enrolling in educational programs, learning a skill or trade, increasing their physical fitness, or using the prison's legal resources to challenge their convictions—we call them **jailhouse lawyers**.

Jailhouse lawyers are inmates who have developed an expertise at challenging their own convictions and those of other inmates. Few of them are actual attorneys, but they have studied the law and have learned how to write court documents. Schwartzapfel (2015, para. 3) says that most "are self-taught, spending long hours in the prison law library. With no access to the internet, they read outdated law books and case law on CD-ROMS." Some law schools and prison advocacy organizations have developed resources to aid inmates in their efforts to overcome mistreatment or bad conditions and the *Jailhouse Lawyer's Manual* has been published by Columbia University since 1978 and the eleventh edition was published in 2017. This book, which is almost 1,400 pages long, is available to prisoners for a reduced price and provides them information about doing legal research, filing a lawsuit, and covers specific areas such as inmate rights.

Some inmates have used their expertise as jailhouse lawyers to occupy a distinct role in prison society. Their efforts sometimes have been resisted by correctional systems as some officials feel threatened by their activities. Some corrections and

PHOTO 3.5
Justices of the Supreme Court, Washington, DC, 30 November 2018. Credit: Kevin Dietsch/Pool via CNP/Alamy Stock Photo.

court officials, for instance, have criticized jailhouse lawyers as they are said to encourage filing frivolous claims (such as the inmate who filed a lawsuit after receiving broken cookies with his meal), creating a division between inmates and staff and exploiting the hopes of newly admitted prisoners (Smilowitz, 2017, p. 512). As a result of the potential threat that jailhouse lawyers pose, some states have attempted to prohibit inmates from providing legal assistance to other inmates. Tennessee was one such state and its policies prohibiting the activities of jailhouse lawyers were challenged before the U.S. Supreme Court in *Johnson v. Avery* (1969). In that case, the Court held that inmates might be restricted but could not be prohibited from helping other inmates file appeals of their convictions or other legal documents. In 1977, the Court's decision in *Bounds v. Smith* expanded prisoners' access to the courts, making law books and other legal materials available to them in the institution and allowing them to consult with attorneys or paralegals who specialize in inmate appeals.

Inmates traditionally have used two legal mechanisms for appealing the conditions of their confinement or their convictions. For much of our history, the primary means of appeal has been the **writ of *habeas corpus***. Under a writ of *habeas corpus* prisoners assert they are being held unjustly and ask the court to require the state to justify their conviction and incarceration. Thus, *habeas corpus* petitions challenge the very fact of incarceration, and a successful challenge means the conviction could be overturned and the prisoner retried or set free. Most inmates who are successful in their *habeas corpus* claims are retried rather than released. Since 2000 there have been a series of legislative changes and Supreme Court decisions that have weakened prisoners' ability to use these claims. Primus (2019, p. i) says that "state prisoners who file federal *habeas corpus* petitions face a maze of procedural and substantive restrictions that effectively prevent almost all prisoners from obtaining meaningful review of their convictions."

One of the primary issues raised by inmates on appeal is access to the courts. Often, this is the most fundamental issue in the appeals process because it alleges that the inmate has been deprived of the legal resources or assistance necessary to prepare whatever the substantive challenge may be. In many instances, access to the courts is really a catchall phrase for lack of counsel or ineffective representation by counsel. The appeal's substance indicates the appropriate remedy: If an inmate alleges that he or she is not receiving adequate legal assistance, the remedy would be to provide the necessary assistance. If the inmate alleges inadequate representation by counsel at trial, and the court finds that to be the case, the appropriate remedy would be a retrial.

Individuals also may challenge the trial procedures that resulted in their conviction. For instance, an inmate might claim that physical evidence or an admission of guilt was improperly admitted at trial. An inmate also could assert that he or she was denied the right to a jury trial or that the jury was improperly constituted. For example, in his appeal to the Supreme Court in *Batson v. Kentucky* (1986), the petitioner, who was a African American man, alleged that African Americans had been systematically excluded from the trial jury. The Court ruled that using race as a basis for excluding a juror is unconstitutional and remanded the case for further action. Another basis for appeal is the state's failure to try the case in a timely manner. The Supreme Court has defined in very broad terms what constitutes a speedy trial; today all of the states and the federal government have laws defining the time within which a suspect must be brought to trial. If the time to trial exceeds the state's limits, many jurisdictions allow the trial court to dismiss all charges.

In appeals of criminal convictions, the appellate court must answer two basic questions: Was there an error? And was the error harmless? If the court finds an error but holds that it was harmless, the conviction is usually allowed to stand. If the error was not harmless, the appellate court may order the conviction overturned and the defendant immediately released or held for retrial. In the case of a retrial, the trial court pays special attention to correcting the original error. This brings us to several important points:

- In general, the basis for appear is an error in law. That is, the judge must have made a mistake of some sort before or during a trial.
- Federal and state courts convict thousands of people each year; yet the percentage of cases appealed is fairly small.
- Of the convictions appealed, about 7% of state court appeals were successful in 2010 (Waters, Gallegos, Green, & Rozsi, 2015, p. 5).
- Most successful appeals result in re-hearings on specific issues or matters or retrials of the case, not outright dismissals of the charges. Therefore, inmates are not leaving prisons in large numbers as a result of overturned convictions.

SENTENCING TRENDS

The use of punishment in the United States has gone in two directions. First, there has been a movement to make sentences less severe for both adults and juveniles who commit minor offenses (see Chapter 4). We are diverting these individuals from the formal adjudication system and expanding the menu of sentences available to judges. These individuals are being sent to first-offender programs and driving while intoxicated (DWI) schools and are being ordered to perform community service in lieu of fines or incarceration.

Second, sanctions have become more severe for adults and juveniles who commit the most serious crimes. The nation's perception of a crime wave (even during a period where crime has been dropping) and the get-tough-on-crime laws passed by legislatures have made it easier to keep individuals behind bars for longer periods of time. Until the early 2000s, the United States was on an imprisonment binge, but the total number of federal and state prisoners peaked in 2007 and has slowly been decreasing (Bronson & Carson, 2019).

And what of the future? Certainly, we expect the leniency shown to first-time offenders to continue. Although penalties for repeat and serious offenders continue to be harsh by international standards, there appears to be some movement to moderate even those punishments. With respect to the death penalty, for example, the Death Penalty Information Center (2020, p. 1) reports that 279 people were sentenced to death in 1999, but that number dropped to 34 in 2019, an 88% reduction. Legislatures are also reducing the severity of some tough-on-crime sanctions, and FAMM (2019) reports that 34 states eased their mandatory minimum sentencing practices in some manner between 2001 and 2019.

There may be a greater reliance on science and technology in correctional interventions in the future (see Chapter 13). Decisions on correctional placements have been made using the results of risk assessments for decades but these instruments are becoming more sophisticated and may be used more extensively if they successfully reduce recidivism. There is also an increased interest in using biological explanations for involvement in crime and responding to biological deficits could be the basis for correctional interventions in the future. Although it is too soon to determine whether those responses will be founded on interventions based on evidence-based therapies or medications the important point is that these factors are being researched, and the outcomes of those studies will shape our future practices.

SUMMARY

In this chapter we examined a broad range of issues dealing with the criminal law and particularly focusing on the sentencing process. Some of the major points covered in this chapter are the following:

- Legislative bodies define criminal behavior. They determine both the substantive law and procedural law. They distinguish felonies from misdemeanors and prescribe the appropriate punishments.
- Throughout the 1980s and 1990s legislators introduced get-tough-on-crime policies, such as mandatory minimum sentences, habitual offender statues such as "three-strikes" and truth-in-sentencing laws that increased the prison time the individual would serve.
- Throughout the 1980s and 1990s prosecutors became even more prominent and powerful actors in the criminal justice system. Their tough-on-crime practices are considered a key driver of mass imprisonment.

- The poor are vulnerable to economic sanctions such as paying fines and fees and failing to pay this debt can lead to their incarceration.
- Sentencing choices range from fines to probation, jail and prison sentences, and the death penalty.
- Although we tend to disregard the importance of misdemeanors, convictions on these minor offenses can have lifelong negative consequences for an individual.
- Prison sentences may be indeterminate or determinate and judges may impose them concurrently or consecutively.
- Offenders can appeal their convictions on writs of *habeas corpus* or through civil rights actions. The method of appeal chosen has implications for the most important form of relief.

Altogether, our review of sentencing shows that judges have a wide array of options available to sanction individuals. The severity of sanctions increased starting in the 1970s and correctional populations swelled: Herring (2015) reports that a new prison was built every 8.5 days between 1984 and 2005. After peaking in 2007, correctional populations have been slowly decreasing and Chapter 4 describes how some of those people are now under community correctional supervision.

KEY TERMS

- aggravating factors
- appeal
- concurrent sentence
- consecutive sentence
- contraband
- courtroom work group
- day fine
- determinate sentence
- fees and surcharges
- felony
- fines
- forfeiture
- going rate
- indeterminate sentence
- jailhouse lawyers
- mandatory minimum sentence
- misdemeanor
- mitigating factors
- pay only probation
- petty misdemeanor
- plea bargaining
- presumption of innocence
- procedural law
- Racketeer Influenced and Corrupt Organizations (RICO)
- sentencing guidelines
- substantive law
- writ of *habeas corpus*

THINKING ABOUT CORRECTIONAL POLICIES AND PRACTICES: WRITING ASSIGNMENTS

1. In a short essay discuss the strengths and weaknesses of electing, rather than appointing prosecutors, as they do in most nations.
2. Incarceration has a crime reduction benefit but list some possible reasons why crime rates in the United Kingdom and Canada dropped at about the same rate as the United States while using only a fraction of the imprisonment rate.
3. Identify some negative outcomes that might occur when fines and forfeiture are used to fund justice system operations.
4. Can you explain why the number of executions has been declining?
5. Many inmates rely on the assistance of jailhouse lawyers to prepare their appeals for court. In a brief essay provide some reasons jailhouse lawyers write writs for other prisoners.

CRITICAL REVIEW QUESTIONS

1. What is meant by the concept of mitigating factors and how does it figure into the types and amounts of punishments that seem appropriate when a sentence is imposed?
2. Define and describe the concept of probation. Based on the numbers provided in this chapter, how important is probation to the field of corrections in the United States?
3. Day fines are described as means-based penalties. What do they mean by this description? Are there reasons why day fines are not used more often in the United States?
4. Explain why we continued to increase the use of imprisonment for over a decade after crime rates started to fall?
5. What are the different types of sentences that can be imposed on convicted offenders? Who decides which offenders get which sentences?
6. What do we mean by intermediate sanctions? Give some examples of punishments in this category.
7. Some say sentencing is the most complex and time-consuming function performed by the courtroom work group. What are the factors that add to the complexity of this process?

8. What kinds of cases are likely to increase public demand for three-strikes-and-you-are-out legislation? Have any of these cases been in the news lately?

9. Why does support for the death penalty stay relatively constant even though homicide rates are the lowest level in four decades?

10. What are some possible reasons why most states and the federal government are reforming criminal justice practices to reduce imprisonment?

CASES

Batson v. Kentucky 476 U.S. 79 (1986)

Bounds v. Smith 430 U.S. 817 (1977)

Johnson v. Avery 393 U.S. 483 (1969)

REFERENCES

Amnesty International. (2019). *Death sentences and executions, 2018*. London, UK: Author.

Arazan, C. L., Bales, W. D., & Blomberg, T. G. (2018). Courtroom context and sentencing. *American Journal of Criminal Justice*, Published online ahead of print at: DOI: 10.1007/s12103-018-9444-8

Blanks, J. (2019). *Book review: Punishment without crime: How our massive misdemeanor system traps the innocent and makes America more unequal. Democracy: A Journal of Ideas*. Retrieved from https://democracyjournal.org/magazine/52/crime-and-misdemeanors/

Bouchard, J., & Wong, J. S. (2018). The new panopticon? Examining the effect of home confinement on criminal recidivism. *Victims & Offenders, 13*(5), 589–608.

Brennan Center for Justice. (2018). *21 principles for the 21st century prosecutor*. New York: Author.

Bronson, J., & Carson, E. A. (2019). *Prisoners in 2017*. Washington, DC: Bureau of Justice Statistics.

Conrad, R. J. Jr., & Clements, K. L. (2018). The vanishing criminal jury trial: From trial judges to sentencing judges. *The George Washington Law Review, 86*(1), 99–169.

Criminal Justice Policy Program at Harvard Law School. (2019). *50 state criminal justice debt reform builder*. Retrieved from https://cjdebtreform.org/

Death Penalty Information Center. (2020). *Facts about the death penalty (March 12, 2020)*. Retrieved from https://deathpenaltyinfo.org/documents/FactSheet.pdf

Dervan, L. C., & Edkins, V. A. (2013). The innocent defendant's dilemma: An innovative empirical study of plea bargaining's innocence problem. *Journal of Criminal Law and Criminology, 103*(1), 1–48.

Eagle Country. (2016, September 2). *Dearborn county justice is focus of New York Times report*. Retrieved from https://www.eaglecountryonline.com/news/local-news/dearborn-county-justice-is-focus-of-new-york-times-report/

Ecenbarger, W. (2012). *Kids for cash: Two judges, thousands of children, and a $2.6 million kickback scheme*. New York: New Press.

FAMM. (2019). *State reforms to mandatory minimum sentencing laws to Jan. 25, 2019*. Retrieved from https://famm.org/wp-content/uploads/Chart-STATE-REFORMS-TO-MANDATORY-MINIMUM-SENTENCING-LAWS-2018.pdf

Hager, E. (2017, Sept. 14). I can't visit my sons in prison because I have unpaid traffic tickets. *The Marshall Project*. Retrieved from https://www.themarshallproject.org/2017/09/14/i-can-t-visit-my-sons-in-prison-because-i-have-unpaid-traffic-tickets

Halpin, J. (2020, Jan. 27). Feds decline to retry Ciavarella for racketeering. *The Citizens' Voice*. Retrieved from https://www.citizensvoice.com/news/feds-decline-to-retry-ciavarella-for-racketeering-1.2587883

Herring, K. (2015). Was a prison built every 10 days to house a fast-growing population of non-violent inmates? *Politicfact*. Retrieved from https://www.politifact.com/truth-o-meter/statements/2015/jul/31/cory-booker/was-prison-built-every-10-days-house-fast-growing-/

Human Rights Watch. (2014). *Profiting from probation: America's "offender funded" probation industry*. Washington, DC: Author.

Human Rights Watch. (2018). *"Set up to fail": The impact of offender-funded private probation on the poor*. Retrieved from https://www.hrw.org/report/2018/02/20/set-fail/impact-offender-funded-private-probation-poor

Indiana Department of Corrections. (2019). *Adult new admissions, by county of commitment*. Retrieved from https://www.in.gov/idoc/2376.htm

Johnson, C., & Waldman, M. (2019). How surcharges punish the poor: New York must combat court fees that many low-income residents cannot pay. *New York Daily News*. Retrieved from https://www.nydailynews.com/opinion/ny-oped-how-surcharges-punish-the-poor-20190131-story.html

Juvenile Law Center. (2018). *Luzerne "kids for cash" scandal*. Retrieved from https://jlc.org/luzerne-kids-cash-scandal

Kaeble, D. (2018). *Time served in state prison, 2016*. Washington, DC: Bureau of Justice Statistics.

Kaeble, D., & Cowhig, M. (2018). Correctional populations in the United States, 2016. Washington, DC: Bureau of Justice Statistics.

Kantorowicz-Reznichenko, E. (2015). Day-fines: Should the rich pay more? *Review of Law and Economics, 11*(3), 481–501.

Keller, J., & Pearce, A. (2016). This small Indiana county sends more people to prison than San Francisco and Durham N.C. combined. Why? *The New York Times*. Retrieved from https://www.nytimes.com/2016/09/02/upshot/new-geography-of-prisons.html

Kilgore, J., & Sanders, E. (2018). Ankle monitors aren't humane. They're another kind of jail. *Wired*. Retrieved from https://www.wired.com/story/opinion-ankle-monitors-are-another-kind-of-jail/

Kohler-Hausmann, I. (2018). *Misdemeanorland: Criminal courts and social control in an age of broken windows policing*. Princeton, NJ: Princeton University Press.

Lavoie, D. (2018, Dec. 31). Reformist prosecutors back major changes in approach. *Houston Chronicle*. Retrieved from https://www.houstonchronicle.com/nation/article/Reformist-prosecutors-back-major-changes-in-13500551.php

Liptak, A., & Dewan, S. (2019, Feb. 20). Supreme Court limits police powers to seize private property. *New York Times*. Retrieved from https://www.nytimes.com/2019/02/20/us/politics/civil-asset-forfeiture-supreme-court.html

Lucas, L. (2018). Public defense litigation: An overview. *Indiana Law Review, 51*(1), 89–109.

Maher, W. (2018). Pay-to-stay jail fees in Wisconsin. *Institute for Research on Poverty*. Retrieved from https://www.irp.wisc.edu/wp/wp-content/uploads/2018/10/Factsheet15-Pay-to-Stay-Jail-Fees-in-WI.pdf

Mays, G. L., & Ruddell, R. (2019). *Making sense of criminal justice, 3rd edition*. New York: Oxford University Press.

Motivans, M. (2019). *Federal justice statistics, 2015–2016*. Washington, DC: Bureau of Justice Statistics.

Natapoff, A. (2018). *Punishment without crime: How our massive misdemeanor system traps the innocent and makes America more unequal*. New York: Basic Books.

Neily, C. (2018). The trial penalty. *Cato*. Retrieved from https://www.cato.org/blog/trial-penalty

Packer, H. (1968). *The limits of the criminal sanction*. Stanford, CA: Stanford University Press.

Pavlo, W. (2018, Oct. 31). Once meant to nail mobsters, RICO sees resurgence in civil cases in 2018. *Forbes*. Retrieved from https://www.forbes.com/sites/walterpavlo/2018/10/31/once-meant-to-nail-mobsters-rico-sees-resurgence-in-civil-cases-in-2018/#a77d95f2421f

Pew Charitable Trusts. (2016). *Use of electronic offender-tracking devices expands sharply*. Retrieved from https://www.pewtrusts.org/-/media/assets/2016/10/use_of_electronic_offender_tracking_devices_expands_sharply.pdf

Pfaff, J. F. (2017). *Locked in: The true causes of mass incarceration and how to achieve real reform*. New York: Basic Books.

Pi, D., Parisi, F., & Luppi, B. (2018). *Quantifying reasonable doubt*. Retrieved from https://papers.ssrn.com/sol3/papers.cfm?abstract_id=3226479

Pimentel, D. (2018). Forfeiture policy in the United States: Is there hope for reform? *Criminology & Public Policy, 17*(1), 129–137.

Primus, E. B. (2019). Equitable gateways: Toward expanded federal habeas corpus review of state court criminal convictions. *Arizona Law Review, 61*(2) 291–324.

Reaves, B. (2013). *Felony defendants in large urban counties, 2009 – Statistical tables*. Washington, DC: Bureau of Justice Statistics.

Riley, K. (2018, June 15). Neither inmates nor counties get out of jail free. *Mackinac Center for Public Policy*. Retrieved from https://www.mackinac.org/neither-inmates-nor-counties-get-out-of-jail-free

Roelof, T. (2016, Dec. 13). We hope you enjoyed your stay at the county jail. Here's your bill. *Bridge*. Retrieved from https://www.bridgemi.com/public-sector/we-hope-you-enjoyed-your-stay-county-jail-heres-your-bill

Rosenmerkel, S., Durose, M., & Farole, D. (2009). *Felony sentences in state courts, 2006 – statistical tables*. Washington, DC: Bureau of Justice Statistics.

Ruback, B. (2018). Economic sanctions. In O. H. Griffin III & V. H. Woodward (Eds.), *Routledge handbook of corrections in the United States* (pp. 63–73). New York: Routledge.

Ruddell, R. (2020). *Exploring criminal justice in Canada*. Toronto, ON: Oxford University Press.

Schierenbeck, A. (2018, April 10). Opinion: A billionaire and a nurse shouldn't pay the same fine for speeding. *New York Times*. Retrieved from https://www.nytimes.com/2018/03/15/opinion/flat-fines-wealthy-poor.html

Schultz, C. (2019, Feb. 1). Misdemeanor court tackles fast-paced flow of cases. *Medill Reports Chicago*. Retrieved from https://news.medill.northwestern.edu/chicago/misdemeanor-court-tackles-fast-paced-flow-of-cases/

Schuppe, J. (2015, Aug. 12). Pennsylvania seeks to close books on "kids for cash" scandal. *NBC News*. Retrieved from https://www.nbcnews.com/news/us-news/pennsylvania-seeks-close-books-kids-cash-scandal-n408666

Schwartzapfel, B. (2015, Aug. 13). What it's like to be a jailhouse lawyer. *Vice*. Retrieved from https://www.vice.com/en_ca/article/3bjaky/what-its-like-to-be-a-jailhouse-lawyer-813

Sentencing Guidelines Resource Center. (2018). *In depth: Sentencing guidelines and discretionary parole release*. Retrieved from https://sentencing.umn.edu/content/depth-sentencing-guidelines-and-discretionary-parole-release

Smilowitz, M. (2017). What happens after the right to counsel ends? Using technology to assist petitioners in state postconviction petitions and federal habeas review. *Journal of Criminal Law and Criminology, 107*(3), 493–520.

Smith, L. J. (2018, Feb. 3). UK speeding tickets – what is the law? How much can you be fined? *Sunday Express*. Retrieved from https://www.express.co.uk/life-style/cars/913806/speeding-ticket-fines-UK-law-points-how-much

Snell, T. L. (2019). *Capital punishment, 2017: Selected findings*. Washington, DC: Bureau of Justice Statistics.

Steiner, B., & Cain, C. M. (2018). Punishment within prison: An examination of the influences of prison officials' decisions to remove sentencing credits. *Law & Society Review, 51*(1), 70–98.

Stephenson, C. (2018, Oct. 24). Fines and failures to appear put pressure on low-income convicts and Madison County jails. *Jackson Sun*. Retrieved from https://www.jacksonsun.com/story/news/local/2018/10/24/fines-and-failures-appear-put-pressure-convicts-and-madison-county-jails/1740512002/

Stevenson, M., & Mayson, S. (2018). The scale of misdemeanor justice. *Boston University Law Review, 98* (3), 731–777.

Tonry, M. (2020). *Of one-eyed and toothless miscreants: Making the punishment fit the crime?* New York: Oxford University Press.

U.S. Department of Justice. (2015). *Investigation of the Ferguson police department*. Washington, DC: U.S. Department of Justice, Civil Rights Division.

U.S. Department of Justice. (2017). *Review of the department's oversight of cash seizures and forfeitures activities*. Washington, DC: U.S. Department of Justice, Office of the Inspector General.

U.S. Department of Justice. (2019a). *Helpful definitions*. United States Attorney's Office, District of Alaska. Retrieved from https://www.justice.gov/usao-ak/helpful-definitions

U.S. Department of Justice. (2019b). *Legal terms glossary*. Offices of the United States Attorneys. Retrieved from https://www.justice.gov/usao/justice-101/glossary#m

U.S. Sentencing Commission. (2018). *Mandatory minimum penalties for firearms offenses in the federal criminal justice system*. Washington, DC: Author.

Walker, S. (2015). *Sense and nonsense about crime, drugs, and communities, 8th edition*. Stamford, CT: Cengage Learning.

Washington State Institute for Public Policy. (2019). *Benefit-cost results: Adult criminal justice*. Retrieved from https://www.wsipp.wa.gov/BenefitCost

Waters, N. L., Gallegos, A., Green, J., & Rozsi, M. (2015). *Criminal appeals in state courts, 2010*. Washington, DC: Bureau of Justice Statistics.

Zeng, Z. (2019). *Jail inmates in 2017*. Washington, DC: Bureau of Justice Statistics.

Chapter 4
Probation and Community Corrections

OUTLINE

- Introduction
- A Short History of Community Supervision
- Diverting Individuals from the Justice System
- Ordinary Probation
- Intermediate Sanctions
- Characteristics of Community Corrections Programs
- Probation Officer Roles and Functions
- Increasing Successful Probation Outcomes
- Summary

OBJECTIVES

After reading this chapter you will able to:

- Describe the contemporary arrangements by which probation is provided, monitored, and revoked

- Explain the differences between diversion, standard probation, and intermediate sanctions

- Describe the different roles and functions of probation officers
- Describe the best practices in reducing probationer recidivism
- Describe the personal and offense-related characteristics of probationers

CASE STUDY

Offender-Funded Probation: Do We Punish Probationers for Being Poor?

Cash-strapped governments in 11 states contract with private firms to monitor hundreds of thousands of misdemeanor probation cases. This practice has been a profitable strategy for the businesses delivering these services and local governments benefit because the probationers pay all of their supervision costs. The trouble with this arrangement is that some poor probationers become trapped in a cycle where they cannot escape the fees and other costs, such as drug testing, that are required to stay on probation. If they are unable to pay their supervision fees—that range between $25 and $100 per month (Human Rights Watch, 2014)—they can be arrested and placed in jail. The costs of their jail incarceration are then added to their debt, so their probationary terms are often extended. The firms supervising their probation, by contrast, continue to receive funds for their supervision. Some probationers have paid thousands of dollars because they could not afford a fine of several hundred dollars. A sheriff in a county that uses offender-funded probation says that "The unfortunate part of our judicial system is once you get caught up in it, it's like a rat wheel you can never get out of because of some of the fines and probation" (Cohen, 2016, para. 7).

Karen McNeil, a disabled Tennessee woman in her fifties on a fixed income, was fined $426 in November 2015 for driving with a revoked license. Unable to pay that amount, she was placed on **pay-only probation** (i.e. the only condition of her supervision was paying her fine and supervision fees) and was ordered to pay an installment on the fine as well as $25 every week in court costs, $45 a month to supervise her probation, and $45 for drug tests ordered by the firm supervising her probation. Loller (2019) observes that she became homeless because all her money was going to pay her fine and fees. After failing to make her payments, she was jailed several times for violating her probation conditions and her probationary term was extended, and additional fines added. She eventually served 65 days in jail in 2017 instead of paying her fine and fees (see *McNeil et al. v. Community Probation Services, LLC et al. 2018*), and on December 23, 2019, the Sixth Circuit determined that the case could proceed, and as this book goes to press the case is ongoing.

McNeil's case shows the plight of misdemeanor offenders supervised by private firms that are rewarded when probationers are unable to pay their court-ordered supervision fees. As the probationary period is often extended by the court, more supervision fees for the company are generated. One way of minimizing practices disadvantaging the poor is to waive supervision fees, and probation officers in some jurisdictions can make that request to the courts (Stevens-Martin & Liu, 2017).

Critical Questions

1. Can you think of an alternative to requiring the poor to pay fines and court fees that have very little chance of being collected?
2. On offender-funded probation, who "wins" when a probationer's term of supervision is extended; who loses?
3. What are the direct taxpayer costs for placing Karen McNeil in jail for 65 days because she couldn't afford to pay a $426 fine? (Hint: The Sycamore Institute estimates it cost $44 per day for jail incarceration in Tennessee). What are indirect costs of pay-only probation such as pushing someone into homelessness?

INTRODUCTION

A number of approaches to community supervision of offenders have been introduced since the mid-1800s, and although several different criminal sanctions exist, the most commonly encountered are diversion, probation, and intermediate sanctions, the latter intended to bridge the gap between probation and incarceration. Each of these approaches is distinctive, although probation has been called the "workhorse of the justice system," given that almost 3.7 million probationers are supervised in the community (Kaeble, 2018). Every year about two million new probation cases are added to officer caseloads, while the sentences of another two million end successfully or they are returned to court with new charges (Kaeble, 2018). In this chapter we examine the reasons why governments at all levels are willing to take the risks associated with non-secure alternatives to jail or prison to sanction offenders, as well as the characteristics of these probationers and community-based corrections programs.

Before we examine those issues, however, we must consider several points. First, community-based programs are key parts of the corrections mission in the United States. They stand as viable—and less costly (fiscally, psychologically, and personally)—alternatives to incarceration. One factor that explains the importance of these programs is their variety: they range from interventions that remove people accused of committing crimes from the justice system without appearing in court, such as diversion, to confinement short of placement in a jail or prison, in an individual's home—known as house arrest—in day reporting centers, and punishments that blend custody and community corrections.

Second, it is important to recognize that community-based programs have both supporters and detractors. Program outcomes—particularly high-profile failures—are a source of disagreement between these two groups. Other points of contention reflect philosophical differences about how society should treat people who have committed crimes. Some even believe that probation is overused and that few probationers threaten public safety (Phelps, 2018). For example, Human Rights Watch (2018) notes examples of individuals being placed on probation for not paying their traffic tickets or engaging in minor misdemeanors.

In Chapter 1 we described the issues of mass incarceration and mass probation, although society tends to pay far less heed to the millions of probationers and parolees supervised in the community (Phelps, 2017). DeMichele and Payne (2018, p. 244) observe that "although mass incarceration has received the bulk of the public's and policymakers' attention, there has been a parallel and nearly hidden growth in community supervision populations." While the public generally believes that probation is basically harmless, Phelps (2017) says that anytime people are under correctional supervision, there is the potential that they will move further into the criminal justice system, and once enmeshed in the system, some individuals find it difficult to escape.

Despite these ongoing debates about community-based alternatives to incarceration we expect these sanctions will continue to dominate corrections. We base this statement on several observations:

- As indicated in previous chapters, prison populations are slowly decreasing, and the practices that led to the high numbers such as mandatory minimum sentences and three-strike laws are slowly being eased or dismantled. As a result, there appears to be a growing interest in keeping offenders in the community.
- Probation and parole populations are also decreasing, having dropped by 11% between 2008 and 2016 (Kaeble, 2018, p. 3). Kaeble also reports that about two million cases are added to probation caseloads every year, and, as previously observed, about another two million probationers either successfully fulfill the terms of probation or accumulate additional charges.
- The behavioral expectations placed on probationers seem to be increasing since the 1990s, especially in terms of requiring them to abide by more conditions and participating in rehabilitative interventions such as education, treatment, and vocational programs.

To summarize, this chapter has two key goals. First, we describe the three main categories of community correctional programs and examine their history, processes, current applications, and their futures. Of key interest is whether these approaches reduce correctional populations or instead act as pathways to increased jail and prison admissions. Second, we describe the officers who implement these programs and the ways that community-based correctional agencies can reduce recidivism. Our examination of community-based alternatives to incarceration for accused and convicted offenders starts with a description of the origins of probation.

A SHORT HISTORY OF COMMUNITY SUPERVISION

Probation is the conditional freedom granted to an offender by a court. It is a test of whether the probationer can live in the community without committing new crimes or violate the conditions of release into the community. Even before probation had evolved into its current form, certain legal remedies allowed accused and convicted criminals alike to prove they deserved a second chance. Those remedies—the forerunners of modern probation—included judicial reprieve, bail, and release on one's own recognizance.

Forerunners of Modern Probation

Judicial reprieve has a direct link to modern probation. A common practice in medieval English courts, judicial reprieve was the suspension of a penal sanction for a fixed time. A reprieve gave an offender time to petition the Crown for mercy, which was the only way a sentence—usually the death penalty—could be permanently set aside. Originally used only as a stay of execution courts used the judicial reprieve to delay any sentence indefinitely.

By the 1700s, English judges began suspending sentences in return for a specified period of good behavior. Once these offenders proved they could live crime-free, they petitioned the Crown for a full or partial pardon. Judicial reprieve was also essential to the English transportation program by enabling the courts to suspend the imposition of sentences for prisoners destined for British penal colonies in Australia (or off the coast of Australia), or the lands that would become the United States, including Maryland, Virginia, and Georgia. A century later, the US judicial system adopted the judicial reprieve. The importance of judicial reprieve cannot be overstated. To give convicted offenders a second chance, judges needed a discretionary means to stop the imposition of a sentence. Judicial reprieve was ideal for this purpose.

PHOTO 4.1
Many bail bonds companies are family owned businesses that provide people who would otherwise be held in custody with the opportunity to return to the community if they can afford to post bail. Bail has come under fire in many jurisdictions and some policymakers are trying to develop alternatives to bail that do not disadvantage the poor. Credit: Duncan Selby/ Alamy Stock Photo.

For hundreds of years, bail and **release on recognizance** (ROR) were the only means by which the accused could avoid confinement. Bail is money or property pledged to or held by the court to ensure that an arrested and charged individual will appear for trial. If someone other than the accused posts the bail, that person (or company) assumes responsibility for ensuring the accused appears in court at the scheduled time.

As practiced for centuries under English common law, ROR operated much like modern bail: the accused posted a bond or surety deposit with the court. Its formalization can be traced to the *Habeas Corpus Act* of 1679, which was introduced by the English parliament and stated that:

> A Magistrate shall discharge prisoners from their Imprisonment taking their Recognizance, with one or more Surety or Sureties, in any Sum according to the Magistrate's discretion, unless it shall appear that the Party is committed for such Matter or offences for which by law the Prisoner is not bailable.

By the 1800s, ROR came to mean release from custody based solely on one's personal word to return for trial. It is highly likely that ROR was used in other US criminal cases prior to that time; however, there are no official records describing this practice. In Massachusetts ROR was used as a sentencing alternative and this became the forerunner of probation. By the 1840s the Massachusetts legislature tied monetary sureties to recognizance, but the foundation for what would become probation had been introduced. However, it remained for a colorful Bostonian, John Augustus, to give the practice its name and a set of operational procedures.

John Augustus: The Origins of American Probation

John Augustus (1785–1859) was a wealthy shoemaker when he began an 18-year association with the Boston courts in a quasi-official role where he supervised individuals convicted by the court but released into his care for a period of time, something he called probation. By his death in 1859, Augustus had "bailed on probation" almost 2,000 individuals (Barnes & Teeters, 1959, p. 554). Augustus believed that preventing crime was the intent underlying society's laws and that sanctions should reform criminals rather than simply punishing them. A member of the temperance movement—a religious and political effort to ban alcohol—Augustus was forever changed after visiting a Boston courtroom where he describes how he bailed out an alcoholic:

> I was in court one morning…in which the man was charged with being a common drunkard. He told me that if he could be saved from the House of Corrections, he never again would taste intoxicating liquors: I bailed him, by permission of the Court.
>
> (Augustus, 1852/1972, pp. 4–5)

After carefully selecting the arrestees he thought needed support, Augustus helped them secure jobs and places to live. He supervised them in the community, giving each one a set of conditions intended to enhance their likelihood of making prosocial changes. Augustus warned them that returning to their old ways would also mean a return to court. At the end of a short supervision period—perhaps as little as two or three weeks—Augustus would give the courts an impartial report on the offender's behavior. He coined the term probation, derived from a Latin word meaning to prove or test, as an apt description of his approach to bailing out and treating these individuals. Augustus was the first to conduct presentence investigations, to set conditions of release, to make supervision mandatory, to report on probationers' progress, and to revoke the conditional release. Revocation was rare: August claimed that only one of his first 1,100 probationers forfeited bail (Dressler, 1962, p. 18).

The Evolution of Probation

After Augustus died, volunteers continued to provide probation for Boston's courts until the city hired a professional probation officer in 1878, the year the Commonwealth of Massachusetts adopted a probation statute. By 1918 adult probation services were authorized in 29 states in some form (e.g. only young, first-time offenders were eligible in some states). Like other justice system innovations in the early 1900s there was inconsistent access to probation in most states and it was more likely to be available in cities than in rural areas (Parsons, 1918). Compared with the Northern and Midwestern states, there was very little access to adult probation services in the Southern states (Chute, 1922).

The field of probation evolved during the **progressive era** (1890–1920), which was a time of social reforms that were driven by a desire to advance social progress founded on professionalism and scientific expertise (Sieh, 1993). Many of the individuals involved in these reforms were middle-class women and activists such as **Jane Addams** who helped establish the first juvenile court in 1899 and advocated for the expansion of juvenile probation. Many women were delivering probation services, and the profession evolved from individuals working in voluntary roles to salaried probation officers who had a higher education and were hired based on their performance on civil service examinations (Knupfer, 1999). Organizations such as the National Probation Association, which was formed in 1907, also wanted to professionalize the practice of probation. That organization later became the **American Probation and Parole Association**, an interest group that advocates for all community corrections agencies, supports research on probation and parole, and offers training to members.

Federal authorities were slow to officially adopt formal probation, although federal judges had been suspending prison sentences in cases where this punishment would be considered an unusual hardship. In 1916, a first-time embezzler made full restitution and avoided prison. When the federal judge in the case, John Milton Killits, suspended a five-year sentence, he referred to the embezzler's otherwise good reputation and high standing in the community. The Supreme Court ruled unanimously in *Ex Parte United States* (1916) that Judge Killits did not have the authority to suspend the sentence. The National Probation Association used this opportunity to lobby Congress to pass legislation that would recognize probation. President Calvin Coolidge signed a probation bill into law in 1925, creating what we know today as the U.S. Probation and Pretrial Services System.

From the 1840s to the present, the practice of probation has evolved and become more professional. The following three sections describe a range of community corrections services and include (a) diversion from the justice system, (b) probation, which involves supervising offenders in the community instead of incarcerating them, and (c) intermediate sanctions, such as **intensive supervised probation** (ISP) and house arrest, which are intended to act as tough alternatives to ordinary probation that fall short of jail or prison incarceration.

PHOTO 4.2
Jane Addams was a prominent social reformer who helped introduce the first juvenile court in 1899 and she also played a role in advancing the practice of juvenile probation. Many progressive women of the era volunteered to make the criminal and juvenile justice systems of the era more humane. Credit: PF-(bygone1)/Alamy Stock Photo.

DIVERTING INDIVIDUALS FROM THE JUSTICE SYSTEM

Origins of Diversion

Diversion was a practice that was originally intended to remove young and first-time or minor offenders from the justice system and is intended to remove the stigma of a criminal conviction and the subsequent labeling as an offender. A common element of such programs is holding the individual accountable for his or her actions (Office of Juvenile Justice and Delinquency Prevention, 2017). The sanctions could be as simple as a written apology to a victim or requiring the individual to make restitution or do some community service work. Other diversionary practices, by contrast, are more formal and occur after the individual has been arrested or occur in specialty courts. This section starts with a brief description of how diversion has evolved.

Diversion is the process of removing individuals from the formal system of prosecution and adjudication and placing them in a less-formal treatment setting. For example, a trial court might agree to suspend proceedings against substance abusers charged with possession of illicit drugs if they complete an in-class addictions education program over a two-month period. If the individual successfully finishes the education program the court will drop all charges. If participants fail to complete the sessions, they will be tried and, if convicted, sentenced.

Diversion is based on a criminological theory called **labeling**, or the process by which individuals adopt a new status as an offender after their formal and informal interactions with the police, courts, and corrections. The concept of labeling has been around since the 1960s, although some criminologists would argue that work completed by sociologists in the early twentieth century described a similar process of tagging and identifying youthful offenders that are problematic. Interventions that reduce labeling are popular because it has an intuitive and common-sense appeal. Some social scientists say that after labeling a person a criminal, the criminal justice system contributes to that individual's negative self-image as they define themselves as a deviant, offender, or criminal. Once defining themselves as an offender (i.e. they take on a deviant self-identity) they are more likely to engage in further deviant or criminal behavior.

The connection between labeling theory and diversion programming is straightforward: if we can suspend proceedings before society labels a person who has committed a criminal act as a delinquent or criminal, we can prevent the negative effects of the label. Many supporters of diversion believe this is possible only if the diversion occurs before the individual appears in court. Once a judge finds a person guilty of some crime, they insist, removing the individual from the criminal justice system is simply a means of minimizing their penetration into the system. At that point, some stigma has already attached to the individual and all that placing him or her in a community corrections programming achieves is keeping them out of jail or prison. Hence the key to successful diversion, claim labeling theorists, is the pre-adjudicatory removal from the system. As a result, in some places the police will play a key role in diverting individuals from the courts while in other jurisdictions the individual will go to court although they will not have the stigma of a criminal record if they fulfill all the court's requirements.

Types of Diversionary Programs

Since the 1970s diversionary programs have been introduced throughout the country and according to the Center for Health and Justice at TASC (2013, p. 11) there are three types of these programs:

- Diversion at the law enforcement phase
- Diversion at the pretrial or prosecution phase
- Diversion at the problem-solving/specialty court phase

Given the thousands of counties there will be significant differences in the way that diversion is carried out. Some local justice systems, for example, place a priority on juvenile diversion programs operated by law enforcement agencies, whereas large urban counties are more likely to operate problem-solving courts for adults. A national survey of these programs carried out by the Bureau of Justice Statistics reveals there were over 3,000 of these courts (Strong, Rantala, & Kyckelhahn, 2016). A common goal of these diversionary programs is their efforts to reduce the likelihood of getting a criminal conviction. Table 4.1 shows the different elements in these programs.

Some diversionary programs operated by law enforcement agencies focus on individuals with mental health problems and are intended to get them into treatment rather than being arrested. In jurisdictions prioritizing this approach the police typically work with social workers in **crisis intervention teams**, also called the Memphis Model, to manage people with special needs (Segal, Winfree, & Friedman, 2019). These initiatives are important given the high volume of police calls for service related to people with mental health problems, and a key goal of these programs is to avoid criminalizing their behaviors (Dewa, Loong, Trujillo, & Bonato, 2018). Although the focus of this chapter is on adult services, many law enforcement agencies also have developed diversionary programs to respond to youth crime.

TABLE 4.1 Characteristics of Diversionary Programs

	Law Enforcement	Pretrial/Prosecution	Problem-Solving/Specialty Courts
Managed By	Municipal Police Departments County Sheriff	Prosecuting attorneys (city, county, state, or federal) Pretrial services	Local courts
Diversion Goals	Street-level safety Reduce jail admissions	Reduce court dockets Reduce jail and court expenses Maximize prosecution resources for serious cases	Reduce recidivism Supervision with rehabilitation
Diversion Practices	Street-level crisis management Partner with behavioral health services	Deferred prosecution Referral to community services Individual conditions for each participant	Deferred adjudication/ sentencing Referral to community services Clear goals/sanctions Multidisciplinary staffing

Source: Center for Health and Justice at TASC (2013).

Diversion can also take place after the individual has had an initial or even subsequent contact with the police, but he or she has not been formally charged with a crime; these programs are typically overseen by prosecutors. Although most of these diversionary activities are delivered by probation officers working for county probation agencies, the U.S. Department of Justice (2011, para. 1) also operates a pretrial diversion program and they observe that:

> A majority of offenders are diverted at the pre-charge stage. Participants who successfully complete the program will not be charged or, if charged, will have the charges against them formally dismissed; unsuccessful participants are returned for prosecution.

According to Vance (2018, p. 30):

> the objectives of pretrial diversion are to ensure that the divertee satisfies the terms of the pretrial diversion agreement and to provide the divertee with support services to help facilitate the divertee's compliance with supervision and reduce the likelihood that the divertee will recidivate.

The third form of diversion involves **specialized courts**, also called **problem-solving courts**. Individuals appearing before these courts have already been arrested and prosecutors have decided to bring their cases before a judge. Most specialty courts address issues related to mental health and substance abuse, although Strong, Rantala, and Kyckelhahn (2016) report there are a growing number of courts to confront domestic violence and driving while intoxicated (DWI) offenders as well as crimes committed by veterans. Some tribal courts also have developed programs that recognize the distinctive cultural needs of Native Americans. This approach has several advantages as court and probation personnel develop an expertise in dealing with these individuals. Moreover, most courts have access to resources and services to aid in their rehabilitation. While individuals appearing in these courts are not formally diverted from the justice system, after they complete their court-ordered treatment their cases do not result in a criminal conviction.

Altogether the original intent of diversionary programs is to respond to first-time, young, and minor offenders who pose little risk to public safety. By holding them accountable for their actions and providing them with support and services it is argued they are less likely to commit further offenses. There are three different approaches to diversion that are defined by how far the individual penetrates the justice system—and an important question is whether they are diverted prior to a court appearance. Diversionary programs can reduce the demands on the courts and corrections and should result in better outcomes for these individuals, but that is not always the case. Like other aspects of the criminal justice system, there is sometimes a disconnection between program intention and what actually occurs, and we now turn our attention to the operations of these programs.

Success and Failure

Although the public supports the diversion of some offenders from the criminal justice system, these programs often suffer from a lack of funding. In most jurisdictions funding from county, municipal, or state governments accounts for the greatest share of community corrections budgets although some programs are receiving funding from the United Way or other community organizations; other organizations ask businesses for donations or engage in fund-raising. In tough economic times, however, government funding for community-based programs is often cut and those funds are used for custody programs. For example, in 2018 West Virginia cut funding to 31 community corrections programs, forcing these agencies to cut staff and services (Snoderly, 2018). This problem is not isolated to a single state and rehabilitative and recreational programs are often the first to be cut during economic downturns (Polson, 2002).

The second issue relating to diversion program effectiveness is **net widening**, which "occurs when these types of programs and tactics create an overall increase in the number of individuals having contact (formal and informal) with the criminal justice system by including those that would otherwise not have had that contact" (International Association of Chiefs of Police, 2018, p. xv). In other words, while diversion is intended to reduce the volume of contacts with the justice system, it can have the opposite effect if more individuals become involved in the system. If diversion programs did not exist, say the critics, then many of their clients would have been warned and released by the police; the prosecutor would have declined to prosecute; or the judges would have put them on standard probation. Concerns of net widening have been an ongoing criticism of diversion programs dating back to the 1970s (Austin & Krisberg, 2002). Some research demonstrates that diversion programs are net widening by their very nature (see Mears, Kuch, Lindsey, Siennick, Pesta, Greenwald, & Blomberg, 2016 for an example from the juvenile court). Ultimately, diversion programs may have the effect of significantly increasing our capacity to punish.

A third possible limitation of diversion programs is that these interventions can be used to worsen the overrepresentation of minorities in the justice system. It has been suggested that Whites may be placed in diversionary programs while members of minority groups are not diverted. Writing about youth diversion programs, the Office of Juvenile Justice and Delinquency Prevention (2017, p. 5) observes that "due to their subjective nature, diversion programs may be contrary to the concepts of fairness and justice."

The fourth limitation related to diversion programs is whether they are effective in reducing future justice system involvement. Although diversion programs often receive praise for their effectiveness they deal with the least serious and in some instances, most highly motivated individuals and so these programs should show high success rates. The evidence about program effectiveness, however, is mixed and some programs are more successful than others. A study undertaken by the International Association of Chiefs of Police (2018) found there is little evidence demonstrating that police diversion programs were successful. Consistent with these results, the Washington State Institute for Public Policy (2019) reports that police diversion for persons with mental illnesses had a higher cost than benefit in reduced crime, although jail diversion programs for individuals with mental illnesses were cost-effective, as were police diversion programs for persons involved in low-severity offenses. Rempel et al. (2018) also found mixed results when they evaluated prosecution-led diversionary programs and while most were found to be effective, some were not.

COMPARATIVE ISSUES IN CORRECTIONS

Mass Probation

We have noted previously that the United States has the world's highest imprisonment rate, and although probation is intended to reduce the use of incarceration, the US probation rate per 100,000 residents is also the highest in the world (Corda & Phelps, 2017). This leads to the question of why the United States has the highest rates of incarceration and probation. Figure 4.1 shows the world's highest probation rates and these statistics show that the average of the European nations is one-fifth the US rate. How can we explain that difference, especially when most European nations also use about one-quarter as much incarceration as America (Walmsley, 2018)?

There are two reasons why the United States leads the world in terms of using probation as a sanction: judges sentence more offenders to probation and their sentences are longer. In the United States, for example, the average probationary sentence is about three years, and ten-year probationary sentences are not uncommon. In Canada, by contrast, the average probationary sentence is one year, and nobody can be sentenced to more than three years on probation. A predictable outcome of imposing lengthy probationary terms is that the longer the sentence (the "time at-risk"), the greater the likelihood a violation of probation will occur. US judges also impose probationary sentences more often than judges in other nations, which suggests that our courts are more punitive or that diversionary programs are not having their desired impact.

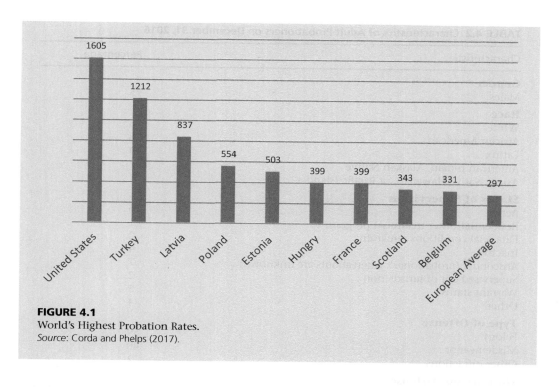

FIGURE 4.1
World's Highest Probation Rates.
Source: Corda and Phelps (2017).

ORDINARY PROBATION

Profile of Probationers

Understanding the demographic and offense-related characteristics of probation populations is important as those factors influence the delivery of probation programs. The information presented in Table 4.2 is based on national-level information on 3.7 million probationers collected by the Bureau of Justice Statistics (Kaeble, 2018). These statistics have remained relatively stable for years, although the proportion of women increased from 22% to 25% between 2000 and 2016 and the proportion of African Americans dropped from 31% to 28% during the same period. Despite those changes, women are still under-represented on probation while African Americans are overrepresented, given that they account for about 13% of the national population (U.S. Census Bureau, 2018). There are fewer Latinx on probation caseloads compared with their prevalence in the national population (14% and 18%, respectively), and the remaining groups, including Native Americans and Pacific Islanders, account for about 2% of all probationers. These statistics are shown in Table 4.2.

Kaeble's (2018) description of probation populations on 31 December 2016 shows that 59% of probationers were felons and that was up from 52% in 2000. This increase could reflect several factors. The first is that probationers convicted of serious offenses in 2016

TABLE 4.2 Characteristics of Adult Probationers on December 31, 2016

Characteristic	Percentage
Gender	
Males	75
Race	
White	55
African American	28
Latinx	14
American Indian, Alaskan Native	1
Asian, Native Hawaiian, or Pacific Islander	1
Status of Supervision	
Active	75
Residential/other treatment program	1
Financial conditions remaining	2
Inactive	4
Absconder (probationer's whereabouts are unknown)	7
Supervised out of jurisdiction	2
Warrant status	5
Other	4
Type of Offense	
Felony	59
Misdemeanor	40
Other infractions	2
Most Serious Offense	
Violent	20
Property	26
Drug	24
Public Order (e.g., DUI, Weapons offenses)	16
Other	13

Source: Kaeble (2018).

were more likely to be placed on probation rather than incarcerating them. It is also possible that prosecutors were more likely to file their cases as felonies in 2016 than they were in 2000. The relatively high proportion of felony probationers has implications for the agencies supervising their cases as high-risk probationers meet with their officer more frequently. Another consideration is that probationers who have committed felonies may be required to participate in rehabilitative endeavors such as substance abuse or anger management courses. With respect to the types of offenses that led to the offender's probationary sentence, these results show they are balanced between violent (20%), property (26%), drug (24%), and public order crimes (16%), with the remaining 13% falling into a category called "other." With respect to the rate of probationers in the state population, Table 4.3 shows that Ohio, Minnesota, and Rhode Island have the highest rates in the nation.

TABLE 4.3 State Probation Rates per 100,000 Adults, December 31, 2016

	Rate
Alabama	1,382
Alaska	1,193
Arizona	1,447
Arkansas	1,347
California	791
Colorado	1,870
Connecticut	1,461
Delaware	2,049
District of Columbia	1,034
Florida	1,288
Georgia	— Not available
Hawaii	1,828
Idaho	2,578
Illinois	1,154
Indiana	2,135
Iowa	1,213
Kansas	758
Kentucky	1,411
Louisiana	1,124
Maine	632
Maryland	1,550
Massachusetts	1,133
Michigan	— Not available
Minnesota	2,280
Mississippi	1,280
Missouri	928
Montana	1,115
Nebraska	937
Nevada	601
New Hampshire	366
New Jersey	2,015
New Mexico	798
New York	628
North Carolina	1,044
North Dakota	1,090

TABLE 4.3 (Continued)

Rate	
Ohio	2,624
Oklahoma	1,129
Oregon	1,127
Pennsylvania	1,783
Rhode Island	2,680
South Carolina	839
South Dakota	1,009
Tennessee	1,209
Texas	1,805
Utah	568
Vermont	969
Virginia	927
Washington	1,565
West Virginia	448
Wisconsin	988
Wyoming	1,046

Source: Kaeble (2018).

Conditions of Probation

There are a number of **standard probation conditions** (also called **general probation conditions**) such as abiding by the law and reporting to the probation officer or the courts that most probationers are expected to follow. In the past, most probationers had to abide by fewer than 10 of these standard conditions, but those numbers have been gradually increasing since the 1990s and Corbett (2015, p. 1710) reports the number of standard conditions in his study of probationers "ran from a low of seven to a high of twenty-four. The average was in the mid-teens." Probationers in Corbett's (2015, p. 710) study were also required to abide by an average of three to five special conditions such as drug testing. His most surprising finding, however, was that probationers were required to abide by an average of 18–20 conditions.

As noted earlier, every jurisdiction is likely to have different standard and special probation conditions, so we provide the ones used by the federal courts as an example. The following standard conditions, described by the Administrative Office of the United States Courts Probation and Pretrial Services Office (2016, p. 94), are monitored by federal probation officers and are summarized as follows:

- You shall not leave the judicial district without the permission of the court or probation officer.
- You shall report to the probation officer and submit a truthful and complete written report within the first 5 days of each month.
- You shall answer truthfully all inquiries by the probation officer and follow their instructions.
- You shall support your dependents and meet other family responsibilities, to include complying with any court order or order requiring the payment of child support.
- You shall work regularly at a lawful occupation unless excused by the probation officer for schooling, training, or other acceptable reasons.
- You shall notify the probation officer 10 days prior to any change of residence or employment.
- You shall refrain from excessive use of alcohol and shall not purchase, possess, use, or distribute any controlled substance or paraphernalia related to such substances.
- You shall not frequent places where controlled substances are illegally sold, used, distributed, or administered.
- You shall not associate with any persons engaged in criminal activity and shall not associate with any person convicted of a felony unless granted permission to do so by the probation officer.
- You shall permit a probation officer to visit at any time at your home, employment, or elsewhere and shall permit confiscation of any contraband observed in plain view by the probation officer.
- You shall notify the probation officer within 72 hours of being arrested, questioned, or upon having any contact with a law enforcement officer.
- You must not own, possess, or have access to a firearm, ammunition, destructive device, or dangerous weapon.
- You shall not enter into any agreement to act as an informant or special agent of a law enforcement agency without the permission of the court.
- If the probation officer determines that you pose a risk to another person or organization, they may require you to notify the person about the risk and you must comply with that instruction.
- You must follow the instructions of the probation officer related to the conditions of supervision.

Judges can also order that probationers abide by additional special conditions such as participating in drug treatment or anger management programs. Some requirements are specific to certain types of offenders or problem behaviors such as sex offenders or probationers with gambling problems. In the federal system, for example, another 20 special

TABLE 4.4 Special Probation Conditions for Federal Probationers

Substance abuse treatment and testing.	Participating in educational services or vocational training.
Mental health treatment.	Location monitoring such as electronic or GPS monitoring.
Financial requirements, including paying outstanding fines.	Residing in a residential treatment center.
Employment restrictions.	Intermittent confinement (e.g. serving a custody sentence on weekends).
Restrictions on contact with others (e.g. gang members).	Submit to search and seizure of one's person, property, residence, or computer.
Place restrictions such as prohibiting sex offenders from being near playgrounds.	Immigration-related requirements including surrendering to Immigration and Customs Enforcement.
Supporting dependents, including children.	
Gambling-related conditions such as requiring treatment.	Restrictions on viewing sexually explicit materials.
Completing community service work.	
Participating in cognitive behavioral treatment.	Submit to polygraph testing for sexual offender management.
Computer-related restrictions, including prohibiting accessing the Internet.	

Source: Administrative Office of the United States Courts Probation and Pretrial Services Office (2016).

conditions can be imposed, and they are described by the Administrative Office of the United States Courts Probation and Pretrial Services Office (2016, pp. 95–99) and summarized in Table 4.4.

The 20 special conditions summarized in Table 4.4 can be modified to fit the specific risk that a probationer poses. For example, when it comes to gambling, the probationer's condition can be written as:

> You must not engage in any form of gambling (including, but not limited to, lotteries, on-line wagering, sports betting) and you must not enter any casino or other establishment where gambling is the primary purpose (e.g., horse race tracks, off-track betting establishments).
>
> (Administrative Office of the United States Courts Probation and Pretrial Services Office, 2016, p. 97)

Judges can also require that probationers pay for their supervision, treatment, or electronic monitoring (EM) in the community.

One of the gaps in our knowledge is whether extra-legal factors that have nothing to do with the actual offense—such as race, class, or gender—influence the number and severity of conditions imposed on probationers. Kimchi (2018) examined the probation conditions of over 3,000 persons sentenced in two urban courts and found that a greater number of conditions were imposed on young African Americans and African American drug dealers. While these results came from a small number of cases, it suggests the issue requires further examination.

Length of Probation Supervision

Probationary sentences can range from less than a year to a lifetime for serious offenses. In 1988, Arizona legislators enacted laws allowing judges to sentence sex offenders to **lifetime probation** (Pullen & English, 1996). However, lifelong probation is rarely imposed and Watts (2016) examined the maximum length of probationary sentences in 21 states, finding that in 12 states the maximum length of sentence was two years for a misdemeanor and five years for a felony. By contrast, judges in California, Minnesota, Pennsylvania, and Wisconsin can impose a probationary sentence that was the equivalent of the maximum incarceration term for felony offenses. Watts (2016, p. 1) explains that "in Minnesota, the maximum felony incarceration term for a very serious crime is 40 years; this would also be the maximum possible length of probation for such an offense."

Sawyer and Bertram (2018, para. 8) argue that lengthy probation terms, strict conditions, and close supervision set probationers up to fail. Moreover, the failure rate of probationers also seems to increase when more conditions are imposed on them. But there are always two sides to every story and many front-line police and probation officers disagree that probationers are set up to fail. Sipes (2018, para. 2) points out that many:

> Violations committed by the average probationer are simply ignored or responded to with warnings. It's been my experience that many (if not most) probationers have scores of technical violations, don't make full restitution, don't complete community service, fail drug or mental health treatment, don't meet family obligations, continue to use drugs, violate stay away orders and abuse women yet "successfully" complete probation.

Sipes (2018) softens this statement somewhat by saying that it is very difficult for some ex-prisoners to reintegrate back into society, especially when community corrections programs are under-funded and provide inadequate supports for participants. Like many of the issues raised in our exploration in corrections, there are no clear black and white answers to overcoming these challenges and both Sawyer and Bertram (2018) and Sipes (2018) raise important points.

Since 2010 several states have placed limits on the length of time individuals can serve on probation or allow probationers to apply to terminate their sentences early. In Georgia, for example, the average probationary sentence was about seven years, which was more than twice the national average (Georgia Council Report, 2011) and 1 in 17 adults in the state was on probation (Council of State Governments, 2018). In 2017 the Georgia legislature amended its laws to allow probationers who were successfully fulfilling their probation conditions to apply to have their sentence terminated. Since that time the number of probationers has decreased and smaller caseload sizes enable probation officers to devote more attention to higher-risk individuals (Council of State Governments, 2018).

Violations of Probation

Probation has several different outcomes, and they are shown in Figure 4.2. According to the Bureau of Justice Statistics, over one-half of probationers successfully complete their sentences (Kaeble, 2018, p. 15). About one-quarter (26%) were incarcerated (either for new charges or violations of their current probation orders) or their exit from probation was considered unsatisfactory. An unsatisfactory exit means that the individual failed to meet all conditions of probation—normally only financial conditions—although none were incarcerated. Of the remaining probationers, about 3% **absconded** (either left the jurisdiction or didn't report to their officer in a specific time frame such as three months), and less than 1% died. One of the largest categories shown in Figure 4.2 is "other" and the Bureau of Justice Statistics was unable to determine the outcomes for those probationers. As a result, this category could include any of the outcomes reported earlier, as well as deportation or transfer to Immigration and Customs Enforcement. Said another way, we don't know why one in five probationers exited probation, which is a serious limitation in our understanding of the issue.

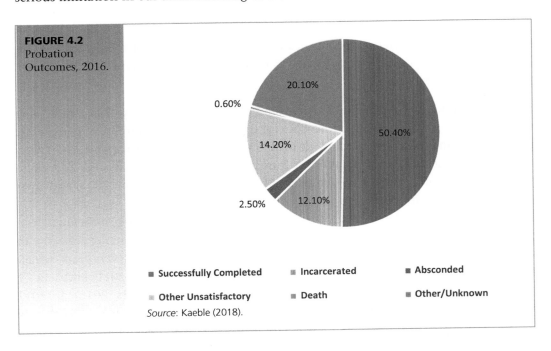

FIGURE 4.2
Probation Outcomes, 2016.

- Successfully Completed
- Incarcerated
- Absconded
- Other Unsatisfactory
- Death
- Other/Unknown

Source: Kaeble (2018).

Although most of us think that successfully completing a term of probation as a relatively easy task, some individuals prefer incarceration to probation. Corbett (2015, p. 1712) reports that probationers in focus groups say that "the stiff enforcement of an impossibly demanding set of requirements will ultimately lead to incarceration. So, they ask, why postpone the inevitable and subject themselves to the steady drip-drip-drip of close monitoring of everyday behavior?" May, Wood, and Eades (2008, p. 193) found that offenders rated probation as being almost twice as punitive as corrections professionals, judges, or members of the public. Given those perceptions some probationers violating their probation conditions ask judges to serve their sentences in jail, a topic covered in the pages that follow.

Many probationers violate their probation conditions, and many are considered a **technical violation**. The Pew Charitable Trusts (2018, p. 3) defines a technical violation as "noncompliance with one or more conditions of supervision, excluding new criminal convictions, that may result in sanctions or revocation." Like other aspects of the corrections system, a probation officer's discretion determines whether the probationer will be cautioned or warned, or whether the case is referred to a prosecutor. As a result, technical violations can be a controversial issue, although it is relatively safe to say that the sanctions for minor violations such as failing to notify the probation officer of a job change, missing a reporting date or a therapy session, or applying for a driver's license without prior consent are more likely to result in a warning than a violation. Technical violations that are more serious, such as possessing a firearm, are more likely to result in a referral to a prosecutor. However, some persons committing relatively minor technical violations can be treated very harshly. *The New York Times* reports about a probationer who received a technical violation after sending a judge a letter requesting to move to a different apartment within her complex because mice had infested her apartment. The judge refused to approve the move, and even though the move never happened "it would take her three and a half months, five court hearings, three letters from her landlord and a copy of her lease to convince the judge" that her probation should not be violated (Dewan, 2015, para. 30).

Some critics argue that violating the conditions of one's probation and the potential for incarceration is much too severe a penalty for minor technical violations (Sawyer & Bertram, 2018). Instead, some scholars suggest that less punitive sanctions be imposed, but few probation agencies have the resources to deal with these violations, so incarceration is seen as the only option (Jacobson, Schiraldi, Daly, & Hotez, 2017). In most cases where the court orders probation revocation, the probationer has a new criminal charge, and not just a technical violation. So, what are the most common types of violations? Gray, Fields, and Maxwell (2001,

p. 548) found that these were most frequently violations in their study of Michigan probationers (that did not result in a new criminal charge):

- Failure to report
- Failed drug test
- Failure to pay fine/restitution
- Program failure (substance abuse)
- Program failure (community service)
- Alcohol violations

Gray and colleagues report that nearly 30% of these violations occurred within 100 days of their sentencing. These researchers also found that although most probationers violated their probation conditions, few committed serious crimes.

In order to streamline the punishment of probationers for their technical violations California, Hawaii, and several other states have developed **flash incarceration**. Neil (2008, para. 2) defines flash incarceration as an "immediate, short-term punishment—in the form of a brief jail term—for virtually any probation violation." Somewhat similar to shock incarceration, flash incarceration of one to two weeks which was followed by the probationer's release was one of the features of Hawaii's Opportunity Probation with Enforcement (HOPE) program. This approach was introduced in other states, but evaluations showed these programs never lived up to their expectations (Schiraldi, 2016).

Ruhland and Robey (2017) asked adults whose probationary sentences had been revoked about why they violated their conditions, and those responses help us better understand probation from an offender's perspective. For instance, when asked about their experiences on probation, many said that abiding by curfews and the financial requirements of being on probation were difficult to meet, especially when the probationer had employment and childcare responsibilities. Some probationers were critical of the probation staff who would not let them bring their children to their interviews. Not only did they have to travel to their probation appointments, but they also had to arrange childcare. Paying for their supervision was a common complaint of three individuals reported below:

PHOTO 4.3
A probation and police officer from Los Angeles arrest a probationer after handguns were found in his home. In many jurisdictions the police and probation staff form partnerships and work together to provide better supervision of these parolees. Credit: ZUMA Press, Inc./Alamy Stock Photo.

The prices [for probation] were too high, the monthly payments...$350 per month. I've got 4 kids. I was able to pay for a while but eventually I couldn't.

(p. 5)

I lost my job. I couldn't find another one. I couldn't make my payments. She revoked me.

(p. 5)

I was going to [court ordered] drug classes but I couldn't pay them. I decided to take state jail for 9 months because I didn't want probation. I didn't try to run. I turned myself in. For the classes I had to pay $50 every Monday.

(p. 5)

The last respondent says it is easier to be incarcerated than being on probation, and that preference is commonly expressed by offenders. Ruhland and Robey (2017) found that some probationers who could no longer follow their conditions would ask to be placed in jail if the judge would end their probation once they were released from custody.

Revoking Probation

When the officer learns that a probationer has violated the conditions of the release order, that officer can take a number of steps, including issuing a verbal or other informal warning or they can arrest the individual and take them into custody. If the probationer is accused of committing a new crime or a technical violation it can trigger a revocation hearing, and most probation agencies have adopted a standardized process for revocations. The probationer receives formal notice of the specific charges and a preliminary hearing date. The preliminary hearing determines probable cause that a violation has occurred. If the probationer fails to show up at the hearing, the court normally issues a failure-to-appear warrant. The warrant adds to the probationer's problems because it is a new charge and a technical violation in and of itself. If the probationer appears and enters a guilty plea, the court has the option of ordering imprisonment or issuing a reprimand, which is something like a stern warning. If the probationer waives the preliminary hearing or enters a plea of not guilty, the next step is a revocation hearing.

Several U.S. Supreme Court decisions have established specific guidelines for revocation hearings. Probationers should have the opportunity to testify and present witnesses. They also should be able to hear and cross-examine the state's witnesses and challenge any other evidence. Unless a compelling state interest exists, the accused also has the right to counsel. Probationers are at some disadvantage in these proceedings as the civil standard of proof, which is a preponderance of evidence, applies rather than standard of guilt beyond a reasonable doubt. Second, evidence that would not normally find its way into a criminal case, including hearsay evidence, often is used at revocation hearings. In reaching their decisions, judges may consider any relevant information, including work records, their progress in any treatment programs, and the probationers' relationships with family or friends.

If the hearing authority finds a probationer had not violated the conditions of their release he or she returns to probation. However, if the decision is that the defendant is guilty, the judge has several options. If the violations were relatively minor, the judge can sentence the offender to continued probation, perhaps with new conditions, such as assignment to a **halfway house** (HH), intensive supervision, or EM. When the violations are more serious or numerous or both, the court usually revokes probation and orders incarceration. In cases where the judge suspended sentencing pending the offender's successful completion of probation, the judge can impose whatever sentence the law allows for the original offense, up to and including the maximum. If the court did impose a sentence before releasing the offender on probation, the judge may choose to execute that sentence once he or she revokes probation.

Meek Mill's 12 Years on Probation

Meek Mill had been incarcerated or on probation for gun and drug charges for almost a decade when he won the 2016 Billboard Music Award for the top rap album. Afterwards he was jailed for five months for recklessly driving his dirt bike and an altercation with an airport employee (Zaru, 2017). Even though the charges were dropped for those offenses, the arrests were enough to violate the conditions of his probation, and he could have served up to four years for these technical violations.

After his release from custody in 2017 Mill said that "A lot of people, they get locked up for technical violations…they lose their jobs, and they lose their family. Their kids go fatherless for months, years at a time, over small mistakes, not committing crimes" (as cited in Bala, 2018, para. 4). Mill was still on probation until August 2019, when his sentence ended as part of a negotiated plea bargain where he pleaded guilty to the misdemeanor firearms offense from 2007. The Philadelphia District Attorney stated that Mill "was unfairly treated in a case that exemplifies the destruction caused by excessive supervision, instances of corruption, and unfair processes in our criminal courts" (as cited in Allyn, 2019, para. 9).

Mill, fellow rapper Jay-Z, and media personality and author Van Jones are co-chairs of the REFORM Alliance, which is an organization they founded to reform America's

PHOTO 4.4
Rapper Meek Mill speaks at a downtown Philadelphia Rally in 2018. Mill served almost a decade on probation before his sentence ended in August 2019. Mill has become involved in the efforts to reform the criminal justice system and is an opponent of people serving long-term probationary sentences. Credit: ZUMA Press, Inc./Alamy Stock Photo.

criminal justice system. They point out that Mills' case is only one in a nation where millions of people become trapped in systems such as probation. Once present in the system, they find it difficult to escape their supervision, which makes them vulnerable to probation officers violating the conditions of their release.

INTERMEDIATE SANCTIONS

Diversion and ordinary probation were originally intended to manage low-risk offenders, although over one-half of probationers today are felons. In response to that change we developed a range of intermediate sanctions, which are community-based punishments intended to bridge the gap between ordinary probation and incarceration. According to a report by the Columbia University Justice Lab (2018), these sanctions emerged along with the "get tough" on crime movement in the 1980s although our review finds that some of these sanctions have been around for over a century. Intermediate sanctions were developed in response to the popular view that probation wasn't very tough on crime. It was also thought that intensive sanctions would reduce correctional overcrowding and be a cost-effective alternative to incarceration. Furthermore, supporters of rehabilitation believed that keeping offenders in the community would make it easier to work toward their reform. Ultimately, these community-based sanctions were intended to hold individuals accountable and reduce the reliance on incarceration and they range across the four approaches described below.

PHOTO 4.5
This woman wears an ankle monitor that transmits information to the probation agency about their client's whereabouts. Electronic monitoring enables some probationers to remain in the community rather than placed in jail. One downside to these programs is the high costs of supervision the probationer must pay, which can exceed $15 per day in some places, making these punishments inaccessible to the poor. Credit: Bob Daemmrich/Alamy Stock Photo.

Intensive Supervised Probation

ISP is based on increasing the supervision that probationers receive and was originally intended for high-risk offenders who might otherwise have been incarcerated. Early forms of these programs have been around since the 1960s and 1970s and briefly fell out of favor before making a comeback in the 1980s in Georgia (Gill, 2018). Caseload sizes for the officers supervising these probationers are often very small (e.g. 20–30 persons) and the probationers may be required to meet weekly or even more often with their probation officer. In addition to more frequent meetings, most of these probationers are required to follow a greater number of standard or specialized probation conditions. These conditions might include frequent drug testing and require the offender to participate in educational or treatment programs.

Some people serving ISP sentences are also required to participate in EM, in which they wear a monitor attached to their ankles or wrists that alerts correctional officials at a central location if the probationer is more than a short distance from their home's landline phone (e.g. 25 yards). Newer versions of EM use global positioning systems (GPS) to continuously track the probationer's whereabouts, and some monitors can also test for alcohol consumption. Advances in GPS technology also make it possible to determine if the individual is in a "no go" zone (e.g. playgrounds for those convicted of sex offenses or a victim's home for a domestic violence offender). GPS also allows offender movements be restricted to an inclusion zone, where the probationer is expected to stay, such as an alcohol treatment center (Latzer, 2017). The Washington State Institute of Public Policy (2019) found that for every dollar spent on EM, there was a $12 return in lower crime. Their results are similar to those reported by Williams and Weatherburn (2019), who found that EM lowered correctional costs over the short- and long-term.

House Arrest

Some probationers are sentenced to house arrest (also called **home confinement**), where they must remain in their residence unless they make arrangements with their probation officer to leave the home. Finding an appropriate and stable home where there is no substance abuse for these individuals is not always an easy proposition, and these homes also require a landline for the EM equipment. Once a home is secured, the probationer will often be required to attend school or treatment programs or work. House arrests have a number of benefits to the offender such as enabling them to take a positive rehabilitative step and take control of their lives. Society also benefits as the costs of incarceration are reduced since in many jurisdictions these probationers are required to pay for their supervision. This brings us back to the problem of funding programs using offender payments as this approach might create an incentive for them to commit crimes to pay for their community-based supervision. Bouchard and Wong (2018) carried out a meta-analysis (where the impact of many studies is considered) and they found that EM reduces recidivism for individuals who are released from custody.

One of the challenges of evaluating house arrest programs is that while EM verifies the individual was at home they could be selling drugs out the back door. As a result, probation agencies conduct home visits to enhance a probationer's supervision (Abt Associates, 2018). Patten, La Rue, Caudill, Thomas, and Messer (2018) describe how EM offenders received more frequent home visits at the start of their sentences and afterwards their visits were matched to their level of risk; lower risk individuals were visited less frequently. Even though these researchers predicted these offenders would think these visits were intrusive, they found that "home visits built relationships with the deputies, created a level of trust and respect with the deputies, and even altered their decision-making behaviors for the positive" (Patten et al., 2018, p. 726).

Community Residential Centers

Community residential centers (CRC) are sometimes called HHs, given that they are intended to bridge the community and incarceration. HHs have been around since 1800s and smaller ones are sometimes found in residential neighborhoods. These CRC are operated by federal, state or county governments, privately owned correctional firms, or by non-governmental organizations. According to Wong, Bouchard, Gushue, and Lee (2019, p. 1020) these facilities share four common elements:

- Temporary housing
- Provided in a community-based residential facility
- Using around the clock supervision
- Offering services to assist with the difficult transition from incarceration to the community (or as an alternative to incarceration)

These places lack the high security features of a jail or prison and are more "home-like" and few have fences surrounding the facility. Unlike prisons, these CRC tend to be small. Because of their low security nature and low staff-to-resident ratio, they are often inexpensive to operate compared with traditional correctional institutions.

PHOTO 4.6
Halfway houses are intended to form a bridge between prison and the community for the ex-prisoner. In this picture a half-way house resident is watering that facility's garden. Produce raised by this halfway house is donated to soup kitchens and local residents. Credit: Jim West/Alamy Stock Photo.

There is no single pathway to an individual's admission to a CRC. Some are sentenced directly into these facilities as a condition of probation, while others are released to a CRC after a jail or prison sentence. Phrased another way, individuals are either "halfway in" to jail or prison or "halfway out" of jail or prison (Latessa, 2012). CRC allow more freedoms than jails or prisons but Hyatt and Han (2018, p. 189) observe that "movements in and out of HH are restricted, residents are permitted to leave for a variety of reasons: medical visits, employment opportunities, and educational and religious services, among others." Can these places reduce recidivism? Wong, Bouchard, Gushue, and Lee (2019) conducted a meta-analysis of studies where ex-prisoners were placed in HHs and they found these individuals were more successful than ex-prisoners released to the community. The Washington State Institute for Public Policy (2019), however, did not find a cost benefit to these programs.

Split Sentences

As the name implies, **split sentences** involve a sentence that is divided between a custody facility and the community. Individuals are sentenced to a period of incarceration that typically ranges from one to six months, followed by a probationary sentence. There are some differences across the country and legislation in California and other states enables judges to impose sentences of several years of incarceration followed by probation (Navratil & Hill, 2017; Nguyen, Grattet, & Bird, 2017). Moreover, there is no single model within some states and Florida has three types of split sentences. The federal government also allows individuals to be sentenced to a split sentence where half the sentence is served in a federal facility and the remainder on home arrest or in a community-based facility.

There are few meaningful differences between split sentences and **shock probation** except that most people sentenced to shock probation serve shorter periods of incarceration: usually less than a month. These interventions are intended for first-time offenders and the short period of incarceration is designed to act as a cost-effective alternative to long-term incarceration. These sanctions have been around since the 1960s, and they were controversial then (Waldron & Angelino, 1977). Supporters of shock probation say the short period of incarceration gives offenders a taste of prison life, which will deter them from engaging in further crimes. Opponents of this approach contend that incarceration disrupts their lives and introducing them to the hostile environment of the prison and more sophisticated offenders may be criminogenic.

Intermediate sanctions that bridge probation and incarceration, such as HHs, have been around since the 1800s, and shock probation has existed since the 1960s. These sanctions are more punitive than ordinary probation and are popular with legislators who want to be seen as being tough on crime. The evidence surrounding their effectiveness, however, tends to be mixed. Some of these interventions—during different eras and places—were seen as effective, but most research has not found that these programs reduce recidivism. This makes it difficult to say with any certainty whether these programs should be abandoned, and new interventions developed. The issue of why some correctional programs are more successful than others is addressed in Chapter 6.

CHARACTERISTICS OF COMMUNITY CORRECTIONS PROGRAMS

As previously noted, probation refers to the practice of conditionally releasing an offender into the community. The releasing authority is the trial court, part of the judiciary. However, either the judicial branch or the executive branch of state or local government provides probation services—distinctions in practice that owe as much to tradition as to policy. In most jurisdictions, responsibility for probation services lies with the executive branch of the state government. In this section we explore who is eligible for probation, the officials who supervise these individuals in the community, and the characteristics of their workloads.

Eligibility for Probation

The Supreme Court ruled in *United States v. Birnbaum* (1970) that probation is a privilege and not a right. The probation-granting authority is under no constitutional or statutory obligation to choose conditional release over incarceration. In fact, both federal and state statutes prohibit probation for certain types of offenses. For example, some states deny probation to individuals convicted of murder, kidnapping, or rape. A review of felony offenders sentenced in large urban courts shows that no homicide offenders were placed on probation, although 8% of convicted rapists were sentenced to probation (Reaves, 2013, p. 29). And while probationary sentences for murderers are very rare, they are sometimes imposed, and Skoloff (2013) describes how an Arizona man was sentenced to two years on probation for his role in the mercy killing of his terminally ill wife. Some women found guilty of killing an abusive partner are also sentenced to probation (Field, Cherukuri, Kimuna, & Berg, 2017).

Probation Officers

The various jurisdictions in the United States take several different approaches to probation work. First, about one-third of the states use probation-only officers (Mays &

Winfree, 2014). This model acknowledges that separate government bodies are responsible for probation and parole. That is, probation officers are sworn officers of the judicial branch, as are judges, attorneys, and even bailiffs. In many of these jurisdictions, judges or court administrators hire, train, and supervise probation officers. The second approach combines probation and parole functions, and this is the model in about two thirds of states, the District of Columbia, and the federal government's U.S. Probation and Pretrial Services System. In these jurisdictions, the officers either have mixed probation and parole caseloads or they specialize in one or the other. Specialization recognizes the different risks and needs that probationers and parolees pose.

A second set of issues involves the arming of probation officers, a practice that has been controversial among probation officers for decades. While probation officers in some states were first issued firearms in the 1970s about three-quarters of agencies now authorize their officers to carry firearms, but practices within states were sometimes mixed, and some counties would allow officers to carry a firearm, but other jurisdictions would not (American Probation and Parole Association, 2014). Furthermore, decisions about carrying firearms are sometimes left to the individual officer. When Rhineberger-Dunn and Mack (2018) asked front-line officers about carrying firearms, they found that support for carrying firearms increased when they were fearful of their safety.

Given the variety of practices and policies, it is difficult to come up with a single way of classifying firearms use. In about one-half of the states and the U.S. Probation and Pretrial Services System, all officers are certified peace officers and must always carry weapons or when performing special duties such as arresting a probationer. Another pattern is where the probation officers are not certified peace officers and may not be armed while on duty, and this accounts for about one-quarter of all states. There are two remaining classifications. The first is that some probation staff are peace officers and are conditionally armed, which occurs in one-quarter of these jurisdictions. An equally rare combination, found in several states and the District of Columbia, is where certified peace officers are not authorized to carry side arms. Although state legislation may authorize probation officers to carry firearms, some local or county agencies may not permit the practice. Unlike traditional law enforcement officers in the United States, there is no single pattern concerning the peace officer and firearms statuses of probation officers.

Presentence Investigation and Reports

A presentence investigation report (PSI) is a detailed examination, prepared by a probation officer, caseworker, or other court officer, of a criminal defendant's life. These reports are ordered by the court and officers are typically given from 30 to 60 days to complete the investigation and write the report. To gather information about the offender, the investigator examines records (school, police, and, with a court order, medical records) and interviews the offender as well as people who have regular contact with them such as family members, friends, coworkers, teachers, coaches, or religious leaders. The PSI can also include interviews with witnesses to the crime, the investigating police officers, and the victims or victims' next of kin. Probation officers also scan the online presence of these people to gain additional insight about them (American Probation and Parole Association, 2014).

Few documents take on a greater significance in a convicted-felon's life than the PSI report. It can spell the difference between probation and incarceration. Moreover, these reports often form the basis of the individual's assessment if incarcerated and can influence their security placement and their access to rehabilitative opportunities while imprisoned. As a result, the PSI can act as a roadmap for their future rehabilitative efforts. Thus, the information contained in these reports can impact an individual's access to services throughout their time in the criminal justice system.

To some extent, the PSI reports are a product of the court's culture and they can vary in length, from short standardized documents to longer examinations of the offender's circumstances. Some probation officers will tailor the report to the offense, and for serious crimes their examination may be more thorough than for an individual convicted of property offenses. In some respects, the courtroom experience of probation officers—especially their understanding of the judge or judges they serve—may well shape the factors they choose to include in PSI reports and even in their recommendations.

The product of this lengthy examination is a PSI report that often includes a recommended sentence. These recommendations may be based on the probation officer's understanding of the local going rate (see Chapter 3). While some jurisdictions may require a recommendation for sentencing some judges might not want such a recommendation. When probation officers make a recommendation, the outcome is often the same: judges follow the PSI recommendations about three-quarters of the time. Leifker and Sample (2010) found that judges followed officer recommendations in 79% of the cases they reviewed, and even when there was a difference between the recommended and actual sentence, those differences were often very minor. Leiber, Beaudry-Cyr, Peck, and Mack (2018) also found a high agreement (78%) between an officer's recommendation for community placement and sentences imposed by judges, while judges were slightly more likely to depart from an officer's recommendation for incarceration (62%).

In the PSI, probation officers answer three questions. First, what circumstances promote a sentence other than incarceration? Second, what aggravating circumstances suggest that jail or prison, rather than a community-based sentence, is the best alternative for this offender? Third, does the defendant—now a convicted criminal—have special needs or problems that can be best resolved in the community rather than behind bars? When answering these questions, the probation officer tends to focus on the offender's threat to public safety. Given the potential risks of making a bad recommendation, with the possibility of the probationer committing a serious violent crime, some probation officers tend to err on the side of being conservative (Ricks, Louden, & Kennealy, 2016). In other words, as some officers are risk-averse they won't take many chances with the recommendations they make in the PSI.

Some of the PSI content is legally hearsay: that is, someone other than the informant either saw or heard the defendant do or say something. As a result, diligent probation officers attempt to crosscheck the accuracy of mitigating and aggravating information before including it in the report. Although officers might tell their sources that their information is confidential, the judge may require that informants testify to confirm the information's reliability (see *Gardner v. Florida*, 1977).

When the Rich Are Sentenced

In Chapter 1 we introduced readers to the work of Reiman and Leighton (2017), who entitled their book *The Rich Get Richer and the Poor Get Prison*. When the rich are prosecuted and sentenced, they can use their resources to reduce the harshness of their sentences. Some well-to-do offenders hire **sentencing consultants** to provide them with information on how to influence the officers preparing presentence investigation reports. Their goal in hiring these consultants is to reduce their likelihood of incarceration as well as making their transition to jail or prison more comfortable if they are incarcerated. These sentencing consultants include former judges or correctional officials as well as ex-prisoners and other officials familiar with prison placements. An online search reveals there are dozens of these consultants. The Prison Professors (2018), for example, provide individuals with information prior to their interviews with the probation officer to "position themselves for the lowest possible sentence" and "ensure the defendant serves the sentence in the best possible environment." They charge individuals up to $5,000 for their advice, but for those who can afford it, this might be money well-spent.

Some middle- and upper-class offenders headed for prison contract with **prison preppers**—most of whom are ex-prisoners—who provide courses called *Prison 101* to smooth the transition from life on the streets to time behind bars. These consultants provide the person headed to jail or prison with tips on how to avoid trouble while incarcerated and help them serve their time with as few difficulties as possible, and to make the most of their incarceration (Albrecht, 2018). Hiring sentencing consultants and prison preppers is another example of how the wealthy can manipulate the system to ease the pains of imprisonment.

RACE, CLASS, AND GENDER

Risk-Management Classifications, Caseload, and Workload Issues

Rather than simply dividing caseloads into felony or misdemeanor probationers most probation departments classify their probationers into different groups based on the risks they pose to public safety and their need for supervision. In addition, almost all large probation agencies place individuals with special needs (such as persons with mental illnesses) or have been convicted of specific offenses such as driving while intoxicated (DWI), sex offenses, or domestic violence into a single caseload. The probation officers supervising these offenders develop specialized knowledge and skills in dealing with these individuals and this may increase their effectiveness.

When it comes to the "generalized" caseloads, four different supervision models have been identified based on the probationer's need for supervision, and the following describes an approach based on those levels of supervision:

- *Administrative* is for the lowest risk individuals, who are assessed as posing no serious public safety threat and are generally first-time offenders. Probation officers' interactions with these probationers are minimal and any contacts might only happen if the probationer contacts them. Some jurisdictions have required low-risk probationers to report at computer terminals (called kiosks) on a scheduled basis and their probation officer will not contact them unless they fail to report (Viglione & Taxman, 2018).
- *Minimum supervision* is for probationers who pose no significant public safety threat and have no history of serious crimes although they often have prior convictions for misdemeanors. These low-risk probationers generally contact their probation officer by mailing postcards or by phone once a month or even less frequently.
- *Medium supervision* is for individuals who pose no significant threat to public safety but do have histories of serious crime. They must report in person at least once a month, and the officer may make occasional visits to their home or places of work.
- *Intensive supervision* is for offenders who have histories of violent behavior. They must report to their probation officer several times a month and are subject to even more frequent workplace and home visits than are probationers under medium supervision.

Agencies may label these classifications differently, and the U.S. Probation and Pretrial Services System also uses four categories, but labels them according to risk: low, low-moderate, moderate, and high-risk (Cohen, Cook, & Lowenkamp, 2016). One factor differentiating probation departments is how these individuals are classified and assigned to **caseloads** (all the probationers supervised by an officer). Some agencies might use the officer's judgment—or gut feelings—to make these classification decisions while other agencies use formal risk assessments. Given the time and expense of carrying out risk assessments, however, they are more likely to be conducted in larger probation agencies and for people with more extensive criminal histories.

A key issue in probation is offender supervision and how many individuals are assigned to each probation officer. There are practical limits to how many individuals an officer can supervise, and those limits are based on the number of clients on their caseloads and the intensity of their supervision. When caseloads are classified according to risk, one officer can typically supervise very large numbers of low-risk probationers as they may have few contacts with the officer. High-risk probationers, by contrast, require frequent face-to-face contact and sometimes these requirements are defined in the agency's policies. As a result, the caseload size of high-risk offenders is generally small. Table 4.5 shows the American Probation and Parole Association (2006) recommendations in terms of caseload size for different classifications of probationers.

When addressing caseload sizes, Baldwin (2018) says that these caseloads do not consider the different expectations of courts and some judges may require more contact with low or medium risk probationers. States also have different reporting requirements and standards requiring a set number of face-to-face meetings per month (e.g. North Carolina Department of Public Safety, 2017). Moreover, the jurisdiction's characteristics might also influence whether those caseload sizes are reasonable. In rural areas, for example, probation officers spend more time traveling to make home or workplace visits, and they have less time to meet with their probationers. This brings us to the issue of specialized and generalized caseloads.

Many small probation agencies might only supervise several hundred probationers, so they cannot take advantage of classifying probationers into different groups. In many of these offices a probation officer may supervise up to 100 individuals in a **generalized caseload** (also called mixed or traditional caseloads), where all probationers are managed, from low-risk misdemeanor offenders to those with extensive criminal histories. When supervising a generalized caseload, the officer will prioritize supervision efforts and spend more time with high-risk offenders and less time (or no time at all) with low-risk

TABLE 4.5 Recommended Caseload Sizes

Supervision Level (Low to High)	Probationers per Officer	Time per Month per Probationer
Administrative	1,000	0.12 hours
Minimum	200	0.61 hours
Medium	50	2.44 hours
Intensive	20	6.04 hours

Source: American Probation and Parole Association (2006).

clients. Specialized probation caseloads, by contrast, typically involve supervising one type of offender, such as sex offenders, or persons who have mental health problems. By having an officer specialize in managing these specific groups of offenders, they can develop an expertise with them and an awareness of the resources available for them. As a result, their interventions with these probationers can be more effective.

So, what is an average caseload? There is considerable variation throughout the country and when Cotton, Mitchell, and Ross (2015, pp. 50–53) surveyed state probation and parole agencies, they found the average numbers of clients for each of the following types of caseloads:

Generalized caseload	Average: 82 cases	(Range: 35–200 cases)
Violent offender caseload	Average: 34 cases	(Range: 15–50 cases)
Sex offender caseload	Average: 42 cases	(Range: 20–70 cases)
Offenders with mental illnesses	Average: 46 cases	(Range: 25–60 cases)

When reviewing these national averages, it is important to remember that there is a range between the states and probably even differences within a state, as some counties or city agencies will have higher (or lower) caseloads.

As noted earlier, **home visits** (also called fieldwork) are used to monitor some medium and many high-risk probationers or individuals on specialized caseloads such as sexual offenders. Although time consuming in terms of travel and less efficient than seeing all of one's probationers in an office, they provide an opportunity to meet with these offenders in their own environment, which can be a more relaxed setting for them. Home visits can also be a valuable tool in terms of supervision as officers can establish rapport with probationers and their family members, and ensure they are complying with their probation conditions (Ahlin, Lobo Antunes, & Tubman-Carbone, 2013). We know relatively little about how often home visits occur, but an Abt Associates (2014) study found that almost all agencies (94%) conducted these visits, and most agencies also had officers who visited probationers at their workplace, in correctional facilities, in educational settings, or in shelters (see also Abt Associates, 2018).

When it came to ensuring officer safety for these out-of-office activities, most agencies provided safety-related training such as being aware of their surroundings, how to deescalate incidents, and self-defense techniques. In order to enhance their safety, officers often make these visits in pairs or are accompanied by police officers (Abt Associates, 2018). Some probation officers also had access to firearms, body armor, radios, and pepper spray, depending on their agency's policies. In many jurisdictions issuing sidearms officers can choose whether they carry a firearm when engaged in fieldwork (Abt Associates, 2014).

PROBATION OFFICER ROLES AND FUNCTIONS

One of the challenges of working in either probation or parole jobs is the conflicting demands placed on the officers, and one of the most pressing is balancing the rehabilitative needs of the offender against their risk to public safety. Researchers who have examined this issue often come up with different classifications of officers based on the amount of time spent on rehabilitative or enforcement-related duties. Although community-based corrections was founded on social work principles, some scholars have argued that the emphasis on enforcement has been prioritized (Phelps, 2018). Yet, there are variations in the styles adopted by probation officers and over the years researchers have identified these different approaches. Hsieh et al. (2015, pp. 21–22), for example, identify four categories of probation officers and the following summarizes their work:

- *Social Worker*: Focusing on Rehabilitation. From its founding in the 1800s until the 1980s the focus of most probation officers was supporting a probationer's rehabilitative efforts. Officers assessed their client's needs and developed strategies with them to meet their basic needs such as housing and employment. Once stabilized, they used individual and group counseling to address prosocial goals such as learning how to develop healthy relationships and building their interpersonal skills.
- *Police Officer*: Emphasizing Law Enforcement Practices. The "get tough on crime" era started in the 1980s and many probation agencies placed more emphasis on the surveillance and control of the individuals on their caseloads. As a result, officers devoted more time and resources into investigation, arrest, assisting law enforcement agencies, and enforcing the laws. There was a growing emphasis on police-probation partnerships and probation officers in some jurisdictions patrol with law enforcement.
- *Case Manager*: Considering Risk Assessment and Individual Needs. There was a greater emphasis from the mid-1990s on ensuring public safety through managing a probationer's risks and needs. Agencies focused on assessing an individual's needs and managed the risk posed to public safety using the Risk, Needs, and Responsivity (RNR) model introduced in Chapter 1. More emphasis was also being placed on victim protection and community reintegration.
- *Synthetic Officer*: Balancing Treatment and Surveillance. After 2000 a growing number of probation agencies tried to balance probation officers' social work and law enforcement functions. Some of this interest in balancing these two roles was based on research that showed that outcomes for probationers who were supervised by strict enforcers were worse than officers who had a greater rehabilitative orientation.

Hsieh et al. (2015, p. 22) summarized their findings regarding the roles of probation officers as:

(1) shifting between conventional dichotomous roles of social workers or peace officers; (2) having a tendency towards case managers who have recognized the need to address both risks and needs in order to reduce future offending; and (3) gradually moving to synthetic officers who have balanced the two conventional narrative roles.

It is important to note that the roles of probation and parole staff are largely shaped by the priorities of their agencies. If a probation department has a law enforcement orientation it will promote that goal and reward officers who devote more of their efforts in the investigation and surveillance of offenders. Moreover, these agencies may prioritize hiring probation or parole officers who have an interest or background in enforcement, rather than hiring graduates of schools of social work who have a more rehabilitative orientation.

When discussing the job activities of probation and parole staff members the term **role conflict** is often raised. That term describes how officers are pulled in two different directions in their efforts at supervising the individuals on their caseloads. In their law enforcement role they are expected to enforce the conditions of their supervision, while at the same time they are expected to carry out a social work role by addressing the offender's unmet needs that leads them to engage in crime. Trying to balance these two roles during a get-tough era can be difficult as officers might believe there are few rewards for rehabilitating an offender, but there is a significant downside if the probationer is not properly supervised and is later involved in a serious crime.

Most recent research shows that many probation officers use a blend of approaches, which is consistent with the synthetic officer role first identified in the 1970s. There is also a growing recognition that probation outcomes are associated with a number of officer characteristics, including their orientation and their skills. The following section describes the strategies probation agencies have introduced to reduce recidivism.

INCREASING SUCCESSFUL PROBATION OUTCOMES

In the past, probationer recidivism was seen as a failure on the part of the probationer, but there is increasing awareness that some probation officers and agencies have lower rates of probationer recidivism. That brings us to the question of why these differences occur and whether changing the way an agency intervenes in the lives of probationers might decrease recidivism. As a result, researchers are taking a closer look at the types of interventions used by different community corrections agencies, as well as the skills and motivations of their workers. One of the outcomes of those studies is that researchers have consistently found that correctional interventions based on the risk-need-responsivity approach reduce recidivism in community and custody settings.

Risk-Need-Responsivity Approach

The RNR approach is founded on an assessment of the probationer's risk and needs and probation officers and their clients then work together to address those issues. James (2018) calls these the "central eight" risk and needs factors in community supervision, which are shown in Table 4.6. Research has shown that individuals with high needs in

TABLE 4.6 The Central Eight Risk and Needs Factors

Risk/Need Factor	Indicator	Target for Intervention
The Big Four		
History of Antisocial Behavior	Early involvement in antisocial behavior such as arrests at a young age, a large number of prior offenses, and history of violating the conditions of previous releases.	History cannot be changed, but targets for change include developing new non-criminal behaviors and building beliefs supportive of prosocial behaviors.
Antisocial Personality Pattern	Individuals with high levels of impulsivity, thrill-seeking, aggression, and disregard for others.	Building skills to improve self-control (e.g. anger management) and problem-solving skills.
Antisocial Cognition	Individuals holding attitudes, beliefs, values, and rationalizations that are favorable to crime (e.g. identifying with criminals, negative attitude toward the justice system, and rationalizations such as "they deserved it").	Reducing antisocial thinking and feelings by building and practicing less risky thoughts and feelings.
Antisocial Associates	When one's friends and associates are crime involved (e.g. gang members) as well as isolation from persons with anti-criminal values.	Reduce association with pro-criminals and increase association with anti-criminal attitudes and beliefs.
The Moderate Four		
Family/Marital Circumstances	Poor-quality relationships between the child and parent (for youthful offenders) or spouses in adults.	Reduce conflict, build positive relationships, and enhance monitoring and supervision.
School/Work	Low levels of involvement in and satisfaction from legitimate pursuits.	Support involvement in education and employment by rewarding positive performance.
Leisure/ Recreation	Low levels of involvement in and satisfaction from non-criminal pursuits in unstructured times.	Enhance involvement in non-criminal leisure activities. Learn how to constructively occupy oneself in unstructured times.
Substance Abuse	Problems with alcohol and drug abuse.	Reduce substance abuse and reduce the influence of individuals who support substance abuse.

Source: Adapted from James (2018).

these areas have higher rates of recidivism, and these factors should be the target of interventions delivered by probation staff (Grieger & Hosser, 2014).

However, there are a number of barriers in working toward a probationer's rehabilitation. Young, Farrell, and Taxman (2013, p. 1071) observe that assessment instruments used by an agency must accurately measure risks and needs, and they must be implemented correctly. Staff members must also receive training that enables them to deliver a quality intervention that is faithful to the rehabilitative model. In other words, if the individual is supposed to receive ten hours of counseling by a trained psychologist, agencies should not try to substitute those requirements with a nurse who provides eight hours of counseling. When agencies reduce the intensity of the intervention or attempt to save money by using less qualified staff, the results are often less effective than the outcomes reported by the developers of the intervention (which is called **program fidelity**, which means being faithful to the rehabilitative model as it is supposed to be delivered).

In addition to ensuring agencies are implementing programs that are faithful to the way they were designed and developed, the relationships that probation officers have with their clients are also important when it comes to probationer outcomes. Earlier we addressed the issue of whether probation officers had a law enforcement or social work orientation. Researchers are finding that officers that endorse rehabilitative values may have less recidivism on their caseloads (Steiner, Travis, Makarios, & Brickley, 2011). In addition, some officers "seemed far more actively engaged in supervision than others, and this seems to flow (in part at least) from caseload characteristics and agency contexts, as well as the personal values and characteristics of probation officers" (Miller, 2015, p. 19). There is a common-sense appeal to this observation, as probationers may find it easier to form relationships with officers who are more approachable and sympathetic (see Kennealy, Skeem, Manchak, & Eno Louden, 2012). This is also consistent with the finding that officers who have better relationships with the individuals they supervise have lower recidivism rates (Chamberlain, Gricius, Wallace, Borjas, & Ware 2018). Less supportive or punitive officers, by contrast, may contribute to feelings of fewer choices and higher levels of anxiety which, in turn, may increase recidivism (Morash, Kashy, Smith, & Cobbina, 2015).

Officer Skills Matter in Reducing Recidivism

In addition to delivering rehabilitative services that are targeted toward a probationer's risk and needs, there is a growing body of research that highlights the importance of probation officer skills in reducing recidivism. Raynor, Ugwudike, and Vanstone (2014) found that probation officers who were more skilled had caseloads with lower recidivism rates. Those findings lend support to the developers of the **Strategic Training Initiative in Community Supervision (STICS)**, which is intended to improve worker skills and knowledge so that they can target probationers' needs and reduce their recidivism (Bonta, Bourgon, & Rugge, 2017).

According to Haas (2014, p. 3), STICS is a training program that helps community corrections workers establish stronger relationships with their probationers, familiarizes officers with the RNR model, and encourages them to challenge the pro-criminal or antisocial attitudes of their clients. Research has shown that the approach has reduced recidivism (Bonta et al., 2017). So, what are the impacts of community-based treatments based on an RNR model? Bonta and Andrews (2017) report that basing these interventions on RNR reduces recidivism by over one-third and that finding is consistent across males and females in adult and youth populations. In addition to an officer's clinical skills, research shows that workers who are more diligent have less recidivism in their caseloads. Gossner, Simon, Rector, and Ruddell (2016) found that some probation officers were more up-to-date on their work (e.g. their assessments were completed on time), had more comprehensive case plans, and made more referrals to community agencies than other workers. The more attentive workers consistently had lower rates of reoffending with their high-risk probationers.

Ruddell (2020) summarizes these findings, and observes that although probationers have barriers to overcome, probation departments can reduce their recidivism by:

- Using interventions that have been proven to be effective with probationers
- Focusing officer time and resources on high-risk offenders
- Confronting attitudes and values that support criminal behavior
- Hiring competent and skilled probation officers
- Ensuring that the case work is comprehensive and up-to-date

Although probation officers may be professional in their interactions with clients and use evidence-based interventions in their work with these individuals, it is important to acknowledge that a large number of probationers will violate their probation conditions. A smaller percentage will be convicted of committing crimes and a very small proportion of them will commit serious and violent crimes.

SUMMARY

Probation and community corrections are similar correctional programs but differ in important ways. From this chapter you should especially note the following.

- Probation carries the major corrections burden for both adults and juveniles.
- The growth of probation services, which expanded tremendously during the 1980s and 1990s, has slowed since peaking in 2007.
- Misdemeanor probationers in 11 states must pay for their own supervision, drug testing, and treatment, and these fees can be a burden for probationers who are poor.

- It is unclear whether increasing the surveillance on probationers will result in lower recidivism. Likewise, supervision that is more intensive tends to yield higher failure rates.
- An average probationary sentence is over two years and an average probationer will have to abide by about 15 standard conditions and some are required to abide by additional special conditions.
- Many, but not all, forms of intermediate sanctions function as forms of diversion from jails and prisons.
- Modern technology and old-fashioned approaches to holding people accountable for their actions permeate the movement toward intermediate sanctions.

Modern criminal justice could not function in the United States without probation services, even though community-based corrections enhance the service delivery; eventually the emphasis remains on traditional forms of supervision long associated with probation.

KEY TERMS

- absconded
- American Probation and Parole Association
- big four risk factors
- central eight risk factors
- crisis intervention team
- diversion
- flash incarceration
- generalized caseload
- halfway house (community residential centers)
- home visits
- house arrest (home confinement)
- intensive supervised probation (ISP)
- judicial reprieve
- labeling theory
- lifetime probation
- moderate four risk factors
- net widening
- pay-only probation (also in 3)
- problem-solving courts (specialized courts)
- program fidelity
- progressive era
- presentence investigation
- presentence report
- prison preppers
- release on recognizance
- role conflict
- sentencing consultants
- shock probation
- specialized courts (problem-solving courts)
- split sentences
- standard probation conditions (general probation conditions)
- Strategic Training Initiative in Community Supervision (STICS)
- technical violation

THINKING ABOUT CORRECTIONAL POLICIES AND PRACTICES: WRITING ASSIGNMENTS

1. Americans volunteer more hours per 100,000 population than almost any other nation. Would probation services benefit from volunteerism? Why or why not? Prepare a one-page paper in response to this question.
2. Write an argument supporting the use of hearsay evidence in the preparation of Pre-sentence Investigation reports.
3. Prepare a one-page essay arguing why the average probation sentence in the United States (about 3 years) is a better or worse crime control strategy than the one-year average probationary sentence in Canada.
4. Complete an essay that starts with the following sentence: "An offender-funded justice system means the poor get a different quality of justice than those who are not poor."
5. Argue why electronic monitoring is a desirable monitoring strategy for probationers or parolees.

CRITICAL REVIEW QUESTIONS

1. What is the history of probation? Go back to Chapter 1 and review the philosophies of punishment. Where does probation fit into this list?
2. Why is the work of probation officers so difficult? What is it about their caseload and workload that adds to the job's complexity?
3. Describe how the imposition of fees and fines for probationers can trap them in the criminal justice system.
4. The standard of proof in the revocation process is different from the standard of proof at a criminal trial. Do you think that is fair?
5. Net widening is a common criticism of diversion programs and other alternatives to incarceration. Briefly describe your understanding of net widening.
6. Labeling theorists believe that people adopt the labels society places on them. Are there interventions that the police, courts, or corrections can carry out that might interrupt or reduce the labeling process?
7. What kinds of cases seem most appropriate for fines and forfeitures? Would you be in favor of applying these sanctions to violent crimes such as aggravated assault, rape, and robbery? Why or why not?

8. Is restitution an idea that looks better on paper than in practice? Do you believe that restitution is effective? What do you think would make it more effective?

9. Is house arrest a punishment? Do you think it works better for certain types of offenders? Would you set a maximum duration for house arrest? Why or why not?

10. Do the practices associated with probation reduce public safety? Defend your answer.

CASES

Ex Parte United States, 242 U.S. 27 (1916).

Gardner v. Florida 430 U.S. 349 (1977)

McNeil et al. v. Community Probation Services. MD Tenn. Case No. 1:2018cv00033

United States v. Birnbaum 421 F.2d 993 (1970)

REFERENCES

Abt Associates. (2014). *Key findings from a national survey on home and field visits policies and procedures*. Retrieved from https://www.appa-net.org/eweb/docs/APPA/pubs/HV_Brief.pdf

Abt Associates. (2018). *Evaluating the impact of probation and parole home visits*. Cambridge, MA: Author.

Administrative Office of the United States Courts Probation and Pretrial Services Office. (2016). *Overview of probation and supervised release conditions*. Washington, DC: Author.

Ahlin, E. M., Lobo Antunes, M. J., Tubman-Carbone, H. (2013). A review of probation home visits: What do we know? *Federal Probation, 77*(3), 32–37.

Albrecht, L. (2018, Mar. 11). When rich 'bros' like Martin Shkreli get sent to prison, they call these wise guys first. *MarketWatch*. Retrieved from https://www.marketwatch.com/story/when-vips-head-to-prison-they-call-these-wise-guys-first-2017-09-30

Allyn, B. (2019, August 27). Meek Mill pleads guilty to misdemeanor gun charge, ends 12-year legal case. *National Public Radio*. Retrieved from https://www.npr.org/2019/08/27/754769378/meek-mill-pleads-guilty-to-misdemeanor-gun-charge-ends-12-year-legal-case

American Probation and Parole Association. (2006). *Caseload standards for probation and parole*. Retrieved from https://www.appa-net.org/eweb/docs/APPA/stances/ip_CSPP.pdf

American Probation and Parole Association. (2014). *Issue paper on the use of social media in community corrections*. Retrieved from https://www.appa-net.org/eweb/docs/APPA/stances/ip_USMCC.pdf

Augustus, J. (1852/1972). *A report of the labors of John Augustus*. Montclair, NJ: Patterson Smith.

Austin, J. F., & Krisberg, B. (2002). Wider, stronger and different nets: The dialectics of criminal justice reform. In J. Muncie, G. Hughes, & E. McLaughlin (Eds.), *Youth justice: Critical readings* (pp. 258–274), London, UK: Sage.

Bala, N. (2018, April 24). Meek Mill is exhibit A of a nation's broken probation system. *USA Today*. Retrieved from https://www.usatoday.com/story/opinion/policing/spotlight/2018/04/24/meek-mill-exhibit-nations-broken-probation-system/488084002/

Baldwin, K. (2018). *How many is too many? Addressing caseload sizes in specialty courts.* Paper presented at the National Association of Drug Court Professionals Annual Meeting, Houston, TX.

Barnes, H. E., & Teeters, N. K. (1959). *New horizons in criminology.* Englewood Cliffs, NJ: Prentice Hall.

Bonta, J., & Andrews, D. A. (2017). *The psychology of criminal conduct, 6th edition.* New York: Routledge.

Bonta, J., Bourgon, G., & Rugge, T. (2017). From evidence-informed to evidence-based: The Strategic Training Initiative in Community Supervision. In P. Ugwudike, P. Raynor, & J. Annison (Eds.), *Evidence-based skills in criminal justice* (pp. 169–192), Chicago: Polity Press.

Bouchard, J., & Wong, J. S. (2018). The new panopticon? Examining the effect of home confinement on criminal recidivism. *Victims & Offenders, 13*(5), 589–608.

Center for Health and Justice at TASC. (2013). *No entry: A national survey of criminal justice diversion programs and initiatives.* Chicago, IL: Author.

Chamberlain, A. W., Gricius, M., Wallace, D. M., Borjas, D., & Ware, V. M. (2018). Parolee-parole officer rapport: Does it impact recidivism? *International Journal of Offender Therapy and Comparative Criminology, 62*(11), 3581–3602.

Chute, C. L. (1922). *The development of probation.* New York: Russell Sage Foundation.

Cohen, S. (2016, Mar. 12). Poor offenders pay high price when probation turns on profit. *The Spokesman-Review.* Retrieved from http://www.spokesman.com/stories/2016/mar/12/poor-offenders-pay-high-price-when-probation-turns/

Cohen, T., Cook, D., & Lowenkamp, C. T. (2016). The supervision of low-risk offenders: How the low-risk policy has changed federal supervision practices without compromising community safety. *Federal Probation, 80*(1), 3–11.

Columbia University Justice Lab. (2018). *Too big to succeed: The impact of the growth of community corrections and what should be done with it.* New York: Author.

Corbett Jr., R. P. (2015). The burdens of leniency: The changing face of probation. *Minnesota Law Review, 99*(4), 1697–1714.

Corda, A., & Phelps, M. S. (2017). American exceptionalism in community supervision. *American Probation and Parole Association Perspectives,* Spring, 20–27. Retrieved from https://pure.qub.ac.uk/en/publications/american-exceptionalism-in-community-supervision

Cotton, P. A., Mitchell, T. A., & Ross, J. I. (2015). *Maryland Department of Public Safety and Correctional Services: Parole and probation agent workload study.* Retrieved from http://dlslibrary.state.md.us/publications/JCR/2014/2014_116(v3).pdf

Council of State Governments. (2018). *Changes to Georgia's probation system yield positive early results.* Retrieved from https://csgjusticecenter.org/jr/georgia/posts/changes-to-georgias-probation-system-yield-positive-early-results/

DeMichele, M., & Payne, B. (2018). Taking officer time seriously: A study of the daily activities of probation officers. *Probation Journal, 65*(1), 39–60.

Dewa, C. S., Loong, D., Trujillo, A., & Bonato, S. (2018). Evidence for the effectiveness of police-based pre-booking diversion programs in decriminalizing mental illness: A systematic literature review. *Plos One.* Retrieved from https://www.ncbi.nlm.nih.gov/pmc/articles/PMC6007921/pdf/pone.0199368.pdf

Dewan, S. (2015, Aug. 2). Probation may sound light, but punishments can land hard. *The New York Times*. Retrieved from https://www.nytimes.com/2015/08/03/us/probation-sounding-light-can-land-hard.html

Dressler, D. (1962). *The theory and practice of probation and parole.* New York: Columbia University Press.

Field, C., Cherukuri, S., Kimuna, S. R., & Berg, D. (2017). Women accused of homicide: The impact of race, relationship to victim, and prior physical abuse. *Advances in Applied Sociology, 7,* 281–304.

Georgia Council Report. (2011). *Report on the special council on criminal justice reform for Georgians.* Retrieved from http://www.legis.ga.gov/Documents/GACouncilReport-FINALDRAFT.pdf

Gill, C. E. (2018). Intensive probation and parole. In G. Bruinsma & D. Weisburd (Eds.), *Encyclopedia of criminology and criminal justice* (pp. 2581–2592). New York: Springer.

Gossner, D., Simon, T., Rector, B., & Ruddell, R. (2016). Case planning and recidivism of high risk and violent adult probationers. *Journal of Community Safety & Well-Being, 1*(2), 32–43.

Gray, M. K., Fields, M., & Maxwell, S. R. (2001). Examining probation violations: Who, what, and when. *Crime & Delinquency, 47*(4), 537–557.

Grieger, L, & Hosser, D. (2014). Which risk factors are really predictive?: An Analysis of Andrews and Bonta's "central eight" risk factors for recidivism in German youth correctional facility inmates. *Criminal Justice and Behavior, 41*(5), 613–634.

Haas, S. M. (2013). Current practice and challenges in evidence-based community corrections. *JRP Digest, 15*(1), 1–17.

Habeas Corpus Act. (1679). *An act for the better securing the liberty of the subject, and for the prevention of imprisonment beyond the seas.* 31 Chapter 2.2.

Hsieh, M., Hafoka, M., Woo, Y., van Wormer, J., Stohr, M. K., & Hemmens, C. (2015). Probation officer roles: A statutory analysis. *Federal Probation, 79*(3), 20–37.

Human Rights Watch. (2014). *Profiting from probation: America's "offender funded" probation industry.* Washington, DC: Author.

Human Rights Watch. (2018). *"Set up to fail": The impact of offender-funded private probation on the poor.* Washington, DC: Author.

Hyatt, J. M., & Han, S. H. (2018). Expanding the focus of correctional evaluations beyond recidivism: the impact of halfway houses on public safety. *Journal of Experimental Criminology, 14*(1), 187–211.

International Association of Chiefs of Police. (2018). *Deconstructing the power to arrest: Lessons from research.* Cincinnati, OH: IACP/UC Center for Police Research and Policy.

Jacobson, M. P., Schiraldi, V., Daly, R., & Hotez, E. (2017). *Less is more: How reducing probation populations can improve outcomes.* Cambridge, MA: Harvard Kennedy School.

James, N. (2018). *Risk and needs assessment in the federal prison system.* Washington, DC: Congressional Research Service.

Kaeble, M. (2018). *Probation and parole in the United States, 2016.* Washington, DC: Bureau of Justice Statistics.

Kennealy, P. J., Skeem, J. L., Manchak, S. M., & Eno Louden, J. (2012). Firm, fair, and caring officer-offender relationships protect against supervision failure. *Law and Human Behavior, 36*(6), 496–505.

Kimchi, A. (2018). Investigating the assignment of probation conditions: Heterogeneity and the role of race and ethnicity. *Journal of Quantitative Criminology.* Published online ahead of print.

Knupfer, A. M. (1999). Professionalizing probation work in Chicago, 1900–1935. *Social Service Review, 73*(4), 478–495.

Latessa, E. (2012). Halfway houses and residential centers. In S. M. Barton-Bellessa (Ed.), *Encyclopedia of community corrections* (pp. 195–197). Thousand Oaks, CA: Sage.

Latzer, B. (2017). Electronic monitoring can be a boon to criminal justice reform. *National Review.* Retrieved from https://www.nationalreview.com/2017/12/electronic-monitoring-key-criminal-justice-reform/

Leiber, M. J., Beaudry-Cyr, M., Peck, J. H., & Mack, K. Y. (2018). Sentencing recommendations by probation officers and judges: An examination of adult offenders across gender. *Women & Criminal Justice, 28*(2), 100–124.

Leifker, D., & Sample, L. L. (2010). Do judges follow sentencing recommendations, or do recommendations simply reflect what judges want to hear? An examination of one state court. *Journal of Crime and Justice, 33*(2), 127–1541.

Loller, T. (2019, Feb. 1). Federal judge considering order on jailing offenders who can't pay. *Tennessean.* Retrieved from https://www.tennessean.com/story/news/2019/02/01/federal-judge-considering-order-jailing-offenders-who-cant-pay /2748188002/

May, D. C., Wood, P., & Eades, A. (2008). Lessons learned from punishment exchange rates: Implications for theory, research, and correctional policy. *The Journal of Behavior Analysis of Offender and Victim Treatment and Prevention, 1*(2), 187–201.

Mays, G. L., & Winfree, L. T. Jr. (2014). *Essentials of corrections, 5th edition.* Malden, MA: Wiley-Blackwell.

Mears, D. P., Kuch, J. J., Lindsey, A. M., Siennick, S. E., Pesta, G. B, Greenwald M. A., & Blomberg, T. G. (2016). Juvenile court and contemporary diversion: Helpful, harmful, or both? *Criminology & Public Policy, 15*(3), 1–29.

Miller, J. (2015). Contemporary modes of probation officer supervision: The triumph of the "synthetic" officer? *Justice Quarterly, 32*(2), 314–336.

Morash, M., Kashy, D. A., Smith, S., & Cobbina, J. (2015). The effects of probation or parole agent relationship style and women offenders' criminogenic needs on offenders' responses to supervision interactions. *Criminal Justice and Behavior, 42*(4), 412–434.

Navratil, A. J., & Hill, J. E. (2017). SB 174 Probation and early release. *Georgia State University Law Review, 34*(1), 115–141.

Neil, M. (2008). Hawaii's fix for the crime problem: Flash incarceration. *ABA Journal.* Retrieved from http://www.abajournal.com/news/article/hawaiis_fix_for_the_crime_problem_flash_incarceration

Nguyen, V., Grattet, R., & Bird, M. (2017). *California probation in the era of reform.* San Francisco, CA: Public Policy Institute of California.

North Carolina Department of Public Safety. (2017). *Legislative report on probation and parole caseloads.* Retrieved from https://www.ncleg.gov/documentsites/committees/JLOCJPS/Reports/FY%202016-17/DPS_Report_on_Probation_and_Parole,_Electronic_Monitoring,_Global_Positioning_Systems.pdf

Office of Juvenile Justice and Delinquency Prevention. (2017). *Diversion from formal juvenile court processing.* Washington, DC: Author.

Parsons, H. C. (1918). Probation and suspended sentence. *Journal of the American Institute of Criminal Law and Criminology, 8*(5), 694–708.

Patten, R., La Rue, E., Caudill, J. W., Thomas, M. O., & Messer, S. (2018). Come and knock on our door: Offenders' perspectives on home visits through ecological theory. *International Journal of Offender Therapy and Comparative Criminology, 62*(3), 717–738.

Pew Charitable Trusts. (2018). *Probation and parole systems marked by high stakes, missed opportunities.* Retrieved from https://www.pewtrusts.org/en/research-and-analysis/issue-briefs/2018/09/probation-and-parole-systems-marked-by-high-stakes-missed-opportunities

Phelps, M. S. (2017). Mass probation: Toward a more robust theory of state variation in punishment. *Punishment & Society, 19*(1), 53–73.

Phelps, M. S. (2018). Ending mass probation: Sentencing, supervision, and revocation. *The Future of Children, 28*(1), 125–146.

Polson, G. (2002). *State budget shortfalls impact correctional recreation; The view from both sides.* Stillwater, OK: Strengthtech.

Prison Professors. (2018). *For defendants who want to show they are more than their criminal charge—but don't know how to get started.* Retrieved from https://prisonprofessors.com/prepare-for-sentencing/

Pullen, S., & English, K. (1996). Lifetime probation in Arizona. In K. English, S. Pullen, & L. Jones (Eds.), *Managing adult sex offenders: A containment approach* (pp. 6.1–6.15). Lexington, KY: American Probation and Parole Association.

Raynor, P., Ugwudike, P., & Vanstone, M. (2014). The impact of skills in probation work: A reconviction study. *Criminology & Criminal Justice, 14*(2), 235–249.

Reaves, B. A. (2013). *Felony defendants in large urban counties, 2009 – Statistical tables.* Washington, DC: Bureau of Justice Statistics.

Reiman, J., & Leighton, P. (2017). *The rich get rich and the poor get poorer.* New York: Routledge.

Rempel, M., Labriola, M., Hunt, P., Davis, R. C., Reich, W. A., & Cherney, S. (2018). *NIJ's multisite evaluation of prosecutor led diversion programs: Strategies, impacts, and cost-effectiveness.* Washington, DC: U.S. Department of Justice.

Rhineberger-Dunn, G., & Mack, K. Y. (2018). Impact of workplace factors on role-related stressors and job stress among community corrections staff. *Criminal Justice Policy Review, 30*(8), 1204–1228.

Ricks, E. P., Louden, J. E., & Kennealy, P. J. (2016). Probation officer role emphasis and use of risk assessment information before and after training. *Behavioral Sciences and the Law, 34*(2–3), 337–351.

Ruddell, R. (2020). *Exploring criminal justice in Canada.* Toronto, ON: Oxford University Press.

Ruhland, E. L., & Robey, J. P. (2017). *Probation revocations.* Minneapolis, MN: Robina Institute of Criminal Law and Criminal Justice.

Sawyer, W., & Bertram, W. (2018). New report shows probation is down, but still a major driver of incarceration. *Prison Policy Initiative.* Retrieved from https://www.prisonpolicy.org/blog/2018/04/26/probation_update-2/

Schiraldi, V. (2016). Confessions of a failed "HOPE-er." *Criminology & Public Policy, 15*(4), 1143–1153.

Segal, A. F., Winfree, Jr., L. T., & Friedman, S. (2019). *Mental health and criminal justice.* Frederick, MD: Wolters Kluwer.

Sieh, E. W. (1993). From Augustus to the progressives: A study of probation's formative years. *Federal Probation, 57*(3), 67–72.

Sipes, L. (2018). Editorial: Is probation set up to fail? *Law Enforcement Today*. Retrieved from https://www.lawenforcementtoday.com/probation-set-fail/

Skoloff, B. (2013). Arizona man, 86, gets probation in mercy killing case. *The Christian Science Monitor*. Retrieved from https://www.csmonitor.com/USA/Latest-News-Wires/2013/0330/Arizona-man-86-gets-probation-in-mercy-killing-case

Snoderly, J. (2018, Sept. 2). Community corrections grants cuts in Harrison, other counties lead to questions about how funds are awarded. *WV News*. Retrieved from https://www.wvnews.com/news/wvnews/community-corrections-grant-cuts-in-harrison-other-counties-lead-to/article_e4856ca1-2dea-5f20-a64b-431e4e7c7728.html

Steiner, B., Travis, L. F., Makarios, M. D., & Brickley, T. (2011). The influence of parole officers' attitudes on supervision practices. *Justice Quarterly, 28*(6), 903–927.

Stevens-Martin, K., & Liu, J. (2017). Fugitives from justice: An examination of felony and misdemeanor probation absconders. *Federal Probation, 81*(1), 41–51.

Strong, S. M., Rantala, R. R., & Kyckelhahn, T. (2016). *Census of problem-solving courts, 2012.* Washington, DC: Bureau of Justice Statistics.

U.S. Census Bureau. (2018). *Population estimates, July 1, 2018.* Retrieved from https://www.census.gov/quickfacts/fact/table/US/PST045218

U.S. Department of Justice. (2011). *Pretrial diversion program.* Retrieved from https://www.justice.gov/jm/jm-9-22000-pretrial-diversion-program

Vance, S. E. (2018). Overview of federal pretrial services initiatives from the vantage point of the criminal law committee. *Federal Probation, 82*(2), 30–34.

Viglione, J., & Taxman, F. S. (2018). Low risk offenders under probation supervision. *Criminal Justice and Behavior, 45*(12), 1809–1831.

Waldron, J. A., & Angelino, H. R. (1977). Shock probation: A natural experiment on the effect of a short period of incarceration. *The Prison Journal, 52*(1), 45–52.

Walmsley, R. (2018). *World prison population list, 12th edition.* London, UK: Institute for Criminal Policy Research.

Washington State Institute for Public Policy. (2019). *Benefit-cost analysis (adult criminal justice).* Retrieved from http://www.wsipp.wa.gov/BenefitCost?topicId=2

Watts, A. L. (2016). *Probation in-depth: The length of probation sentences.* Minneapolis, MN: Robina Institute of Criminal Law and Criminal Justice.

Williams, J., & Weatherburn, D. (2019). *Can electronic monitoring reduce reoffending?* Bonn, Germany: IZA Institute of Labor Economics.

Wong, J. S., Bouchard, J., & Gushue, K., & Lee, C. (2019). Halfway out: An examination of the effects of halfway houses on criminal recidivism. *International Journal of Offender Therapy and Comparative Criminology, 63*(7), 1018–1037.

Young, D. W., Farrell, J. L., & Taxman, F. S. (2013). Impacts of juvenile probation training models on youth recidivism. *Justice Quarterly, 30*(6), 1068–1089.

Zaru, D. (2017, Nov. 11). Meek Mill's prison sentence draws outrage, sparking a criminal justice debate. *CNN*. Retrieved from https://www.cnn.com/2017/11/10/politics/meek-mill-prison-sentence-judge-jay-z/index.html

Chapter 5
Jails and Detention Facilities

OUTLINE

OBJECTIVES

After reading this chapter you will able to:

- Describe the differences between jails and other types of detention facilities

- Explain the challenges of incarcerating female inmates in jails

- Describe the characteristics of special needs jail populations

- Explain how the new-generation jail concepts differ from traditional designs and operations

- Describe some of the key challenges confronting jails in the twenty-first century

CASE STUDY

Corruption in the Baltimore City Detention Center (BCDC)

In 2013, a jail scandal in Baltimore received national attention as dozens of correctional staff and inmates were charged with crimes taking place in both the facility and local community. Although it took several years for these cases to work their way through the courts, 40 of them, involving 24 correctional officers and 16 inmates, ultimately resulted in convictions. Other BCDC personnel were fired, quit, or retired. Police and FBI investigations revealed that members of the Black Guerilla Family gang were running some of the jail operations. Gang members were having sexual relationships with the correctional officers, and in return the officers smuggled contraband items such as cellphones and drugs into the facility. Jendra (2015, para. 2–3) writes that "Correctional officers were rewarded for facilitating this underground economy with payments, gifts, or a share of the profits... Police say the conspiracy allowed gang members to run their criminal enterprise within and outside the jail." Inmates also profited from the **underground economy** and one ringleader was recorded saying he made nearly $16,000 in one month from his gang activities within the jail (Zoukis, 2015).

The crimes occurring at the BCDC have been called one of the biggest sex scandals in US corrections and one inmate fathered five children with four different officers (Schaffer, 2016). Ralph Johnson, a former BCDC supervisor, says that gang members would threaten other inmates to follow the rules, and one of the ringleaders:

> was able to operate freely because of what he was bringing to the table ... He was bringing non-violence to the correctional facility. He was bringing a lot of money to the correctional facility. You even had correctional officers saying they enjoyed coming to work because they knew they were going to have a peaceful day.
>
> (As cited in Schaffer, 2016, para. 18)

Johnson makes it clear that some officers attempted to correct these problems, but these ethical officers were transferred, or their concerns ignored.

One question comes to mind when we hear about these scandals: Why do officers engage in this misconduct? Knezevich (2013) notes that some were very young when hired and questions whether 18- and 19-year-old correctional officers had the maturity to work with gang members and older inmates. Many of these gang-involved inmates have a lifetime of experience in manipulating other people, and all correctional officers have to be aware of that threat (see Cornelius, 2009). After the 2013 scandal became public, BCDC took steps to reduce officer misconduct by providing more training, carrying out more searches of staff members entering the facility, requiring some officers to undergo polygraph testing, and increasing the severity of punishments for staff members engaging in misconduct.

Maryland Governor Larry Hogan, who expressed frustration because the inmates were running the facility, shut down the BCDC in 2015. The impact of the closure is still felt today as some defendants awaiting their trials are now being held in state facilities hundreds of miles away from the city, making it difficult for them to maintain contact with their attorneys or get family visits (Oppenheim, 2019).

Critical Questions

1. What traits differentiate staff members who report the illegal or unprofessional behaviors of their co-workers compared to those who ignore or engage in those activities?
2. Why would a jail administrator hire an 18- or 19-year-old person with very little life experience to supervise sophisticated inmates such as 30-year-old gang members?
3. How can you use this case example to prepare yourself for a public service, correctional or law enforcement career?

INTRODUCTION

As we noted in Chapter 2, jails were part of this nation's earliest history, dating back to the Jamestown settlement in the Colony of Virginia in the 1600s. By the time of the Revolutionary War, many villages and towns had what was often called a common jail. Even in colonial times, jails were built, financed, and operated locally. The buildings were simple, small, and sturdily built. Few had the room to separate inmates—hence the name common jail. Males and females, adults and children, hardened criminals and undesirables were all typically housed in a single room or a small number of cells.

As with so many other elements of the US criminal justice system, English settlers brought the institution of the local or county jail with them, including administration by a sheriff who collected fees. Jails today fulfill several functions, but early English jails existed primarily to hold individuals until they could be tried or punished, which in many cases meant execution. Like their English counterparts, most of the individuals held in American jails were awaiting trial or punishment and incarceration was not itself considered a punishment. By the mid-1800s though, the colonists had broken with this English tradition. Jails in this country were now housing three types of individuals: people awaiting trial, those convicted but awaiting sentencing, and those sentenced to serve jail time.

This was the role jails continued to play in the United States throughout the 1800s and most of the 1900s. They evolved differently throughout the country and the jail administration and operations in the Northeastern states differed from the practices in the South. By the 1900s, however, American jails were growing in number, and they increased in size, but jails still performed the same basic functions. These jails experienced some growing pains as the administrators often failed to meet the inmate's basic needs (Fishman, 1923). Although living conditions have improved since Fishman's book, some jails are noisy, chaotic, overcrowded, and dangerous places that are home to gang members, the poor, and persons with unresolved mental health and addictions issues. These inmate characteristics shape the way that jails are operated today as most of them are austere, high-security facilities intended to provide only basic care for people serving short periods of incarceration.

CONTEMPORARY JAIL AND DETENTION FACILITIES

Many of the challenges related to jail operations are due to under-funding, overcrowding, and having to accommodate a diverse range of people who are admitted to jails with a host of unmet needs. Often these individuals are in some type of crisis and they may be under the influence of drugs and alcohol when admitted. If drug- or alcohol-addicted, they may go through withdrawal during their incarceration. After being booked into the jail, they can be under a high degree of stress due to the uncertainty of their circumstances. Some recently admitted individuals think about suicide because they believe they have disappointed their families and friends. In addition to experiencing high levels of stress a lot of inmates suffer from physical health problems ranging from the injuries they received being arrested to chronic health conditions, such as diabetes, although some have serious health conditions and many women are mothers or are pregnant. Moreover, a wide range of mental health problems either emerge during incarceration or existing ones are exacerbated by confinement. Clearly, life in jail is not for the faint of heart.

What Is a Jail?

Any number of facilities can be used to house inmates. What makes jails different from the rest? In its definition, the Bureau of Justice Statistics notes that jails:

> [i]nclude confinement facilities operated under the authority of a sheriff, police chief, or city or county administrator. They are intended for adults but may hold juveniles before or after they are adjudicated. Facilities include jails, detention centers, city or county correctional centers, special jail facilities (such as medical centers and pre-release centers) and temporary holding or lockup facilities.
>
> (Zeng, 2018, p. 8)

Most jails come under either city or county government administration, although six states—Alaska, Connecticut, Delaware, Hawaii, Rhode Island, and Vermont—and the District of Columbia have integrated jail-prison systems. The U.S. Federal Bureau of Prisons

(BOP) also operates metropolitan jails or detention centers in larger cities and one in Puerto Rico. Several dozen jails are also operated by tribal authorities in Indian Country (Minton, 2017). Last, there are a small number of privately operated jails that contract with local governments to hold their inmates. Regardless of who funds these operations, they hold a diverse population of pretrial detainees, convicted misdemeanants serving short sentences, and convicted felons either serving their sentences in some states or awaiting transportation to prison.

The American Jail Association (2018, para. 6) reports that in 2007 there were 3,163 jail facilities; these operations range in size from facilities holding fewer than 10 individuals to the large urban jails such as the Cook County facility in Chicago that holds over 6,500 inmates. The box below shows the range of responsibilities of contemporary jails. The American Jail Association (2018, para. 7) differentiates between jails and **lockups**, which they define as a "temporary holding facility" that "are generally operated by the local police or sheriff's office and are located in police headquarters, station houses, or a designated area if in the jail building." Lockups are also called detention facilities, and some call them drunk tanks. While an inmate might spend several days in a jail, most individuals are only held a few hours in a lockup while they are charged, processed, or before they are transported to their court appearance or jail, or released after individuals arrested for public drunkenness are sober.

Functions Served by Jails

Among the functions served by jails, as defined by Zeng (2018), are the following:

- Receive individuals pending arraignment and hold them awaiting trial, conviction, or sentencing.
- Readmit probation, parole, and bail bond violators and absconders.
- Temporarily detain juveniles pending their transfer to juvenile authorities.
- Hold mentally ill persons pending their movement to appropriate mental health facilities.
- Hold individuals for the military, for protective custody, for contempt, and for the courts as witnesses.
- Release inmates to the community on completion of their sentences.
- Transfer inmates to federal, state, or other authorities.
- House inmates for federal, state, or other authorities because of crowding of their facilities.
- Operate community-based programs as alternatives to incarceration.

A CLOSER LOOK

One of the functions listed earlier is when jails hold witnesses to crimes to ensure their court appearances using material witness warrants. Shen (2018, para. 3) says they are "meant to be used in extraordinary circumstances, such as for when a prosecutor suspects that a critical witness in a case might flee." Pishko (2018, para. 17) adds that as these individuals are not accused of committing crimes, they may be unable to qualify for public defenders, and "innocent witnesses and victims of crimes have spent days and even weeks in jail. Many had bond amounts higher than the person accused of the crime." In a case highlighted by Shen, a witness was required to post a $150,000 bond, which means she would have to give a bail bondsman $15,000 to secure her release from jail, and she had not been accused of committing a crime.

Jails are so interesting to study because they defy an easy description, but they do share some common features. They occupy a distinctive place in the criminal justice system as they are the gateway to that system. In other words, most individuals who end up in the criminal justice system are first booked into jails before their court appearances. For example, in 2017 jails admitted about 10.6 million individuals (Zeng, 2019, p. 1). One common mistake that reporters and others often make is calling jails and prisons by the same name, and, except for the six states and Washington D.C. operating combined jail-prison systems, jails are primarily in the business of holding individuals until their next court dates. Other inmates are awaiting a transfer or are serving custody sentences of less than one year. However, in several states, including California and Texas, state prisoners are held in county jails to reduce crowding in their prison systems. Most jails are relatively small, as 55% of jail inmates are held in facilities with 99 or fewer beds. Phrased another way, there are over 1,000 jails with fewer than 49 beds, and many of them are in rural counties or sparsely populated towns or cities. Hundreds of these facilities may have ten or fewer beds. In contrast to these smaller facilities, jails with 1,000 or more beds are members of the National Institute of Correction's **large jails network**, a group that has existed since 1998.

We can identify four factors that distinguish jails from prisons. First, a local jail must house a diverse population of convicted and unconvicted individuals. Unlike prisons, which tend to house convicted felons of a single gender, jails hold all kinds of people, males and females (and members of sexual minorities), young and old, misdemeanants and felons. Often between half and two-thirds of a jail's average daily population (ADP) are pretrial detainees who do not have the money to make bail. Probation and parole violators can also be detained in jail while they await judicial or administrative hearings, and convicted felons on their way to state or federal prisons may spend several weeks in jail until bed space becomes available in a secure facility. Jails also house individuals sentenced to periods of incarceration of less than a year and some of them are supervised in the community using electronic monitoring or they participate in work-release programs where they work during the day and return to the facility in the evening. Jail populations are also transient; Zeng (2019, p. 7) notes the average jail stay is about 26 days, while the average state prisoner serves a 30-month sentence. As a result, jail populations are always changing while prison populations are more stable.

A second factor distinguishing jails from prisons is location. Jails traditionally have been constructed in an urban area's central business district, often in the same building as, or immediately adjacent to, the county courthouse. Prisons, by contrast, are frequently situated in rural locations and they have traditionally held individuals from urban areas—although the number of rural people sentenced to prison terms has been increasing (see Chapter 6).

A third factor distinguishing jails and prisons is the way they are administered. Most US prisons are operated by state corrections departments or the BOP. The National Center for Jail Operations (2019, para. 1) says that 85% of the nation's jails are operated by sheriffs, and almost all US sheriffs are elected. In Alaska, Connecticut, and Hawaii, however, there are no sheriffs, and sheriffs are appointed by the governor in Rhode Island, and by county executives in several Colorado and Florida counties. Sheriffs typically come from law enforcement backgrounds and few are excited about jail administration. For most sheriffs, jail management is a responsibility that is incidental to the office. This means that jails are both financially and operationally subordinate to law enforcement.

The fourth key difference between jails and prisons is that jails are more numerous. There are fewer than 2,000 state and federal prisons in the United States (Stephan, 2008) and 3,163 jails (American Jail Association, 2018). The number of jails has been dropping over time, and Ruddell and Mays (2006) attributed that drop to smaller facilities (fewer than 50 beds) either being closed or consolidated into regional jails, where several counties cooperate and build a single facility that replaces smaller jails. Some smaller facilities within a single county also have been closed so that all jail operations can be delivered in a single facility. Whereas all prisons are part of a larger system or network, most jails are stand-alone facilities.

ALTERNATIVE DETENTION ARRANGEMENTS

Several options other than county or regional jails are available to local, state, and federal authorities for short-term incarceration. Although at some point we may witness more alternatives to incarceration, the introduction of these approaches will balance the public's frustration with paying for incarceration and their desire for safety. As noted in Chapter 1, the public seems more supportive of using less punishment today, although those perceptions can sometimes change quickly.

Minimum Security Facilities

One category of alternatives to traditional jails is minimum security facilities. Virtually all jails are built to maximum-security standards. This approach is inefficient because maximum-security space is the most expensive to construct and few inmates require maximum-security confinement. As a result, a growing number of jurisdictions are constructing sections of new jails or completely separate facilities—called satellite jails—to house low-risk inmates or distinctive populations such as women. This option seems particularly appropriate for certain inmates. For example, individuals charged with shoplifting and other minor property crimes seldom warrant anything more than minimum-security custody. The same is probably true for most of those charged with driving while intoxicated (DWI), especially those sentenced to serve weekend terms (e.g. intermittent sentencing).

There is a growing number of **sobering centers** being introduced throughout the nation. These facilities hold people who are found drunk in public and these facilities take the approach that public intoxication is a public health rather than law enforcement issue. When picked up by the police, intoxicated individuals were traditionally taken to city jails until they were sober. The advantages to taking intoxicated persons to sobering centers are threefold. First, these facilities reduce the demands on city jails, and in Houston, for example, the annual number of intoxicated jail admissions dropped by almost one-half between 2010 and 2017 (Jarvis, Kincaid, Weltge, Lee, & Basinger, 2019). The second advantage is that the staff working in these facilities are better able to respond to any health-related concerns of these people than jail officers, including providing counseling to address issues of long-term substance abuse. Third, placing individuals in these facilities decriminalizes their behavior, as public intoxication in some jurisdictions is considered a misdemeanor offense.

Police Lockups

One of the most pervasive detention facilities in the United States is the police lockup. There are so many, in fact, that we do not have an exact count, although estimates run as high as 15,000 facilities around the country. This is based on the estimated number of police units at all levels, each of which is assumed to have at least one lockup. Hounmenou (2012, p. 275) says these facilities are "operated for the detention of persons awaiting processing, booking, court appearances, and transportation to jail or for other administrative procedures, within a period of arraignment not exceeding 48 hr. in most places or 72 hr. in others." Several features distinguish lockups from other forms of detention facilities:

- Most lockups are in police buildings.
- Lockups temporarily detain suspects until they can be interrogated or fully processed by the police and then transferred to the county jail.
- Lockups tend to be dangerous places because they are temporary holding structures where inmate activities are not always carefully monitored, and detainees are at high risk of physical and sexual victimization (Just Detention International, 2015).

As lockups are often small and intended for holding individuals only for a few hours, they tend to receive very little scrutiny from researchers. When it comes to corrections, however, a lack of attention sometimes results in negative outcomes.

Hounmenou (2010, p. 1) has examined conditions in police lockups in different nations, and he identified the common set of shortcomings in these places, including:

> Overcrowding and long stays for persons in police cells, substandard physical conditions and design faults, lack of access to health and mental health care, vulnerable persons being inappropriately held in police cells, abuse of detainees, poor sanitary conditions, lack of adequate accommodation, juveniles being held with adults, and absence of consistent training in duty of care and custodial role of police lockup staff.

As we describe conditions in local corrections throughout this chapter, we see that many of the shortcomings reported for lockups are occurring in jails as well.

In some cases, the risks to inmates come from staff. In February 2019 an individual who had been detained in a Buffalo, New York lockup was awarded $300,000 in damages after being assaulted by a cellblock attendant. The arrestee was handcuffed at time of the assault, and the incident was witnessed by two police officers, and captured on the lockup's surveillance cameras. The cellblock attendant "pleaded guilty in federal court to a felony: deprivation of constitutional rights under color of law" and was sentenced to 18 months in prison (Spina & Michel, 2019, para. 15). The cellblock

PHOTO 5.1
Inmates admitted to jails must be searched and their possessions documented and then held in a secure area. This Brownsville, Texas sheriff's deputy is recording the property of an individual who was arrested with 230 pounds of marijuana in his vehicle. Credit: Bob Daemmrich/Alamy Stock Photo.

attendant attributed his behavior to the stress of working 80 hour-weeks and the medications he was taking after being bitten by another detainee were making him feel sick. While staff-on-inmate assaults are rare, it is important to learn why they happen as most of these acts can be prevented by properly training the staff members, providing them with the supports they need to carry out their work, and ensuring they are not overworked and experiencing excessive stress.

State-Run Jails

Throughout this chapter, we describe jails as being locally operated and funded facilities that are distinct from prisons, but there are some exceptions. While most jails are operated by cities, counties, and regions (where several counties engage in partnerships to run a single jail), state governments may also provide funding to those local governments for corrections. Alaska, Connecticut, Delaware, Hawaii, Rhode Island, Vermont—and the District of Columbia—operate their own jail systems. In these states and the District, either the state size or sparse populations led to the development of state-run jails. For example, Delaware has only three counties and instead of each county operating its own jail the state combined prison and jail operations into a single network. Alaska has a somewhat distinctive approach as that state has an integrated jail-prison system and they also have 15 small locally operated jails (Zeng, 2019).

Most jail systems throughout the world are operated and funded by state (provincial) or national governments and one advantage to these arrangements is that the cost of detaining individuals is spread to a greater number of taxpayers, which reduces the burden on any local government. In addition, because they are operated by higher levels of government, there is less local political interference in their operations. Because local politics are removed from jail operations, state-operated jails are constructed where they are needed, a smaller number are required, and they can be run using a common set of standards overseen by a single state agency. Reducing the number of facilities can also save costs by centralizing administrative services. Last, jail conditions also can be improved through merit hiring and standardizing jail services (Mays & Thompson, 1988).

Federal Detention Facilities

As previously observed in this chapter, the BOP detains individuals accused of committing federal crimes and defendants awaiting their court dates, and their facilities are all located in large cities. The BOP operates three Metropolitan Correctional Centers (Chicago, New York, and San Diego), five Federal Detention Centers (Honolulu, Houston, Miami, Philadelphia, and Seattle), and two Metropolitan Detention

Centers (Brooklyn and Los Angeles) in the continental United States and one facility in Puerto Rico. These facilities range in size from about 400 to 1,600 beds and hold pretrial detainees, although some also hold individuals serving short sentences, or prisoners awaiting transfers to federal facilities. Due to the limited number of federal detention facilities in the nation, the U.S. Marshals Service contracts with local jails to hold their arrestees and those awaiting their court dates. Moreover, the federal government also makes arrangements with local jails to hold immigration detainees awaiting deportation.

PROFILE OF JAIL INMATES

Jails are busy places and on any given day they held almost three-quarters of a million inmates; about 10.6 million individuals were booked into jails in 2017 (Zeng, 2019). We must be careful when using the figure of 10.6 million individuals as some people are arrested and booked numerous times in a single year. Fischer (2018), for example, reports that a 57-year-old Miami man had been arrested 344 times, and most of those arrests would have included a trip to a police lockup or jail admission. Booking officers in jails often call these inmates **frequent flyers** due to their repeated admissions and discharges. Many frequent flyers are suffering from chronic mental health problems or addiction issues and they may place significant demands on the health system as they are often admitted to emergency rooms (Akins, Burkhardt, & Lanfear, 2016). The existence of these frequent flyers shows that shortcomings in other social systems—such as a lack of community mental health services—can become a problem for the criminal justice system.

When it comes to jail admissions, we find that the rich and famous like Lindsay Lohan are sometimes admitted to jails although they are seldom behind bars for more than a few hours and they quickly make bail and are released. Most jail inmates, by contrast, are poor, homeless, and many of them have chronic alcohol and drug or mental health problems (or both problems together). Table 5.1 shows a profile of jail inmates including their conviction status, their drug use, and health-related problems using national-level information retrieved from Bureau of Justice Statistics reports released between 2015 and 2019. We can summarize this list by defining a typical jail resident as an unconvicted male facing felony charges who is struggling with substance abuse and is likely to have physical and mental health problems. Although women account for about one in six jail inmates, they typically have a greater need for health and addictions treatment than their male counterparts.

Over three decades ago, John Irwin (1985) called the individuals living within American jails "the rabble." He included among the rabble members of the permanent urban underclass, as well as the disorderly or unruly segments of society. Do these jail inmates

TABLE 5.1 Characteristics of Jail Inmates

Characteristic	Percentage
Gender	
• Males	85
Race	
• White	50
• African American	34
• Latinx	15
• American Indian, Alaskan Native	1
• Asian, Native Hawaiian, or Pacific Islander	1
Conviction Status	
• Convicted	35
• Unconvicted	65
Most Serious Offense	
• Felony	69
• Misdemeanor	26
• Other	5
Drug Use (Sentenced jail inmates)	
• Dependency (Males)	62
• Dependency (Females)	72
• Regularly use drugs	75
• Used drugs at time of offense	37
• Committed current offense to get money to obtain drugs	21
• Drug use in month prior to current offense	54
Mental Health Status (All jail inmates)	
• Serious psychological distress (Males)	26
• Serious psychological distress (Females)	32
• History of mental health problem (Males)	41
• History of mental health problem (Females)	68
Prevalence of Disabilities (Any disability)	
• Males	39
• Females	50
Medical Problems	
• Chronic health condition (e.g. Asthma, high blood pressure)	45
• Infectious disease (e.g. Hepatitis or sexually transmitted infection)	14

Sources: Bronson and Berzofsky (2017); Bronson, Maruschak, and Berzofsky (2015); Bronson, Stroop, Zimmer, and Berzofsky (2017); Maruschak, Berzofsky, and Unangst (2015); Zeng (2019).

differ from the general population? Figure 5.1 shows that they are far more likely to be drug dependent and have physical and health-related problems, including disabilities, chronic health conditions, or serious psychological disorders. Given those facts, do you believe that jails are the right place for these individuals?

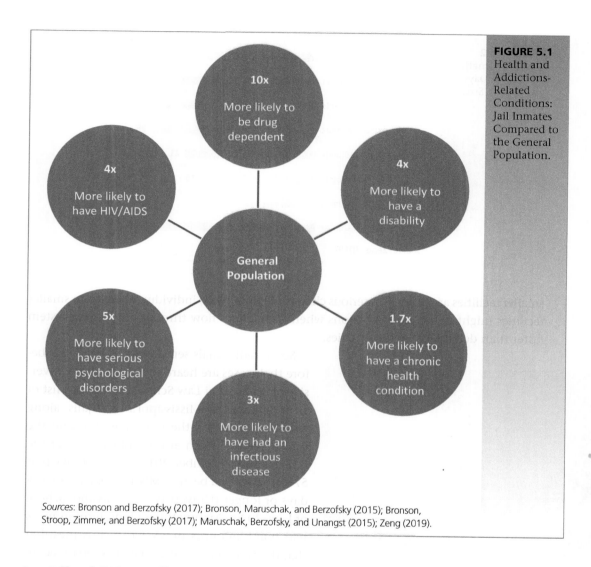

FIGURE 5.1 Health and Addictions-Related Conditions: Jail Inmates Compared to the General Population.

Sources: Bronson and Berzofsky (2017); Bronson, Maruschak, and Berzofsky (2015); Bronson, Stroop, Zimmer, and Berzofsky (2017); Maruschak, Berzofsky, and Unangst (2015); Zeng (2019).

Length of Stay—Jails

When it comes to their time behind bars, Zeng (2019, p. 8) reports that the average stay for all jail inmates is about 26 days, but that is a national average. We must be careful about using that statistic as it masks the differences in facilities of various sizes and jails in different locations, as well as detained and sentenced populations. Figure 5.2 shows that as facility size increases, so does the time served and individuals in a 2,500-bed facility will spend almost three times longer than inmates housed in a jail with fewer than 50 beds. There is no single reason for this difference, and it is possible that the individuals in the

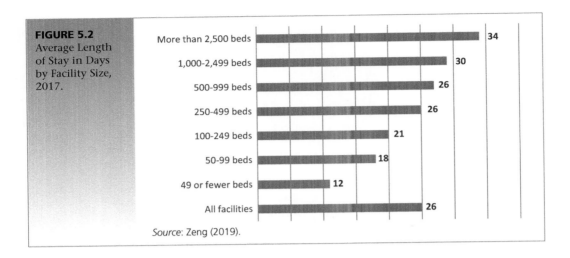

FIGURE 5.2
Average Length of Stay in Days by Facility Size, 2017.

Facility Size	Average Length of Stay (Days)
More than 2,500 beds	34
1,000-2,499 beds	30
500-999 beds	26
250-499 beds	26
100-249 beds	21
50-99 beds	18
49 or fewer beds	12
All facilities	26

Source: Zeng (2019).

smaller facilities are facing less serious charges. Alternatively, individuals housed in smaller facilities might reside in jurisdictions where individuals flow through the justice system faster than defendants in larger cities.

PHOTO 5.2
The Los Angeles Twin Towers Correctional Facility is one of the largest US jails, and has been called the largest mental health facility because it holds so many people with mental health problems. Credit: ZUMA Press/Alamy Stock Photo.

Some individuals serve years in local jails before their cases are heard in a court. The University of Mississippi Law School publishes a list of all individuals in Mississippi's local jails, along with their charges, the bond amount, and the time served between arrest and the date of the census. The December 2019 census shows that 578 inmates had been in Mississippi jails for 365 days or longer (University of Mississippi School of Law, 2020). Many of these long-term inmates had bond amounts of $5,000 or less meaning that they could not come up with $500 to secure their release during that year. Sixteen of these inmates had served more than five years in the local jail. Although some of these long-term inmates could be state prisoners, most are awaiting a court date, trial, or sentencing. While we do not know the longest time any defendant waited for their day in court, Kharon Davis of Dothan, Alabama, was held without bail for over ten years on a murder charge before he was convicted (Cassens Weiss, 2017). What can we learn from this information? Whenever we see a national average, we must remember that there are likely many outlying or extreme cases in those averages.

Sentenced jail inmates tend to serve short periods of incarceration. Reaves (2013) found that the median jail sentence in large urban courts was about four months. Yet, most sheriffs allow inmates to earn some time off for good behavior. When Ruddell and Mays (2006) surveyed jail administrators about the actual time served their respondents indicated that inmates served about 75% of their sentence, although there was considerable variation. In New York, for instance, individuals typically serve about 66% of a misdemeanor sentence and 70% of a felony sentence after they earn good time credits, and people receiving very short sentences—such as 14 days—might only serve three days (Rempel, Kerodal, Spadafore, & Mai, 2017, p. x). Sometimes the nature of the offense influences the time served. Like the practice in New York, most inmates serving a sentence in the Los Angeles County Jail serve a fraction of their sentence, but offenders who used a gun in their crimes serve 100% of their sentence (Granda, 2018).

Women Jail Inmates

On 31 December 2016 there were about 100,000 women jail inmates, and their numbers have been increasing. While they represented 11.4% of all inmates in 2000 that proportion increased to 15.3% by 2017 (Zeng, 2019). This growth was not consistent with what is happening in state prisoners as the number of female prisoners has been slowly decreasing (Bronson & Carson, 2019).

Although comprising only a fraction of the entire jail population, the characteristics reported in Table 5.1 show that women are booked into jails with more serious health-related problems, including drug dependency and serious mental health problems. Most have experienced victimization and Figure 5.3 shows the proportion of female jail inmates reported having experienced sexual, partner, or caregiver violence (Swavola, Riley, & Subramanian, 2017). Being victimized may contribute to the high prevalence of these inmates with mental health problems and they may worsen those problems by using alcohol and drugs to self-medicate. Regardless of the cause, the need to provide services for these women increases the jail's costs.

Maruschaak (2006) found that about 5% of women inmates are pregnant, and that finding suggests there are about 6,000 pregnant inmates at any given time, although most of them are thought to be in the early stages of their pregnancies. Pregnancy poses challenges for the inmate and the jail personnel. Many of these women received poor prenatal care in the community although about one-half reported receiving an

RACE, CLASS, AND GENDER

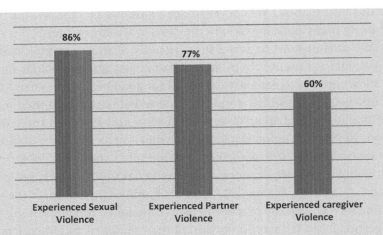

FIGURE 5.3
Self-reported victimization: Women jail inmates.
Source: Swavola, Riley, and Subramanian (2017).

obstetrics exam after their admission to the jail and about one-third received some pregnancy care (Maruschak, 2006, p. 7). Yet, many of these women contend their treatment fails to meet their needs. A lawsuit filed by inmates of the Alameda (CA) County jail say they received "grossly inadequate nourishment, warmth, sanitation, medical care, and other necessities of pregnancy" (p. 1) and they claimed these conditions harmed their unborn children and led to miscarriages (*Alameda County Women Prisoners et al. vs. Alameda County Sheriff's Office et al.*, 2018).

There is no shortage of examples where local jails failed to provide appropriate care to pregnant inmates and some delivered their infants in jail cells or in vehicles while being transported to hospitals. One controversial practice is requiring inmates in labor to be handcuffed or shackled to their hospital beds. While the BOP as well as many state correctional systems has banned this practice, it is still happening in some state prisons and jails. Dorwart (2018, para. 7) says the licensing body for obstetricians and gynecologists has called "the practice of restraint demeaning and unnecessary, as no incarcerated women have been reported to attempted escape during childbirth." Such opposition led to bans on the practice in 26 states (Southall & Weiser, 2018).

One questions whether these practices are occurring in women-only jails, but single-gender facilities are rare, and most jails house both men and women. Of the thousands of American jails, there were only 13 that were single-gender facilities in

1999 and that number has been decreasing (Stephan, 2001). The problem for some women is that correctional practices such as strip searches and being supervised by male correctional officers while showering, dressing, or using the bathroom can be traumatizing (Swavola, Riley & Subramanian, 2017, p. 14). Moreover, the ongoing exposure to conflict and jail violence also can be stressful and may contribute to **post-traumatic stress disorder (PTSD)**.

Altogether, we are coming to realize that many women jail inmates require additional supports in order to survive their time behind bars. This observation is especially relevant given their unmet needs regarding mental health and addictions, their prior histories of experiencing abuse and violence, as well as their physical care needs. The problem is that recognizing these needs is only the first step in solving these problems, and there has been a reluctance to increase jail funding to provide better care for these women.

JAIL DESIGN

The jail's physical layout shapes how inmates are supervised. With advances in technology, and new tools for supervising inmate activities, the configuration of jails has evolved through at least three phases. The most traditional jail design, shown in Figure 5.4 is called a **linear design**, with cells opening onto long straight hallways, an approach first used in Eastern State Penitentiary in the 1830s. In facilities with a linear design, correctional officers work outside the cells and make periodic rounds. To see what any inmate is doing the officer has to look into the individual's cell. This pattern of inmate management is called **intermittent supervision**, and one downfall of this approach is that the officer's ability to know what is going on is limited by blind spots caused by the design.

Second-generation jails make use of closed-circuit television cameras (CCTV) or other devices to increase an officer's ability to supervise the inmates. The basic layout of these facilities is still linear, and officers have to walk down a hallway and look into cells to check on individual inmates, but monitoring devices allow remote supervision of inmates and the staff members at jail entrances (called sally ports), in booking areas, in drunk tanks, and in corridors. This form of supervision allows a relatively small number of correctional officers to supervise large numbers of inmates.

A third-generation design is commonly found in **new-generation jails**, which first emerged in the 1970s (Tartaro, 2006). The **podular design** departs from linear design

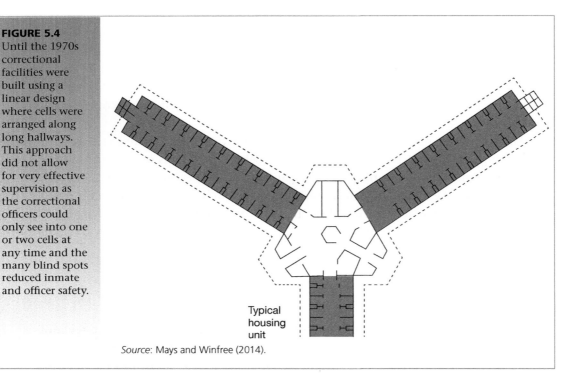

FIGURE 5.4
Until the 1970s correctional facilities were built using a linear design where cells were arranged along long hallways. This approach did not allow for very effective supervision as the correctional officers could only see into one or two cells at any time and the many blind spots reduced inmate and officer safety.

Typical housing unit

Source: Mays and Winfree (2014).

by housing inmates in pods, which are sometimes called living units. These pods can be shaped using triangles or quadrangles where the inmate's cells are built into the perimeter and those rooms overlook a central courtyard, which are often constructed in two levels. These units are intended to have a more home-like feel to them as the security features are built into the architecture and are not as obvious as the iron bars and cages that dominated jail and prison construction from the 1830s to the 1970s. Moreover, it was envisioned that various rehabilitative programs would be offered in the common areas of these living units (Wener, 2005). Last, officers are removed from closed in control rooms and are assigned to work stations that are directly in the units. As a result, they have a much better view of inmate activities and this design is shown in Photo 5.3.

The new-generation design was intended to contribute to a new form of inmate management where officers and inmates would have a higher degree of interaction, especially since the correctional officers were no longer supervising from control rooms. In new-generation jails the inmates are under the direct and constant supervision of the corrections officers. This allows the staff members to have a greater interaction with and control over the inmates. This supervision model is based on the idea that officers would help inmates to develop better interpersonal and problem-solving skills. It was thought that after increasing those skills, inmates would be less likely to engage in misconduct. Increasing the interactions between inmates and officers has never been as fully accepted as many correctional managers hoped. One reason for this implementation failure was that it required both groups to make significant changes in their traditional roles, but inmates did not want to be seen associating with the officers and officers were reluctant to become involved in the lives of inmates.

PHOTO 5.3
This Florida facility was built using the podular design, where the inmate rooms are built around a courtyard and the rooms are built into the perimeter walls. The multipurpose area on the ground floor is used for dining, education, and recreation. This facility design is safer for the inmates and the correctional officers because there are few blind spots. Credit: Ron Buskirk/Alamy Stock Photo.

Tartaro (2006) surveyed jail administrators that were using a new-generation approach and she found that few county governments delivered the model as originally developed. While a cornerstone of the approach was to reduce the institutional feel of these living units and promote a more home-like environment, most facilities used furniture and fixtures that were designed for corrections: an example is a dining table made of steel or aluminum and bolted to the floor. Tartaro (2006, p. 293) also found that few of these facilities fully implemented the direct supervision model and delivered rehabilitative services such as educational programs, drug treatment, non-drug therapy, or employment-related programs directly in the units. Nor did these facilities deploy the college-educated officers that were supposed to serve as positive role models and help inmates develop their problem-solving skills. Thus, the full implementation of the new-generation approach that was originally envisioned has not taken place.

One of the issues related to the implementation of all criminal justice programs is that there is often a disconnection between what is originally proposed by administrators, researchers and policymakers and the services actually delivered by the front-line staff. Often the elements of the intervention that are not fully delivered are considered expensive or they depart from the traditional operations. Moreover, some interventions are threatening to the staff or, in the case of new-generation jails, threatening to the correctional officers and the inmates. Tartaro (2006) calls this a partial implementation and throughout the chapters that follow we describe similar cases where various types of treatment programs fail to have the desired impacts because they are "watered down."

JAIL PERSONNEL

As noted earlier sheriffs' departments operate almost all US jails and in almost all the remaining states, elected sheriffs are responsible for jail operations. There are some different arrangements existing throughout the country including the following:

- Kentucky jails are operated by elected officials called jailers (Kentucky Jailer's Association, 2019).
- In some counties jail administration is a county department, and the head of that department is appointed by the county government. Under this arrangement the jail administrator reports to the county manager, the county judge, or the board of supervisors.
- Some jails fall under the control of the chief of police. This is the most common in police departments in large cities that operate their own jails.
- In several large urban areas—Dade County (Florida), Los Angeles County, and New York City, for example—the jails are part of a local corrections department. In these cities, each facility may be designated for a special use as part of a local jail network: possibly one jail for females, another for pretrial detainees, and another for sentenced inmates.

The administrative arrangement often indicates the significance of the jail's operating budget. Administration-by-sheriff can mean money and attention goes to law enforcement instead of jails. In addition, the type of jail administration can influence salaries, status, and how the jail is staffed. We now turn our attention to the personnel working within these places.

Jail Employees

Although jail layout and administration are critical to mission performance, the greatest influence on the jail's day-to-day operations is the skills and abilities of the people working there. Working with jail inmates is a challenging job given the constant flow of people being admitted and discharged. Moreover, inmate behaviors tend to be unpredictable as most people booked into jails are under the influence of alcohol or drugs, and many are uncertain and fearful about their prospects. These fears and uncertainty can contribute to impulsive behaviors ranging from self-harm to violence. This lack of predictability creates stressful working conditions, and that stress is enhanced when working in overcrowded and understaffed facilities (Ricciardelli, Power, & Simas Medeiros, 2018). Other administrative shortcomings also can contribute to job-related stress, including inadequately trained staff, poor leadership, or inadequate resources to meet the inmate's needs such as a lack of mental health services.

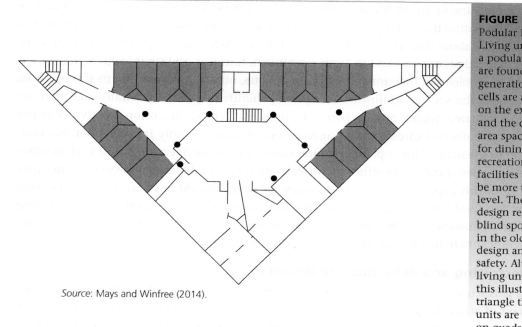

Source: Mays and Winfree (2014).

FIGURE 5.5
Podular Design. Living units using a podular design are found in new generation jails. The cells are arranged on the exterior walls and the common area space is used for dining and recreation. In larger facilities there will be more than one level. The podular design reduces the blind spots found in the older linear design and increases safety. Although the living unit shown in this illustration is a triangle these living units are also based on quadrangles.

There are several common problems relating to jail staffing and they relate to recruiting officers who are effective in working with inmates, reducing turnover (when employees leave their jobs), and how jail officers are assigned and supervised. Many of the challenges are related to inadequate funding, which is a key reason why it is difficult to recruit and retain good jail officers. In the traditional approach to jail staffing, custodial personnel are simply sheriff's deputies assigned to work in the jail. In this approach, there is one career track within the sheriff's department and personnel move in and out of jail assignments. These employees tend to come from five groups:

1. New hires awaiting the start of a training-academy class.
2. Newly trained deputies awaiting assignments to road patrol or what is frequently called paying one's dues.
3. Deputies who have requested a jail assignment, which is not uncommon among older deputies who have become tired of the rigors of patrol.
4. Deputies on limited duty because of accidents or injuries.
5. Deputies who are being disciplined.

One outcome of an integrated patrol-jail role for deputies is that many of them may be working within the jail for some other reason than their personal choice, and not all of them are happy about their placement. Stohr and her colleagues (2012, p. 379) observe that dissatisfied jail officers can lead to "staff resentment, turnover, and stress" which, in turn, can lead to problems in their interactions with inmates, other employees, and their supervisors.

Under the second administrative system, sheriffs or jail administrators develop two separate career tracks: one for patrol deputies and one for detention facility personnel. These are distinct career options and personnel cannot simply transfer from one function to the other. This approach ensures continuity in jail operations, and staff members who are better trained in either their role as patrol or jail deputies. One significant difference in this approach is that jail deputies are typically paid less than their patrol counterparts, and this reflects the value sheriffs place on correctional officers. Paying lower salaries, however, makes it difficult to recruit and retain high-quality officers, which is a significant challenge for most jail administrators.

Recruiting and Retaining Jail Officers

In jails where there is no overlap between patrol and correctional deputies, there are two ways of attracting jail personnel who are better motivated: paying higher salaries and offering more training. In some states, there are no formal training standards for jail officers, and their training might be minimal. In small facilities, for example, officers might learn on the job prior to receiving any formal training. Academy or on-site training programs typically provide an overview of the technical aspects of facility operations such as using physical restraints, writing reports, and how to discipline inmates. Less attention, however, is paid to the human relations functions such as enhancing the trainee's interpersonal communications skills and teaching them how to resolve disputes or conflicts without escalating situations. Training that is related to better understanding the distinctive characteristics of jail inmates such as their mental health and addictions-related issues often receives less attention. In the end, jail training is distinctive to the populations being booked into the jail and there is usually some orientation training about the risks of self-harm, suicide, withdrawal from aditions, and likelihood of engaging in aggressive behavior.

The nature of jail training is one reason some sheriff's departments have decided to separate the law enforcement and custody career paths. Law enforcement officers generally receive between 400 and 800 hours of academy training whereas jail officers typically receive 80–120 hours of training prior to working their first shifts. These differences may explain why jail personnel are paid less and why they are often perceived to have second-class status when compared to patrol deputies.

When it comes to salaries for correctional officers, they may be paid less than other law enforcement positions, and jail officers are often paid less than officers working in state prisons or for the BOP. Table 5.2 shows the starting salary for a deputy in the Butte County, California jail and a correctional officer employed by the California Department of Corrections and Rehabilitation (CDCR). Not only is the state salary higher but also the benefits are sometimes much better working for state governments. California correctional officer salaries are among the highest in the nation. Some rural counties in the Southern states, by contrast, pay much less and the starting annual salary for a jail deputy for the Caddo Sheriff's office in Louisiana is $27,720 (Caddo Parish Sheriff's Office, 2019). Issues related to officer salaries are important as deputies who were more satisfied with their pay tend to be more involved and committed to their organization (Paoline, Lambert, Hogan, & Keena, 2018).

PHOTO 5.4
Writing about jails, Paoline and Lambert (2012, p. 247) say that "staff are the heart and soul of these institutions," and "Satisfied, committed staff, who do not suffer from undue job stress, are critical in ensuring that a jail is successful, whereas highly stressed, unhappy, and uncommitted staff can result in disaster." Credit: David R. Frazier Photolibrary, Inc./Alamy Stock Photo.

Retaining jail deputies can be a challenge for jail administrators; moreover replacing officers who resign is expensive because new officers must be recruited and trained before starting their work. Another challenge related to turnover is that jails tend to lose the officers with the best set of knowledge, skills, and abilities, what a former Missouri correctional official calls the cream of the crop (Lewis-Thompson 2019, para. 26). Several researchers have looked into the issue of why jail officers leave their jobs, and the results show that salaries are not always a main factor in the decision to quit. For example, Lambert and Paoline (2010) found that supervisors and officers who had been in their jobs longer were less likely to think about quitting, while officers with a degree were more likely to consider quitting. This research also suggests that deputies who liked their work, who were committed to the organization, and were involved in their work (e.g. those agreeing with statements such as "I live, eat, and breathe my job") were less likely to think about leaving.

With respect to jail employees, Zeng (2019, p. 9) reports that there were almost one-quarter million jail staff and almost four out of five (79.5%) were correctional officers; the

TABLE 5.2 Jail Deputy and State Correctional Officer Pay

	Starting Salary	Maximum Salary
Butte County Jail Deputy	$45,006	$60,320
State CDCR Correctional Officer	$53,218	$88,932

Sources: Butte County Department of Human Resources (2019); CDCR (2019).

remainder worked in various support roles. There is a diverse range of support personnel who are not employed as officers and this includes administrators, clerical, housekeeping, kitchen staff, maintenance, health workers (e.g. nurses), and therapeutic staff. In a small jail all those functions might be undertaken by one or two persons, while hundreds of staff members oversee the different aspects of the jail's operations in the largest facilities.

Jail Officer Burnout and Stress

There is growing concern about the long-term effects of job-related stress on all correctional officers, and jail officers may work in more stressful conditions than their state prison counterparts. The constant turnover of jail populations, for example, presents significant challenges for officers as they are seldom aware of the threats a new jail admission will pose. Inmates admitted to state prisons, by contrast, may live in the same housing units for years and their conduct (both positive and negative) is well-known to the staff and the other prisoners. Moreover, as we noted earlier, many jail inmates are suffering from psychological and addictions-related issues and may be acting unpredictably as they are going through withdrawal, or because they are failing to take their medications. As a result, some jail officers report feeling fearful while on the job and this can contribute to job dissatisfaction (Lambert, Gordon, Paoline, & Hogan, 2018).

Jail officers will also witness disturbing incidents that can lead to PTSD such as acts of self-harm, suicide, and inmate-on-inmate or inmate-on-staff assaults (Carleton et al., 2019). Responding to those acts is also stressful and can be demoralizing to the worker. Long-term exposure to these incidents can result in staff members developing psychological disorders such as PTSD, depression, anxiety, and alcohol abuse. When various public safety staff members were screened for these psychological problems, Carleton and colleagues (2018, p. 59) found that over one-half of correctional personnel tested positive for these disorders and they had higher rates of PTSD, depression, anxiety, social anxiety, panic disorder, and alcohol use than police officers, paramedics, or firefighters. The long-term outcomes for officers suffering from these disorders can be grim, and especially when they receive inadequate training on the long-term effects of stress on their well-being or if they continue working in overcrowded, chaotic, or underfunded facilities. Researchers are now examining the outcomes of long-term exposure to trauma and stressful working conditions in corrections. One goal of these researchers is to help correctional officers develop better resiliency to these conditions.

MAJOR JAIL CHALLENGES

By design, jails deal with society's entrenched social issues, which may be one of the reasons they exhibit so many problems themselves. Next, we address ten of the most significant problems affecting jail operations. Although these challenges are diverse, the one underlying factor is that they are all resistant to change.

Local Politics

A major problem facing contemporary jails is that they are a product of their local political environment. Most are administered by a sheriff's department; at the same time, they are subject to the policy directives and funding controls of a city council, a county commission, or a county board of supervisors. Sometimes, jails are caught in the middle of a standoff between a sheriff from one political party and a coalition of county commissioners from another. This can result in a policy stalemate. The political problems of jails become all too apparent in the budget process. Jails must compete in budget negotiations with schools, parks, and recreational programs, and those programs are far more popular with voters than are jails.

One significant challenge when policymakers or academics discuss the issue of reforming jails is that sheriffs are elected officials and operating a jail gives them considerable influence. Historically, after new sheriffs were elected, they would fire many of the jail staff who were working in the previous administration, and they would appoint their own family members and supporters. While this practice has ended, the ability to appoint one's supporters to positions as they become vacant is a powerful incentive for keeping the *status quo*. As a result, state officials often point out that jails could be operated more efficiently and at lower costs if several counties combined their detention services under one roof, what is called **regionalization**. To date, these efforts have largely been unsuccessful unless state governments can overcome resistance by providing funding to regionalize jails, like they did in Ohio.

Funding

A second problem jails face is local financing, and jails can be an expensive proposition. The National Association of Counties estimates that counties spend about $26 billion on local jails (Ortiz, 2016, p. 7). When we combine political conservatism ("Lock 'em up and throw away the key") with fiscal conservatism ("Public money shouldn't be wasted on bad people and the jails that house them"), we find that most local jails suffer from a lack of funding. As a result, jail administrators are expected to manage inmates in aging facilities that are poorly maintained, inadequately staffed, and sometimes unable to provide for inmates' basic needs such as care for their chronic health conditions. Given those shortcomings jails can become unpredictable and violent places. Although jail inmates are not a sympathetic population with the public, we have to remember that more than one-half of them have not been convicted of a crime, and many people are in jail because their families cannot scrape together a few hundred dollars to obtain bail.

The lack of jail funding has led some local governments to seek revenue from state and federal governments for new jail construction, as well as obtaining funding for different projects such as introducing programs to serve persons with mental illnesses. Martin (2002, p. 18) provides a list of other sources of funding, including:

- Inmate fees and copays (e.g. jail booking fees and charging these people for their room and board while incarcerated).
- Contracts to hold inmates from other jurisdictions, such as federal detainees, or holding detainees for Immigration and Customs Enforcement.
- Profits from inmate purchases of food or other goods from the jail's commissary.
- Fees from inmate telephone calls, as fees are charged for most outgoing calls.

Although cash-strapped governments cannot be blamed for trying to fund their jail operations their search for revenue creates problems for their inmates.

Charging individuals booked into the jail a series of fees, for example, has been criticized because it can create a cycle of debt some poor individuals can never overcome and may lead to further incarceration if they cannot pay those fees (Human Rights Watch, 2018). Moreover, almost all jails charge inmates to make collect phone calls and their families pay for those calls. Wagner and Jones (2019, Appendix 2) collected information from 1,800 jails and they found that most charged more than $1 per minute to make calls, and a 15 minute in-state call from the Mississippi County Detention Center in Arkansas costs $24.82. These high fees, however, make it difficult for inmates to maintain family contacts, arrange bail, or receive some reassurance or support from friends. Last, while some sheriffs have profited from holding inmates for other local, state, or the federal government, there are problems associated with that approach as well, and they are described in our review of jail privatization.

Jail Locations and Structures

Many jails are overcrowded or rely on aging facilities and some of the problems they confront can be solved only through their expansion, construction, or relocation. Expansion often is the least costly alternative when the issue is simply one of needing more space. But expansion may not be feasible in a jail's present location, or it may not be possible to expand capacity in an older building. For some counties, the issue is not the size of the jail, but its suitability. Although many counties have replaced their antiquated jails with newer facilities, hundreds of aging and run-down jails are still admitting inmates. Some have suffered a great deal of wear and tear from the large number of inmates being admitted and discharged as well as vandalism and neglect. Moreover, older correctional facilities are more expensive to operate given their high rates of energy consumption and requiring a greater number of officers to supervise inmates. In these places it might be necessary to build a new facility. Some jail administrators have used the National Institute of Corrections (NIC) as a resource because they can provide "training, technical assistance, and information related to new jail planning" (NIC, 2019, para. 1).

When it comes to the location for a new jail the preferred site for these facilities usually is at or near a jail's current location. Often the courthouse and jail-related services such as lawyers' offices and bail-bonding businesses are located near the jail and they have a vested interest in keeping the jail where it is. In addition to requiring space for a new facility, the local government might also have to purchase additional land for a yard and parking for staff and visitors. Land development can be expensive and construction costs increase because most jail facilities are constructed as maximum-security space. This means building jails out of indestructible materials such as reinforced concrete and steel.

Most counties faced with a major jail expansion or relocation project are forced to look for property away from a city's central business district. Remote locations are more feasible today because of video arraignments, which allow the courtroom work group to be in one place while the inmates are in another. Yet, there is often widespread community opposition to relocating a jail from neighboring landowners, who have nothing against a jail as long as it's not in their backyard. Another challenge is that moving the jail further from the downtown district might lead to fewer attorney and family visits. In the face of organized opposition, politicians have been known to back down from a jail relocation decision.

Managing Crowding

Overcrowded correctional facilities pose challenges for inmates and jail personnel. Jail officers report that crowded and understaffed conditions increase feelings of danger and stress and are associated with increased violence (Ricciardelli et al., 2018). Inmates living in crowded conditions are also exposed to a higher risk of assault and they often express feelings of fear. For some counties, the problem of jail crowding is ongoing while other jails are faced with periodic overcrowding such as weekends when the police are more active and judges unavailable to conduct bail hearings. About one in five of all US jails are overcrowded on any given day, and the problem is more serious in facilities with 250–999 beds (Zeng, 2019, p. 8).

In counties with chronic overcrowding one solution is to add more beds. While some counties have constructed larger facilities to manage overcrowding some jurisdictions added beds by constructing **jail annexes** or **satellite jails** to manage overflow at high demand times or to develop space for women or special needs inmates such as persons with mental illnesses. An annex is simply an extension to the existing structure whereas a satellite jail is a new jail structure. Satellite jails may be more likely to be encountered in large cities. For example, the Los Angeles County jail system has seven different facilities, and they have approved the construction of a 4,000-bed facility that will hold inmates with mental health problems.

Interestingly, the Sheriff's Department will relinquish control of operations of that facility and those inmates, and it will be run by the Department of Health Services (Lau, 2019).

Some counties have established various community-based programs to supervise low-risk individuals and "jail authorities supervised 55,900 persons at mid-year 2017 in programs outside the jail, including weekend programs, electronic monitoring, home detention, day reporting, community service, alcohol or drug treatment programs, and other pretrial and work programs" (Zeng, 2019, p. 9). Although it is much cheaper to house a low-risk individual in the community jail administrators seem reluctant to take advantage of this approach, and there are fewer jail inmates in these community programs today than there were in 2006 (Zeng, 2019).

Crowded correctional facilities are an outcome of mass imprisonment policies and two groups oppose adding additional jail beds. Some contend that expanding capacity increases our ability to punish. That is, when counties can add jail beds quickly and relatively inexpensively, they do not have to address the underlying issues, such as: Whom are we jailing? Why are we jailing these individuals, and are there alternatives to incarcerating them? The second group argues that what jail administrators call "temporary solutions" or community-based options tend to be enduring because crowding is a chronic problem. They insist that the use of alternative structures keeps decision makers from focusing on the root of the problem, which is the jail's place in the criminal justice system.

Jones (2019) developed a guide to help jail administrators address the need for jail expansion, and encourages them to look at: (a) whether pretrial populations can be reduced; (b) reducing the number of inmates incarcerated for failing to pay fines and fees; (c) finding alternatives to the incarceration of persons with substance abuse and mental health problems; (d) consider releasing misdemeanants incarcerated for low-level offenses; (e) cutting the number of inmates held for federal or state authorities such as the immigration detainees or prisoners; and (f) determining if there are alternatives to incarcerating probationers or parolees for technical violations of their community releases. Although tackling any of these issues may lower jail populations there is seldom a political willingness to make those changes, as policymakers would have to confront the vested interests of prosecutors, bail bondsmen, probation and parole authorities, and county administrators who receive funding when local jails rent out cells to federal or state authorities.

Contracting to Hold Prisoners and Detainees for Other Jurisdictions

Hundreds of local jails are holding state prisoners and immigration detainees for the federal government. Copp and Bales (2018, p. 107) observe that "many rural facilities have added capacity to take in out-of-county boarders… [and] the influx of state prisoners and undocumented immigrants has brought in money to help sustain struggling jurisdictions."

Kang-Brown and Subramanian (2017a, p. 14) report that 84% of jails hold inmates for other authorities, and some jurisdictions rented out more beds than they used for their own inmates. These researchers found that about a dozen county jails rented out 87% or more of their beds. In other words, only about one in ten of their total jail population were local inmates (Kang-Brown & Subramanian, 2017b).

Adding these inmates can change the jail dynamics and reduce facility safety. Placing state prisoners in the jail population, for example, might require the facility to develop and deliver rehabilitative programs for these individuals. Moreover, these state prisoners might include a higher number of gang offenders, who may pose additional risks to facility security. Most jail administrators would probably prefer to hold immigration detainees for Immigration and Customs Enforcement (ICE). The Department of Homeland Security (2018, p. ICE-14) reports they housed 51,379 immigrant detainees and the average direct cost to the department was $122 for each day to hold them (Department of Homeland Security, 2018, p. ICE-O&S 127). Although costs vary somewhat across the country, if a jail can house an individual for $50 a day and bill the federal government for $122, it can be a money-maker for the jail, especially when the average detainee was held for 44 days. Although paying these costs can be expensive for a state or the federal government, it saves them money as they do not have to expand the number of beds or staff members and, in some cases, a local jail is able to house state prisoners or federal detainees at a lower cost.

Some local jails expanded their capacity to house inmates but shrinking prison populations in some states have cut the number of prisoners being sent to these jails. As a result, some jails have unused beds they financed to build, which strains county budgets. Burnett (2011, para. 22) explains that:

> The packages look sweet. A town gets a new detention center without costing the taxpayers anything. The private operator finances, constructs and operates an oversized facility. The inmates pay off the debt and generate extra revenue.

While the growing number of immigration detainees being held has also increased revenue for some county jails, local operations must compete for contracts with large correctional corporations such as the GEO Group and CoreCivic. However, small jails may not be as effective at lobbying governments as the large prison firms, and they may receive fewer inmates and receive less money for them.

One controversial practice that received considerable media attention in 2018 and 2019 was separating the family members of immigration detainees and sending the adults to jails or privately operated detention facilities and the children to separate places. Although this practice had been going on for some time, federal officials often attempted to keep family members together. One of the challenges of keeping families together if the only confinement option is a jail is that these facilities lack the ability to house family members together in units that are apart from the other inmates. Some non-jail detention facilities do have units that enable families to await their deportation together, and the Department of Homeland Security (2020, p. 3) budgets for 2,500 beds for these family units. Jervis and Gomez (2019, para. 2) report that since a federal judge banned the practice in 2018, the number of these separations has decreased, but has not ended.

Jail Standards

The American Correctional Association (ACA) has been pushing for national-level standards for correctional facilities since the 1950s. Today, there are voluntary standards for juvenile and adult facilities including standards for jails and prisons, community-based corrections programs and for health-care operations within correctional facilities. Becoming an accredited facility has some significant implications for jails, including their ability to charge fees for holding prisoners or detainees for the federal government. The BOP or ICE will not, for example, place inmates or detainees in non-accredited facilities. Accredited facilities tend to be safer and the ACA (2019) says these operations are often given discounts for their liability insurance. While the ACA has the gold standard for correctional accreditation, some facilities also obtain accreditation for their health care services offered by the National Commission on Correctional Health Care.

So, what is accreditation and how does a facility become accredited? The ACA (2019, para. 2) describes their standards as a:

> National benchmark for the effective operation of correctional systems throughout the United States and are necessary to ensure that correctional facilities are operated professionally. They address services, programs and operations essential to good correctional management, including administrative and fiscal controls, staff training and development, physical plan, safety and emergency procedures, sanitation, food service, and rules and discipline. Standards reflect practical, up-to-date policies and procedures that safeguard the life, health and safety of staff and offenders.

The accreditation process is time-consuming and expensive. Correctional administrators are given guidelines showing hundreds of standards they must meet. In order to ensure that the jail meets those standards, the ACA sends a team of evaluators to ensure the guidelines are being met through a series of audits, facility inspections, reviews of the agency's documents, and hearings.

In addition to ACA standards, at least 32 states have some form of jail standards overseen by the state government (Martin, 2007). Black-Dennis (2011) notes that many of these standards are voluntary and some states have no formal inspection or audits. There is some debate about the effectiveness of state oversight of jails. For example, as Patrick (2018) observes, there are only four jail inspectors in Texas, and they are responsible for evaluating a total of 250 facilities. Consequently, "the state's jail standards...are simply not enforced"

(Patrick 2018, para. 2). The outcomes of a jail's inspection might also depend on who carries them out. As Ferrise and Astolfi (2018, para. 1) point out:

> State jail inspectors failed to uncover routine inhumane treatment of inmates in the Cuyahoga County Jail [in Cleveland, OH] during their four inspections of the facility in the last three years. Yet, the U.S. Marshals Service found dozens of instances of inmate mistreatment, including the denial of food, water and constitutional rights.

Given the growing number of inmate lawsuits being filed for jail conditions, we are likely to see more states adopt standards and undertake more vigorous inspections and enforcement. As many jail administrators have learned, however, having jail standards does not keep a jail from being sued, but having standards and adhering to them can greatly reduce both the mishandling of inmates and the rates at which lawsuits are brought and won.

Removing Juveniles from Adult Jails

Since the 1970s, and some would say even earlier, there has been ongoing debate about placing youths in adult jails. One of the major provisions in the *Juvenile Justice and Delinquency Prevention Act* of 1974 was the removal of juvenile detainees from adult jails. That has yet to happen although the number of juveniles held in adult jails declined by about half between 2000 and 2017, and that drop is shown in Figure 5.6. There is a distinction in the two lines as persons under 18 years of age can be held as adults, or as juveniles. In New York and North Carolina anybody older than 16 years was considered an adult, but both states changed their laws in 2019 to raise the age of criminal responsibility to 18 years of age. Other youths have been charged with serious offenses and may be held in adult jails, and they are also considered adults.

Zeng (2019, p. 5) reports that about 3,500 youths were detained in adult jails in 2017. That number can be a bit misleading because it does not reflect the total number of youngsters booked into jails and then released throughout the year. If we use the same formula for youths as adults (14.5 admissions times the average daily inmate population), we came up with an estimate of over 50,000 youths booked into jails every year. Most people assume these are the worst of the worst juvenile offenders but that is a shaky assumption at best as few sparsely populated rural counties have a juvenile detention center, and so the only two options to hold juveniles in those places are the local jail or to release them. As a result, some of these jails may be holding youth who have been accused of committing relatively minor crimes as no local alternative options exist.

Jail administrators are reluctant to house juveniles in their facilities under any circumstances. The issue is liability. Juvenile detainees must be housed out of sight and sound of adult inmates. The result is these youngsters often end up placed in isolation, which is detrimental to their psychological well-being and may contribute to a higher

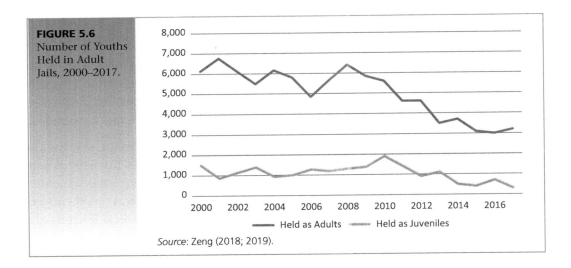

FIGURE 5.6
Number of Youths
Held in Adult
Jails, 2000–2017.

Source: Zeng (2018; 2019).

involvement in self-harm or suicide. Copp and Bales (2018) also report that juveniles in adult facilities are at high-risk of sexual victimization from the other inmates and staff members. In a Bureau of Justice Statistics study Carson and Cowhig (2020, p. 7) reports that between 2009 and 2016, two or three persons 17 years or younger died in adult facilities every year. More than two-thirds (71%) of the youths who died between 2000 and 2016 committed suicide while the remainder died of illnesses, drug or alcohol intoxication, and two youth were murdered (Carson & Cowhig, 2020, p. 11).

Increasing Rural Jail Populations

Ruddell and Mays (2006) observed that the number of jails with fewer than 100 beds decreased by over 1,000 facilities between 1982 and 2003 and most of these operations were in sparsely populated or rural areas. They speculated that the administrators in smaller jails had two choices if they wanted to survive: to expand their capacities by regionalizing or hold inmates from other jurisdictions. A growing number of news accounts and studies by advocacy groups published since 2010 show that jail administrators are expanding operations. Whereas the population of the largest urban jails has been decreasing, rural jail populations are increasing. This change is occurring during a time when "[r]ural counties have property crime rates that are three-quarters, and violent crime rates that are two-thirds, that of urban areas" (Kang-Brown & Subramanian, 2017a, p. 17). This brings us to the question of why incarceration is increasing during a time when crime rates in the countryside are less than in the cities.

Between 1970 and 2014 jail incarceration rates grew fourfold, but most of this growth was occurring in counties with fewer than 250,000 residents and this is shown in

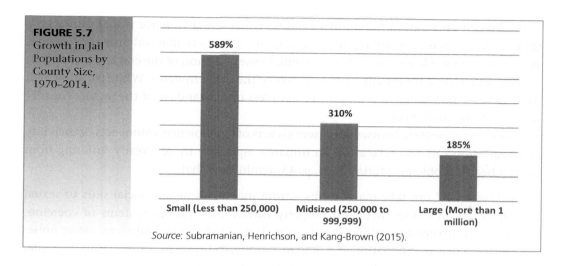

FIGURE 5.7 Growth in Jail Populations by County Size, 1970–2014.

Small (Less than 250,000) — 589%
Midsized (250,000 to 999,999) — 310%
Large (More than 1 million) — 185%

Source: Subramanian, Henrichson, and Kang-Brown (2015).

TABLE 5.3 Number of Inmates Held by Rural County Jails for Other Authorities

Region	Percentage of Total Jail Population Held for all Other Authorities
Midwest	33
Northeast	25
South	57
West	41

Source: Kang-Brown and Subramanian (2017a).

Figure 5.7. Whereas the largest 40 counties used to hold over one-third of all inmates (38%), they now hold less than a quarter, while the 2,625 smallest counties went from holding 28% to 44% of all jail inmates. So, what accounts for the increased use of incarceration in smaller counties? Levin and Haugen (2018, p. 3) identify three possible causes: (a) a growth in pretrial jail populations, (b) economic incentives to build jail capacity, and (c) rising drug abuse. Yet, the number of non-county inmates held for other local jails, state prison systems, or the federal government can represent a large percentage of the jail's population. Kang-Brown and Subramanian (2017a, p. 16) examined jail populations and found that rural jails in the South had the highest proportion of inmates held for other authorities, and this is presented in Table 5.3.

Jail Violence

Although some jails report statistics on inmate-on-inmate or inmate-on-staff assaults we have very little information about the extent of jail violence for the entire nation. One of the biggest obstacles in fully understanding correctional violence is that only a fraction of these acts is formally reported. As a result, it is likely that only the most serious assaults are reported, and the rest never come to the attention of the correctional officers or they are handled informally by the officers or the other inmates. While we know that some jails are very dangerous places, we have less understanding of the factors contributing to those differences.

Although this section focuses upon serious acts of jail violence, minor acts of incivility and aggression can also take a toll on inmates, especially those already suffering from mental health problems. Morin (2016, p. 45) reminds us that:

> jail 'violence' can take many forms – from mental abuse and racial slurs to sexual predation and rape, theft and property damage, ubiquitous systems of coercion, constant surveillance, stimuli deprivation, lack of privacy, crowding, excessive noise, the 'violence' of resignation and despair, perceived threats to bodily harm – to actual beatings, stabbings, and other types of physical assaults.

Morin's definition makes the issue of studying jail violence very complicated as many of those acts are an everyday occurrence that would never be recorded. As a result, we can only focus on acts that are counted such as serious assaults, sexual assaults, and murders. Not only are we interested in how often these acts occur but also the factors that contribute to inmates acting violently.

Researchers examining jail violence find that increasing the number of maximum-security inmates in a jail leads to more assaults (Kellar & Wang, 2005). Tartaro and Levy (2007), by contrast, found that urban jails are more violent places than rural or suburban jails. They also reported that facilities with a higher proportion of non-White residents and places where each officer supervised a greater number of inmates were also more violent. Caudill and colleagues (2014) also found that importing state prisoners into California's county jails increased rates of jail violence. These results suggest it is inmate characteristics, rather than the jail, that influence assaults, but what about other serious offenses?

Since the introduction of the *Prison Rape Elimination Act* in 2003 the federal government has been collecting information about sexual assaults in correctional facilities. Rantala (2018) reports that the number of allegations (unproven) and substantiated (proven) acts of sexual misconduct and harassment in jails and prisons has been increasing. However, we don't know if that is a result of actual increases in these acts, or whether these individuals are now more likely to report their victimization. Table 5.4 shows the number of alleged and substantiated acts per 1,000 jail and prison inmates. This table shows that when it comes to acts that were proven to have happened, jail inmates are at higher risk than state or federal prisoners, although the risks of harassment are the same in both types of facilities.

TABLE 5.4 Sexual Victimization in Jails and Prisons, Rate per 1,000 Inmates, 2015

Type of Incident	Rate per 1,000 inmates
Allegations of Sexual Victimization	
• Jails	8.0
• Prisons	12.6
Substantiated Incidents of Sexual Victimization	
• Jails	0.8
• Prisons	0.6
Substantiated Incidents of Sexual Harassment	
• Jails	2.55
• Prisons	2.25

Source: Rantala (2018).

Research reported by the Bureau of Justice Statistics shows that almost 1,100 jail inmates die in custody every year: about one-half these deaths are due to health-related problems and one-third are from suicides (Carson & Cowhig, 2020). Neither of those causes is surprising given the large numbers of inmates suffering from physical health and psychological problems. In addition to death from suicide and natural causes, about 30 jail inmates are murdered every year (which accounts for about 3% of all deaths). Carson and Cowhig's review of 389 homicide victims from 2000 to 2016 shows that almost all of them were male and African American inmates were over-represented. Most jail homicide victims were younger than 45 years, were awaiting a court date, and about half were being held on a violent offense.

Carson and Cowhig (2020) report that the homicide rate for jail inmates between 2000 and 2016 was 3 per 100,000 inmates, which is 50% less than the rate for community (4.5 murders per 100,000 US residents). The jail suicide rate of 43 per 100,000 inmates, however, was over three times greater than the suicide rate in the community, which was 13.4 suicides per 100,000 US residents. When the characteristics of the individuals who committed suicide were examined 91% were male, and they tended to be White inmates who had been convicted and were being held on a violent crime. Carson and Cowhig's study shows that the suicide mortality rate has been relatively stable since 2000, fluctuating between one-quarter and one-third of all deaths.

Rehabilitating Jail Inmates

Earlier we said that more than one-half of individuals booked into jails are in psychological distress, have unmet health needs, or are alcohol and/or drug addicted. Many of them live at society's margins even when they are not incarcerated. They tend to be drawn disproportionately from racial and ethnic minorities and, in general, from the lowest socioeconomic classes. In addition to their special needs, many are unemployed.

PHOTO 5.5
One of the challenges for jail personnel is to keep the inmates constructively occupied, and because there are so few inmates participating in rehabilitative programs, most watch television. Credit: David R. Frazier Photolibrary, Inc./ Alamy Stock Photo.

In other words, these people have problems outside jail, and when they come to jail, they bring those problems with them.

Any number of programs are available to address the physical, emotional, and socioeconomic problems of jail inmates. But three factors limit their implementation in jails. The first is time. The jail population is transient and many will leave within a few days or weeks. Even those who are serving time measure their sentences in months: recall that the median jail sentence is about four months, and that is before the inmate receives good time credits, which generally reduce their sentences by a quarter or more. This is not an excuse for a lack of programming, but it means that jail administrators must make constructive use of whatever time they have with these inmates. A second factor is that most jail inmates have not been convicted of a crime. The third factor that limits program participation is a lack of money.

There is no shortage of correctional-based interventions that have shown that the benefits outweigh the costs (Washington State Institute for Public Policy, 2019). Most of those programs, however, require a long-term commitment and must be delivered by trained counselors. Most jail-based interventions, however, are short-term interventions that are delivered by jail officers, and are typically intended to enhance the inmate's life or social skills. These programs generally fall into four broad classifications that include:

- *Medical treatment*: These interventions respond to acute (immediate or emergency) and chronic health conditions, from an individual's needs for emergency dental care to long-term care for HIV/AIDS. Once people are admitted into correctional facilities, the government takes responsibility for their care, and many jail administrators express frustration over the high cost of inmate care.

- *Counseling programs*: Given the high proportion of inmates with psychological problems, there is no shortage of demand for counseling and support. Some jailers point out that their facilities have become society's primary mental health centers, as there is a lack of community-based mental health programs, and the daily cost for providing in-patient psychiatric care might be four or five times greater than jailing individuals. The problem for the jail administrators is that while community-based programs can refuse to help some individuals, the jail must accept everybody who is booked into their facility. Getting inmates the help they need is another challenge. For example, a Nebraska jail administrator reports the average waiting time to get an inmate to a psychiatric center for an assessment is 85 days (Farrell, 2018).

- *Rehabilitative services*: These programs range from religious and recreational programs to offering anger management and parenting classes. These efforts are intended to help inmates develop the skills and abilities that are relevant in the outside world.
- *Education and vocational training*: Many jail inmates are unemployed when they are arrested. Some are virtually unemployable due to their substance abuse and mental health problems, and their involvement in the justice system. All jails provide work opportunities for inmates in the kitchen or cleaning and maintaining the facility, although some of these efforts might only take an hour or so per day. By contrast, some jails do offer opportunities for academic upgrading.

While jail-based rehabilitative programs can provide participants with some opportunities to develop their skills, these efforts are generally hamstrung by the short periods of incarceration, the unwillingness to participate in these programs, and a lack of meaningful rehabilitative programs that challenge the individual's antisocial thinking and criminal beliefs. However, by failing to respond to the unmet needs of these inmates some become caught in a revolving door of corrections where they will be readmitted to the jail dozens or even hundreds of times.

Pretrial Detention in Other Nations

Jails—short-term incarceration facilities administered and operated locally—are relatively rare outside the United States. What happens in other countries to people awaiting arraignment or to post-conviction misdemeanants? In most European nations, those accused of crimes are taken as quickly as possible before a magistrate, who advises them of the charges and their right to pretrial release. Most are simply released at that point on a money or property bond or on their word they will return for trial. Except for those accused of serious and violent crimes detention is usually the last resort.

In some nations—France is one example—the police, with judicial approval, can temporarily detain a person accused of what the French describe as flagrant felonies or misdemeanors for as long as 24 hours although prosecutors can sometimes extend that detention for another day. In Poland, by contrast, pretrial detention—called preliminary detention—is an option only if there is probable cause that the suspect committed the offense and one or more of the following conditions exists: (a) the accused is a flight risk or has no permanent residence; (b) there is reason to believe that the accused may attempt to obstruct justice, for example, by suborning

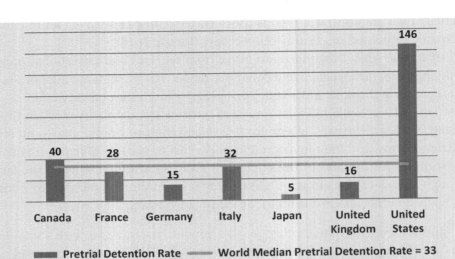

FIGURE 5.8
Pretrial Detention Rate per 100,000 National Residents, G7 Nations.
Source: Walmsley (2017).

perjury; (c) the penalty for the charge is at least an 8-year sentence (or the individual has been convicted and the sentence is more than three years); or (d) there is reason to believe the accused will commit another crime. Japan has a distinctive approach to pretrial detention. In theory, accused persons can be detained for as long as 23 days without bail unless they confess. Not surprisingly, most suspects confess; only rarely are people detained for the entire 23 days.

These different practices result in fewer persons per capita being detained until their court dates than in the United States, and this is shown in Figure 5.8. This figure illustrates that pretrial detention is a rare occurrence compared to its use in the United States, where heavy reliance on monetary bail ensures that the poor are detained before trial. One question that emerges from that observation is whether our high rates of pretrial incarceration makes us any safer than in the other G7 nations.

The types and forms of jails also differ, and some nations have no equivalent structure as US jails. So, where are pretrial detainees housed in those countries? They are usually housed temporarily—from a few hours to a few days—in a police lockup, just like in the United States. If a decision is made to detain them longer, they often go to a state-run correctional facility. The Prague city jail in the Czech Republic (also called Pankrac Prison), for example, is both a jail and a prison and this facility houses accused and convicted misdemeanants and felons, men and women, and children and adults.

SUMMARY

There are more jails and detention facilities in this nation than any other kind of correctional facility. Jails and detention facilities admit and discharge about 10.6 million people a year, keeping them for as little as a few hours to a year or longer. In reviewing the nature and functions of local jails, keep the following points in mind:

- Jails are distinct from prisons in a variety of ways, although they may serve similar functions.
- Jails house males and females, adults and juveniles, pretrial detainees and convicted offenders.
- Many jail inmates have significant unmet needs with respect to their physical and psychological health.
- Most jails are locally funded and operated, often by law enforcement agencies. Some states assist with the funding or operations of local jails, and six states have state-run jail systems.
- We identified ten challenges of jail operations and most of them can be traced to a lack of funding or a lack of community-based alternatives to jail incarceration.
- The average number of jail inmates increased dramatically starting in the 1980s but peaked in 2008 and has been slowly decreasing.
- The incarceration of women has outpaced the male incarceration rate and the largest growth in jail populations is happening in rural America.

Because most jails are locally operated stand-alone facilities that draw from a limited tax base they are often underfunded, and there is little political willingness to provide more funding to these operations. Jails have been called catch all facilities because they can manage individuals who are not served by other community services. Thus, jails cannot refuse admissions from the police or courts, and many of them hold large numbers of persons who have serious mental health and substance abuse problems because there are no other places for them. Jails are further disadvantaged because as many as one in five inmates in some jurisdictions are incarcerated because they are unable to pay their fines or fees. Moreover, in any given year, jails admit a million or more probationers or parolees who have violated their conditions but as community correctional agencies lack any alternatives to incarceration, there is no other option for them. Prison administrators have fewer of these problems, and the next chapter explores the key issues surrounding prison operations.

KEY TERMS

- federal detention facilities
- frequent flyers
- intermittent supervision
- large jails network
- linear design
- lockups (police lockups)
- new-generation jails
- podular design
- post-traumatic stress disorder (PTSD)
- regionalization
- sobering centers
- underground economy

THINKING ABOUT CORRECTIONAL POLICIES AND PRACTICES: WRITING ASSIGNMENTS

1. Describe the characteristics that distinguish jails and prisons.
2. In a one- to two-page essay, discuss the status of jails in the criminal justice system.
3. Provide arguments why (or why not) jails can benefit from expanded inmate programming. In your paper, clearly state the reasons for the position you have taken.
4. Rank the three issues confronting jails that you feel are the most in need of resolution. Justify your response.
5. Go to the following website and search for the number of inmates held for other authorities for your local jail. How does your local jail compare to the others listed in this table? [https://www.vera.org/publications/out-of-sight-growth-of-jails-rural-america#jailPopulationHeldForOtherAuthorities]

CRITICAL REVIEW QUESTIONS

1. Briefly describe the range of functions served by local jails.
2. Jail inmates have been called society's "rabble" or permanent members of the underclass. What kinds of people make up jail populations?
3. What impact do jail inmates have on jail operations?
4. Describe the basic designs used in the construction of US jails. How does the design of these facilities influence staff and inmate interactions?

5. Describe some of the special challenges of housing females in jails.

6. Sheriffs are responsible for administrating most US jails. How does this arrangement help or hinder the operations of local corrections?

7. The average jail inmate is incarcerated for 26 days. How does that length of stay influence the types of rehabilitative programs a jail can offer or deliver?

8. What are some of the most significant challenges of recruiting and retaining jail officers?

9. Why are other nations less dependent upon pretrial incarceration than in the United States?

10. What impact would an average jail stay (26 days) have on your life in terms of your work, education, and family relationships?

CASE

Alameda County Women Prisoners and Former Prisoners and Pregnant Prisoners v. Alameda County Sheriff's Office et al. (3:18-CV-00050).

REFERENCES

Akins, S., Burkhardt, B. C., & Lanfear, C. (2016). Law enforcement response to "frequent fliers": An examination of high-frequency contacts between police and justice-involved persons with mental illness. *Criminal Justice Policy Review, 27*(1), 97–114.

American Correctional Association. (2019). Benefits of accreditation. Retrieved from http://www.aca.org/ACA_Prod_IMIS/ACA_Member/Standards___Accreditation/Seeking_Accreditation/ACA_Member/Standards_and_Accreditation/Seeking_Accreditation_Home.aspx?hkey=ed52ffa0-24e4-4575-9242-1aa9d7107e69

American Jail Association. (2018). *Jail statistics*. Retrieved from https://www.americanjail.org/jail-statistics

Black-Dennis, K. (2011). *Core jail standards*. Presented at the Compliance and Accreditation Managers Association Annual Meeting.

Bronson, J., & Berzofsky, M. (2017). *Indicators of mental health problems reported by prisoners and jail inmates, 2011–12*. Washington, DC: Bureau of Justice Statistics.

Bronson, J., & E.A. Carson (2019). *Prisoners in 2017*. Washington, DC: Bureau of Justice Statistics.

Bronson, J., Maruschak, L. M., & Berzofsky, M. (2015). *Disabilities among prison and jail inmates, 2011–12*. Washington, DC: Bureau of Justice Statistics.

Bronson, J., Stroop, J., Zimmer, S., & Berzofsky, M. (2017). *Drug use, dependence, and abuse among state prisoners and jail inmates, 2007–2009*. Washington, DC: Bureau of Justice Statistics.

Burnett, J. (March 28, 2011). "Private prison promises leave Texas towns in trouble." National Public Radio: Morning Edition. Retrieved from https://www.npr.org/2011/03/28/134855801/private-prison-promises-leave-texas-towns-in-trouble.

Butte County Department of Human Resources. (2019). *Salary ordinance and position allocation*. Retrieved from https://www.buttecounty.net/Portals/17/LaborRelations/Salary_Ordinance.pdf

Caddo Parish Sheriff's Office. (2019). *Careers*. Retrieved from https://www.caddosheriff.org/content.php?c=42

California Department of Corrections and Rehabilitation. (2019). *Pay and benefits*. Retrieved from https://www.cdcr.ca.gov/career_opportunities/por/pay.htmlCarleton, R. N., Afifi, T. O., Taillieu, T., Turner, S., Krakauer, R., Anderson, G. S.,…McCreary, D. R. (2019). Exposure to potentially traumatic events among public safety personnel in Canada. *Canadian Journal of Behavioural Science, 51*(1), 37–52.

Carleton, R. N., Afifi, T. O., Turner, S., Taillieu, T., Duranceau, S., LeBouthillier, D.M.,…,Asmundson, G. J. G. (2018). Mental disorder symptoms among public safety personnel in Canada. *Canadian Journal of Psychiatry, 63*(1), 54–64.

Carson, E. A., & Cowhig, M. P. (2020). *Mortality in local jails, 2000–2016 – Statistical tables*. Washington, DC: Bureau of Justice Statistics.

Cassens Weiss, D. (2017, June 6). Man in jail for 10 years awaiting murder trial wants court to toss the charge. *ABA Journal*. Retrieved from http://www.abajournal.com/news/article/man_in_jail_for_10_years_awaiting_murder_trial_wants_court_to_toss_the_char/

Caudill, J. W., Trulson, C. R., Marquart, J. W., Patten, R., Thomas, M. O., & Anderson, S. (2014). Correctional destabilization and jail violence: The consequences of prison depopulation legislation. *Journal of Criminal Justice, 42*(6), 500–506.

Copp, J. E., & Bales, W. D. (2018). Jails and local justice system reform: Overview and recommendations. *The Future of Children, 28*(1), 103–124.

Cornelius, G. F. (2009). *The art of the con: Avoiding offender manipulation, 2nd edition*. Alexandria, VA: American Correctional Association.

Department of Homeland Security. (2018). *U.S. Immigration and Customs enforcement budget overview. Fiscal year, 2018*. Washington, DC: Author.

Department of Homeland Security. (2020). *FY 2020: Budget in brief*. Washington, DC: Author.

Dorwart, L. (2018, Jan. 16). Giving birth in jail can traumatize women for decades. *Vice*. Retrieved from https://tonic.vice.com/en_us/article/kznxav/giving-birth-in-jail-can-traumatize-women-for-decades

Farrell, J. (2018, Oct. 22). Managing mental health in area jails. *Fremont Tribune*. Retrieved from https://fremonttribune.com/news/local/crime-and-courts/managing-mental-health-in-area-jails/article_4a9d5488-7655-5173-98d2-838bc12482e3.html

Ferrise, A., & C. Astolfi (December 5, 2018). "How did the U.S. marshals and Ohio corrections inspectors reach such different conclusions for the Cuyahoga County Jail." Cleveland Plain Dealer. Retrieved at https://www.cleveland.com/metro/2018/12/how-did-the-us-marshals-and-ohio-corrections-inspectors-reach-such-different-conclusions-for-the-cuyahoga-county-jail.html.

Fischer, S. (2018, Jan. 24). Man arrested more than 300 times lands back in jail. *WPLG*. Retrieved from https://www.local10.com/news/weird-news/man-arrested-more-than-300-times-lands-back-in-jail

Fishman, J. F. (1923/2010). *Crucibles of crime: The shocking story of the American jail*. Richmond, KY: Newgate Press.

Granda, C. (2018, Sept. Sept. 13). LA County sheriff announces maximum jail time for those convicted of gun violence. *KABC News*. Retrieved from https://abc7.com/la-co-sheriff-announces-max-jail-time-if-convicted-of-gun-violence/4235474/

Hounmenou, C. (2010). *Standards for monitoring human rights of people in police lockups*. Retrieved from https://pdfs.semanticscholar.org/66a2/085f6e4a0aeef527da11efee275262dfad57.pdf?_ga=2.79451735.2133594142.°1584557700-1206208776.1566412987

Hounmenou, C. (2012). Monitoring human rights of persons in police lockups: Potential role of community-based organizations. *Journal of Community Practice, 20*(3), 274–292.

Human Rights Watch. (2018). *"Set up to fail": The impact of offender-funded private probation on the poor*. Washington, DC: Author.

Irwin, J. (1985). *The jail: Managing the underclass in American society*. Berkeley: University of California Press.

Jarvis, S. V., Kincaid, L., Weltge, A. F., Lee, M., & Basinger, S. F. (2019). Public intoxication: Sobering centers as an alternative to incarceration, Houston, 2010–2017. *American Journal of Public Health, 109*(4), 597–599.

Jendra, C. (2015, July 11). Forty-four charged in Baltimore jail scandal; here's how cases ended. *Baltimore Sun*. Retrieved from https://www.baltimoresun.com/news/maryland/sun-investigates/bs-md-sun-investigates-jail-20150711-story.html

Jervis, R., & Gomez, A. (2019, May 2). Trump administration has separated hundreds of children from their migrant families since 2018. *USA Today*. Retrieved from https://www.usatoday.com/story/news/nation/2019/05/02/border-family-separations-trump-administration-border-patrol/3563990002/

Jones, A. (2019). Does our county really need a bigger jail? *Prison Policy Initiative*. Retrieved from https://www.prisonpolicy.org/reports/jailexpansion.html#substanceusequestions

Just Detention International. (2015). *PREA and police lockups*. Los Angeles, CA: Author.

Kang-Brown, J., & Subramanian, R. (2017a). *Out of sight: The growth of jails in rural America*. New York: Vera Institute of Justice.

Kang-Brown, J., & Subramanian, R. (2017b). *Jail populations held for other authorities*. Retrieved from https://www.vera.org/publications/out-of-sight-growth-of-jails-rural-america#jailPopulationHeldForOtherAuthorities

Kellar, M., & Wang, H. (2005). Inmate assaults in Texas county jails. *The Prison Journal, 85*(4), 515–534.

Kentucky Jailers Association. (2019). *Duties of elected jailer*. Retrieved from http://www.kyjailers.com/legislation-resources/duties-of-elected-jailer.aspx

Knezevich, A. (2013, June 15). After jail scandal, spotlight on growing role of women officers. *Baltimore Sun*. Retrieved from https://www.baltimoresun.com/news/maryland/crime/bs-md-female-officers-20130615-story.htmlLambert, E. G., Gordon, J., Paoline III, E. A, & Hogan, N. L. (2018). Workplace demands and resources as antecedents of jail officer perceived danger at work. *Journal of Crime and Justice, 41*(1), 98–118.

Lambert, E. G., & Paoline III, E. A. (2010). Take this job and shove it: An exploratory study of turnover intent among jail staff. *Journal of Criminal Justice, 38*(2), 139–148.

Lau, M. (2019, Feb. 13). In landmark move, L.A. County will replace men's central jail with mental health hospital for inmates. *Los Angeles Times*. Retrieved from https://www.latimes.com/

local/lanow/la-me-jail-construction-20190212-story.htmlLevin, M., & Haugen, M. (2018). *Open roads and overflowing jails: Addressing high rates of pretrial incarceration.* Austin: Texas Public Policy Foundation.

Lewis-Thompson, M. (2019, Feb. 14). Missouri aims to boost correctional officers' low pay to help fill vacancies. *St. Louis Public Radio.* Retrieved from https://news.stlpublicradio.org/post/missouri-aims-boost-correctional-officers-low-pay-help-fill-vacancies#stream/0

Martin, M. D. (2002). *Budget guide for jail administrators.* Washington, DC: National Institute of Corrections.

Martin, M. D. (2007). *Jail standards and inspection programs.* Washington, DC: National Institute of Corrections.

Maruschak, L. M. (2006). *Medical problems of jail inmates.* Washington, DC: Bureau of Justice Statistics.

Maruschak, L. M., Berzofsky, M., & Unangst, J. (2015). *Medical problems of state and federal prisoners and jail inmates, 2011–12.* Washington, DC: Bureau of Justice Statistics.

Mays, G. L., & Thompson, J. A. (1988). The political and organizational context of American jails. In J. A. Thompson & G. L. Mays (Eds.), *American jails: Public policy issues* (pp. 3–21). Chicago: Nelson-Hall.

Mays, G. L., & Winfree, L. T. (2014) *Essentials of Corrections,* fifth edition. Chichester: Wiley Blackwell.

Minton, T. (2017). *American Indian and Alaska Natives in local jails, 1999–2014.* Washington, DC: Bureau of Justice Statistics.

Morin, K. M. (2016). The late-modern American jail: Epistemologies of space and violence. *The Geographical Journal, 182*(1), 38–48.

National Center for Jail Operations. (2019). *Jail resources.* Retrieved from https://nsajails.org/jail-resources/

National Institute of Corrections. (2019). *New jail planning.* Retrieved from https://nicic.gov/new-jail-planning

Oppenheim, T. (2019, Feb. 1). Baltimore has a detention problem. *Washington Post.* Retrieved from https://www.washingtonpost.com/opinions/baltimore-has-a-detention-problem/2019/02/01/f48f0596-2403-11e9-ad53-824486280311_story.html?noredirect=on&utm_term=.d08d6d65306d

Ortiz, N. R. (2016). *Priorities in America's counties, 2016.* Washington, DC: National Association of Counties.

Paoline, E. A., & Lambert, E. G. (2012). Exploring potential consequences of job involvement among jail staff. *Criminal Justice Policy Review, 23*(3), 231–253.

Paoline, E. A., Lambert, E. G., Hogan, N. L., & Keena, L. D. (2018). The effects of the workplace on jail staff: The issue of perceptions of pay fairness. *Corrections, 3*(3), 203–224.

Patrick, W. (2018, Aug. 1). State jail standards can't protect employees, prisoners. *Palestine Herald-Press.* Retrieved from https://www.palestineherald.com/columnists/state-jail-standards-can-t-protect-employees-prisoners/article_469db654-95c8-11e8-9ffc-cf893ca83a5c.html

Pishko, J. (2018, July 13). Why this mother and daughter were jailed without being charged with a crime. *The Appeal.* Retrieved from https://theappeal.org/material-witness-warrants-new-york/?utm_source=The+Appeal&utm_campaign=6e5b5c2ce4-EMAIL_CAMPAIGN_2018_07_03_03_52_COPY_01&utm_medium=email&utm_term=0_72df992d84-6e5b5c2ce4-58408803

Rantala, R. R. (2018). *Sexual victimization reported by adult correctional authorities, 2012–2015.* Washington, DC: Bureau of Justice Statistics.

Reaves, B. A. (2013). *Felony defendants in large urban counties, 2009 – Statistical tables.* Washington, DC: Bureau of Justice Statistics.

Rempel, M., Kerodal, A., Spadafore, J., & Mai, C. (2017). *Jail in New York City: Evidence-based opportunities for reform.* New York: Center for Court Reform.

Ricciardelli, R., Power, N., & Simas Medeiros, D. (2018). Correctional officers in Canada: Interpreting workplace violence. *Criminal Justice Review, 43*(4), 458–476.

Ruddell, R., & Mays, G. L. (2006). Expand or expire: Jails in rural America. *Corrections Compendium, 31*(6), 1–5, 20–21, 27.

Schaffer, C. (2016, October 5). Former Baltimore corrections officer pens book on prison sex scandal. *WMAR Baltimore.* Retrieved from https://www.wmar2news.com/news/region/baltimore-city/former-baltimore-corrections-officer-pens-bookon-prison-sex-scandal

Shen, A. (2018, May 21). 'Like a bad dream': In New Orleans, witnesses are going to jail instead of perpetrators. *The Appeal.* Retrieved from https://theappeal.org/like-a-bad-dream-in-new-orleans-witnesses-are-going-to-jail-instead-of-perpetrators-604243d9faff/

Southall, A., & Weiser, B. (2018, Dec. 6). Police forced Bronx woman to give birth while handcuffed, lawsuit says. *The New York Times.* Retrieved from https://www.nytimes.com/2018/12/06/nyregion/pregnant-inmate-shackled-lawsuit.html

Spina, M., & Michel, L. (2019, Feb. 23). Video: Buffalo police watch as handcuffed defendant is beaten. *The Buffalo News.* Retrieved from https://buffalonews.com/2019/02/21/video-buffalo-police-watch-as-handcuffed-defendant-is-beaten/

Stephan, J. J. (2001). *Census of jails, 1999.* Washington, DC: Bureau of Justice Statistics.

Stephan, J. J. (2008). *Census of state and federal correctional facilities, 2005.* Washington, DC: Bureau of Justice Statistics.

Stohr, M. K., Hemmens, C., Collins, P. A., Iannacchione, B. Hudson, M., & Johnson, H. (2012). Assessing the organizational culture in a jail setting. *The Prison Journal, 92*(3), 358–387.

Subramanian, R., Henrichson, C., & Kang-Brown, J. (2015). *In our own backyard: Confronting growth and disparities in American jails.* New York: Vera Institute of Justice.

Swavola, E., Riley, K., & Subramanian, R. (2017). *Overlooked: Women and jails in an era of reform.* New York: Vera Institute of Justice.

Tartaro, C. (2006). Watered down: Partial implementation of the new generation jail philosophy. *The Prison Journal, 86*(3), 284–300.

Tartaro, C., & Levy, M. P. (2007). Density, inmate assaults, and direct supervision jails. *Criminal Justice Policy Review, 18*(4), 395–417.

University of Mississippi School of Law. (2020). *Mississippi jail records (December 2019 Raw Data in Excel Format).* Retrieved from https://msjaildata.com/

Wagner, P., & Jones, A. (2019). *State of phone justice: Local jails, state prisons and private phone providers.* Washington, DC: The Prison Policy Initiative.

Walmsley, R. (2017). *World pretrial/remand imprisonment list.* London, UK: Institute for Criminal Policy Research.

Washington State Institute for Public Policy. (2019). *Benefit-cost analyses.* Retrieved from https://www.wsipp.wa.gov/BenefitCost

Wener, R. (2005). The invention of direct supervision. *Corrections Compendium, 30*(2), 4–7, 32–34.

Zeng, Z. (2018). *Jail inmates in 2016*. Washington, DC: Bureau of Justice Statistics.

Zeng, Z. (2019). *Jail inmates in 2017*. Washington, DC: Bureau of Justice Statistics.

Zoukis, C. (2015, April 9). Forty defendants, including 24 guards, convicted in widespread corruption scandal at Baltimore city jail. *Prison Legal News*. Retrieved from https://www.prisonlegalnews.org/news/2015/apr/9/forty-defendants-including-24-guards-convicted-widespread-corruption-scandal-baltimore-city-jail/

Chapter 6
Institutional Corrections

OUTLINE

- Introduction
- Prisoner Management
- Institutional Controls
- Prison Types and Functions
- Inmate Classification
- Federal Prison System
- State Prison Systems
- Private Prison Systems
- Summary

OBJECTIVES

After reading this chapter you will able to:

- Describe the challenges of prison management and operations

- Describe the history and evolution of institutional corrections at both the state and federal levels

- Explain the differences in the types and functions of prisons, penitentiaries, and other correctional institutions for long-term confinement
- Describe how the efforts of prison personnel are intended to reduce violence within a facility and recidivism once released

CASE STUDY

What Happens When a Natural Disaster Hits a Prison?

Providing a safe and secure environment are key priorities of staff in correctional facilities. Over the past century, everything from a prison's design, the technology used by correctional officers (COs), a facility's policies and procedures, and the activities of the correctional personnel have evolved to promote those priorities. First-time visitors to a prison are unlikely to recognize how these efforts and initiatives work together to provide a safe and secure environment. Visitors sometimes question the reasons for rules or procedures that don't seem to make sense to them, but decades of trial and error have led to such practices as a way to make the staff, visitors, and prisoners safer. For the most part prison wardens and their staff are successful in the day-to-day operations of these facilities, but sometimes unforeseen acts disrupt those carefully laid-out plans.

After Hurricane Harvey hit southeast Texas in September 2017, six state and federal prisons were flooded and living conditions for some prisoners were grim. Owing to reduced staffing—as officers could not get to their jobs due to the flooded highways, the power (and, as a consequence, air conditioning) failed in some facilities and inmates had limited access to drinking water, food, or medical care; some inmates drank from their toilets as they had no alternative (Banks, 2017). Unlike those of us in free society, prisoners are at the mercy of decisions made by COs about their well-being and sometimes these officials make mistakes.

Correctional institutions are clearly vulnerable to breakdowns of both good order and proper functioning when natural disasters occur. As another example, after Hurricane Katrina hit New Orleans in 2005, some Orleans Parish jail inmates lived for days in dark cells (as the power was cut and the generators failed) in neck deep water filled with sewage, and hundreds had to be rescued by sheriff's deputies in boats (Welch, 2015). Welch (2015, para. 7) reports that many jail officers deserted their posts, and he quoted one jail officer as saying: "The prisoners thought we were all planning to leave them to die locked in there...and I can't say I blamed them for thinking that." To prevent officers from deserting some were locked in the jail and they also had to be rescued (ACLU, 2006a).

The prisoners, including some children housed in the facility, claimed they received no food or drinking water for several days and violence broke out among the inmates, and some tried to escape. In the aftermath of this disaster, the inmates initiated lawsuits alleging that jail officials acted with deliberate indifference. Speaking about the Orleans Parish jail, an attorney said that "The Louisiana Society for the Prevention of Cruelty to Animals did more for its 263 stray pets than the sheriff did for the more than 6,500 men, women and children left in his care" (ACLU, 2006b, para. 6).

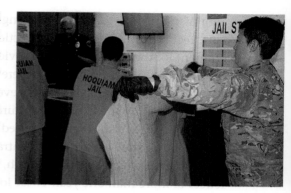

PHOTO 6.1
Natural disasters can create unique problems for both prisons and jails. Specialist Jennifer Staley of the Washington National Guard's 506th Military Police Detachment looks for contraband as she shakes out the blankets of inmates at the Hoquiam jail, 9 June 2016, while police chief Jeff Meyers oversees the evacuation of the jail's inmate population. The inmate movement exercise was part of a drill designed to test the security procedures and speed at which the Hoquiam Police Department could evacuate the jail should a tsunami hit the city. Prisons would face similar problems in the wake of a natural disaster. Credit: U.S. Air National Guard photo by Captain Colette Muller, Western Air Defense Sector/Alamy Stock Photo.

Readers interested in what happens when a disaster hits a prison are encouraged to read Mitchel Roth's (2019, p. 2) *Fire in the Big House*; a book describing the 1930 fire on Easter Monday at the Ohio State Penitentiary in Columbus that claimed the lives of 320 prisoners "from toxic smoke and flames in a little less time than it took to eat dinner."

Critical Questions

1. After the mayor ordered the evacuation of New Orleans due to Katrina the sheriff said that prisoners would stay "where they belong" rather than moving them. Does this statement show indifference to the plight of these people?

2. As a local official with limited resources, how would you prioritize evacuating prisoners and the public in your plans? How would you defend your decision to the media or to the public? Where would you place jail inmates if they could not stay in the facility?

3. It has been said that we can judge a society by the way prisoners are treated. Given the two examples described earlier, do you agree with that statement? Why or why not?

4. What happens to those in prison, both the inmates and the staff, when a national emergency hits, such as the COVID-19 pandemic of 2020? What if the staff refuses to come to work? What if a prison has a significant outbreak of a disease such as COVID-19?

INTRODUCTION

This chapter focuses on institutional corrections and we examine the nation's prisons and prison systems, what are essentially the "bricks and mortar" element of modern corrections. Although jails and detention facilities are also correctional institutions, prison administrators face different challenges than the sheriffs who oversee most American jails. Technically, a prison is a correctional facility operated by a state or the federal government for the confinement of convicted felons serving sentences longer than one year. As of the last prison census, there were about 2,000 state and federal prisons in the country, although that number changes every year as some are closed; of those facilities, 122 were operated by the U.S. Federal Bureau of Prisons ([hereafter BOP] Bureau of Prisons, 2018). There are also several hundred privately operated facilities holding inmates under federal or state government contracts. Military prisons, including the United States Disciplinary Barracks at Leavenworth, Kansas, held roughly 1,100 prisoners serving sentences of more than one year. These long-term correctional facilities go by several different names, including penitentiaries or correctional facilities, although we use the term prisons throughout this chapter.

On 31 December 2017 there were about 1.5 million men and women living in state or federal prisons (Bronson & Carson, 2019). They ranged in age from under 18 years of age to a growing number of elderly prisoners who will in all likelihood die behind bars. Furthermore, prisons are also holding over 2,600 inmates sentenced to death, and officials in these agencies are tasked with carrying out their executions (Death Penalty Information Center, 2020). Not only did these 1.5 million prisoners come from a diverse range of national, ethnic, and racial backgrounds, but they also committed a wide range of offenses, from driving under the influence to homicide.

One of the challenges of correctional administration is that prisons have no control over who will be sentenced to their care and there are a growing number of inmates with special needs. Researchers at the Bureau of Justice Statistics report that over one-half of state prisoners meet the criteria for drug dependence or abuse (Bronson, Stroop, Zimmer, & Berzofsky, 2017); about one-half suffered from current or prior mental health problems (Bronson & Berzofsky, 2017) and about one-third had at least one disability (Bronson, Maruschak, & Berzofsky, 2017). Moreover, pregnant women are also admitted to prisons, as are veterans with post-traumatic stress disorder (PTSD), members of sexual minorities, and juveniles as well as elderly prisoners. Regardless of their conditions or needs, prison officials are tasked with providing a safe and humane environment for them.

PRISONER MANAGEMENT

Prisons are **total institutions**, where correctional officials exert control over every aspect of a prisoner's day-to-day activities. Inmates are told when and where to eat, work, exercise, and sleep. In the highest security prisons, inmates cannot move about the facility without being placed in restraints and escorted by staff members, and those in the most restrictive housing units will live alone and have almost no contact with other prisoners. The greater the control exercised over the inmates, the more total the institution. Like other issues described in this book, there are both positive and negative aspects of placing high levels of control on prisoners. If prison personnel did not place the appropriate restrictions on inmates' freedom, they would be failing at perhaps the most important assigned task, protecting society.

As suggested earlier, those staff members operating prisons must assume responsibility for virtually all phases of the inmates' lives. This is a complex task, for inmates commonly resist what they view as efforts at external control. Indeed, it is the combination of the operational goals of a given prison, the security levels provided within the facility, and the classification levels assigned to its inmates that determines the methods and severity of control used by prison administrators. We begin our look at prisoner management with a critical examination of two organizational goals fulfilled by all prisons—custody and treatment, moving next to a review of prison security levels, and finally examine inmate classification systems that facilitate the attainment of these goals within the available security levels.

For the most part, efforts at providing an environment that enables prisoners to work toward their return to the community have been successful. With respect to violence reduction, a review of Federal Bureau of Investigation and Bureau of Justice Statistics data for deaths in jails and prisons, summarized in Table 6.1, suggests that living in a jail is somewhat safer than living in the community, although one is at a higher risk of homicide while residing in a federal or state prison. That fact represents a remarkable achievement, given that every prison inmate is a convicted felon and over one-half of them are sentenced on violent offenses, and this is shown in Figure 6.1. Yet, as we noted in the case example, almost every staff activity is designed around ensuring the safety and security of the facility, and the fact that COs can manage inmate violence is a result of good management rather than luck.

TABLE 6.1 Homicide in Community and Correctional Populations, 2016

Location	Homicide Rate (2016)
Community	5.3
Local Jails	3.0
State Prisons	8.0
Federal Prisons	9.0

Sources: Federal Bureau of Investigation (2017); Carson and Cowhig (2020a, 2020b).

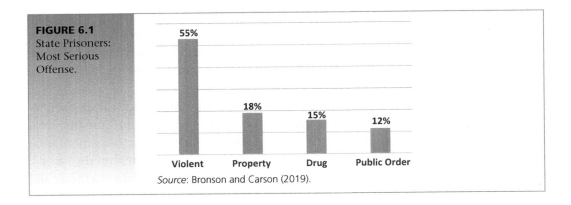

FIGURE 6.1
State Prisoners: Most Serious Offense.

Source: Bronson and Carson (2019).

For the remainder of the chapter it is important to note there is a formal set of written policies and rules guiding the behavior of the COs and the inmates they supervise. However, there is also an informal set of rules that shapes behaviors. For example, inmates need to know which prisoners have greater status within a facility and must learn how to manage interactions with gang members and why they should not become indebted to other prisoners. Understanding these informal expectations and the subcultures of both the officers and inmates may be just as important as the formal rules when one is trying to understand how correctional facilities actually function (Skarbek, 2014).

INSTITUTIONAL CONTROLS

Prisons have two widely acknowledged and—some would argue—somewhat conflicting goals: custody and treatment. **Custody** is the legal or physical control of people. Prison authorities are responsible for both the inmates' legal *and* physical control. This fact means they have an obligation to provide for inmates' basic needs; however, that obligation is second to public safety. **Treatment** is a term borrowed from medicine by early penal reformers and refers to interventions associated with a particular diagnosis, including a prison's rehabilitative programs. As noted earlier, about one-half of inmates have medical or psychiatric and psychological needs, ones they possessed upon entry into the facility and others they developed in response to institutional life. Most large prison systems have **reception centers** (sometimes called **diagnostic centers**), where newly sentenced prisoners are screened for medical, emotional, and psychological problems, as well as their risks to themselves or others. Some prison systems also assess for the psychological factors associated with criminal behavior, including their risks and criminogenic needs (Andrews & Bonta, 2017). Altogether, these assessments, which are sometimes carried out over a period of weeks, form the foundation of correctional **classification**. Classification enables prison officials to place inmates in the housing unit, specific security level, and institutional programs that are the most appropriate for their current offense, criminal history, and their treatment needs.

Whether custody or treatment is the most important goal depends on who you ask. As Craig (2004, p. 968) notes:

> The goal of controlling inmates subsumes all other goals. Even rehabilitative programming, which may involve time away from the prison routine or better quarters than can be had in the general population, is a privilege that may be granted or taken away.

There is sometimes a tension between the staff responsible for ensuring facility security or custody, which is the primary responsibility of COs, and those who deliver the treatment or rehabilitative programs. The following paragraphs describe the sources of that tension.

Correctional Officers

One objective guides COs: to ensure institutional safety and security for its staff, visitors, contractors, and then, once these groups have been provided for, its inmates. On its face, that would appear to be a relatively simple task, but given the characteristics of the inmate population it is a very difficult proposition. Given that their primary job role is ensuring security, COs tend to be suspicious, and they are constantly on the lookout for unusual exchanges—verbal or physical—occurring among inmates and, in some situations, between inmates and staff members. COs must be on the lookout for contraband, including cellular phones, illegal drugs, tobacco, home-brewed liquor, and weapons. Officers are also continuously assessing whether there have been any breaches in the facility's physical security such as inmates who are trying to escape by trying to exit through non-secure ceiling tiles or windows. Some CO duties involve searching the facility, prisoners' cells, patting down individuals, ensuring that the perimeter fences have not been tampered with, and counting inmates. These security-related activities are more difficult to achieve today. One emerging problem is that drones are used to drop contraband into prison yards and helicopters have been used in escape attempts (Associated Press, 2018). Cohen (2020), for example, describes how two New Jersey men were charged after their drone dropped cell phones, SIM cards, syringes, and saw blades into a low-security federal facility.

Another aspect of COs' jobs is the judicious use of their power and authority to maintain order within the facility. At times that task involves acting on behalf of inmates to help them achieve their goals or meet their needs, which could be as simple as arranging contact with family members or making a medical appointment. Shannon and Page (2014, p. 634) say that COs can grant or withhold privileges, help inmates meet their basic needs, provide guidance (including how to get things done in the prison bureaucracy), obtain information, and ensure their safety. In return for this help, the officers expect inmates to comply with their orders. One potential negative outcome of these relationships is that some officers lose their boundaries with inmates and engage in unprofessional relationships or illegal conduct such as bringing contraband into the facility or having sexual relationships with prisoners.

Treatment Staff

While the COs have the keys to the facility, front-line officers are often assigned to a specific post and, in many respects, they are as confined as the prisoners. After several years on the job, this work can become monotonous and, combined with the stress of supervising inmates, officers often express feelings of cynicism, frustration, and few of them feel appreciated by their managers, topics we explore in greater detail in Chapter 7. COs tend to have an orientation based on rule enforcement and they often develop a generalized distrust for inmates because it is their job to be suspicious. There are good reasons for those suspicions, as many jail and prison inmates will test their boundaries of and attempt to compromise them. Books written by COs describe the games criminals play (Allen & Bosta, 1981) and how offenders attempt to manipulate them (Cornelius, 2009).

In regard to treatment staff, there are two pathways to these jobs. Some treatment staff come from the ranks of COs and may receive very little formal training about working with incarcerated people prior to working in those jobs. Other treatment staff are hired directly into these roles and most of them have college degrees in fields such as social work, education, or psychology. Depending on the requirements of those positions, these personnel will fulfill several roles, including acting as counselors, caseworkers, case managers, psychologists and psychiatrists, social workers, activities coordinators, chaplains, educators, nurses, and physicians.

There is sometimes a tension between the treatment and custody personnel, and this can be due to a number of factors. In addition to being paid more than COs, treatment staff working conditions are often more desirable. While COs supervise a relatively large number of offenders in cellblocks or yards (it is not unusual for one CO to be posted to a unit with 100 or more prisoners during the daytime and more at night), treatment staff typically work on a one-to-one basis, in small groups, or teaching equally small classes. Their activities usually take place in semi-private offices or classrooms and they often have more time to prepare for teaching classes and take breaks between appointments. The roles of security and treatment staff are also differentiated based on their apparel and most COs wear military-style uniforms, while treatment staff generally wear their street clothes.

Another key difference between custodial and treatment staff is philosophical. Whereas the key role of the CO is security and control, treatment providers cannot force inmates to learn or to deal with their psychological problems. As a result, the success of treatment programs often rests on establishing trust relationships between providers and inmates. Given the different roles, job activities and philosophies, it is not surprising that there is sometimes a tension between the custody and treatment staff. In fact, the closed nature of correctional facilities, with the staff and inmates living and working within the confinement imposed by fences, walls, and locked units, can intensify conflict. Given those conditions the custody and treatment staff often try to find common ground, and to some degree each group depends on the other. The treatment staff need the security that COs provide and the COs benefit from the hope that the treatment staff can inspire in the inmates. Moreover, the treatment staff can play a powerful role in reducing the risks posed by some prisoners.

While we have described two distinct job roles, a growing number of prison systems are enabling their officers to play a greater role in correctional rehabilitation. Moreover, the relationships between custody and treatment staff may also be less pronounced in prisons with lower security levels (a topic addressed in the next section). In the lowest security prisons—ones that have no bars, fences, or imposing security—there may be a greater blend in job roles. This blended role can occur in programs developed for specific types of inmates such as those with mental illnesses, addiction problems, or sex offenders. Furthermore, some COs are also working within a **therapeutic community (TC)**, where officials create a separate housing unit in which treatment staff and officers deliver a 6- to 12-month rehabilitative program that prepares inmates for their eventual release. TCs are

PHOTO 6.2
A correctional officer talks with an inmate in the yard of the Lincoln Correctional Center (LCC) in Nebraska. The LCC, with a capacity of 500 adult male beds is a medium/maximum security facility, which was opened in 1975 and is situated next to the state's Diagnostic and Evaluation Center. Credit: Philip Scalia/Alamy Stock Photo.

popular interventions for substance abusers and inmates generally feel positive about the interventions, as well as the separation from the general prison population (Kreager et al., 2018). Not only are they popular with staff and inmates, but research shows these interventions provide $5.09 benefit for each dollar invested (Washington State Institute for Public Policy, 2019).

What do we know about COs' views on the goals of corrections? Similar to other professions, not all COs will share a common vision of their organization's primary goal. Gordon (2006), for example, found that all officers expressed some support for correctional rehabilitation, although African American and female officers, and evening shift workers had the highest levels of support for correctional rehabilitation. Other researchers have also looked at the factors associated with support for rehabilitation or punishment. Lambert, Hogan, Barton, and Elechi (2009, p. 113) report that older officers, as well as COs who were more involved in their work ("I live, eat and breathe my job"), were strongly attached to their employer, or expressed pride in their work (traits the researchers called organizational commitment), had greater support for rehabilitation. Furthermore, Shannon and Page (2014, p. 647) found that officers who believed their prisons had sufficient staff and high-quality programs also expressed less punitive attitudes.

Taken as a group, these studies suggest that COs do not hold consistent attitudes toward rehabilitation or punishment, and, given those findings, Gordon (2006, p. 236) says prison administrators should try to balance custodial and rehabilitative approaches, as:

> Some inmates will benefit from a more humanistic approach while others may not. Some inmates are not interested in treatment, and therefore, a more custodial approach may be the only way to achieve compliance. Some officers may be more inclined to use one approach over the other depending on the time, place, setting, and situation.

There has been increasing interest in the role that front-line officers are playing in correctional rehabilitation. Schaefer (2017, p. 4) contends that COs should carry out more rehabilitative interventions with inmates, and they ought to employ strategies such as **core correctional practices** where staff use their authority in an appropriate manner, encourage problem-solving, engage in advocacy, and reinforce positive behaviors. According to the GEO Group (2019, p. 12), a for-profit company that provides a range of services and programs in the corrections field, officers using core correctional practices receive training in:

- Principles of effective interventions
- Relationship skills
- Effective use of reinforcement
- Effective use of disapproval
- Effective use of authority
- Pro-social modeling
- Cognitive restructuring

- Social skills training
- Problem-solving skills
- Principles of effective behavior management systems

Being able to use these skills enables officers to reinforce inmates' positive behaviors, address their negative conduct, and act as a role model for the prisoners they supervise. As Kifer, Hemmens, and Stohr (2003, p. 67) observe COs "hold the power to either carry out or destroy the institutional mission."

PRISON TYPES AND FUNCTIONS

As we noted earlier, there are roughly 1.5 million prisoners in about 2,000 US state, federal, and private prisons. Correctional officials must manage their misconduct, the possibility of escape, and their risks to other prisoners, correctional staff, and the public. Incapacitating these prisoners is one of the primary goals of corrections and, like other tasks undertaken by prison administrators, it is very difficult. For example, many of these inmates could live free in the community, and no one would be in any greater danger than before their release. By contrast, other prisoners have been assessed so dangerous that they are held in their cells up to 23 (or more) hours a day and they have very little or no interaction with other inmates, and only limited contact with the staff. To manage these individuals, correctional officials have designed prisons and housing units to reflect their diverse security needs.

Placing prisoners in the housing units or prisons that best match their security and treatment needs is a critically important task, and a cornerstone of classification which is covered in the section below. Placing a nonviolent offender who has been assessed to pose little risk to others or risk of escape in a high security prison, for example, is expensive (given that the ratio of officers to inmates increases with security levels). It also may be **criminogenic** (lead to higher recidivism) as the low-risk offender may be negatively influenced by higher-risk prisoners (Gaes & Camp, 2009). Over one-half of prison facilities hold fewer than 500 inmates, as shown in Figure 6.2 and most facilities are minimum-security institutions (see Figure 6.3).

At this point it is important to distinguish between static and dynamic security as described by the United Nations (2015a). **Static security** refers to the physical design of a correctional facility that is intended to produce a secure environment, including the fences, hardened steel doors and thick polycarbonate (break-resistant) windows, and the fixtures such as stainless-steel toilets and tamper-resistant lighting. Another aspect of static security is that beds, tables, and chairs (in cells and common areas) are often permanently attached to the floor so they cannot be used as weapons. Many developments in static security are related to the introduction of new technologies such as

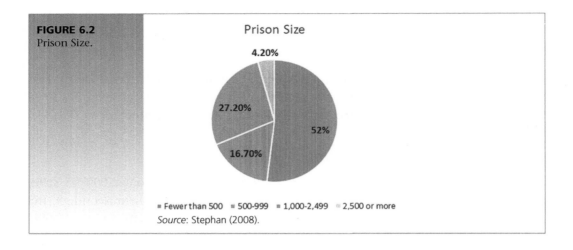

FIGURE 6.2
Prison Size.

Prison Size

4.20%

27.20%

52%

16.70%

- Fewer than 500　- 500-999　- 1,000-2,499　- 2,500 or more

Source: Stephan (2008).

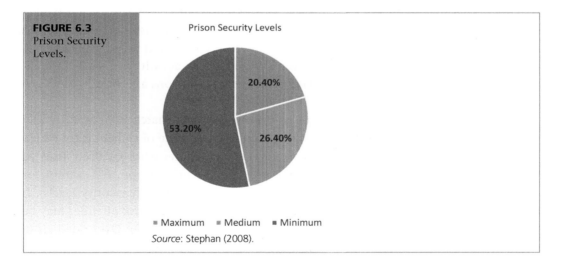

FIGURE 6.3
Prison Security
Levels.

Prison Security Levels

20.40%

53.20%

26.40%

- Maximum　- Medium　- Minimum

Source: Stephan (2008).

the use of electric locks and fixtures that enable COs to lock or unlock an inmate's cell door—or all the doors on a unit—from centralized and protected workstations. COs in most modern facilities also have the ability to override the lighting or plumbing in an individual inmate's cell. Furthermore, closed circuit television (CCTV) cameras are present in most correctional institutions both inside and outside the facility and CCTV coverage increases along with the facility's security level. These cameras are intended to deter inmate and staff misconduct, and while not always successful the visual records they capture are used in investigations and prosecutions.

A correctional facility's physical design, which was described in more detail in Chapter 5, also influences the amount of mischief that takes place, and new generation designs (with inmate cells arranged around a center court) have less misconduct than traditional prisons where inmate cells are arranged in tiers (Morris & Worrall, 2014).

Dynamic security, by contrast, refers to the actions correctional staff take in order to reduce misconduct, including searches of the facility and inmates, and inmate counts. Dynamic security also refers to the relationships that COs develop with the inmates and helping them learn problem-solving strategies. As in life outside the secure facility, by solving minor problems, such as helping an inmate arrange a visit with a family member, staff members sometimes reduce the risk of larger problems later on, such as responding to a suicide attempt or act of violence, because prisoners could not arrange a visit on their own. The degree to which the COs and inmates engage in problem-solving, or even voluntarily speak with each other, varies by the level of security and institutional culture, and there will be differences in these conditions even in prisons that are on the same grounds. The following sections describe different prison security levels.

Minimum Security

About one-fifth of US inmates are housed in **minimum-security** facilities, and they are the least restrictive form of prison custody (Stephan, 2008). Many minimum-security facilities constructed after 1990 look like college campuses, ranches and farms, or work camps. There are few bars or signs of security, and many are surrounded with a perimeter fence that might be only four or six feet tall; some will not even have a fence. There are some differences that accommodate male versus female inmate needs and interests. For example, minimum-security facilities for women in some states often look like cottages, and these arrangements are based on decades-old thinking that a homelike environment better serves women's needs. Inmates in a minimum-security facility have been assessed as exhibiting low-to-little security risk. They have often been convicted of engaging in nonviolent offenses (e.g. white-collar criminals) or first-time offenders, are serving short sentences, or were transferred from medium-security facilities and are about to be released from custody.

Although our description of minimum security suggests that inmates have it easy, some inmates experience problems living in these facilities. Minimum-security facilities may be less oppressive and restrictive than higher security prisons, but inmates are not free to come and go as they please and they must follow institutional rules and routines. Inmates can also be subject to abuse from other inmates and given that the ratio of staff to inmates is very low, there is less likelihood aggressors will be punished. Not surprisingly, however, rates of inmate misconduct tend to be the lowest in minimum security (Steiner, Butler, & Ellison, 2014). Another challenge for inmates is the urge to walk away from the facility and some prefer to live in a higher security level facility as there is less temptation in those places. However, if inmates engage in serious misconduct, they are generally transferred to a facility with a higher security level.

Medium Security

Medium-security prisons are more restrictive and regimented than minimum-security institutions. Unlike the fortress-style prisons of the past with their high cement or stone walls, most modern minimum-security institutions are enclosed by a double chain-link fence topped with razor wire. The area between the fences may have electronic sensors or other devices that warn of escape attempts. Most of these prisons also have strategically located gun towers, and COs provide roving security around the perimeter on foot or in vehicles.

In some medium-security prisons, housing units may be arranged like dormitories, with 50 or more inmates sleeping in a huge open area. In podular-design facilities, inmates may have individual cells with shared toilet and shower areas, and they are able to access common areas where they eat, recreate, and take classes. Medium-security prisons have more safety-oriented rules than do minimum-security facilities, including placing more restrictions on a prisoner's ability to move around the facility. Inmate counts and searches of the inmates, cells, and common areas occur with more regularity than in minimum-security facilities.

Depending on the prison system, most newly admitted prisoners are placed in medium-security facilities, although this depends on their criminal history—including prior escapes—and seriousness of their current offenses. Their future correctional placements depend on their behavior, and future engagement in misconduct may result in their placement in a maximum-security prison. By contrast, a history of good conduct and no involvement in misconduct typically results in a move to minimum security.

Maximum Security

Maximum security is the highest security level found in most but not all prison systems, as some systems have developed super-max units or prisons (see below). Correctional authorities reserve it for inmates who represent the greatest threat to society, the institution, and other inmates. Homicide offenders in some states are automatically placed in maximum security, even though many of them present a low risk to others. While large fortress style prisons with high stone walls used to be the standard type of maximum-security institution, almost all facilities built since the 1970s are surrounded with chain link fences topped with razor wire. Some prison systems use fences that can deliver an electric shock (these electric fences are sandwiched between two taller fences to ensure nobody is accidently injured). While prison architects designed facilities to include gun towers in the center of some facilities and along the perimeter, many of these towers are unmanned today, as it is cheaper to use electric fences topped with razor wire and embedded remote sensors compared with placing an armed officer in an observational post staffed 24/7. Prisons also utilize officers in vehicles who patrol the perimeter of their facilities and act as the first line of defense for the security operations.

The buildings within a maximum-security prison are typically constructed using stone, reinforced concrete, or cinder block structures. In older prisons, visitors could see the physical security with iron bars and gates, but modern prison architects have created designs where the security is hidden; specifically, thick layers of polycarbonate glass have replaced iron bars and cell windows are narrow and tall, which prevents escapes. The design of these modern facilities also reduces privacy, but this in turn increases safety. Moreover, in addition to the CCTV cameras monitoring the buildings and grounds, many newly constructed facilities have listening devices incorporated into the building's design. Unarmed COs move about the corridors. Finally, depending on a facility's design and capacity, an inmate may share a cell with other prisoners.

Officers working in maximum-security facilities monitor all visitations electronically or by direct supervision, except when the visitation is with the prisoners' attorneys. Because meetings between prisoners and their lawyers are confidential, the officers cannot monitor these visits. COs may prohibit physical contact between inmates and visitors, and prisoners may be required to communicate through a barrier or by a telephone or intercom system, both of which are subject to monitoring. Prison security staff also monitor the conversations occurring on external telephone calls. Inmates in some facilities also have limited access to email communication, and they are often arranged through service providers who are required to share the content of these communications with the security staff. Altogether, the intent of these security measures is to prevent inmates from forming escape plans, smuggling in contraband, and committing crimes inside or outside the prison.

PHOTO 6.3
The Indiana State Prison, located 50 miles east of Chicago and opened in 1860, currently holds over 2,300 inmates. Although classified as a maximum-security facility, the complex also contains minimum-security housing. Death row inmates live inside this walled unit. Credit: Philip Scalia/Alamy Stock Photo.

Death Row Units

Supervising condemned inmates presents a set of distinctive challenges and concerns. Death row housing units are generally located within maximum-security prisons and these inmates are often held in single cells in a special wing of the facility, where living conditions are usually very austere. For example, consider the Human Rights Clinic (2017, p. 5) description of the conditions in Texas, where all condemned prisoners are held in solitary confinement, which involves:

> [t]otal segregation of individuals who are confined to their cells for twenty-two to twenty-four hours per day, with a complete prohibition on recreating or eating with other inmates. An average cell is no bigger than 8 feet by 12 feet, and contains only a sink, a toilet, and a thirty-inch-wide steel bunk with a thin plastic mattress. Inmates are rarely provided with adequate blankets and often suffer from ongoing physical pain due to the mattress provided. The majority of cells include a small window, but inmates are only able to see out by rolling up the mattress and standing on it. This fact, paired with the lack of adequate outdoor recreation time, means that daily exposure to natural light is rare. Every individual on Texas' death row thus spends approximately 23 hours a day in complete isolation for the entire duration of their sentence, which, on average, lasts more than a decade.

With respect to the death row population, the Death Penalty Information Center (2020, p. 2) reports there were over 2,600 condemned inmates in March 2020. Almost one-half of them were held in California, Florida, and Texas. Both the numbers of death sentences imposed and carried out have been decreasing since 2008–2009 and the long-term placement of inmates on death row—prisoners can serve decades on death row before the sentence is carried out—creates unique challenges for prison officials. One emerging challenge for prison administrators is managing these prisoners if restrictions are placed on the use of solitary confinement. Missouri, for example, has abandoned their death row and they place condemned inmates in the general population in a maximum-security prison, although that practice is the exception to the norm (Aldape et al., 2016).

Administrative Segregation (Super-Max)

Almost every correctional facility has a small unit of restrictive housing, which is commonly called solitary confinement or segregation. These cells are intended to provide a safe and secure environment for prisoners who are disruptive or dangerous to the other inmates and staff. In addition to removing these prisoners from the general population, the presence of these units is also thought to have a deterrent effect on misconduct. Inmates assigned to these units live in austere conditions, have few amenities, and may be isolated as much as 24 hours per day. Historically, most prisoners placed on these units were there for less than a month. Since the 1980s, however, the practice of placing the most dangerous inmates or gang-involved prisoners has been occurring in some states. So, who ends up in restrictive housing? Labrecque and Mears (2019, pp. 206–208) report that prisoners with histories of violent behavior outside and inside of the prison, as well as gang members, persons with mental illnesses, and younger, male, and African American inmates were more likely to be placed in segregation.

In response to this need for restrictive housing, many larger prison systems, such as the California Department of Corrections and Rehabilitation or the Federal BOP, introduced high-security institutions for the highest risk offenders. There are about 55 of these facilities throughout the nation, and they go by various names, including super-max or administrative segregation. There are two basic models: the first is the free standing super-maximum facility such as Pelican Bay in California, and the second is the very high-security housing unit that is usually attached to maximum-security facilities. Frost and Monteiro (2016) found that about 2.6% of inmates in 34 prison systems were in administrative segregation. If we apply that average to the nation's 1.5 million prisoners, there are about 39,000 prisoners living in these units on a long-term basis. Frost and Monteiro (2016) contend that administrative segregation placement is important for correctional systems in order to manage high-risk prisoners such as gang members, those assessed as being too dangerous or disruptive to the other inmates or staff, and those at high risk of escaping—in other words the "worst of the worst."

Placement in super-max facilities, however, is becoming increasingly controversial given the psychological harms associated with long-term solitary confinement (Haney, 2018). Labrecque and Mears (2019, p. 199) point out that "the harsh conditions and idleness of restrictive housing cause offenders to become more disturbed, disruptive, and difficult to manage when they return to the general prison population and the community." Given those findings, a growing number of states are banning the placement of juveniles in long-term solitary confinement and restricting the placement of persons with mental health problems in solitary confinement. A number of prisoner advocacy and civil libertarian organizations, such as Amnesty International, the American Civil Liberties Union, and Human Rights Watch, support restrictions on long-term solitary confinement; they suggest that the placement of a prisoner in solitary for more than 15 days constitutes torture (Mendez, 2016). Given those strong positions, it is likely that we will see further restrictions on the use of this practice.

Banning Books in Prison

Some people become avid readers while incarcerated as reading is a constructive way to pass time and provides a positive escape from prison life. Access to books and magazines can be limited by the size of a prison's library and popular titles become worn over time. As a result, many prison libraries depend on the donations of new and used books from non-profit organizations such as the Prison Book Program, Books Through Bars, or Books to Prisoners. Family members can also arrange for reading materials to be sent to prisoners although there are restrictions. Most of us would agree that inmates should not have access to every

A CLOSER LOOK

book or magazine they might want to read. Books explaining how to pick locks or magazines that educate readers how to subdue other people could be used to engage in misconduct. There is less agreement, however, on what novels or non-fictional works are acceptable. Ujiyediin (2019) quotes a Kansas prison official as saying that "We censor based on the impact, or potential impact, on the security and operations of a correctional facility."

So what types of books and magazines are banned? In Kansas, magazines such as *Bloomberg Business*, *US Weekly*, or *Elle* are banned, as are some technical books such as *Excel for Dummies* (Ujiyediin, 2019). The issue becomes more controversial when it comes to novels and books relating to historical or current events. Novels such as *Fifty Shades of Grey* are banned in Kansas because of its sexual content, while books about slavery, race, and African American history are banned in Illinois, presumably as they could inflame racial tensions (Nickeas, 2019).

Bala (2018) says that there is an increasing amount of censorship happening in corrections that she calls a war on books, and especially if they are related to criminal justice policies such as mass imprisonment. Some states have created additional barriers to accessing books. Department of Corrections officials in Pennsylvania, for example, restricted the flow of books into prisons by requiring inmates to have a tablet that costs $147, and making them pay for each electronic book they buy from a private company (Lincoln, 2018). The move toward e-books was taken to prevent the introduction of contraband drugs into their facilities. The problem is that most inmates earn less than $1 per day and few can afford the tablets or purchasing e-books. As a result, their ability to increase their reading skills, constructively use their leisure time, or learn about the world is further restricted.

INMATE CLASSIFICATION

By the middle of the nineteenth century prison reformers were lobbying for the classification of inmates into broad categories, owing to the fact that men and women, as well as adults and children, the sick and healthy, and violent criminals and debtors, were often housed in the same facilities and, indeed, sometimes in the same cells. In response, prison administrators started to separate inmates by gender, age, their health status, and involvement in offenses. Up until the 1980s classification was often an informal process, and the COs who handled prison admissions made decisions to place inmates in specific housing units and rehabilitative programs based on their professional opinions (commonly called "gut feelings") or what is called **subjective classification**. These officers considered their prior criminal histories, their current offense(s), any assessments that had been done (such as psychological testing), and after interviewing the individual, they would decide on the most appropriate placement.

More formal classification systems were introduced as prison populations began growing in the 1970s and critics expressed concern over the arbitrary nature of subjective classification. As these classification decisions were based on hunches, it was difficult for prison officials to defend challenges when inmates complained about being placed in housing units or prisons that seemed inappropriate such as placing a youthful nonviolent first-time offender in a maximum-security unit with gang members or offenders with long histories of violence. In the wake of a series of court decisions, Craddock (1996, p. 20) found that classification systems had to meet three goals:

1. Classification staff must assign inmates to the least-restrictive security level possible to provide for the safety of the community at large, the staff, and other inmates.
2. The system must incorporate the assessment of inmates' needs on a regular and recurring basis, while not excusing inmates from responsibility for their own behavior.
3. Staff members should encourage prosocial change by extending positive incentives to those inmates who exhibit control over their own behavior.

The next generation of classification instruments percolated up from well-deserved criticisms of subjective classifications. They became the basis of, not surprisingly, **objective classification**, as these emergent instruments relied upon numerical scores and were used to predict an inmate's risk of misconduct or escape. Typically, the higher the inmate's score, the greater the risk, and this helps determine placement in the most appropriate prison and housing unit. With the passage of time and increased application across the nation, the purposes of classification instruments were expanded to include determining the prisoner's treatment needs, suitability for different correctional programs, and potential for recidivism.

A wide range of instruments are used to assess risk, and Austin and McGinnis (2004, p. 20) observe there is a set of commonly used factors when assessing institutional risk, and they are:

- Age (current age, age at first offense or conviction)
- Criminal history (arrests, convictions, incarcerations)
- Prior institutional conduct (disciplinary record, program participation)

- Prior performance on probation or parole (technical violations, arrests)
- History of alcohol or drug use
- Time served in current and prior imprisonment (actual time, percentage of time served)
- Parole/release plans (employment, residency)
- Mental and physical health

Assessing a prisoner's potential for future criminality is more involved and requires extensive training, and some of these tests can only be administered by licensed psychologists, social workers, or therapists.

As the classification process became more formalized and complex it also took longer to conduct. As a result, newly sentenced offenders in larger prison systems often went to reception centers. For an inmate facing a long sentence, assessment might take weeks or even months to complete. This enhanced and expanded classification process also created the need for the COs admitting these inmates to have a greater range of skills, and these personnel were retitled classification officers in some states and case managers or case workers in other jurisdictions. Like other aspects of correctional work, there is considerable diversity among different prison systems, and in some states these jobs go to COs who have experience on the job, while other systems require a bachelor's degree or higher.

Classification officers conduct initial intake assessments, review test results and inmate records, and make recommendations for institutional placement. They also work with additional team members, including psychologists, social workers, nurses, and other health professionals. The range of their responsibilities depends on the size of the employing prison system. For example, in the BOP, California, Florida, and Texas prison systems, their roles would be limited to carrying out assessments on newly sentenced prisoners (or those returned for technical parole violations). In smaller prison systems, by contrast, these officers may also perform rule-enforcement functions in addition to their jobs conducting assessments, and they might review rule infractions and recommend sanctions for those found guilty. They may also consult with inmates to find appropriate work or living assignments, assist with educational goal attainment, and facilitate engagement in rehabilitation programs such as anger management courses or addictions counseling (see Chapter 7). One emerging issue being addressed by all correctional administrators is the growing number of sexual minorities in jail and prison populations, and the box below shows that members of these groups are at higher risks of victimization. Effective classification is intended to reduce some of the risks these inmates may experience.

Sexual Minorities Behind Bars

Corrections officials have responded to gay, bisexual, transgender, and intersex prisoners (hereafter **sexual minorities**: see Meyer et al., 2017 for a formal definition) since the first prisons were built. However, there was little formal recognition that many of these individuals received discriminatory treatment, were targets of abuse by staff and other inmates, and many of their medical and rehabilitative needs were unmet.

In their national survey of state prisons, Meyer et al. (2017, p. 234) found that sexual minorities were disproportionately incarcerated: "9.3% of men in prison, 6.2% of men in jail, 42.1% of women in prison, and 35.7% of women in jail" and this is much higher than their prevalence in the general population. Researchers from the Bureau of Justice Statistics interviewed former state prisoners (believing that group would provide more valid responses than incarcerated inmates) and found that bisexual, gay, and lesbian inmates were at much higher victimization risk than heterosexual prisoners, and these results are shown in Table 6.2.

It is important to note that the definitions of victimization used in the Beck and Johnson (2012) research are quite broad, and the staff sexual misconduct category was split into willing activity (about 86% of cases) and unwilling contacts with staff (14%). Even though an act between a staff member and prisoner might be willing, these acts are illegal in most states as the power relationship between the individuals is unequal: given the CO's role, inmates cannot legally give consent for sexual activities. While the Beck and Johnson study sheds light on some sexual minorities, they did not track the victimization of transgender inmates.

TABLE 6.2 Percentage of Former State Prisoners Reporting Sexual Victimization

Sexual Orientation	Inmate-on-Inmate (%)	Staff Sexual Misconduct (%)
Heterosexual males	3.5	5.2
Bisexual males	33.7	17.5
Gay males	38.6	11.8
Heterosexual females	13.1	3.7
Bisexual females	18.1	7.5
Lesbian	12.8	8.0

Source: Beck and Johnson (2012).

Although transgender inmates represent a very small number of prisoners, most states have established policies in order to manage these cases better (Routh et al., 2017). These prisoners pose a special dilemma for correctional officials as inmates had historically been placed on housing units based on their genitalia at birth. But a problem arises when the individual does not identify with that classification and some prisoners might be assigned to a housing unit that places them at higher victimization risk (Carlino & Franklin, 2018). Moreover, many transgender prisoners have special medical needs and discontinuing hormone treatment, for example, might lead to serious health problems. More controversial are the seven states in 2017 that will pay for an inmate's sex reassignment surgery. These can be contentious issues and Routh and colleagues (2017, p. 662) observe that states require "clear treatment criteria to guide correctional staff and medical personnel who are dealing with transgender inmates. Following such criteria will reduce the likelihood of lawsuits and improve the quality of life for transgender inmates."

FEDERAL PRISON SYSTEM

In 1891, the U.S. Congress authorized the *Three Prisons Act*, which led to the construction of facilities in Atlanta, Georgia; Leavenworth, Kansas; and McNeil Island, Washington although it took more than a decade before any of these facilities opened. Prior to the opening of the first federal prison, state prisons and local jails housed federal prisoners in return for a fee. The size of the federal prison system grew along with the nation, and the number of prisons built increased from 14 institutions in 1930—when the BOP was established and had its first director—to 24 institutions in 1940. The federal prison system became more professional as concepts such as classification and security levels were introduced and refined. These operations were also centralized in Washington, DC to increase consistency among the facilities, and this central monitoring was intended to provide more humane care. The number of inmates housed by the BOP between 1940 and 1980 experienced almost no growth and the entire system housed less than 25,000 inmates in 1980 (BOP, 2017a, 2017b, 2017c). Changes in the federal antidrug policies, parole policies, and sentencing mandates led to a huge increase in the number of federal prisoners in the 1980s. In 1986, for example, the entire population was 40,000 inmates, but this population increased to about 175,000 prisoners with about 36,500 employees in March 2020 (BOP, 2020a). The increase in the federal prison population from 1980 to 2017 is shown in Figure 6.4.

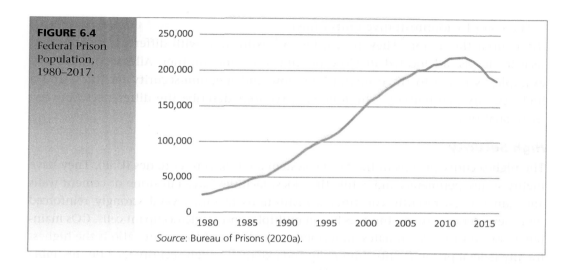

FIGURE 6.4
Federal Prison Population, 1980–2017.

Source: Bureau of Prisons (2020a).

Federal Facilities Profile

The Bureau of Prisons is the nation's largest prison system. Of its 175,000 prisoners almost 30,000 were held in privately managed or other types of facilities (BOP, 2020a). The federal government operates 122 institutions, six regional offices, their headquarters in Washington, DC, two staff training centers, and 25 residential re entry management offices (BOP, 2020b). It is important to acknowledge the complexity of operating such a large nation-wide prison system, particularly one that employs about 36,500 personnel in a variety of roles, from accountants to training instructors, many of whom will never actually interact with an inmate.

Like state prison systems, the BOP operates institutions with varying security levels and classifies its facilities by high-, medium-, low-, and minimum-security levels. The Bureau also operates a number of administrative facilities that include jail operations in Chicago, Los Angeles, and New York, mental health and medical facilities, and the administrative maximum facility in Florence, Colorado. Bureau personnel assign these security designations by weighting, in order of importance, the impact of seven features: external patrols, gun towers, external security barriers, external detection devices, type of housing, internal security features, and staff-to-inmate ratios. We provide a detailed look at the different types of federal facilities below. In March 2020, less than one-fifth (16%) of prisoners were in minimum-security facilities, 37% were housed in low-security institutions, 31% in medium-security institutions, and almost 12% were in high-security institutions (BOP, 2020c).

There are 15 administrative units called **federal correctional complexes** (FCC) throughout the nation. They are clusters of institutions with different missions and security levels, all located in close proximity to one another. Allenwood-FCC, for example, is home to three institutions: low and medium-security facilities, and a high-security penitentiary. The following sections describe the differences between these facilities.

High Security

The high-security prisons in the federal system are U.S. Penitentiaries (USP). They have highly secure perimeters and, while the oldest facilities have tall stone or cement walls and gun towers, recently constructed institutions feature several strongly reinforced multi-level fence systems. Inmates live in multiple- and single-occupant cells. COs maintain close control over inmates' movements, and the staff-to-inmate ratio is the highest for any federal prison facility. Internally and externally, high-security facilities resemble the maximum-security prisons found in most state systems.

There were 22 USPs in 2020 and two, USP Atlanta (Georgia) and USP Leavenworth (Kansas), are over 100 years old, and only hold medium-security prisoners today. The growth in federal prison populations also increased the number of high-security facilities and this number more than tripled between 1993 and 2007. Two facilities, on the same grounds, have the greatest degree of security: the Florence, Colorado USP and the Florence ADX. Federal executions, including those of military personnel, are carried out at the Special Confinement Unit at USP Terre Haute. Between 1976 and 2020 the US government executed three prisoners and almost 70 more, including four military prisoners, are awaiting execution (Death Penalty Information Center, 2020).

Medium Security

More than half of all facilities operated by the BOP are **federal correctional institutions** (FCI). At this security level, the perimeters are double fenced, often strengthened by the addition of electronic security devices. Inmates live in one-, two-, or three-person cells. Internal controls are not as tight as they are in high-security facilities, but they are strict. This security ranking is comparable to the medium-security level in state prison systems.

Low Security

All low-security federal facilities—20 in 2020—are FCIs. In these facilities, perimeters are double fenced; 20–30 or more residents live in dormitories or cubicles; and the staff-to-inmate ratio is lower than in medium-security facilities. Inmates must have less than 20 years to serve in their sentences to be placed in a low security facility, and few inmates have histories of violence.

Minimum Security

The BOP operates seven Federal Prison Camps (FPCs) and they are all minimum-security facilities. These camps have limited or no perimeter fencing, house inmates in dormitories, and have a very low staff-to-inmate ratio. Campers are the lowest risk of all federal prisoners and most are white-collar criminals or other nonviolent (and often first-time) offenders with no histories of escape. Two of these facilities hold only women: FPC-Alderson (West Virginia), opened in 1927, is the oldest functioning federal women's facility while FPC-Bryan (Texas) was opened in 1989. Together, they held about 2,000 women in 2020. Several facilities have minimum-security satellite camps that generally hold 100–200 individuals, and an example is the **Federal Medical Center** (FMC) in Lexington, Kentucky.

Administrative Facilities

Administrative facilities are special-use institutions that provide a range of security conditions or services for inmates. These facilities house inmates at all risk levels. Examples include the five FMC that altogether hold about 7,000 prisoners. One of these, the Carswell FMC, holds only women (about 1,600 in 2020). The Carswell program is distinctive given the reproductive health needs of these inmates and some are pregnant when admitted to custody. Sufrin and colleagues (2019, p. 802) found that the BOP admitted about 16 pregnant women a month, and there were about 38 pregnant women in these prisons on any given month. These women are given pre-natal care and childbirth takes place at a regular hospital; and because no newborns are admitted to the facility, the prisoner must arrange care for the child. The **Federal Transfer Center** (FTC) is also a distinctive facility and the individuals staffing this facility are responsible for coordinating the movement of male and female inmates among facilities using the BOP's fleet of aircraft. This facility is located adjacent to the Will Rogers Airport in Oklahoma City.

PHOTO 6.4
The Federal Medical Center (FMC), in Lexington Kentucky, which sits on 1,000 acres, first opened its doors to inmates in 1935 as the United States Narcotic Farm. The FMC is designated as an administrative facility, meaning that it holds inmates at all security classification levels. There are nearly 1,500 inmates housed at this facility, including about 200 in an adjacent minimum-security satellite camp for women. Credit: Jim Lane/Alamy Stock Photo.

Detention Facilities

As noted in Chapter 5, the BOP also operates **metropolitan correctional centers** (MCC) and **metropolitan detention centers** (MDC) that function much like large local jails.

These facilities range in size from about 400 to 1,800 inmates, and only hold federal inmates awaiting their court dates, those serving short-term sentences, or prisoners awaiting transfers. The BOP opened the first MCC/MDC facilities in the mid-1970s, and prior to that time they contracted with local sheriffs to temporarily hold federal prisoners. The BOP still contracts with sheriffs in communities that are not close to an MCC or MDC. They operate five federal detention centers (FDC), which are administrative security facilities that primarily confine male and women offenders for short terms.

Programs Profile

The federal government operates many programs at its 122 facilities. Four emphases are clear: work, education, vocational and occupational training, and drug treatment.

Work

Work is important for at least three reasons. First, it keeps inmates busy for extended periods, and all able-bodied federal inmates have a job. Second, good work habits, combined with vocational training, can lead to a successful post-release job placement. Third, inmates provide a ready labor pool for the institutional jobs.

Federal facilities operate two main work programs. The first, the Federal Prison Industries (FPI), also known as **UNICOR**, was established in 1934. According to the BOP (2017b), UNICOR has the following vision statement:

> To protect society, reduce crime, aid in the security of the Nation's prisons and decrease taxpayer burden, by assisting inmates with developing vital skills necessary for successful re-entry to society. Through the production of market-priced quality goods and services, FPI provides job training and work opportunities to inmates, while minimizing impact on private industry and labor.

There are FPI factories in 52 prisons and some of the products produced by inmates are used for federal government operations which reduces government costs. UNICOR (2017, pp. 4–5) describes how inmates are engaged in five business groups:

- *Clothing and Textiles*. Inmates produce uniforms for the military and household items such as towels and bags, as well as textiles for commercial applications (e.g. mail bags).
- *Office Furniture*. Prisoners construct desks and workstations for a variety of offices, as well as filing and storage cabinets, and industrial shelving.
- *Electronics*. Inmates manufacture a wide range of cables and electrical components used for military and civilian applications, and in some cases, they build specialized products such as solar panels and vehicle parts.
- *Recycling*. Prisoners recycle used computers and electronic goods.

- *Services Business.* Inmates are employed in customer support roles such as working for help desks or contact centers, and other business-related services such as printing and manufacturing signs.

Inmates working in UNICOR receive wages, but the maximum pay is $1.15 per hour. Many inmates use this money to make restitution to victims and pay court costs or fines.

The second work program—known as facility support services—supports the ongoing maintenance and operations of BOP facilities. About three-quarters of federal inmates work at institutional jobs, in health or food services, educational and recreational services, or support functions such as libraries, business offices, and facility maintenance. Inmates in these roles make less than half as much per hour as the UNICOR workers. Ring and Gill (2017, p. 7) conducted a survey of 2,000 federal prisoners for the advocacy group Families Against Mandatory Minimums where they found that some inmates only work a few hours a week in facility support services, while others worked 40 or more hours in placements such as UNICOR. Writing about UNICOR programs, Richmond (2014) found that there was no difference in future arrests or return to federal prison for participants compared to prisoners who did not participate. While these research findings are discouraging, they suggest that not all inmates benefit from these vocational programs.

Education

All BOP institutions offer literacy classes, English as a Second Language (ESL), adult continuing education, parenting classes, library services, wellness education, and instruction in leisure time activities (BOP, 2017c). Prisoners who have not finished their high school education or general educational development (GED) are required to participate in literacy programs until they finish their GED. Without a GED, inmates cannot participate in UNICOR jobs. Ring and Gill (2017, p. 8) found that educational classes could be taught by prison staff or volunteers, but said that "in practice, the vast majority of educational offerings are taught by other inmates" and that the "quality and availability of educational programs differ from prison to prison and sometimes even within the same prison compound" (p. 9).

Vocational and Occupational Training

The BOP supports hundreds of occupational, apprenticeship, and advanced occupational education programs, and they are available in almost all of the facilities. On any given day about 10,000 prisoners participate in these programs. Inmates also have access to courses offered by a broad range of technical schools, community colleges, and four-year colleges and universities. Apprenticeship programs include dozens of short- and long-term opportunities for conventional trades such as baking and welding, but also for more specialized careers such as biomedical equipment repair. Although some programs serve thousands of inmates, other programs are small and distinctive, and are only offered at a limited number of facilities. A review of the BOP (2016) training directory reveals a number of training offerings focused on "the new economy" such as recycling and solar energy. Because of the large numbers of inmates interested in participating in these programs, those who are closer to release are given a priority, which can be discouraging for those serving long sentences and are unable to access these opportunities.

Drug Treatment

Over one-half of federal prisoners have been convicted of a drug-related offense, whereas these offenders represent less than one-fifth of state prisoners. As a result, all federal facilities provide drug treatment, as well as psychological and psychiatric counseling, whereas these services are not as accessible in state or private facilities (Stephan, 2008). The BOP offers three drug treatment programs, and they are typically taken in steps, starting with **drug abuse education**. Drug abuse education involves classes that inform inmates about substance abuse and its physical and psychological effects. This course also screens participants for further treatment. Graduates of this program can participate in **nonresidential drug abuse treatment**, which is a 12-week program offered in a group setting that "addresses criminal lifestyles and provides skill-building opportunities in the areas of rational thinking, communication skills, and institution/community adjustment." This program is offered to prisoners with short sentences, are awaiting more intensive treatment, are preparing for their release to the community, or have tested positive for drug use (BOP, 2017d).

A third option for drug treatment is the **residential drug abuse program** (RDAP), and this intervention is promoted as a pathway to an early release. RDAP is an intensive 500-hour course delivered in living units separate from the general population. Inmates typically participate in RDAP activities for one-half their workday, and services are delivered over a 9–12-month period. RDAP is akin to the TC approach where inmates live in an environment that promotes prosocial values. Approximately 20,000 inmates participate in RDAP programs each year, and successful program completion makes prisoners eligible for a sentence reduction. In addition to a sentence reduction these inmates could also receive financial awards, special consideration for community placements, preferred living arrangements, and special recognition (Arons et al., 2014). These researchers also point out that prisoners who are eligible for RDAP but decline to participate may be ineligible for the best facility jobs and opportunities for community placements.

Groh (2013, p. 402) says that prison industries, such as UNICOR, have been criticized as being "anticompetitive and undercut labor and the private sector, especially small businesses" as small companies cannot afford to compete against inmate labor, and the costs of prison built items do not include manufacturing costs such as management, electricity, or facility rent. Some small businesses have been unable to compete with operators that employ prisoners who are often paid less than $1 per hour (*The Economist*, 2018). Supporters of prison industries, by contrast, point to the benefits of such programs, as prisoners are keeping busy and learning employment skills, and government agencies that pay less for items such as furniture.

Advocates for prisoners are becoming increasingly critical of inmates who are required to work in correctional industries with little compensation. In 2017 Washington State's Attorney General Bob Ferguson sued the GEO Group—a large private prison operator—as they were paying their inmates only $1 per day, which violates the state's minimum wage laws. Shapiro (2017, para. 3) cites Ferguson as saying that "Let's be honest about what's going on," "GEO has a captive population of vulnerable individuals who cannot easily advocate for themselves. This corporation is exploiting those workers for their own profits." While Ferguson makes an important point, the Thirteenth Amendment prohibiting slavery specifically exempts those being punished for a crime.

STATE PRISON SYSTEMS

There are about 1,700 state prison facilities in the United States, and there is incredible diversity within the 50 state systems: on 31 December 2017, the smallest systems—Montana, North Dakota, and Vermont—held fewer than 2,000 inmates, while both Texas and California each housed over 100,000 prisoners (Bronson & Carson, 2019). Within these systems there is a mix of minimum to maximum security facilities. Some will be operated by correctional leaders that have a very strong rehabilitative orientation, while others will be more focused on security and control. Furthermore, some of these agency leaders will be innovative, while others will be more focused on the day-to-day operations and maintaining the *status quo*.

There is also some diversity in terms of the types of prisoners these systems hold, and in Alaska, Connecticut, Delaware, Hawaii, Rhode Island, and Vermont, the jail and prison systems are integrated and operated by the state government. Like what happened in federal prisons, the number of state inmates grew rapidly starting in the early 1980s and continued until about 2008, when numbers first started their slow decrease. This trend is shown in Figure 6.5. While many critics of mass incarceration are optimistic about the decreased use of imprisonment, the annual drop is very small and Ghandnoosh (2018) questions whether we can wait 75 years to cut the prison population by one-half.

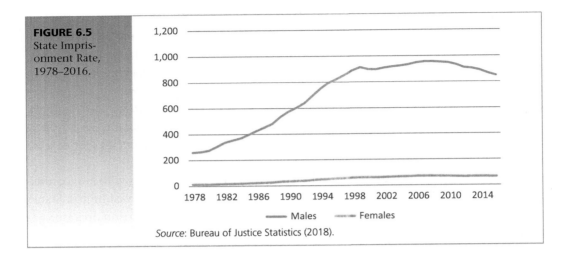

FIGURE 6.5
State Imprisonment Rate, 1978–2016.

Source: Bureau of Justice Statistics (2018).

The male and female imprisonment rate changes over time shown in Figure 6.5 raise a number of questions. The Bureau of Justice Statistics (2018) notes that in 1978 the incarceration rate for male inmates was 235 for every 100,000 US male residents; by 31 December 2016 the rate was 847 per 100,000 adult males. The rate for women in 1978 was 9 for every 100,000 US female residents; by 2016, that had increased to 64 per 100,000 adult women. One interesting observation is that while the men's imprisonment rate grew by 228%, the women's rate increased by 540% from 1978 to 2016, and those results are shown in Table 6.3. That finding leads us to the question why the women's imprisonment grew at such a high rate: were more women becoming more involved in crime? Or, are women today being treated more similar to men? It is likely that a number of factors are responsible for this growth. Moreover, these changes are more apparent in some states, and in Oklahoma, for example, the women's imprisonment rate is twice the national average. Regardless of the answers to these questions, correctional officials were expected to manage these changes, and they introduced a number of work, educational and vocational training, and treatment programs much like their federal counterparts.

TABLE 6.3 Changes in Adult Imprisonment Rates by Gender, 1978–2016

Gender	Imprisonment Rate Increases (%)
Males	↑ 228
Females	↑ 540

Source: Bureau of Justice Statistics (2018).

Programs Profile

Work

Jobs are important to state prison systems, but the factory work opportunities like those offered by UNICOR are not as prevalent. Results from the most recent (2005) prison census shows that work programs are available in 87% of the nation's state prisons (Stephan, 2008). There is a long history of inmate work programs and, as highlighted in Chapter 2, they have always been a cornerstone of prison programs. In the past it

PHOTO 6.5
A prison inmate trims weeds and grasses alongside a road in rural Nebraska. Credit: Mikael Karlsson/Alamy Stock Photo.

was said that inmate work programs exploited their labor and most fortress-style prisons built in the 1800s and 1900s were built by prisoners. Moreover, prisoners on chain gangs also worked on railroads, road construction, and other public works projects throughout the South (LeFlouria, 2016). While prisoners are treated in a less harmful manner today, there has been an increasing debate whether inmates are being treated fairly.

Bozelko (2017) describes two types of prison jobs. The first are facilities support services which are work programs where inmates clean and maintain the prison's buildings, cook the meals, care for the grounds, and in almost all prisons (except for super-max facilities, or in restricted staff areas where prisoners are not allowed) the inmates will do most of this work. These jobs, like their parallel positions in the federal system, are necessary for facility operations and an important way to keep prisoners occupied, although some of these duties require only a few hours a week. A department of corrections can keep operational costs low by paying inmates a few dollars a week for doing this work. Sawyer (2017) calculated prisoner earnings from the policies of state correctional agencies, and she found that regular jobs (such as cooks) earned an average of 14–63 cents per hour. Several prison systems, primarily in Southern states such as Alabama and Texas, do not pay inmates any salary.

State prisoners are also employed in **Prison Industry Enhancement (PIE)** programs, where the inmates work for private businesses that contract with the state correctional system (Bozelko, 2017). There is a wide variety of private-corrections partnerships and inmates have worked to produce garments for Victoria's Secret, as well as software companies or operating phones for call centers. Sawyer (2017) found that about four-fifths of state correctional systems were involved in these partnerships. Inmate-employees were unpaid in states such as Arkansas, Georgia, and Texas, but could earn up to $5.15 in Nevada with the low average at 33 cents per hour and the high average at $1.41 per hour for all the states.

Whether they are paid by the prison for their efforts in maintaining the facility or work in a prison industry benefiting a corporation, these prisoners rarely get to keep all their earnings. They are often required to use their salaries to pay room and board, outstanding fines and court costs, compensate victims, and support their families (Sawyer, 2017).

Do these programs work? That is, do they achieve their intended goals of reducing prison misconduct, constructively occupying inmate time, providing work experience, and reducing recidivism? By several benchmarks, the impact of such work on inmate re entry appears to be significant. A National Institute of Justice (NIJ) study revealed that participants in traditional prison industries found work sooner had lower recidivism rates after release than inmates who did something other than work while incarcerated; moreover, PIE program participants faired even better than those employed in traditional prison jobs (Smith, Bechtel, Patrick, Smith, & Wilson-Gentry, 2006). Not only was their recidivism lower, but inmate labor also benefited taxpayers (by lowering prison operating costs) and an inmate's income supported his or her release back into the community.

Is the use of prison labor a good idea? The answer depends on who you ask. Busy inmates are certainly happier than ones who have nothing to do other than wait for the time to pass. They tend to be more tired and less prone to get into trouble looking for ways to entertain themselves. Having made those observations, it is important to recall that the proportion of the total inmate population engaged in meaningful and financially rewarding employment is very small. The potential for work-related abuses can be high given that few of these prisoners have individuals who will advocate for them. Montoya-Barthelemy (2019, p. 74) observes that inmates are sometimes involved in hazardous work, such as recycling, exposing them to heavy metals (such as lead) that can range from 40 to 500 times above the recommended levels.

There is reason to be concerned about the rights of prison laborers, as they enjoy few legal protections and are susceptible to the same market forces as workers in the free society. For example, after the economic downturn that started in 2008, inmate jobs also decreased (Kirklin, 2011). A number of advocacy organizations are critical of prison labor and call it "dressed-up slavery" where inmates:

> are forced to do grueling, backbreaking, and dangerous work for nickels and dimes, while corporations rack up billions of dollars off the cheap labor. They are put to work under the guise of rehabilitation, but the reality is that few people leave prison with the skills, knowledge, or resources to succeed professionally.
>
> (Townes, 2016)

A national prisoner's strike in September 2016—where some 24,000 prisoners in 12 states did not show up for work—drew attention to the issue (Schwartzapfel, 2016). There was a similar three-week strike in 2018 that involved prisoner sit-ins, hunger strikes, prison yard protests, and work slowdowns and stoppages. The inmates had ten broad demands that included ending prison slavery, rescinding tough on crime sentencing, enabling prisoners to vote, and improving the conditions of confinement (see Incarcerated Workers Organizing Committee, 2018).

Educational and Vocational Training

Educational and vocational training programs are commonly offered in state corrections (Stephan, 2008). About two-thirds of state-operated facilities provide at least adult basic education (ABE), usually leading to a GED. About one-half of prisons operate technical, pre-release, or job-readiness training. Roughly one-third (32%) of state prisons have special education programs, including opportunities for people with learning disabilities. College programs are also available in 32% of public facilities for inmates who can pay for their classes. Fewer than 8% operate study-release programs, where prison inmates leave their facilities and attend classes at nearby institutions of higher learning.

Although prison rehabilitation programs only account for 1–3% of all prison expenditures, there is concern about getting the best value for those investments. Writing for California's Legislative Analyst's Office, Taylor (2017, pp. 1–3) recommends that prison-based rehabilitation programs should:

- *Be evidence-based*: Funding should only be given to correctional interventions that have been demonstrated by research to be effective. These programs should be regularly evaluated to ensure they remain effective.
- *Demonstrate their cost-effectiveness*: Independent researchers should evaluate the costs and benefits of correctional interventions to determine whether the benefits exceed the costs.
- *Target programs to the highest-risk and highest need inmates*: Inmates who have been assessed as having the highest risks of recidivism and have the greatest needs for rehabilitation should be prioritized for treatment.
- *Utilize existing resources*: Existing prison programs should be assessed to determine how to introduce new interventions and use existing resources most efficiently.
- *Improve performance measures*: Rehabilitative programs must use performance measures such as reduced prison misconduct and the percentage of prisoners being released who completed rehabilitative interventions.

Throughout this book we have used similar lists and they all boil down to the fact that legislators are reluctant to commit taxpayer dollars for prisoner rehabilitation. Thus, prison administrators must use those funds to get the best return on investment by placing the prisoners with the highest needs in programs that work, and those programs must be regularly evaluated to ensure they are effective.

Treatment Programs

One of the most pressing needs among state prisoners is substance abuse treatment (Bronson, Stroop et al., 2017). Drug, alcohol, mental health, and sex-offender programs receive varying degrees of attention—and resources—in state corrections systems. Nine out of ten state-operated facilities offer inmates counseling services. The most common of these, found in about three-quarters (72%) of public facilities, focus on drug and alcohol dependence, substance abuse, and drug awareness programs (Stephan, 2008). Psychological or psychiatric counseling is less common, and found in about 55% of public facilities, roughly the same percentage having training in life skills, community adjustment, and employment skills (Stephan, 2008).

While almost everybody would be in favor of prison-based substance abuse treatment, the problem is that few individuals get any formal treatment. Researchers at the Pew Charitable Trusts (2015a, p. 8) report that "In 2010, roughly 65 percent of incarcerated adults in jails or prisons met the medical criteria for a substance use disorder." About one-quarter million of the nation's 2.1 million jail and prison inmates were involved in some form of treatment in 2013 and that total includes participating in self-help groups such as Alcoholics Anonymous (Pew Charitable Trusts, 2015, p. 4). While Alcoholics Anonymous programs can be an important support for individuals with alcohol problems, more intensive treatment is often needed. With respect to formal substance abuse treatment, the National Center on Addiction and Substance Abuse (2010, ii) estimates that only 11% of inmates received these more intensive services during their imprisonment.

Costs and Benefits of Prison-Based Programs

The Washington State Institute for Public Policy regularly studies the costs and benefits of these drug treatment and other prison-based programs. In their 2019 report they stated that most of these programs were good investments in crime reduction. The list of correctional programs in Table 6.4 shows the positive benefits for each dollar spent.

TABLE 6.4 Benefits of a $1 Expenditure in Correctional Programming

Prison-Based Program	Benefits for Each Dollar in Program Costs
Correctional education (post-secondary)	$19.74
Employment counseling and job training	$18.21
Vocational education in prison	$11.94
Correctional education (basic skills)	$9.64
Therapeutic communities (substance abuse treatment)	$5.09
Correctional industries	$12.68

Source: Washington State Institute for Public Policy (2019).

It is important to acknowledge that not every program will be effective for every incarcerated person, just like some of us learn better in lectures, while others prefer to learn by participating in group-based exercises. Yet, the evidence is strong that prison-based programming is a good investment to lower recidivism. Given those benefits, we question why more inmates do not participate in these programs.

PRIVATE PRISON SYSTEMS

Bronson and Carson (2019, p. 27) report that over 120,000 inmates or about 8% of all federal and state prisoners are held in facilities operated by private firms, a figure that does not include individuals held under an Immigration and Customs Enforcement order. The Bureau of Prisons and 28 state governments contract with these for-profit corporations to hold their inmates due to overcrowding in those systems. Two companies, CoreCivic (formerly the Corrections Corporation of America) and the GEO Group, operate the largest private prison systems. CoreCivic operates or manages 122 different facilities, and that total includes jails, detention centers (mostly to hold immigration detainees for the US government), and community re entry facilities. CoreCivic operates a subsidiary company called TransCor America that provides inmate transportation across the nation. This corporation, which claims to operate the fifth largest corrections system in America, was founded in 1983 and houses about 70,000 inmates and has 13,000 employees (CoreCivic, 2019). The GEO Group (2020), by contrast, operates 130 facilities in the United States and has a total capacity of almost 96,000 beds, including re entry facilities for parolees, and employs approximately 23,000 personnel. Given those numbers these two organizations are larger than most state prison systems.

Both CoreCivic and the GEO Group provide a full range of correctional services, from the transportation of inmates to housing them in minimum-, medium-, and maximum-security facilities, although most of their prisoners are held in lower security facilities. The types and amounts of correctional services delivered by private operators are specified in the contracts with the federal or state governments. In other words, the private operator will deliver whatever services the government wants, but at a price. Most of these basic services are fairly routine, such as specifying the number of calories an inmate must receive each day, the conditions of confinement (e.g. space per resident), and the amount of rehabilitative programming per day per inmate (e.g. two hours of education). Some of these services are more distinctive: Hawaiian prisoners in a CoreCivic facility in Kentucky, for instance, had to be provided with a meal containing fish at least two times a week. Moreover, in some jurisdictions the private firm is required to pay prevailing wages for the area, so the state specifies the COs' salaries.

The leadership of CoreCivic and the GEO Group is often former executives of federal and state corrections departments, and they have extensive knowledge of prison operations. In order to ensure that inmates receive quality care, most contracts with private-corrections firms specify that facilities must be accredited by the American Correctional Association (ACA). Correctional facilities awarded accreditation have met standards relating to "services, programs and operations essential to good correctional management, including administrative and fiscal controls, staff training and development, physical plant, safety and emergency procedures, sanitation, food service, and rules and discipline" (ACA, 2020). In addition to requiring accreditation, all employing governments, whether state or federal, use **contract monitors** who conduct site visits and audits of the private prisons to ensure they are meeting all of the obligations of their contracts.

The fact that corporations are profiting from punishment has been controversial since the 1980s and advocacy organizations such as the American Civil Liberties Union, the Equal Justice Initiative, the Sentencing Project, and the Vera Institute of Justice strongly oppose these operations. Officials from these organizations believe that the presence of private operators makes it easier for states to maintain high imprisonment policies, and they argue that conditions in privately operated prisons are less humane than their federal and state counterparts. By contrast, some scholars say that privatization only accounts for about 8% of all prisoners and is only one contributing factor in mass imprisonment policies (Eisen, 2018; Pfaff, 2017). Debates over the pros and cons of privatizing correctional facilities have been conducted at the highest levels of government. While President Obama took steps to reduce the number of federal inmates and immigration detainees in privately operated facilities, President Trump reversed that decision.

While we have described the two largest private prison systems, there are also dozens of smaller firms that might operate only one or two facilities, and those operations lack the depth of expertise provided by CoreCivic or the GEO Group. Moreover, other aspects of corrections are also privatized such as delivering food services, operating inmate commissaries, transporting inmates, or delivering correctional health care. Given the reliance on private operators to manage federal and state prison overcrowding these private operators will continue to deliver services but their role in corrections will remain controversial.

The existence of corporations delivering correctional services for local, state, and federal governments returns us to the issue of vested interests and the difficulty in ending a profitable practice once it is well-established. Not only are profits important for the owners and shareholders of these firms but also these operations are important for communities. A private prison established in a rural county, such as the Big Spring prison in Texas operated by the GEO Group, holds inmates for the Bureau of

Prisons. This facility employs hundreds of hard-working employees and their families depend on those salaries. Moreover, the community of almost 30,000 residents relies on those salaries to keep businesses afloat in tough economic times. We question how many of these employees or their families would support the *First Step Act*, that is intended to reduce the federal prison population and could possibly jeopardize their future livelihoods?

What Can We Learn From Norway's Prisons?

Norway operates what has been called the world's most humane prison system. Weller observes how the highest security living units closely resemble a college dorm room with attached bathrooms, common recreation areas, and amenities such as gyms with rock climbing walls and one facility has a recording studio. Weller (2017) further observes that Norwegian correctional philosophy is based on sentiments such as "Allow people, even dangerous people, to feel like humans and they'll behave more civilly than if treated like forces of evil" (para. 11). Does their approach work? Slater (2017, para. 11) says that "violence is rare and assaults on guards are unheard of. Solitary confinement is almost never used."

Berger (2016) describes how Norwegian policymakers believe "life inside prison while serving a sentence must resemble life outside of prison as much as possible" (p. 4). Rehabilitation is a core goal of Norway's approach through education, job training, and therapy. While the costs of holding a prisoner in Norway are approximately three times as much as in the United States, recidivism rates are much lower.

Could a Norwegian approach be imported to the United States? Some state governments have looked to Norway's prison system for ideas about rehabilitating their inmates. Officials from Washington State's Department of Corrections, for example, have toured these facilities to find ways of reducing recidivism (Show & Show, 2020). North Dakota's Department of Corrections and Rehabilitation (2016) reports that after a 2015 visit to Norway, their administrators began to question their practices and introduced several reforms to make their facilities more humane including introducing cookouts, planting more gardens, and making it easier for families to visit inmates. One of the more extensive reforms was adding a minimum-security facility—that is based on the Norwegian model (without some of their amenities)—that prepares inmates nearing the end of their sentences for their release. Slater (2017) says that preparing inmates for release is important and "Once you accept that these people will one day be your neighbors, you might feel more invested in making sure they have the skills to get by on the outside" (para. 7).

So, what can we learn from Norway's prisons? Obviously, their correctional systems are more comfortable for inmates and their approach is costly, but affordable for that country as the entire nation imprisoned fewer than 3,500 prisoners in 2018, which represents an imprisonment rate that is one-tenth that of the United States (Walmsley, 2018). Given that most states are having trouble paying for their current correctional systems, few American policymakers will advocate for adopting Norwegian imprisonment practices. Yet, the changes undertaken in North Dakota show us we can make our prisons a bit more humane without increasing costs, and these efforts may result in places that are safer for staff and inmates. They may also reduce recidivism once these prisoners return to the community.

SUMMARY

Correctional institutions play an essential role in the protection of society from some of its more dangerous law-breakers. Whether the state or federal governments operate them, the facility administrators must balance multiple goals, including custody and treatment, although the former tends to outweigh the latter. Some of the key points presented in this chapter include the following:

- A prison is a total institution specifically designed for punishment, but the punishments rendered must be humane and follow guidelines based on the U.S. Constitution and defined by federal and state laws and court decisions.
- Security arrangements—especially those found in maximum-security or supermax prisons—can and do create bleak living conditions for those subjected to them.
- There is a dynamic tension between inmates' rights and the need to protect society, the institution, and the inmates.
- Prison administrators have no control over who will be sentenced to their care and there are a growing number of special needs inmates including those with medical, substance abuse, or psychological problems, as well as those with disabilities, elderly prisoners and pregnant women requiring specialized care.

- The safety of correctional facilities is not an accident as prison officials have developed systems to reduce the risks posed by the most difficult to manage inmates, including gang members. The COs play a significant role in ensuring safe and secure facilities.
- Today, prisons are an economic force as they represent jobs that are nonpolluting, renewable, and, except for private prisons, protected by civil service regulations.

Altogether, prisons are complex social institutions that house 1.5 million people who society has defined as being the "worst of the worst." Yet, most of them living in prison today will return to our communities within the next two or three years. Whether their re entry is successful is shaped by the skills of the correctional personnel and the resources we have invested in their community reintegration. These are the topics of the next two chapters.

KEY TERMS

- administrative segregation (super-max)
- classification
- contract monitors
- core correctional practices
- criminogenic
- custody
- death row
- diagnostic centers
- drug abuse education
- dynamic security
- federal correctional complexes (FCC)
- federal correctional institutions (FCI)
- federal medical centers
- federal transfer center
- maximum security
- medium security
- metropolitan correctional center
- metropolitan detention centerminimum security
- nonresidential drug abuse treatment
- objective classification
- prison industry enhancement (PIE)
- reception centers
- residential drug abuse program? Or treatment?
- segregation
- sexual minorities
- static security
- subjective classification
- super-max (administrative segregation)
- therapeutic communities (TC)
- total institutions
- treatment
- UNICOR

THINKING ABOUT CORRECTIONAL POLICIES AND PRACTICES: WRITTEN ASSIGNMENTS

1. You are a mid-level unit manager at a state prison and have been asked to prepare a short policy brief on why prisoners should not be placed in solitary confinement for more than 15 days. What would you say?
2. Access your state's department of corrections website and review the security levels of the prisons and the goals for inmates (this may be in the mission statement). Prepare a one-to-two-page paper summarizing each element: security level, and institutional goals for inmates. If you cannot find a website for your state, use the one for the Federal Bureau of Prisons.
3. In this chapter, we presented information about prison security levels. In the previous chapter, you learned about jail security levels. In a one-to-two-page paper, compare and contrast life in prisons and jails in terms of security levels. How are they similar? How do they differ? Where would you rather spend a year and why?
4. In a page or two, describe why female prisoners are sometimes disadvantaged when compared with their male counterparts.
5. In a page or two describe some reasons why classification makes prisons safer.

CRITICAL REVIEW QUESTIONS

1. Describe some reasons why sexual minorities in prison are at higher risk of victimization.
2. Briefly summarize the main conflicts between custody and treatment as institutional goals for prisons, paying close attention to the role of staff. In what other kinds of total institutions might attempts to attain these goals be less difficult?
3. Why is classification essential to the smooth functioning of prisons?
4. Describe prison growth throughout the twentieth and twenty-first centuries. What do you make of the overall trends and the trends for female prisoners?
5. The federal prison system has grown tremendously since changes in sentencing laws in the 1980s. What characteristic of federal prisons is most instructive about these changes?
6. Contrast the approach to corrections in the United States and Norway. What would Americans gain or lose by adopting a more humane approach to imprisonment?
7. Describe why many inmates feel powerless while imprisoned. How might these feelings affect their community re entry?

8. Why are work and rehabilitative programs important for reducing prison misconduct?
9. What are the key differences between federal or state prisons and their privately operated counterparts?
10. Prisoners were engaging in a series of "strikes" between 2016 and 2018. Are these protests an indicator that US prisons might undergo a series of more serious uprisings similar to the ones in the 1970s and 1980s?

REFERENCES

Aldape, C., Cooper, R. Haas, K. Hu, A., Hunter, J., & Shimizu, S. (2016). *Rethinking death row: Variations in the housing of individuals sentenced to death*. Yale Law School: Arthur Liman Public Interest Program.

Allen, B., & Bosta, D. (1981). *Games criminals play: How you can profit by knowing them*. New York: Rae John Publishing Company.

American Civil Liberties Union. (2006a). *Abandoned and abused: Orleans Parish prisoners in the wake of Hurricane Katrina*. New York: Author.

American Civil Liberties Union. (2006b). *National Prison Project calls for immediate action by President, Congress and Justice Department*. Retrieved from https://www.aclu.org/news/aclu-report-details-horrors-suffered-orleans-parish-prisoners-wake-hurricane-katrina

American Correctional Association. (2020). *Standards and accreditation: Frequently asked questions*. Retrieved from http://www.aca.org/ACA_Prod_IMIS/ACA_Member/Standards___Accreditation/About_Us/FAQs/ACA_Member/Standards_and_Accreditation/Standards__FAQ.aspx?hkey=b1dbaa4b-91ef-4922-8e7d-281f012963ce

Andrews, D. A., & Bonta, J. (2017). *The psychology of criminal conduct, 6th edition*. New York: Routledge.

Arons, A., Culver, K., Kaufman, E., Yun, J., Metcalf, H., Quattlebaum, M., & Resnik, J. (2014). *Dislocation and relocation: Women in the federal prison system and repurposing FCI Danbury for men*. New Haven, CT: Yale Law School.

Associated Press. (2018). *Drones delivering contraband to Florida prisons becoming a budding problem*. Retrieved from https://www.abcactionnews.com/news/science-and-technology/drones-delivering-contraband-to-florida-prisons-becoming-a-budding-problem

Austin, J., & McGinnis, K. (2004). *Classification of high-risk and special management prisoners. A national assessment of current practices*. Washington, DC: National Institute of Corrections.

Bala, N. (2018, February 8). There's a war on books in prisons. It needs to end. *Washington Post*. Retrieved from https://www.washingtonpost.com/opinions/theres-a-war-on-books-in-prisons-it-needs-to-end/2018/02/08/c31cd122-02b3-11e8-8acf-ad2991367d9d_story.html

Banks, G. (2017). Texas prisons take hit from Harvey, complaints of water, sewage problems surface. *Houston Chronicle*. Retrieved from http://www.chron.com/news/houston-texas/article/Texas-prisons-take-hit-from-Harvey-complaints-of-12172438.php#photo-14048019

Beck, A. J., & Johnson, C. (2012). *Sexual victimization reported by former state prisoners, 2008*. Washington, DC: Bureau of Justice Statistics.

Berger, R. (2016). *Kriminalomsorgen: A look at the world's most humane prison system in Norway*. Retrieved from https://papers.ssrn.com/sol3/papers.cfm?abstract_id=2883512

Bozelko, C. (2017). Give working prisoners dignity – and decent wages. *National Review*. Retrieved from http://www.nationalreview.com/article/443747/prison-labor-laws-wages-make-it-close-slavery

Bronson, J., & Berzofsky, M. (2017). *Indicators of mental health problems reported by prisoners and jail Inmates, 2011–2012*. Washington, DC: Bureau of Justice Statistics.

Bronson, J., & Carson, A. E. (2019). *Prisoners in 2017*. Washington, DC: Bureau of Justice Statistics.

Bronson, J., Maruschak, L. M., & Berzofsky, M. (2015). *Disabilities among prison and jail inmates, 2011–2012*. Washington, DC: Bureau of Justice Statistics. Retrieved from https://www.bjs.gov/content/pub/pdf/dpji1112.pdf

Bronson, J., Stroop, J., Zimmer, S., & Berzofsky, M. (2017). *Drug use, dependence, and abuse among state prisoners and jail inmates, 2007–2009*. Washington, DC: Bureau of Justice Statistics.

Carlino, R. M., & Franklin, A. (2018). *Out of sight: LGBTQ youth and adults in Texas' justice systems*. Austin, TX: Texas Criminal Justice Coalition.

Carson, E. A., & Cowhig, M. P. (2020a). *Mortality in state prisons, 2001–2016 – Statistical Tables*. Washington, DC: Bureau of Justice Statistics.

Carson, E. A., & Cowhig, M. P. (2020b). *Mortality in local jails, 2000–2016 – Statistical Tables*. Washington, DC: Bureau of Justice Statistics.

Cohen, N. (2020, March 13). Duo used drones to smuggle drugs, cell phones to inmates at federal prison in N.J., officials say. *Hudson County News*. Retrieved from https://www.nj.com/hudson/

CoreCivic (2019). *Who we are*. Retrieved from http://www.correctionscorp.com/who-we-are

Cornelius, G. F. (2009). *The Art of the con: Avoiding offender manipulation*. Alexandria, VA: American Correctional Association.

Craddock, A. (1996). Classification systems. In M. McShane & F. P. Williams (Eds.), *Encyclopedia of American prisons* (pp. 87–96). New York: Garland.

Craig, S. C. (2004). Rehabilitation versus control: An organizational theory of prison management. *The Prison Journal, 84*(4_supplement), 92s–114s.

Death Penalty Information Center. (2020). *Fact sheet (March 12, 2020)*. Retrieved from https://deathpenaltyinfo.org/documents/FactSheet.pdf

Eisen, L. B. (2018). *Inside private prisons: An American dilemma*. New York: Columbia University Press.

Federal Bureau of Investigation. (2017). *Crime in the United States, 2016*. Washington, DC: Author.

Frost, N. A., & Monteiro, C. E. (2016). *Administrative segregation in U.S. prisons*. Washington, DC: National Institute of Justice.

Gaes, G. G., & Camp, S. D. (2009). Unintended consequences: Experimental evidence for the criminogenic effect of prison security level placement on post-release recidivism. *Journal of Experimental Criminology, 5*(2), 139–162.

GEO Group. (2019). GEO continuum of care: 2018 annual report. Retrieved from https://www.geogroup.com/Portals/0/CoC%20Annual%20Report%20020719%20FINAL.pdf

GEO Group. (2020). The GEO group declares quarterly cash dividend of $0.48 per share. Company Release Retrieved from http://investors.geogroup.com/file/Index?KeyFile=402605699

Ghandnoosh, N. (2018). *Can we wait 75 years to cut the prison population in half?* Washington, DC: The Sentencing Project.

Gordon, M. S. (2006). Correctional officer control ideology: Implications for understanding a system. *Criminal Justice Studies, 19*(3), 225–239.

Groh, M. C. (2013). Gone: A proposal to maintain the benefits of prison work programs despite the restructuring of Federal Prison Industries' mandatory source status. *Public Contract Law Journal, 42*(2), 391–410.

Haney, C. (2018). The psychological effects of solitary confinement: A systematic critique. *Crime and Justice, 47*, 365–416.

Human Rights Clinic. (2017). *Designed to break you: Human rights violations on Texas' death row*. Austin: University of Texas School of Law.

Incarcerated Workers Organizing Committee. (2018). *Prison strike 2018*. Retrieved from https://incarceratedworkers.org/campaigns/prison-strike-2018

Kifer, M., Hemmens, C., & Stohr, M. K. (2003). The goals of corrections: Perspectives from the line. *Criminal Justice Review, 28*(1), 47–69.

Kirklin, J. T. (2011). Title VII protections for inmates: A model approach for safeguarding civil rights in America's prisons. *Columbia Law Review, 111*, 1048–1089.

Kreager, D. A., Bouchard, M., De Leon, G., Schaefer, D. R., Soyer, M., Young, J. T. N., & Zajac, G. (2018). A life course and networks approach to prison therapeutic communities. In D. F. Alwin, D. H. Felmlee, & D. A. Kreager (Eds.), *Social networks and the life course* (pp. 433–451). New York: Springer.

Labrecque, R. M., & Mears, D. P. (2019). Prison system versus critics' views on the use of restrictive housing: Objective risk classification or ascriptive assignment? *The Prison Journal, 99*(2), 194–218.

Lambert, E. G., Hogan, N. L., Barton, S. M., & Elechi, O. O. (2009). The impact of job stress, job involvement, job satisfaction, and organizational commitment on correctional staff support for rehabilitation and punishment. *Criminal Justice Studies, 22*(2), 109–122.

LeFlouria, T. L. (2016). *Chained in silence: Black women and convict Labor in the new South*. Chapel Hill: University of North Carolina Press.

Lincoln, J. (2018, October 11). Incarcerated Pennsylvanians now have to pay $150 to read. We should all be outraged. *Washington Post*. Retrieved from https://www.washingtonpost.com/opinions/incarcerated-pennsylvanians-now-have-to-pay-150-to-read-we-should-all-be-outraged/2018/10/11/51f548b8-cbd9-11e8-a85c-0bbe30c19e8f_story.html?noredirect=on

Mendez, J. E. (2016). *Seeing into solitary: A review of the laws and policies of certain nations regarding solitary confinement of detainees*. New York: United Nations.

Meyer, I. H., Flores, A. R., Stemple, L., Ruomero, A. P., Wilson, B. D. M., & Herman, J. L. (2017). Incarceration rates and traits of sexual minorities in the United States: National Inmate Survey, 2011–2012. *American Journal of Public Health, 107*(2), 234–240.

Montoya-Barthelemy, A. (2019). The occupational health of prison inmates: An ignored population and an opportunity. *Journal of Occupational and Environmental Medicine, 61*(2), 74–76.

Morris, R. G., & Worrall, J. L. (2014). Prison architecture and inmate misconduct: A multilevel assessment. *Crime & Delinquency, 60*(7), 1083–1109.

National Center on Addiction and Substance Abuse. (2010). *Behind bars II: Substance abuse and America's prison population*. New York: Author.

Nickeas, P. (2019, August 15). 'It's the racial stuff': Illinois prison banned, removed books on black history and empowerment from inmate education program. *Chicago Tribune*. Retrieved from https://www.chicagotribune.com/news/ct-illinois-prison-books-removed-inmate-education-20190815-6xlrmfwmovdxnbc3ohvsx6edgu-story.html

North Dakota Department of Corrections and Rehabilitation. (2016). *The Insider*. Retrieved from https://www.nd.gov/docr/media/newsletter/archive/July2016.pdf

Pew Charitable Trusts. (2015). *Substance use disorders and the role of the states*. Washington, DC: Author.

Pfaff, J. F. (2017). *Locked in: The true causes of mass incarceration and how to achieve real reform*. New York: Basic Books.

Richmond, K. M. (2014). The impact of federal prison industries employment on the recidivism outcomes of female inmates. *Justice Quarterly, 31*(4), 719–745.

Ring, K., & Gill, M. (2017). *Using time to reduce crime: Federal prisoner results show ways to reduce recidivism*. Washington, DC: Families Against Mandatory Minimums.

Roth, M. (2019) *Fire in the big house: America's deadliest prison disaster*. Athens, OH: Ohio University Press.

Routh, D., Abess, G., Makin, D., Stohr, M. K., Hemmens, C., & Yoo, J. (2017). Transgender inmates in prison: A review of applicable statutes and policies. *International Journal of Offender Therapy and Comparative Criminology, 61*(6), 645–666.

Sawyer, W. (2017). How much do incarcerated people earn in each state? *Prison Policy Initiative*. Retrieved from https://www.prisonpolicy.org/blog/2017/04/10/wages/

Schaefer, L. (2017). Correcting the "correctional" component of the corrections officer role: How offender custodians can contribute to rehabilitation and reintegration. *Corrections: Policy, Practice and Research, 3*(1), 38–55.

Schwartzapfel, B. (2016). A primer on the nationwide prisoners' strike. *The Marshall Project*. Retrieved from https://www.themarshallproject.org/2016/09/27/a-primer-on-the-nationwide-prisoners-strike?ref=collections#.PNx2GbFzI

Shannon, S. K. S., & Page, J. (2014). Bureaucrats on the cell block: Prison officers' perceptions of work environment and attitudes toward prisoners. *Social Science Review, 88*(4), 630–657.

Shapiro, N. (2017) State AG Ferguson sues firm that operates Tacoma detention center for immigrants over $1 a day wages. *The Seattle Times*. Retrieved from https://www.seattletimes.com/seattle-news/state-ag-bob-ferguson-files-lawsuit-against-company-that-operates-northwest-detention-center/

Show, G., & Show, U., (2020, Feb. 28). Washington state prisons look to Norway for ways to curb prolific offenders. MYNorthwest. Retrieved from https://mynorthwest.com/1739860/washington-norway-prisons-guidance/?

Skarbek, D. (2014). *The social order of the underworld: How prison gangs govern the American penal system*. New York: Oxford University Press.

Slater, D. (2017). North Dakota's Norway experiment. *Mother Jones*. Retrieved from http://www.motherjones.com/crime-justice/2017/07/north-dakota-norway-prisons-experiment/

Smith, C. J., Bechtel, J., Patrick, A., Smith, R., & Wilson-Gentry, L. (2006). *Correctional industries preparing inmates for re-entry: Recidivism and post-release employment*. Washington, DC: US Department of Justice. Steiner, B., Butler, H. D., & Ellison, J. M. (2014). Causes and correlates of prison inmate misconduct: A systematic review of the evidence. *Journal of Criminal Justice, 42*(6), 462–470.

Stephan, J. J. (2008). *Census of state and federal correctional facilities, 2005*. Washington, DC: Bureau of Justice Statistics.

Sufrin, C., Beal, L., Clarke, J., Jones, R., & Mosher, W. D. (2019). Pregnancy outcomes in US prisons, 2016-2017. *American Journal of Public Health, 109*(5), 799–805.

Taylor, M. (2017). *Improving in-prison rehabilitation programs*. Sacramento, CA: Legislative Analyst's Office.

The Economist. (2018). How convict labour increased inequality. *The Economist*. Retrieved from https://www.economist.com/news/united-states/21740468-forcing-prisoners-work-lowered-wages-and-increased-unemployment-how-convict-labour

Townes, C. (2016). America's shadow workforce rises up against prison labor. *Think Progress*. Retrieved from https://thinkprogress.org/its-just-dressed-up-slavery-america-s-shadow-workforce-rises-up-against-prison-labor-e8ee1b5a8738/

Ujiyediin, N. (2019, June 17). 7,000 books and magazines are banned in Kansas prisons. Here are some of them. *KCUR*. Retrieved from https://www.kcur.org/post/7000-books-and-magazines-are-banned-kansas-prisons-here-are-some-them#stream/0

UNICOR. (2017). *Discover UNICOR*. Washington, DC: U.S. Bureau of Prisons.

United Nations. (2015a). *Handbook on dynamic security and prison intelligence*. New York: Author.

United Nations. (2015b). *United Nations minimum rules for the treatment of prisoners* (Mandela rules). New York: Author.

U.S. Bureau of Justice Statistics. (2018). *Corrections statistical analysis tool (CSAT) –Prisoners*. Retrieved from https://www.bjs.gov/index.cfm?ty=nps

U.S. Bureau of Prisons. (2016). *Inmate occupational training directory*. Washington, DC: Author.

U.S. Bureau of Prisons. (2017a). *Historical information*. Retrieved from https://www.bop.gov/about/history/

U.S. Bureau of Prisons. (2017b). *UNICOR program details*. Retrieved from https://www.bop.gov/inmates/custody_and_care/unicor_about.jsp

U.S. Bureau of Prisons. (2017c). *Education programs*. Retrieved from https://www.bop.gov/inmates/custody_and_care/education.jsp

U.S. Bureau of Prisons. (2017d). *Substance abuse treatment*. Retrieved from https://www.bop.gov/inmates/custody_and_care/substance_abuse_treatment.jsp

U.S. Bureau of Prisons. (2018). *Our locations*. Retrieved from https://www.bop.gov/locations/

U.S. Bureau of Prisons. (2020a). *Inmate statistics*. Retrieved from https://www.bop.gov/about/statistics/population_statistics.jsp

U.S. Bureau of Prisons. (2020b). *About our facilities*. Retrieved from https://www.bop.gov/about/facilities/

U.S. Bureau of Prisons. (2020c). *Prison security levels*. Retrieved from https://www.bop.gov/about/statistics/statistics_inmate_sec_levels.jsp

Walmsley, R. (2018). *World prison population list, 12th edition*. London, UK: Institute for Criminal Policy Research.

Washington State Institute for Public Policy. (2019). *Benefit-cost results: Adult criminal justice*. Retrieved from http://www.wsipp.wa.gov/BenefitCost?topicId=2

Welch, M. P. (2015, Aug. 28). Hurricane Katrina was a nightmare for inmates in New Orleans. *Vice*. Retrieved from https://www.vice.com/en_ca/article/5gjdxn/hurricane-katrina-was-a-nightmare-for-inmates-in-new-orleans-829

Weller, C. (2017). Photos of maximum-security prisons in Norway and the US reveal the extremes of prison life. *Business Insider*. Retrieved from http://www.businessinsider.com/norway-and-american-prisons-reveal-how-each-country-sees-punishment-2017-1/#opened-in-2010-halden-prison-has-been-called-the-worlds-most-humane-prison-despite-its-official-status-as-maximum-security-1

Chapter 7
Correctional Personnel

OUTLINE

- Introduction
- Corrections Officers
- Corrections Counselors
- Community-Based Corrections: Probation and Parole Officers
- Administrative and Support Staff
- Employee Ethics
- Well-Being and Corrections Work
- Summary

OBJECTIVES

After reading this chapter you will able to:

- Describe the three main correctional job roles (administrative, institutional, and community-based corrections)

- Describe the typical hiring and training requirements for correctional officers

- Describe the job-related challenges that some women correctional officers confront

- Describe the different types of correctional officer misconduct

- Explain why it is difficult to maintain correctional officer well-being

CASE STUDY

Preventing Prison Riots

Throughout the 1970s and early 1980s, US prisons were rocked with a series of riots resulting in numerous deaths and assaults on inmates and correctional personnel; some institutions were severely damaged. A list of the most dangerous and disruptive riots in US history would have to include the 1971 Attica uprising in upper New York State that claimed 43 lives—including ten correctional officers (COs)—the destruction of four barracks at an Arkansas immigration holding facility at Fort Chaffee by frustrated Cuban detainees in 1980—and the New Mexico State Penitentiary riot, where 33 inmates died. Since the mid-1980s, however, the number of riots and inmate uprisings decreased substantially. Changes in prison design, improvements in inmate classification and programming, and better trained and equipped staff members reduced the number of these events. In addition, when major incidents have occurred, the loss of lives, injuries, and damage have decreased. Although happening less often than in the past, these uprisings still occur and they result in deaths, injuries, damage, and significant disruptions to institutional life.

On 15 April 2018 seven inmates were killed and nearly two dozen others seriously injured in a seven-hour riot at the Lee Correctional Institution in Bishopville, South Carolina. This riot claimed more lives than any American prison riot in the previous 25 years, and some reporters were quick to point out that unresolved gang conflicts, understaffing, and management problems led to this disaster. Thompson (2018b) attributes the riot to tensions resulting from mixing inmate gangs (also called security threat groups by prison administrators) on the same living units, deteriorating living conditions, and serving insufficient and unappetizing food. Reilly (2018) points out that South Carolina prioritizes cost-savings in its prisons and operates facilities with inadequate staffing, cutting prison programs and inmate amenities, and failing to monitor and suppress gang activities. While South Carolina has one of the lowest costs of state imprisonment, it is also one of the most violent prison systems. These administrative and management practices, Reilly (2018) observes, led to South Carolina inmates launching over 160 lawsuits from 2015 to 2018 to address the treatment they received in prison.

Although the public does not consider prison inmates a sympathetic population, the inmates themselves look forward to the same things all of us desire such as safe and clean surroundings, decent meals, access to healthcare, and constructive activities to occupy their time, including access to rehabilitative or recreational programs. While few Americans advocate for the living conditions that inmates in many European and Scandinavian prisons experience (which might be nicer than some US college student dorms), many pundits are questioning whether we can afford decent living conditions for the people behind bars due to the additional fiscal burden taxpayers would assume. The problem with placing inmates in dangerous and unhealthy prison conditions is they are sometimes returned to the community worse than when they went to prison, and that, ultimately, reduces public safety. One alternative to our current practice is to maintain correctional spending at current levels, but decreasing the inmate population, enabling us to provide safer, more humane, and rehabilitative prisons.

Critical Questions

1. Can you think of some reasons why prisoners might riot?
2. Why would prison gang leaders want to have fewer murders, riots, and escapes?
3. Correctional leaders in South Carolina have developed a number of innovative violence reduction programs, including recruiting ex-prisoners turned advocates to work with current inmates (Jackson, 2019). Is involving ex-prisoners in violence reduction programs a good idea? Defend you answer.

INTRODUCTION

When we ask veteran COs about their jobs, we often find that correctional work was seldom their first career choice. Until the 1970s, the salaries and benefits for COs were low and the profession lacked the status or desirability of, for example, policing. During that era, selection standards for hiring were also low, and some officers lacked even high school diplomas. Most new recruits received training on the job rather than attending pre-service training academies. Furthermore, jails and some prison systems were often managed by political appointees who had little correctional experience before becoming senior-level administrators. As a result of a lack of training and professional leadership, some of the front-line officers engaged in misconduct that led to stereotypes of COs as cruel, apathetic, or unethical. Ross (2012, p. 418) suggests that the public perception of COs is driven by myths such as their brutality, incompetence, low intelligence, or uncaring nature. Much has changed since those times. Today, the officers working within jails and prisons are better educated and trained; moreover, they are more likely to be led by correctional professionals. In response to the excesses of the past, the courts have established minimum requirements for correctional care. These changes have increased the effectiveness of correctional operations, and inmates and officers benefitted from these changes.

As correctional populations increased nationwide throughout the 1980s, the need for personnel grew and the opportunities within the profession also expanded. Salaries and benefits increased, and administrators were able to recruit and retain more professional officers. At the same time the corrections field was also evolving; organizations such as the American Correctional Association (ACA), American Jail Association, and the **National Association of Wardens and Superintendents** sought to professionalize corrections through their efforts at accreditation, education, and training. Over the long term, their efforts made positive changes in the culture of correctional agencies to one that is more focused on accountability and best practices intended to increase public safety.

The Bureau of Labor Statistics (2019a) reports that about 450,000 individuals are working in corrections today. Their pathways to correctional careers—whether they are working in jails, prisons, or community corrections agencies—have changed. In the past, an individual's entry to a correctional career was often encouraged by his or her friends and family members who were already working in jails or prisons. Others drifted into correctional work based on where they lived. For instance, prisons in some rural counties are often the largest local employer. To some extent things have changed today, as a growing number of individuals use their post-secondary educations to prepare for working with correctional populations, especially in the subfields of community corrections and youth justice.

Despite the increased demand for correctional personnel, we find that the front-line staff working with inmates generally fall into two groups. Many officers will stay for a year or two and then use their experience to move on to other law enforcement or government careers. For these officers, correctional work is a steppingstone to other criminal justice career opportunities. The remaining individuals tend to stay in their correctional careers for the long term. In smaller local or county operations the opportunities for career growth and advancement tend to be limited, whereas individuals working for a state or the federal prison system can take advantage of different work assignments within a larger facility or can transfer to different jobs throughout the entire prison system, including community corrections.

Correctional personnel working for local or county governments are typically employed in jails, juvenile facilities, in courts (as bailiffs), or probation and other community corrections agencies. Opportunities for promotions or career development in these agencies tend to be limited (e.g. working in a 50-bed jail, or a six-person probation agency). In large urban counties or cities, by contrast, there may be 1,000 officers working within a regional jail complex, and hundreds in community corrections roles. Given these latter numbers, there is a need for officer specialization, such as working on units for people with mental health problems, and many take advantage of these opportunities throughout their careers to develop new skills. In addition to career growth, there are also more promotional opportunities in larger agencies, and the pay and benefits tend to be higher.

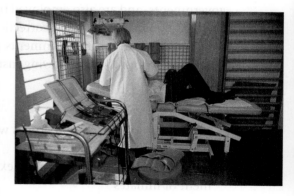

PHOTO 7.1
A physiotherapist examines an inmate in a prison medical clinic. Physiotherapists help people afflicted by injury, illness, or disability using movement and exercise, manual therapy, and education. Credit: BSIP SA/Alamy Stock Photo.

When we are considering correctional personnel, we often forget that there is a demand for administrative staff members who ensure that jails and prisons keep running. A modern prison can have the same population as a small town, and the facility must provide all the inmates' basic needs, from food and laundry services to their dental, medical, and psychological care. To fulfill these goals there may be hundreds of support staff from accountants to doctors. So, what does this all mean? Despite a generally downward trend nationally in correctional populations, there will continue to be career opportunities in institutional and community corrections roles as well as front-line and administrative positions that have virtually no contact with the inmates.

In the sections that follow we shed light on the issue of correctional personnel and take a closer look at the roles and duties of the staff members working directly with inmates as well as those who support their efforts. Their working environments in custodial and community-based settings are also described. We then examine some of the workplace challenges correctional personnel must confront and highlight the key issues related to CO ethics. By the end of this chapter you will have a greater appreciation for the work that officers and support staff carry out in their efforts to increase public safety.

CORRECTIONS OFFICERS

Institutional work is one of the major employment areas in corrections and officers account for about four of five positions. These officers work for federal, state, and local governments, and are also employed by private correctional firms such as CoreCivic and the GEO Group. Institutional corrections involves employment in any facility in which federal, state, and local governments hold people accused or convicted of committing crimes. COs work in the following institutions:

- Prisons and penitentiaries
- Jails
- Institutions confining individuals with mental health problems considered not criminally responsible
- Institutions and facilities for the examination, evaluation, classification, and assignment of inmates
- Facilities for the confinement, treatment, and rehabilitation of persons with substance abuse problems

Roughly 60% of all state and local corrections workers in the United States are employed in facilities, and they worked in all manner of jobs, from uniformed COs to administrators such as superintendents or wardens. Bear in mind, however, that about two-thirds of all institutional correctional employees work in custody or security positions.

Correctional Officers

Most people working in secure facilities started out as COs, the staff members directly responsible for monitoring the security of the facility, and for supervising inmates and ensuring the facility's safety and security. The following job-related duties of COs were identified by the Bureau of Labor Statistics (2019a) and CorrectionalOfficer.Org (2019):

- Enforce rules and keep order within jails and prisons, including settling disputes between inmates and preventing inmate misconduct such as assaults or escapes. To maintain order, the officers enforce prison regulations and address inmate misconduct.
- Directly supervise activities of inmates on their living units and while being transported within facilities. Some officers may monitor inmate behavior on closed circuit television (CCTV) in control rooms.
- Supervise the transportation of inmates being transported to other jails or prisons, courts, and medical facilities.
- Inspect facilities to ensure that they meet security and safety standards by monitoring the physical plant or fences as well as carrying out formal inspections of the living units. Officers look for evidence of inmates trying to breach security, such as interfering with the windows or doors, and look for contraband (e.g. drugs) and rule violations.
- Some officers maintain the security of the prison's perimeter and that can involve vehicle and foot patrols or working in a "gun tower"; although most facilities have reduced the number of officers working in towers.
- Reduce the flow of contraband items into the facility by conducting searches of staff and visitors coming into the facilities, as well as searching inmates and their living units.
- Report on inmate behavior including documenting rule violations or major incidents (e.g. after a serious crime or breach of security occurs). Officers are also responsible for carrying out and documenting inmate counts and writing reports.
- Activities related to correctional rehabilitation are carried out by a relatively small proportion of all officers and some may deliver interventions such as anger management or addictions programs to inmate groups.
- In some institutions, COs might refer inmates on their living units to various rehabilitative programs and are responsible for assigning their institutional work.

Most of these duties are related to ensuring safety and security and those duties account for most of a CO's role, and in virtually every institution most COs are in direct contact with inmates. They are responsible for taking head counts and making rounds on the living units and in their travels through the institution.

Work Environment

To understand the CO's job more fully, one must examine the environment where they work. Our starting point is that jails and prisons operate using a paramilitary hierarchy, which is shown in Figure 7.1, where there is a clear **chain of command** with COs at the bottom of the organizational pyramid and a warden at the top position. The assignment of these roles depends on facility size. Generally, COs report to sergeants, who might supervise a living unit or a program area (such as the kitchen), who then report to lieutenants and captains, who are responsible for the institution during a shift or may have specific assignments such as overseeing the **corrections emergency response team** (CERT) or **special operations response teams** (SORT) in a larger facility. Lieutenants and captains report to the deputy wardens, and larger organizations may have deputy directors who oversee security operations, rehabilitative and treatment programs, and support services such as the prison administration. Figure 7.1 presents a simplified version of a chain of command and these hierarchies are more complex in larger organizations. All the deputies in a small jail, for example, might be supervised by one sergeant who reports to the sheriff. As correctional organizations grow in size, there is a similar increase in the number of specialized roles in the chain of command, and very large organizations can add additional ranks including majors and colonels, although these administrators might also be known as directors or deputy wardens.

The realities of the prison work environment can be both positive and negative. For instance, one of the most positive and challenging is direct contact with inmates. Face-to-face contact with inmates can give some officers a sense of accomplishment and the feeling they are making a difference in their lives. It also can result in high levels of

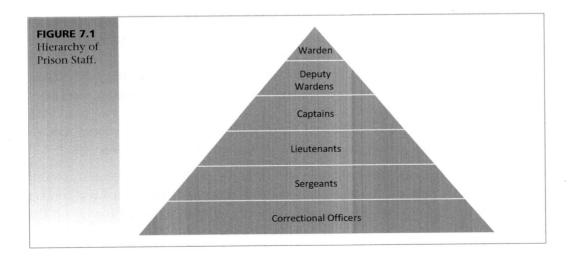

FIGURE 7.1
Hierarchy of
Prison Staff.

Warden

Deputy
Wardens

Captains

Lieutenants

Sergeants

Correctional Officers

anxiety and job-related stress, and a cynical attitude toward life. Indeed, some officers express feelings of despair, fear, frustration, and hopelessness. More than any other institutional corrections employees, COs have the greatest impact on inmates' day-to-day lives. As a result, their outlooks and attitudes are very important in prison operations, including working toward a well-run and healthy workplace.

Shift work is a second key element of the CO's employment. Institutions must staff CO posts 24/7. Fewer officers are on duty at night, and the staff-to-inmate ratio increases when the prisoners are out of their cells. More desirable shifts, such as working weekdays, typically go to officers with more seniority or who are involved in specialized roles such as delivering rehabilitative programs, admitting or transporting inmates, or scheduling and assigning inmate work. New officer-recruits, by contrast, are often required to work the less desirable days and times such as holidays and weekends, and during the evenings or nights for the first year or two of their careers. Work duties are typically structured in 8-, 10-, or 12-hour shifts. Given the large number of institutions throughout the nation, there is considerable diversity in terms of shift rotations, and while most individuals are assigned to rotating shifts, officers in some facilities work permanent day or night shifts. Officers working in front-line roles may be required to work overtime. While most officers appreciate the extra money they earn, these shifts often occur on the days they least want to work such as weekends during summer vacations.

Training

Several factors determine the quality and quantity of training new officers receive, although the most important is funding. As noted earlier, deputies assigned to work in a cash-strapped rural jail might receive very little or no formal training prior to their first day working with inmates and most of their training will be on the job. But, as the size of the jail grows the likelihood of receiving academy training also increases. In addition, a growing number of states also have mandatory hiring and training requirements (Kowalski, 2020). For example, a jail officer-cadet in Georgia must complete two weeks (80 hours) of training (Georgia Public Safety Training Center, 2020), whereas Florida requires jail deputies to have 420 hours of instruction (Tallahassee Community College, 2020).

The federal and state prison systems generally require officers to complete more hours of training compared with local jails. Training has values beyond learning how to do the job, and a key benefit of training is increasing the new officer's confidence. Burton, Lux, Cullen, Miller, and Burton (2018) surveyed 44 state correctional systems about their recruitment and training strategies. First, when it comes to state prison systems, almost all require officers to receive training at a central facility and in the three states lacking a training facility officers were trained at the institution where they worked. Prior to starting their academy training, officers in more than four-fifths of the states were required to spend time learning on the job, in what they called **job shadowing**. For example, the Indiana Department of Corrections (2019, para. 1) observes that:

> Job shadowing allows a student, employee, or intern to gain comprehensive knowledge about what an employee who holds a particular job does…Job shadowing allows the observer to see and understand the nuances of a particular job. The job shadowing employee is able to observe how the employee does the job, the key deliverables expected from the job, and the employees with whom the job interacts.

During this shadowing period the new officer learns how institutions operate. More importantly, this period also allows the facility supervisors to see how that individual interacts with other staff and inmates, and also gives prospective officers an exposure to corrections and helps them determine whether they want to pursue a career in this field. The results of the national survey show that the average time spent on job shadowing was about 40 hours (Burton et al., 2018).

With respect to the actual correctional academy training, only one state required less than 100 hours. Indeed, Burton and colleagues (2018, p. 30) found that:

- 11 states require 100–199 hours of training
- 20 states require between 200 and 299 hours of training
- 12 states require 300 or more hours of correctional academy training

States place different priorities on the topics taken during an officer's academy training, but the most important is the steps COs must take to ensure a safe and secure environment. Each jurisdiction will have its own set of priorities in terms of the importance they place on different training topics. To illustrate one example, Florida requires that cadets receive the 420 hours of training before they can work in a jail or prison. Broward College (2019) instructs Floridian cadets on the following topics:

• Introduction to Corrections	32 hours
• Communications	40 hours
• Officer Safety	16 hours
• Facility and Equipment	8 hours
• Intake and Release	18 hours
• Supervising in a Correctional Facility	40 hours
• Supervising Special Populations	20 hours
• Responding to Incidents and Emergencies	16 hours
• First Aid	40 hours

- Firearms   80 hours
- Defensive Techniques   80 hours
- Officer Wellness and Physical Abilities   30 hours

Total   420 hours

After starting their prison assignments, officers in most states serve a probationary period of up to one year. During that time, they will typically receive more mentoring and support from senior officers and some states have correctional field training officers, who provide additional instruction, support, and mentoring. According to the Idaho Department of Corrections (undated, p. 5) this post-academy or in-service training "is intended to give the new recruit instruction, direct supervision, guidance and experience so that the officer may develop good judgment, efficiency, and good habits of conduct and appearance."

In addition to the new officer orientation and training, every state requires that COs receive ongoing training to ensure their skills are up to date. The Burton and colleagues (2018, p. 30) survey of state correctional systems found that officers are required to attend about one week—the national average was 39 hours—per year of ongoing training.

Many states require that skills such as first aid and firearms be certified every one or two years. Training is also used to respond to challenges such as ensuring a healthy workplace. For example, Texas requires COs have mandatory discrimination training twice a year (Blakinger, 2018). Officers may also be required to have instruction about changing policies and practices, as well as new technologies and emerging threats. After 2015, for instance, there were a growing number of COs who required hospitalization due to unintentional exposure to fentanyl that was smuggled into jails

Photo 7.2
Future correctional officers receiving training at the Nebraska Department of Corrections Staff Training Academy. Everyone hired by the Department of Correctional Services or a service provider must attend at least 100 hours of new-hire training. Academy in the Nebraska Department of Corrections. Credit: Mikael Karlsson/Alamy Stock Photo.

and prisons and officers need to learn about how to minimize their risks of exposure to these substances. Furthermore officers also need training to manage emerging threats, such as developing ways to respond to the spread of the COVID-19 virus (Calams, 2020).

Officers who are moving into a new specialized job may also be required to have additional training before assuming their new positions. As we noted earlier, there is considerable job diversity in larger correctional agencies, and COs are able to apply for specialized assignments, including canine (K9) officers who use dogs to search for contraband and escapees. Some officers are interested in becoming members of CERT or SORT teams while other officers apply for intelligence officer positions who collect information on security-threat groups or gangs. Most prison systems also provide additional training for officers who are being promoted into supervisory and management positions. Some COs aspire to correctional counselor jobs in order to change their relationships with the inmates—or take advantage of their college education—as well as working a Monday to Friday workweek. These positions are described in the following section.

Women Corrections Officers' Experiences of Harassment

Prisons and jails have been historically male-dominated institutions and until the late 1800s most women employed in these places worked as matrons, working with juveniles and female inmates. Although some women, such as Katherine Bement Davis—profiled in Chapter 2—made significant inroads in corrections in the early 1900s, but these pioneering women were the exceptions. Most women worked in support positions such as clerical careers. Like their counterparts in policing women started playing an increasingly more important role in the delivery of correctional services in the 1970s. Today over one-half of prison employees are women in some states and they account for over one-quarter of the Bureau of Prisons workforce. Despite making these inroads there are ongoing media accounts of women who have had to overcome mistreatment carried out by the inmates and their male officer counterparts.

The behaviors that some women COs have had to endure are difficult to read about. Some prisoners make unwanted and demeaning sexual comments and make masturbatory gestures toward them and some express verbal threats. They will also intentionally expose themselves to female staff members or openly masturbate when the officers are making their rounds (Jones, Cathcart, & Cooksey, 2019). Prisoners may throw bodily fluids at women staff members, grope them, and some women officers have been sexually assaulted. A number of female officers claim they endured this treatment throughout their careers.

All facilities have mechanisms enabling officers to sanction inmate behavior. But as one women officer told Santo (2017, para. 8) about sexual harassment: "If I wrote an incident report every time, I would literally write hundreds a day." Writing about inmates who intentionally masturbated in front of her Carter (2018, para. 32) observed that "I soon realized that for some men housed in isolated segregation, the punishment they would get—another day or so in [segregation]—was no deterrent for this kind of misconduct." A growing number of states are enacting new laws to deter inmate sexual misconduct and some have received additional prison time because of their harassing behaviors such as intentionally masturbating in front of staff members. Like other examples of discretion we have described in previous chapters, some acts are more likely to end in formal sanctions. Yet, there may be no deterrent effect of adding another year of confinement for a person already serving a life sentence. As Carter (2018) further notes, regardless of the consequences, these acts can have a lifelong impact on an individual:

> Four years ago, I left the jail to go to grad school. But this stays with me: I was a female corrections officer who had to figure out how to do my job while inmates masturbated to my presence, my voice, even my scent. That was the job. And there is nothing at all that will help me forget it.

(para. 42)

When it comes to harassment from their male coworkers, women officers have reported being bullied and experiencing unwanted propositions and verbal abuse about their sexuality. Some receive emails containing obscene pictures or videos from their coworkers. Dickerson (2018, para. 6) notes that some complainants "face retaliation, professional sabotage and even harassment" [while] "the careers of many harassers and those who protect them flourish."

Why does this happen? Blakinger (2018) says that it has to do with a "boys club" mentality and a culture of indifference. Many women are fearful of complaining about their treatment as "There is a code of silence, and women who come forward face retaliation for breaking that code" (Blakinger, 2018, para. 52). When the complaints of women officers reporting harassment and assaults by their coworkers have been ignored by senior managers, they launched individual and class-action lawsuits (Dennison, 2019). Newspaper accounts detail how these COs are winning these lawsuits throughout the country. Sometimes the harassers are terminated after the women officers win their lawsuits, although others carry on with their careers.

In addition to being embarrassing and humiliating, experiencing verbal harassment and assaults have a number of negative outcomes for the individual and the agency. Exposure to harassment can cause a series of psychological and other health-related problems. Depression, low self-esteem, shame, having a negative body image, and anxiety are commonly reported psychological impacts for victims of these attacks. Victimization is also associated with physical health problems such as high blood pressure and insomnia and may have long-term impacts on heart health. Intolerable working conditions push these women into quitting their jobs and this can lower their lifelong earnings.

Organizations also pay a high price for workplace harassment and bullying, including employees requiring higher levels of sick time and employee turnover. When experienced staff members quit, they have to be replaced which increases costs associated with recruiting new officers and training them. It also takes a year or longer before officers fully develop their knowledge and skills to the point where they are effective working with inmates. Failing to address a toxic workplace has also resulted in lawsuits being launched by jail and prison personnel throughout the country. As a result jail and prison systems have paid out millions of dollars in lawsuits in response to the claims of unwanted attention directed toward these women (Tolbert, 2018).

CORRECTIONS COUNSELORS

Counselors working in secure facilities can operate in a number of different roles. Some correctional counselors carry out screening, risk and needs assessments, security ratings, and other psychological testing to determine the most appropriate security classification and treatment programs for newly admitted inmates to state or federal prisons. Admitting officers in larger jails can also carry out a series of similar tasks, although most of their focus is on inmate security and suicide risks. There is a range of job classifications related to these roles, and they can include psychological technicians or psychological diagnosticians. In some state corrections departments, psychological technicians or treatment specialists are called classification officers; in the federal Bureau of Prisons they are called case managers. Whatever the label, essentially these people serve as frontline counselors.

The specific job duties of correctional counselors or case managers will vary depending on their role within a facility, but we use an example of an entry-level corrections case manager position from the Missouri Department of Corrections. Their duties are as summarized as follows:

- Serves on a classification team; evaluates the individual's institutional adjustment, attitude toward society, and release plans; and makes recommendations relative to job assignments, facility transfers, and disciplinary actions.
- Secures and verifies information from incarcerated adults concerning their home life, family relationships, work history, and other pertinent personal and social factors; develops, maintains, and reviews classification plans.
- Assesses classification status and helps to determine program eligibility using different classification instruments.

- Acts as a grievance officer; processes and responds to Informal Resolution Requests; and holds disciplinary hearings on conduct violations.
- Processes offenders by completing initial file review and protective custody assessment; enters enemy waivers and updates enemies' lists.
- Maintains open-door office policy; handles the inmates' laundry, property, and financial concerns, as well as mail and censorship notices; and notifies persons on their caseloads of the critical illness/death of immediate family members.
- Participates and assists in the vocational, educational, and social adjustment planning for all assigned offenders; facilitates offender programs.
- Evaluates civilian visiting applications and determines whether to approve or deny the individual's request to visit with an offender.
- Cooperates with public and private agencies and law enforcement agencies in matters relating to assigned offenders; arranges and facilitates calls to attorneys, public agencies, and law enforcement agencies.
- Provides pre-release counseling; researches and identifies community resources and services prior to processing these individuals for release.

(Missouri Office of Administration Division of Personnel, 2016)

A review of these duties shows there are three key roles of case counselors working in Missouri prisons. The first is maintaining facility safety by ensuring that inmates are correctly classified and managing their behavior within the institution by addressing misconduct and responding to grievances they have filed. The second role is to ensure that they take advantage of rehabilitative opportunities that are appropriate for their risks and needs. The third role is helping these people manage the day-to-day challenges they encounter, from arranging visits with family members to ensuring that monies sent by family members are deposited in the correct inmate account. Altogether, the main role of these counselors is to help prisoners reduce their likelihood of misconduct, aid in their rehabilitation, and help with their transition to the community.

Many of a case manager's duties are focused on helping prisoners solve their problems. One of the challenges of living behind bars is that inmates lack access to telephones or the Internet (although their use of unauthorized cell phones is rampant). Moreover, few inmates have the background knowledge of the law or various government programs to solve problems on their own. Some inmates lack the interpersonal skills to successfully resolve their problems. As a result, they depend on their case manager or COs to help them solve the day-to-day challenges that all of us confront.

There are two ways to obtain case manager positions. The first is on-the-job training. Many case managers started as COs and developed their knowledge, skills, and abilities on the job. The second pathway to case management work is when individuals are hired directly into these positions; the typical job requirement is a bachelor's degree in social work, psychology, or a related social science.

In Chapter 4 we observed there was sometimes a tension between probation officers who primarily identified with their roles as a law enforcer compared with those who had a social work orientation. A similar tension exists in corrections between the security staff and counselors or other behavioral mental health specialists. One of the challenges is the orientation of these two positions: most COs are primarily concerned with ensuring institutional safety and security whereas counselors have a rehabilitative orientation. Lazzaretto-Green et al. (2011, p. 109) found that behavioral and nursing staff soon learn that security trumps caring in correctional settings. Some professional staff are labeled by the COs with terms such as "con lovers" who are seen as naïve and who may identify more closely with the inmates than the correctional staff. Security staff see con lovers as prone to manipulation. Despite the tension that can sometimes arise between different correctional workgroups, during crisis times these groups can very quickly become united.

At a higher level in most institutional settings is a **clinical psychologist**, the person who is responsible for supervising the psychological technicians and for approving treatment plans. The work responsibilities and job duties of correctional psychologists are directly related to their education and experience. Bierie and Mann (2017, p. 479) observe they carry out three main functions which are summarized as follows:

- Engage in clinical work, including designing, engaging, and supervising treatment programs, crisis intervention, and therapeutic sessions for inmates. They may also provide clinical programming or other assistance to staff.
- Act as researchers and translators of correctional science by evaluating treatment programming, test hypotheses, and contribute to policymaking, including writing scientific reports or articles for the prison system.
- Creating, refining, or using forensic tools such as risk-screening instruments, polygraphs, interviews, and similar applications.

Most of the duties of a front-line psychologist focus on reducing prison misconduct, recidivism, self-harm, and suicide (Bierie & Mann, 2017). Individuals in these careers will have a graduate degree in clinical or counseling psychology. Some psychologists are generalists who work with all different types of inmates, an arrangement more common in smaller facilities. Other psychologists will specialize in working with specific offender types such as sex offenders or inmates suffering from chronic or severe mental health problems.

Buche, Gaiser, Rittman, and Beck (2018) note that prisons also hire several other behavioral health personnel, including social workers, nurses, marriage and family therapists, addictions counselors, as well as physicians and psychiatrists. However, prison and jail administrators often find it difficult to recruit and retain these personnel. Buche and colleagues say that a number of factors make it difficult to recruit these workers, including inadequate pay, competition from other fields, and the nature of delivering care in jails and prisons (including the administrative burdens), as well as the stigma of working in corrections.

Hiring Requirements

Although the baseline hiring requirement for most jails and prisons is a high school diploma, having a college degree can increase one's likelihood of obtaining a CO position, and having such a degree opens doors to a greater range of positions at earlier stages of an officer's career. In addition to the educational requirement, most states restrict these jobs to applicants who are 18 years of age or older and are US citizens, and have passed a background check (Kowalski, 2020). Almost all state departments of corrections require applicants to pass a written test (Burton et al., 2018), and several states, including New Jersey, require applicants to be state residents. Residency requirements are also a common requirement for jail positions.

PHOTO 7.3
Ongoing training of a correctional institution's professional staff is crucial to the timely and proper delivery of services. Patricia Sollock, the Chief of Mental Health for the Montgomery County Department of Corrections and Rehabilitation in Bethesda, MD, presents a seminar on "Symptoms and Management of Depression" at the Naval Hospital Galley at the Guantanamo detention camp. Credit: PJF Military Collection/Alamy Stock Photo.

The New Jersey Department of Corrections (2019) screens applicants using the following criteria:

- High school diploma or its equivalent. Candidates must read and write English sufficiently to perform duties of the position.
- Must be a minimum of 18 years of age.
- Must be a citizen of the United States and a New Jersey resident. Institutions located in certain municipalities also have residency requirements, which require candidates to provide proof of residency.
- Applicants must possess a valid state driver's license.
- Candidates must be eligible to possess a firearm in accordance with state and federal laws.
- Background: Investigation of candidates' employment history, driving history, domestic violence history, and criminal history are conducted.
- Candidates will be given a thorough medical and psychological examination. They must provide urine samples for analyses to determine drug use.

One potential obstacle for employment in the criminal justice field is that applicants cannot have convictions for domestic violence, as a conviction of this nature can make them ineligible to legally possess firearms. When reviewing the requirements for applying for correctional positions we found that some state corrections departments will hire individuals who have criminal histories, but almost all exclude applicants who have been convicted of serious offenses, or individuals with recent convictions (e.g. within the prior two or three years).

Applicants for correctional work often express frustration with the wait between the time they submit their application and when they start their academy training, which is often a year or more. Again, this gap will depend somewhat on where one is applying for work and the number of positions the corrections department requires. In order to gain a better understanding of why it takes so long to obtain a job, we take a closer look at the process used by the New Jersey Department of Corrections (2019), and the four steps to employment are summarized below:

Phases 1 and 2: Completion of employment application, computer background check, written psychological examination, fingerprinting for background investigation, and urinalysis testing for drug screening.

Phase 3: Background investigation that includes personal interviews and visits to the candidate's residence and/or place of work.

Phase 4: When vacancies occur, those candidates who have successfully completed Phases 1–3 are required to report for Phase 4 processing, which includes a medical exam (e.g. blood, vision, hearing test, chest X-ray, and EKG). An interview conducted by a psychologist is carried out based on the results of the written examination competed during Phase 2.

In addition to these four phases, many states require some form of physical agility test, and many jurisdictions use the CO's physical abilities test (COPAT), which includes a timed test where the candidate must lift and drag a 150-pound dummy, along with timed sit ups and pushups. While these physical tests can exclude physically unfit individuals, a growing number of corrections departments publish guides on their websites on how to get into shape to pass these tests. Furthermore, an Internet search will produce video examples of these testing requirements. In other words, given several months to prepare, almost any CO candidate can meet these physical test requirements.

Working in the Private Sector

The final issue we examine here is the likelihood of private sector employment. There is a diverse range of privately operated agencies that deliver correctional services, including:

- Prisons holding federal and state inmates
- Jails holding inmates for local governments
- Detention facilities holding immigrant detainees

- Halfway houses holding probationers and ex-prisoners
- Behavioral health facilities holding juveniles or adults with addictions or mental health problems
- Juvenile facilities
- Probation agencies

The number of private correctional facilities in the United States has increased sharply since the 1980s. About 8% of all prisoners live in facilities operated by private firms, and these for-profit firms operate in about half of the states (Bronson & Carson, 2019). There are also several dozen privately operated jails in the United States, but there is very little information on these operations.

Privatization also extends to providing specific services to correctional systems, and some of these firms hire former COs or other personnel to work in these enterprises. Some examples include:

- *Prisoner transportation services*: Firms that transport inmates from courts to jails and prisons, carry out transfers between correctional facilities, or transport inmates to medical appointments.
- *Commissary services*: Some firms run inmate commissaries, which are the "stores" where inmates can obtain food, hygiene supplies, and other amenities.
- *Health services*: Private operators provide medical and dental care as well as behavioral mental health support (e.g. psychological services) for jails and prisons.
- *Food services*: Food services in some jails and prisons are provided by contractors; many of the larger contractors, such as Aramark, also deliver food services on college campuses.
- *Video visitation*: Visits are conducted by video in over 500 facilities: in some facilities family members can pay from $5 to $12.99 for a 20-minute visit (Coleman, 2018).
- *Email*: Where family members can send emails to jail inmates or state prisoners for a set price, such as $0.25 per message.
- *Inmate care packages*: Where family members arrange to send packages of food, hygiene supplies, or clothing from suppliers that are approved by the jail or prison.
- *Phone services*: Where the caller to a jail inmate or prisoner is charged a rate per minute to talk to that person.
- *Financial services*: Money transfer services, such as JPay, which operates in roughly 35 states, or Western Union, allow families to deposit money directly into an inmate's account.

The Urban Justice Center (2019, p. 3) identified 3,905 privately operated firms that profited from corrections. As a result, there are thousands of job opportunities with these firms. Some of these services are based within the actual correctional facility, and these employees may have considerable interactions with inmates such as the individuals working in prisoner transportation services. As correctional personnel have insight into the operations of jails and prisons, they are sometimes recruited into these jobs.

The salary of officers working in privately operated facilities depends on the contracts with the state or federal government. Most front-line COs working for private prisons are paid less than their state or federal prison counterparts and frequently enjoy fewer associated benefits of employment. Some jurisdictions, however, require officers to be paid prevailing wages, and those salaries are more competitive. The Montana Department of Labor and Industry (2018, p. 11), for instance, requires that corrections and detention officers be paid a minimum of $17.13 an hour plus $9.78 in benefits, and those wages increase for counties with a higher cost of living. Reporting on a Texas jail run by private contractors, Coyne (2018, para. 8) cites an official as saying that "Since we're privatized and we have federal inmates, then we have to pay federal wages whenever those individuals aren't segregated or cannot be segregated by our workforce."

But not every state requires that COs be paid the prevailing wage. Bauer (2019), a reporter for *Mother Jones*, worked in a private prison for four months and wrote a critically acclaimed book about his experiences. Bauer contends that in the Louisiana prison where he worked, the officers were paid only slightly more than minimum wage and most of them were poor and had few other career options. The screening and training these officers received were less comprehensive than officers working in state prison systems, and they tended to hire very young workers. Executives in the private prison industry, by contrast, are paid quite well. Bloomberg (2019) reports that their average compensation was about $1.1 million (counting bonuses and stock options). Many executives in these private firms have extensive career experiences in state and federal corrections and are considered experts in the field.

COMMUNITY-BASED CORRECTIONS: PROBATION AND PAROLE OFFICERS

Community corrections is difficult to describe for several reasons. First, job titles are not uniform from state to state. As we noted in Chapter 4, in some states the probation and parole functions are delivered by a single agency, while in most states, probation services are delivered by local or county employees and parole officers are state personnel. The federal government also employs the equivalent of probation and parole officers in the U.S. Probation and Pretrial Services System. A second factor preventing us from making a clear definition of these services is whether the clients are adults or juveniles. These differences make it hard to describe the day-to-day job activities of probation and parole officers or gain a reasonably accurate perspective on the job market for these community-based employees of the criminal justice system.

In Chapter 4 we describe how most probation officers fall into four roles depending on their orientation including social worker, police officer, case manager, and those who balance the enforcement and social work options, the latter being the so-called synthetic officer (Hsieh et al., 2015). As also noted in that chapter officers might find themselves engaging in all of these roles with some cases. When these workers were, asked about their work roles and personalities most indicated they were most like the synthetic officer.

Some aspects of a probation or parole officer's (PPO) orientation are related to the population supervised. Remember that probationers generally are first-time offenders. If an officer is supervising a large caseload of low-risk probationers convicted of non-violent crimes, he or she might provide virtually no individual counseling, supervision, or support. As the levels of risk of the probationers increase, the caseload size decreases, meaning the officers spend more time supervising, monitoring and counseling these individuals. Probationers who are on specialized caseloads, such as sex offenders, may receive more individual attention and those assessed as high-risk often receive more enforcement-related scrutiny.

Parolees, having endured longer terms of incarceration and having experienced longer histories of criminal involvement, tend to present more adjustment problems than probationers and nationwide statistics generally show lower rates of success with parolees. For example, in 2016, almost one-third (30.3%) of all parolees were incarcerated or had some other unsatisfactory outcome, including individuals who absconded or disappeared (Kaeble, 2018, p. 22). The biggest challenge facing parole officers is helping former prisoners in their reintegration into the community, a topic described more comprehensively in Chapter 10. In particular, however, parole officers are expected to ease ex-prisoners' transition into the community, including helping them find housing, employment, and ensuring they are complying with their parole conditions, which may include attending counseling and treatment.

The PPO's job, not surprisingly, has both positive and negative aspects. Many probation and parole officers are able to point to success stories. Unfortunately, those successes never make the newspaper headlines. Fully one-third of parolees disappear or are returned to prison, and a very small proportion of them are involved in serious and violent crimes. Among the negative aspects of probation and parole work three issues

PHOTO 7.4
Male and female corrections officers place shackles (also called leg irons) on two teenage male residents at the Orange County Juvenile Hall. The Orange County Juvenile Hall is a 434-bed facility for male and female juvenile law violators between the ages of 12 and 18. Residents are being detained pending Juvenile Court hearings, being tried as adults in Superior Courts, or who remain in custody by order of the Juvenile or Adult Superior Court. Credit: Spencer Grant/Alamy Stock Photo.

seem especially prominent. First, probation and parole work can be emotionally taxing. When PPOs become overinvolved in their clients' lives and problems, it can be hard to leave their problems at the office. Burnout and stress-related injuries can also be a problem for officers, especially after being directly exposed to traumatic events (including in their previous roles as COs). Some individuals are also affected by indirect exposure to traumatic events, and examples include hearing about these acts from family members, witnesses, or offenders, or viewing or reading about traumatic incidents in offender files.

A second negative aspect of community corrections is that workers seldom receive much positive feedback or recognition from the people they supervise or other personnel working within the criminal justice system. A third negative aspect of their work many officers soon come to realize is that some of their clients seem doomed to fail despite an officer's best intentions and efforts to help. This realization can slowly sap a worker's optimism and enthusiasm with which most officers start their careers. Ultimately, some of the individuals supervised by community COs are so damaged that it is almost impossible to respond to their unmet needs. These individuals might pose the greatest risk of recidivism.

Women Corrections Officers: A Cross-National Comparison

Nink (2008) describes women working in corrections as an asset to the profession that has been overlooked in the past. As noted earlier, the first women officers were matrons working with juveniles and female jail and prison inmates in the 1800s, but they have been making significant inroads and in some jails and state prison systems they account for more than one-half the correctional workforce. These women officers can be found in all job classifications and about one-fifth of state corrections systems are led by female executives (Collica-Cox & Schulz, 2018). Collica-Cox and Schultz (2020, p. 18) noted that these women executives reported they had to work harder than their male counterparts to earn their promotions, but despite that challenge, 94% of them recommended corrections as a career for women.

One question we were curious about was how the proportion of women COs in the United States is compared with other nations. Figure 7.2 shows a comparison of the proportion of women officers in the United States and selected European nations. Interestingly, the proportion of female officers in the United States (28%) is slightly higher than the average for all 28 European nations (25%

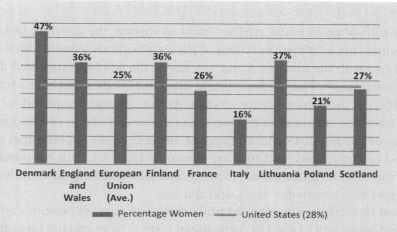

FIGURE 7.2

Proportion of Women Corrections Officers in the United States and Selected European Nations, 2016.

Sources: Bureau of Labor Statistics (2017); Eurostat (2019).

of officers in 2016) and while only 16% of officers in Italy are women almost one-half of Denmark's prison personnel are women. As a result, when it comes to women in corrections, they are more likely to be found in US facilities compared with jails and prisons in European nations.

What are the benefits of hiring more women? Whereas male COs are often described as being hyper-masculine, women bring a different set of skills and abilities to corrections work. Nink (2008) observes how women often have a different approach to problem-solving than men and they are more likely to consult and collaborate with others. Moreover, Zimmer (1987, p. 424) reminds us that it has long been recognized that women have a calming influence when it comes to resolving conflicts with inmates as they are less likely to encourage "ego showdowns" with inmates. Women can also be more successful in verbally de-escalating volatile situations. Mann (2016, para. 14) says that "a balanced approach with inmates can create a calm atmosphere within a housing unit. This type of presence and authority makes for establishing mutual respect and compliance from the inmate." As a result, nations employing higher proportions of female officers may benefit from more smoothly operating facilities.

ADMINISTRATIVE AND SUPPORT STAFF

About one-fifth of correctional staff are hired to support the activities of the officers. These personnel are employed in dozens of job classifications requiring little or no face-to-face contact with the inmates. Again, the size of the administrative staff depends on the correctional facility's population. A rural jail with 25 beds might have a single person who provides all the administrative services. As the size and complexity of the jail or prison increase, the organization requires a greater number of non-officer positions. The U.S. Bureau of Prisons (2019a) lists a range of different career opportunities in addition to COs and case managers, and they are shown in Table 7.1. This list provides only a basic overview and there are dozens of additional jobs requiring different levels of academic preparation, knowledge, skills, and abilities.

Regardless of their classification, administrative and support positions are critical to the effective operations of a jail or correctional system, from making sure inmates have enough food to ensuring officers are paid on time. Many individuals graduating from criminal justice programs overlook these types of opportunities when seeking careers and that is unfortunate as correctional agencies are looking for well-educated and motivated workers for these administrative roles. Ultimately, their work is important as it allows the correctional staff to focus on the primary correctional goals: to provide a safe and secure environment and prepare inmates for their eventual return to the community.

TABLE 7.1 Non-Correctional Officer Job Classifications, Bureau of Prisons

Inmate Custody and Programs	Health Services
• Chaplain	• Clinical Director
• Clinical Psychologist	• Dentists and Dental Hygienists
• Drug Treatment Specialist	• Physicians
• Recreation Specialist	• Health System Administrator
• Safety Compliance Specialist	• Medical Records Technician
• Teacher	• Nurse
• Training Instructor	• Pharmacist
Support and Administration	**Operational Readiness**
• Accountant	• Automotive mechanic
• Attorney	• Carpenter
• Contract Specialist	• Electrician
• Human Resource Specialist	• Food Service Supervisor
• Information Technology Specialist	• Painter
• Clerical Support	• Plumber

Source: Bureau of Prisons (2019a).

EMPLOYEE ETHICS

No discussion of correctional personnel would be complete without touching on the topic of ethics. Like every aspect of the criminal justice system, correctional employees regularly face ethical dilemmas. In fact, most of the chapter case studies so far have shown the challenges that COs must confront, as well as their failures to abide by ethical behavior or engage in criminal conduct. In this section we briefly address the key ethical issues in corrections.

Abuse of Authority

Much like police officers, correctional employees are required to use a great deal of discretion in the performance of their duties and inmates' powerlessness can lead to their abuse. COs can play favorites and decide to ignore misconduct by some inmates, or they can write reports on any number of disciplinary infractions for inmates they dislike. Ross (2013, p. 114) observes that COs can intentionally humiliate prisoners or make their lives more difficult by:

> confiscating inmates' possessions, destroying their belongings, playing with the thermostat settings, arbitrarily denying privileges, placing inmates who hate each other in the same cell, repeatedly tossing (searching) cells, repetitively strip-searching inmates, and frequently transferring inmates to different correctional jobs.

Likewise, probation and parole officers can keep their clients on a "short leash" and initiate technical violations for very minor breaches of their conditions of probation or release on parole such as being out after their curfew because they were required to work extra hours. Supervisors may review these decisions, but some decisions may be unknown to them. Although discretion is a value-neutral term, it can lead to discrimination and work to the detriment of some inmates or clients relative to others.

Misuse of Force

Although the misuse of authority occurs throughout corrections, the misuse of force is more likely to occur in institutional settings. COs are taught when and how to use force lawfully, and many police lockups, jails, and prisons use closed circuit television to record the activities occurring in most common areas. Moreover, the planned use of force, such as cell extractions of uncooperative inmates, is video recorded by officers. Nevertheless, prisons can cover large areas and not every spot is under camera surveillance. Therefore, it is possible that a CO or groups of these workers could physically abuse inmates identified as troublemakers.

Code of Silence

In every segment of the criminal justice system and most professional organizations—from air traffic controllers to college professors, there is a strong sentiment toward coworker loyalty, and this is ingrained in an organization's culture. In previous coursework, you have probably come across the term **code of silence**, which happens when police or correctional officers are reluctant to report the mistakes, unethical behavior, or misconduct of their colleagues. In some cases, officers are reluctant or refuse to fully cooperate in investigations of staff misconduct or lie when asked about incidents. This code exists, in some extent, in all correctional facilities and undermines the legitimate organizational mission.

Improper Relationships with Offenders

Both institutional and community corrections personnel can have improper relationships with inmates or clients. These relationships can involve exchanging favors (including sex), smuggling contraband in and out of jails and prisons, and accepting gratuities. A long-term problem for institutional corrections is inappropriate sexual relationships between correctional personnel and inmates, and because of the power differential between these parties even consensual relationships can result in criminal charges in most states. Despite the threat of criminal charges, these acts still happen. In an ongoing national study for the Bureau of Justice Statistics, Rantala (2018, p. 6) found that allegations of staff sexual misconduct increased by 191% between 2011 and 2015, although few of these acts were ever proven to have happened.

Deviance against the Institution

Ross (2013, p. 113) raises the issue of deviance against the institution, including the improper use of the agency's resources for personal benefit such as taking office supplies home or using the agency photocopier to duplicate personal documents. Officers have also used government credit cards to buy gas for their personal vehicles, while others steal food or other items of value from their institutions. Additional forms of deviance against the organization include officers who intentionally destroy agency equipment when it is old or does not work properly so it can be replaced with new equipment. Some correctional leaders also engage in deviance. As Sheets (2019, para. 9) reports, outgoing Alabama sheriffs who lost elections, "pocketed public money, fudged financial reports, wasted sheriff's funds and destroyed or stole public property."

Ross (2013) also identifies the abuse of sick time as deviance against the institution, and this activity is rampant in some organizations. Officers in some jails or prisons will engage in conspiracies with their coworkers to call in sick on specific days to generate opportunities for overtime work for their partners. Officers will also shirk their duties or sleep on the job, or surf the Internet on their work computers instead of doing their rounds.

Conflicting Loyalties

Among some professional employees, including psychologists and counselors, there can be conflicting loyalties. For example, professional codes of conduct generally dictate that in a counseling setting, staff must treat certain information the client discloses with confidentiality. However, concerns for jail and prison security might necessitate the disclosure even if the client-related information he or she believed had an expectation of confidentiality. In effect, employees in these positions may find themselves torn between competing sets of ethical mandates.

Deviance against Other Corrections Personnel

COs engage in discriminatory behavior against their coworkers, resulting in differential treatment of identifiable "classes" of staff members, including women, personnel from different racial or ethnic groups, and members of sexual minorities such as gay officers. Perhaps the most destructive acts of discrimination happening today are the acts of harassment occurring against female personnel described earlier. Acts of discrimination can also lead to unfair practices within the agency if some individuals are excluded from highly sought-after jobs. These acts may be so subtle that it is difficult for COs to launch a successful complaint or grievance of this misconduct.

Ross (2013) also identifies drinking on the job and other substance abuse, including the overuse of prescription drugs, as a deviant practice. Drug-impaired officers are unable to carry out their job duties, placing additional demands on their coworkers and reducing the institution's safety. Shepherd, Fritz, Hammer, Guros, and Meier (2018) found that alcohol use in COs was high and was associated with burnout. As a result, excessive drinking may be part of the occupational culture, and overlooked by the other officers.

Corruption

There is a general concern with corruption. We identify six types of corruption based on the work carried out by Banks (2020, pp. 217–221) and Goldsmith, Halsey, and de Vel-Palumbo (2018, pp. 12–15):

1. Theft of items from inmates.
2. Trafficking in contraband may involve correctional staff members at all levels, and the contraband items can include drugs, alcohol, money, cellular phones, and weapons.
3. Embezzlement is when prison employees (perhaps with inmate help) convert money or materials from government accounts and supplies to their own use.
4. Misuse of authority relates to accepting gratuities or favors from inmates or clients, and/or their families in violation of agency rules.

5. Misuse of prisoner information, which can range from workers who access information without a legitimate work-related need (e.g. an officer who "checks out" a famous serial killer's file information) to personnel who sell this information to others.

6. "Procurement corruption concerns the misuse of one's position to engage in activities such as bribery, extortion, receipt of kickbacks, theft, fraud, abuse of discretion, [and] exploitation of conflicts of interests" (Goldsmith et al., 2018, p. 14).

The key issue underlying these different forms of corruption is that most inmates are powerless and they can be exploited by corrupt correctional personnel for their personal gain. While it is relatively easy to describe correctional corruption, like many of the problems identified in this book, it has proven very difficult to eliminate.

A CLOSER LOOK

The American Correctional Association Code of Ethics

COs are often portrayed in films and television as "brutal, corrupt, ignorant bullies who take advantage of unfortunate inmates with no civil rights" (Pearson, 2010, para. 2). As the public has very little exposure to what happens in jails and prisons, they are more likely to believe those stereotypes are accurate. Corrections professionals have been working for decades to overcome those negative labels and most jails and departments of corrections send messages to the public that they are professionals doing difficult jobs. The ACA has worked to change the public's image of COs and the practice of corrections since it was founded—as the National Prison Association—in 1870. One expectation for COs is that they engage in ethical behavior and treat inmates and their family members in a respectful, just and fair manner. The following section that defines the ethical principles of the ACA (2020) was taken from their website:

- Members shall respect and protect the civil and legal rights of all individuals.
- Members shall treat every professional situation with concern for the welfare of the individuals involved and with no intent to personal gain.
- Members shall maintain relationships with colleagues to promote mutual respect within the profession and improve the quality of service.
- Members shall respect the importance of all disciplines within the criminal justice system and work to improve cooperation with each segment.
- Members shall honor the public's right to information and share information with the public to the extent permitted by law subject to the individual's right to privacy.

- Members shall respect and protect the right of the public to be safeguarded from criminal activity.
- Members shall refrain from using their positions to secure personal privileges or advantages.
- Members shall refrain from allowing personal interest to impair objectivity in the performance of duty while acting in an official capacity.
- Members shall refrain from entering into any formal or informal activity or agreement which presents a conflict of interest or is inconsistent with the conscientious performance of duties.
- Members shall refrain from accepting any gifts, services, or favors that is or appears to be improper or implies an obligation inconsistent with the free and objective exercise of professional duties.
- Members shall report to appropriate authorities any corrupt or unethical behaviors in which there is sufficient evidence to justify review.
- Members shall refrain from discrimination against any individual because of race, gender, creed, national origin, religious orientation, age, disability, or any other type of prohibited discrimination.
- Members shall preserve the integrity of private information; they shall refrain from seeking information on individuals beyond that which is necessary to implement responsibilities and perform their duties; members shall refrain from revealing non-public information unless expressly authorized to do.
- Members shall make all appointments, promotions, and dismissals in accordance with established civil service rules, applicable contract agreements, and individual merit, rather than furtherance of personal interests.
- Members shall respect, promote, and contribute to a workplace that is safe, healthy, and free of harassment in any form.

Organizational Culture and Ethical Officer Behavior

Many of the issues related to correctional personnel misconduct are associated with the culture of the jail, prison, or community-based agency. What is an agency or **organizational culture**? Writing about corrections, Smith and Yarussi (2007, p. 10) observe that: "Agency culture is an organization's sum of attitudes, values, norms, beliefs, prejudices, history, personality and ethics of staff—both past and present. It is the organization's character and the way it does business." In correctional agencies, there are often two types of culture:

- *Ideal*: the values held in principle such as an organization's mission statement, policies and procedures, formal incentives and sanctions.
- *Real*: the way an agency actually works, the hidden, informal chain of command, how things get done, and who has the power and leadership (Smith & Yarussi, 2007, p. 10).

Dysfunctional correctional organizations often have high occurrences of unethical behaviors and employees may fear being shunned or retaliated against when they are contemplating reporting the misconduct of others. In these situations, many employees simply say nothing, like the example from the Baltimore City Detention Center that starts Chapter 5. These staff members may rationalize their lack of action with the qualifier: "At least I'm not doing anything illegal or unethical."

Correctional organizations with a healthy workplace culture are more positive places to work. Mei, Iannacchione, Stohr, Hemmens, Hudson, and Collins (2017, p. 249) identified the following characteristics of correctional workplaces with a supportive culture:

> organizational fairness and supervision, the existence of caring supervisors, an employee-friendly culture, letting the employees know that they are responsible for their behavior, providing staff with opportunities to have operational input into the organization and their work, and rewarding those who do the job well.

In correctional agencies with a favorable workplace culture the staff members are more content, less stressed out, are more satisfied and committed to their work, and less likely to quit. Mei and colleagues (2017) say that most of these factors relate to good leadership.

There are also examples of organizational failures that require significant reform. A number of correctional personnel have raised issues about the inappropriate treatment of juveniles, jail inmates, immigration detainees or prisoners. Two physicians who were responsible for overseeing the conditions of detention for the children of immigrant detainees, for example, spoke out against the care these children received in 2016 and 2017 (Shoichet & Bracho-Sanchez, 2019). While these doctors received support from their professional associations for their actions, some COs have been fired for identifying shortcomings or problems in their jails or prison systems. Other officers keep their jobs but may be shunned by their supervisors and coworkers as the organizational culture conveys the message that being a "rat" or "snitch" is disloyal. One of the challenges for correctional administrators is changing the workplace culture as both the officers and inmates are sometimes very resistant to changes.

In concluding this section on employee ethics, we want to emphasize two points. First, as should be apparent from the ACA Code of Ethics, some issues are distinct to certain employee or supervisory groups, and others cut across all ranks and types of agencies. Second, research with jail and prison employees indicates that most at least overtly express a strong ethical orientation (Stohr, Hemmens, Kifer, & Schoeler, 2000) and experience teaches us that many correctional employees act in a manner consistent with their agency's stated mission. However, a few act unethically or illegally and their behavior reflects on others who work in the same profession.

WELL-BEING AND CORRECTIONS WORK

Successful correctional administrators are concerned that the officers working within their facilities are mentally and physically healthy. Healthy, professional, and well-motivated officers are better able to manage their workloads and are less likely to engage in misconduct or quit. Facilities with a higher proportion of healthy officers seem to run better and keeping valued employees on the payroll is important to reduce disruption to the correctional facility when good officers leave their jobs. Every CO that quits has to be replaced, requiring a considerable investment in recruiting and training new officers.

Few appreciate the challenges of correctional work. Working conditions can be stressful as many correctional facilities are overcrowded, understaffed, and underfunded. Inmates can be manipulative and disrespectful and some may act violently and unpredictably. These factors can place great demands on the employees and these stressors are intensified in jails and prisons with poor leadership. In this section we identify the biggest challenges that COs face in terms of their well-being or wellness. Like many of the issues raised in the previous chapters, these factors are often linked together and it is difficult to disentangle one of these issues from the others. A CO who is assaulted, for example, might go on to experience post-traumatic stress disorder (PTSD), which may, in turn, have a serious impact on his or her physical wellness.

Inmate-on-Officer Assaults

In the absence of reliable nationwide information, it is difficult to describe accurately the number of officers assaulted every year by jail or prison inmates. The U.S. Bureau of Prisons (2019b) reports the monthly number of serious assaults on staff, and these data show there was an average of about one serious assault per month for every 50,000 inmates between 2015 and 2019. These assaults are unlikely to happen in low-security facilities, as most occur in the medium- and high-security institutions. Consequently, COs in some maximum-security facilities express fear of being injured on the job. One of their biggest worries is being caught in a riot, although they also expressed concern about the presence of contraband, working with disruptive inmates and gang members (Ferdik, 2016). These feelings of fear and dread about their workplace may contribute to stress that results in psychological disorders (see below).

A review of prison data shows that most of the injuries occurring in inmate-on-officer assaults are minor. The New York State Department of Corrections and Community

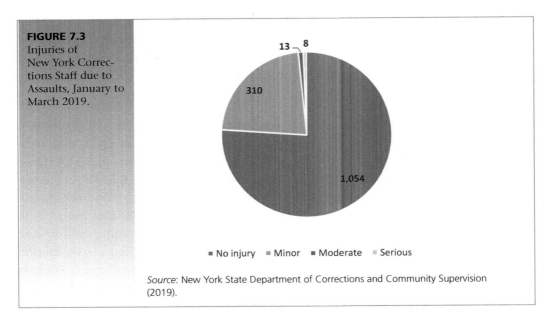

FIGURE 7.3
Injuries of
New York Correc-
tions Staff due to
Assaults, January to
March 2019.

310

13 — 8

1,054

■ No injury   ■ Minor   ■ Moderate   ■ Serious

Source: New York State Department of Corrections and Community Supervision (2019).

Supervision (2019, p. 2) reveals that of the 1,385 staff assaults that happened from January to March 2019, over three-quarters resulted in no injury. Of the remaining attacks, there were 13 moderate injuries (such as lacerations, concussions, serious sprains, or muscle damage) and eight serious injuries requiring a hospital visit but were not considered life-threatening. A break-down of these different injuries is shown in Figure 7.3.

A review of Bureau of Labor Statistics (2019b) reports shows that an average of nine COs were killed on the job every year between 2009 and 2017. That works out to a fatality rate of two per 100,000 officers, which is about one-third of the murder rate for the general population (5.3 murders per 100,000 population; see Federal Bureau of Investigation, 2018). It is important to acknowledge, however, that these deaths are from all causes including officers killed in traffic accidents and overexertion. Thus, although COs work with the most dangerous people in America, the likelihood of being seriously injured because of an assault, or killed, is very low, and law enforcement officers in the community are at a higher risk of serious injury or death while at work.

Despite the fact that officers might be at a relatively low risk of being seriously injured or killed on the job in an assault, COs perceive their work as dangerous. Worley, Barua Worley, and Hsu (2018, p. 338) asked officers about their risks of injury on the job. There was strong agreement they worked in a more dangerous job than other careers and their risks of being hurt were high. Inconsistent with those perceptions, however, these officers report that few people they worked with were actually hurt on the job. Feelings that one's workplace is dangerous can increase an officer's fear of being victimized. Gordon and Baker (2017, p. 476) found that non-White male officers who were frustrated with the organization, had less education, and worked in higher security units with a higher inmate-to-staff ratio were more fearful. Their study also reveals that fear is higher for minority female officers working on male units in dysfunctional facilities. It is important for researchers to look into these issues as fearful officers may be less effective in their duties and long-term feelings of fear are stressful and contribute to psychological problems such as anxiety and depression.

Psychological Injuries

Many injuries COs experience are invisible and related to witnessing acts of violence or self-harm and suicide; these experiences are worsened by the everyday stress associated with correctional work. Brower (2013, p. 1) notes that COs experience four different types of stressors, including:

- *Inmate-related*: Threat of violence/injury, having to confront gang activities, working in overcrowded facilities, responding to inmates with mental illness and other emotional problems, witnessing and having to respond to incidents of inmate violence (including physical and sexual assaults), and self-harm and/or suicide. Inmates can also engage in harassing, threatening, and disrespectful behavior and this takes an emotional toll on workers who are greatly outnumbered. For every officer, for example, there are often 50–100 inmates. Inmates are also manipulative and some actively try to compromise employees in order to get them to ignore their criminal behavior within the facility or smuggle in contraband. Inmates are generally unappreciative or uncooperative of a CO's efforts to provide a safe and stable environment.
- *Occupational-related*: In many respects, officers are as confined as the inmates they supervise. They are locked in a closed and austere environment for 8–12 hours. With respect to their surroundings, facilities are often poorly lit and the background noise from the heating and ventilation systems can be taxing over the long term. Whether working in a jail or prison, officers are continually exposed to the inmate subculture—including gang attitudes and behaviors. COs also experience role ambiguity, such as the priorities placed on security and rehabilitation, abiding by a macho "code of silence" that rejects getting help for stress-related illnesses, and having to be hyper-vigilant (e.g. being constantly aware of their surroundings).
- *Organizational-related stressors*: Most COs express frustration about their employer as well as their supervisors and managers, whether those perceptions are accurate or not. Research shows that working in a poorly led or mismanaged and understaffed facility that has high levels of conflict is stressful. It is not surprising that officers also find

it irritating working in facilities where they have little input into decision-making, or don't receive feedback on their job performance, or are forced to work with inadequate or poorly operating equipment. Low pay, being required to work overtime shifts, and shiftwork also contribute to stressful working conditions.

- *Psycho-social stressors*: These are individual-level factors such as an officer's fear of workplace violence or being anxious about going to work. Not all officers experience these factors in the same way and Brower (2013) explains that conflict with an inmate may produce dread in one officer and excitement in another. Mistrust of one's coworkers also contributes to workplace stress (Worley et al., 2018). Some of these stressors are related to factors outside the workplace. For example, a lack of family support, such as work/family conflict, can reduce their effectiveness in the workplace. The presentation of COs in the entertainment media (such as programs like *Orange Is the New Black*) can also influence how they are perceived by friends and family members.

Brower (2013) observes that wardens and other correctional administrators are placed in stressful roles and female officers are sometimes harassed by inmates and prison staff. Most administrators are on-call and expected to respond to emergencies around the clock. Where COs are responsible for confronting inmates, jail and prison administrators are responsible for confronting officer misconduct, including sanctioning them. Wardens, their deputies, and other managers may become the focal point for officer complaints over which they might have little control such as facility overcrowding or requiring them to work overtime as the state has not approved hiring additional officers.

PHOTO 7.5
A Georgia prison tower officer holds his weapon at the ready. The strain of constantly watching for violent inmate misbehavior within a prison or attempted escapes, and being ready to use deadly force, can be the source of much stress in a correctional officer's life. Credit: Ken Hawkins/Alamy Stock Photo.

Females have to confront the same challenges as male officers, but as described earlier some must also contend with harassment from the inmates they supervise and their coworkers. Responding to those acts can be humiliating, stressful, and demoralizing. Long-term exposure to these incidents can have a corrosive effect on an individual's well-being. Many individuals experiencing long-term harassment suffer in silence because they might have few other career options and cannot afford to quit or transfer to a job with less salary and benefits.

COs are prone to becoming cynical and this trait is common to front-line workers in policing, courts, and corrections. Officers are continually exposed to the inmate subculture which is often antisocial and promotes criminogenic thinking. Gangs are very prevalent in some jails and prisons, and they play a significant role in the informal operations of some facilities (Pyrooz & Decker, 2019; Skarbek, 2014). As a result, inmates may attempt to manipulate officers into crossing some type of boundary, such as a prison rule, in order to compromise them. If the officer succumbs to breaking minor rules the inmates will threaten to report the officer unless they commit a more serious boundary violation (Elliot & Verdeyen, 2002).

There are some long-term outcomes of working in stressful workplaces and a number of psychological disorders can form after COs witness or are exposed to traumatic incidents such as assaults or acts of self-harm and suicide. A study of California COs, for example, reveals they were exposed to violence at almost the same rates as military veterans (Lerman, 2017). As a result of that exposure Carleton and colleagues (2018, p. 59) found that correctional personnel had higher rates of PTSD, depression, anxiety, social anxiety, panic disorder, and alcohol use than police officers, paramedics, or firefighters. In order to cope with these psychological affects, some COs use alcohol and prescription drugs to self-medicate. Alcohol or drug use, however, can worsen feelings of anxiety or depression.

High rates of depression are associated with self-destructive behaviors. The suicide rates for COs are higher than the general population and women officers were at double the risk as the average for all other occupations (Violanti, 2017, p. 61). The problem of suicide is severe in some jails and correctional systems. In the California Department of Corrections and Rehabilitation, for example, there were 96 confirmed or suspected suicides between 1999 and 2015 (Thompson, 2018a, para. 3) and during that time one officer was killed on the job due to an inmate-on-officer assault (Officer Down Memorial Page, 2019). The topic of CO suicide has been a taboo subject that was seldom acknowledged, but a growing number of jails and prison systems are trying to reduce these deaths by openly talking about the issue and encouraging healthier lifestyles. An important first step in solving any health-related problem that is related to the workplace is to recognize the risks and work toward a better work-life balance.

Physical Well-Being

Like other workplaces, there are some very unhealthy as well as very physically fit officers. Fit officers are often better able to resist psychological problems than officers who have unhealthy lifestyles. However, there are a number of factors that work against CO wellness. Not only is their work environment stressful but also sleep problems and fatigue associated with shift work and a poor diet can have long-term health consequences (Ferdik & Smith, 2017). The corrections work environment is not conducive to healthy living such as standing on concrete floors for their entire shift. As a result, some researchers found that COs have a shorter lifespan than members of the general public although that research has produced conflicting results.

When it comes to officer fitness Ferdik and Smith (2017, p. 13) observe that:

> COs also disproportionately experience higher rates of physical health problems such as chronic neck, back and knee injuries; heart disease; diabetes; high cholesterol; and hypertension, compared with crisis counselors and law enforcement personnel. [And that] Much of this can be attributed to the demanding nature of this line of work, including prolonged work hours, irregular sleep patterns due to constantly changing shift assignments, and being tasked with extra duties.

As a result a large proportion of supervisors in correctional facilities were overweight, sleep deprived, ate unhealthy diets, and were physically inactive (Buden et al., 2016). Lerman's (2017, p. 4) study of California officers found that a large proportion of them who did not feel safe at work reported suffering from "headaches, digestive issues, high blood pressure, diabetes, and heart disease."

Jail inmates and state or federal prisoners are very unhealthy populations and a high proportion of them have communicable diseases (Maruschak, Berzofsky, & Unangst, 2015; Maruschak & Bronson, 2017). As a result, COs are exposed to infectious diseases from this group given the close confinement of correctional facilities, and some died after exposure to the COVID-19 virus (Marcius, 2020). In addition, officers encounter used syringes or life-threatening drugs such as fentanyl that have been smuggled into their facilities. Some prisoners also engage in "gassing" COs by throwing their bodily fluids at them.

COs are at high risk of non-fatal injuries. The Bureau of Labor Statistics (2019b) reports that in 2017, 98 individuals for every 10,000 workers were injured on the job. The rate for COs, by contrast—418 for every 10,000 workers—was more than four times higher. The number of COs injured on the job (and involving more than one day away from work) is shown in Figure 7.4. Although COs often express concern about being injured on the job, the data show these injuries are decreasing at the national level.

A review by the Bureau of Labor Statistics (2019b) shows that of the 15,490 officers who lost at least one day for a job-related injury in 2017, less than half of these injuries (45%) were the result of an assault, which was followed by overexertion (22%) and slips or falls (18%). The rest were from all other causes (including traffic collisions). When it came to time away from work for these injured COs, the median time was 11 days (compared with nine days for workers from all other industries). Of all the COs injured at work, about one-third were away from their jobs for 31 or more days, suggesting they received very serious injuries.

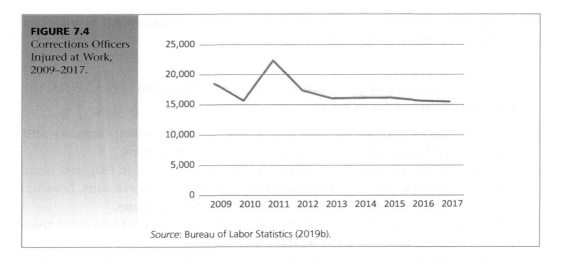

FIGURE 7.4
Corrections Officers Injured at Work, 2009–2017.

Source: Bureau of Labor Statistics (2019b).

Increasing Officer Well-Being

Many COs are reluctant to seek help for their health-related problems as admitting one has a problem runs against the officer's masculine personality. There are a number of standard approaches that correctional agencies use to respond to a staff member who is having problems or ways to enhance their well-being. The primary response is to use Employee Assistance Plans (EAP), which are employer-funded services that provide psychological supports for correctional personnel. These initiatives are often delivered by service providers contracted by the agency. Due to their expense, these services may be more likely to be offered by state governments and less available for jail personnel or workers in private corrections. One of the challenges of EAP programs is that many officers do not trust that the information they provide to these programs will be held in confidence. Lerman's (2017) study of California officers, for example, found that less than one-in-five officers had used EAP programs and officers expressed concern that participating in these programs would result in negative consequences including being seen as weak by their coworkers or losing their job.

Agencies are taking steps to make their workplaces healthier. New York State, for example, has established a division for Chaplaincy and Staff Wellness and in 2019 they opened an employee wellness center. Described as a place of respite, the facility "offers employees the opportunity to de-stress through exercise, meditation, religious worship, and counseling services" (Johnson, 2019, para. 1). A growing number of jails and prison systems are now providing training for COs to help them recognize the health-related risks of their work and to develop lifestyle changes that will increase their physical and mental health. Ultimately, a well-run correctional organization will put these programs in place to reduce the harms to their employees. One of the challenges for these organizations is that researchers have not yet identified any single strategy that has proven effective in increasing CO well-being (Evers, Ogloff, Trounson, & Pfeifer, 2020).

SUMMARY

In this chapter we examined the working environment of the world of corrections. The key points of interest are the following:

- Correctional personnel are employed in a diverse range of positions working with local, state, and federal governments, as well as private corporations.
- Institutional corrections typically have one employment entry point: COs, and many counselor positions are filled by experienced COs. A growing number of states, however, are requiring that counselor positions are filled by university graduates.
- The hiring process for COs is often lengthy given the background checks and screening that has to be done before a cadet starts their training.
- Salaries and benefits for COs vary across the country and working for the Bureau of Prisons or state department of corrections often pay better than in jails or privately owned facilities.
- Secure facilities employ people to provide rehabilitative and educational services, as well as dozens of administrative careers that have few or no interactions with inmates.
- Some COs engage in misconduct and there is a movement to improve the ethical behavior of correctional personnel.
- Among the greatest concerns expressed by many prospective employees is an injury or death on the job, but the greatest risks are related to managing job-related stress and their psychological well-being.
- More correctional agencies are focusing on improving the work-life balance and well-being of correctional and probation/parole officers.

Much is expected of the women and men working in community and institutional corrections. Although their efforts are seldom formally recognized by the public, these officers receive support and recognition from their peers.

KEY TERMS

- abuse of authority
- American Correctional Association (ACA)
- chain of command
- clinical psychologist
- code of silence
- conflicting loyalties
- corrections emergency response team (CERT)
- corruption

- deviance against the institution
- improper relationships with offenders
- job shadowing
- misuse of force

- National Association of Wardens and Superintendents
- organizational culture
- psychological injuries
- special operations response team (SORT)

THINKING ABOUT CORRECTIONAL POLICIES AND PRACTICES: WRITING ASSIGNMENTS

1. Prepare a one-page summary for a correctional administrator addressing the issue of whether a college degree should be required for a position as a corrections officer in a jail or prison. Does a degree really make a difference? What about the applicant's major in college? Carefully explain and be prepared to defend your position.
2. This exercise involves two parts: First interview someone in your community who currently works in some capacity in corrections. Think about a series of five to six questions that you want to ask before you schedule your interview. After the interviews, write a summary of the information you gathered and share it with the other members of your class.
3. Prepare a one-page paper that describes two actions corrections officers can take to minimize the likelihood of a successful lawsuit will be brought against them. Can you think of other preventative actions? Explain.
4. In a two-page paper describe the steps individuals must take to obtain a job in a state prison and explain why the hiring process takes so long to complete.
5. Write a one-page paper describing the steps you would take to reduce the harassment of women COs in your state's prison system.

CRITICAL REVIEW QUESTIONS

1. Whose salaries are typically higher, jail personnel or prison correctional officers? If there is a pay disparity between these groups, why does it exist?
2. Describe the positive and negative aspects of working in a CO position.
3. Why are front-line corrections personnel in the private sector paid less money? What are the implications of paying low salaries for recruiting and retaining highly motivated, ethical, and competent personnel?

4. What is the purpose of the background check for employment in corrections? Why is a polygraph or drug test required? What kinds of activities might disqualify a person from a correctional career?

5. You are the warden of a 1,000-bed medium security prison. At a staff meeting, someone raises the issue of salaries. A representative from the state personnel office mentions that your director of corrections is considering a plan to pay your clinical psychologists more than you make: What is your reaction?

6. What is the most damaging type of officer misconduct? Why did you select that type?

7. What are the most significant threats to employee wellness? Explain your answer.

8. How does the correctional officer work culture shape ethical behaviors?

9. Suppose you have a strong rehabilitative orientation. Select one of the following job settings as a preferred place to work: community corrections, jails, or prison.

10. What are the challenges female COs confront on the job?

REFERENCES

American Correctional Association. (2020). *ACA code of ethics (1994)*. Retrieved from http://www.aca.org/ACA_Prod_IMIS/ACA_Member/About_Us/Code_of_Ethics/ACA_Member/AboutUs/Code_of_Ethics.aspx?hkey=61577ed2-c0c3-4529-bc01-36a248f79eba

Banks, C. (2020). *Criminal justice ethics, 5th edition*. Los Angeles: Sage.

Bauer, S. (2019). *American prison: A reporter's undercover journey into the business of punishment*. New York: Penguin Random House.

Bierie, D. M., & Mann, R. E. (2017). The history and future of prison psychology. *Psychology, Public Policy, and Law, 23*(4), 478–489.

Blakinger, K. (2018, May 30). Still a 'boys club': Texas prison system faces allegations of harassment, discrimination. *Houston Chronicle*. Retrieved from https://www.houstonchronicle.com/news/houston-texas/houston/article/Still-a-boys-club-Texas-prison-system-12954409.php#photo-1102028

Bloomberg. (2019). Company overview of *CoreCivic*. Retrieved from https://www.bloomberg.com/research/stocks/private/people.asp?privcapId=166457

Bronson, J., & Carson, E. A. (2019). *Prisoners in 2017*. Washington, DC: Bureau of Justice Statistics.

Broward College. (2019). *Institute of public safety. Corrections officer academy basic recruit training*. Retrieved from http://www.broward.edu/academics/programs/Program%20Sheet%20Library/5270.pdf

Brower, J. (2013). *Correctional officer wellness and safety literature review*. Washington, DC: U.S. Department of Justice.

Buche, J., Gaiser, M., Rittman, D., & Beck, A. J. (2018). *Characteristics of the behavioral health workforce in correctional facilities*. Ann Arbor, MI: Behavioral health workforce research center.

Buden, J. C., Dugan, A. G., Namazi, S., Huedo-Medina, T. B., Cherniack, M. G., & Faghri, P. D. (2016). Work characteristics as predictors of correctional supervisors' health outcomes. *Journal of Occupational and Environmental Medicine, 58*(9), 325–334.

Bureau of Labor Statistics. (2017). *Women in the labor force: A databook (Table 11)*. Retrieved from https://www.bls.gov/opub/reports/womens-databook/2017/home.htm

Bureau of Labor Statistics. (2019a). *Correctional officers and bailiffs*. Retrieved from https://www.bls.gov/ooh/Protective-Service/Correctional-officers.htm#tab-2

Bureau of Labor Statistics. (2019b). *Occupational injuries/illnesses and fatal injuries*. Retrieved from https://www.bls.gov/iif/

Burton, A. L., Lux, J. L., Cullen, F. T., Miller, W. T., & Burton, V. S. (2018). Creating a model correctional officer training academy: Implications from a national survey. *Federal Probation, 81*(1), 26–36.

Calams, S. (2020, March 18). 5 things jails, prisons can do to get ahead of COVID-19. *Correctionsone.com*. Retrieved from https://www.correctionsone.com/products/infection-control/articles/5-things-jails-prisons-can-do-to-get-ahead-of-covid-19-SW8g1FcIiKxphylp/

Carleton, R. N., Afifi, T. O., Turner, S., Taillieu, T., Duranceau, S.,...Asmundson, G. J. G.. (2018). Mental disorder symptoms among public safety personnel in Canada. *Canadian Journal of Psychiatry, 63*(1), 54–64. doi: 10.1177/0706743717723825

Carter, T. J. (2018). My sexual harassers were behind bars. I was their guard. *The Marshall Project*. Retrieved from https://www.themarshallproject.org/2018/02/08/my-sexual-harassers-were-behind-bars-i-was-their-guard?utm_medium=email&utm_campaign=newsletter&utm_source=opening-statement&utm_term=newsletter-20180209-950

Coleman, E. (2018, Oct. 29). Prisons are using video visitation as punishment. *Slate*. Retrieved from https://slate.com/technology/2018/10/video-visitation-prison-inmates-punishment.html

Collica-Cox, K., & Schulz, D. M. (2018). Of all the joints, she walks into this one: Career motivations of women corrections executives. *The Prison Journal, 98*(5), 604–629.

Collica-Coz, K. & Schulz, D. M. (2020). A token for your thoughts? Perceptions of tokenism among female corrections executives. *Criminal Justice Review*. Available online ahead of print at: doi 10.1177/0734016820902259.

CorrectionalOfficer.Org (2019). *Correctional officer duties*. Retrieved from https://www.correctionalofficer.org/faq/correctional-officer-job-description

Coyne, C. (2018, April 27). County jailers underpaid for years, feds investigating. *Weatherford Democrat*. Retrieved from https://www.weatherforddemocrat.com/news/local_news/county-jailers-underpaid-for-years-feds-investigating/article_bfcbdd8e-1047-5fbc-ad45-b9850b9a21e0.html

Dennison, M. (2019, September 24). Former state corrections employee sues, alleging sexual harassment by department director. *KPAX*. Retrieved from https://www.kpax.com/news/montana-news/former-state-corrections-employee-sues-alleging-sexual-harassment-by-department-director

Dickerson, C. (2018, Nov. 17). Hazing, humiliation, terror: Working while female while in federal prison. *New York Times*. Retrieved from https://www.nytimes.com/2018/11/17/us/prison-sexual-harassment-women.html

Elliot, B., & Verdeyen, V. (2002). *Game over: Strategies for redirecting inmate deception*. Alexandria, VA: American Correctional Association.

Eurostat. (2019). *Personnel in adult prisons (share of women), average 2014–2016*. Retrieved from https://ec.europa.eu/eurostat/statistics-explained/index.php?title=File:Personnel_in_adult_prisons_(share_of_women),_average_2014_-_2016.png

Evers, T. J., Ogloff, J. R. P., Trounson, J. S., & Pfeifer, J. E. (2020). Well-being interventions for correctional officers in a prison setting: A review and meta-analysis. *Criminal Justice and Behavior, 47*(1), 3–21.

Federal Bureau of Investigation. (2018). *Crime in the United States, 2017*. Washington, DC: Author.

Ferdik, F. V. (2016). An investigation into the risk perceptions held my maximum security correctional officers. *Psychology, Crime, & Law, 22*(9), 832–857.

Ferdik, F. V., & Smith, H. (2017). *Correctional officer safety and wellness literature synthesis*. Washington, DC: National Institute of Justice.

Georgia Public Safety Training Center. (2020). *Basic jail officer training program*. Retrieved from https://www.gpstc.org/about-gpstc/training-divisions/basic-training-division/basic-jail-officer-training/

Goldsmith, A., Halsey, M., & de Vel-Palumbo, M. (2018). *Literature review: Correctional corruption*. Adelaide: Flinders University Center for Crime Policy & Research.

Gordon, J., & Baker, T., (2017). Examining correctional officers' fear of victimization by inmates: The influence of fear facilitators and fear inhibitors. *Criminal Justice Policy Review, 28*(5), 462–487.

Hsieh, M., Hafoka, M., Woo, Y., van Wormer, J., Stohr, M. K., & Hemmens, C. (2015). Probation officer roles: A statutory analysis. *Federal Probation, 79*(3), 20–37.

Idaho Department of Corrections. (undated). *Field training officer manual for corrections officers*. Retrieved from https://www.post.idaho.gov/Forms/documents/COFTO_Manual.pdf

Indiana Department of Corrections. (2019). *Job shadowing*. Retrieved from https://www.in.gov/idoc/2820.htm

Jackson, A. (2019, May 27). After deadly riot, SC prison officials hope program can reform gang members behind bars. *The Post and Courier*. Retrieved from https://www.postandcourier.com/news/after-deadly-riot-sc-prison-officials-hope-program-can-reform/article_e4311b56-710d-11e9-8f12-4b841c71f619.html?utm_source=The+Marshall+Project+Newsletter&utm_campaign=1df8cce5f6-EMAIL_CAMPAIGN_2019_05_30_11_27&utm_medium=email&utm_term=0_5e02cdad9d-1df8cce5f6-174432429

Johnson, L. (2019, May 7). NYC DOC's employee wellness center is an investment in officer well-being. *Correctionsone.com*. Retrieved from https://www.correctionsone.com/ptsd/articles/482609187-NYC-DOCs-employee-wellness-center-is-an-investment-in-officer-well-being/

Jones, S. J., Cathcart, K., & Cooksey, S. (2019). Management of the sexually abusive/harassing actions of inmates directed towards correctional staff: The impact of policy and training upon exposure and the corrections workplace culture. *Women & Criminal Justice*. Published online ahead of print at: doi:10.1080/08974454.2019.1697793

Kaeble, D. (2018). *Probation and parole in the United States, 2016*. Washington, DC: Bureau of Justice Statistics.

Kowalski, M. A. (2020). Hiring and training requirements for correctional officers: A statutory analysis. *The Prison Journal, 100*(1), 98–125.

Lazzaretto-Green, D., Austin, W., Goble, E., Buys, L., Gorman, T., & Rankel, M. (2011). Walking a fine line: Forensic mental health practitioners' experience of working with correctional officers. *Journal of Forensic Nursing, 7*(2), 109–119.

Lerman, A. E. (2017). *Officer health and wellness: Results from the California correctional officer survey*. Berkeley: University of California.

Mann, M. (2016). Women in corrections face a number of obstacles. *CorrectionsOne.com*. Retrieved from https://www.correctionsone.com/women-in-corrections/articles/210396187-Women-in-corrections-face-a-number-of-obstacles/

Marcius, C. R. (2020, March 16). 'One of the best men on earth': Coronavirus kills NYC correction department official. *New York Daily News*. Retrieved from https://www.nydailynews.com/coronavirus/ny-coronavirus-department-correction-employee-dies-from-coronavirus-20200316-akeai6gop5alledhzhi7u3pivm-story.html

Maruschak, L. M., Berzofsky, M., & Unangst, J. (2015). *Medical problems of state and federal prisoners and jail inmates, 2011–12*. Washington, DC: Bureau of Justice Statistics.

Maruschak, L. M., & Bronson, J. (2017). *HIV in prisons, 2015 – Statistical tables*. Washington, DC: Bureau of Justice Statistics.

Mei, X., Iannacchione, B., Stohr, M. K., Hemmens, C., Hudson, M., & Collins, P. A. (2017). Confirmatory analysis of an organizational culture instrument for corrections. *The Prison Journal, 97*(2), 247–269.

Missouri Office of Administration, Division of Personnel. (2016). *Corrections case manager 1*. Retrieved from https://oa.mo.gov/personnel/classification-specifications/5116#class-spec-compact2

Montana Department of Labor and Industry. (2018). *Prevailing wage rates for nonconstruction services 2019*. Retrieved from http://erd.dli.mt.gov/Portals/54/Documents/Labor-Standards/5bedfad55f005-NCS%20Prelim%202019.pdf?ver=2018-11-15-164432-883

New Jersey Department of Corrections. (2019). *Careers in corrections*. Retrieved from https://www.state.nj.us/corrections/pages/careers2.shtml

New York State Department of Corrections and Community Supervision. (2019). *DOCCS fact sheet, June 1, 2019*. Albany, NY: Author. Retrieved from https://doccs.ny.gov/FactSheets/PDF/DOCCS%20Fact%20Sheet%20March%202019.pdf

Nink, C. (2008). *Women professionals in corrections: A growing asset*. Centerville, UT: MTC Institute.

Officer Down Memorial Page. (2019). *California department of corrections and rehabilitation*. Retrieved from https://www.odmp.org/agency/499-california-department-of-corrections-and-rehabilitation-california

Pyrooz, D. C., & Decker, S. H. (2019). *Competing for control: Gangs and the social order of prisons*. New York: Cambridge University Press.

Rantala, R. R. (2018). *Sexual victimization reported by adult correctional authorities, 2012–2015*. Washington, DC: Bureau of Justice Statistics.

Reilly, S. (2018, April 30). Bloodied bodies stacked in a prison yard: What happens when states slash prison spending. *USA Today*. Retrieved from https://www.usatoday.com/story/news/2018/04/30/prison-riots-and-killings-rising-states-slash-budgets-guards/545299002/

Ross, J. I. (2012). Debunking the myths of American corrections: An exploratory analysis. *Critical Criminology, 20*, 409–427.

Ross, J. I. (2013). Deconstructing correctional officer deviance: Toward typologies of actions and controls. *Criminal Justice Review, 38*(1), 110–126.

Santo, A. (2017). The unique sexual harassment problem female prison workers face. *The Marshall Project*. Retrieved from https://www.themarshallproject.org/2017/11/09/the-unique-sexual-harassment-problem-female-prison-workers-face?utm_medium=email&utm_campaign=newsletter&utm_source=opening-statement&utm_term=newsletter-20171110-889

Sheets, C. (2019, June 12). Wasted funds, destroyed property: How sheriffs undermined their successors after losing reelection. *Propublica*. Retrieved from https://www.propublica.org/article/alabama-sheriffs-undermine-successors-after-losing-reelection?utm_source=The+Appeal&utm_campaign=fc4408e4aa-EMAIL_CAMPAIGN_2018_08_09_04_14_COPY_01&utm_medium=email&utm_term=0_72df992d84-fc4408e4aa-58408803

Shepherd, B. R., Fritz, C., Hammer, L. B., Guros, F., & Meier, D. (2018). Emotional demands and alcohol use in corrections: A moderated mediation model. *Journal of Occupational Health Psychology, 24*(4), 438–449.

Shoichet, C. E., & Bracho-Sanchez, E. (2019, May 23). These doctors risked their careers to expose dangers children face in immigration family detention. *CNN*. Retrieved from https://www.cnn.com/2019/05/23/health/ice-family-detention-whistleblowers-doctors/index.html?fbclid=IwAR2XnmMj902eouQJkhhN7GAyzeMeUkAjJNcNwvor29r8FTDzvBtqgblyzps

Skarbek, D. (2014). *The social order of the underworld: How prison gangs govern the American penal system.* New York: Oxford University Press. Retrieved from https://www.amazon.com/Social-Order-Underworld-Prison-American/dp/0199328501

Smith, B. V., & Yarussi, J. M. (2007). *Breaking the code of silence: Correctional officers' handbook on identifying and addressing sexual misconduct.* Washington, DC: National Institute of Corrections.

Stohr, M. K., Hemmens, C., Kifer, M., & Schoeler, M. (2000). We know it, we just have to do it: Perceptions of ethical work in prisons. *The Prison Journal, 80*(2), 126–150.

Tallahassee Community College. (2020). *Corrections.* Retrieved from http://www.tcc.fl.edu/about/locations/florida-public-safety-institute/programs/corrections/

Thompson, D. (2018a, January 9). California examines prison guards' high suicide rate. *Associated Press*. Retrieved from https://apnews.com/ 96fdc27aea0c401ea590b1c74162c43a

Thompson, H. A. (2018b, April 28). How a South Carolina prison riot really went down. *New York Times*. Retrieved from https://www.nytimes.com/2018/04/28/opinion/how-a-south-carolina-prison-riot-really-went-down.html

Tolbert, W. (2018, June 11). Female correctional officers win lawsuit for hostile work environment. *San Quentin News*. Retrieved from https://sanquentinnews.com/female-correctional-officers-win-lawsuit-hostile-work-environment/

Urban Justice Center. (2019). *The prison industrial complex: Mapping private sector players.* New York: Author.

U.S. Bureau of Prisons. (2019a). *Job opportunities.* Retrieved from https://www.bop.gov/jobs/opportunities.jsp

U.S. Bureau of Prisons. (2019b). *Prison safety.* Retrieved from https://www.bop.gov/about/statistics/statistics_prison_safety.jsp?month=May&year=2019

Violanti, J. M. (2017). Suicide behind the wall: A national analysis of corrections officer suicide. *Suicidology Online, 8*(1), 58–64.

Worley, R. M., Barua Worley, V., & Hsu, H. (2018). Can I trust my co-worker? Examining correctional officers' perceptions of staff-inmates inappropriate relationships within a Southern penitentiary system. *Deviant Behavior, 39*(3), 332–346.

Zimmer, L. (1987). How women reshape the prison guard role. *Gender and Society, 1*(4), 415–431.

Chapter 8
Prisoners and Prison Life

OUTLINE

OBJECTIVES

After reading this chapter you will be able to:

- Explain why prisonization occurs

- Describe how jail and prison culture has been changing over time

- Describe the deprivations of prison life

- Explain why it is important to know about prison effects if we intend on rehabilitating offenders

- Describe how the roles of gangs in US prisons have been changing since the 1980s

CASE STUDY

Keri Blakinger: From State Prisoner to Crime Reporter

There are over two million Americans behind bars; while few of us think about their personal histories or their friends and family in the community, all have a story. Most jail and prison inmates come from poor families and have few social supports. Their prison admissions are usually the product of substance abuse, traumatic experiences, poor choices, a lack of opportunity, and other causal forces. Yet, not all people admitted to prison are from marginalized populations. Consider one case in point: Keri Blakinger. As a former competitive figure skater who graduated from a private high school and attended Cornell University, Keri Blakinger had more pre-conviction advantages than most prison inmates described in this book. Despite those differences, her pathway to prison is all too familiar. She says her descent into drug use started after breaking up with her figure skating partner when she was 17 years old; however, even prior to the break-up, she struggled with depression and a self-destructive streak (Stein, 2013). Despite her drug use she functioned well, earning a place on the Dean's List for several semesters and serving as an editor of the university's newspaper.

Blakinger was arrested in 2010, at 26 years of age, for possessing six ounces of heroin. Her case was widely reported in the media and resulted in her expulsion from Cornell and shortly thereafter, she was sentenced to 2½ years in a New York prison. Blakinger (2015) explains that she benefitted from being sentenced in a very liberal county, and doubts she would have received such lenient treatment if sentenced in any of the surrounding counties, where ten-year prison terms were the norm for similar amounts of heroin possession. Moreover, New York's drug laws were rolled back the previous year, which also reduced her potential sentence length. She served 21 months in prison. During that time, Blakinger reports that she was exposed to prisoners with mental illness, was married in a visiting room, observed the racist treatment of minority prisoners, was placed in solitary confinement, and became sober (Bentz, Seavy-Nesper, & Hensley, 2018; Blakinger, 2015; Stein, 2013).

Blakinger's return to the community on parole was made easier by the support of family, friends, and former professors. While serving her first years on parole, she worked at the *Ithaca Times* and *New York Daily News* newspapers; she also successfully petitioned for readmission to Cornell, having convinced a dozen supporters, including her parole officer, to write letters to the university supporting her return. Once re-admitted, she finished her remaining classes, graduated in 2014 and continued working as a crime reporter. Blakinger now works with the Marshall Project, a non-profit news organization, where she writes about criminal justice issues. Her life experiences give her considerable insight into jail and prison issues and readers can follow her work on Twitter: @keribla.

Critical Questions

1. Describe the advantages Blakinger had when re entering the community after her prison term.
2. Do you have more in common with Blakinger than prisoners coming from inner-city America? Does that change your ideas about the seriousness of her crimes?
3. Why would Blakinger be a good (or bad) choice as a reporter covering the crime beat for a major newspaper?

INTRODUCTION

For most of American correctional history, the public knew very little about what happened in prisons, as they were closed systems that had little interaction with other organizations or the public. In the 1930s and 1940s, the public knew that incarcerated people were worked hard and were flogged if they did not abide by institutional rules. For the most part, people were fine with treatment of that sort for convicted offenders. Most prisons were in rural areas, and they were both out-of-sight and out-of-mind.

Most of our historical knowledge of jail and prison operations comes from newspaper reporters and prison tourists (like Charles Dickens) who wrote accounts of the conditions of confinement. Furthermore, dozens of best-selling books about prison life have been written by correctional officers (COs) and former prisoners. While those accounts have helped us better understand the day-to-day aspects of prison life, they could not always convey the grittiness of life behind bars.

Television reality shows such as *Lockup* added another layer to our understanding of prison life. *Lockup* showed the living conditions and operations of jails and prisons in 237 episodes airing between 2005 and 2017. Yet, some critics have questioned whether that depiction of jail or prison life is very accurate. Specifically concerning *Lockup*, Cecil and Leitner (2009, p. 186) say that it takes about eight days of filming to produce an hour-long episode. In order to get the content that most interests the viewers, the producers often focus on what is happening in special handling units (SHU) or death row—which may only hold 1% of all US prisoners—and their one-hour documentaries focus on violence, gangs, and sex. But does that focus on maximum security units accurately portray American corrections?

In addition to admitting a larger number of inmates, some jail and prison administrators have opened their operations to public scrutiny. Some correctional administrators, such as Sheriff Joe Arpaio, who ran the Maricopa County (Phoenix, AZ) jail from 1993 to 2016, actively seek out publicity, especially with the media. For example, Santos (2012) reports that every month Arpaio gave about 200 interviews on local television, and he was profiled by

PHOTO 8.1
Inmates from one of Sheriff Joe Arpaio's Maricopa jails are shackled together with nine feet of spacing between each prisoner before being put to work outside the facility. Highly controversial, the chain gangs were reintroduced by Arpaio in 1995. Forced to wear pink underwear, black and white prison outfits, and "paraded" in shackles along highways and other public places while doing hard labor, the chain gang was only one of many contentious actions in the sheriff's bid to be tough on crime. Arpaio was sheriff for 22 years, losing a re-election bid in 2016. Litigation tied to his "get tough" practices cost Maricopa county millions of dollars. Credit: Orjan Ellingvag/Alamy Stock Photo.

news organizations around the globe. His "tough-on-criminals" approach was popular with the public, who supported him when he placed jail inmates in tents, fed them baloney sandwiches, cracked down on undocumented immigrants, started chain gangs for women, and gave male inmates pink underwear. Despite that popularity, he was not re-elected sheriff in 2016. Arpaio, a former DEA agent, was eventually convicted of contempt and sentenced to a federal prison term, although he was pardoned by President Donald Trump.

What lessons can we learn from Sheriff Joe? Ultimately, whether we are viewing reality television shows like *Lockup* or following the publicized exploits of law enforcement officers such as Sheriff Joe, we have to remember that what we see on television or access online shapes our ideas about public policies such as the use of jails and prisons. We also have to be careful to scrutinize such messages carefully because the people making those claims may have some interest in promoting a biased viewpoint.

One way we can learn about jail or prison life is to ask people who have been there, including Keri Blakinger. Until the 1980s, correctional populations were small, and jails or prisons did not touch the lives of many Americans. Today, things are much different, as every year there are about 10.6 million admissions to jails (Zeng, 2019) and over 600,000 prison admissions (Carson, 2018). As a result, there is no shortage of inside accounts of jail and prison life published in various blogs, reports, and online sources, including the Marshall Project's *Life Inside* series. Moreover, some of the individuals caught in the nation's mass incarceration movement are our friends, coworkers, and family members, and we can hear from them what happens in these places. In order to better understand jail and prison life researchers have also asked current inmates and ex-prisoners about their experiences, and these studies have broadened our understanding of American corrections.

Not only is it difficult to separate the everyday jail or prison life from what we view on television or see online, we can't forget that there is incredible diversity in correctional facilities. What we view on an episode of *Lockup* might not be very applicable to what happens in another facility 100 miles away. There is a similar diversity in American jails. Media portrayals of what is happening in jails in Chicago, Los Angeles, or New York—where an average spaghetti lunch requires 3,000 pounds of ground beef to feed the inmates—might represent an accurate portrayal of those facilities, yet bears little resemblance to what happens in a 20-bed facility in rural Nebraska or Montana. As a result, we must be careful that we don't apply what we see in any one facility to correctional operations in the rest of the country.

As we have mentioned previously, the types of behaviors one might expect in jail or prison are related to the characteristics of the inmates. Younger inmates with histories of violent crime and gang involvement will present a different set of challenges than elderly inmates who were admitted to prison decades ago. Moreover, if the people being admitted to jail and prison are overwhelmingly afflicted with alcohol, drug, and mental health problems, the correctional system will have to develop responses to manage those inmates. It can be easier for large jails or prison systems to manage these special needs inmates as administrators can develop programs that target the needs of large groups, whereas administrators in small facilities might have too few of these inmates, not to mention far fewer resources, to develop specialized programs.

In the sections of this chapter that follow, we describe how jail and prison inmates have developed ways of surviving their sentences. In those efforts, we provide, among other things, a description of the inmate subculture, prison sex, and how the convict code—that was intended to reduce tension and violence—is being replaced by the informal rules imposed by prison gangs. Members of these latter groups, including street-gang members, have developed strategies to survive their prison stays. These strategies address a wide array of day-to-day deprivations associated with institutional life and prison effects, including overcrowding, the use of solitary confinement, and the impact of **trauma** on people who are already suffering from mental health, addictions, and other physical health problems.

EVOLUTION OF JAIL AND PRISON CULTURE

Prison films from the 1940s or 1950s typically portray smoothly running facilities where murders and riots were relatively rare events. Imprisonment during that time was used sparingly, and individuals placed in prisons generally had extensive criminal histories. People admitted to prison entered places that had a distinct and powerful **prison subculture**, which is to say a culture within the larger culture. Prison subcultures were first systematically described by Donald Clemmer (1940), a former Illinois CO, in his book *The Prison Community*. This groundbreaking work inspired other scholars, such as sociologist Gresham Sykes (1958), to carry out similar studies of prison life.

The prison subculture these scholars described had rules and regulations, values, and prejudices. Newly incarcerated people learned about the prison subculture in a process Sykes called **prisonization**, which was itself based on a **convict code** (also called an inmate code).

The convict code is a set of unwritten rules that guides inmate behavior. These rules have at their core certain values such as being tough, avoiding talking with the COs, minding their own business, and not informing on other inmates. Like any other deviant social group, the convict code espouses an "us versus them" mentality, which helps to bolster their solidarity and group identity. Sykes, working with Sheldon L. Messinger (1960), identified the five basic principles of the code:

- *Never interfere with the interests of other inmates.* Above all else, this means do not betray another inmate, particularly to the authorities; however, it also means keeping out of the other inmates' business and generally being loyal to other cons.
- *Don't lose your head.* In other words, play it cool and do not get involved in matters that have nothing to do with you.
- *Don't exploit other inmates.* Specifically, keep your word, pay your debts, and do not steal from other inmates.
- *Don't be weak.* If you whine or look for special privileges from guards or other authority figures, or are easily exploited by others, you deserve what you receive.
- *Punish violators quickly and severely.* Proof beyond a reasonable doubt is not necessary; suspicion is enough to set the inmates' wheels of justice in motion.

Sanctions for inmates who broke these rules were harsh and most violations resulted in beatings or death in rare cases. There is no appeals process. As proposed by Sykes and Messinger, if an inmate believes that a violation of some provision of the code has occurred, then that person is generally free to act as he sees fit.

Although scholarly representations of the convict code emerged over 75 years ago, these rules have lost much of their relevance since the emergence of prison gangs in the 1970s and 1980s, a topic covered below. Yet, vestiges of the old convict code remain. Mitchell (2018, pp. 94–98) interviewed over 800 Texas prisoners and found that their convict code is based on four factors, which are summarized as follows:

- *Social distance:* Inmates should maintain and preserve the distance between themselves and the COs, including never sharing personal information with them.
- *Masculinity:* Prisoners need to be tough, show no fear, maintain their reputation, and be willing to use violence.

- *Invisibility*: Inmates are encouraged to keep to themselves, avoid trouble, do their own time, mind their own business, and do not **snitch** (inform) on other inmates.
- *Strategic survival*: Prisoners need to learn how to live in the prison environment where they are responsible for their own survival and being loyal to other inmates, but not dependent upon them.

Mitchell found that some prisoners were more attached and committed to the convict code, including even some who were involved in gangs. While this is important research, two factors need to be considered. The first is that there may be factors that are distinctive to Texas that might be different in other states. The second is that incarcerated women have a different correctional experience than their male counterparts, which is described in Chapter 11.

Inmates new to prison life typically are called **fish**, a term that indicates their low and easily exploited status. After their admissions, more experienced inmates could take them aside and explain the facts of prison life. If these newly admitted inmates are weak or fail to understand the code, other inmates exploit them. If they are strong or learn to use the system for their own benefit, they will have more status in the prison hierarchy. Prisoners with more conventional values often prefer to stay out of trouble and do their own time. Regardless of how committed they were to the prison's subculture, being incarcerated tends to reshape the individual's outlook on life, including norms, values, culture, and even language.

Living in a total institution such as an asylum or prison powerfully influences the resident's attitudes and behaviors (Goffman, 1961). Throughout the process of prisonization members develop a way of interpreting the world and form their own terms to describe aspects of their daily lives. Moreover, Clemmer (1940, p. 302) contends that prisonization is highest among inmates with the following characteristics:

- A long sentence
- An unstable personality in pre-prison life
- Few positive relationships outside the prison walls
- A readiness for integration into the inmate subculture
- Complete acceptance of an inmate code as well as those norms and values
- Living in the same cell or in close proximity with others of like persuasion
- Participating in gambling or homosexual behavior

The world Clemmer describes was largely unseen except by those who lived or worked in it, and because there were relatively few people locked up—especially when compared with today—prison life did not touch the lives of many Americans.

Inmate Language

Every subculture develops a set of terms to describe their world and this jargon seldom makes sense to outsiders. In his book on surviving one's first imprisonment Fuller (2013) describes a generic set of terms used by jail and prison inmates, and although they might not be applicable to all regions of the country they shed light on a world most of us will never experience:

- *All day*: A life sentence ("I'm doing all day")
- *Back door parole*: To die in prison
- *Brake fluid*: Psychiatric medications
- *Bug*: A prison staff member considered untrustworthy or unreliable
- *Cowboy*: New CO
- *Diesel therapy*: A lengthy bus trip or transfer to a faraway facility used as punishment or to get rid of troublesome inmates
- *Fish*: New inmate
- *Fish kit*: New inmate's blanket, bedroll, and sheets
- *Free world*: What inmates call the rest of the world outside prison
- *Gassing*: Throwing feces at a CO or prison employee
- *Hats and bats*: The prison's emergency response team that is used to extract inmates from cells or respond to prison riots
- *Hooch*: Inmate-made alcohol made by mixing sugar, yeast, and fruit or fruit juice and ferments in a container for several days (also called *pruno*)
- *Jackrabbit parole*: To escape from a facility
- *Jungle*: Prison recreation yard
- *Lock in a sock*: When locks or other heavy objects are placed in a sock and used as a weapon
- *Money*: Postage stamps that are substituted for cash
- *On vacation*: When an inmate is placed in solitary confinement
- *Packing the rabbit*: Inserting contraband into a body cavity
- *Robocop*: CO who writes inmates up for any possible rule infraction
- *Shank*: Any object an inmate has made into a knife/shiv/sharpened point
- *Shot caller*: An inmate who represents and speaks for a group within a prison such as a gang, dorm, or racial group
- *Stainless steel ride*: Death by lethal injection
- *Walk in*: to allow membership into a gang without initiation
- *Yolked*: A muscular inmate

Over time, COs will also adopt and use many of these terms. In some respects, officers are as imprisoned as the inmates they supervise, although officers often refer to their time behind bars as being served in eight-hour installments.

Prisoner Values

As in the conventional world, prisoners have different levels of status, and their standing in that world is often associated with their criminal histories. Individuals sentenced to prison for a series of armed robberies, for example, have more status than a drunk driver who was involved in a fatal crash. These values differ somewhat throughout the country, but regardless of where one is imprisoned, being a sex offender has the lowest status, rankings that apparently transcend the location of the prison (see, e.g., Winfree, Newbold, & Tubb, 2002). Today, however, much of one's status in jail or prison depends on gang affiliation, but prior to the 1970s, one had to earn status by abiding by the convict code.

Regardless of the era when one is imprisoned, the relationships between the COs and inmates tend to be reserved. Inmates are reluctant to being seen with officers or cooperate with them for fear of being labeled an informer. While the expression "snitches get stitches" emerged after 2010, there has been scorn for informers for over a century, and that label is tied to an inmate's credibility and status. Despite the hatred of informers, the practice is widespread and snitching is sometimes purposeful such as intentionally trying to get another inmate punished by the COs. Wilkerson (2018) also explains that snitching can be inadvertent, a careless word or behavior that attracts the attention of the officers and results in another inmate being punished. Fuller (2013) calls this "dry snitching" by talking loudly, behaving suspiciously, or supplying general information to COs without naming anybody.

Once labeled a snitch, that label might follow the inmate through their jail or prison stay. There are hazards of being labeled a snitch, foremost being assaulted, although the extent of an inmate's punishment depends on the outcomes of the information shared with the COs. An informant whose information resulted in another inmate receiving additional criminal charges may be killed. Informants are especially vulnerable in a riot, and many of the people killed in the 1980 New Mexico State prison riot had "snitch jackets" or official files identifying them as informers.

Fuller (2013), a **prison consultant** who was imprisoned 11 for years applies the convict code to a list of ten rules he calls commandments. He maintains that people with no prior histories of incarceration must follow these commandments to survive a stay in jail or prison. Although these unwritten and informal inmate rules differ throughout the country, they are intended to reduce conflict among inmates. Routine tasks, such as using the toilet in a cell can become very complicated when two people are locked inside a cell originally designed for one person. Fuller's (2013) commandments are summarized as follows:

1. *Do not stare at other inmates.* This might be misunderstood as sizing up the other prisoners or trying to exert dominance over them, which can result in violence.

2. *Do not trust your fellow inmates.* Fuller describes them as predators who cannot be trusted and most have ulterior motives when offering their advice or help. Gang-involved inmates, substance abusers, smokers, and gamblers should be avoided.

3. *Respect your cellmate.* One's roommate, and property, must be respected and permission should be asked before touching any items or even using the cell toilet.

4. *Mind your business.* There are strict rules on watching television (and changing channels without permission), where one is permitted to sit in a recreation area or in the cafeteria, and there can be violent consequences for cutting into a line or reaching across a table without first asking permission.

5. *Respect the staff.* Abide by the orders of the COs even if they seem unreasonable, as few officers cause trouble intentionally but they will sometimes retaliate for non-compliance.

6. *Do not steal.* Stealing another prisoner's possessions can result in immediate physical punishment, although stealing from the COs is seen as acceptable by the other inmates.

7. *Don't be a snitch.* Avoid talking to the COs and do not help them with their investigations. Not only can snitching result in violence but few prisoners will associate with a snitch.

8. *Avoid prison gangs.* Inmates should resist joining a gang to increase their safety. Fuller says that most prison violence is related to gang activities and a prisoner's family members in the outside community can also be victimized. Prison gang involvement can also lead to crimes that can result in longer sentences and some gangs require a lifelong commitment.

9. *Stay away from drugs.* Drug use can result in losing privileges, additional charges, overdoses, and debt if a prisoner cannot pay for them.

10. *Do not gamble.* Losing a bet and refusing to pay will end in violence, and it may be one's own gang members who beat the individual for failing to pay up (as the gang does not want conflict with another gang holding that inmate's debt).

Fuller's (2013) commandments are intended to reduce victimization for new prisoners in an austere and uncaring environment surrounded by people with extensive criminal histories. All prisoners live in an environment that is defined by deprivation, and that is the focus of the next section.

THE PAINS OF IMPRISONMENT

The increasing interest in understanding prisons and prison life led Sykes (1958) to identify the pains of imprisonment in his classic book *The Society of Captives*. These deprivations were previously identified by Charles Dickens in his tours of American prisons, including Pennsylvania's Eastern State Penitentiary, in the 1830s, although they were not presented as concisely or articulately as Sykes (Shammas, 2017). While Sykes identified these deprivations decades ago, they are reported in every corrections textbook because they are still true today. Sykes' main contribution was clearly defining the five main deprivations of imprisonment, including:

- *Liberty*: Prisoners are held apart/excluded from society and few have access to the community. Inmates are further restricted by a facility's regulations, which can restrict them to specific areas within the jail or prison, including being segregated. Some inmates saw themselves as social outcasts and adopted what Clemmer (1940) calls an inferior social role.
- *Goods and services:* Prisoners live in austere environments where they have very little legitimate access to desirable goods or services. Although inmates can purchase goods at the prison's commissary, the selection is limited and access is limited (e.g. once per week), and few have money in their inmate accounts. Because of the bans placed on alcohol, tobacco, drugs, or cellular phones there is a thriving underground economy in jails and prisons to meet the demand for these items.
- *Heterosexual relationships*: Few prisons house both males and females, and even in such "co-ed" prisons, they restrict inmates' contact with the opposite sex (we also acknowledge the presence of sexual minorities). As a result, most inmates wanting sexual intimacy must choose between celibacy or same-sex relationships. Conjugal visits (also called extended family visits), where a prisoner's family would visit in a private setting on the prison grounds, have gradually disappeared. Presently, conjugal visits are only available in four state prison systems (CA, CT, NY, and WA) and are banned in federal prisons.
- *Autonomy*: Residents of total or near-total institutions have few choices to act independently in their daily routines: they are told when to wake up, leave their cells, eat their meals, and go to educational, recreational, or job-related duties. While the prison's routine provides a structure for inmate success because it is consistent and increases predictability, it also diminishes their decision-making abilities or skills. Haney (2012, p. 5) says that "some prisoners lose the capacity to initiate activity, to use their own judgment to make effective decisions, or to engage in planful behavior of any kind." Losing these skills can hamper their successful return to the community.

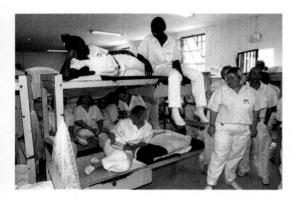

PHOTO 8.2
Alabama's Tutwiler Prison for Women was built in 1942 and intended to house 417 inmates. In January 2020 the facility and its minimum-security annex held nearly 900 inmates, including five women condemned to death (Alabama Department of Corrections, 2020). Ironically, the facility was named for Julia S. Tutwiler, called the "angel of the stockades," as she championed inmate education, classification, and treatment. In 2016, after a series of scathing reports on conditions at Tutwiler, the governor of Alabama announced that the state would begin the decommissioning of the prison within the year. However, in April 2020, the prison was still holding inmates. Credit: ZUMA Press Inc./Alamy Stock Photo.

- *Security*: Inmates not associated with a group or gang have little security, and often they are afraid of being assaulted by the COs or other inmates, and almost all are fearful of riots. As noted below, the risks of victimization increase along with prison security levels, as living conditions are safer in minimum-security facilities.

Although first identified over a half-century ago, the content and context of these deprivations are equally applicable today. One factor that received less attention decades ago was the issue of being separated from their families and especially their children. While applicable to both male and female prisoners, being apart from one's children is especially difficult for mothers, a topic addressed in more detail in Chapter 11.

The pains of imprisonment identified by Sykes are often felt more intensely during the first years of one's sentence, as prisoners adapt to their confinement. In order to better understand the psychological effects of imprisonment, researchers have asked prisoners about the most severe problems associated with being incarcerated. Hulley, Crewe, and Wright (2016, p. 780) summarized the responses expressed by the people they surveyed about their long-term imprisonment, to include:

- Missing somebody
- Worrying about people outside
- Feeling that you are losing the best years of your life
- Having to follow other people's rules and orders
- Feeling that your life has been wasted

These findings can be summed up in two themes: a prisoner's concerns about the passage of time and their powerlessness. The inmates in Hulley and associates' (2016) study said that feeling sorry for themselves, being worried about their safety, or being angry with the world or thinking about suicide were the least serious problems they confronted.

Sex and Institutional Life

Regardless of where or when researchers have examined the deprivations of prison life, the issue of lacking access to heterosexual relationships is always identified as one of the most significant pains of imprisonment. While the issue of a lack of heterosexual sex in jails and prisons has always been important for the field of corrections, there were only a handful of articles written about the topic prior to the publication of Fishman's (1934) book about sexuality in male prisons. In the 1930s, Fishman saw an inmate's predatory behavior as an outcome of depriving them of "normal" sex. He was critical that some inmates were being victimized, and he described the existence of predator-prey relationships where passive inmates—many of whom were imprisoned because of the homosexuality laws of the era—and young prisoners were vulnerable to assault. In this section we focus primarily on sex in male facilities, but turn our attention to sex in women's facilities in Chapter 11.

Much of the public's knowledge about the criminal justice system, including sex in prisons, is based on television series, movies, or folklore (Fleisher & Krienert, 2009). Fleisher and Krienert contend that the prison's culture shapes perceptions about sexuality, and they describe how a single act can be interpreted in several ways. For example, acts that might be interpreted in the free world as a rape might be seen in prison as a consensual act, an economic exchange identical to prostitution in the free world, or a forced act of intimidation and violence. Forced acts can be between an aggressor and a victim, a form of rape. Even consensual acts between inmates involve aspects of coercion if one inmate gives the other three choices: "fight, flee, or fuck." Some inmates see forcing sex on others as a show of strength and masculinity. Others, by contrast, engage in prostitution for survival, that is, they exchange sex for protection. Inmates can also achieve status from their work as male prostitutes and obtain access to contraband such as drugs, alcohol, and food through their sex work.

In 2003 Congress passed the *Prison Rape Elimination Act* (PREA). This legislation was intended to give prison authorities and others a better understanding of the nature and extent of the sexual victimization of inmates in adult and youth, and male and female facilities. One significant issue that became apparent to the researchers conducting these studies was that inmates made thousands of allegations of these crimes, but only a small proportion of these acts were ever substantiated as occurring. In her analysis for the Bureau of Justice Statistics, Rantala (2018) reveals that 58% of the reported incidents occurred between inmates and staff. Sexual relationships between inmates and correctional staff occur, and they are illegal in most states as they are based on unequal power relationships. Inmates may feel they have very little choice but to submit to the staff member's advances if they believe the officer will make things difficult for them by refusing.

How do staff members feel about inmates having sexual relationships? There are no clear answers to this question as they may depend on one's role in the prison hierarchy.

Studies carried out before the PREA statistics were available found that most wardens believed inmates were not very sexually active (Hensley & Tewksbury, 2005). Even after the first PREA reports, wardens still believed sexual assaults were rare (Moster & Jeglic, 2009). Prison wardens may be somewhat insulated about the extent of these acts, given that most of the information they receive about prison rapes are official reports. Front-line COs, by contrast, would have a better understanding of acts that occurred but were never reported. Alternatively, some wardens may have a vested interest in choosing not to acknowledge these offenses, and this is a short-sighted perspective given the threats posed by infectious diseases and the traumatic effects of violent victimizations.

Correctional line-staff can provide additional insights. It is important to note that their attitudes toward non-heterosexual sex, like those of the public, vary greatly. There seems to be a contradiction between what officers say and do about inmates' sexual habits. That is, most COs indicate they would report such acts, but few are reported. Unlike prison administrators who appear to underestimate prison inmate sexual activity, officers may overestimate it, including the incidence of rape and especially when compared with the inmate self-report information.

Perhaps COs, in jails or prisons, simply chose not to "see" rapes and other sexual assaults for several reasons. Personal estimates about the prevalence of these acts, then, may be based on what they have heard from their coworkers and even inmates rather than what was observed, hence the overestimates. Beyond indifference to the fate of inmates or being coerced to look the other way, both of which could get the COs in trouble if the results are serious injury or death, officers may view such acts as consensual or may have difficulty determining whether these acts were consensual. Other officers may believe the inmate-endorsed idea that inmate-on-inmate homosexual sex is a functional and situational alternative to other sexual outlets. Finally, some COs view the inmate-victims of forced sexual encounters as getting what the inmates deserve (Eigenberg, 2000).

Prisoners also have ideas about sex and those engaging in non-consensual sex have little status. In researching their book on sex in prison Fleisher and Krienert (2009, p. 3) interviewed over 500 inmates and they considered prison rapists to be weak and cowardly. Even though some scholars say there is relatively little risk of prison sexual violence, inmates express fear of being victimized, especially in the first weeks of their sentences. During that time, they will often isolate themselves to reduce their risks of victimization. While most newly admitted jail or prison inmates believe that violence is a random occurrence, they learn that most assaults are for violations of the convict code: snitching, unpaid debts, or payback for bad drug deals (Fleisher & Krienert, 2009).

Are Prisons Hotbeds for Prisoner Radicalization?

Ever since the 11 September 2001 attacks there has been concern that some former prisoners are engaging in terrorist acts, and some ex-prisoners have been involved in very high-profile terrorist attacks. One example from the United Kingdom was the London Bridge attack in December, 2019. One of the challenges for prison staff is that many of the individuals who become radicalized did not have terrorist sympathies prior to their imprisonment. So, what is radicalization, and why and how does it occur?

Hunter and Heinke (2011) use the Federal Bureau of Investigation definition of **radicalization** as "the process by which individuals come to believe their engagement in or facilitation of non-state violence to achieve social and political change is necessary and justified." One can become radicalized to violence in religious institutions, schools, prisons, and online sites where people with similar values share ideas or attempt to influence others. Prison may be an ideal recruiting ground for potential terrorists as inmates are often discouraged, depressed, and isolated from positive influences. Hamm (2008) also points out that inmates may be radicalized more easily in overcrowded maximum-security prisons with gang problems and a lack of positive supports such as rehabilitative programs or chaplains to provide religious guidance. Moreover, the likelihood of radicalization may increase when there is a lack of moral or social supports.

In many respects, the process of radicalization is similar to joining a gang. In trying to understand their incarceration these people may be searching for meaning in their lives through a higher power or trying to form an identity beyond the label of criminal. Charismatic leaders might target the most vulnerable prisoners for special attention and attempt to recruit them into a group that provides safety, security, and support. Although the focus of this section is what happens to Islamist inmates Hamm (2008) says that it is fairly common for people with Judeo-Christian backgrounds to convert to religions such as Islam and other faiths while imprisoned.

We know very little in terms of the actual numbers of convicted terrorists behind bars, but the total is most likely under 300, and that total includes the 40 enemy combatants held at Guantanamo Bay and the 49 prisoners held on national security offenses by the U.S. Bureau of Prisons (2020) in March 2020. The remainder are housed in state prisons and some are held in local jails awaiting their court dates. Hamm (2008) divides our responses to radicalization into two groups: (a) policymakers and scholars believing there is relatively little risk, and (b) members of groups believing that prisons are hotbeds of radicalization. Like many of the issues addressed throughout this book the real position rests in the middle and while radicalization has not been a significant problem in the United States so far, a relatively small number of radicalized offenders can lead to a significant loss of life. LaFree, Jiang, and Porter (2019) found that former prisoners who had been radicalized were twice as likely as non-radicalized ex-prisoners to engage in politically motivated violent crimes. Given the relatively small numbers of these individuals it is safe to say that US prisons are not hotbeds of radicalization although prison officials are taking these risks seriously, especially in light of LaFree, Jiang, and Porter's findings.

PHOTO 8.3
US Army soldier stands guard as a detainee spends time in the exercise yard of Camp Five at the Guantanamo Bay Naval Base. The facility consists of six maximum-security facilities like Camp Five that house the most noncompliant and hostile detainees held as enemy combatants in the War on Terror. Many of the facilities associated with these six camps have been the subject of negative reports by groups such as Human Rights Watch and several are objects of federal litigation about prisoner rights. Credit: Everett Collection Historical/Alamy Stock Photo.

PRISON EFFECTS

There is little doubt that prisoners live in conditions of deprivation or that most feel powerless about their circumstances. There is a growing awareness that imprisonment has a number of costs borne by prisoners, especially with respect to their long-term well-being. While state prison administrators will sometimes talk about rehabilitation, only about 2–3% of most state corrections budgets are dedicated to rehabilitative programs. Instead of receiving rehabilitative programming most incarcerated people live in warehouse prisons, where the state meets only their basic needs. As prisoners are not a sympathetic population, the public mostly approves of that treatment.

In line with Clemmer's (1940) observations, Haney (2012, p. 2), writing over 70 years later, also contends that incarceration shapes how inmates think, feel, and act. It is not surprising that prison has such a powerful influence as inmates are confined in what we have previously called a total institution, one governed by sets of formal rules, which are enforced by the prison staff, as well as a more powerful set of informal rules, which are developed *and* enforced by the inmates. The COs give tacit approval to these informal rules as they know they exist but do not challenge them, largely since they are instrumental for the overall management of the institution. That is, formal rules alone could not maintain the level of social stability needed to operate a facility housing hundreds—if not thousands of humans—some of whom have committed horrific crimes on the outside, if not the inside. Haney (2012) also defines the process of prisonization as socialization into the norms of the prison. It is the means by which inmates adapt to an austere, impoverished, and deprived environment. Haney says that prison confinement is driven by two extremes: solitary confinement and overcrowding, and these effects are often experienced by people with long histories of trauma, which can worsen the effects of prisonization.

Solitary Confinement

Solitary confinement, also called segregation or administrative segregation (Ad Seg), has been used for almost 200 years. For example, inmates placed in Philadelphia's Eastern State Penitentiary in the 1800s served their entire stay in isolation. Sentences, however, were shorter two centuries ago, and as the time served by prisoners increased, so did the use of solitary confinement. Validated gang members in California and several other states are often placed in solitary confinement, and some of these individuals, after their sentences expire, are returned directly to the community after having served years in solitary. Some death row inmates are also placed in Ad Seg, while condemned prisoners in some states are housed in the facility's general population.

Solitary is often used as a short- and long-term punishment. Spencer (2018) writes about serving 17 days for having unauthorized food—two onions—in her cell. She reports experiencing feelings of anxiety and depression during that time. The experience changed her life for the worse, as she became hardened and started talking to herself. Most jails and prisons reserve placement in segregation for inmates involved in serious incidents, and some of these placements can last for years. Maurice Wallace, an Illinois prisoner serving life without parole, assaulted a CO in 2006 and, as of 2018, he was still in segregation. Wallace launched a lawsuit in that year in an attempt to get the federal courts to order his release from segregation, arguing that it was a cruel and unusual punishment to segregate him for over 11 years, especially given his mental health problems. In his appeal to the Seventh Circuit (*Wallace v. Baldwin et. al.*, 2018, pp. 4–5), the judge noted that:

> The core of Wallace's complaint is that solitary confinement has intensified his mental illness, including post-traumatic stress disorder, causing nightmares, severe anxiety, and most relevant here, suicidal thoughts. He describes his segregation as "akin to being sealed inside a coffin." He spends 23 to 24 hours a day alone in a cell that is "significantly smaller" than 50 square feet. The cell is dark, noisy, infested with insects, freezing in the winter, and hot in the summer. Because of his segregation, he cannot attend educational or religious classes, visit the law library used by the general population or earn income from a prison job.

This extreme isolation for more than a decade has taken a toll on Wallace's mental health. He takes antidepressants for post-traumatic stress disorder. But despite this medication he still experiences depression, anxiety, panic attacks, difficulty sleeping, and auditory hallucinations.

The Court of Appeals believed that Wallace faced imminent danger and should be allowed to proceed with his lawsuit, although the case had not been resolved by March 2020.

A review of news reports reveals that some individuals have served more than a decade in segregation. Woodfox (2019, para. 4) describes being imprisoned for 40 years in a closed cell restricted (CCR) unit in Louisiana's Angola prison:

> We were locked down 23 hours a day. There was no outside exercise yard for CCR prisoners. There were prisoners in CCR who hadn't been outside in years. We weren't allowed books, magazines, newspapers, or radios. There were no fans on the tier; there was no access to ice, no hot water in the sinks in our cells. There was no hot plate to heat water on the tier. Needless to say, we were not allowed educational, social, vocational, or religious programs; we weren't allowed to do hobby crafts (leatherwork, painting, woodwork). Rats came up the shower drain at the end of the hall and would run down the tier.

Hundreds of people are held in solitary confinement indefinitely as they have no way of earning their way back to the general population, even when their last acts of prison misconduct occurred a decade or more in the past. The Association of State Correctional Administrators' (2016, p. 7) survey of state prison systems found almost 3,000 individuals had been segregated between three and six years, and over 2,900 had served more than six years in solitary confinement. Some of those long-term prisoners have no plan for reentry into the general prison population. Ewing and Stroud (2018), for example, describe how there are over 100 people in Pennsylvania prisons serving indefinite terms in solitary confinement. As a result, unless there is some change in state prison policy, they will likely die in a segregated housing unit.

Overcrowding

While long-term solitary confinement has harmful effects on inmates, having too many inmates in a confined space also presents its own set of problems. Overcrowding occurs when the number of inmates exceeds the facility's design to house them (e.g. the number of cells and beds), a state captured by the term "rated capacity." A given prison's or jail's rated capacity is defined by the U.S. Department of Justice (2019, n.p.) as "the number of beds or inmates assigned by a rating official to institutions within the jurisdiction." Exceed the "highest rated capacity," and a facility is technically overcrowded. On 31 December 2017, 13 states and the federal government exceeded the highest "rated capacity" of their prison systems (Bronson & Carson, 2019, p. 25). Furthermore, about one-fifth of all US jails are operating at more than 100% of their rated capacity (Zeng, 2019, p. 8). Phrased another way, about one-fifth of US jails and prison systems are overcrowded.

Packing too many people into spaces designed for fewer inmates reduces correctional security and inmate safety. As the number of inmates in a jail or prison exceeds the number of beds, facility administrators typically come up with a number of solutions. Some of these include placing two inmates in cells originally designed for one (double-bunking) or using cots in gyms and other spaces not intended for inmate housing such as classrooms. If crowding does not decrease, these make-shift solutions can sometimes become long-term practices. There are negative outcomes of using gyms or classrooms to house inmates. These arrangements greatly limit inmates' ability to exercise or attend classes, increasing their idle time, which, in turn, can lead to more misconduct. Moreover, as gyms and classrooms (or other spaces) were not designed to hold prisoners they lack the appropriate electronic surveillance measures or other security elements, it can become difficult for the COs to monitor inmate behavior.

Crowding can lead to staff shortages, as the number of correctional personnel is watered down by the larger number of inmates. If no new positions are added, the remaining officers are expected to work more overtime shifts, which leads to fatigue and increases stress. Not only are there fewer officers to supervise the inmates, but some junior COs are expected to carry out more supervisory duties. While this practice presents a career opportunity for these officers, some are not ready for these responsibilities, and they can make poor decisions due to their inexperience.

While overcrowding is stressful for officers, it is harmful for the inmates. Crowding has been associated with increases in violence, as the greater the number of individuals in a confined space, the greater the opportunities for negative interactions (Haney, 2012). Crowded conditions also makes it easier to transmit communicable diseases such as COVID-19. Finally, inmates can be harmed by overcrowding if the jail or prison does not increase the medical, mental health, and rehabilitative resources. As those resources tend to be fixed, the inmates receive less than they did before the crowding started. Local corrections, such as jails, may be more vulnerable to providing these rationed services because their tax base is limited. State prison administrators, by contrast, may be more successful in obtaining more resources when their facilities are crowded. However, there is often a lag of a year or more between the time the problem is identified and when extra funding to manage the problem is received.

Ultimately, one of the most serious shortcomings of overcrowding is that the time, energy, and resources of the jail or correctional system are invested in managing crowding. As a result, they have less time to devote to solving other challenges such as improving opportunities for inmate rehabilitation, enhancing correctional health care, or ensuring that the facilities are safe and secure. Moreover, working in overcrowded conditions increases CO stress. Martin, Lichtenstein, Jenkot, and Forde (2012) found that COs working in the most crowded facilities expressed a higher fear of victimization than their counterparts working in less crowded prisons. These fears can harm their job performance, and one officer explains that: "This is a hostile and dangerous environment. We are spread thin, sometimes we have to monitor several hundred inmates by ourselves. We have become prey" (Martin et al., 2012, p. 99).

Trauma and Re-Traumatization

There is increasing attention being paid to the short- and long-term effects of trauma on people involved in the criminal justice system. Trauma is defined as the experiencing of a deeply disturbing event; the most serious and damaging forms include exposure to serious accidents, natural disasters, violence, terrorism, and war. The most commonly encountered types for most children and young persons are related to physical, sexual, and psychological abuse. There are also "less harmful" forms of trauma that include the death of a loved one, family dysfunction, interpersonal conflict, and stressful life events such as bankruptcy or divorce. Not surprisingly, inmate populations tend to have experienced a higher degree of these stressful life events than members of the general public. Stensrud, Gilbride, and Bruinekool (2019) found that about one-half of male

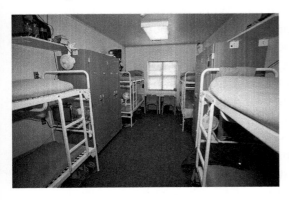

and over three-quarters of female prisoners had experienced childhood traumas. This was several times the likelihood of experiencing trauma in members of the general population. They contend that these high levels of trauma need to be addressed while they are incarcerated and after their release.

Imprisonment itself can be a traumatizing experience. As noted throughout the first chapters in this book, the victimization of jail inmates and state or federal prisoners is common; individuals who are not directly harmed in an incident can be traumatized by witnessing an assault or the aftermath of accidents, acts of self-harm (such as cutting one's body—known as slashing—and other forms of self-mutilation), and suicides. Other factors might worsen the effects of experiencing or witnessing a traumatic act. Inmates are also subject to abuse from other prisoners and the officers. Everyday prison routine is sometimes broken by unannounced and disruptive actions, such as

PHOTO 8.4
Prison and jail crowding, is a potential source of trauma and re-victimization for both male and female inmates. Work-release programs, too, suffer from crowding, as revealed in this photo of a minimum-security cell designed for four inmates but double-bunked for eight. Credit: Mikael Karlsson/ Alamy Stock Photo.

moves to new cells (with new cellmates), as well as transfers to different units within the facility or other prisons. Inmates are frequently strip searched; they may find themselves physically restrained by COs and placed in mechanical restraints (such as handcuffs and shackles) or in solitary confinement after engaging in misconduct. For these reasons, Haney (2012, p. 13) describes prisons as impoverished environments that are cold and uncaring places.

As a result, correctional administrators have begun to place more attention on **trauma-informed care (TIC)** and trauma-informed correctional care (TICC). A first step in working toward TIC is acknowledging the prior trauma most prisoners have experienced and helping them to rebuild a sense of control and empowerment. Some aspects of prison life, such as working toward a safe, secure, and predictable environment, are important first steps in moving toward that goal. Attempting to limit re-traumatization is another important step. Some prisoners also benefit from focused interventions such as individual or group therapy that enable them to build their skills. Like many other attempts to change correctional practices, there is resistance to implementing TIC, a resistance that is rooted in the inmate culture and also requires the buy-in of correctional staff (Levenson & Willis, 2019). The goal of TIC, however, is to help these people become more resilient and make a more successful transition from the prison to community life. We return to the topic of TIC in our review of women's programs in Chapter 11.

Inmate Social Systems and Prisonization Around the World

Prisonization has proved to be one of the most enduring and persistent concepts in corrections as it emerges wherever jails and prisons are built. The existence of an inmate social system, the convict code, and prison slang has been identified in studies in corrections in Canada, England, Germany, Israel, Mexico, New Zealand, Scandinavia, South Korea, Spain, and Ukraine. Those studies reveal that the more rigid the prison structure, the stronger the inmates' social system, and the less conventional their attitudes. Almost without exception, prisonization is associated with antisocial behavior and strong resistance to authority.

Researchers examining the existence of convict codes in other nations often find similar results to what American scholars report. Ricciardelli (2014), for instance, interviewed formerly incarcerated people in Canada and found results very similar to Mitchell's (2018) interviews with Texas prisoners. Ricciardelli (p. 234) identifies five main inmate rules in Canada including (a) never rat on a con, (b) be dependable (not loyal), (c) follow daily behavior rules, (d) abide by an "I don't see you,

COMPARATIVE ISSUES IN CORRECTIONS

you don't see me, and shut up already" philosophy, and (e) be fearless or at least act tough. Like the results from research carried out in prisons in the US and New Zealand, Canadian prisoners also have a hierarchy where child molesters had the lowest status and career criminals had the highest status.

The extent of prisonization might depend on the nature of the prison system. Prisons in Denmark, Norway, and Sweden are smaller and have nicer living conditions and amenities than US facilities. Sentences in these nations tend to be short and there are fewer restrictions on inmate movement. As a result, most of us would say there are bound to be some differences in prisonization and the inmate subculture. Yet, when Minke (2014) asked newly admitted inmates in Denmark about their introduction to prison life they described a code of conduct that discouraged interacting with COs and forbade stealing from other prisoners. Violating these rules results in being shunned or physically punished by the other inmates. Like in the United States, informing on other inmates or telling the staff if another prisoner was being exploited was sometimes punished with violence, and seldom were these assaults reported to the COs.

Inmate or convict codes are necessary to provide a structure for prisoners in their relationships with their peers and the prison staff. While the officers enforce the formal rules, the inmates create a set of informal rules to regulate each other's behavior in order to live in a more predictable environment with less volatility and violence (Winfree, Newbold, & Tubb, 2002). In order to better understand the issue, Symkovych (2018) interviewed prisoners in Ukraine. He found evidence of a convict code and observes that they "evolve along with the changing needs and profile of prisoners to sustain a predictable and relatively tolerable environment in a dehumanizing and inherently volatile place" (Symkovych, 2018, p. 1088).

JAIL AND PRISON GANGS: SECURITY THREAT GROUPS

The Evolution from the Convict Code to Prison Gang Code

Until the mid-1960s the inmate code dominated both academic and practitioner insights into the prison culture. The existence of this code lent a degree of stability to prison life and this approach was able to work given the relatively small numbers of prisoners and their lack of turnover. Prisoners generally knew each other, and they could predict how the other inmates would act. Older and more experienced prisoners had status within these facilities and younger inmates followed their advice. As a result, these inmates were relatively successful in self-regulation and reducing violence.

Other factors led to the prison's stability. There were fewer inmates with serious mental health problems, as they were still being placed in large asylums apart from prisons. By the 1970s, however, the nature of American corrections was changing. The numbers of individuals admitted to prison began to increase, and the characteristics of the prison population were also changing. In part, these changes were due to the experiment with the de-institutionalization of the mentally ill, which was not supported by subsequent expansions of community-based support programs and services. Consequently, a growing number of ex-mental patients ended up in jails and prisons. Moreover, the war on drugs, at least the version that started in the 1970s, also contributed to a growth in prison populations. The inmates incarcerated beginning in the mid- to late-1970s were younger and more ethnically and racially diverse than was previously the case. The older, Whiter, and more established convicts were often unable to exert much control on these younger, more racially and ethnically diverse prisoners. Taken together, these changes disrupted prison stability, and violence increased. Prison riots and other uprisings of the late 1970s and early 1980s were very visible reactions to these changes.

In fact, by the late 1960s, prison gangs had started to emerge, and like today they were based on racial and ethnic lines. Jacobs (1973, p. 399) describes how African American gangs were gaining footholds in Midwestern prisons. These gang members, many from large cities like Chicago, Los Angeles, and New York, saw themselves as political prisoners who advocated for revolution against White racism. Latinx gangs, by contrast, were also emerging in California and the states along the Mexican border.

The previously dominant informal inmate or convict code was slowly replaced. As Jacobs (1973) describes it, these gangs, which may have originated in the large cities, evolved in prison; they had new formal written rules that governed their members' behaviors, ones that defined gangs and gang behavior on the streets. Jacobs points out that inmates also brought with them their gang's organization, roles, and norms in a process he called **importation**. There is an opposing position: Skarbek (2014) says that some California street gangs originated within corrections. Once established, they were exported to the streets. Regardless of where these prison gangs originated, they became entrenched in American correctional facilities, and gangs such as the Aryan Brotherhood, Mexican Mafia, Nazi Lowriders, Nuestra Familia, and Black Guerilla Family have a significant presence in the community and in prisons.

Wood (2014, para. 7) says that "understanding how prison gangs work is difficult: they conceal their activities and kill defectors who reveal their practices." That one sentence summarizes why there is sometimes so much conflicting information about prison gang operations and their contributions to violence, CO corruption, their day-to-day influence on correctional operations, and the role they play in crime and violence on the streets. Not only have gang members become increasingly sophisticated, but their reach undeniably extends into the streets, given their access to contraband smart phones and social media.

Since the 1980s, prison officials have voiced increased concern about the prevalence of jail and prison gangs, mainly expressed in the development of interventions in the community and within correctional institutions to control them. Gangs are responsible for increased rates of correctional violence, and their influence in the underground prison economy is well-documented (Skarbek, 2014). As most prison gangs form along racial or ethnic lines, they also contribute to increasing racial tensions. Some researchers report their presence can undermine cooperative efforts with the prison administration (Skarbek, 2014). One of the problems that correctional administrators have had to overcome is that the presence of gangs has changed the culture within many correctional institutions, but researchers do not know the full extent of their influence, and it varies in different prison systems. Pyrooz and Decker (2019) say that gangs play a key role in the social order of prisons, although they also contend that gangs have lost some of the influence they once had.

Even the nature of prison gangs has changed significantly since the 1970s, as they have become less political and more concerned with profiting from the underground economy (Hunt, Riegel, Morales, & Waldorf, 1993). Most jail or prison gangs are loosely affiliated with at least one street gang, although the gang organization and leadership in jails and prisons tend to be more formal and sophisticated. For example, the Aryan Brotherhood, a White supremacist group, maintains ties with motorcycle gangs in the community, many of which are involved in the importation of contraband into correctional facilities and the distribution of illicit drugs on the streets.

Prison and Jail Gang Members

As viewed by most academics familiar with the topic, prison gangs are criminal organizations, although most corrections professionals refer to them as security threat groups (STGs), which are defined by the Arizona Department of Corrections (2019) as:

> Any organization, club, association or group of individuals, either formal or informal (including traditional prison gangs), that may have a common name or identifying symbol, and whose members engage in activities that would include, but are not limited to planning, organizing, threatening, financing, soliciting, committing or attempting to commit unlawful acts that would violate the department's written instructions, which detract from the safe and orderly operations of prisons.

Some definitions of STGs are more legalistic. The National Gang Intelligence Center (2015, p. 4) indicates that these groups must have a minimum size (usually three persons) who have a group identity, and whose main purpose is to (a) engage in crime, (b) their motivation is to maintain or perpetuate the gang, and (c) they have a set of ongoing characteristics such as a written charter or holding regular meetings.

Definitions of gang involvement become important when prosecutors are seeking harsher sentences based on an individual's gang activities. That is, many states have sentencing enhancements, essentially a sentence add-on, for persons known to be affiliated with a criminal gang (Caldwell, 2015). Furthermore, correctional officials must also validate the person's status as a gang member in order to manage their behaviors while incarcerated. The **validation** process determines that the prisoner is gang-involved and includes physical markers such as gang tattoos, reviewing the inmate's official records such as court documents and pre sentence investigation reports, and their admission that he or she is gang-involved.

Once validated as a gang member, the security rating might be increased and restrictions placed on internal movements and access to prison programs. These sanctions might include placing the gang member-inmate on a gang-only housing unit, and some state correctional systems—such as California—place validated gang members in restricted or segregated housing. These practices can be controversial, as these prisoners are placed in restricted housing not because they have engaged in misconduct, or because they are at-risk of victimization from other offenders, but because of the potential risks they pose (Pyrooz & Mitchell, 2019). Given those potential consequences validating gang involvement requires a thorough investigation generally carried out by the institution's security staff.

Given their secretive nature, it is difficult to estimate the true number of gang-involved inmates. Academic and government researchers have surveyed jails and prisons and asked the administrators of those facilities how many of their inmates belonged to gangs. More than a dozen years ago, Ruddell, Decker, and Egley (2006) found that 13.2% of jail inmates were gang-involved, while Pyrooz and Mitchell (2019) found that 18.5% of prisoners were gang members. By applying those numbers to the entire correctional population, we can estimate there are almost 400,000 gang-involved jail and prison inmates (see Table 8.1). However, because gang activities are so secretive,

TABLE 8.1 Estimated Prison Gang Population, 2017

Inmate Population (2017)	Percentage Gang Involved (Estimate)	Estimated Gang Population
Jails: 745,200	13.2	98,366
Prisons: 1,489,363	18.5	275,532

Sources: Bronson and Carson (2019); Zeng (2019).

TABLE 8.2 Distinctions between Prison and Street Gangs

Prison Gangs	Street Gangs
Blood in/Blood out: Prisoners have to kill to join and death is the only exit in hard core STGs such as the Aryan Brotherhood (e.g. life membership).	Jump in/Jump out: New recruits submit to a beating to join or leave the gang.
Unite under the banner of one name and identify with one set of signs and symbols such as art and tattoos.	Unite under the banner of one name and identify with one set of signs and symbols such as art and tattoos.
Conflict management: Controlled by leaders.	Chaotic approach to conflict management.
Identifiable leadership such as a "shot caller" in a prison gang (who directs a group of prisoners). Rigid membership is hierarchical, and leadership must be earned.	Leadership can be fluid and can be purchased.
Operate according to bylaws, written rules, and an organizational structure. Strict control of members given the confined space of a prison.	Loosely structured and less rigid organizational stçructures. Less control exerted over members given the lack of boundaries in the community.
Form almost exclusively on racial or ethnic lines.	May have a racially or ethnically diverse composition.
Criminally more sophisticated: Purpose of the gang is to further its power, reputation, and resources.	Less sophisticated: Street gangs commit offenses on behalf of prison gangs.
Often invisible to law enforcement.	Visible to law enforcement and the general public given their dress (e.g. "colors").
Originated in prisons and expanded throughout state and federal prison systems due to inmate transfers.	Typically, territorial and limited to one city, region, or state.

Sources: Arizona Department of Corrections (2019); National Gang Intelligence Center (2015); Ortiz (2018).

it is impossible to come up with a true total. Nevertheless, these estimates provide us with a reference point in our discussion on gangs.

The term gang is very broad, and that label is often used to describe prison and street gangs, as well as terrorist and traditional criminal organizations, including the Italian Mafia. However, definitions of gang often will vary across the nation. When it comes to different types of these groups, the Arizona Department of Corrections (2019), National Gang Intelligence Center (2015, p. 17), and Ortiz (2018, p. 102) provide a further breakdown between the characteristics of street and prison gangs, and this is presented in Table 8.2.

Gang Problems

The presence of STGs can undermine the authority of COs, along with the value of the rehabilitative programming offered within a prison. Ruddell, Decker, and Egley (2006) observe that gang-involved inmates "contribute to higher rates of prison violence, increase racial tensions within prisons, challenge rehabilitative programming by supporting antisocial values or beliefs, and engage in criminal enterprises within prisons." This assessment was confirmed by Winterdyk and Ruddell's (2010) survey of prison administrators, who indicated that the number of gang members in their facilities was increasing, and these gangs were more sophisticated, engaged in violence, increased disruptive behaviors within their facilities and undermined rehabilitative programs. Being involved in gangs also contributes to higher rates of recidivism once they are returned to the community (Dooley, Seals, & Skarbek, 2014). That finding has a common-sense appeal, as those former prisoners are still members of criminal organizations and have not changed their pro-criminal thinking.

The prison administrators surveyed by Winterdyk and Ruddell said that about one-fifth of their prison populations were gang involved, and about one-half of them were not affiliated with a gang when they were admitted to prison (see also Pyrooz & Decker, 2019, p. 192). When asked the most important reasons inmates joined prison gangs, these administrators reported that the primary reasons were due to fears of victimization and to benefit from a sense of belonging. These administrators were least likely to report that prisoners joined gangs in order to profit or to access contraband: these results are shown in Table 8.3. Inmates' obligations to their gang also vary, and some prison gangs require a "blood in-blood out" commitment—and members are prepared to die for their gang—whereas some prisoners informally associated with the gang may not have much loyalty to the group and will never become full members.

Ross and Richards (2002, p. 127) take it a step further, claiming that, "Some penitentiaries are literally run by gangs. In those pens, if you don't join one faction or another,

TABLE 8.3 Reasons for Joining Prison Gangs: Order of Importance

Fear of other inmates/gangs
Sense of belonging
Increase their status
Access to contraband
Economic benefits (least important reason)

Source: Winterdyk and Ruddell (2010).

you may not be able to defend yourself." One of the ironies of joining a prison gang for safety is that research shows that joining gangs exposes members to more violence. In order to enhance their status and wealth gang leaders manage the prison environment by reducing the number of random or unplanned acts of violence carried out by prisoners. As Ortiz (2018, p. 113) says:

> Prison gang members must maintain strict daily routines, which dictate their every movement. Within prisons, gang members must obey these rules of conduct or face violent disciplinary action from their organization [and] Prison gang members must acquire permission to attack or retaliate against another inmate, even inmates from rival gangs. This requirement is due to a mutual need to reduce the level of violence within the prison. Any form of violence committed by one inmate may result in the loss of privileges for both his organization and all inmates within the facility.

PHOTO 8.5

A Mara Salvatrucha (MS-13) gang member shows off gang tattoos in prison. While associated with El Salvador, where it is one of the most dangerous and violent gangs in the world, MS-13 actually began as a street gang in southern California in the 1970s and 1980s. MS-13 gang members are found in many US prisons; however, in El Salvador there is a special prison "reserved" for them that is allegedly run by gang members. US prisons often segregate gang members, what they call security threat group (STG) members, in separate housing units, but not entire prisons. Credit: Jan Sochor/Alamy Stock Photo.

While gang members may be less vulnerable to unplanned or random violence, their efforts at managing prison violence benefit the entire gang. The reason why goes to the heart of why they are tolerated: correctional officials are less likely to investigate or interrupt the underground economy when things are running smoothly.

The correctional gang problem varies throughout the country, and some jurisdictions may have a relatively small population of gang-involved inmates (Winterdyk & Ruddell, 2010). There are also differences in the prevalence of gang members within prison systems, and there may be very little pressure for people admitted to low-security facilities to join a STG. Rural and youth gangs, for instance, tend to have a shorter lifespan than gangs from urban areas. Some gangs, such as the Black Guerilla Family, have an intergenerational membership that remains active. In addition, some of these groups are involved in the drug trade with some individual members becoming very wealthy, while other gangs are transient and poorly led and disorganized. All these factors will have an impact on the types of interventions that correctional officials use to respond to these groups.

Gangs and Corrections Operations: Do STGs Run Some Jails and Prisons?

It was earlier claimed by at least one researcher that gangs ran some prisons. Most of us believe that prison gang members act randomly and violently without giving much thought to the outcomes of their actions. Like the members of any other informal or formal organization, however, the individuals who establish and run prison gangs tend to act very methodically and out of self-interest. For example, in June 2019, reporters explained how gangs were openly running some jails and prisons, and these investigators used an example from a privately run Mississippi prison to illustrate their point. This is not a new problem, and the case study in Chapter 5 describes how gang members were running the Baltimore City Detention Center with only minor interference from the correctional personnel. Unlike what happened in Baltimore, where the number of drug-related crimes happening within these gang-operated facilities increased with little reported violence, the 950-bed Mississippi facility described by Neff and Santo (2019) became a violent place. It had two homicides per year, which is many times higher than the national average for prison murders. While most prison research shows that less than one-quarter of all prisoners are gang-involved, Gates (2019, para. 1) says that more than 80% of the prisoners in the Mississippi facility were gang-involved.

It is troubling that correctional administrators in some facilities are openly working with the gang leaders to manage the day-to-day operations on the living units. Neff and Santo (2019, para. 8) say that the warden of the Mississippi prison "turned to gang leaders to keep the inmates under control." An audit of the facility carried out by the Management Training Corporation (2018, p. 6) found that:

> The prevalence of not only STG activity, but staff's tolerance of it, cannot be understated. Gang graffiti is evident throughout the facility. STG leaders are surrounded by their "security" at all times…STG leaders control who gets jobs and other preferential treatment… [And]… it never felt like staff were in control of the offender population. It was evident from observations and interviews that staff do not enforce rules or perform routine duties consistently.

The auditors investigating the living conditions in this prison were concerned about the gang leaders who were given these powers, and they point out that:

> When inmates exert power over other inmates, they can use this to coerce, manipulate, control, or threaten individuals to get what they want and satisfy their own needs. Not only does this have safety implications but it is not conductive to a

healthy, pro-social environment and can interfere with rehabilitative efforts. Gang leaders will reinforce behaviors they value – these behaviors are most likely antisocial and criminal.

(Management Training Corporation, 2018, p. 6)

Neff and Santo (2019) say that the correctional administrators lost control of the Mississippi facility because of a lack of staff. Over one-third of the positions were vacant and almost nine out of ten COs quit every year. Ultimately, few people want to work in a violent and gang-infested environment for only slightly more than minimum wage.

A question arising from these observations is whether the practice of gangs running correctional facilities is widespread. In an influential book, Skarbek (2014) describes the behind-the-scenes influence that prison gangs enjoy. He claims that their existence is totally rational as individuals join gangs to increase their safety and security in a hostile and unpredictable environment that is fueled by distrust and where the inmate's needs are not being met by staff in the formal operations of the prison system. When things are operating efficiently, gang leaders enable their members to informally resolve disputes and solve problems without outbreaks of violence. Thus, they operate in the background, although COs give tacit approval for some of their behaviors.

Gangs enable their members and other inmates to access scarce resources, including smart phones, illicit drugs, and alcohol. Because such items are banned, the demand is high, as is the profit in their supply. Gangs can draw upon their internal resources and street connections to increase the flow of contraband into facilities. The danger is that the links between the prison and street gangs are becoming more powerful, and feuds that start in within the prison can continue onto the streets. In addition, some prison gangs operate protection rackets where members of rival or unaffiliated street gangs admitted to jails or prisons are required to pay protection or they are victimized.

One of the hazards of the expansion in the number of gang-involved prisoners is that their values are antisocial and criminogenic. As a result, they may have very little interest in prison-based rehabilitative programs. Moreover, these former prisoners are at higher risk of recidivism given their ties to the criminogenic gangs. Some, for example, may believe that they are unable to leave their gang and stay alive, even if this belief is in part myth (Pyrooz & Decker, 2019). Ultimately, the survival skills that protected them while incarcerated may increase their likelihood of engaging in crime.

Throughout this book we have addressed the issue of vested interests. In this case, officials profiting from their roles in the criminal justice system seldom advocate for reforms that would result in downsizing the mass imprisonment industry, as these changes may jeopardize their careers and status. A similar case exists for prison gang leaders. As gangs become more established and control more of the underground prison economy, it is not in the interest of the members to discontinue or downsize their illicit operations. In addition to the revenue from the prison economy, gang leaders are also awarded power, influence, and status. This clout transfers onto the streets as prisons are increasingly open given the inmates' access to contraband smart phones.

Responding to Gangs

Several strategies have been developed to respond to STGs. Among the most common gang-intervention techniques in prisons are intelligence sharing (between correctional institutions and community-based law enforcement agencies) and aggressive prosecution of crimes that gang members commit in prison. Other strategies to reduce gang influence include isolating or segregating these inmates or preventing them from communicating with other members. In California, for example, validated or verified gang members are placed in segregated units or facilities and are held in their cells up to 23 hours a day, sometimes for years.

In a somewhat pessimistic assessment, Lessing (2016, pp. 2–3) says that prison gangs might be almost impossible to eradicate, and his three observations are summarized as follows:

- Anti-gang crackdowns, which often raise incarceration rates, lengthen sentences, and worsen prison conditions, can help prison gangs establish authority outside prison, organize criminal markets, and lead to mass violence and protest.
- Mass imprisonment policies helped prison gangs establish their authority, both within prison and on the street, and reducing correctional populations or improving prison conditions might not change those conditions, especially given the formality of prison gangs with their written constitutions and formal structures.
- Reducing or undermining gang authority—which might be impossible given their entrenched nature—might only result in outbreaks of violent infighting and/or a chaotic scramble for power.

Given those realities, Lessing (2016, pp. 3–4) advocates for acknowledging the true extent of the gang problem (rather than minimizing it), creating incentives for gang leaders to avoid violence and antisocial behavior, and investing in strategies that counter the expansion of prison gangs in non-criminal enterprises.

Prison administrators are currently using gang management strategies to suppress or manage inmate gangs. Some states experimented with gang-free prisons to reduce the influence of gangs and cut the number of unaffiliated inmates or people who joined their first gang after their admission to prison. That practice, however, never caught on with most prison systems. Winterdyk and Ruddell (2010, p. 733) asked correctional administrators about the strategies they thought were most effective in responding to gangs, and these officials reported the following list of effective strategies:

- Restricted housing (e.g. segregation/isolation or specialized housing units for gang members)
- Restrictions on a gang member's privileges such as visits, program participation, commissary, access to communication or employment
- Increase the security classification/ratings of gang members (e.g. which places inmates in higher security units, restricts their privileges, and may slow a release to the community)
- Delay parole eligibility for gang members
- Loss of good time credits for gang members

Before any of these strategies can be implemented, jails and prisons must determine whether an individual is a gang member, and COs are hired specifically in these intelligence gathering roles. A foundation for any prison system's gang management strategy is to gather and share intelligence about STGs, and administrators identified the following investigative strategies as very effective: monitoring STG phone conversations, searching their mail, analyzing their phone records, and tracking their involvement in misconduct (Winterdyk & Ruddell, 2010). Over three-quarters (78%) of the prison administrators in their study report that sharing information on gang members was a very effective gang-management strategy, and these officials also thought that sharing information with other prison systems and law enforcement was an effective practice.

Pyrooz and Decker (2019) observe that some correctional officials try to get gang members to renounce their gang membership (**gang renunciation**). Gang members can sometimes be persuaded to make significant changes in their lives after some sort of crisis such as being victimized or if they feel abandoned by their gang. Many people age out of gang life as the excitement of being involved in gang activities in one's teen years or 20s can seem different when they are in their 40s. Exiting can be difficult or impossible in prison gangs with "blood-in, blood-out" practices. Gutierrez (2019, para. 30) is an exception and he joined his first gang as a juvenile living in northern California, but became disenchanted by his gang involvement as he aged:

> I've since left the gang, and plan on removing all of my tattoos. I became disillusioned over time. Lost faith in the leadership. Hypocrites, most of them. The whole experience, I realized, was like a strange mix between junior high school and the Roman Senate. Petty. Treacherous. Although I rose through the ranks myself, and

ended up in the infamous Security Housing Unit at Pelican Bay State Prison, I knew in my heart that it was over.

Despite being tired of his gang activities, Gutierrez (2019, para. 35) says that:

Walking away was difficult. Not only did I instantly become an anathema to many of the people I now had to be segregated from a different yard...I'd also identified as a gangster my entire life. It was the perspective through which I saw the world. If I was no longer that, then what was I?

Like other challenges we have identified in the previous chapters, there are no easy answers to some of these problems. If a prison gang members' identities provide them with status, influence, and wealth, how can we get them to renounce their illicit activities?

SUMMARY

In this chapter we explored prison life. Today's inmate shares much in common with his or her counterparts of 50 years ago because many of the challenges they confront—deprivations or the pains of imprisonment—have not changed, and some may have become more painful. However, in other important ways, prisoners are changing to meet a new prison world. Key points of interest to consider in this chapter are as follows:

- Prisoners today face the same pains of imprisonment that confronted jail and prison inmates decades or even centuries ago.
- The pains of imprisonment can be worsened by overcrowding, the use of solitary confinement, and being traumatized while incarcerated.
- The inmate subculture is evolving and while the convict code still exists, prison gang members now have the wealth, power, and status that older convicts enjoyed prior to the 1970s.
- The inmate subculture may be universal, as researchers have found that the informal culture in American jails and prisons is remarkably similar to that of other nations.
- Never a pleasant living environment, current conditions in the nation's jails and prisons may be worse than they were in the 1950s, largely due to mass imprisonment and a lack of services to respond to the larger prison population.
- Inmate gangs have been gaining more power and influence, and they play a significant role in the operations of some correctional facilities with the tacit support of the staff.

While this chapter has focused upon the living conditions and prison life, the next chapter focuses on some of the negative outcomes in American corrections: violence, self-harm and suicide, and unrest.

KEY TERMS

- convict code (inmate code)
- fish
- gang renunciation
- importation
- prison consultant
- prison subculture
- prisonization

- radicalization
- security threat group (STG)
- snitch
- trauma
- trauma-informed care (TIC)
- validation

THINKING ABOUT CORRECTIONAL POLICIES AND PRACTICES: WRITING ASSIGNMENTS

1. In a one-page essay explain one of these positions: (a) jail and prison inmates are the same because…or (b) jail and prison inmates are different because….
2. Explain how new prisoners are socialized into prison life.
3. In a brief essay describe steps prison administrators could take to reduce the number of people who become gang-involved after their admission to jail or prison.
4. Prepare a one-page paper on the negative impacts of trauma on the health of jail and prison inmates.
5. Explain why the convict code can make an individual's prison stay safer and more predictable.

CRITICAL REVIEW QUESTIONS

1. What is the hazard of giving prison gang leaders the authority to run parts of the prison routine?
2. What are the factors that would increase the likelihood of an inmate's prisonization?
3. Is the inmate subculture driven by internal or external factors?
4. Describe the difference between the importation and deprivation approaches to the inmate social culture.
5. How are Fuller's (2013) commandments for new prisoners related to the convict code?

6. Which of the three prison effects is the most stressful for inmates?
7. What are the main differences between a street and prison gang?
8. Which of the five deprivations of prison life has the least impact on an inmate's life?
9. Describe some of the issues that complicate our understanding of sex in jails or prisons.
10. A similar convict code emerges in prisons around the world: provide some reasons why this might happen.

CASE

Wallace v. Baldwin Case No. 17-CV-0576-DRH (S.D. Ill. Jul. 5, 2017)

REFERENCES

Alabama Department of Corrections. (2020). *Alabama Department of Corrections monthly statistical report (January 2020)*. Retrieved from http://www.doc.state.al.us/docs/MonthlyRpts/DMR%2001%20January%202020PUB.pdf

Arizona Department of Corrections. (2019). *What is a security threat group?* Retrieved from https://corrections.az.gov/public-resources/inspector-general/security-threat-group-unit/security-threat-group-faqs

Association of State Correctional Administrators. (2016). *Aiming to reduce time-in-cell*. New Haven, CT: Arthur Liman Public Interest Program, Yale Law School.

Bentz, B., Seavy-Nesper, M., & Hensley, S. (2018). From convict to criminal justice reporter: 'I was so lucky to come out of this." *National Public Radio*. Retrieved from https://www.npr.org/sections/health-shots/2018/12/12/676041064/from-convict-to-criminal-justice-reporter-i-was-so-lucky-to-come-out-of-this

Blakinger, K. (2015, Jan. 21). Heroin addiction sent me to prison. White privilege got me out and to the Ivy League. *The Washington Post*. Retrieved from https://www.washingtonpost.com/posteverything/wp/2015/01/21/heroin-addiction-sent-me-to-prison-white-privilege-got-me-out-and-to-the-ivy-league/?utm_term=.a5a3742a466b

Bronson, J., & Carson, E. A. (2019). *Prisoners in 2017*. Washington, DC: Bureau of Justice Statistics.

Caldwell, H. (2015). Reeling in gang prosecution: Seeking balance in gang prosecution. *University of Pennsylvania Journal of Law and Social Change, 18*(4), 341–376.

Carson, E. A. (2018). *Prisoners in 2016*. Washington, DC: Bureau of Justice Statistics.

Cecil, D. K., & Leitner, J. L. (2009). Unlocking the gates: An examination of MSNBC investigates – Lockup. *The Howard Journal, 48*(2), 184–199.

Clemmer, D. (1940). *The prison community*. New York: Holt, Rinehart and Winston.

Dooley, B. D., Seals, A., & Skarbek, D. (2014). The effect of prison gang membership on recidivism. *Journal of Criminal Justice, 42*(3), 267–275.

Eigenberg, H. M. (2000). Corrections officers' definitions of rape in male prisons. *Journal of Criminal Justice, 28*(5), 435–449.

Ewing, M., & Stroud, M. (2018). Over 100 Pennsylvania prisoners are held in solitary confinement – with no end in sight. *The Appeal*. Retrieved from https://theappeal.org/over-100-pennsylvania-prisoners-are-held-in-solitary-confinement-with-no-end-in-sight-3c680de29b50/

Fishman, J. F. (1934). *Sex in prison: Revealing sex conditions in American prisons*. New York: National Library.

Fleisher, M. S., & Krienert, J. L. (2009). *The myth of prison rape: Sexual culture in American prisons*. New York: Rowman & Littlefield.

Fuller, J. (2013). *The ten prison commandments*. Secaucus, NJ: Prison Coach Speaking & Consulting LLC.

Gates, J. E. (2019, June 26). Private Mississippi prison operator denies gangs are in charge. *Mississippi Clarion Ledger*. Retrieved from https://www.clarionledger.com/story/news/politics/2019/06/26/private-prison-company-addresses-report-gangs-severe-problems/1559071001/

Goffman, E. (1961). *Asylums: Essays on the social situation of mental patients and other inmates*. New York: Anchor.

Gutierrez, B. (2019, January 31). Why I quit my California prison gang. *The Marshall Project*. Retrieved from https://www.themarshallproject.org/2019/01/31/why-i-quit-my-prison-gang

Hamm, M. S. (2008). Prisoner radicalization: Assessing the threat in U.S. correctional institutions. *National Institute of Justice Journal, 261*, 14–19.

Haney, C. (2012). Prison effects in the era of mass incarceration. *The Prison Journal*. Retrieved from https://journals.sagepub.com/doi/abs/10.1177/ 0032885512448604

Hensley, C, & Tewksbury, R. (2005). Wardens' perceptions of prison sex. *The Prison Journal, 85*(2), 186–197.

Hulley, S., Crewe, B., & Wright, S. (2016). Re-examining the problems of long-term imprisonment. *British Journal of Criminology, 56*(4), 769–792.

Hunt, G., Riegel, S., Morales, T., & Waldorf, D. (1993). Changes in prison culture: Prison gangs and the case of the "Pepsi generation." *Social Problems, 40*(3), 398–409.

Hunter, R., & Heinke, D. (2011). Radicalization of Islamist terrorists in the western world. *FBI Law Enforcement Bulletin*. Retrieved from https://leb.fbi.gov/articles/perspective/perspective-radicalization-of-islamist-terrorists-in-the-western-world

Jacobs, J. B. (1973). Street gangs behind bars. *Social Problems, 21*(3), 395–409.

LaFree, G., Jiang, B., & Porter, L. C. (2019). Prison and violent political extremism in the United States. *Journal of Quantitative Criminology*. Published online ahead of print at: doi:10.1007/ s10940-019-09412-1

Lessing, B. (2016). *Inside out: The challenge of prison-based criminal organizations*. Washington, DC: Brookings Institution.

Levenson, J. S., & Willis, G. M. (2019). Implementing trauma-informed care in correctional treatment and supervision. *Journal of Aggression, Maltreatment & Trauma, 28*(4), 481–501.

Management Training Corporation. (2018). *Audit of Wilkinson County Correctional Facility*. Retrieved from: https://www.themarshallproject.org/documents/ 6162195-MTC-Audit-STG-Section

Martin, J. L., Lichtenstein, B., Jenkot, R. B., & Forde, D. R. (2012). "They can take us over any time they want": Correctional officers' responses to overcrowding. *The Prison Journal, 92*(1), 88–105.

Minke, L. K. (2014). A study of prisonization among Danish prisoners. *Prison Service Journal, 211*, 37–42.

Mitchell, M. M. (2018). *The convict code revisited: An examination of prison culture and its association with violent misconduct and victimization*. Dissertation retrieved from file:///C:/Users/ruddell/Downloads/MITCHELL-DISSERTATION-2018.pdf

Moster, A. N., & Jeglic, E. L. (2009). Prison warden attitudes toward prison rape and sexual assault. *The Prison Journal, 89*(1), 65–78.

National Gang Intelligence Center. (2015). *National gang report, 2015*. Washington, DC: Author. https://www.fbi.gov/file-repository/stats-services-publications-national-gang-report-2015.pdf/view

Neff, J., & Santo, A. (2019). Corporate confession: Gangs ran this private prison. *The Marshall Project*. Retrieved from https://www.themarshallproject.org/2019/06/26/corporate-confession-gangs-ran-this-private-prison

Ortiz, J. M. (2018). Gangs and environment: A comparative analysis of prison and street gangs. *American Journal of Qualitative Research, 2*(1), 97–117.

Pyrooz, D. C., & Decker, S. H. (2019). *Competing for control: Gangs and the social order of the prison*. New York: Cambridge University Press.

Pyrooz, D. C., & Mitchell, M. M. (2019). The use of restrictive housing on gang and non-gang affiliated inmates in U.S. prisons: Findings from a national survey of correctional agencies. *Justice Quarterly*. Printed online ahead of print.

Rantala, R. R. (2018). *Sexual victimization reported by adult correctional authorities 2002–2015*. Washington, DC: Bureau of Justice Statistics.

Ricciardelli, R. (2014). An examination of the inmate code in Canadian penitentiaries. *Journal of Crime and Justice, 37*(2), 234–255.

Ross, J. I., & Richards, S. C. (2002). *Behind bars: Surviving prison*. Indianapolis, IN: Delta Press.

Ruddell, R., Decker, S. H., & Egley, A. (2006). Gang interventions in jails: A national analysis. *Criminal Justice Review, 31*(1), 33–46.

Santos, F. (2012, Aug. 1). When a taste for publicity bites back. *The New York Times*. Retrieved from https://www.nytimes.com/2012/08/02/us/an-arizona-sheriffs-fondness-for-publicity-may-bite-back.html?pagewanted=all

Shammas, V. L. (2017). Pains of imprisonment. In K. R. Kerley (Ed.), *The encyclopedia of corrections* (pp. 1–5). New York: John Wiley and Sons.

Skarbek, D. (2014). *The social order of the underworld*. New York: Oxford University Press.

Spencer, T. (2018). I spent 17 days in solitary for having two onions in my cell. The isolation changed me. *Publicsource*. Retrieved from https://www.publicsource.org/i-spent-17-days-in-solitary-for-having-two-onions-in-my-cell-the-isolation-changed-me/

Stein, J. (2013, April 24). Released from prison after $50K heroin bust, fmr. Cornell student gets clean, writes book. *The Cornell Daily Sun*. Retrieved from https://cornellsun.com/2013/04/24/released-from-prison-after-50k-heroin-bust-fmr-cornell-student-gets-clean-writes-book/

Stensrud, R. H., Gilbride, D. D., & Bruinekool, R. M. (2019). The childhood to prison pipeline: Early childhood trauma as reported by a prison population. *Rehabilitation Counseling Bulletin, 62*(4), 195–208.

Sykes, G. M. (1958). *The society of captives: A study of a maximum security prison*. Princeton, NJ: Princeton University Press.

Sykes, G. M., & Messinger, S. (1960). The inmate social code and its functions. InR. A. Cloward, D. R. Cressey, G. H. Grossner, R. McCleary, L. E. Ohlin, G. M. Sykes, & S. L. Messinger (Eds.), *Theoretical studies in the social organization of the prison* (pp. 5–19). New York: Social Science Research Council.

Symkovych, A. (2018). The 'inmate code' in flux: A normative system and extralegal governance in a Ukrainian prison. *Current Sociology, 66*(7), 1087–1105.

U.S. Bureau of Prisons. (2020). *Offenses*. Retrieved from https://www.bop.gov/about/statistics/statistics_inmate_offenses.jsp

U.S. Department of Justice. (2019). Terms and definitions: Corrections. Retrieved from https://www.bjs.gov/index.cfm?ty=tdtp&tid=1

Wilkerson, G. T. (2018). Its surprisingly tough to avoid snitching in prison. *The Marshall Project*. Retrieved from https://www.themarshallproject.org/ 2018/07/19/it-s-surprisingly-tough-to-avoid-snitching-in-prison

Winfree, L. T., Jr., Newbold, G., & Tubb, S. H. (2002). Prisoner perspectives on inmate culture in New Mexico and New Zealand: A descriptive case study. *The Prison Journal, 82*(2), 213–233.

Winterdyk, J., & Ruddell, R. (2010). Managing prison gangs: Results from a survey of U.S. prison systems. *Journal of Criminal Justice, 38*(4), 730–736.

Wood, G. (2014). How gangs took over prisons. *The Atlantic*. Retrieved from https://www.theatlantic.com/magazine/archive/2014/10/how-gangs-took-over-prisons/379330/

Woodfox, A. (2019). After 40 years in solitary, activist Albert Woodfox tells his story of survival. *The Guardian*. Retrieved from https://www.theguardian.com/us-news/2019/mar/04/after-40-years-in-solitary-activist-albert-woodfox-tells-his-story-of-survival

Zeng, Z. (2019). *Jail inmates in 2017*. Washington, DC: Bureau of Justice Statistics.

Chapter 9
Living and Dying in Prison

OUTLINE

OBJECTIVES

After reading this chapter you will be able to:

- Describe the challenges posed by life-sentenced prisoners for prison systems

- Explain why the pains of imprisonment are worsened for long-term prisoners and lifers

- Explain why women experience long-term imprisonment differently than men

- Describe how litigation has changed the use of the death penalty

- Provide some reasons why the numbers of death sentences and actual executions have been decreasing

- Describe the living conditions for death row inmates

CASE STUDY

Jeffrey Epstein's Suicide

Jeffrey Epstein committed suicide in New York's Metropolitan Correctional Center (MCC)—a facility operated by the Bureau of Prisons (BOP)—on 10 August 2019. Epstein, a 66-year-old who had previously been convicted of committing sex offenses, was awaiting trial on federal charges for the sex trafficking of minors. Epstein's death was not unusual, as Bureau of Justice Statistics reveals that about one inmate dies every day in an American jail due to suicide, and that number has been increasing since 2000 (Carson & Cowhig, 2020a). Epstein's case drew national attention simply because he was a high-profile inmate who moved in the same social circles as former President Clinton and President Trump, as well as other prominent individuals, including Britain's Prince Andrew.

In addition to his high-profile status, the circumstances of Epstein's death were controversial, but probably not all that unusual. He allegedly tried to hang himself several weeks before his death and after being assessed by a psychologist he was taken off a suicide watch. The investigation carried out after his death alleged that both officers responsible for supervising Epstein's unit had not checked on him for several hours and failed to do the 30-minute checks required by policy (Benner & Ivory, 2019). There were also irregularities associated with the facility's staffing when Epstein died. One of the officers supervising Epstein's unit was a former correctional officer who was employed in another role within the facility but had volunteered to work overtime. The second officer had been required to work overtime as the facility was understaffed.

Attorney General William Barr (2019), who administratively oversees the BOP, has expressed his anger with Epstein's death. Barr has pledged to "get to the bottom of what happened at the MCC and we will hold people accountable for this failure." In November 2019 the two BOP employees who were working on Epstein's unit were charged with falsifying records and engaging in a conspiracy. According to Allyn (2019) these officers were browsing the Internet and were sleeping on the job while Epstein died in his cell about 15 feet from their post.

Few jail inmates who die in custody get more than a line or two in the local newspaper because most of them are homeless, poor, beset by mental health problems, and often members of minority groups. Their deaths are not surprising, given the health-related problems of these jail inmates (see Chapter 5). Yet, there are also critics who contend that many of these deaths are preventable, and correctional staff are indifferent to their plight. Gonnerman (2019) quotes a doctor who worked in New York City's Correctional Health Services as saying the following about jail operations: "Because jails are chaotic and concealed from outside view, we only become aware of them when very bad outcomes occur, such as deaths."

Critical Questions

1. Although only about one-third of jail inmates have been found guilty, explain why we seem to be indifferent to their plight.
2. Do you agree that there are systemic problems, such as short-staffing or under-funding, that underlie many of the problems highlighted in the case studies presented in these chapters? Why or why not?
3. Explain why it is important for the public to have a full understanding of what happens behind the closed doors of America's jails and prisons.

INTRODUCTION

The topic of this chapter is different than the preceding ones as there is very little reference to rehabilitation or helping prisoners making a safe transition back into the community. Instead, our focus is on the growing number of inmates who will spend the rest of their lives behind bars. Stearns, Swanson, and Etie (2019) question whether this population should be called the **walking dead**, given that they can become forgotten as a consequence of their "social death." Although the average time served in prison is about three years, the number of long-term prisoners has been steadily increasing since the 1990s. The Sentencing Project (2018, p. 1) estimates that over 200,000 of the nearly 1.5 million state and federal prisoners—or about one in seven prisoners—will be incarcerated for decades or never be returned to the community.

In addition to the life-sentenced prisoners—called **lifers** in this chapter—there are over 2,600 people condemned to die (Death Penalty Information Center, 2020). As we described in Chapter 1, federal and state prison systems are responsible for carrying out executions of death-sentenced individuals. Prior to the 1940s, the responsibility for these **condemned prisoners** was typically undertaken by sheriffs and many executions took place at the local jail. As the death penalty is falling out of favor, the number of people sentenced to die and their executions have been dropping since their peak in 1999.

Renaud (2018) reminds us that the numbers of long-term prisoners are more than statistics; they are human beings living out their lives in cages. Although about 90% of them have engaged in violent crimes, Renaud (2018, para. 3) says that "people should not spend decades in prison without a meaningful chance of release." In the sections that follow we describe their living conditions and adjustment to long-term sentences.

There are several challenges associated with housing so many people serving lengthy sentences or who will die in prison. One of the foremost is when inmates age, they place a significant burden on a prison's capacity to provide constitutionally mandated health care. Some have questioned the wisdom of imprisoning 75- and 80-year-olds as few of them pose any serious risk to the public (The Osborne Association, 2018). The enactment of the *First Step Act* in 2018 enabled some federal prisoners to be returned to the community under compassionate release polices if their circumstances were extraordinary and compelling (Samuels, La Vigne, & Thomson, 2019). Within seven months of enacting the legislation, however, the Bureau of Prisons reported that only 51 *First Step Act* applications had been approved (U.S. Department of Justice, 2019).

State prison systems are also grappling with the challenges of housing a growing number of elderly, infirm, or chronically ill individuals, including those with life-threatening illnesses. Handtke, Bretschneider, Elger, and Wangmo (2017) observe that releasing these prisoners sends two messages to the public. The first relates to fiscal responsibility, where the financial costs of caring for them shift from the prison system to community health. The second message is one of compassion as these terminally ill people can then spend their last days with family members. Although the first message is appealing to the public, there is a reluctance to send these prisoners home, and compassionate releases are rarely granted (Thompson, 2018). Forty-six states have some form of compassionate release policies for elderly prisoners or those in ill-health, but four states (Illinois, Iowa, Nebraska, and Utah) have no written policies (Holland, Prost, Hoffman, & Dickinson, 2018).

Some inmates suffer from chronic illnesses such as heart disease, and their long-term prospects are grim. As we noted in Chapters 5 and 6, people living in jails and prisons tend to be less physically and psychologically healthy than the general population. The delivery of satisfactory medical care for these inmates is always the leading cause of prisoner lawsuits (see Chapter 12). These prisoners tend to have the worst of both worlds, as they are sick, and they are unable to access adequate care. As a result, mortality rates are high in jails and prisons. In 2016, there were almost 1,100 jail deaths and over 4,100 prison deaths (Carson & Cowhig, 2020a, 2020b). Carson and Cowhig found that illnesses, including cancer and heart disease, account for about two-thirds of these deaths.

With respect to unexpected deaths, as noted in the Epstein example, almost 350 jail inmates kill themselves every year, while about 250 state or federal prisoners die from completed suicides (Carson & Cowhig, 2020a, 2020b). About 125 jail inmates and state prisoners are murdered every year and those numbers have been increasing. However, some jail administrators have been accused of manipulating their information about inmate deaths to intentionally undercount the number of fatalities (Wilson, Schick, Jenkins, & Brownstone, 2019). One approach jail administrators use to reduce their deaths-in-custody statistics is to transfer inmates who are ill or have been severely injured in an assault or accident to a community hospital. If that inmate dies, the death is not counted as occurring "in custody" as they were formally released from the jail.

In this regard, Wilson et al. (2019) describe how a Spokane County Jail inmate hanged himself and was transported to a local hospital after the suicide attempt. While this inmate was on life support at the hospital, he was officially released from custody. After he died in hospital, his death was not considered an in-custody death. As a result, the jail would not include this death in its annual report to the Bureau of Justice Statistics on prisoner mortality. We question how many times the manipulation of statistics happens throughout the country every year. Like other examples presented in previous chapters, we are not always aware of the true scope of the problem or the accuracy of the government data. This limits our understanding of what actually happens in US correctional facilities, and whether conditions of living (and dying) in prisons and jails are getting better or worse.

Photo 9.1
On 10 August 2019, financier Jeffery Epstein, who had pled not guilty to both sex trafficking and conspiracy charges and was being held without bail, died in his cell at the Metropolitan Correctional Center in New York City. The medical examiner ruled that Epstein's death was a suicide which may have been the result of staff misconduct. Epstein's suicide caused a shakeup in both the facility and the Bureau of Prisons, which oversees the facility's operation (see page 336). Credit: MediaPunch Inc./ Alamy Stock Photo.

We start our discussion of long-term correctional populations with a description of the challenges posed by inmates sentenced to life imprisonment, including women and people who were juveniles when their crimes occurred. People sentenced to lengthy prison terms inevitably age, and elderly prisoners place significant demands on many prison systems. Last, we describe how the number of people sentenced to be executed has increased death row populations and how they wait for decades before their sentences are carried out.

LIFE-SENTENCED PRISONERS

Although, as noted earlier, the average prisoner in the United States will serve abouta three year sentence, about one in seven of them serve very lengthy or even life sentences. Figure 9.1, which uses data from the Sentencing Project (2018, p. 1), shows a 376% growth in such sentences since 1984. What is remarkable about this trend is that violent and property crime rates, as reported by the Federal Bureau of Investigation (2019), peaked in 1992 and then declined by half between 1993 and 2017 (Gramlich, 2019). Although crime rates decreased during that time, the number of lifers almost doubled.

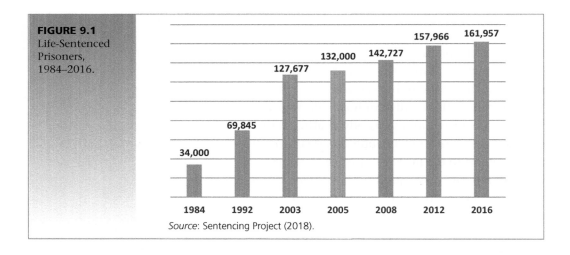

FIGURE 9.1
Life-Sentenced Prisoners, 1984–2016.

Source: Sentencing Project (2018).

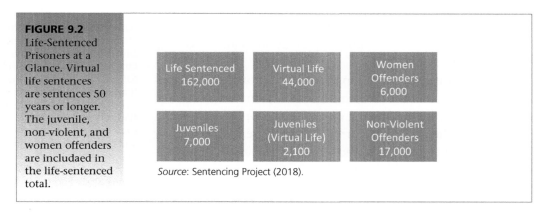

FIGURE 9.2
Life-Sentenced Prisoners at a Glance. Virtual life sentences are sentences 50 years or longer. The juvenile, non-violent, and women offenders are includaed in the life-sentenced total.

Source: Sentencing Project (2018).

Figure 9.2 summarizes the demographic and offense-related characteristics of life-sentenced prisoners. Most (59%) violent-crime lifers are sentenced on homicide offenses with the remainder being sentenced on sex crimes (17%) or aggravated assault, robbery and kidnapping offenses (15%), and about one in ten were convicted of non-violent offenses. Thus, the lengthy sentences are not surprising. So, how does one get a life sentence for a non-violent offense? In 2011 Jody Butler, a New Orleans resident, pled guilty to possessing marijuana and five cocaine rocks. Sledge (2018, para. 12) reports that Butler had previously been convicted of "simple robbery, purse snatching and drug possession" and those prior convictions enabled prosecutors to have him sentenced as a habitual offender—a classification similar to the three-strikes punishments in other states. However, Butler was given a life sentence, which was later upheld by the Louisiana Supreme

Court. Attorneys working on Butler's behalf were able to convince the New Orleans D.A. that the sentence was too severe, and this ultimately led to a shorter sentence. Sledge (2018) believes that the New Orleans D.A. has subsequently softened his stance on harsh punishments for people convicted of drug crimes

Prison Adjustment of Life-Sentenced Prisoners

Correctional systems have developed most of their programs based on the risks and programmatic needs of prisoners serving fewer than five years. Almost all the challenges lifers pose, by contrast, relate to coping with sentences that are measured in decades rather than years. People serving **life without the possibility of parole (LWOP)** sentences have different ideas about the future than prisoners who will be released after a few years. Ruddell, Broom, and Young (2010, pp. 325–326) observe that some lifers have a difficult adjustment to prison and may develop a "nothing to lose" perspective. Those beliefs may push them into committing acts of self-harm or involvement in misconduct during the first years of their sentences. Penal Reform International (2018) provides the following insightful comments from life-sentenced prisoners:

> [Life in prison is] a slow, torturous death. Maybe it would have been better if they had just given me the electric chair and ended my life instead of a life sentence, letting me rot away in jail. It serves no purpose. It becomes a burden on everybody.
>
> (p. 1)

> A life sentence means that, in effect, you're dead. It's just another form of a death sentence. Instead of having the gall to do it in one fell swoop, you die one day at a time.
>
> (p. 7)

> I am alive, and I really don't want to be. I have nothing to live for. I'm serving life without the possibility of parole, and that might as well be a death sentence. I will never leave this place, and the thought of that forces any sliver of hope out of me.
>
> (p. 8)

The despair lifers experience is understandable; they will spend the rest of their lives attempting to manage the pains of imprisonment described in Chapter 8; Leigey and Ryder (2015) refer to this as the pains of permanent imprisonment. Some escape their pain by committing suicide. Indeed, Tartaro (2019) reports that longer sentences are a good predictor of prison suicide.

The pains that lifers experience change over time. LWOP inmates who had served less than ten years of their sentences were more likely to report having psychological problems such as depression, anxiety disorders, and PTSD, and having attempted suicide than were lifers who had served longer than ten years (Leigey, 2010). Leigey also found that most people serving LWOP sentences developed coping mechanisms to adjust to prison life, and few of them found the prison mental health services helpful. An individual's prison adjustment was also related to his or her prior experiences. For instance, lifers who had previously served a prison term had a smoother adjustment to their sentence than did individuals whose first correctional experience was a life sentence.

What do lifers say are their most significant pains of imprisonment? Leigey and Ryder (2015, p. 733) asked LWOP prisoners who had served 20 or more years about their deprivations and the following is their top 10 list:

- Missing little "luxuries" (e.g. favorite food, or wearing their own clothes)
- Missing social life and feeling lonely
- Missing somebody such as separation from their loved ones
- Feeling that their life is being wasted
- Wishing for more privacy, and many preferred a single cell to double-bunking
- Getting annoyed or irritated with other prisoners
- Longing for a time in the past
- Being afraid of dying before their release
- Wishing that time would pass faster
- Boredom

Although many lifers express feelings of depression, loss, and anger, they gradually settle into a routine and most try to make the most of their lives. Herbert (2018) says that some lifers realize they have much to lose, including internal privileges and extended family visits (e.g. unsupervised visits in separate housing units with their family members) in the four states that still have those options. Johnson and McGunigall-Smith (2008, p. 337) describe how prison life becomes increasingly lonely for lifers permanently separated from their families, friends, and loved ones. Those contacts wither over time. Friends move away, their parents and other relatives die, and they gradually become more isolated and forgotten.

Some lifers are reluctant to engage in positive activities that constructively occupy their days. Others are prevented from participating in any programs, given that state officials prioritize rehabilitative programming for people who will be returning to the community. Nellis's (2012, p. 24) survey of lifers found that about two-thirds of them were not participating in any rehabilitative programs. The reasons varied but included their ineligibility to participate, a lack of such programs, and the fact that the inmate simply was not interested in participating. A breakdown of their reasons for non-participation is shown in Figure 9.3.

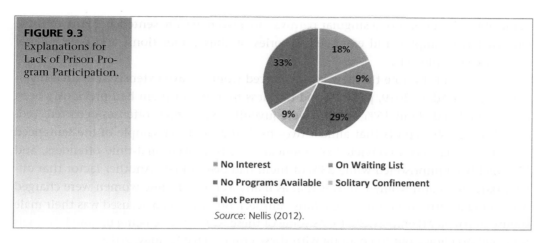

FIGURE 9.3
Explanations for Lack of Prison Program Participation.

33%   18%
9%
9%   29%

- No Interest
- On Waiting List
- No Programs Available
- Solitary Confinement
- Not Permitted

Source: Nellis (2012).

Lifers often become more positive about their imprisonment as they age, and they can become a stabilizing influence on their living units (Herbert, 2018). These individuals are motivated to make the prison environment comfortable and predictable which, in turn, reduces their pains of imprisonment and makes their lives more meaningful. Herbert found that many lifers reached out to the younger inmates, trying to mentor them or to provide guidance and support by encouraging them to avoid the mistakes the lifers had made. Some lifers wanted to find ways of making up for the harms they had caused. One of their frustrations, however, is that while their efforts are seen as positive by prison staff and parole boards, they are rarely granted parole because their lives are defined by offenses that happened decades earlier.

Women Lifers

Women are one of two distinct groups of lifers that deserve special attention. The second, examined in the next section, are juvenile lifers, children who were sentenced for crimes they committed prior to their 18th birthdays. With respect to women lifers, the Sentencing Project (2018, p. 2) estimates there are about 6,000 of them, and their numbers have been increasing faster than for males. The offenses these women committed differ somewhat from their male counterparts. Dye and Aday (2019, p. 10) report that about one-half of them were being abused by their partners, and some killed their abusive partners. They describe one such case:

> In a state without self-defense laws, women who tried to protect or defend themselves against victimization and abuse were left with a life sentence, and anger: "I was mad as hell because I was being raped and I took the life of the man who was raping me. The state paid me back by taking my life away."
>
> (Dye & Aday, 2019, p. 62)

Being abused is often not a singular pathway to a woman's life sentence. Many of these women have complex and extended histories of abuse, addictions, and poor mental health (see Chapter 11).

It is important to note that few life-sentenced women have extensive criminal histories. Dye and Aday (2019, p. 10) found that less than 9% of them had previously been incarcerated and about 15% of them were juveniles when their offenses occurred. Fedock (2018, p. 69) reports that almost two-thirds (62%) of her sample of life-sentenced women—all had been convicted of homicide offenses—were first-time offenders, and 15% had been imprisoned while 23% of them had been in jail. Another factor that differentiates men and women lifers is that as many as 60% of these women were charged with being a party to a crime (e.g. felony murder); often their co-accused was their male spouse or partner (Lempert, 2016). As some of these women were being battered they felt they had no choice but to go along with these crimes (Dye & Aday, 2019).

Another factor differentiating women and men life-sentenced prisoners is the higher need for physical and mental health care needs for these women. In Chapter 11 we noted that about two-thirds of women come to prison with chronic physical health conditions, histories of mental health problems, and substance abuse. Research examining the pathways to women's life imprisonment also shows that many have extensive histories of emotional, physical, and sexual abuse (Dye & Aday, 2019). Thus, in addition to having to cope with the other pains of imprisonment, they must also manage serious health-related problems.

Our final factor differentiating women's imprisonment is that upwards of two-thirds of them are parents (Dye & Aday, 2019; Lempert, 2016). How often do they get visits from their children? We don't have specific statistics for lifers, but 57.7% of all state prisoners reported they never received any personal visits from their children (Glaze & Maruschak, 2008, p. 18). Like their male counterparts, these women can become invisible, isolated, and shunned by the free world.

Juvenile Lifers

The United States is the only nation where youths are routinely sentenced to life in prison (Rovner, 2019). There are about 7,000 inmates who were sentenced to life terms for crimes that happened prior to their 18th birthdays and about another 2,100 are serving **virtual life sentences** (50 years or longer). In Chapter 14 (online resource) we describe how the sentences of young people historically have been mitigated because judges have realized that they are not as mature as adults, and some youths make very poor decisions in their rush to test adult roles, including participating in risky behaviors, experimenting with drugs and alcohol, and involvement in crime. Researchers have reported that some of these behaviors can be explained by their brain development, and there is a growing body of evidence showing that the regions in the brain that are responsible for making good decisions are not fully developed until individuals are in their twenties. Those scientific findings were used by reformers in their successful efforts to ban the death penalty for juveniles in 2005 (*Roper v. Simmons*, 2005). Juvenile life sentences without the possibility of parole for homicide offenses were also banned in *Graham v. Florida* (2010), and the Supreme Court later extended that ban to any offense (*Miller v. Alabama,* 2012). Although juveniles are still sentenced to life sentences, they must have the opportunity to appear before a parole board.

Life-sentenced juveniles are admitted to prisons with the same set of challenges and problems as their older counterparts, but they are less able to cope with those sentences given their immaturity (Nellis, 2012). Although some have committed serious and violent crimes, these lifers are not always hardened or sophisticated offenders. In some cases, the crimes that triggered their life sentences were their first offenses (Human Rights Watch, 2005). As a result, their imprisonment might be their first non-detention experience in custody. Kolivoski and Shook (2016, p. 1243) summarized the research literature and observe that:

> In general, research on the prison experiences of juveniles has found that they are subject to higher rates of victimization, experience different types of programs and services than those offered in juvenile facilities, are less likely to form positive relationships with staff in adult facilities, suffer from higher levels of depression, and are more likely to attempt suicide in adult prisons.

Overall, the research shows that youths imprisoned at earlier ages have a higher involvement in misconduct. Kolivoski and Shook speculated that juveniles might engage in misconduct to avoid stressful or threatening situations; consequently, such acts might be their way of self-protection. A similar argument might be made for suicide, as youths who are fearful may try to take their own lives to escape physical or sexual abuse.

The National Prison Rape Elimination Commission (2009) points out that youngsters incarcerated with adults are at the highest risk of sexual victimization. The Prison Rape Elimination Act (PREA), which was introduced in 2003, sought to reduce prison sexual assaults. To determine the prevalence of these crimes the Bureau of Justice Statistics collects information from inmates using surveys. When Beck, Berzofsky, Caspar, and Krebs (2013, p. 6) examined the PREA data, they found that about 1.8% of juveniles in adult jails and prisons were victimized by other inmates, and about 3.2% had been victimized by staff members. Those rates were comparable with the sexual assaults of adults in the same facilities. Given their immaturity, however, the physical and psychological effects of these assaults can be more harmful than those experienced by adults.

Managing Life-Sentenced Inmates

The Council of Europe ([COE] 2016, p. 5) made a number of recommendations for managing life-sentenced prisoners. They contend that prison officials should provide opportunities for:

- *Individualization*: The individual characteristics of life-sentenced prisoners—such as their risk, needs, and responsivity—should be considered in case planning.
- *Normalization*: Life-sentenced prisoners should be subject only to the restrictions that are necessary for their safe and orderly confinement and should not be placed in indefinite maximum-security placements. They should have full access to work, education, sports, and cultural activities to pass the time (COE, 2016, p. 7).
- *Responsibility*: Life-sentenced prisoners should have opportunities to exercise personal responsibility in their daily lives, including participating in their sentence planning. They should be able to join the general inmate population unless they pose specific risks to others.

- *Security and safety*: One of the goals of the COE (2016) is to transition these life-sentenced prisoners to lower levels of prison security and their introduction to the community if allowed by the terms of the sentence.
- *Non-segregation*: Life-sentenced prisoners should not be segregated based only on their sentence and they should be allowed to associate with other prisoners unless they pose a risk to others.
- *Progression principle*: Life-sentenced prisoners should be encouraged and allowed by the prison's regulations to move through their sentence to less restrictive living conditions based on their behavior and cooperation with prison staff and other prisoners.

PHOTO 9.2
Sandra Patient holds a picture of her murdered uncle, Bucky Arthur Barrett, as she hugs a friend following the sentencing of James "Whitey" Bulger to two life sentences in prison plus five years. Bulger had previously been convicted of 31 counts, including racketeering charges and complicity in 11 murders. Hours after he was transferred to the United States Penitentiary, Hazelton (WV), 89-year-old Bulger was found unconscious and unresponsive in his wheelchair. He later died a homicide victim. Credit: Zuma Press Inc./ Alamy Stock Photo.

These recommendations are based on the assumption that most lifers will eventually be returned to the community, which is not necessarily the case in the United States.

There is, however, a recent movement to restrict the use of LWOP and life sentences in the United States and to provide lifers with more opportunities to return to the community on parole. Few inmates who have served two or three decades behind bars pose much risk to the public, and their continued imprisonment is costly. Research shows that few life-sentenced prisoners released from custody ever commit further crimes (Liem, 2016). The Bureau of Justice Statistics indicates that former prisoners who were convicted of homicide offenses had the lowest rates of re-arrest of all types of offenders (Durose, Cooper, & Snyder, 2016). Given those findings, the Sentencing Project (2018) has proposed that homicide offenders serving life sentences be eligible for parole after serving 15 years. Although the public has rejected some tough on crime strategies, we question if they are ready for lifers serving only 15 years prior to being eligible for parole. By contrast, other than being tough on crime, is there a good reason for continuing to imprison people who are assessed as being low risk decades after their trials and sentencing?

Life Imprisonment Practices across the Globe

Where does the United States stand in terms of life-sentenced prisoners when compared to the rest of the world? Van Zyl Smit and Appleton (2019, p. 87) report that life sentences are used in 183 of 216 separate nations and territories. That means that 33 nations do not impose life sentences. Moreover, most countries using life sentences provide prisoners with some ability to access parole, while only 65 countries impose LWOP sentences. The increased use of life sentences seems to be commonplace across the globe, as most developed nations have abandoned capital punishment in favor of lengthy sentences, the latter showing the public their government is not "soft on crime." Even China, a nation with a very high use of capital punishment, introduced LWOP sentences in 2015, although Smith and Jiang (2019) found that this sanction is rarely used and primarily for cases of corruption.

While about one in seven US prisoners is life-sentenced, a review of Figure 9.4 shows that the proportion of lifers in some other nations is higher. Van Zyl Smit and Appleton (2019, p. 93) found that over one-half of India's prison population (54%) are sentenced to life, while South Africa and the United Kingdom have about the same percentage of lifers as the United States. As a result, we find that lifer populations are growing throughout many nations. Although the proportion of life-sentenced prisoners can be high, in some nations they might have more access to the community than in the United States. For example, in Canada about one-third of the persons serving a life sentence are supervised in the community (Public Safety Canada, 2019). However, these life-sentenced prisoners must serve a period of parole eligibility that ranges from 10 to 25 years. They are under correctional supervision for their entire life and these parolees can be returned to prison indefinitely for a technical violation or committing a new crime.

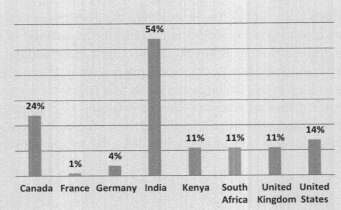

FIGURE 9.4
Life-Sentenced Prisoners in Selected Nations
Sources: Public Safety Canada (2019); Sentencing Project (2018); Van Zyl Smit and Appleton (2019).

The European Union (EU) places limits on severe punishments for member states. No EU nation, for example, can impose the death penalty, and a lifer's continued imprisonment must be reviewed prior to serving 25 years. These reviews are intended to ensure that the lifer's continued imprisonment is needed to safeguard public safety (Leigey & Schartmueller, 2019). Some non-EU nations do not have life sentences or the death penalty, and some tough cases have fallen through the cracks of those justice systems. In Norway, the mass murderer who killed eight people in a van bombing and 69 young people at a summer camp in 2011 was given the maximum sentence of 21 years in prison for these crimes. That sentence can be extended in five-year increments in preventative detention if he is assessed as being a danger to society.

Requiring a nation's criminal laws to conform to EU policies as a condition of membership in the EU raises interesting questions about a country's sovereign ability to punish offenders. For instance, should a nation be bound by regulations made by a body of unelected officials? Many Americans would oppose these practices. Moreover, in most European nations there is less political attention paid to justice system operations. Instead, senior government bureaucrats, rather than elected officials, play a greater role in the development of criminal justice policies, and they are more likely to be influenced by research results rather than public opinion. Points to ponder: Should research findings drive our treatment of offenders? Or, should public opinion play a greater role in deciding how people who commit crimes are managed by the criminal justice system?

ELDERLY PRISONERS

It has been said that prison is no place for old men or women. One outcome of imposing decades-long sentences is that correctional populations are aging. The American Civil Liberties Union (ACLU) (2012, p. i) estimates there will be 400,000 persons 50 years and older behind bars by 2030. That possibility poses significant challenges for prison administrators, including managing health care costs, reducing their likelihood of being victimized, and the possibility of offering meaningful correctional programming to them. There is also a growing acknowledgement that elderly prisoners should be provided with dignity if they are dying in prison, including placement in a prison **hospice** to provide end-of-life care. A movement to return critically ill prisoners to the community on a compassionate release has also gained traction in the past few decades. As previously mentioned, releasing federal prisoners on these releases was authorized in *First Step Act*.

The definition of elderly is at the heart of this problem. Many correctional researchers define elderly inmates as being persons 50 and older, as these individuals have often lived more difficult lives in the community, in jail, and in prison. As a result, most 50-year-old inmates have a greater set of health-related problems compared to the average person in the community of the same age. Regardless of whether one defines an elderly inmate as somebody who is 50 or 65 years old, their numbers have been increasing since the nation enacted tough on crime policies in the 1980s. Between 1993 and 2013, for example, the number of state prisoners 55 or older grew 400%: from 26,300 to 131,500 prisoners (Carson & Sabol, 2016, p. 2) and there has been a modest increase since then. The growth of this population from 1993 to 2016 is shown in Figure 9.5.

Many elderly prisoners were sentenced through tough on crime sanctions such as LWOP, truth in sentencing, or three-strike laws. There were about 200,000 life-sentenced inmates or persons serving virtual life sentences in 2016 (Sentencing Project, 2018).

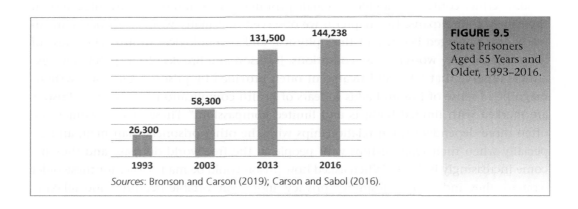

FIGURE 9.5
State Prisoners Aged 55 Years and Older, 1993–2016.

Sources: Bronson and Carson (2019); Carson and Sabol (2016).

Unless these individuals' sentences are commuted, most will die in prison. Prisoner advocacy groups want correctional administrators to provide an environment where these people are safe and can die with some dignity in a prison or community hospice.

Challenges of Incarcerating Elderly Inmates

One of the most pressing challenges of incarcerating the elderly is managing their health care needs. The ACLU (2012, p. ii) estimates the health care costs for these people are twice as high as for younger inmates. For example, Bronson, Maruschak, and Berzofsky (2015) found that 44% of state and federal prisoners and 60% of jail inmates over 50 had at least one disability. An additional challenge in managing this population is that jails and prisons are designed for holding and managing younger populations and:

> Older inmates have difficulty coping with the typical routines of the prison day and feel more agitated when they cannot escape from the continuous noise and distracting activities of other inmates. They tend to be uncomfortable in large groups and need more privacy and time alone. Older inmates also need more orderly conditions, emotional feedback, and familial support than younger prisoners.
>
> (Blowers & Blevins, 2015, p. 98)

Elderly inmates are also less mobile than younger prisoners and are slower in conducting the basic activities of daily living, including eating, showering, or keeping up with a group when being escorted within a facility. As a result, they can upset the younger inmates. Kuhlmann and Ruddell (2005) found that elderly jail inmates were more likely to be victimized than other inmates, and the same finding holds true for prisoners. Almost all (91%) of the elderly prisoners in Blowers and Blevins's study report being intentionally injured in prison, whereas less than one-fifth of younger inmates reported similar injuries.

Some critics contend that elderly female prisoners are even more disadvantaged than their male counterparts. In Chapter 6 we observed that many women prisoners are already disadvantaged because of their physical and psychological health. The stress of incarceration may worsen those conditions. Johnson and Brooks (2011, p. 885), for example, observe that "the cold treatment often provided by prison health care systems magnifies a sense of loss and adds to fears of health complications as they age. Prisons are marked with limited budgets and limited compassion." These elderly women are often more dependent upon relationships with the other prisoners than men, and especially when their relationships with people in the free world decrease and they become increasingly isolated. When asked how prison could be made easier for these older women, they indicated a desire for privacy, more comfortable bedding, and relaxing rules obviously intended for younger, fitter prisoners such as requiring them to stand in line for extended periods of time.

Many elderly prisoners, regardless of gender, express frustration with the boredom of prison and their inability to seek activities that might provide meaning in their lives. Blowers and Blevins (2015) found that inmates over 55 were more likely to participate in prison-based work programs, but less likely to attend vocational or educational programs than their younger counterparts. When their likelihood of engaging in misconduct was examined, Blowers and Blevins found that elderly prisoners were less likely to engage in rule violations than younger inmates. Moreover, when they did engage in misconduct, they were typically involved in the least serious acts (see also Sheeran, Hilinski-Rosick, Richie, & Freiburger, 2018).

Prison systems have developed several strategies to manage elderly inmates and some are employing **gerontologists** (specialists in aging) to develop correctional programs for these people. Others have adapted the prison's physical environment to accommodate older inmates by installing ramps, improving lighting, and placing railings in the showers. Taking these steps is important to reduce the likelihood of falls, which are a leading cause of injuries and premature deaths for elderly people.

One group with unmet needs is the growing percentage of prison inmates with different forms of psychological disorders related to aging, including **dementia**. These ailments may reduce an inmate's reaction time, which might lead to accidents or falls, and their impulse control, which could increase conflicts with the staff members or other prisoners. A review of the literature shows that between 0.8% and 18.8% of all prisoners are suffering from this condition (Brooke, Diaz-Gil, & Jackson, 2018). In some cases, their psychological functioning can worsen before their needs are observed, diagnosed, and addressed.

The increasing number of inmates dying in prison has created a need for prison hospices. Ollove (2016) describes how over 75 prison hospices provide care to inmates suffering from terminal illnesses, which is generally defined as having a life expectancy of six months or less. Hospice care, whether in the community or a prison, is based on making the patients comfortable, but there are no attempts to prolong life. Inmates admitted to a prison hospice receive care from the medical staff as well as inmate volunteers. Cloyes and associates (2017) describe a hospice program at Louisiana State Penitentiary where prisoner-volunteers working on this unit are given 40 hours of training to learn about providing basic health care and emotional support to the dying. The inmates providing care to these patients stay with them around the clock in the last three days of their lives to ensure they do not die alone, what they call sitting vigil. In addition to providing support for these prisoners, the hospice staff are flexible when it comes to enforcing security and visiting rules to accommodate family visits.

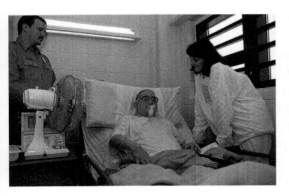

PHOTO 9.3
An elderly inmate in a maximum-security prison is attended by a nurse under the watchful eye of a correctional officer. Many elderly prisoners, typically considered inmates 55 and older, enter the prison hospital never to return to their cells. Credit: Mikael Karlsson/ Alamy Stock Photo.

As most hospice patients are bedridden and represent very little risk to the community, some prison systems have been paroling inmates directly to nursing homes. Ollove (2016), however, says these transfers are sometimes opposed by the public. In 2020, for example, Bernie Madoff, who was sentenced to a 150-year federal sentence for swindling thousands of investors, applied for a compassionate release after being diagnosed with a terminal kidney disease. The opposition to his release has been broad and vocal. While well-to-do prisoners receiving a compassionate release can return home, other ex-prisoners have a difficult time finding a place that will take them. Some nursing homes refuse to take inmates who were convicted of committing serious crimes, even though their offenses may have occurred decades ago and the person has shown exemplary behavior since their prison admission.

Sanders and Stensland (2018) found that dying inmates expressed some frustration with the lack of control about where they would die. The federal government and most states enable terminally ill prisoners to apply for compassionate releases, and these applications are screened by the state parole board or equivalent releasing body. Although states have been introducing policies intended to ease the early release of these inmates, applicants often die before the board or governor approves their requests. Compassionate releases are often seen as "win-win" for the inmate and the prison system. Prisoners are returned home and can spend their last days with friends and family. Moving these people into the community, by contrast, cuts correctional costs.

CAPITAL PUNISHMENT

The Current State of the Death Penalty

The media are the main source of information about crimes and punishments for the average citizen, including the use of the death penalty. One limitation of relying on the Internet or other mass media accounts as our primary sources of information about issues of crime and justice is that they tend to boil down very complex issues into reports of a minute or two. As you recognize by now, many of the practices intended to rehabilitate or punish offenders can be very complicated and difficult to administer under the best of circumstances. In this section, we outline some facts about the use of the death penalty. This information will increase your ability to debate the use of capital punishment, regardless of your feelings about it.

One way the public can influence criminal justice policies and practices is to elect politicians whose campaigns are based on being tough on crime or, conversely, those who argue that sanctions in the justice system should be more humane or rehabilitative. In contemporary society, this false choice seems to dominate the political landscape. While politicians traditionally have been reluctant to be perceived as soft on crime, throughout 2018 and 2019 a number of reformist prosecutors—who campaigned on reducing harsh punishments for people who had committed minor offenses—were elected throughout the country. Criminal justice policies, including ones related to corrections, such as capital punishment, are often controversial. The death penalty evokes strong reactions in those who oppose it under any circumstances and those who support it for all first-degree murders and, in some instances, for other crimes as well. The groups adopting these extreme positions constitute small but vocal minorities. Most Americans favor the death penalty for first-degree murder—or at least are not opposed to it—but are more ambivalent than the vocal advocates. The public's support for the death penalty has been measured by the Gallup organization since the 1930s. As shown in Figure 9.6, that support has changed over time. Four-fifths (80%) of Americans supported the use of capital punishment in 1994, but support has been dropping ever since. According to the most recent poll, only 56% of respondents supported the use of the death penalty by 2018.

Why has support for capital punishment been dropping? One possible reason is due to our awareness of the number of people who have been wrongfully convicted. That is, since 1973, 167 death row inmates were found to be innocent and were exonerated (Death Penalty Information Center, 2020). After the use of DNA evidence became more widespread in the 1990s, the number of these exonerated death row inmates increased.

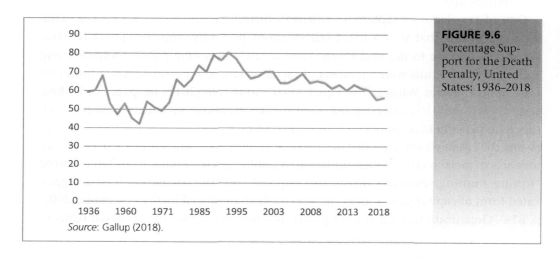

FIGURE 9.6
Percentage Support for the Death Penalty, United States: 1936–2018

Source: Gallup (2018).

Many received millions of dollars in compensation because of their wrongful convictions and imprisonment. Discouraged with the large number of death row inmates who were released back to the streets because they were innocent, Illinois Governor George Ryan placed a moratorium on capital punishment in 1999, and it was abolished in 2011. Ryan later said that the system was "haunted by a demon of error" and to reduce the likelihood of innocent persons being executed, he commuted the sentences of 164 death row prisoners to life imprisonment (Chicago Tribune, 2018).

Moreover, there is increasing criticism of the death penalty as discriminatory, as it has been applied disproportionately to people of color. The Death Penalty Information Center (2020) cites several recent studies showing the disproportionate number of African Americans who are executed, and the likelihood of execution is much higher for African Americans who kill Whites, than for Whites who kill African Americans, the basic definition of the racist application of a legal practice.

RACE, CLASS, AND GENDER

Race and Illegal Executions

In the next section, we describe how executions have become more humane and are carefully managed affairs. In contemporary executions condemned individuals are given a number of supports to lessen the psychological pains of their executions. Those supports include access to the courts to ensure that their sentences were fairly imposed, and their punishments are not cruel and unusual. While there is no shortage of critics who contend the practice of capital punishment in America is deeply flawed, there is a degree of procedural fairness and legitimacy that was not present even a half-century ago.

One of the darkest chapters in America's history is lynching, which are extra-legal executions that were carried out by mobs primarily from the post-Civil War Reconstruction era to the mid-1900s. Most of these acts were public spectacles, and almost all the victims were members of racial or ethnic minorities, while the mobs were almost always Whites. The Equal Justice Initiative (2017, no page) calls these acts terror lynchings and defined them as "horrific acts of violence whose perpetrators were never held accountable." They also define public spectacle lynchings as events that were widely attended by the White community and conducted as celebratory acts of racial control and domination. A public spectacle lynching often involved "torture, burning, dismemberment, and display," and "the lynchers created an aggravated form of capital punishment, more terrible than official justice" (Garland, 2005, p. 814). Organizations such as the Equal Justice Initiative reject the view that many of these acts were examples of mob justice, as they occurred in places with functioning justice systems and often happened in broad daylight. Lynchings often took place near the local courthouses, and sometimes with the tacit approval of the local law enforcement, who did little to stop these illegal executions.

The Equal Justice Initiative (2017, no page) documented a number of key findings in their study of these illegal executions and they are summarized as follows:

- Racial terror lynching was more prevalent than previously thought, with about 4,500 of these acts occurring between 1877 and 1950.
- These acts were more likely to occur in Mississippi, Florida, Arkansas, and Louisiana than in other states.
- Lynchings were used to maintain racial control by attempting to threaten the entire African American community. Few lynchings were related to serious crimes and most were carried out because the person had committed a minor social transgression or for demanding basic rights and fair treatment.
- The presence of lynchings resulted in a migration of African Americans out of the South to the northern states.
- There has been a reluctance to acknowledge, discuss, or address lynching and there are few monuments to the history and legacy of lynching.
- Lynchings were often related to fears of interracial sex, minor social transgressions, and allegations of serious violent crimes, and sometimes targeted ministers and community leaders who opposed the mistreatment of African Americans.
- The decline of lynching was replaced by the increased use of capital punishment that was often followed by a speedy trial that resulted in an execution that happened a month or two after the sentence was imposed.

Garland (2005) believes that these illegal executions were related to the insecurities Whites were experiencing as African Americans gained more economic and political clout. He also contends that legally imposed death sentences were intended to replace lynchings, and that researchers need a better knowledge of the relationships between illegal and legal executions in order to understand fully the modern use of capital punishment.

Although about three-quarters of the victims of these lynchings were African Americans, Urbina and Alvarez (2018) contend that the illegal executions of Latinx peoples have been overlooked. Research reveals that Mexican residents in the United States were also at risk of violence from the 1880s to the 1930s (Carrigan & Webb, 2003). Similar to Garland's analysis, Urbina and Alvarez (2018, p. 243) say that these illegal

PHOTO 9.4
Not all "terror lynchings" occurred as a result of a hanging. In the summer of 1955, 14-year-old Chicago-born Emmett Till visited relatives in rural Mississippi. Till, an African American youth, talked to Carolyn Bryant, the White owner of a local store. According to court documents, Bryant's husband Roy and Roy's half-brother J.W. Milam beat Till to death and threw his body into the Tallahatchie River. Even though his face was unrecognizable, Till's mother insisted on an open casket so that the world could see what had happened to her son. At trial, Bryant and Milam were acquitted after the jury deliberated for 67 minutes. A marker placed at the site of Till's murder has been repeatedly vandalized, the most recent such act taking place in 2018. Credit: Everett Collection Historical/Alamy Stock Photo.

executions were "used to intimidate, oppress, control, and silence Mexicans and other Latinos." Similar arguments have been used to explain the differential use of imprisonment with ethnic or racial minority defendants. Do you think that race matters when it comes to imposing a prison or death sentence?

The Death Penalty Today

We have previously noted that the number of executions peaked in 1999 with 98 of them and have been declining ever since, and in 2019 there were 22 executions. Besides those executed in a given year, another issue related to death row populations is how many new people are sentenced to death row. In 1998, for example, death sentences were imposed on 295 people and that number decreased to 34 in 2019 (Death Penalty Information Center, 2020). Figure 9.7 shows the rate of executions per ten million US residents for each decade from the 1930s to 2018. Both death sentencing and actual executions are concentrated in a relatively small number of states. Indeed, 29 states and the US government authorize capital punishment, while it is banned in 21 states and the District of Columbia. Of the 29 states retaining the death penalty, four had moratoriums on this punishment in 2019 (California, Colorado, Oregon, and Pennsylvania). Of the 1,516 executions between 1976 and March 2020, most happened in the Southern states ($n = 1,242$) and this region was followed by Midwestern ($n = 186$) and Western ($n = 85$) states, and only four occurred in the Northeast.

Figure 9.8 summarizes the information about death row populations and executions. One of the challenges for correctional administrators is that people are still being sentenced to death, but few executions are actually being carried out. Figure 9.9 shows the average time it takes between the time sentences are imposed and when they are carried out. Snell (2019) found that the time increased from 71 months in 1985 to 243 months

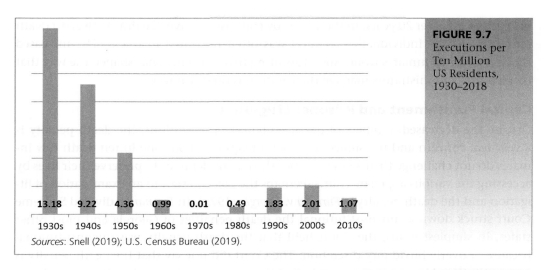

FIGURE 9.7
Executions per Ten Million US Residents, 1930–2018

| 13.18 | 9.22 | 4.36 | 0.99 | 0.01 | 0.49 | 1.83 | 2.01 | 1.07 |

1930s 1940s 1950s 1960s 1970s 1980s 1990s 2000s 2010s

Sources: Snell (2019); U.S. Census Bureau (2019).

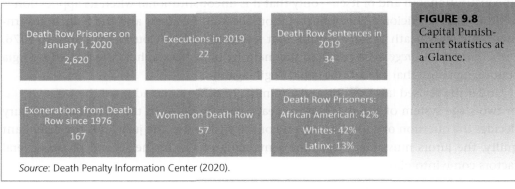

FIGURE 9.8
Capital Punishment Statistics at a Glance.

Death Row Prisoners on January 1, 2020
2,620

Executions in 2019
22

Death Row Sentences in 2019
34

Exonerations from Death Row since 1976
167

Women on Death Row
57

Death Row Prisoners:
African American: 42%
Whites: 42%
Latinx: 13%

Source: Death Penalty Information Center (2020).

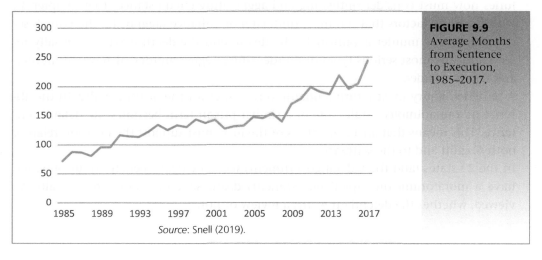

FIGURE 9.9
Average Months from Sentence to Execution, 1985–2017.

Source: Snell (2019).

in 2017, or just over 20 years. In the 1930s, by contrast, the average time between a death sentence and the individual's execution was often measured in weeks. The increased time condemned inmates would spend awaiting their sentences has shaped the way that correctional administrators manage the conditions on death row.

Capital Punishment and Prisoner Litigation

Despite the decreased numbers of death sentences or executions, the death penalty is a very real concern and the subject of much litigation. About one in ten death row inmates do not challenge their sentences, but the remainder fight to preserve their lives by accessing the various appellate courts. Perhaps the place to start in an examination of litigation and the death penalty is *Furman v. Georgia* (1972). In *Furman*, a divided Supreme Court struck down as unconstitutional the death penalties of Georgia and most other states. In simplest terms, the Court held that the death penalty was unconstitutional because of overly broad jury discretion. The Court did not say that the death penalty is unconstitutional in and of itself—only that it is unconstitutional when its application is arbitrary and capricious. This interpretation allowed the states and the federal government to redraw death penalty statutes that responded to the Court's criticisms. In 1976, the Court heard *Gregg v. Georgia*, and the majority of justices upheld the revised Georgia statute, meaning that executions could begin again.

Under the revised law Georgia and a number of other states adopted the **bifurcated** or two-stage system of adjudication for death penalty cases. In the trial phase, the jury decides the question of guilt. If at the end of this first phase, the jury finds the defendant guilty, the jurors must then begin the sentencing phase. In the second phase, several factors come into play:

- Juries now must consider mitigating and aggravating circumstances (see Chapter 3), which are any factors that diminish (mitigate) or enhance (aggravate) the crime's seriousness. Only murder is punishable by death, and the death penalty is usually reserved for the most serious types of murder—first-degree murder, aggravated murder, and felony murder.
- A sentencing jury must return a unanimous verdict for the death penalty. In the absence of a unanimous verdict, life or a similar prison term becomes the default sentence. This means that all 12 members of the jury must support the decision relating both to guilt and to the sentence.
- In the 29 states (and the federal government) with the death penalty (four of which have a moratorium on capital punishment) death sentences are automatically reviewed, whether the defendant wants a review or not.

Death Penalty Cases

Cases coming before the Supreme Court in the 2000s have seldom raised the issue of the death penalty's constitutionality. Instead, the Court has been asked to deal with technical issues: When is the death penalty appropriate? Are there individuals for whom capital punishment is not appropriate? Are the procedures employed by state and federal trial courts in imposing death sentences adequate? The following list briefly outlines some of the landmark cases and issues coming before the Court. A review of these cases suggests that the Court has been limiting the population of individuals eligible for execution by banning capital punishment for juveniles, non-homicide offenders, and persons with developmental and psychological impairments.

- *Atkins v. Virginia* (2002): The Court found it unconstitutional to execute persons suffering from developmental disabilities based on the concept of evolving standards of decency. The Court held that "executions of persons with these disabilities are 'cruel and unusual punishments' prohibited by the Eighth Amendment."
- *Ring v. Arizona* (2002): The jury in Ring's trial was deadlocked on the charge of premeditated murder but found him guilty of felony murder, the result of an armed robbery. To sentence a defendant to death under these circumstances, Arizona law requires the trial judge to conduct a separate hearing to decide whether there were aggravating or mitigating circumstances. Ring's appeal was based on the constitutionality of entrusting the judge with fact-finding concerning the capital sentence. The Court held in *Ring* that judicial fact-finding in relation to capital sentences is not insurance against arbitrariness, and that most states entrust those kinds of decisions to juries. In simplest terms, judges cannot be the decision makers in cases where the death penalty can be imposed.
- *Roper v. Simons* (2005): This is perhaps one of the most significant death penalty cases to be decided by the Supreme Court since *Gregg v. Georgia* (1976). A series of appeals that came before the Court in the 1980s had questioned the constitutionality of the death penalty for individuals whose crimes had been committed before they turned 18 years old. The Court allowed capital sentences for 16- and 17-year-olds and at the time of this decision, 14 states still allowed the juvenile death penalty. However, in this case the Supreme Court held that because of "evolving standards of decency" the death penalty could no longer be imposed on persons whose crimes took place before they were 18 years old.
- *Panetti v. Quarterman* (2007): The Court ruled on the issue of persons with mental illnesses (as opposed to those who were developmentally disabled). The question in

this case was "Does the Eighth Amendment permit the execution of an inmate who has a factual awareness of the state's stated reason for his execution, but who lacks, due to mental illness, a rational understanding of the state's justification?" The Court ordered a stay of execution and returned Panetti's case back to the courts of Texas to allow them to decide more fully the claims of incompetence, but declined to establish a new standard for mental competence.

- *Baze v. Rees* (2008): This was another of the technical issue cases decided by the Supreme Court. The case challenged the use of **lethal injection** by Kentucky in carrying out death sentences. The Supreme Court ruled that nothing in the Constitution prohibits states from employing lethal injection as a means of capital punishment.
- *Kennedy v. Louisiana* (2008): The Court held that the death penalty is unconstitutional for non-homicide crimes.
- *Madison v. Alabama* (2019): Madison killed a police officer in 1985 and during his stay on death row he had a number of strokes and suffered from dementia. As a consequence, he was unable to remember the offense. Given that finding the Court ruled that executing Madison would be a cruel and unusual punishment.

Altogether these decisions have banned the executions of persons who were juveniles at the time of the offense, non-homicide offenders as well as persons with developmental disabilities or mental illnesses, or who are suffering from dementia.

Life on Death Row

The supervision of over 2,600 condemned individuals poses a set of challenges for the staff members working on these specialized units. That is, in most states, these people are housed in solitary confinement, and some of the condemned refer to themselves as the living dead or dead men walking. Robert Johnson (2016), a scholar who has been conducting death row research since the 1970s, calls these places human warehouses, and he argues that these people live in dehumanizing conditions that are akin to torture. Earlier we defined warehouse prisons as correctional facilities providing little or no rehabilitative opportunities and inmates as receiving only their basic needs ('three hots and a cot'), but little else. Johnson is suggesting that death units are something far more sinister. Toch, Acker, and Bonventre (2018) add another layer to this idea, writing that death row inmates are often treated as the most violent and volatile prisoners and their status seldom changes, even after they have displayed a decade or longer of stable behavior. Most death row cells are identical to segregation cells. They are small, austere single rooms with beds made from steel or concrete with stainless-steel toilets and writing desks bolted to the floor.

Death row inmates are typically locked away from 22 to 24 hours a day. They have very little access to areas outside the death row unit or much face-to-face contact with other prisoners. Few death row inmates are able to access any sort of prison programming including religious services, and some go years without any exposure to the outdoors. If they receive any visitors, they are typically separated by barriers preventing any physical contact. As a result, these inmates are said to experience years of deprivation, isolation, and inactivity, or what the ACLU (2013) calls punishment on top of punishment. These experiences lead to despair and the ACLU contends that these conditions contribute to high rates of suicides on death row. Johnson (2016, p. 1217) relates the words of one death row inmate:

> Not a day passes that I do not fight just to get out of bed. And in the late hours of the night, it takes much strength just to keep a grip on my sanity. I have spent many hours, at my window, standing on my toilet at the air vent, pleading with men who were considering suicide... I have been on that very edge myself.

Death row can become unbearable. Scott Dozier, for example, was a 48-year-old individual who had served over a decade on Nevada's death row and then abandoned all of his appeals in order to facilitate his execution. He even sent a letter to a district judge requesting his death sentence to be carried out. A reporter covering Dozier's case reveals that "I don't want to die," he told me. "I just would rather be dead than do this" (Chammah, 2019, para. 3). Even though he had an execution date, the state's attorney general postponed his execution as the drugs Nevada was planning on using for the execution were not authorized. Discouraged with the delays, Dozier committed suicide by hanging himself in his cell.

There are several different approaches to managing condemned individuals. Robles (2017, para. 4) observes that Arizona, California, Colorado, Louisiana, Nevada, North Carolina, Tennessee, and Virginia permit them to live in the general population if they have clean disciplinary records. Other states enable death row inmates to socialize together within the unit, and they will play cards or board games and watch television together (Johnson, 2016). Taking these steps to improve their living conditions can reduce the psychological hardships they experience. Improving the quality of life for these people can be uplifting for correctional officers (Toch et al., 2018). Rates of despair among officers are high. For example, Link (2019) describes how working on Pennsylvania's death row exposed him to the suffering of the inmates who will wait decades before their sentences are carried out. After a 16-year gap since the last execution, the governor of Pennsylvania placed a moratorium on executions in 2015. Many Pennsylvania death row inmates will likely die before their executions.

Even a Prisoner's Last Meal Can Be Controversial

Death row inmates are often given their choice of a last meal, which offers them a reprieve from standard prison food. What do these people usually eat? Prison diets are often based on starchy foods—bread, potatoes, and pasta—inexpensive cuts of meat such as pork and other processed foods, and the cheapest fruits and vegetables available. The quality and quantity of meals vary across the country and inmates living on death row receive the same meals as the other prisoners. Monk (2019) describes meals on South Carolina's death row:

> A typical breakfast is grits, eggs, biscuits and juice. For lunch they get a meal such as turkey, rice and gravy, a vegetable and juice or tea. Supper is something like spaghetti with meat sauce, green beans, salad, bread, cake and juice or tea. Over and over and over.

Prison systems try to provide basic food at a low cost that meets the minimum nutritional requirements for an adult, but seldom is food quality a priority. Prison Voice Washington (2016)—a prisoner advocacy organization—found that almost all food served in Washington prisons is processed with high levels of sugar and sodium and inmates seldom receive fresh or natural foods.

The practice of giving condemned inmates their choice for a final meal dates back hundreds of years. Given the dismal options for regular food, many condemned prisoners look forward to their final meal, and the public is fascinated by their choices. A number of researchers have studied what they order and eat, and Wansink, Kniffin, and Shimizu (2012) found that the average death row prisoner requests high calorie meals that include meat—chicken, steak, and hamburger are popular choices—French fries and other fried foods, desserts (ice cream, pie, and cake are the most commonly requested), and soft drinks. Some prison systems allow foods to be bought from restaurants for a last meal, and hamburgers and fried chicken are the most requested foods. There are some limits to what the prison system will provide for a last meal, and the spending is limited to $20–$40.

One controversy arising from last meals is that many prisoners do not eat them. Wansink and associates (2012) found that about one in five inmates did not request a last meal. Other prisoners do not eat the food they requested, either because they lost their appetite or because they want to send a statement to the prison administrators. Texas legislators were so upset that one death row inmate did not eat the food he ordered that they ended the practice of providing last meals for all condemned prisoners. As with many other issues related to corrections, no issue is ever simple to resolve.

Executions

Methods of executing condemned inmates have arguably become less punishing to the body. Hangings and electrocution were largely abandoned with the return of the death penalty in the late 1970s, although Utah still has the firing squad as an option for the condemned. The introduction of lethal injections was intended to reduce the pains those being executed experienced, but especially the number of **botched executions**. Executions employing the gas chamber or electrocution were prone to errors if done incorrectly. Hangings sometimes resulted in the person's decapitation or their slow strangulation if their neck was not broken. Sarat (2014) describes how some inmates were re-hanged after the first attempts failed. With death by electrocution, which was introduced in the late 1800s because it was thought to be more efficient and less painful than hanging, some condemned inmates suffered burns and witnesses to several botched electrocutions could see flames coming from the prisoner's body (Denno, 2000). Death by lethal gas, introduced in the 1930s, was also thought to be more humane than other methods as it was supposed to result in an instantaneous death. Sarat, however, notes that it took upward of ten minutes for some executions using lethal gas to achieve the desired results.

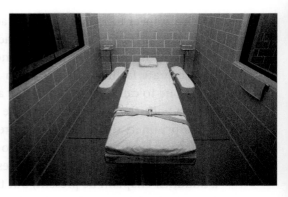

PHOTO 9.5
Arizona's death chamber, located at the Arizona State Prison in Florence, is where inmates receive a lethal concoction of deadly drugs called a three-drug cocktail. Thirty-seven people in Arizona were executed between 1976 and 2020 although none have been executed since 2 014. Credit: Norma Jean Gargasz/ Alamy Stock Photo.

Lethal injection was introduced to provide a quick and painless death. This method involves the injection of one or more drugs which causes the individual's death. Sarat (2014), however, examined all the executions from 1890 to 2010 and he says this method has the highest rate of botched executions. Of the 8,776 executions carried out prior to 2010, Sarat found that lethal injection had the highest botched rate (7%), followed by lethal gas (5%), hanging (3%), and electrocution (2%). In order to reduce the potential for pain a three drug cocktail was injected into the individual, but a growing number of states started to use only pentobarbital. This medication is seen as causing death more quickly and less painfully than the three drugs used in the first lethal injection executions. One obstacle prison administrators have to overcome, however, is that manufacturers of pentobarbital will not sell these drugs to a prison if they are used for executions. As a result, prison systems have arranged for pharmacies to manufacture small batches of pentobarbital, and the pharmacies where these drugs are made are a closely guarded secret in fear that death penalty protestors will use demonstrations to shame these pharmacists.

With respect to carrying out the actual death sentence, inmates are typically moved from their death row cell to a room adjacent to the execution chamber a day or two prior to the scheduled date of their sentence, although in some prisons executions take place in a separate facility, called a death house. Prison rules such as visiting and using the telephone to call friends and family are often relaxed. Some prison administrators place officers with the inmate around the clock to provide a measure of emotional support. These prisoners do have access to religious officials such as prison chaplains or other authorized spiritual advisors prior to the execution. Their presence in the actual execution chamber, however, is sometimes restricted. For example, a Texas inmate requested a Buddhist chaplain be present, but the state only employs Christian and Muslim chaplains. As the Supreme Court decided this was religious discrimination, the execution was postponed, and Texas now forbids any chaplain from being present in the execution chamber (McCullough & Byrne, 2019).

Unlike in the past, when executions were public spectacles, executions today are quiet affairs reserved for government officials, the media, selected witnesses, and family members of the victim(s). Family members of the condemned inmate are also invited to witness the execution. These events are typically very reserved, and few inmates make any struggle. The prison's warden or an official from the corrections department often presides over the execution and most states allow these individuals to make a statement. A Texas reporter who witnessed hundreds of executions wrote about their last words, and said that they included "anguished apologies and outlandish claims of innocence, as well as Biblical passages, quotes from rock songs, even the occasional joke" (Dirs, 2018, para. 25).

SUMMARY

Unless they obtain some form of early release about one in seven of all federal and state prisoners incarcerated today will die in custody. That number will continue to grow as more life sentences are imposed since the death penalty has fallen out of favor. The costs of incarcerating these aging prisoners can be two times greater than their younger counterparts and advocates argue that most elderly prisoners could be released with little risk to community safety. From this chapter, you should especially note the following:

- There are about 200,000 state and federal prisoners who are life-sentenced or are serving virtual life sentences.
- Over 2,600 death-sentenced individuals are living on death rows in conditions of deprivation and isolation.
- There are a growing number of elderly prisoners who will require expensive health care as they age.
- About 3,000 prisoners and 500 jail inmates die each year due to illnesses such as cancer or heart disease.

- The death penalty is slowly falling out of favor as the number of people sentenced to die has dropped as has the number of actual executions.
- Women may experience long-term imprisonment more harshly than men given their status as parents and their relationship needs.
- The United States is the only developed nation that sentences juveniles to life imprisonment.

With respect to older inmates, there has been a political reluctance to allow early or compassionate releases as many of them have committed violent offenses, and politicians do not want to be seen as being soft on crime. As a result, the challenge of managing these populations will continue into the future.

KEY TERMS

- bifurcated
- botched execution
- condemned prisoner
- dementia
- gerontologists
- hospice
- lethal injection
- life without the possibility of parole (LWOP)
- lifer
- lynching
- public spectacle lynchings
- terror lynchings
- virtual life sentence
- walking dead

THINKING ABOUT CORRECTIONAL POLICIES AND PRACTICES: WRITING ASSIGNMENTS

1. Rovner (2019) estimates that it costs taxpayers about $2.25 million to sentence a juvenile to life in prison. Is this a good investment of taxpayer dollars? Why or why not?
2. Why might juveniles or females sentenced to life imprisonment have a more difficult time adjusting to prison than adult males?
3. Nellis (2012) says that about one-third of prison systems restrict lifers from participating in rehabilitative programs. In a one page paper, defend this position.
4. Prepare a brief essay on the challenges of managing long-term prisoners within prisons.
5. Provide some reasons why the death penalty is falling out of favor.

CRITICAL REVIEW QUESTIONS

1. Why would a local jail administrator or sheriff deliberately try to undercount the number of inmates who killed themselves in their facilities?
2. What are the advantages and disadvantages of releasing terminally ill prisoners on compassionate releases?
3. Why is health care so important for the populations described in this chapter?
4. Provide some possible reasons why the number of life-sentenced prisoners more than doubled during a time when violent crimes decreased.
5. What are some typical challenges a life-sentenced prisoner confronts after their admission to prison?
6. Why would the outlook of a life-sentenced prisoner change over time? Explain your answer.
7. What factors differentiate the experiences of life-sentenced men and women prisoners?
8. Summarize the key decisions of the Supreme Court that have limited the types of offenders who can be executed.
9. Why are we fascinated by a death row inmate's last words and meal choices?
10. What makes Jeffrey Epstein's suicide different than the average inmate who commits suicide in a jail?

CASES

Atkins v. Virginia, 536 U.S. 304 (2002)

Baze v. Rees, 553 U.S. 35 (2008)

Furman v. Georgia, 130 S. CT. 2011 (2010)

Graham v. Florida, 130 S. CT. 2011 (2010)

Gregg v. Georgia, 428 U.S. 153 (1976)

Kennedy v. Louisiana, 554 U.S. 407 (2008)

Madison v. Alabama, 139 S. Ct. 718 (2019)

Miller v. Alabama, 567 U.S. 460 (2012)

Panetti v. Quarterman, 551 U.S. 930 (2007)

Ring v. Arizona, 536 U.S. 586 (2002)

Roper v. Simmons, 543 U.S. 551 (2005)

REFERENCES

Allyn, B. (2019, Nov. 19). Jeffrey Epstein's prison guards are indicted on federal charges. *National Public Radio*. Retrieved from https://www.npr.org/2019/11/19/780794931/prosecutors-charge-correctional-officers-who-guarded-jeffrey-epstein-before-his-

American Civil Liberties Union (ACLU). (2012). *At America's expense: The mass incarceration of the elderly*. Washington, DC: Author.

American Civil Liberties Union (ACLU). (2013). *A death before dying: Solitary confinement on death row*. Washington, DC: Author.

Barr, W. (2019, August 12). Attorney General William P. Barr delivers remarks at the Grand Lodge Fraternal Order of Police's 64th national biennial conference. *Justice News*. Retrieved from https://www.justice.gov/opa/speech/attorney-general-william-p-barr-delivers-remarks-grand-lodge-fraternal-order-polices-64th

Beck, A. J., Berzofsky, M., Caspar, R., & Krebs, C. (2013). *Sexual victimization in prisons and jails reported by inmates, 2011–12*. Washington, DC: Bureau of Justice Statistics.

Benner, K., & Ivory, D. (2019, August 13). Jeffrey Epstein death: 2 guards slept through checks and falsified records. *The New York Times*. Retrieved from https://www.nytimes.com/2019/08/13/nyregion/jeffrey-epstein-jail-officers.html

Blowers, A. N., & Blevins, K. R. (2015). An examination of prison misconduct among older inmates. *Journal of Crime and Justice, 38*(1), 96–112.

Bronson, J., & Carson, E. A. (2019). *Prisoners in 2017*. Washington, DC: Bureau of Justice Statistics.

Bronson, J., Maruschak, L., M., & Berzofsky, M. (2015). *Disabilities among prison and jail inmates, 2011–2012*. Washington, DC: Bureau of Justice Statistics.

Brooke, J., Diaz-Gil, A., & Jackson, D. (2018). The impact of dementia in the prison setting: A systematic review. *Dementia*. Available online ahead of print at: doi:10.1177/1471301218801715.

Carrigan, W. D., & Webb, C. (2003). The lynching of persons of Mexican origin or descent in the United States, 1848–1928. *Journal of Social History, 37*(2), 411–438.

Carson, E. A., & Cowhig, M. P. (2020a). *Mortality in local jails, 2000–2016 – Statistical tables*. Washington, DC: Bureau of Justice Statistics.

Carson, E. A., & Cowhig, M. P. (2020b). *Mortality in state prisons, 2001–2016 – Statistical tables*. Washington, DC: Bureau of Justice Statistics.

Carson, E. A., & Sabol, W. J. (2016). *Aging of the state prison population, 1993–2013*. Washington, DC: Bureau of Justice Statistics.

Chammah, M. (2019, June 1). The volunteer. *The Marshall Project*. Retrieved from https://www.themarshallproject.org/2018/01/18/the-volunteer

Chicago Tribune. (2018). How the death penalty was abolished in Illinois. *Chicago Tribune*. Retrieved from http://www.chicagotribune.com/news/ct-met-illinois-death-penalty-timeline-gfx-20180514-htmlstory.html

Cloyes, K. G., Rosenkranz, S. J., Supiano, K. P., Berry, P. H., Routt, M., & Llanque, S. M. (2017). Caring to learn and learning to care: Inmate hospice volunteers and the delivery of prison end-of-life care. *Journal of Correctional Health Care, 23*(1), 43–55.

Council of Europe. (2016). *Situation of life-sentenced prisoners*. Retrieved from https://rm.coe.int/16806cc447

Death Penalty Information Center. (2020). *Facts about the death penalty (March 12, 2020)*. Retrieved from https://files.deathpenaltyinfo.org/documents/pdf/FactSheet.f1564498881.pdf

Denno, D. W. (2000). Adieu to electrocution. *Ohio Northern University Law Review, 26*(3), 665–688.

Dirs, B. (2018, May 7). The woman who watched 300 executions in Texas. *British Broadcasting Corporation*. Retrieved from https://www.bbc.com/news/world-us-canada-43995866

Durose, M. R., Cooper, A. D., & Snyder, H. N. (2016). *Recidivism of prisoners released in 30 states in 2005: Patterns from 2005 to 2010*. Washington, DC: Bureau of Justice Statistics.

Dye, M. H., & Aday, R. H. (2019). *Women lifers: Lives before, behind, and beyond bars*. Lanham, MD: Rowman & Littlefield.

Equal Justice Initiative. (2017). *Lynching in America: Confronting the legacy of racial terror*. Retrieved from https://lynchinginamerica.eji.org/report/

Federal Bureau of Investigation. (2019). *Table 1 (Crime 1998–2017)*. Retrieved from https://ucr.fbi.gov/crime-in-the-u.s/2017/crime-in-the-u.s.-2017/tables/table-1

Fedock, G. (2018). Life before "I killed the man that raped me": Pre-prison life experiences of incarcerated women with life sentences and subsequent treatment needs. *Women & Criminal Justice, 28*(1), 63–80.

Gallup. (2018). *Death penalty*. Retrieved from https://news.gallup.com/poll/1606/death-penalty.aspx

Garland, D. (2005). Penal excess and surplus meaning: Public torture lynchings in twentieth-century America. *Law & Society Review, 39*(4), 793–833.

Glaze, L. E., & Maruschak, L. M. (2008). *Parents in prison and their minor children*. Washington, DC: Bureau of Justice Statistics.

Gonnerman, J. (2019, February 20). Do jails kill people? *The New Yorker*. Retrieved from https://www.newyorker.com/books/under-review/do-jails-kill-people

Gramlich, J. (2019, January 3). 5 facts about crime in the U.S. *Pew Research Center*. Retrieved from https://www.pewresearch.org/fact-tank/2019/01/03/5-facts-about-crime-in-the-u-s/

Handtke, V., Bretschneider, W., Elger, B., & Wangmo, T. (2017). The collision of care and punishment: Ageing prisoners' view on compassionate release. *Punishment & Society, 19*(1), 5–22.

Herbert, S. (2018). Inside or outside? Expanding the narratives about life-sentenced prisoners. *Punishment & Society, 20*(5), 628–645.

Holland, M. M., Prost, S. G., Hoffman, H. C., & Dickinson, G. E. (2018). U.S. department of corrections compassionate release polices: A content analysis and call to action. *OMEGA—Journal of Death and Dying*. Published online ahead of print at: doi:10.1177/0030222818791708.

Human Rights Watch. (2005). *The rest of their lives: Life without parole for child offenders in the United States*. Washington, DC: Author.

Johnson, R. (2016). Solitary confinement until death by state-sponsored homicide: An eighth amendment assessment of the modern execution process. *Washington and Lee Law Review, 73*(3), 1213–1242.

Johnson, R., & Brooks, A. (2011). Cold comfort: Woman aging in prison (book review), *The Gerontologist, 51*(6), 887.

Johnson, R., & McGunigall-Smith, S. (2008). Life without parole, America's other death penalty: Notes on life under sentence of death by incarceration. *The Prison Journal, 88*(2), 328–346.

Kolivoski, K. M., & Shook, J. J. (2016). Incarcerating juveniles in adult prisons. *Criminal Justice and Behavior, 43*(9), 1242–1259.

Kuhlmann, R., & Ruddell, R. (2005). Elderly jail inmates: Problems, prevalence, and public health. *Californian Journal of Health Promotion, 3*(1), 50–61.

Leigey, M. E. (2010). For the longest time: The adjustment of inmates to a sentence of life without parole. *The Prison Journal, 90*(3), 247–268.

Leigey, M. E., & Ryder, M. A. (2015). The pains of permanent imprisonment: Examining perceptions of confinement among older life without parole inmates. *International Journal of Offender Therapy and Comparative Criminology, 59*(7), 726–742.

Leigey, M. E., & Schartmueller, D. (2019). The fiscal and human costs of life without parole. *The Prison Journal, 99*(2), 241–262.

Lempert, L. B. (2016). *Women doing life: Gender, punishment and the struggle for identity*. New York: New York University Press.

Liem, M. (2016) *After life imprisonment: Reentry in the era of mass incarceration*. New York: New York University Press.

Link, C. (2019, July 16). The death penalty punishes PA's corrections workers, too. Opinion. *Penn Live*. Retrieved from https://www.pennlive.com/opinion/2019/07/the-death-penalty-punishes-pas-corrections-workers-too-opinion.html

McCullough, J., & Byrne, E. (2019, April 3). Texas bans chaplains from its execution chamber. *The Texas Tribune*. Retrieved from https://www.texastribune.org/2019/04/03/texas-ban-chaplains-execution-chamber-death-row/

Monk, J. (2019, July 12). SC death row inmates in new (and nicer) home after quiet, high security move. *Greenville News*. Retrieved from https://www.greenvilleonline.com/story/news/2019/07/12/sc-death-row-inmates-new-facility-after-quiet-high-security-move-department-corrections/1714794001/

National Prison Rape Elimination Commission. (2009). *Report*. Washington, DC: Author.

Nellis, A. (2012). *The lives of juvenile lifers: Findings from a national survey*. New York: The Sentencing Project.

Ollove, M. (2016). Elderly inmates burden state prisons. *Pew Charitable Trusts*. Retrieved from https://www.pewtrusts.org/en/research-and-analysis/blogs/stateline/2016/03/17/elderly-inmates-burden-state-prisons

Penal Reform International. (2018). *Life imprisonment: A policy briefing*. London, UK: Author.

Prison Voice Washington. (2016). *Correcting food policy in Washington prisons*. Mountlake Terrace, WA: Author.

Public Safety Canada. (2019). *Corrections and conditional release statistical overview, 2018*. Ottawa: Author.

Renaud, J. (2018). Eight keys to mercy: How to shorten excessive prison sentences. *Prison Policy Initiative*. Retrieved from https://www.prisonpolicy.org/reports/longsentences.html

Robles, G. (2017, July 23). Condemned to death – And solitary confinement. *The Marshall Project*. Retrieved from https://www.themarshallproject.org/2017/07/23/condemned-to-death-and-solitary-confinement

Rovner, J. (2019). *Juvenile life without parole: An overview*. New York: The Sentencing Project.

Ruddell, R., Broom, I., & Young, M. (2010). Creating hope for life-sentenced offenders. *Journal of Offender Rehabilitation, 49*(5), 324–341.

Samuels, J., La Vigne, N., & Thomson, C. (2019). *Next steps in federal corrections reform*. Washington, DC: Urban Institute.

Sanders, S., & Stensland, M. (2018). Preparing to die behind bars: The journey of male inmates with terminal health conditions. *Journal of Correctional Health Care, 24*(3), 232–242.

Sarat, A. (2014). *Gruesome spectacles: botched executions and America's death penalty.* Stanford, CA: Stanford University Press.

Sentencing Project. (2018). *The facts of life sentencing: 1 in 7 people in prison is serving a life sentence.* Retrieved from https://www.sentencingproject.org/wp-content/uploads/2018/12/Facts-of-Life.pdf

Sheeran, A. M., Hilinski-Rosick, C. M., Richie, M., & Freiburger, T. L. (2018). Correlates of inmate misconduct: A comparison of younger, middle-age, and elderly inmates. *Corrections.* Published online ahead of print at doi:10.1080/23774657.2018.1549965

Sledge, M. (2018, August 18). 'It means the world to him': New Orleans man serving life for pot possession gets lighter term. *Nola.com.* Retrieved from https://www.nola.com/news/courts/article_2045d7b0-4e82-512b-9f25-acc0f9d9d89a.html

Smith, T., & Jiang, S. (2019). Making sense of life without parole in China. *Punishment & Society, 21*(1), 70–88.

Snell, T. L. (2019). *Capital punishment, 2017: Selected findings.* Washington, DC: Bureau of Justice Statistics.

Stearns, A. E., Swanson, R., & Etie, S. (2019). The walking dead? Assessing social death among long-term prisoners. *Corrections, 4*(3), 153–168.

Tartaro, C. (2019). *Suicide and self-harm in prisons and jails.* Lanham, MD: Lexington Books.

The Osborne Association. (2018). *The high costs of low risk: The crisis of America's aging prison population.* Retrieved from http://www.osborneny.org/resources/the-high-costs-of-low-risk/the-high-cost-of-low-risk/

Thompson, C. (2018, July 3). Old, sick and dying in shackles. *The Marshall Project.* Retrieved from https://www.themarshallproject.org/2018/03/07/old-sick-and-dying-in-shackles

Toch, H., Acker, J. R., & Bonventre, V. M. (2018). Introduction. In H. Toch, J. R. Acker, & V. M. Bonventre (Eds.), *Living on death row: The psychology of waiting to die.* Washington, DC: American Psychological Association.

Urbina, M. G., & Alvarez, S. E. (2018). *Hispanics in the U.S. criminal justice system: Ethnicity, ideology, and social control, 2nd edition.* Springfield, IL: Charles C. Thomas.

U.S. Census Bureau. (2019). *Population estimates.* Retrieved from https://census.gov/programs-surveys/popproj/data.html

U.S. Department of Justice. (2019). *Department of Justice announces the release of 3,100 inmates under First Step Act.* Retrieved from https://www.justice.gov/opa/pr/department-justice-announces-release-3100-inmates-under-first-step-act-publishes-risk-and

Van Zyl Smit, D., & Appleton, C. (2019). *Life imprisonment: A global human rights analysis.* Cambridge, MA: Harvard University Press.

Wansink, B., Kniffin, K. M., & Shimizu, M. (2012). Death row nutrition. Curious conclusions of last meals. *Appetite, 59*(3), 837–843.

Wilson, C., Schick, T., Jenkins, A., & Brownstone, S. (2019, April 2). Booked and buried: Northwest jail's mounting jail toll. *OPB.* Retrieved from https://www.opb.org/news/article/jail-deaths-oregon-washington-data-tracking/

Chapter 10
Parole and Prisoner Reentry

OUTLINE

- Introduction
- Origins of Parole
- The Administration of Parole
- Conditions of Release
- Violations of Parole
- Community Reentry
- Summary

OBJECTIVES

After reading this chapter, you will be able to:

- Describe how the evolution of parole in the United States shapes parole and prisoner reentry today

- Identify the mechanisms by which parole is provided, monitored, and revoked

- Explain the differences between release based on states with determinate and indeterminate sentencing

- Describe the challenges of prisoner reentry

- Explain why collateral consequences can serve as a barrier to prisoner reentry

CASE STUDY

Accidental Reentry: A Colorado Prisoner Is Mistakenly Released 88 Years Early

In 2000, 21-year-old Rene Lima-Marin was sentenced to serve a 98 year prison term in the Colorado Department of Corrections for his role in the armed robbery of two video rental stores. Although he was involved in only two robberies, the prosecutor separated the crimes into a series of eight different offenses, including two counts of kidnapping (as the employees were moved from one room in the store to another) and six counts of robbery (one for each employee in the two stores). Taken together, these eight convictions resulted in the lengthy prison term. When imposing the sentence, the judge expressed his discomfort with the way the crimes were prosecuted, but he followed the sentencing guidelines. The clerk admitting Lima-Marin to prison, however, made a mistake calculating his release date. Specifically, the sentences were supposed to run consecutively, but the clerk erred and calculated them to run concurrently—so all would run at the same time. As a result of this error, the Department of Corrections showed he had to serve a 16-year sentence.

Lima-Marin's time behind bars was uneventful and he was described as a model inmate (Kolker, 2015). Because of his good conduct, he was paroled in 2008, after serving eight years. While on parole he got married to a woman he knew before his imprisonment, fathered two boys and started working. He eventually obtained a well-paying union job installing windows on skyscrapers, enabling him to buy a home for his family. On his time off-work he regularly attended church and coached soccer. He was living the American dream and the dream of many ex-prisoners. After serving five years on parole without incident, however, prosecutors discovered the mistake and Lima-Martin was returned to prison. His new parole date was in 2054, when he would be 75 years old (Simpson, 2016).

Because Lima-Marin had such a successful community reentry, the case drew national attention and over 250,000 people signed a petition calling for his release. His lawyers worked on his behalf for several years to obtain his freedom, arguing that he had rehabilitated himself. In May 2017, a judge granted his release saying that further imprisonment would be unjust. More importantly, Lima-Marin was pardoned by Colorado's governor (Sallinger, 2018).

Lima-Marin's troubles were not over for another year as he was detained in an immigration detention facility upon his release from prison. Although he legally immigrated to the United States with his parents when he was two years old, his immigration status was in jeopardy because of his criminal convictions (Simpson, 2018). Tabachnik (2020) reports that since his release from immigration detention, Lima-Martin's life has returned to normal, and he is back at his job of installing windows, and he continues to coach his son's soccer team and stay involved in his hobbies.

Bronson and Carson (2019) observe there are about 600,000 prison admissions every year. There are bound to be mistakes when new prisoners' sentences are calculated, although errors do not always work in the inmate's favor. For example, O'Sullivan and Brunner (2019) report that a software problem resulted in at least ten Washington State inmates being held after their release dates. Washington State had mistakenly early released as many as 3,200 prisoners over a ten-year period due to a similar problem where staff relied on a computer that calculates a prisoner's sentence length. Similar mistakes occur in almost every adult and juvenile correctional facility, and this is one reason why inmates carefully review the sentence calculation sheets they are given.

Critical Questions

1. Was justice served when Lima-Marin was released by the judge and pardoned by the governor? Why or why not?
2. Should public opinion, such as 250,000 signatures on petitions to free Lima-Marin (after his successful community reentry was publicized) be a factor in the decision to release a prisoner? Would your answer change if the victim(s) of his crimes wanted him released?
3. What is the best way to hold prison officials accountable when they make mistakes calculating an individual's sentence?

INTRODUCTION

Many members of the public consider it an injustice that ex-prisoners are returned to the community before the end of their prison sentences, free to commit new crimes before they have fully paid their debt to society for the old ones. It does not seem fair to many crime victims and their families that these criminals are roaming the streets when they should be locked up for every day of their prison sentence. Owing to our almost innate fear of crime, most of us take precautions to reduce our risk: we don't walk alone after dark; when we do venture outdoors, we stay in well-lit places and avoid certain neighborhoods. When we return home, we double-check the locks on our doors and bars on the windows and ensure the alarms are set. Because criminals are free, goes this way of thinking, the rest of us become prisoners in our own homes.

Is this what you think too? Even if you do not agree with those who would like to see all criminals locked up until they no longer pose a threat to society, you must admit their arguments lead to other important questions that we address in this chapter. Consider Todd Clear and James Austin's (2009, p. 312) **iron law of prison populations**, which states that prison populations are first and foremost determined by the number of people sent to prison and second by the amount of time they serve behind bars. They contend there is no way to reduce the prison population without tackling either of these factors: we must reduce the number of prison admissions or cut their time served; we could even do both and maximize our change results. We can view changes in sentencing as managing the *front end* of corrections. Alternately, we can reduce prison populations by shortening the time prisoners serve through early release or parole, which is considered making changes to the *back end* of corrections. Beyond these two considerations, however, lies a third: correctional populations are impacted by ex-prisoners who are on parole or some other form of early release who violate their release conditions and are readmitted to jail or prison.

Indeed, the numbers of persons moving in and out of prison can be staggering. For instance, in 2017 there were over 600,000 new admissions to prison and almost 625,000 prisoners released (Bronson & Carson, 2019, p. 13). That number is almost the same as the entire population of Wyoming or Vermont flowing in and out of American prisons every year. The average sentences are relatively short—as most inmates will serve about three years, and most released prisoners will be supervised in the community by parole officers.

Travis (2005) also writes about an **iron law of imprisonment**, but his perspective focuses on the observation that except for a small percentage of inmates who will die in prison (either from natural causes, being murdered, or executed), almost all of them are eventually be released. This observation has several implications. First, these ex-prisoners will be our neighbors and the people we encounter in our everyday lives. As a result, it is in our best interest if they return to the community less damaged than when they were admitted to prison. About 95% of prisoners will eventually earn their releases and be returned to the community, and every year the 625,000 people released from prison will join another quarter-million former prisoners already on parole or other release (Kaeble, 2018). Of those leaving prison, about 160,000 will have **maxed out**, meaning that their entire sentence is served and, as a consequence, no one will oversee their release (Bronson & Carson, 2019). The remaining 875,000 ex-prisoners are supervised by parole officers or, in states with very small parole populations, by probation officers. Some states, such as Arizona, can also impose probationary sentences to follow an individual's prison sentence. As Campbell (2017, para. 3) explains it, "a **probation tail** means an offender receives a prison term on one charge and a probation term to be served immediately after on a second charge. Under that model, probation essentially takes the place of community supervision."

The fact that so many individuals are returned to the community raises some important questions, including the following:

1. How much time will they serve?
2. What are the conditions of their releases?
3. What is society doing to help these ex-prisoners make a safe transition to the community?
4. Does parole act as a backdoor feeder of correctional populations when parolees are returned to custody because of a technical violation or a new charge?

In this chapter, then, we look at the important idea of prisoner reentry into the community and the primary mechanism by which inmates accomplish this reentry is parole. Parole is one of the oldest and most widely practiced means of re entering society, but since the 1980s and 1990s federal and state authorities have instituted other means of reentry. We turn first to an examination of parole, starting with its origins.

ORIGINS OF PAROLE

Parole is a conditional release from prison, which means what it sounds like: inmates are released back into the community for as long as they abide by certain restrictions on their conduct. Like other correctional practices we can trace its existence back several centuries to Europe, and the term comes from *parole d'honneur*, a French phrase meaning "word of honor." In medieval times, a defeated knight could give his word of honor that he would withdraw from combat and leave the battlefield. Promises to withdraw from battle were also commonly used in the US Civil War by both the Union and Confederate armies as captured soldiers would give their word not to re enter the hostilities. These practices established the idea that a captured soldier or imprisoned person could be freed in exchange for a promise to behave in accordance with a set of agreed-on conditions. It took many years, however, before the practice was introduced to the penal system, and those changes started in the early 1800s in the Australian and New Zealand penal colonies, where convicts from the United Kingdom were transported.

Parole: From an English Practice to US Law

Captain Alexander Maconochie (1787–1860) is considered the father of parole. As the superintendent of two British penal colonies off the coast of Australia, he was shocked by the living conditions he observed upon his arrival at the colony on Van Diemen's Land. Maconochie set out to humanize the facility, and he was well-suited as a prison reformer because he served several years as a prisoner-of-war. As a result, he had a good understanding of correctional life and what motivated inmates to abide by prison rules. Maconochie introduced a plan to prepare his inmates for their return to the community but was fired from his position before fully implementing his reforms.

PHOTO 10.1

Alexander Maconochie 1787–1860 had been a prisoner of war prior to becoming the superintendent of two prison colonies off the coast of Australia. He used his knowledge of incarceration to encourage his prisoners to work toward a system of rewards, which could eventually earn them a return to their homelands. Credit: UtCon Collection/ Alamy Stock Photo.

Maconochie was more successful in his reforms after his transfer to the penal colony of Norfolk Island where he developed a system of rewards—or **marks of commendation**. These rewards were given to inmates for their good behavior, and they could use these marks to earn more freedoms on the island. When entering the colony, all prisoners were at the lowest level of classification—the penal stage—where they were closely supervised and required to do hard labor. After a period of demonstrating good behavior, prisoners could earn enough marks to move to the social stage. At this level, prisoners would have better living conditions in a smaller group setting with less supervision. Prisoners reached the final stage ("individual") through even more marks and earned the privilege of living in a cottage. All the while, they were working toward conditional release, which was called a **ticket of leave**. Maconochie's system also called for the loss of marks—and status—if the inmates violated the rules. This carrot-and-stick system gave the prisoners incentives for good behavior in the penal colony and punished misconduct. Prior to the introduction of the marks system, the most common punishment for misconduct was flogging.

Maconochie's ideas about reform and preparing inmates for their return to the community proved popular in the United Kingdom and led to prison reforms. One of these reforms, the establishment of parole, was a key goal in the **Penal Servitude Act of 1853**. Walter Crofton (1815–1897), chair of the Board of Directors of Convict Prisoners for Ireland from 1854 to 1862, introduced a four-stage process called the **Irish ticket of leave system**. Under the terms of this system, inmates serving three or more years could earn their early release. The first two stages involved solitary confinement on a reduced diet for the first three months, followed by placement on an island where hard work and good behavior had to be maintained in order to return to the mainland. The third stage was an open prison setting that offered inmates the opportunity to earn trust and demonstrate their reformation. Fourth-stage inmates were granted a conditional release and supervised in the cities by civilian employees (called ticket-of-leave men) or by the police in rural Ireland. These practices based on the gradual and earned transition from prison to the community proved successful in Ireland and were adopted throughout the United Kingdom.

Although prisons had been around for less than half-a-century by the late 1800s, critics voiced concerns that penal sanctions were heavy-handed and costly. Some recognized that the prison experience damaged some inmates. As a result, the notion of earned parole became popular. It is important to acknowledge, however, that parole in the United States did not originate from a single program or experiment, but it evolved out of many different practices. These early efforts resulted in the development of early release programs that started in Massachusetts and New York, and then were gradually adopted throughout the nation. These experiments with parole were informal and, as Klingele (2013, p. 1027) reports:

> a prisoner who exhibited good conduct was permitted to leave the prison under the supervision of a guardian (usually a family member or employer), who would vouch for the person's good conduct during the period immediately following release. By 1942, all states and the federal government had adopted parole legislation.

Parole in the Twenty-First Century

Like other aspects of the corrections system, as time passed the practice of parole evolved and became more formalized. Agencies were established that oversaw the supervision of parolees, and college-trained parole officers carried out that supervision. The introduction of parole was embraced with enthusiasm in most jurisdictions, although over time policymakers realized that parolees did not always have positive outcomes, as some parolees went on to commit serious crimes. As a result, like other correctional interventions, parole went through periods of crisis and reform. Indeed, some lawmakers became disillusioned with the practice and in 1976 Maine was the first state to disband their parole system. Fifteen states joined Maine, today relying on determinate sentencing schemes where the prisoner's sentence is set, but prisoners can earn an early release based on their good behavior. Today parole continues to evolve in response to changes in legal and political decisions, the influence of technology, and changing ideas about correctional rehabilitation and public safety.

One important contemporary change is that many state and federal prisoners leave correctional institutions under a mandatory early release system, bypassing the traditional parole system. Most parole programs do not even pretend to meet inmates' rehabilitative needs. Their objective is to give overburdened prison systems a way to control their inmate population. That is, as a prison system becomes overcrowded, prison administrators begin to release prisoners who are close to their release dates and who have presented few disciplinary problems. However, relying solely on backdoor methods to reduce the nation's prison populations in the twenty-first century may not be enough, especially considering the iron law of prison populations.

Many members of the public are skeptical about the ability of prisoners to reform themselves, and the evidence suggests their perceptions are correct. Alper, Durose, and Markman (2018, p. 1) found that over four-fifths (83%) of state prisoners released in 2005 were re-arrested within nine years. While acknowledging that an arrest is not a conviction—and an actual conviction on a non-violent offense might not be very threatening to public safety—these statistics do not bode well for the practice of parole. The high re-arrest rate for parolees raises several questions, including why these outcomes are so dismal and how can we improve the success of these ex-prisoners in their transition back to their communities. In the sections that follow we identify some promising practices to increase parolee success, but we first direct your attention to the different types of releases from confinement.

Release Types

Unless an inmate dies in prison or jail, he or she reenters society in one of five ways: **commutation of sentence** is an extraordinary action by the executive branch of government, either the president of the United States or a state's governor. Legally, commutation literally means exchanging one punishment for another less severe one. Practically, it means an inmate's release from prison in consideration for time served. The chief executive can commute sentences for illness, impending death, or other compassionate reasons. In some states, an inmate's early release is possible if the inmate is very ill or debilitated by disease or is terminally ill. Such releases, which go by many names that reflect their extraordinary nature, are rare and self-serving for the institution. They save huge medical costs and, in most cases, pass them along to cities and counties where these ex-prisoners reside until their deaths or recoveries. Such releases are generally permanent.

The First Step Act, a law signed into effect in December 2018, now allows sick or elderly federal prisoners to go before a federal judge if the Bureau of Prisons does not act on their request for a compassionate release (Johnson, 2019). Holland, Grace Prost, Hoffmann, and Dickinson (2018) report that 46 state corrections departments also have the ability to release elderly, and terminally or seriously ill inmates. The application process for these releases, however, can be lengthy and some prisoners die before their applications are approved. Most inmates who are granted these releases are placed on parole, which is sometimes called medical parole. Compassionate release practices are important to prisoners and their families as over 3,100 federal and state prisoners die every year from illnesses (Carson & Cowhig, 2020, p. 5).

A second form of executive clemency or mercy, and equally as rare as the commutation, is a **pardon**. Under the US and various state constitutions, the chief executive may grant a pardon or forgiveness for some or all past criminal deeds. In some instances, pardons restore some or all rights taken away from convicted felons; in others, pardons cause the convicted felon's immediate release from confinement. In some jurisdictions, including the federal government, a pardon board reviews all requests for executive clemency and makes recommendations to the chief executive. However, it is ultimately within the power of the chief executive to pardon quite literally any convicted felon under his or her legal authority. Prisoners can also be released after a pardon, and the case study that started this chapter showed that Colorado's governor pardoned Lima-Marin, shortening his prison sentence by more than 50 years.

Presidential clemency takes three forms: *pardon*, which is a form of presidential forgiveness and usually granted after individuals have paid their debt to society or in the case of a miscarriage of justice; **clemency**, which reduces an individual's sentence but does not change the fact of the conviction; and **remission**, which removes the individual's financial obligations such as a fine. The number of presidential pardons issued over the past four decades has generally been decreasing, except for President Obama's use of clemency for people who had been convicted of federal drug offenses, most of whom were serving mandatory minimum terms. It is important to remember that presidents can only grant clemency to persons convicted of federal offenses, and they do not have jurisdiction to pardon individuals sentenced in state courts. Table 10.1 shows the number of pardons, clemency, and remissions issued between 1977 and 2020.

The issuing of pardons by state governors is different from presidential pardons, and in some states, they are rarely granted. In South Carolina, by contrast, they are regularly issued for former prisoners who have served their sentences and lived crime-free in the community. South Carolina's parole board approves almost two-thirds (64%) of the applications it receives, even from murderers and sex offenders (Self, 2018). Some reformist governors have used their powers to grant mass clemency, such as Governor Ryan of Illinois, who commuted all the sentences of death row inmates to life imprisonment without the possibility of parole in 2003.

In some cases, inmates simply leave prison, under no terms of supervision. This practice, called **expiration release**, is an unconditional release from prison when the individual's sentence—minus any good-time credits—ends. It is not a form of parole: inmates released

TABLE 10.1 Presidential Pardons, Commutations, and Remission Granted: 1977–2020

President	Term	Pardons/Commutations and Remission Granted per Year
Jimmy Carter	1977–1981	11.8
Ronald Reagan	1981–1989	4.2
George H. W. Bush	1989–1993	1.6
William J. Clinton	1993–2001	4.8
George W. Bush	2001–2008	2.1
Barack Obama	2009–2017	240.9
Donald Trump	2017–March 2020	11.6

Source: U.S. Department of Justice (2020).

at the end of their term are not under supervision and do not have to meet any other conditions for release. This practice is also known as "maxing out." The Pew Charitable Trusts (2014, p. 1) reports that more than one in five state inmates max out. That proportion, however, varies by state, and less than 10% max out in eight states, among them Arkansas, California, and Wisconsin, while more than 40% max out in nine states, including Florida, New Jersey, and Utah. The Pew Charitable Trusts (2014, p. 9) contend that the lack of supervision for these ex-prisoners contributes to a higher rate of reconvictions and returns to custody, and advocate for post-prison supervision on parole for all prisoners.

Correctional authorities can initiate a **discretionary release** when they believe an inmate is ready for life on the outside. This system is found in states that have retained some elements of indeterminate sentencing. Another government entity, usually a parole board, must concur and authorize the parole, although the ultimate authority may rest with the state's chief executive. Typically, inmates released under this system must adhere to certain restrictions including limitations on their movement in the community, types of persons with whom they can associate, and even where they live or whether they can buy or drive a car.

Many inmates today leave custody under **mandatory release**. Once an inmate has served a statutorily defined minimum length of time, his or her release is nearly automatic. The prison authority simply informs the paroling or releasing authority that the person has served this statutorily defined limit, and the supervised release begins. In some cases, the releasing authority can deny release if the individual is deemed to pose a public safety risk. In such systems a fixed set of guidelines governs the actual release. In some states and the federal government this method is referred to as a supervised release, as it extends supervision upon exiting the state's prison system to as much as one-third of the original sentence. In many jurisdictions using this type of release mechanism, probation officers provide post-release supervision.

THE ADMINISTRATION OF PAROLE

Every state, the District of Columbia, and the federal government have developed mechanisms to determine how parole is granted, who makes the decisions to parole a prisoner, and who will supervise these parolees in the community. As noted earlier, 16 states, the District of Columbia, and the federal government do not have parole, and they use good-time credits to manage inmate behavior. Many of those jurisdictions, however, still have some parolees either under community supervision, or are still holding offenders who were sentenced to prison prior to abolishing parole. Some of them may be able to apply for parole at some point.

Table 10.2 shows the characteristics of the US parole population on 31 December 2016. In the previous chapters, we described the demographic and offense-related

TABLE 10.2 Characteristics of Adult Parolees, 2016

Characteristics/Legal Status/ Offense Type	Percentage of Total Parole Population
Males	87
Race	
White	45
African American	38
Latinx	15
All others	2
Status of Supervision	
Active	82
Inactive	5
Absconder	7
Supervised out of state	4
All other	2
Most Serious Offense	
Violent	30
Property	21
Drug	31
Weapon	4
Other	13

Source: Kaeble (2018).

characteristics of the probation, jail, and prison populations. Understanding the characteristics of the individuals the parole system must manage is important because the risks they pose should shape the nature of community supervision and intervention services. The information presented in Table 10.2 shows that males and African Americans are over-represented in the parole population, and Whites and women are under-represented, while Latinx parolees are represented very close to their prevalence in the general population. Whereas Bronson and Carson (2019) find that over one-half of state prisoners have at least one conviction for a violent offense, the proportion of parolees convicted of violent crimes is less than one-third. This underrepresentation in parole populations suggests fewer violent offenders are granted a discretionary parole, and many of them could have maxed out and are not supervised in the community.

Table 10.3 contains a summary of the parole status of the states breaking them down into two groups. The first column represents the 34 states with indeterminate sentencing, where the upper sentence limits are specified by the courts, but the actual time served by the prisoner depends on their prison conduct and rehabilitative efforts. The time served by inmates with determinate sentences, by contrast, can be predicted relatively closely as inmates earn good-time credits (e.g. 54 days per year in the federal system).

TABLE 10.3 Status of Parole Boards by State and Sentencing Structure

State	Parole Release: Indeterminate Sentencing	No Parole Release: Determinate Sentencing	Year Parole Abolished
Alabama	X		
Alaska	X		
Arizona		X	1994
Arkansas	X		
California		X	1977
Colorado	X		
Connecticut	X		
Delaware		X	1990
Florida		X	1983
Georgia	X		
Hawaii	X		
Idaho	X		
Illinois		X	1978
Indiana		X	1977
Iowa	X		
Kansas		X	1993
Kentucky	X		
Louisiana	X		
Maine		X	1976
Maryland	X		
Massachusetts	X		
Michigan	X		
Minnesota		X	1982

TABLE 10.3 (Continued)

State	Parole Release: Indeterminate Sentencing	No Parole Release: Determinate Sentencing	Year Parole Abolished
Mississippi	X		
Missouri	X		
Montana	X		
Nebraska	X		
Nevada	X		
New Hampshire	X		
New Jersey	X		
New Mexico		X	1979
New York	X		
North Carolina		X	1994
North Dakota	X		
Ohio		X	1996
Oklahoma	X		
Oregon		X	1989
Pennsylvania	X		
Rhode Island	X		
South Carolina	X		
South Dakota	X		
Tennessee	X		
Texas	X		
Utah	X		
Vermont	X		
Virginia		X	1995
Washington		X	1994
West Virginia	X		
Wisconsin		X	2000
Wyoming	X		
Total	34	16	

Source: Rhine, Mitchell, and Reitz (2019).

Eligibility for Parole

In many jurisdictions the key to understanding parole is an inmate's parole eligibility date, the earliest point at which he or she can leave prison. Calculating this date varies by jurisdiction and release model. First, the inmate must be eligible for parole. In some jurisdictions, those convicted of first-degree murder or aggravated homicide must serve a natural life sentence. As a result, they will not leave prison unless they are pardoned or receive a commutation of their sentence. Five states exclude prisoners serving life imprisonment from being paroled, including Iowa, Illinois, Maine, Pennsylvania, and South Dakota; collectively, these prison systems hold almost 8,000 lifers (NYU Law, 2019, p. 2).

The second criterion depends on whether the jurisdiction uses a discretionary or mandatory release approach, as summarized by Renaud (2018):

- The federal government and states with determinate sentencing are called **mandatory release states** as they base release decisions on the time served by prisoners, and they are released at a "predetermined point and supervised in the community for the remainder of the sentence." The federal government and most states offer some form of good-time credits which enables inmates to earn an early release for their good conduct, and some jurisdictions also reduce the time served for successfully completing rehabilitative programs. Some states have a post-release review board or commission that may examine pending releases, and these entities can delay release if they are concerned about the potential for post-release failure.
- States with indeterminate sentencing have **discretionary-parole** systems where inmates can be granted their release from prison by a parole board. Prisoners become eligible for parole after serving a set amount of their sentence, although Alper (2016) found there is no minimum term in several states. In discretionary-release jurisdictions, inmates are automatically eligible for a parole board hearing after serving a specified portion—often expressed as a percentage of the minimum or maximum sentence, depending on the nature of their most recent offense. However, there is no guarantee that parole will be granted, and some inmates may not be released until their sentence expires. Figure 10.1 shows how discretionary parole is administered.

Until 2011, the question of "the right to parole" was unclear, in spite of the fact that nearly all states' websites devoted to parole or early release eligibility declare it to be a privilege and not a right. The Supreme Court addressed this issue in a straightforward and rare unanimous decision about a California prisoner denied parole because of his potential risks. The Court found that parole *can be a right* extended at the state level, but

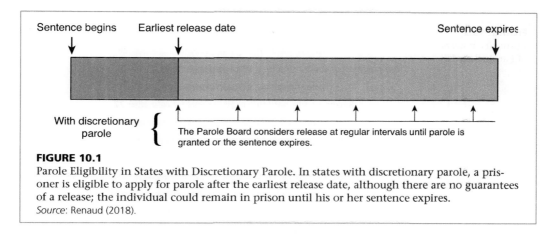

FIGURE 10.1

Parole Eligibility in States with Discretionary Parole. In states with discretionary parole, a prisoner is eligible to apply for parole after the earliest release date, although there are no guarantees of a release; the individual could remain in prison until his or her sentence expires.

Source: Renaud (2018).

there is no US constitutional right to parole. In *Swarthout v. Cooke* the Court's majority held that "There is no right under the Federal Constitution to be conditionally released before the expiration of a valid sentence, and the States are under no duty to offer parole to their prisoners." In other words, if your state says in its constitution that parole is a right, you have that right. If you are held in a federal facility for a federal offense, there is no such right.

Granting Parole: The Parole Board

There has been some variation in the way that parole administration has evolved throughout the country. While in this section we describe some shortcomings with the operations of parole boards, these agencies are becoming more professional and accountable to the public. Ruhland, Rhine, Robey, and Mitchell (2017) surveyed all US states about the organization of their parole boards (they called them releasing authorities). Of the 45 states that responded to their survey, parole boards or similar bodies in 40 states (89%) answer to the executive branch, but there are a number of different administrative arrangements throughout the country:

- In 20 states (44%) these boards are independent but are attached to the Department of Corrections;
- In nine states (20%), the board is an independent and autonomous agency;
- In seven states these boards are independent but attached to an agency other than the Department of Corrections;
- In five states these boards were a division, bureau, or office within the Department of Corrections.
- In four states, the arrangements were listed as "other" (Ruhland et al., 2017, p. 17).

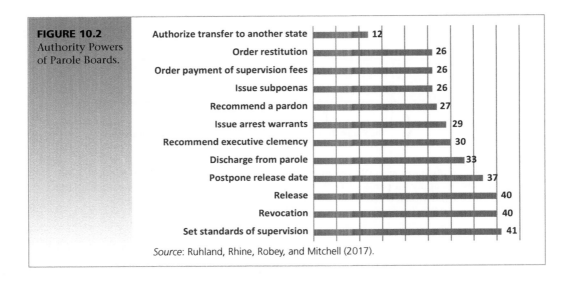

FIGURE 10.2 Authority Powers of Parole Boards.

Source: Ruhland, Rhine, Robey, and Mitchell (2017).

In addition to how these agencies are administered, there are differences in their powers, and they are displayed in Figure 10.2. Most of these agencies set the standards of supervision which includes making the decision to release and setting the conditions the parolee must follow.

Board members wield considerable power. Rhine, Petersilia, and Reitz (2015, p. 96) report that "340 parole board members in 46 states granted 187,035 discretionary entries to parole" in 2013. They also note how these board members "determine the amount of time offenders spend in confinement, conditions of post-release supervision and whether violations will result in revocation" (Rhine et al., 2015, p. 96). These board members "are vested with almost unlimited discretion to make decisions on almost any basis. Hearsay, rumor and instinct are all fair game" (Schwartzapfel, 2015). The workloads placed on these boards can be very demanding, especially when we consider the magnitude of the decisions they make about people's lives. McVey, Rhine, and Reynolds (2018) surveyed board members and found that workloads are high. These board members complain that the lack of both support staff and the time to consider their cases can lead to poor-quality decisions.

Governors are granted the sole authority to appoint board members in most states, although the director or commissioner of the Department of Corrections can appoint members in four states, and the president appoints members to the U.S. Parole Commission (Ruhland et al., 2017). Historically, parole board members were political appointees who typically did not know much about corrections, parole, or prisons before they became members, and many lacked a formal education. In sharp contrast to those past practices, board members today tend to be well-educated. In particular, Ruhland

and colleagues (2017, p. 21) found that 89% of board members had a bachelor's degree or higher, and about half of these members had a master's degree, law degree, or Ph.D. Many of these board members also had experience working with people involved in the justice system prior to their appointments to these boards.

After the appropriate authority makes the decision to consider an inmate for early release the parole board assesses all relevant information. Given the emphasis on treatment and suitability for release in these states, the board may consider evidence of the inmate's progress toward rehabilitation. Ruhland et al. (2017, p. 26) found that board members considered the following factors:

- Nature of the present offense
- Prior adult criminal record
- Institutional program participation
- Psychological report
- Inmate's disciplinary record
- Risk assessments or reports
- Previous parole adjustment
- Victim input
- History of illegal drug use
- Inmate's disposition or demeanor at hearing
- Previous probation adjustment
- Inmate family input
- Inmate testimony
- Prior juvenile criminal record
- Age at first conviction
- Treatment reports or discharge summaries
- Prosecutor input
- Offender's case plan as prepared by institutional staff
- Sentencing judge input

In states using mandatory-release procedures the board's decision to release is based on three criteria once an individual is statutorily eligible for parole:

1. The inmate generally must have followed the correctional institution's rules and regulations.
2. The inmate must not pose a significant public safety risk.
3. The inmate must not have committed a crime so serious that his or her release would lead citizens to question the validity of the criminal justice system or to disrespect the law.

Consider the third item in the list. How do the members decide whether a specific criminal's release is going to anger the public? In some cases, the public's reaction is relatively easy to predict—the release of a convicted child molester, for instance, is likely to be met with protest—but there is no way to be sure how the community is going to respond in every case. As a result, these decisions remain largely subjective.

Parole Decisions: Risks and Remedies

A parole decision that angers the public is largely a political mistake; a parole decision that compromises public safety could well be a life-threatening mistake. For example, the Maine parole board was the first to be disbanded and parole ceased in 1976 because of a lack of public confidence in both the board and parole. Within two decades, another 15 states would follow Maine's lead in permanently ending parole. To minimize a parole decision's adverse risk to public safety, 36 states use some form of risk assessment to inform the decision-making (Ruhland et al., 2017). Berk (2017) observes that different types of risk assessments have been used in parole decision-making since the 1920s, although the versions used today are more sophisticated than the ones introduced a century ago.

Decisions about the risks that offenders pose are increasingly based on assessments that were developed using studies that explored recidivism in tens of thousands of cases. The goal behind these methods is that researchers will be able to determine the patterns, trends, and relationships that emerge when looking at a large volume of cases. In light of these insights, goes the logic, parole boards and other releasing authorities should be able to make better decisions about returning an individual to the community based on identified risk factors. Researchers examining the success of different risk assessments for use in parole-making decisions have achieved mixed results. Desmarais, Johnson, and Singh (2016) looked at the effectiveness of 19 different risk-assessment methods used in corrections; they say that no single assessment tool was the best, although some were more effective in predicting future recidivism. How can these results be used? Berk (2017) describes how information that predicted inmate risks of future involvement in non-violent and violent crime was given to Pennsylvania parole board members considering applications for parole. Berk contends that accessing this information led to better decision-making and considerably fewer subsequent arrests.

Despite research showing the effectiveness of some risk-assessment instruments, a growing number of scholars and civil libertarians are critical of making any decisions about individuals based on software that uses a set of well-defined procedures to calculate outcomes, including recidivism. Tashea (2017) says that an increasing number of risk assessments used for bail, sentencing, and parole decisions are being challenged in the courts. Tashea points out that many software programs are developed by corporations, and the creators of these programs are unwilling to disclose how they were developed. They essentially become "black boxes," where someone enters the data and out pops a recommendation. How those data about offenders shaped that decision, say the vendors, is a proprietary secret. If the risk assessment was constructed using the criminal histories of middle-aged White male offenders, for example, would it accurately predict the recidivism of young African American women? The big question these critics ask is whether these tools are used fairly and whether they accurately predict the risk to reoffend. If they don't predict risk accurately, we can hold prisoners longer than they should be held, which is not an efficient use of a correctional bed (and unjust to the individual), or release them too early, which reduces public safety.

In the end, most parole board members use a variety of methods in their decision-making, relying upon the results of risk assessments and the insights of the prisoner's case managers, as well as their own perceptions about the inmate. These hearings are quite short—usually less than ten minutes—and in some jurisdictions these hearings are discretionary. There need be no formal hearing, and board members are not required to tell inmates why they were granted or denied release. Some parole boards are more diligent when it comes to highly visible cases. For example, New York parole board members interviewed a 67-year-old woman for seven hours over two days before unanimously denying her parole. She had served 35 years in prison after acting as the driver in the robbery of a Brink's armored car that left two police officers and a Brink's employee dead. Law (2017) notes that 35 years after the crime, the board received almost 10,000 letters opposing her release.

PHOTO 10.2

This prisoner is facing a Nebraska Parole Board. Parole boards wield a considerable amount of power over the lives of these people and research shows that their members have higher levels of education and more related experience than the parole boards of the past, making them more professional. Credit: Mikael Karlsson/ Alamy Stock Photo.

In jurisdictions where parole board members still have much discretion, members try to reduce the number of what statisticians call false positives, parolees who looked to be good risks but later committed a crime. Rather than subject the public to danger and themselves to embarrassment, members of parole boards tend to deny parole to people by what statisticians would call false negatives, inmates who would have made a success of their parole, but were kept in prison. Where mandatory release is the law, unless there are competing reasons not to grant parole, early release is nearly automatic.

Parole boards have always had to consider the release of prisoners who were involved in highly publicized cases. Given the swift responses of the media and social media when something goes wrong, the potential outcomes for a bad decision—where a parolee goes on to commit a violent offense upon his release—make board members risk averse (Reitz, 2018). In an era where a mistake can go viral on social media in a few hours, there appears to be less risk-taking, and there is a feeling that nobody will lose their position on the parole board because they made conservative decisions.

Parole Officers

Chapter 4 related how US jurisdictions take several different approaches to probation and parole work. The emphasis here is on release from prison. In jurisdictions where they are used, parole officers receive their authority from the executive branch. Most **parole officers** or **parole agents**, therefore, are state-level civil service employees. Others are combination of probation/parole officers (PPOs), and may either be local or state employees. As noted previously, 16 states and the federal government no longer offer parole. As some inmates in these jurisdictions were eligible for parole before the laws changed there may be so few parolees that local probation officers supervise their release.

Table 10.4 summarizes field supervision service providers. The state-level corrections department is the most common pattern of employment for post-release agents/officers, found in 36 states. Those agents or officers who supervise prison releases in five states work directly for the parole board. In two states supervisory staff are employed by the state-level Department of Community Corrections. The courts oversee parole in the federal system, the District of Columbia, and Iowa. Finally, six states have other patterns of employment, but in most of them, the agents/officers work for a public safety department.

The number of clients assigned to a given parole officer—much like the caseload of probation officers—varies widely. Reliable estimates of the actual ratios for parole officers to clients served, as was the case for probation officer-probationer ratios, are rare. In many jurisdictions, parole officers or probation officers who supervise parolees typically oversee smaller caseloads than do probation officers working entirely with probationers. This difference owes much to the fact that parolees are often viewed as posing a higher risk to the community than probationers (DeMichele & Payne, 2007). However, over the past several decades the differences in risk between lower risk parolees and higher risk probationers may have disappeared, as probationers' characteristics increasingly

TABLE 10.4 Field Supervision Service Providers

Type	Jurisdiction	
Parole Board	Alabama	Pennsylvania
	Georgia	Tennessee
	New Jersey	
Department of Corrections	Arizona	Montana
	California	Nebraska
	Colorado	New Hampshire
	Connecticut	New Mexico
	Delaware	New York
	Florida	North Dakota
	Idaho	Ohio
	Illinois	Oklahoma
	Indiana	Oregon
	Kansas	Rhode Island
	Kentucky	South Dakota
	Louisiana	Utah
	Maine	Vermont
	Michigan	Virginia
	Minnesota	Washington
	Mississippi	West Virginia
	Missouri	Wisconsin
		Wyoming
Department of Community Corrections	Arkansas	South Carolina
Courts	District of Columbia	Federal System
	Iowa	
Others	Hawaii	Nevada
	Maryland	North Carolina
	Massachusetts	Texas

Source: Robina Institute (2018).

mirror the prison population, given that more than one half of them are convicted felons (Kaeble, 2018).

Several scholars have looked into the issue of parole officer workloads, and their research sheds some light on their activities. Some of their tasks are driven by their organizational culture and the priorities placed on rehabilitation or surveillance, as well as whether their work is based in the office or the field. Matz, Conley, and Johanneson (2018, p. 300) examined the workloads of community corrections officers in Montana. Table 10.5 shows their primary case-related activities and the amount of time for each of these interactions. These totals do not include time engaged in matters unrelated to offender supervisions such as attending meetings, supervising other officers or training. The first case-related item, which was contact with clients, accounted for 18% of the officers' time, and the average interaction was 24 minutes. Officers also spent consider-able time responding to offender requests for information, report writing, and entering data. As these Montana officers supervise probationers and parolees, some were assigned to prepare pre-sentence investigations, and those duties would be carried out by proba-tion officers. The amount of time an individual officer spent on these activities varied by their primary job duties, and some officers assigned to specialized caseloads would spend more or less time on the activities reported in Table 10.5. As noted in Chapter 4, officers working in community corrections have different supervisory styles and some of their priorities are driven by their agency's philosophies and missions. Klingele (2013, p. 1036) says that "in some jurisdictions, particularly those in which agents carry heavy caseloads, officers have become little more than glorified bureaucrats who spend their days completing paperwork and conducting periodic check-ins with offenders in the agents' offices."

Matz and his colleagues (2018) found that officers spent over three-quarters of their time in the office, and only 4% of their time was spent on home visits. Even when these home visits take place, they tend to be short-term events. Meredith and colleagues (2020, p. 12) found that home visits to Georgia parolees ranged from one minute to two hours, although the average visit lasted only eight minutes. These researchers found that during these visits officers typically focused on two key themes. The first was topics related to abiding by rules, such as reminding the parolees about the conditions of their release, making inquiries about their drug and alcohol use, and whether they had any contact

TABLE 10.5 Top 10 Case-Related Activities, and Average Time per Interaction, Montana Probation/Parole officers

Case-Related Activities	Percentage of Time	Amount of time per interaction (minutes)
Standard offender contact/interviews	18	24
Responding to offender inquiries	7	13
Report writing/data entry	6	27
Pre-sentence investigations (PSI)	5	72
Discharge activities	4	17
Transition planning	4	24
Violation investigation	3	35
Drug testing (urinalysis)	2	17
Referral procedures	2	30
Court appearances	2	81

Source: Matz, Conley, and Johanneson (2018).

with law enforcement. The second key theme of these visits was related to the parolee's needs, including seeking employment, their progress with substance abuse treatment, and their physical and mental health. What were the outcomes of these visits? Meredith et al. (2020) reported that parolees who received more home visits were less likely to be arrested or have their parole revoked.

CONDITIONS OF RELEASE

The official parole agreement generally lists a state's standard parole conditions; these conditions are often indistinguishable from the conditions states or the federal government set for probationers (see Chapter 4 for a list of the federal probation conditions). If an inmate has special needs, his or her special parole conditions also become part of the parole agreement. Consider, for example, the list of standard conditions for parolees drawn from the state of West Virginia in the following list:

- Must report (to their parole officer) within 24 hours of release
- Stay within a certain area
- Obtain permission before changing residence or employment
- Obtain and maintain employment
- Maintain acceptable, non-threatening behavior
- Must not possess firearms or weapons
- Report any arrest within 24 hours
- Complete monthly written report
- Report as instructed
- Must not use drugs or alcohol or enter drinking establishments
- Must not break any state or local laws
- Abide by other written requirements
- Pay $40 supervision fee monthly
- Sex offenders of children cannot live with anyone under 18
- Sex offenders must register with West Virginia State Police within three days
- Allow contacts at home or employment without obstruction
- Submit to search of person, residence, or motor vehicle at any time by parole officers

Source: West Virginia Division of Corrections and Rehabilitation (2019)

The above-mentioned list of 17 parole conditions is insightful, but does not tell the entire story. Travis and Stacey (2010) identified 127 different conditions used by state parole boards across the nation. Several unusual conditions included prohibiting parolees from possessing dangerous animals and requiring a parole officer's permission to get married in several states.

Similar to probationary conditions, parolees may be required to abide by additional special conditions. These conditions are typically related to the individuals' criminal histories or factors that led to their criminal conduct such as problems with anger or substance abuse. Some special conditions restrict parolees from associating with specific individuals such as gang members who were involved in the offenses that led to the parolee's imprisonment. Once imposed by a parole board, most states allow the agencies supervising these parolees to modify the conditions somewhat, either on their own, or with board approval (Ruhland et al., 2017).

Length of Supervision

State and federal laws govern the duration of parole. Some serious and violent crimes may merit very long paroles, and sexual offenders can be subject to lifelong supervision, as is the case in Indiana (Black, 2016) and Iowa (Boden, 2017). Individuals who were sentenced to life imprisonment—including juveniles—can also be required to remain on parole for the rest of their sentence or, in other words, they will die under correctional supervision (Diatchenko, 2015). In jurisdictions employing mandatory release, a parolee may leave prison after serving a portion of his or her sentence and be required to continue parole for the rest of the sentence that was imposed. Most states empower the parole authority to discharge parolees before the end of the mandated supervision period once the minimum has been satisfied. Again, there is considerable variation among the states in terms of how much time on parole is enough.

Like our discussion of probation in Chapter 4, the length of parole supervision, and the conditions of release can determine the success of any given parolee's community reentry. Klingele (2013) argues that if we want parolees to succeed, legislators, judges, and parole boards should attempt to limit the number of conditions and restrict the length of supervision. As Rhine, Petersilia, and Reitz (2017, p. 324) observe:

> Conditions should be imposed sparingly and only when they correspond with offenders' risk and needs. [And] with the exception of predatory offenders [t]he maximum supervision period should be limited to no more than 5 years for higher risk levels and for a period not to exceed 12 months for lower risk levels.

Releasing Sex Offenders to the Community: A Special Case

Because of our fears of their possibility of reoffending, sex offenders are typically required to abide by several special conditions, including where they live, their contact with children, and reporting requirements; as most are placed on sex offender registries, they must abide by state requirements (e.g. registering annually). Some states, such as Arizona, also require different types of public notification when these individuals are released from prison, and these efforts may include press releases and flyers sent to neighborhoods where they will reside as well as to surrounding schools, community groups, and prospective employers (Arizona Department of Public Safety, 2019).

Sex offenders are often required to abide by residency requirements. For instance, Florida laws, among others, restrict parolees from living within 1,000 feet of playgrounds or childcare centers, and Miami-Dade County further restricts them from living within 2,500 feet of a school. Federal laws also prevent these ex-prisoners from living in public housing. While these restrictions have a common-sense appeal, one of the problems is that most large cities have so many of these facilities that these people cannot live within the city boundaries. Schwartzapfel and Kassie (2018, para. 5) observe that these restrictions have made many sex offenders into nomads who are driven into homelessness, but either local laws or their parole conditions prevent them from living in homeless shelters and forbid them from camping on public property.

Not having suitable living arrangements violates the conditions of a sex offender's release in some states. Hundreds of Illinois sex offenders, for example, were being held in prison years past their sentence expiration dates as they could not start their mandatory supervised release until securing a community residence. Because they were poor or lacked family members or other supporters who could provide a place to live, they remained in prison. Green (2019, para. 7) reports that one Illinois prisoner served eight years beyond his release date and that:

> He couldn't afford his own apartment, so he turned to his family for help. But their living situations disqualified them under state law. He said his father lived too close to a park, his mother had a computer and smartphone with internet access, his sister had small children, and his dad's girlfriend's home was too close to a day care center – all violations of the state's housing rules.

In April 2019, a federal judge found such restrictions unconstitutional, ordering the Department of Corrections to come up with a solution. As Judge Virginia Kendall wrote: "At the very heart of the liberty secured by the separation of powers is freedom from indefinite imprisonment by executive decree" (*Murphy v. Raoul,* No. 16-C-11471 (N.D. Ill 2019) p. 2). Advocates who want to reduce recidivism say that homelessness and unstable living conditions increase the likelihood of any ex-prisoner's recidivism, including sex offenders. The following section describes how Canadian volunteers pioneered a strategy that works toward the safe transition of high-risk sex offenders into the community.

Sex Offender Community Reentry Canadian Style: Circles of Support and Accountability

After reviewing the research literature, King and Roberts (2017) confirm what most of us already suspected: the public has little sympathy for sex offenders and polls show that we want them punished harshly. Harper says that many of our fears about these people are based on stereotypes and the media is sometimes guilty of exaggerating the risks they pose. But, as we noted in the iron law of imprisonment—described in the introduction—almost all prisoners return to the community. As a result, it is in everybody's interest if these ex-prisoners have a safe and orderly transition to the community to lower their risks of recidivism. Our example of comparative corrections describes a volunteer-based intervention called **Circles of Support and Accountability** (CoSA) that was started in Canada due to a lack of options for high-risk sex offenders who had maxed out and had to be released.

CoSA started with one high-risk sex offender named Charlie Taylor, who was returned to the community after serving his entire prison sentence, so he would not be supervised by a parole officer (Wilson, 2018). Taylor was well-known to the police and his release drew widespread news coverage as nobody wanted him living in their neighborhood. A prison psychologist encouraged Henry Nigh, who was the pastor of a church that Taylor once attended, to support his return to the community. Nigh put together a group of volunteers in what they called a circle to provide assistance and support in Taylor's efforts to return to community life. These volunteers met frequently with Taylor and gave him encouragement and advice. Wilson (2018) says that the group reduced his isolation from the rest of the world with their friendship. This approach responded to Taylor's unmet needs; when Charlie Taylor died in 2006, he had been crime-free since his release from prison 12 years earlier.

CoSA has been implemented throughout Canada and each circle is comprised of the ex-prisoner (called a core member) and three to five volunteers who commit to a long-term relationship with that individual. It is not unusual for these groups to exist for years. The circle volunteers are, in turn, supported by the CoSA organization, and this support often includes an "outer circle" where trained professionals mentor and provide training to the volunteers (Chouinard & Riddick, 2014). These volunteers work with only a fraction of the sex offenders released from prison because it is so difficult to recruit people who can commit to working with these individuals for years. Figure 10.3 shows the relationship between the core member, volunteers, and the professionals who support them.

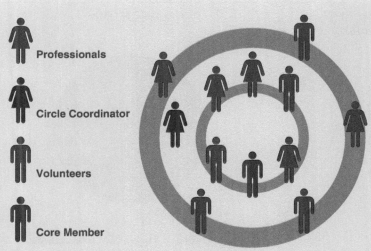

FIGURE 10.3
Circles of Support and Accountability.
Note: COSA is a volunteer-based program that provides supports for high-risk sexual offenders, called core members, who are released from prison. These volunteers are supported by professionals who provide support and advice to the volunteers.
Source: Wilson and McWhinnie (2013).

Neither the volunteers nor the local CoSA organizations are associated with the police or parole authorities, although volunteers are required to inform the police if the core member has talked about committing a crime. Evaluations of the approach consistently demonstrate that CoSA is a low-cost intervention that reduces recidivism (Azoulay, Winder, Murphy, & Fedoroff, 2019). This approach is gaining in popularity and has been adopted throughout Europe, the United Kingdom, and the United States (Azoulay et al., 2019; Harper, 2018).

VIOLATIONS OF PAROLE

Parole has two possible outcomes: success and continued residence in the free society or failure and a possible return to prison. In 2016, 57% of the parolees successfully completed the term of supervision and earned unconditional release, a figure that has increased from 45% where it had stood in the mid-1990s (Glaze & Bonczar, 2011, p. 9). Failure is a complex term, covering several different outcomes. For example, among the 30% of parolees who were unsuccessful, most (90%) were returned to prison, while the remainder absconded. The unknown category includes individuals who transferred to

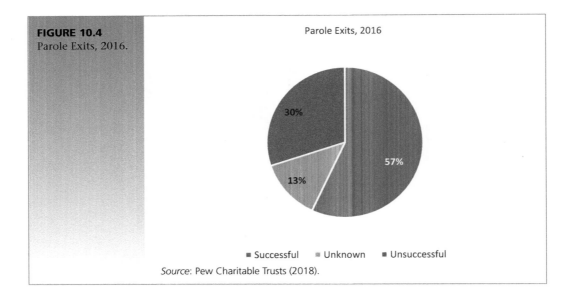

FIGURE 10.4
Parole Exits, 2016.

Parole Exits, 2016

30%

57%

13%

■ Successful   ■ Unknown   ■ Unsuccessful

Source: Pew Charitable Trusts (2018).

another jurisdiction from supervision, died, absconded, or otherwise exited from parole. These success rates are consistently lower than those reported for probationers and these parole exits are shown in Figure 10.4.

Parolees who fail commit new offenses and technical violations. Klingele (2013, p. 1037) says that parole officers become aware of these violations from failed drug tests, calls from community agencies, and sometimes directly from the parolee. Once the parole officer learns of an alleged offense he or she often confers with a supervisor about the next step. If the alleged offense is a minor rule violation, "such as missed appointments, late-filed report forms, or curfew violations may be disregarded entirely or handled with an informal reminder or admonition" (Klingele, 2013, p. 1039). Officers in some jurisdictions are also able to implement a range of intermediate sanctions that are more serious than a warning but fall short of a return to custody. The conditions of release, for example, can be amended and the parolee can be referred for treatment, placed on more intensive supervision, including electronic monitoring, and subjected to flash incarceration, or a short jail sentence. Yet infractions most of us would consider minor can also result in a return to prison. Schiraldi (2019, para. 1) reports that:

> A man nine years out of a New York prison proposes marriage to his girlfriend, who also has a criminal record. Because it is against the rules to associate with someone with a prior record, his parole is revoked and he is returned to prison for a year—after which he marries the same person, this time with his parole officer's permission.

Hager (2017) calculated there are at least 61,000 parolees who were returned to prison for technical violations, and many advocates question whether all of those re-admissions to prison were necessary. We have to acknowledge, however, that for every one of these minor cases that result in a parolee's incarceration, there are also very serious violations of a parolee's release where imprisonment is warranted.

When more serious violations or crimes occur, the parole officer asks the court of jurisdiction to issue an arrest warrant for the parolee. Once in custody, the parolee is likely to remain there until the issue is resolved as few states allow them to post bail. If the offense is not serious, the parole officer, after assessing their threat to the community and flight risk, may ask the court to issue a **citation**, a legal document roughly equivalent to a traffic ticket. The citation orders the parolee to appear at a violation hearing. In most states, a parole officer who observes a violation in person can immediately take the parolee into custody, an act called a summary arrest.

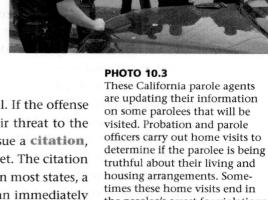

PHOTO 10.3
These California parole agents are updating their information on some parolees that will be visited. Probation and parole officers carry out home visits to determine if the parolee is being truthful about their living and housing arrangements. Sometimes these home visits end in the parolee's arrest for violations of the conditions of their release. Credit: ZUMA Press Inc./Alamy Stock Photo.

The Preliminary Parole Revocation Hearing

In *Morrissey v. Brewer* (1972) the Supreme Court ruled that parolees have limited due process rights. The Court did not mandate that a preliminary hearing take place before the parole board and its only stipulation was that hearings occurred before a neutral party. Often a **hearing officer**, typically a supervisory-level or senior member of the parole agency staff, conducts the preliminary hearing. Here, too, the preliminary hearing is to determine probable cause. The parolee's case officer presents the government's case. Should the officer fail to make the case for a violation, the parolee returns to supervision. If the hearing officer finds that probable cause exists for one or more violations, he or she may remand the parolee to jail until the revocation hearing.

A Missouri class-action lawsuit, launched by a group of parolees, questions whether they obtain the due process protections they are entitled to receive. Schwartzapfel (2019, para. 4) says that:

> The state pressures people to waive hearings, doesn't provide them with lawyers they're entitled to and presents them with paperwork that is so confusing sometimes they don't even know what they're accused of, the suit said. The parole board sends too many people to prison for petty violations and holds them there for too long.

Ruhland et al. (2017) found that in only one state was the public or the media allowed to be present at these hearings. One of the points we have raised in the previous chapters is that due process protections in low-visibility events, such as these hearings, can erode over time.

The Revocation Hearing

The makeup of the hearing board varies from state to state, although in more than one-half (55%) of the states they are conducted by parole board members, and in over one-quarter of states (29%) they are carried out by hearing officers or examiners, while in the rest of the states they are conducted by judges, administrative law judges, or some combination of board members and hearing officers (Ruhland et al., 2017, p. 40). The due process protections granted to parolees at these hearings vary somewhat across the country. While almost all states allow the parolee to be heard in person and present evidence, about one-quarter of the states do not allow the parolee to be represented by counsel (Ruhland et al., 2017). Although the revocation hearing is more exhaustive and comprehensive than the preliminary hearing, many legal niceties are missing. Again, if the preponderance of the evidence supports the alleged violation, the board has several options, including continuing parole with restricted freedom or incarcerating the parolee. When the hearing board, functioning as a quasi-judicial body, finds in the parolee's favor, supervision continues.

RACE, CLASS, AND GENDER

The Community Reentry of Native Americans

Native Americans account for about 1% of the national population although over-represented in the state populations of Alaska, Arizona, Montana, New Mexico, North and South Dakota, and Oklahoma, and similarly over-represented in their correctional populations. Because many of them live on tribal lands that fall under the federal government's jurisdiction, the Native American federal prison population is also growing and increased 18% between 2016 and 2017 (U.S. Sentencing Commission, 2018, p. 1).. There were over 4,100 Native Americans in federal custody in March 2020 and their average sentence was about four years (Bureau of Prisons, 2020). Often, they are not eligible to receive good-time credits. Franklin and Henry (2018, p. 126) found that Native Americans serving federal prison sentences were 152% more likely to be denied access to good-time credits at sentencing compared to White offenders when judges meted out either 365 or 366 day sentences. People sentenced to one year were ineligible for the 15% good-time credits, whereas individuals sentenced to one year and one day were eligible for those good-time credits.

When it comes to individual states, Native American parolees were more likely to be returned to Montana prisons for a technical violation and Mehta and Gomila (2018, p. 16) found that about one-quarter (26%) of Whites were returned to prison whereas over one-third (35%) of Native Americans were returned. Shames and Subramanian (2016, p. 2) report that 44% of all Native American parolees in South Dakota are returned to prison for a parole violation, although only accounting for less than one-quarter of all parolees. Wodahl and Freng (2017, p. 161) found similar results from research examining parole violations in Alaska, California, and Oklahoma, but also acknowledge the lack of national-level statistics makes it difficult to make generalizations about these violations. As we mentioned in Chapter 1, the population of Native Americans is very small (i.e. a bit more than 1% of the national population in 2019), and about 30% live in out-of-the-way places that researchers cannot easily access. There are, however, a growing number of these people moving to cities for better opportunities (Williams, 2013).

Why are the statistics so grim when it comes to parole outcomes with this population? A review of U.S. Census Bureau (2019) statistics shows that a higher proportion of American Indians and Alaska Natives live in poverty than non-Native Americans, unemployment rates are higher, and median family income and educational attainment are also lower. Moreover, many Native American ex-prisoners returning to the community were convicted in local or state courts and live on tribal lands. One of the challenges these ex-prisoners must confront is that many reservations are in rural areas and lack the educational, health, or social services they require for successful reentry. Even when community reentry is supported by a placement in a halfway house, that halfway house may be hundreds of miles from the reservation where they will settle, which minimizes the effectiveness of that intervention (Reentry Council, 2014).

Shames and Subramanian (2016) say that some of the strategies intended to improve public safety with Native American ex-prisoners actually work against them. They observe that conditions of their release requiring them to continuously look for work force them to urban areas that are away from their support networks. Living on tribal lands, however, can make it difficult for parolees to receive services and their parole officer might be based 100 or more miles away from them, making it difficult to form relationships with them. Establishing effective working relationships may also be difficult given their distrust of the justice system and discrimination that many of them have experienced. Last, county or state parole officials have limited jurisdiction on tribal lands and often the only option for dealing with a parole violation is either doing nothing or issuing a warrant for their arrest, and parole officers often opt for the arrest.

Given those challenges, researchers and policy analysts have suggested the following recommendations for improvement:

- Taking a holistic approach to offender reentry, where all of the services responding to their needs for housing, treatment, transportation, and community-based treatments or correctional interventions are provided.
- Recruiting a greater number of Native American staff in parole and treatment positions (e.g. social services or mental health and addiction programs).
- Shortening community supervision terms.
- Requiring cultural competency training for corrections workers, allowing them to understand and respect the distinctive culture and traditions of Native peoples.
- Establishing better working relationships between tribal governments and state or federal correctional and parole authorities.
- Acknowledging the importance of traditional/cultural activities to some Native American parolees.
- Providing services to parolees that are developed by tribal authorities rather than government agencies to reduce distrust.

Given the diversity in Native American populations in terms of their political, linguistic, and cultural traditions, it is unlikely there will ever be a "one-size-fits-all" approach to improving their outcomes on parole. But, given their overrepresentation in the justice system, it is an issue worthy of our attention.

COMMUNITY REENTRY

Most prisoners have good intentions when they are released from custody. Their goals are the same as ours: a clean, safe, and affordable place to live, a job that pays well, and stable relationships with their friends and families. Their pathway to those goals, however, is often challenging given their histories of psychological problems and substance abuse, a lack of employment histories, and the stigma of being labeled an ex-prisoner. Finding a job is hard for anybody, but it is doubly intimidating when applicants have to tell their interviewer they were just released from prison. Moreover, many people are impoverished when released from custody. They have no money for rent or security deposits, funds to fill their prescriptions, or the means to buy a bus pass for public transportation. Many lack credentials such as photo identification or a driver's license that are required to do something as simple as opening a bank account or cashing a check.

Ex-prisoners also lack social resources, such as a network of positive relationships, which is called **social capital**, and is the trust, friendship, and goodwill we develop in our positive relationships with other people. We develop our social capital when we assist other individuals, keep our promises to others, and earn their trust. We use that social capital when we ask our family members, friends, mentors, or our bosses and teachers for advice or help finding a job, writing recommendation letters, or when we need their emotional support. Being incarcerated reduces one's social capital as most prisoners are cut off from the positive supports in the community. Bellair, Light, and Sutton (2019) say that increasing social capital in the months before their release from prison can increase inmates' success as they reenter society.

The long-term success of prisoners released into the community leaves a lot to be desired and we noted earlier that 83% of state prisoners released in 2005 were re-arrested within nine years (Alper, Durose, & Markman, 2018, p. 1). Some parolees find it hard to stay away from their old criminal associates or gang members—despite their best intentions. As a result, some fall back into the same behaviors they carried out before their imprisonment, and find themselves in the revolving door of corrections: entering, exiting, and reentering prison in a cycle that seems to continue until they "age out" of criminality or they are eventually sentenced to a very long prison sentence due to habitual offender laws such as three-strike laws.

Of the 1.5 million prisoners currently behind bars about 1.3 million of them will eventually return to society. The challenge of reentry has received more attention in the corrections community since the mid-1990s and a key question is how we can create a more successful inmate reentry system. The fact that discretionary parole was being replaced by release systems over which the prison and parole authorities had little control suggests to many correctional policymakers that the nation needed a new perspective on reentry. We turn our attention to the factors associated with a prisoner's successful return to the community.

Elements of Successful Community Reentry

What are the elements of a successful reentry system? Researchers have identified a number of factors, and they include:

- *Developing a correctional plan*: Establishing a long-term case plan with individuals soon after their prison admission provides a roadmap for their rehabilitation while incarcerated, and a series of assessments identify their strengths and weaknesses, and how to build on those strengths and overcome the weaknesses.
- *Address criminogenic thinking*: The risk-needs-responsivity (RNR), or similar prison-based approach, is used to confront criminogenic thinking prior to their release from

prison. This approach involves intensive interventions that are carried out over a long period of time and are delivered by skilled instructors who remain faithful to the program.

- *Substance abuse treatment*: Substance abuse is a key predictor of parole failure and prison programs should address this need and must be supported by community-based intervention programs after the prisoner's release. While programs such as Alcoholics and Narcotics Anonymous are available in prison, there is a shortage of intensive prison-based programs, and only about 11% of addicted inmates receive this treatment (National Center on Addiction and Substance Abuse, 2010).
- *Mental health treatment*: Should start soon after the individual is incarcerated and must be supported by community-based agencies once released from prison.
- *Employment*: The risks of recidivism increase when ex-prisoners are unemployed and, as a result, they should have access to prison-based programs that build their knowledge, skills, and abilities, although most lack the social capital to overcome the stigma of their imprisonment. As a result, many ex-prisoners have few options other than taking jobs that few others want to perform.
- *Education*: One-quarter of prisoners have not finished high school, while more than half hold a high school diploma or GED (Couloute, 2018a, para. 1). As having more years of formal education is associated with obtaining better jobs and lower recidivism rates, offering educational opportunities in prison is a minimum step that can increase their likelihood of post-release employment.
- *Housing*: Having a stable, safe, and affordable place to live is central to the ex-prisoner's successful reentry. Rates of homelessness for ex-prisoners are about ten times the average for the general population, and homelessness or unstable housing, such as couch surfing, increases their likelihood of recidivism (Couloute, 2018b).
- *Surveillance plans*: After release the parole officer must attempt to balance surveillance and treatment, and while most officers prioritize surveillance immediately after the offender's reentry, there should also be a focus on treatment and a gradual reduction in surveillance.
- *Graduated problem-solving responses to violations*: Responses to technical violations should be based on graduated sanctions, where minor infractions are dealt with informally using warnings and cautions, while serious acts are addressed more formally—including requiring the parolee to participate in additional community-based interventions (e.g. additional addictions education and drug testing for a parolee who failed a drug test)—and may involve referrals to prosecutors.

Different jurisdictions prioritize some of these interventions over the others. Although we generally focused on the RNR approach, there are similar correctional interventions that have different priorities. The Fresh Start Prisoner Reentry Program, for example, prioritizes linking their clients with the resources they need (Hunter, Lanza, Lawlor, Dyson, & Gordon, 2016). The Good Lives Model is another strength-based approach that proposes that criminogenic thinking inhibits parolees' ability to achieve their goals in a prosocial manner. These approaches generally have more similarities than differences. James (2015, p. 48) identified at least four common themes with reentry programs that research has proven to be effective, which are mentioned as follows:

1. They start during institutional placements, but take place mostly in the community.
2. They are intensive in nature, lasting typically at least six months.
3. They focus services on individuals determined to be at high risk of recidivating through the use of risk-assessment classifications.
4. If they are treatment programs, they use cognitive-behavioral treatment techniques, matching particular therapists and programs to the specific learning characteristics of the offenders.

Unfortunately, almost all correctional interventions have been based on the needs of male prisoners, and there is a growing awareness that women have different pathways to imprisonment, as well as a different set of risks and needs than male prisoners. As a result, there is increasing interest in **gender responsive** interventions, which are correctional programs that are intended to respond to the distinctive needs of women offenders.

There is considerable evidence that women prisoners have different pathways to crime than their male counterparts and most have histories of emotional, physical, and sexual abuse. Coping with the trauma from this abuse can place these women at higher risk of social withdrawal, substance abuse, and involvement in crime (see Brennan, Breitenach, Deiterich, Salisbury, & Van Voorhis, 2012; Joosen et al., 2016). Moreover, many of these prisoners are parents with limited work histories and few financial resources. As

PHOTO 10.4
Women come to prisons with a different set of unmet needs, including their role as parents, compared with their male counterparts. As a result, they require a different set of prison-based interventions prior to their return to the community. Research shows that participating in gender-informed correctional programming reduces recidivism once they are released to the community. The individual in this picture is talking with a psychologist, and receiving counseling can be an important step in their community reentry. Credit: Mikael Karlsson/Alamy Stock Photo.

a result, these women's greatest immediate needs upon release from prison are public health insurance, financial assistance, mentorship, and help obtaining credentials such as a driver's license, in addition to receiving support for their education, employment, and job training (Garcia & Ritter, 2012). Researchers find that women participating in gender-informed interventions had lower recidivism rates than women participating in traditional gender-neutral correctional programs (Gobeil, Blanchette, & Stewart, 2016, p. 316).

While correctional officials working with academics and researchers have developed a series of rehabilitative programs, members of the legislative branch of government have developed a series of civil consequences that are intended to deter people from committing crimes. These consequences, however, create additional barriers for ex-prisoners by placing restrictions on their employment, residency, and ability to access health, education, and social service benefits. The following section describes how these collateral consequences affect everyone who has been convicted of a crime, and their toll on ex-prisoners.

A CLOSER LOOK

Civil Commitment of Sexual Offenders

Fears over the reentry of sex offenders to the community have resulted in a number of different strategies to reduce the risks they pose. One approach is to prevent prisoners assessed as being at high risk to reoffend from returning to the community altogether. Twenty states and the federal government have enacted sexually violent predator (SVP) laws enabling them to indefinitely confine some of these ex-prisoners in mental health facilities after their sentences expire in a process known as **civil commitment**. Washington was the first state to introduce a SVP law in 1990 and Koeppel (2018, para. 5) observes that:

> The new laws sparked legal battles, and in 1997 the U.S. Supreme Court (in *Kansas v. Hendricks*) ruled that sex offenders who complete their prison terms can be locked away again. No new crime. No trial. No set time limits. Double jeopardy? The Court said no.

The process of civilly committing an individual varies somewhat across the country. Koeppel (2019) explains that typically two or more psychologists are required to assess whether the ex-prisoner might commit a new crime, and a judge must review these assessments in a hearing prior to committing them to stay in a mental health facility. Yung (2019, p. 26) says that because the process is a civil rather than a criminal matter, the government is required to demonstrate that the person is sexually dangerous using a lower standard of proof (a preponderance of the evidence rather than proof beyond a reasonable doubt).

Our review of the literature found that somewhere between 5,000 and 6,500 ex-prisoners are civilly committed in the entire country. While more of them are admitted into mental health facilities each year few are released. Koeppel (2018, para. 9) observes that:

- Minnesota committed 720 men in 24 years, and only one was fully released (62 died in custody).
- In Kansas, of 263 civilly committed ex-prisoners, 36 died and three were released.
- New Jersey committed 755 people and 235 were released and 58 died in custody.

Koeppel (2019) says that there is little incentive to release these civilly committed men as the mental health facilities holding them invoice the state for each person they hold. Because they are in mental health facilities, the average cost for their care is three or four times as costly as regular imprisonment, and this has turned into a money making opportunity for some of these facilities. Because so few of these civilly committed sex offenders are ever released they get discouraged and many stop taking any form of treatment (which, in turn, reduces the likelihood they will ever be released).

Collateral Consequences

There are numerous barriers to the community reentry of ex-prisoners, and some sanctions are known as **collateral consequences**. Collateral consequences are restrictions placed on individuals because of their criminal convictions. The American Bar Association (2018, p. 8) observes that many defendants are not aware of these sanctions when pleading guilty and "Defendants often are never notified that their guilty plea can affect social services, employment, professional licensure, immigration status, volunteer opportunities, and more." While the individuals who pled guilty may have paid their debt to society, some criminal convictions have long-term and even lifelong consequences.

In their book entitled *Invisible Punishment: The Collateral Consequences of Mass Imprisonment*, Mauer and Chesney-Lind (2003) called collateral consequences **invisible consequences**, and they explain how these sanctions affect ex-prisoners and their families. Silva (2015, p. 800), for example, describes how a San Francisco family was evicted from their public housing because their son was convicted of possessing drugs in their home.

Millions of Americans are affected by these policies and the following categories are identified by the Collateral Consequences Resource Center (2019):

- *Education*: Many post-secondary institutions require potential students to report their convictions on their applications, and government sponsored student aid for some types of offenders is restricted.
- *Employment*: Individuals with criminal convictions can be restricted from working in professions requiring licenses such as barbering, hairdressing, dog handling, and driving taxis. Criminal convictions can also make individuals ineligible for government jobs. There are over 27,000 state laws restricting the ability of ex-prisoners to access occupational licenses (Love, Roberts, & Logan, 2018). In Texas, for example, there are over 100 occupations where anybody with a felony conviction is automatically banned from those jobs, and misdemeanor offenses committed decades ago can still exclude an individual from working in some professions (French-Marcelin, 2019).
- *Firearms*: Federal laws restrict persons convicted of misdemeanor domestic violence offenses from possessing firearms, and some states have enacted laws restricting individuals convicted of non-violent offenses from legally owning or using firearms.
- *Government Benefits*: Some states impose lengthy and even lifelong bans on people who have committed some types of crime from receiving food stamps (supplemental nutrition assistance program or SNAP) or Temporary Assistance for Needy Families (TANF). Many of these sanctions are imposed for convictions of non-violent offenses such as drug crimes.
- *Housing*: Federal laws ban access to public housing for individuals convicted of certain crimes, and an entire family can be evicted when one member of the household is arrested or convicted. Landlords can also screen out individuals with criminal records from living in their housing.
- *Immigration*: Lawful permanent residents can be deported after their convictions, even though they have legally lived in the United States for decades. In addition, thousands of military veterans have been deported (U.S. Department of Veterans Affairs, 2018; for an example see Associated Press, 2020).
- *Sex Offender Registration*: Individuals convicted of some sexual offenses can be required to register with the police and their information is accessible on state databases. Registration can result in losing of friends (and subsequent social isolation), being fired, being physically assaulted, and having their property damaged (Craun & Bierie, 2014).
- *Voting*: Over six million persons convicted of felonies are prohibited from voting due to felon disenfranchisement laws.

This list does not include all possible examples. The National Inventory of the Collateral Consequences of Conviction (2019) identified nearly 45,000 such consequences—but they tend to fall within these same general classifications. Individuals violating these restrictions can be punished harshly. A Texas woman who had served a five-year prison sentence for tax fraud was banned from voting due to the state's disenfranchisement laws. She was subsequently convicted of violating the law by voting in the 2016 presidential election. Despite claiming she was unaware of her ineligibility to vote, she was sentenced to another five years in prison (Garcia, 2018).

PHOTO 10.5
There is a growing movement to reduce the number of restrictions placed on ex-prisoners called collateral consequences. Members of the Drug Policy Alliance in New York City were calling attention to the issue of reducing the collateral consequences of being convicted for marijuana possession. Credit: Pacific Press Agnecy/ Alamy Stock Photo.

Some collateral consequences make sense. Few of us would agree that a person who has been convicted of committing crimes against children should work in a day care or drive a school bus. But it doesn't make much sense to restrict all felons, including people convicted of non-violent offenses from working as dog handlers or barbers. Moreover, restricting an individual's access to certain licenses might make sense while the individual is on probation or parole, but many critics question why that sanction should remain after they served all their formal punishments. This raises the question of whether an individual be banned from voting for their entire lifetime for a non-violent crime they committed as a young adult.

A growing number of states are easing the collateral consequences of criminal convictions. McLeod (2018) observes that between 1997 and 2018 almost one-half of the states reduced the restrictions on disenfranchised offenders. Nerbovig (2018) says that between 2016 and 2018, 14 states eased the licensing restrictions on employing ex-prisoners. Policymakers in these states may have realized that some of these consequences may *reduce* rather than *enhance* public safety.

SUMMARY

Parole fulfills two main objectives for corrections. First, parole is a form of supervised release intended to promote the safe transition of the ex-prisoner back to the community. The second objective is to act as a type of safety valve that reduces correctional overcrowding for the 34 states still using discretionary parole. Some activists question whether parolees are set up to fail. The expectations on some of them are so high—such as multiple conditions of supervision over a long period of time—that their possibility of success is reduced. Jones (2018) says that parole can hurt the people it is intended to help and about one-half of parolees are returned to prison in what she calls a revolving door between community supervision and incarceration. From this chapter, you should especially note the following:

- Parole allows the executive branch to exercise a measure of control over correctional populations considered more dangerous than probationers.
- Parole or supervised release gives the individual an opportunity to show that he or she can live lawfully and productively in the free community.
- Parole allows prison systems to relieve the pressure of crowding.
- The War on Drugs and other legislative initiatives, along with state and federal movements to restrict or eliminate parole (through determinate sentencing), have swelled the number of prison inmates, resulting in an increased use of parole and supervised release.
- The number of people entering the criminal justice funnel is unlikely to decrease in the near future. This means that parole and other means of prisoner reentry are likely to remain important alternatives to incarceration.
- Contrary to the position widely endorsed prior to 2000, parole is not dead. States have abandoned it, only to reconstitute it, often in response to pressures created by the iron law of prison populations.
- Research is showing that success on parole is linked to the use of evidence-based correctional practices and acknowledging how collateral consequences can create barriers to an ex-prisoner's safe transition to the community.

KEY TERMS

- citation
- collateral consequences
- commutation of sentence
- discretionary parole
- discretionary release
- expiration release
- gender responsive
- hearing officer
- invisible consequences (collateral consequences)
- iron law of imprisonment
- iron law of prison populations
- Irish ticket of leave system
- mandatory release
- mandatory release states
- marks of commendation
- maxed out (maxing out)
- pardon
- parole officers (parole agents)
- Penal Servitude Act of 1853
- preliminary parole revocation hearing
- probation tail
- revocation hearing
- social capital
- ticket of leave

THINKING ABOUT CORRECTIONAL POLICIES AND PRACTICES: WRITING ASSIGNMENTS

1. Criminal justice has very few "laws" that give us greater insights into the system's component parts. This chapter references two in the Introduction. What are they? How can knowledge of these laws help us deal with the challenges of prisoner reentry?

2. The use of parole varies widely from state to state and from region to region. Speculate as to the reasons why these differences exist. Do the states with the highest use of parole also have the highest use of probation, jail, and prison?

3. In an era where the numbers of ex-prisoners on a mandatory release have been growing, and the decline of discretionary release, provide at least two reasons why the states and the federal government may want to return to the use of parole boards and discretionary prisoner release. Is this likely to happen? Why or why not?

4. Prepare a brief essay on the total exclusion of technical violations in the consideration of parole revocation so that former prisoners could only be returned to custody for a new offense. Is this a good or bad idea?

5. Discuss why collateral consequences, which are introduced to increase our safety, may push some ex-prisoners into committing new offenses.

CRITICAL REVIEW QUESTIONS

1. What does the history of parole suggest about the practice? Explain that history and its linkages to current methods of prisoner reentry.

2. Which type of parole board or other releasing authority seems better equipped to render the most equitable decisions about releasing prisoners? Explain your answer.

3. The demise of discretionary release from prison was predicted in the 1980s and 1990s. What is the basis of this prediction? What is its current status? Include in your answer an appreciation for the professional parole commission as an alternative to the parole board.

4. The federal government has created one of the nation's largest prison systems since the war on drugs and sentencing reforms in the 1980s. Describe how the *First Step Act,* which came into effect in 2018, might reduce federal imprisonment.

5. Would you rather be a probation officer or a parole officer? Why? Explain your answer.

6. Summarize the trends in parole from 1990 to 2017. Which single fact do you find most interesting and why?

7. Provide a summary of what you see as the main argument against early release.

8. What legal changes to the criminal justice system would you support to reduce the number of individuals entering the parole system? How would these changes affect other elements of the justice system, or even community services such as health care and social services?

9. Discuss how the adoption of evidence-based practices can change the practice of corrections.

10. What collateral consequence do you see as creating the biggest barrier to community reentry?

CASES

Gasca v. Precythe, No. 17-CV-04149-SRB

Murphy v. Raoul, No. 16-C-11471 (N.D. Ill 2019)

REFERENCES

Alper, M. (2016). *By the numbers: Parole release and revocation across 50 states.* Minneapolis, MN: Robina Institute of Criminal Law and Criminal Justice.

Alper, M., Durose, M. R., & Markman, J. (2018). *2018 update on prisoner recidivism: A 9-year follow-up period (2005–2014).* Washington, DC: Bureau of Justice Statistics.

American Bar Association. (2018). *Collateral consequences of criminal convictions: Judicial bench book.* Washington, DC: Author.

Arizona Department of Public Safety. (2019). *Sex offender compliance.* Retrieved from https://www. azdps.gov/services/public/offender

Associated Press. (2020, March 5). Wrongly deported veteran returns to Arizona 20 years later. *KGUN.* Retrieved from https://www.kgun9.com/news/local-news/wrongly-deported-veteran-returns-to-arizona-20-years-later

Azoulay, N., Winder, B., Murphy, L., & Fedoroff, J. P. (2019). Circles of support and accountability (CoSA): a review of the development of CoSA and its international implementation. *International Review of Psychiatry, 31*(2), 195–205.

Bellair, P. E., Light, R., & Sutton, J. (2019). Prisoners' personal networks in the months preceding prison: A descriptive portrayal. *International Journal of Offender Therapy and Comparative Criminology, 63*(3), 383–405.

Berk, R. (2017). An impact assessment of machine learning risk forecasts on parole decisions and recidivism. *Journal of Experimental Criminology, 13*(2), 193–216.

Black, V. (2016, Jul. 31). Life parole lacks active monitoring. *South Bend Tribune.* Retrieved from https://www.southbendtribune.com/news/local/life-parole-lacks- active-monitoring/article_8c0216b5-0494-5f1e-b43d-183c8a6f6233.html

Boden, S. (2017, May 25). State's high court says lifetime parole for juvenile offender is not cruel and unusual. *Iowa Public Radio.* Retrieved from https://www.iowapublicradio.org/post/states-high-court-says-lifetime-parole- juvenile-offender-not-cruel-and-unusual#stream/0

Brennan, P., Breitenach, M., Deiterich, W., Salisbury, E. J., & Van Voorhis, P. (2012). Women's pathways to serious and habitual crime: A person centered analysis incorporating gender responsive factors. *Criminal Justice and Behavior, 39*(11), 1481–1508.

Bronson, J., & Carson, A. E. (2019). *Prisoners in 2017.* Washington, DC: Bureau of Justice Statistics.

Bureau of Prisons. (2020). *Inmate race (March 7, 2020).* Retrieved from https://www.bop.gov/about/statistics/statistics_inmate_race.jsp

Campbell, K. (2017). Probation practice swamps justice system, leads to higher risk offenders. *Detroit Legal News.* Retrieved from http://legalnews.com/detroit/1441781

Carson, E. A., & Cowhig, M. P. (2012). *Mortality in state prisons, 2001–2016 – Statistical tables.* Washington, DC: Bureau of Justice Statistics.

Chouinard, J. A., & Riddick, C. (2014). *An evaluation of the circles of support and accountability demonstration project: Final report.* Regina, SK: Collaborative Centre for Justice and Safety.

Clear, T. R., & Austin, J. (2009). Reducing mass incarceration: Implications of the iron law of prison populations. *Harvard Law Policy Review, 3*(2), 307–324.

Collateral Consequences Resource Center. (2019). *Types of consequences.* Retrieved from http://ccresourcecenter.org/topics/topics/cctypes/

Couloute, L. (2018a). Educational exclusion and attainment among formerly incarcerated people. *Prison Policy Initiative.* Retrieved from https://www. prisonpolicy.org/reports/education.html

Couloute, L. (2018b). Nowhere to go: Homelessness among formerly incarcerated people. *Prison Policy Initiative.* Retrieved from https://www.prisonpolicy.org/reports/housing.html

Craun, S. W., & Bierie, D. M. (2014). Are the collateral consequences of being a registered sex offender as bad as we think? A methodological research note. *Federal Probation, 78*(1), 28–31.

DeMichele, M., & Payne, B. K. (2007). Probation and parole officers speak out—Caseload and workload allocation. *Federal Probation, 71*(3), 30–35.

Desmarais, S. L., Johnson, K. L., & Singh, J. P. (2016). Performance of recidivism risk assessment instruments in U.S. correctional settings. *Psychological Services, 13*(3), 206–222.

Diatchenko, G. (2015). Why it's hard to be a lifer who's getting out of prison. *The Marshall Project.* Retrieved from https://www.themarshallproject.org/2015/12/04/why-it-s-hard-to-be-a-lifer-who-s-getting-out-of-prison com/politics/article/Gov-Jerry-Brown-sets-record-for-pardons-13487741.php

Franklin, T. W., & Henry, T. S. (2018). One day makes all the difference: Denying federal offenders access to "good time" through sentencing. *Crime & Delinquency, 64*(1), 115–140.

French-Marcelin, M. (2019). *Need not apply: How occupational licensing authorities automatically lock out people with criminal histories from growing professions.* Austin, TX: Texas Criminal Justice Coalition.

Garcia, S. E. (2018, June 13). Texas woman sentenced to 5 years in prison for voter fraud loses bid for new trail. *The New York Times.* Retrieved from https://www.nytimes.com/2018/06/13/us/texas-woman-voter-fraud.html

Garcia, M., & Ritter, N. (2012). Improving access to services for female offenders returning to the community. *National Institute of Justice Journal, 269,* 18–23.

Glaze, L. E., & Bonczar, T. P. (2011). *Probation and parole in the United States, 2010.* Washington, DC: Bureau of Justice Statistics.

Gobeil, R., Blanchette, K., & Stewart, L. (2016). A meta-analytic review of correctional interventions for women offenders. *Criminal Justice and Behavior, 43*(3), 301–322.

Green, M. (2019, April 1). Federal judge finds Illinois rules on sex offenders unconstitutional. *WBEZ.* Retrieved from https://www.wbez.org/shows/wbez-news/ federal-judge-finds-illinois-rules-on-sex-offenders-unconstitutional/fdea1372-1b00-44b1-b0e6-2501bc082378

Hager, E. (2017). At least 61,000 nationwide are in prison for minor parole violations. *The Marshall Project.* Retrieved from https://www.themarshallproject.org/2017/04/23/at-least-61-000-nationwide-are-in-prison-for-minor-parole-violations

Harper, C. A. (2018). The role of the media in shaping responses to sexual offending. In H. Elliott, K. Hocken, R. Lievesley, N. Blagden, B. Winder, & P. Banyard (Eds.), *Sexual crime and circles of support and accountability* (pp. 127–150). New York: Palgrave Macmillan.

Holland, M. M., Grace Prost, S., Hoffmann, H. C., & Dickinson, G. E. (2018). U.S. departments of corrections compassionate release policies: A content analysis and call to action. *OMEGA-Journal of Death and Dying.* Published online ahead of print at: doi:10.1177/0030222818791708

Hunter, B. A., Lanza, A. S., Lawlor, M., Dyson, W., & Gordon, D. M. (2016). A strength-based approach to prisoner reentry: The fresh start prisoner reentry program. *International Journal of Comparative Criminology, 60*(11), 1298–1314.

James, N. (2015). *Offender reentry: Correctional statistics, reintegration into the community, package and recidivism.* Washington, DC: Congressional Research Service.

Johnson, C. (2019, Mar. 15). Seriously ill federal prisoners freed as compassionate release law takes effect. *National Public Radio.* Retrieved from https://www.npr.org/2019/03/15/703784886/seriously-ill-federal-prisoners-freed- as-compassionate-release-law-takes-effect

Jones, A. (2018). Correctional control 2018: Incarceration and supervision by state. *Prison Policy Initiative.* Retrieved from https://www.prisonpolicy.org/ reports/correctionalcontrol2018.html

Joosen, K. J., Palmen, H., Kruttschnitt, C., Bijleveld, C., Dirkzwager, A., & Nieuwbeerta, P. (2016). How "gendered" are gendered pathways to prison? A latent class analysis of the life experiences of male and female prisoners in the Netherlands. *Journal of Developmental and Life-Course Criminology, 2*(3), 321–340.

Kaeble, D. (2018). *Probation and parole in the United States, 2016.* Washington, DC: Bureau of Justice Statistics.

King, L. L., & Roberts, J. J. (2017). The complexity of public attitudes toward sex crimes. *Victims & Offenders, 12*(1), 71–89.

Klingele, C. (2013). Rethinking the use of community supervision. *Journal of Criminal Law & Criminology, 103*(4), 1015–1069.

Koeppel, B. (2018, May 4). Sex crimes and criminal justice. *The Washington Spectator.* Retrieved from https://washingtonspectator.org/koeppel-sex-crimes-and-criminal-justice/

Koeppel, B. (2019, June 4). Modern-day gulag in the golden state. *The Washington Spectator.* Retrieved from https://washingtonspectator.org/koeppel-gulags/

Kolker, R. (2015). Unfreed: The man who was accidently released from prison 88 years early. *The Marshall Project.* Retrieved from https://www.themarshallproject.org/2015/04/07/unfreed?utm_medium=email&utm_campaign=newsletter&utm_source=opening-statement&utm_term=newsletter-20180529-1061

Law, V. (2017, June 5). New York's parole system is 'broken,' but Cuomo can help fix it. *The Village Voice*. Retrieved from https://www.villagevoice.com/2017/06/05/new-yorks-parole-system-is-broken-but-cuomo-can-help-fix-it/

Love, M. C., Roberts, J., & Logan, W. A. (2018). *Collateral consequences of criminal conviction: Law, policy and practice, 2018–2019*. Eagan, MN: Thomson Reuters.

Matz, A. K., Conley, T. B., & Johanneson, N. (2018). What do supervision officers do? Adult probation/parole officer workloads in a rural Western state. *Journal of Crime and Justice, 41*(3), 294–309.

Mauer, M., & Chesney-Lind, M. (2003). *Invisible punishment: The collateral consequences of mass imprisonment*. New York: The New Press.

McLeod, M. (2018). *Expanding the vote: Two decades of felony disenfranchisement reforms*. New York: Sentencing Project.

McVey, C., Rhine, E. E., & Reynolds, C. V. (2018). *Modernizing parole statutes: Guidance from evidence-based practice*. Minneapolis: University of Minnesota Robina Institute of Criminal Law & Criminal Justice.

Mehta, S., & Gomila, R. (2018). *Set up to fail: Montana's probation and parole system*. Helena, MT: ACLU of Montana.

Meredith, T., Rene Hawk, S., Johnson, S., Prevost, J. P., & Braucht, G. (2020). What happens in home visits? *Criminal Justice and Behavior*. Published online ahead of print at: doi:10.1177/0093854820910173

National Center on Addiction and Substance Abuse. (2010). *Behind bars II: Substance abuse and America's prison population*. New York: Columbia University.

National Inventory of the Collateral Consequences of Conviction. (2019). *Collateral consequences inventory*. Retrieved from https://niccc.csgjusticecenter.org/

Nerbovig, A. (2018, July 10). License to clip. *The Marshall Project*. Retrieved from https://www.themarshallproject.org/2018/07/10/license-to-clip

NYU Law. (2019). *The demise of clemency for lifers in Pennsylvania*. New York: NYU Center on the Administration of Criminal Law.

O'Sullivan, J., & Brunner, J. (2019, Feb. 25). Washington corrections officials scrambling after new sentencing errors uncovered. *The Seattle Times*. Retrieved from https://www.seattletimes.com/seattle-news/times-watchdog/washington-corrections-officials-scrambling-after-new-sentencing-errors-uncovered/

Pew Charitable Trusts. (2014). *Max out: The rise in prison inmates released without supervision*. Retrieved from https://www.pewtrusts.org/~/media/assets/2014/ 06/04/maxout_report.pdf

Pew Charitable Trusts. (2018). *Community supervision a leading driver of incarceration*. Retrieved from https://www.pewtrusts.org/en/research-and-analysis/ articles/2018/12/19/community-supervision-a-leading-driver-of-incarceration

Reentry Council. (2014). *Reservation communities*. Washington, DC: Author.

Reitz, K. R. (2018). *American exceptionalism in crime and punishment*. New York: Oxford University Press.

Renaud, J. (2018). Eight keys to mercy: How to shorten excessive prison sentences. *Prison Policy Initiative*. Retrieved from https://www.prisonpolicy.org/reports/longsentences.html#parolesystems

Rhine, E. E., Mitchell, K. L., & Reitz, K. R. (2019). *Levers of change in parole release and revocation*. Minneapolis, MN: Robina Institute of Criminal Law and Criminal Justice.

Rhine, E. E., Petersilia, J., & Reitz, K. R. (2015). Improving parole release in America. *Federal Sentencing Reporter, 28*(2), 96–103.

Rhine, E. E., Petersilia, J., & Reitz, K. R. (2017). The future of parole release. *Crime and Justice, 46*(1), 279–338.

Robina Institute. (2018). *Parole boards with indeterminate and determinate sentencing structures.* Retrieved from https://robinainstitute.umn.edu/news-views/parole-boards-within-indeterminate-and-determinate-sentencing-structures

Ruhland, E. L., Rhine, E. E., Robey, J. P., & Mitchell, K. L. (2017). *The continuing leverage of releasing authorities.* Minneapolis, MN: Robina Institute of Criminal Law and Criminal Justice.

Sallinger, R. (2018, Oct. 26). Gunman and victim square off with unexpected ending. *CBS4.* Retrieved from https://denver.cbslocal.com/2018/10/26/rene-lima- marin-crime-victim-restorative-justice/

Schiraldi, V. (2019, Jan. 24). Do we really need probation and parole? *The Crime Report.* Retrieved from https://thecrimereport.org/2019/01/24/do-we-really-need-probation-and-parole/

Schwartzapfel, B. (2015, July 11). How parole boards keep prisoners in the dark and behind bars. *The Washington Post.* Retrieved from https://www.washingtonpost.com/national/the-power-and-politics-of-parole-boards/2015/07/10/49c1844e-1f71-11e5-84d5-eb37ee8eaa61_story.html?noredirect=on&utm_term=.e102c0c53864

Schwartzapfel, B. (2019). Parole process puts too many people back behind bars, Missouri lawsuit says. *ABA Journal.* Retrieved from http://www.abajournal.com/news/article/want-to-shrink-the-prison-population-look-at-parole

Schwartzapfel, B., & Kassie, E. (2018). Banished. *The Marshall Project.* Retrieved from https://www.themarshallproject.org/records/184-sex-offender

Self, J. (2018, Oct. 21). How to win, or lose, a pardon for your crimes in SC. *The State.* Retrieved from https://www.thestate.com/news/local/crime/ article219716780.html

Shames, A., & Subramanian, R. (2016). *Bridging the divide: Improving parole outcomes for Native Americans in South Dakota.* New York: Vera Institute of Justice.

Silva, L. R. (2015). Collateral damage: A public housing consequences of the "war on drugs." *UC Irvine Law Review, 5,* 783–811.

Simpson, K. (2016, December 22). How an inmate's second chance was yanked away after officials discovered 88-year sentencing mistake. *The Denver Post.* Retrieved from https://www.denverpost.com/2016/06/12/how-an-inmates-second-chance-was-yanked-away-after-officials-discovered-88-year- sentencing-mistake/

Simpson, K. (2018, March 26). Rene Lima-Marin walks free after immigration ruling caps twisting legal saga. *The Denver Post.* Retrieved from https://www. denverpost.com/2018/03/26/rene-lima-marin-immigration-appeal-ruling/

Tabachnik, S. (2020, February 23). He was once sentenced to 98 years behind bars. Now Rene Lima-Marin is forging a new path. *Denver Post.* Retrieved from https://www.denverpost.com/2020/02/23/rene-lima-marin-life-after-prison/

Tashea, J. (2017, March 1). Risk-assessment algorithms challenged in bail, sentencing and parole decisions. *ABA Journal.* Retrieved from http://www.abajournal.com/magazine/article/algorithm_bail_sentencing_parole/?

Travis, J. (2005). *But they all come back: Facing the challenges of prisoner reentry*. Washington, DC: Urban Institute.

Travis, L. F., & Stacey, J. (2010). A half century of parole rules: Conditions of parole in the United States, 2008. *Journal of Criminal Justice, 38*(4), 604–608.

U.S. Census Bureau. (2019). *American fact finder. Selected population profile in the United States, 2017*. Retrieved from https://factfinder.census.gov/faces/nav/jsf/pages/index.xhtml

U.S. Department of Justice. (2020). *Clemency statistics (March 6, 2020)*. Retrieved from https://www.justice.gov/pardon/clemency-statistics

U.S. Department of Veterans Affairs. (2018). *Report of the advisory committee on minority veterans*. Washington, DC: Author.

U.S. Sentencing Commission. (2018). *Quick facts: Native Americans and the federal offender population*. Washington, DC: Author.

West Virginia Division of Corrections and Rehabilitation. (2019). *Conditions of parole*. Retrieved from https://dcr.wv.gov/aboutus/parole-services/Pages/ conditions-of-parole.aspx

Williams, T. (2013, April 13). Quietly, Indians reshape cities and reservations. *The New York Times*. Retrieved from https://www.nytimes.com/2013/04/14/us/ as-american-indians-move-to-cities-old-and-new-challenges-follow.html

Wilson, C. A. (2018). A history of the development of circles of support and accountability. In H. Elliott, K. Hocken, R. Lievesley, N. Blagden, B. Winder, & P. Banyard (Eds.), *Sexual crime and circles of support and accountability* (pp. 1–24). New York: Palgrave Macmillan.

Wilson, R. J., & McWhinnie, A. J. (2013). Putting the "community" back in community risk management of persons who have sexually abused. *International Journal of Behavioral Consultation and Therapy, 8*(3), 72–79.

Wodahl, E. J., & Freng, A. (2017). The challenges of prisoner reentry faced by Native American returning prisoners. *Journal of Ethnicity in Criminal Justice, 15*(2), 160–184.

Yung, C. R. (2019). Civil commitment of sex offenders. In W. T. O'Donohue & D. S. Bromberg (Eds.), *Sexually violent predators: A clinical science handbook* (pp. 21–34). New York: Springer.

Chapter 11
Gender Issues in Corrections

OUTLINE

OBJECTIVES

After reading this chapter you will be able to:

- Explain how gender shapes the corrections environment

- Describe the range of correctional experiences that are affected by gender

- Explain the pathways to women's involvement in the justice system

- Describe the special needs of women offenders

- Describe the special issues confronting corrections in accommodating a growing number of women offenders

CASE STUDY

Giving Birth in Jail: "She Was Forced to Crouch Down and Just Catch the Baby"

Tammy Jackson, a Broward County Florida jail inmate, gave birth by herself in an isolation cell on 10 April 2019. At about 3:00 am she told the staff that she was in labor, and they called a doctor several times but he did not arrive until seven hours later. Before his arrival, Ms. Jackson gave birth. As her lawyer described it: "She was forced to crouch down and just catch the baby" (Garcia, 2019, para. 3). Others noticed her ordeal and according to Barszewski (2019, para. 4):

> [t]wo other pregnant women being held in the same facility later reported they were able to hear Ms. Jackson screaming and watch through the Plexiglas as she bled and suffered for hours, giving birth by herself while jail staff ignored her pleas for help.

Despite her screaming and cries for help, the jail officers were not aware Ms. Jackson had delivered the baby until 10:00 am—over seven hours after notifying them she was in labor. Once the baby was delivered, the doctor and two nurses attended to her needs, and both Jackson and her baby were transported to a hospital by ambulance. The jail staff had the option of calling 911 prior to the doctor's arrival; however, they did not make that call.

Jackson, a 34-year-old African American, had been arrested in January 2019 for cocaine possession and was subsequently released. She did not report to pretrial services. Later, Jackson was charged with failing to report, as well as trespassing, sleeping on a public street, and possession of drug paraphernalia (Rabin & Smiley, 2019). Jackson previously had been placed in a psychiatric facility. Given her problems with mental illness and apparent homelessness, the authorities felt that jail was the only option for Ms. Jackson.

Like other jails and some state prison systems, Broward County contracts with for-profit-healthcare providers to care for their inmates; in Broward County's case it was Wellpath, a large national corporation. Balaban and Kuhik (2019, para. 7) observe that: "Wellpath has a long and sordid history of being sued for endangering and neglecting pregnant prisoners in their care," and they maintained that the "dehumanizing treatment that pervades correctional facilities render them incapable of ever providing the full spectrum of minimal treatment that people with mental illnesses need" (para. 12). Balaban and Kuhik question why Jackson was even in the jail: Are there better places to house pregnant women with serious mental health problems?

What were the outcomes in this case? In the months after the birth, jail administrators carried out an investigation and Wellpath fired two of their staff and implemented plans to curb similar incidents (Barszewski, 2019). Public outrage about this case also led to Florida legislators to pass legislation restricting the placement of pregnant women in solitary confinement, as well as restricting staff from conducting cavity searches or handcuffing or shackling them. The legislation, which is called the *Tammy Jackson Healthy Pregnancies for Incarcerated Women Act* became law on July 1, 2020 (Sun Sentinel Editorial Board, 2020). The long-term national impacts of this incident are more difficult to predict: Can one incident in Florida involving a uniquely "female issue" reduce the callous or uncaring attitudes of some correctional officers in similar situations in other states?

Critical Questions

1. Will the national publicity about the Tammy Jackson case lead to changes that prevent similar incidents? Why or why not?
2. Are there better places to house pregnant, crime-involved women with mental health problems, or are jails always going to be the places that handle these cases because there are no alternatives?
3. Why do you think that some jail or prison staff can become callous or uncaring? What would differentiate you from the Broward County officers who failed to act professionally?

INTRODUCTION

Despite changes in the gender makeup of the various correctional client populations, females seldom receive the same level of services, programs, and other resources routinely offered to males (Harris, 2018). This is a long-standing problem that was first acknowledged more than three decades ago by the U.S. General Accounting Office (1980). And despite efforts directed at developing correctional programs accounting for the special needs of women for almost four decades, a review of the Bureau of Prison's programs found that the agency "has not fully considered the needs of female inmates, which has made it difficult for inmates to access key programs and supplies" (U.S. Department of Justice, 2018, p. i).

The finding of shortcomings in the federal prison system is consistent with the observations of researchers examining women's programs in state prison systems. King and Foley (2014) found that most correctional policies are gender-neutral, although a growing number of states are developing some gender-specific programs for women. Granted, as correctional clients, women do have many of the same short- and long-term problems and daily concerns as men. However, they also have special psychological, medical, and physical needs that often go unrecognized or unmet in a gender-neutral correctional environment. For example, mothers may feel the loss of their children in ways that differ from those of incarcerated fathers. Moreover, those who are pregnant or have gynecological problems often cannot get needed medical services. In many cases, corrections administrators even fail to acknowledge those gender-specific needs.

The treatment of women inmates has been a form of benign neglect. There is no specific intent to create disparities in treatment, services, and programming; rather, they happen largely by default, as the incarcerated females compared to their male counterparts simply get far less attention—and resources—from local, state and federal legislators and policymakers. Why? Consider the number of female inmates, the lack of jails and prisons exclusively for women, and the relatively small number of bed spaces allocated to women in facilities. Moreover, criminal courts tend to convict women of less serious crimes than men, even if the initial charges are nearly identical. Then there is the entrenched sexist perspectives attributed to many policymakers within the criminal justice system: women who have committed crimes somehow deserve what they get because they have betrayed society and other women by their misdeeds. Other experts claim that women adjust to prison somewhat better than men, as they are seldom involved in riots and other inmate uprisings. In spite of these claims, Pupovac and Lydersen (2018) reported that women have higher rates of disciplinary offenses in prison than males. When these reporters looked at the data, they found that most of these offenses were for low-level acts such as being insolent, disobedient, making derogatory comments, or acting disrespectfully. These examples show that, indeed, women present distinct challenges to the nation's corrections systems, challenges that are often unmet.

PHOTO 11.1

Female inmate nurtures her infant child. A parenting program is available for inmates who meet a specific set of criteria at the Nebraska Correctional Center for Women. Very few correctional facilities for women have any programs for new mothers and their newborns are often placed with family members or in state care. Credit: Mikael Karlsson/Alamy Stock Photo.

Before addressing issues related to women in corrections, we look at the nature and extent of female criminality, which is universally regarded as less prevalent and less serious than that of males. Exactly how and to what extent remains important, since many of these people eventually become the female clients of the nation's correctional systems.

NATURE AND EXTENT OF FEMALE CRIMINALITY

Women are arrested less often than men and generally for less serious crimes, although the range of offenses is identical to that for men. For example, look at Table 11.1. Notice that in 2017 women made up 27.2% of the almost seven million adult arrestees. The message is clear: given that women make up roughly 50% of the nation's adult population, they are arrested at a significantly lower rate than the proportion of females in the general population. This table also illustrates an interesting gender difference in arrests

TABLE 11.1 Female and Male Arrests, 2008 and 2017

	male			Female			
	2008	2017	Percent Change	2008	2017	Percent Change	Percent Female
Total	6,684,673	5,006,416	−25.1	2,183,085	1,872,513	+14.4	
Murder and NN Man	6,727	6,407	−4.8	817	935	+14.4	12.73
Rape[a]	13,445	14,341	—	153	418	—	2.83
Robbery	68,320	48,568	−28.9	9,132	8,450	−7.5	14.82
Aggravated Assault	219,276	195,513	−10.8	59,873	58,972	−1.5	23.17
Burglary	172,133	105,800	−38.5	30,796	24,815	−19.4	19
Larceny-Theft	485,729	378,305	−22.1	350,042	265,548	−24.1	41.24
Motor Vehicle Theft	48,194	44,239	−8.2	10,162	12,964	+27.6	22.66
Arson	7,987	4,908	−38.6	1,460	1,194	−18.2	19.57
Violent Crime	307,768	264,829	−14.0	69,975	68,775	−1.7	20.62
Property Crime	714,043	533,252	−25.3	392,460	304,521	−22.4	36.35
Other Assaults	612,453	491,125	−19.8	213,142	199,319	−6.5	28.87
Forgery/Counterfeit	36,845	24,342	−33.9	22,947	12,888	−43.8	34.62
Fraud	86,861	52,167	−39.9	68,796	31,487	−54.2	37.64
Embezzlement	6,948	5,201	−25.1	7,529	5,300	−29.6	50.47
Stolen Property	59,620	51,469	−13.7	15,782	14,567	−7.7	22.06
Vandalism	154,800	98,927	−36.1	31,493	28,204	−10.4	22.18
Weapons	101,938	92,702	−9.1	8,195	9,869	+20.4	9.62
Prostitution	11,333	7,705	−32.0	23,154	10,427	−55.0	57.51

TABLE 11.1 (Continued)

	male			Female			
	2008	2017	Percent Change	2008	2017	Percent Change	Percent Female
Drug Abuse Violation	843,915	813,824	–3.6	200,143	263,816	+31.8	24.48
Gambling	2,035	1,083	–46.8	396	357	–9.8	24.79
Offense against Family	55,945	39,753	–28.9	18,376	17,024	–7.4	29.98
Driving under the Influence	763,493	488,769	–36.0	211,475	166,006	–21.5	25.35
Liquor Laws	293,557	94,685	–67.7	117,198	43,144	–63.2	31.3
Drunkenness	342,258	182,844	–46.6	67,886	47,517	–30.0	20.63
Disorderly Conduct	322,117	163,874	–49.1	117,293	69,062	–41.1	29.65
Vagrancy	12,512	10,594	–15.3	3,527	3,359	–4.8	24.07
All others (Excluding Traffic)	1,869,437	1,549,710	–17.1	569,560	569,306	[b]	26.87
Suspicion	623	150	–75.9	182	51	–72.0	25.37
Curfew/Loitering	41,386	10,788	–73.9	20,278	5,331	–73.7	33.07

[a]Rape is not compared for 2008 due to a changing definition of this offense.

[b]Difference is less than 1/10%.

Source: Federal Bureau of Investigation (2018).

as the proportion of women arrested between 2008 and 2017 *increased* by 14.2%, but the rates for men *dropped* by 25.1% for the same period.

However, if we find women's percentage of a given arrest category higher than 27%, then this is a crime where the number of female arrestees is disproportionately higher, given their contribution to the entire arrestee population. If it is below 27%, then the reverse is true: the arrest rate for women is disproportionately lower than we would expect. Certain economic crimes represent several examples of the former, as women's arrest rates are higher than we might expect for overall property crime, larceny-theft, fraud, and forgery and counterfeiting. For embezzlement the number of women arrested for this offense exceeded male arrests. In the arrest category of prostitution and commercialized sex, women dominate. In 2017 the proportion of women's arrests for offenses higher than 27% was as follows:

- Larceny-theft (41.2%)
- All property crime (36.4%)
- Other assaults (28.9%)
- Forgery/Counterfeit (34.6%)
- Fraud (37.6%)
- Embezzlement (50.5%)
- Prostitution (57.5%)
- Offenses against the family and children (30%)
- Disorderly conduct (30%)
- Curfew/Loitering (33.1%)

The arrest statistics presented earlier show that compared with men, women are under-represented in all but embezzlement and prostitution offenses. A review of other points in the criminal justice system shows that women are under-represented in every subsequent category, from court appearances to imprisonment and even the use of the death penalty. Figure 11.1 shows the proportion of women involved at different points in the justice system. Some have called this a gender gap. This gender gap increases along with the seriousness of the crimes.

We can draw several conclusions from these figures. First, they suggest that one of two driving forces is behind them. Either women commit fewer crimes than men or the police arrest women less frequently than they arrest men (or possibly both). Second, male and female offenders are predisposed to commit different offenses, with men more prone to commit the more serious Index Crimes (especially violent crimes) and women are disproportionately more likely to be arrested for crimes of financial gain. The question then becomes, how much attention do female offenders get from the criminal justice system in

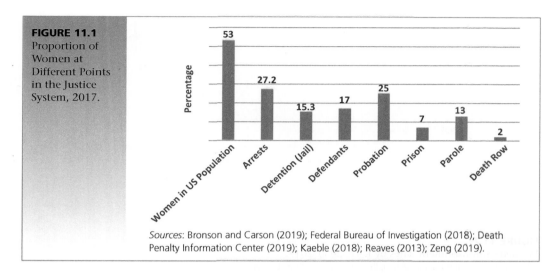

FIGURE 11.1 Proportion of Women at Different Points in the Justice System, 2017.

Sources: Bronson and Carson (2019); Federal Bureau of Investigation (2018); Death Penalty Information Center (2019); Kaeble (2018); Reaves (2013); Zeng (2019).

general and corrections systems in particular? Moreover, what accounts for the differences between men's and women's outcomes after arrest? The evidence suggests that women are second-class citizens in a system that places a great premium on status. To gain a more complete perspective on this phenomenon, we briefly return to criminological theories specifically developed to explain female criminality.

Imprisonment Rates: Dropping for African American Women but Increasing for White Women

Most of our discussions about race, class, and gender have examined how people of color are disproportionately imprisoned, and the relative disadvantage of the poor when it comes to their interactions with the justice system compared with the middle and upper classes. In Chapter 1, however, we observed that African American imprisonment rates have been decreasing, while the imprisonment rates for Whites were increasing. In this chapter, we take a closer look at women's imprisonment rates. Figure 11.2 shows that between 31 December 2000 and 31 December 2017, the African American women's imprisonment rate dropped by 55% while the White women's imprisonment rate increased by 44%. The imprisonment rate for Latinx had a modest increase of 10% during that time.

While describing these changes over time is relatively straight-forward, explaining why the number of White women is increasing is a more complex matter. Hager

RACE, CLASS, AND GENDER

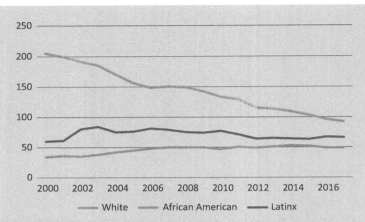

FIGURE 11.2
Women's Imprisonment Rates by Race, 2000–2017.
Sources: Bronson and Carson (2019); Bureau of Justice Statistics (2019).

(2017, p.1) provides four possible reasons why this is occurring, and the following summarizes his observations:

- Crime, arrests, and incarceration are declining overall, and this benefits African Americans the most as they are the most incarcerated group.
- The war on drugs has shifted its focus from crack and marijuana to methamphetamines and opioids. As meth and opioids are more likely to be used by Whites, this has resulted in more of them becoming involved in the justice system.
- White people are experiencing declining socioeconomic prospects such as jobs lost to automation, the aftereffects of the 2008 financial crisis, decreasing wages, and union membership. Many arrests are for so-called crimes of poverty such as burglary, theft, motor vehicle theft, forgery, counterfeiting, and selling or buying stolen property.
- Criminal justice reform has been happening in cities, where more African American live, but not in rural areas, where Whites are more likely to live. Thus, rural Whites might not have access to adequate public defender services, bail reform, pretrial services, or other diversionary practices.

Like other national criminal justice statistics that we have reported in the previous chapters, the average sometimes masks outlying cases (i.e. states or areas within states with very high or low rates). Bronson and Carson (2019, p. 11), for instance, note that Oklahoma had the nation's highest imprisonment rate for women (157), which was almost three times the national average of 57 female prisoners per 100,000 residents. Women's imprisonment rates are the highest in states with high rural populations such as Oklahoma, Kentucky, South Dakota, and Idaho. Some have attributed these high imprisonment rates to lengthy sentences meted out to people convicted of drug crimes who were using and trafficking methamphetamine (Branstetter, Herrera, Rowan, & Sagara, 2018). Oliver (2018) says that the rise in rural imprisonment might also be associated with concentrated White poverty and lower levels of formal education. Oliver also contends that we should look at the impact of local politics on changes in the use of imprisonment, including rural county prosecutors who are waging wars on drugs and crime that urban taxpayers will pay for (see Chapter 3).

We have less knowledge of the female jail population. Like what is happening with male imprisonment, we know that between 2005 and 2017, the female jail population grew by one-fifth (20%), while the male jail population dropped by 3% (Zeng, 2019, p. 6). We do not, however, have a breakdown of the female inmate population by race. The research carried out by Subramanian, Henrichson, and Kang-Brown (2015), and reported in Chapter 5, shows that jail populations in the smallest counties grew three times greater than the larger urban jails. Again, while not explaining all of these population increases, these findings enable us to ask better questions about jails, prisons, and the increasing number of women in these places. We must consider that small changes over a long period of time can have a significant impact on jail or prison populations, and Table 11.2 shows the growth for the entire United States between 1978 and 2017.

TABLE 11.2 Jail and Prison Population Growth Rates, 1978–2017

Male Prison Population 1978–2017	Female Prison Population 1978–2017	Male Jail Population 1978–2017	Female Jail Population 1978–2017
221%	530%	328%	1125%

Source: Bureau of Justice Statistics (2019).

EXPLAINING WOMEN'S INVOLVEMENT IN CRIME

Most explanations of criminality were developed by men to explain why other men commit crimes—what some women call **malestream criminology**. Those explanations were either gender-neutral or gender-negative. That is, either they do not make a distinction between men and women or they simply do not address gender. This failure on the part of criminologists to provide more detailed insights into the female criminal (as contrasted to the male) has been a point of contention for centuries, and not everyone agrees that crime theories are or should be gender-neutral. For example, some biologic theorists—those who look to the influences of biology on criminal behavior, or so-called biogenic criminology—might look to female biochemistry for answers about the presence or absence of crime propensities.

Selman and Dunn (2018, p. 257) observe that when women were included in gender-neutral theories "their engagement in crime and deviance [was presented] in distorted and stereotyped ways." Many early theories of women's criminality were based on sexist stereotypes about women. Italian prison doctor Lombroso (1876), for example, believed that women criminals were an aberration; they were basically masculinized women. A half-century later Freud (1933) considered female criminals to be women who lacked proper maternal instincts.

By the 1960s female scholars began to introduce new ideas about women's involvement in crime that considered the paternalist treatment of women by officials within the justice system, as well as their changing place, roles, and status in society (Adler, 1975; Simon, 1975). They argue that we consider the power-sharing arrangements or lack of them in society as yielding insights into involvement in crime. Furthermore, these scholars, part of an emergent feminist criminology, advanced ideas about male power and privilege and how these factors define all social relations and are the primary cause of social inequities—two factors related to women's criminality. Scholars such as Chesney-Lind (1973) also added to these debates by expanding our understanding of girl's and women's crime as outcomes of their efforts to flee abusive or intolerable living situations. As a result, their crimes—running away from home, incorrigibility, and even prostitution—were simply **survival strategies**, as these women were often powerless and had few other alternatives. These observations greatly expanded our understanding of female criminality.

Perhaps the most important contribution of feminist criminologists has been to focus research on gender differences. After all, the best single predictor of involvement in crime and delinquency is a person's gender. Most social scientists would agree that women are different from men, and these differences are reflected in the kinds and volume of crimes they commit. For example, research on the **pathways to crime** that first emerged in the late 1980s is gaining more acceptance. These notions are popular because they explain gender involvement in crime and acknowledge the different ways that women can become involved in crime. Knowing why women commit crime is also important for corrections because it enables officials to develop policies and tailor practices that enable their facilities to operate more effectively, as well as deliver rehabilitative programs that can reduce recidivism.

Women's Pathways to Crime

Daly (1992) introduced the idea that there were pathways to women's involvement in crime, and they became involved in crime because of weak parental supports, they were battered by intimate partners, had run away from home (because they were neglected or abused), they abused drugs and alcohol, or because they were poor (Lilly, Cullen, & Ball, 2019). Daly's work inspired other scholars to take a closer look at the factors that push women toward crime. There is no agreement that any specific pathway framework does the best job of explaining involvement in crime. Nevertheless, one strength of this approach is that these frameworks help us understand the factors that contribute to an individual's criminality. As a result, they provide the field of corrections with a roadmap to providing **gender-responsive** interventions that address the unmet needs of women in community and institutional corrections. When considering pathways to crime, it is important to remember that many women will experience the factors described in these pathways but never commit any crime.

Brennan (2015, pp. 2–4) identifies the different pathways to serious crime, and they are summarized as follows:

1. *Quasi-normal non-violent women with drug/alcohol issues*: These women have extensive criminal histories of drug and non-violent offenses and most suffer from chronic substance abuse. They tend to have higher levels of educational achievement and employment histories than other women offenders and are unlikely to have been homeless. These women typically do not have histories of serious psychological problems and are less likely to have histories of physical or sexual abuse than women in the other pathways.

   Treatment goals: Address substance abuse and help these women reduce their social and economic marginalization.

2. *Lifelong victims*: These women have extensive criminal histories involving drug offenses and non-violent crimes. They tend to be more socially marginalized and often lack their grade 12, have poor work histories, and most live in poverty. Many of these women have abusive and violent partners with criminal records who tend to be domineering and may push these women into committing crime. Many of them have suffered from physical and sexual abuse as children and adults. These women are likely to express feelings of anger, suffer from depression and other psychological impairments. Having children may increase their involvement in domestic violence offenses.

   Treatment goals: Reduce substance abuse; confront issues related to past and present abuse and trauma and respond to mental health issues such as depression and post-traumatic stress disorder (PTSD).

3. *Socialized subcultural pathways*: These women have above average involvement in crime and often fail to comply with probation or parole conditions. They are often involved in drug trafficking and criminal networks, which can increase their likelihood of being negatively influenced by pro-criminal peers, family members, and significant others. Many were raised in poverty, received inconsistent parenting, and lived in disadvantaged neighborhoods. Few of these women have very extensive employment histories and many lack a complete formal education. These women are less likely to have been abused as adults or children than the lifelong victim group. Although some of these women have antisocial personalities, they are about average in terms of psychological problems or suicidal ideation. Having children may increase their levels of anxiety and stress.

   Treatment goals: Address issues related to poverty, inadequate housing, and bolster educational skills and employability. Reduce substance abuse and confront their antisocial or criminogenic thinking.

4. *Aggressive and antisocial*: These women have the highest involvement in criminal behavior, noncompliance with conditions of community corrections, and substance abuse. They tend to have a high involvement in fighting and misconduct when incarcerated. These women were the most likely to have experienced homelessness, poverty, and socioeconomic marginalization living in high-crime areas. They often have a lifelong histories of physical and sexual victimization. Many suffer from serious mental health problems including suicidal ideation, PTSD, and hostile personality disorders.

   Treatment goals: Address issues related to poverty, inadequate housing, and enhance their educational and vocational skills. Reduce substance abuse and challenge their antisocial beliefs or criminogenic thinking. Respond to mental health issues.

5. *Not classified*: A small percentage of cases fall outside the previous four categories and may include one of a kind individuals. Other women might bridge the boundaries of two or more categories.

   Treatment goals: Are identified by a counselor on a case-by-case basis.

One of the strengths of pathways models is that they provide a starting point for delivering correctional interventions that target the factors that lead to their involvement in crime. Pathways approaches have been criticized, however, as they are often based on samples of Americans and these categories do not neatly fit into classifications for people living in other developed nations such as England.

Brennan's (2015) work is not the final word on pathways research, and one limitation is the lack of explanations for involvement in violent crimes. DeHart (2018, p. 1461) also identified a pathways system that had five different groups, including:

"aggressive career offenders, women who killed or assaulted persons in retaliation or self-defense, women who maltreated children, substance-dependent women experiencing intimate partner violence (IPV), and social capital offenders," where social capital refers to growing up in impoverished conditions with a low likelihood of childhood victimization.

There are several factors that are common to most of these pathways, including the recognition that many women have experienced high levels of emotional, physical, and sexual abuse at different points in their lives. Confronting the aftereffects of these experiences is at the heart of trauma-informed care (TIC), and such interventions fit into a model of gender-responsive services that are increasingly evidence-based. The second factor present in most of these pathways classifications is the issue of chemical and behavioral addictions, and most incarcerated women have struggled with one or more forms of substance abuse. As Covington and Bloom (2007, p. 19) point out: "Nearly one in three women serving time in state prisons reports having committed her offense in order to obtain money to support a drug habit. About half of the incarcerated women describe themselves as daily drug users."

Another issue linked to the pathways research is acknowledging the importance of relationships in women's lives, which is a cornerstone of **relational theory**. Supporters of this approach contend that women desire strong family, friendship, and romantic relationships. Having stronger and healthier connections with others can improve their psychological health, as well as reduce their involvement in substance abuse and crime. Women who are unable to form very strong connections with others are more likely to suffer from depression, abuse drugs and alcohol and, consequently, they may become more socially isolated. When Kreis and associates (2016) looked at this issue more closely, they found that some women experiencing problems in their relationships may be more likely to become substance abusers. Conversely, women who have strong and healthy relationships might find it easier to resist alcohol and drugs and make a crime-free transition to the community (Walt, Hunter, Salina, & Jason, 2014). These issues are described later in the section on operating women's correctional facilities; however, before addressing TIC, we take a closer look at the history of women's corrections.

PHOTO 11.2
These women are participating in a drug treatment seminar. Drug use, from alcohol or heroin, is a significant challenge for more than one-half of women jail inmates. Credit: Art Directors & TRIP/Alamy Stock Photo.

A BRIEF HISTORY OF WOMEN'S INCARCERATION

Historically, women—as was the case with their male counterparts—were rarely imprisoned for long periods of time. Specialized facilities for females were uncommon in late medieval and early Renaissance England, which was the inspiration for much of America's early correctional philosophy and practice. In the eighteenth century, European philosophers of the era opposed keeping male and female prisoners in the same cells, although this was a common practice for another 100 years. One of the first specialized prisons for women was Amsterdam's *Spinhuis*, a former convent that opened its doors in 1597. Women labored in this workhouse prison in appalling conditions that approached slavery; nonetheless, the workhouse became an equally popular practice in England beginning at about the same time. Women in colonial America were often placed in the stocks or the pillory for petty crimes or in more serious cases—including accusations of witchcraft—they were burned at the stake or hanged, although the death penalty was rarely imposed (Newman, 2008).

After the Revolutionary War, individual states took on more responsibility for punishing serious women offenders. From the early 1800s to the 1870s, most women were placed in male facilities. New York's Auburn prison, for example, first admitted women in 1825, four years after the prison was opened (Harris, 1998). Pennsylvania's Eastern State Penitentiary admitted women almost from the day it opened in 1829. At Auburn, officials housed these inmates above the penitentiary kitchen, where they were subjected to neglect, abuse, and outright indifference. In the Pennsylvania facility, where isolation and repentance were the order of the day, the women languished in their cells, suffering the same physical and psychological distress as the men.

In addition to scandals where the victimization of women by the male guards was reported, the poor living conditions for women in these facilities were becoming widely known and this encouraged prison reformers to advocate for change, including establishing women's only prisons that were intended to reform the inmates rather than punishing them. Rafter (1985, p. 236) describes that:

> Crusaders for women's reformatories surveyed existing prisons for adults and concluded that these were unsuitable for the care and treatment of women. In search of an alternative to the maximum security penitentiary, they turned for their model to institutions for juveniles. From the juvenile system they adopted the cottage plan, according to which institutions should be located in rural areas and consist of a number of smallish, homelike residences.

Between the 1830s and 1870s, several women's only facilities were introduced, although they were slow to be accepted in some states. By 1940, for example, only 23 states had separate women's prison facilities; by 1975 that number had only increased to 34. Many of the states lacking a women's facility contracted with other states, county sheriffs, or the private sector to house female prisoners. The following timeline shows some of the notable events in the history of women's punishment in America:

1632	Jane Champion is executed for committing murder: Streib (1990) reports that another 397 women were executed until 1989, and 16 women were executed between 1989 and 2020 (Death Penalty Information Center, 2020).
1825	Rachel Welch became pregnant at Auburn prison while living in a solitary cell. She was flogged by a guard when she was five months pregnant and died several days later. The guard who whipped her was fined $25 but allowed to keep his job.
1835	New York opened the Mount Pleasant Female Prison in 1835. This prison, which operated for 33 years, was the first separate women's facility in the United States.
1848	Laws were enacted enabling Louisiana to sell the children born to enslaved women inmates in the State Penitentiary. Derbes (2013) found evidence that 11 children were sold into slavery at public auction prior to 1862.
1873	The Indiana Reformatory for Women and Girls—the first prison run by women that only housed women—opened in Indianapolis. Despite being operated by women, Jones (2015) describes the abusive treatment of women inmates, which culminated in an investigation carried out in 1881 that led to the resignation of the warden and several other staff.
1879	The Industrial School for Girls was founded in Evanston, IL. A 1911 news account in the *Chicago Tribune* reports that youths were being placed for days in a four feet square windowless "dungeon" and fed a diet of bread and water.
1901	The Bedford Hills Reformatory for Women was founded using a campus design that featured separate cottages.
1914	Katharine Bement Davis was appointed Corrections Commissioner for New York. Prior to this appointment, she had been the superintendent of the New York State Reformatory for Women.
1904	Over 13,300 women are committed to US prisons. Over one-fifth (21.3%) were described as Negro, whereas only 15.3% of male prisoners were African American (Kaba & Russo, 2014).
1927	The first federal prison for women, the Federal Women's Reformatory, opened in West Virginia: the first warden was Dr. Mary Belle Harris.
1935	Susie Lattimore, a 15-year-old, was prosecuted and convicted of first-degree murder for killing a teenage girl she had been drinking with at a bar. Because of this case, Illinois' laws were changed to give adult court jurisdiction to anybody 10 years and older.
1945	Lena Baker, a maid and mother of three children, is the only woman ever executed using electrocution in Georgia's history.

1954	Prisoners at the state women's facility in Raleigh, NC riot after an 18-year-old inmate, who had been living in solitary, died of injuries inflicted by correctional staff.
1974	Two hundred women prisoners seized control of several buildings at the Bedford Hills Correctional Facility after a woman prisoner was restrained by male correctional officers.
1975	Joanne Little, an African American prisoner, was acquitted of killing the White prison guard who had raped her.

The women's **reformatory** movement lasted from the 1870s until the 1930s (Rafter, 1985). Reformatory officials treated some inmates as wayward children, while others were seen as beyond redemption. As suggested earlier in this chapter, the general thinking of the day was that these women, by breaking the law, had betrayed their gender. The notion of betrayal was particularly strong in the nineteenth century in the American West, where women often lived in men's penitentiaries:

> The woman prisoner may have appeared divorced from the gender dynamics that affected womanhood, but that perception rested on a shallow foundation. The incarcerated female of the nineteenth century bore a double identity—woman and criminal. Conversely, noncriminal women, although they often denied it, shared commonality with the incarcerated woman; if the slender thread of social acceptability—a sometimes frayed and tangled line—snapped, a woman's existence changed in an instant.
>
> (Butler, 1997, p. 21)

Women of color in the Old West often faced even more desperate conditions when they conflicted with the law than their White counterparts. This fate was shared by African American women in the eastern states (Young, 2001).

The late nineteenth-century philosophy that guided women's prisons stressed at its core that the ideal woman was "pure, honest, and innocent on the one hand, and... deceitful, designing, and susceptible to corruption on the other" (Harris, 1998, p. 76). This violation of society's notion of the ideal woman offended the moralists of the era (Abrams & Curran, 2000). As a result, the task of women-only prisons was to instill in inmates an appreciation for their proper roles and tasks in society. Consistent with that set of beliefs, prison staff taught women domestic skills and available vocational programs were often based on stereotypical ideas about appropriate careers for women such as clerical work and hairdressing. One of the shortcomings of that approach is that few such careers enabled these women to be financially independent, an issue we explore after an overview of the characteristics of women in local jails and state prisons.

WOMEN IN CORRECTIONS

A Portrait of Women in Local Jails

In Chapter 5 we pointed out that women have been one of the fastest growing populations in local corrections. When it comes to jail inmates, in 1978 there were almost 13,000 adult women in American jails. Zeng (2019) reports that by 2017 that number was 113,700, representing a growth of 1125%. In the same time frame, the male jail population tripled. As a result, there are about 5.5 male inmates for every woman in jail today. But the trends show that ratio might be changing, and while the male jail population decreased between 2005 and 2017 the women's jail population has been increasing. Surprisingly, in 2017 the number of women jail inmates was greater than the 105,000 women in state and federal prisons (Bronson & Carson, 2019).

Most jails—roughly 85%—hold both males and females, although by policy and practice, all jails try to maintain sight and sound segregation between these two groups. Another 13% held only men. There are less than two dozen women-only facilities. Generally, these women-only operations are part of networks found in large cities such as Chicago, Los Angeles, or New York.

Not only are the number of women jail inmates increasing, but as reported in Chapter 5, many of these women have significant health and addictions-related problems, as shown in Figure 11.3. A review of this figure reveals that about two-thirds of sentenced female jail inmates have a history of mental health problems, almost three-quarters are drug dependent, and 46% were using drugs at the time of their offense. With respect to physical health problems, one-half suffered from a disability and two-thirds had a chronic health condition such as high blood pressure, heart-related problems, cancer, or asthma. When compared with their male counterparts, these women had higher levels of these challenges in every category.

These addictions and health-related issues pose major challenges for jail administrators. Jails in rural and sparsely populated counties, for example, often lack addictions and mental health treatment programs. As a result, some female inmates fall through the cracks of the system, receiving very little treatment. We must also acknowledge that the average jail inmate is released within a month. The likelihood that an individual's risks and needs can be assessed and treated in that time window is very low. Failures to intervene, however, can lead to missed opportunities, as individuals in crisis are sometimes very motivated to make changes in their lives such as seeking substance abuse treatment. Alternatively, when people with mental illnesses do not receive treatment and are merely warehoused their conditions can worsen, and they can become disruptive within the facility (Segal, Winfree, & Friedman, 2019).

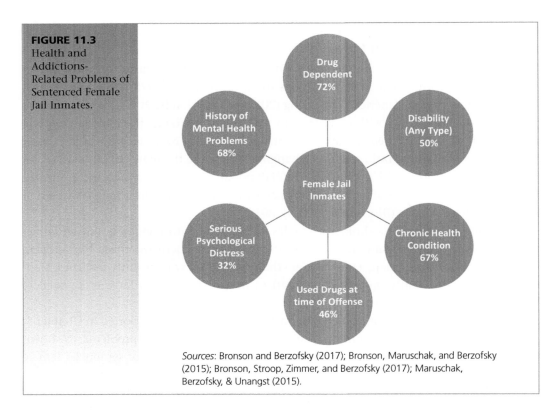

FIGURE 11.3
Health and Addictions-Related Problems of Sentenced Female Jail Inmates.

Sources: Bronson and Berzofsky (2017); Bronson, Maruschak, and Berzofsky (2015); Bronson, Stroop, Zimmer, and Berzofsky (2017); Maruschak, Berzofsky, & Unangst (2015).

Gender-Based Differences in Jail Inmate Populations

Scholars have identified four distinct differences in the characteristics of female and male jail inmates, and these distinctions may play important roles in women inmates' adjustment to life in and out of jail. The net result is that a larger proportion of women than men have problems adjusting to both the jail experience and the stigma of jail. Adjusting to jail life, with its intrusions on privacy and focus on security, is very difficult for some women given their pathways to incarceration that include their prior victimization, mental health problems, substance abuse, and problems with relationships.

1. *Gender-Specific Differences*: Offense-specific programming in jails generally targets the needs of the largest resident group—male inmates. As a result, there are far fewer jail-based interventions that address women's specific needs. For example, Green and associates (2005, pp. 142–143) found that 92% of the women jail inmates in their sample had been pregnant at least once, almost one-half had miscarriages or a sexually transmitted infection (STI), and 60% reported having at least one abortion. Over three-quarters of jail inmates are mothers, and about 150,000 pregnant women are

admitted to jail every year (Sawyer & Bertram, 2018). Given those findings, there seems to be a need for jail-based educational programs that provide information about reproductive health and parenting. In addition, jails could be used to screen for reproductive health problems and providing basic prenatal care Providing these services, however, falls outside the jail's mandate.

One topic that has received considerable media attention is the need for access to free hygiene products for incarcerated women. Many jails and some prison systems do not provide tampons or sanitary napkins; or, they are only available on specific days and may be rationed to all the women on a living unit. As a result of these practices, women in some facilities have no alternative other than buying these products at the facility commissary at a high cost. Most of these women are poor and cannot afford these products, so they are forced to use toilet paper or other makeshift alternatives. As a result, organizations such as the American Civil Liberties Union are launching lawsuits to force jails and prison systems to provide these products free-of-charge.

While providing menstrual care products is a relatively non-controversial issue, women jail inmates have asked for access to contraceptive care and abortions, both of which are far more value-laden practices. Swavola, Riley, and Subramanian (2017) say that information about these issues is rarely offered to jail inmates. Kasdan (2009) contends that female inmates—whether in jail or prison—have a constitutional right to receive an abortion. There are no statistics on how many jail inmates receive abortions or other pregnancy outcomes and that is a significant shortcoming in our understanding of the issue (see Bronson & Sufrin, 2019). Sufrin (2019, p. 35) says that policies vary greatly and "some carceral institutions explicitly prohibit abortion at any point, some allow it only in the first trimester, others permit it only when there is a threat to the woman's health, and some allow it under most circumstances."

2. *The Gender-Specific Role of Drugs*: Drugs play a proportionately larger role in the illegal activities of women than they do for men, and this drug use adds more to the legal and social stigma of women than it does for men. This means that their treatment needs may be different than for male inmates. When Rodda and Beichner (2017) asked women jail inmates about their needs for services most described their long-term histories of drug use and their need for help with addictions. Rodda and Beichner note that the short-term nature of jail incarceration (e.g. most inmates are held for less than 30 days) works against providing meaningful rehabilitative programs.

3. *The Emotional, Physical, and Sexual Abuse Histories of Female Inmates*: As noted in the pathways literature, many women involved with the justice system have histories of emotional, physical, and sexual abuse. Karlsson and Zielinski (2020, p. 326) looked at 28

different studies that asked women prisoners about their prior victimization. They found that 50–66% were victimized as children, 26–68% were victims of adult sexual abuse, and the lifetime likelihood of sexual assault for all the women in these studies ranged from 56% to 82%. Although most of these studies were with prison populations, the results can be applied to local corrections, given that jails are the gateways for prisons.

Jailed women are also vulnerable to victimization by their peers, as well as the jail personnel. Rantala (2018) reports there were almost 6,000 allegations of sexual victimization made in 2015 by jail inmates. This total has increased every year since 2005. When it comes to women in jails, Beck, Rantala, and Rexroat (2014, p. 12) report that 79% of the 356 females in local jails whose allegations of abuse were substantiated were victimized by males, many of whom were correctional officers. Women are also victimized by their fellow inmates. Ellison, Steiner, and Wright (2018, p. 1733) found that the odds of female inmates being victimized were 120% higher than for their male counterparts.

4. *Gender Differences: From Pregnancy to Parenting.* In terms of expectant mothers, about 5% of jail inmates are pregnant (Maruschak, 2006), and Lambert (2019) estimates that about 1,400 children are born to jail inmates every year. Some facilities allow the mother and child to spend a day or two together. Afterward, the infants are placed with relatives or in foster care; other infants are voluntarily given up for adoption. These post-partum separations can be very difficult for some women. In order to provide better care for these mothers and their children, a handful of nursery programs exist in jails where the inmate and her infant can spend longer periods of time together. Swavola, Riley, and Subramanian (2017) describe how the Cook County (Chicago) jail has a nursery unit, while the Rose M. Singer Center on Rikers Island (New York) has a jail-based program for pregnant inmates and mothers. In addition to providing services and support to these expectant inmates and new mothers, both also have an educational component that teaches effective parenting.

One controversial issue that was briefly described in Chapter 1 is the practice of shackling pregnant women to infirmary or hospital beds when they are giving birth. Most women who are in labor are escorted by correctional officers to a hospital and the officers use mechanical restraints such as handcuffs or shackles to reduce their likelihood of escape. At midyear 2019, only about one-half of the states had policies prohibiting this practice. Yet, even when these practices are banned, some women have given birth while physically restrained. A New York woman endured 30 hours of labor handcuffed and shackled to her bed despite her doctor's pleas to remove the restraints. As New York had banned the practice in 2009 she was awarded $610,000 in a federal lawsuit (The Crime Report, 2019).

Since three-quarters of women jail inmates are mothers, the separation from their children can be devastating. Swavola, Riley, and Subramanian (2017) observe that one of the problems of separating children from their incarcerated mothers is weakened family ties. Family calls and visits can be limited by financial barriers such as transportation costs, as well as fees for video visitation or phone calls. Jail policies such as separating the mother and children by a thick glass partition might make it physically and psychologically uncomfortable to visit for both the mothers and their children. Even after the parent is released from jail, there are no guarantees that the family will reunite. As Swavola, Riley, and Subramanian (2017, p. 18) note, "[c]aregivers, child protection agencies, and family court judges may be reluctant to return children to their mother's custody." As a result, even a short period of incarceration might disrupt the mothers' employment, treatment, or educational activities, which may place their parental custody in jeopardy. Yet, how do we best balance the needs of these children for a stable home and the desire of these jail inmates to reunite with their children?

These four factors, combined with the general lack of treatment programs for women in jails, make the incarceration experience potentially more damaging than for their male counterparts. The experiences of being arrested and incarcerated also re-victimize some women, largely through security procedures that can create feelings of powerlessness such as pat downs and **strip searches**. There is growing recognition of the negative impact that these acts can have on women with long histories of trauma, especially when they are confined in group settings or when the officers carrying out searches act unprofessionally. Tchekmedyian (2019, paras. 2–3) summarizes the account of a woman who was strip searched with a group of about 60 women in a bus garage used by the Los Angeles County jail to receive new jail admissions:

PHOTO 11.3
Females in Maricopa County (Arizona) Jail await a turn to be strip searched for contraband. This process is often dehumanizing, embarrassing, and traumatizing for many women. Credit: Scott Houston/Alamy Stock Photo.

> The inmates, some of whom were menstruating, were told to remove their clothes and lift and spread their body parts, in full view of one another. Deputies yelled degrading comments and profanities as they made their orders. Some laughed. [An ex-inmate said] "They wanted us to feel powerless" [and] "Whatever they said went, even if it meant making you feel like you're not human."

Practices changed in Los Angeles after the county purchased scanners as fewer strip searches were necessary. Moreover, the group searches were prohibited, and curtains were installed to increase privacy. There was also a financial incentive for these changes, as ex-inmates who challenged these group strip searches were awarded $53 million to settle a lawsuit.

COMPARATIVE ISSUES IN CORRECTIONS

The United Nations and Women's Imprisonment: The Bangkok Rules

The United Nations (UN) has established several standards for prisoner treatment including a separate set for female prisoners. The UN established its first standards for prison operations in 1957 with the introduction of the Standard Minimum Rules for the Treatment of Prisoners (SMR). These guidelines are intended to promote the appropriate and humane care of prisoners. In 2015, they were renamed the Mandela Rules after Nelson Mandela, the former President of South Africa who was imprisoned for 27 years.

According to a report by Penal Reform International (2016, p. 5), the **Mandela Rules** promote the following principles:

- Prisoners must be treated with respect for their inherent dignity and value as human beings.
- Torture or other ill-treatment is prohibited.
- Prisoners should be treated according to their needs, without discrimination.
- The purpose of prison is to protect society and reduce reoffending.
- The safety of prisoners, staff, service providers and visitors at all times is paramount.

In order to fulfill those goals the UN provides guidelines for categories such as medical services, disciplinary measures, investigating correctional staff misconduct, prisoner access to legal representation, staff training, and protecting vulnerable prisoners.

In 2010 the UN introduced 70 guidelines for the treatment of women who had committed crimes which were known as the Bangkok Rules. The first guideline is to keep women out of prison. When they are incarcerated, Penal Reform International (2013) provides some broad guidelines for their care:

- Provide appropriate health care, including care for mental health and substance abuse, and preventative screening for physical health conditions.

- Treat women humanely and with dignity by rejecting the use of mechanical restraints such as shackles while giving birth and reducing or eliminating the use of solitary confinement.
- Preserving the woman's dignity during pat down or strip searches (e.g. when searching for contraband), and that searches should be carried out by female staff.
- Protection from violence, including acts of harassment, humiliation, and sexual misconduct.
- Provide for prisoners' children whether those children are being cared for within the community or inside a correctional facility with their parent.

A review of the previous and current chapters suggests that our efforts to provide safe and humane jails and prisons that uphold an inmate's dignity often fall short of the UN standards. Nevertheless, reviewing the Mandela and Bangkok Rules reminds us that governments can work toward more favorable outcomes with their correctional populations.

A Portrait of Women in Prisons

In Table 11.2 we learned about changes in the long-term use of imprisonment. Specifically, while the male prison population grew by 221%, the female population increased by 530%. Although the long-term trend shows a substantial increase, the changes since 2000 have been less dramatic. With respect to state and federal prisoners, the number of men decreased by 7.1% between 2007 and 2017, whereas the number of women dropped by only 2.6%.

Like their counterparts in jails many women prisoners have significant health and addictions-related issues, as shown in Figure 11.4. According to the statistics summarized in this figure, about two-thirds of sentenced female state prisoners have a history of mental health problems, over two-thirds are drug dependent, and almost one-half were using drugs at the time of their offense. With respect to physical health problems, 40% suffered from a disability and almost two-thirds (63%) had a chronic health condition such as high blood pressure, heart-related problems, cancer, or asthma. Given that the average prison stay is about three years, those conditions pose long-term costs for these prison systems, especially in terms of scarce health care resources.

Bronson and Carson (2019) report that on 31 December 2017 there were about 105,000 federal and state female prisoners. Slightly less than one-half were White, whereas about one-fifth were either African American or Latinx (the remainder were classified as "other," which excludes Latinx but includes Asians and American Indians). Female prisoners were somewhat younger than males, as 46% were less than 34 years old, which

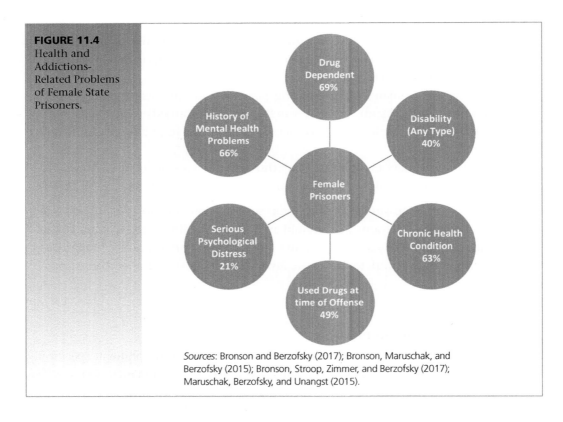

FIGURE 11.4
Health and Addictions-Related Problems of Female State Prisoners.

Drug Dependent 69%

History of Mental Health Problems 66%

Disability (Any Type) 40%

Female Prisoners

Serious Psychological Distress 21%

Chronic Health Condition 63%

Used Drugs at time of Offense 49%

Sources: Bronson and Berzofsky (2017); Bronson, Maruschak, and Berzofsky (2015); Bronson, Stroop, Zimmer, and Berzofsky (2017); Maruschak, Berzofsky, and Unangst (2015).

was slightly less than the 42.1% of men who were under 34 years of age. Moreover, there were fewer elderly (those over 55 years of age) women inmates compared with men (7.8% and 12.2%, respectively).

With respect to the most serious offense, women prisoners were also less violent than their male counterparts: 57% of males had sentences that included violent offenses, whereas only 38% of women had committed a violent offense. Women were more likely to be property or drug offenders compared with men, and about equally likely to have convictions for public order offenses such as driving while intoxicated (DWI) or weapons offenses. The proportion of men and women prisoners is presented in Figure 11.5. In general, women receive substantially lighter sentences than men. When Doerner and Demuth (2014) looked at sentencing in the federal courts, they found that women received shorter sentences than their male counterparts. Women were less likely to be imprisoned and if they were sentenced to prison, they received shorter sentences for similar crimes. These analyses supported many prior studies that found similar results in both state and federal courts (see Nowacki, 2019).

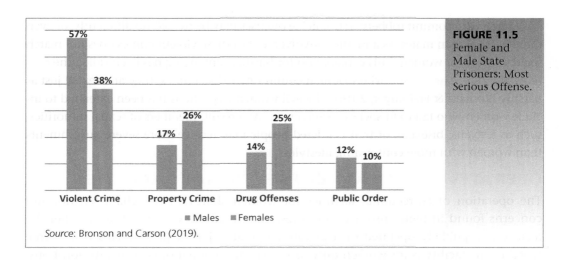

FIGURE 11.5
Female and Male State Prisoners: Most Serious Offense.

Source: Bronson and Carson (2019).

Does being a parent or the type of offense one commits make a difference in an individual's sentencing? Cho and Tasca (2018) examined the criminal and social histories of imprisoned women, focusing on factors that appeared to influence sentencing outcomes. They found that women drug offenders are sentenced less harshly than women who committed violent, property, or public order crimes. Furthermore, Cho and Tasca report that mothers living with their children receive shorter sentences than mothers who were uninvolved with their children.

The reasons for such leniency at sentencing are difficult to explain. Some scholars believe that it is related to the types of offenses they commit, combined with society's views of women. Perhaps our views of women, especially how the legal establishment holds them accountable, are changing. For example, one explanation is based on the concept of **chivalry**. Franklin and Fearn (2008, p. 279) say that "chivalry/paternalism suggests women are awarded leniency in sentencing as a result of their inherent biological weaknesses and consequently, their need to be protected and coddled both as offenders and as victims." These views stress stereotypical perspectives of women as being passive and less responsible for their actions than males. If the officials in the criminal justice system see women in this way, they may treat them in a more lenient manner: police may be less likely to arrest them, prosecutors may be less apt to bring those matters to court, and if they do, judges mete our less severe sentences. When Kim, Wang, and Cheon (2019) looked at these factors, they found support for the chivalry explanation for the lenient treatment of women before the courts. Other researchers, however, have found that the police had intensified their efforts on the aggressive enforcement of women (Winfree & DeJong, 2015). As a result, there are no simple answers to the question of differential treatment based on gender.

Women who commit robbery or homicide offenses may be treated no differently, or even more harshly than males because their involvement in these violent crimes does not match society's views of women. This explanation for harsher sentencing has been called the **evil woman hypothesis**, and when women commit male-like crimes, they are treated just as harshly (Romain & Freiburger, 2016). The evil women hypothesis has been extended to include women who fail to fit society's stereotypes. As a result, members of sexual minorities, such as lesbians, bisexual, or transgendered people may receive more severe punishments than women with more conforming lifestyles.

OPERATING WOMEN'S CORRECTIONAL FACILITIES

The operation of correctional facilities for women shares all the characteristics and concerns found in men's prisons, plus a few additional ones. This is true whether the facility is a publicly operated or a privately operated jail or prison. This is also true whether the facility is for women only or is a co-correctional or coed institution housing both men and women. In this section we highlight four issues that are increasingly important in women's jails and prisons, including (a) gender-responsive strategies, (b) trauma-informed correctional care, (c) evidence-based correctional practices, and (d) inmate classification.

Gender-Responsive Strategies

The term gender-responsive or gender-informed has been part of the correctional literature since the 1990s, and the terms recognize that women come to corrections with a different set of life experiences than men, and their pathways to crime are different, as are their risks and needs. As a result, effective correctional programs should be developed using our knowledge of these critical differences. King and Foley (2014, p. 2) define gender-responsive policies or interventions as those that address:

> ...the specific circumstances of women's lives, their unique risk and need factors, and research on women that guides policy/practice. These programs take into consideration the unique pathways that lead women to commit crimes and are trauma-informed, strengths-based, and **culturally competent**.

Bloom, Owen, and Covington (2003) present a vision for developing gender-responsive strategies. Their six factors were summarized by Mays and Ruddell (2019, pp. 168–169) as follows:

1. *Acknowledge that gender makes a difference*: Correctional programming for women cannot be based on models developed for males, as these groups have different pathways to criminal involvement, have different needs, require different approaches to supervision, and women pose different risks.

2. *Create an environment based on safety, respect, and dignity*: Most women are admitted to jail or prison with histories of emotional, physical, and sexual abuse, and require a safe and supportive environment that reduces the possibility of further victimization.

3. *Develop policies, practices, and programs that are relational and promote healthy connections to children, family, significant others, and the community*: Focusing upon developing healthy relationships is a key to overcoming adversities such as discrimination and victimization as well as problems with substance abuse and mental health.

4. *Address substance abuse, trauma, and mental health issues through comprehensive, integrated, and culturally competent services and appropriate supervision*: Effective correctional programs cannot exist in a vacuum, and they should be based on interventions that rely upon well-trained staff members who provide a safe environment and who implement programs that lead to a safe and seamless transition to the community.

5. *Provide women with opportunities to improve their socioeconomic conditions*: Most of the women admitted to correctional facilities have lived on society's margins and have poor work histories. As a result, they require skills training and vocational support in order to enter a career that provides them with a living wage once returned to the community.

6. *Establish a system of community supervision and reentry with comprehensive collaborative services*: The transition from a correctional institution to the community can be very difficult unless agencies support the efforts of ex-prisoners to find shelter, meet their basic needs, reunite with their family, as well as access to transportation and employment.

These six priorities are easier to describe than deliver. There are several challenges when comprehensive rehabilitative programs based on gender-responsive priorities are being promoted and the foremost is funding: these comprehensive programs are expensive to deliver, and taxpayers are reluctant to see more of their dollars going to corrections.

Trauma-Informed Correctional Care

Earlier we noted that traumatization can include experiencing disturbing events, including accidents or natural disasters, violence, terrorism or war or being emotionally, physically, or sexually victimized. Other forms of personal trauma include experiencing the death of friends or loved ones, family conflict and divorces, or other stressful life events including financial problems. Exposure to trauma typically occurs earlier in one's life and usually decreases as we age. Trauma can involve exposure to one serious event, but we can also be traumatized by ongoing exposure to what some may consider less serious incidents (Reid & Loughran, 2019). In addition to the psychological effects of being traumatized, there are also physical effects of traumatization as our bodies prepare a response to threats, including increased blood pressure and heart rates, and changes in our blood flow within our bodies.

So how many inmates are affected by prior traumatization? According to Stensrud, Gilbride, and Bruinekool (2019), about one-half of male prisoners and over three-quarters of female prisoners report experiencing childhood trauma. This finding comports well with other researchers who maintain that between 65% and 80% of women prisoners report a childhood victimization, which was about twice the rate of non-incarcerated women (Tripodi, Mennicke, McCarter, & Ropes, 2019, p. 281).

Given the high proportion of people who have experienced traumatizing events, we should assume that every person admitted to a jail or prison has a history of being traumatized, which is a cornerstone of trauma-informed correctional care (TICC). In addition to acknowledging that prior history, the correctional staff must also understand how those experiences can affect an individual's behavior years later. Some psychological outcomes of trauma include a higher likelihood of suffering from substance abuse, PTSD, depression, as well as impaired interpersonal and coping skills (Tripodi et al., 2019). Many forms of self-destructive behaviors, such as eating disorders, running from conflict, and substance abuse, may also be related to our prior exposure to trauma.

PHOTO 11.4
Sparse and sterile, segregation units can serve to further stigmatize and isolate all inmates. Credit: Mikael Karlsson/ Alamy Stock Photo.

A second priority of TICC is ensuring that correctional personnel do not **re-traumatize** inmates in their care. Avoiding this re-traumatization can be more difficult than most of us think, especially given that many security-related practices—such as strip searches upon admission to a facility or after the contact visit of a family member or friend—can cause inmates to relive previous sexual abuse. However, these security-related practices are important means of reducing the flow contraband in and about a facility. Some negative responses can be triggered if the women feel their safety is jeopardized by having their rooms searched by COs, being placed in handcuffs or shackles, or requiring the inmate to change rooms without notice (Substance Abuse and Mental Health Services Administration, 2013). Many of these practices, however, are standard procedures required to ensure facility safety and security.

The following steps can be taken by correctional personnel to reduce re-traumatizing jail inmates or prisoners (Arisco,

2014; Kubiak, Covington, & Hillier, 2017; the National Resource Center on Justice Involved Women, 2014):

- Correctional staff require training in order to better understand the prevalence of trauma in jail and prison populations and the steps they can take in reducing re-traumatization.
- Provide a highly structured, safe, and predictable institutional environment with consistent boundaries, limits, and incentives for all the inmates.
- Screening new inmates for their histories of trauma and helping them understand how those prior experiences influence their current behaviors.
- Making the physical environment less threatening, more comfortable, and install screens or walls to increase privacy.
- Increasing respectful relationships between inmates and correctional personnel such as sanctioning officers who yell at or demean inmates.
- Treating inmates in ways respecting their dignity and eliminating opposite-sex pat downs, exams, and strip searches.
- Develop correctional practices that promote healthy relationships with an inmate's children, family members, and significant others.
- Developing—whenever possible—alternatives to placing women in segregation.

This is far from a comprehensive list, and most of these steps require changing the culture of the jail or prison, along with introducing new policies and practices. Those reforms require a long-term commitment to change involving all the staff members. However, many correctional reforms fail, which raises another question: Why is it so difficult to make changes in correctional facilities?

We can provide a partial multi-level answer. Any changes in a jail or prison must be initiated and supported by the organization's leaders, who must obtain the support or "buy-in" of the officers. Organizational reforms are often slow to achieve, taking years before they are fully accepted or implemented. Among the non-institutional barriers to change is a lack of funding, signaling a low commitment by public officials and even, in some cases, voters. Such reforms are often thwarted by the officers and inmates who are threatened by the prospect of something different. As a result, it is often necessary to educate the staff about how they can benefit from these changes, including making working conditions more positive—such as reducing inmate misconduct which increases safety and job satisfaction. The inmates, by contrast, might be more motivated to participate in programs that will reduce their recidivism or increase their access to positive rewards, both of which hold the promise of making their stay in corrections and release to the community more positive.

Evidence-Based Correctional Practices

In Chapter 1 we mentioned that many correctional systems were placing a priority on introducing evidence-based programs or practices (EBP). According to Gleicher (2017, p. 1), "EBP incorporate objective and reliable research and data to guide policy and practice decisions, with the aim of improving outcomes." Gleicher (2017) also notes that EBP include the "skills, techniques, strategies, policy initiatives, or core intervention components that have accumulated a significant amount of supporting research through high-quality process and outcome evaluations" (p. 1). Evidence-based programs provide a framework that target a specific problem such as controlling anger and violent or gang-related behavior in youths. Gleicher (2017, p. 1) uses the example of an EBP intended to reduce anger and aggression called Anger Replacement Training, "which is made up of three evidence-based practices: social skills training, anger control, and moral reasoning."

When it comes to corrections desirable outcomes include reducing misconduct or recidivism. The movement to make government programs more effective started in the 1980s although mentions of these correctional practices became more widespread only after 2000. While almost everybody supports strategies that evidence has proven are effective, their acceptance into correctional practice has posed some challenges. One of the foremost challenges is that researchers have carried out few formal evaluations of different correctional programs. This problem is not isolated to corrections, as there is a similar lack of evaluation research for policing and court operations. In the absence of formal evaluations, many jurisdictions are relying on cost-benefit analysis, which compares the costs of delivering a correctional intervention, and then calculates the benefits in reduced recidivism (or some other outcome).

We do know, however, there are sometimes very high costs of doing nothing. In Chapter 1 we described the practice of warehousing, where inmates receive their basic needs and either very limited or no formal rehabilitative programming. This is the norm in most states and earlier we reported that rehabilitation only accounts for 2% to 3% of state correctional budgets. However, there is a cost to not responding to the risks and needs of inmates. Duwe (2017, p. 9) says that the odds of recidivism increase by 13% when inmates are warehoused, whereas involving inmates in one effective rehabilitative program decreased their risks of recidivism by 12% and when they were involved in two effective programs their risks decreased by 26%. These figures represent a 25% to nearly 40% shift between doing nothing (i.e. warehousing) and doing something (i.e. participation in one or more effective programs). When Gobeil, Blanchette, and Stewart (2016) compared the results of 37 studies of women's correctional treatment programs, they found that participants had lower recidivism rates than non-participants. Not surprisingly, women who participated in gender-neutral or gender-informed correctional programs also had lower recidivism rates than those participating in male-oriented programs.

A logical question, then, becomes what benefits can we gain when we implement correctional programs with qualified and motivated personnel? Cost-benefit analyses carried out by the Washington State Institute for Public Policy (2019) are shown in Table 11.3 and they reveal the following benefits in reduced crime from each dollar spent on the following five of the most successful correctional programs. Altogether, research shows us that correctional rehabilitation is a good investment in crime reduction. As more of these programs are introduced, offered, and evaluated using male and female populations, correctional officials will be able to get the best return on each dollar in rehabilitative spending.

As a follow-up question, consider the following: What is an effective correctional program, and are there programs that are more effective with women? A number of gender-responsive correctional interventions have been developed and Van Voorhis (2013) says that evaluation research has demonstrated their effectiveness. King (2017) also found that some of these interventions were promising, although she questions whether some of these programs have been evaluated very extensively. Table 11.4 presents seven programs and their targets for treatment. Column one provides the program's name and column two shows the treatment targets. Thus, the "beyond trauma" intervention targets how women cope with trauma and working with the woman to improve her cognitive skills, which is carried out in cognitive behavioral therapy (CBT). CBT is a short-term intervention where unhelpful or destructive ways of thinking are challenged by a therapist and better ways of coping with those negative thoughts are developed.

The gender-responsive interventions identified by Van Voorhis (2013) target issues that were presented in the pathways model, including substance abuse, the effects of trauma, poor self-images (e.g. one's body image), and decreased motivation and/or self-efficacy (e.g. one's confidence in achieving goals) that can arise after one is traumatized or victimized. These approaches also address the importance of inmates' relationships, including their role as mothers. Altogether, the seven different programs listed in this table seek to reduce the factors that can be harmful and build on the clients' strengths

TABLE 11.3 Benefits in Reduced Crime for Each $1 Spent on Correctional Programming

Program Name	Benefit
Post-secondary education	$19.74
Employment counseling and job training (beginning in prison)	$18.21
Vocational education	$11.94
Correctional industries	$12.68
Drug treatment (outpatient or non-intensive during incarceration)	$14.05

Source: Washington State Institute for Public Policy (2019).

TABLE 11.4 Evidence-Based, Gender-Responsive Correctional Interventions for Women

Program	Treatment Targets
Beyond Trauma	Coping with trauma, cognitive skills, healthy relationships, increasing self-efficacy, sexuality, body image, spirituality, support systems
Dialectical Behavioral Therapy	Coping, motivational enhancement
Forever Free	Substance abuse, healthy relationships, PTSD, anger management, parenting, self-efficacy
Helping Women Recover	Substance abuse, coping with trauma, healthy relationships, self-worth, sexuality, body image, spirituality, support systems
Moving On	Healthy relationships, self-efficacy, self-defeating thoughts, antisocial attitudes, cognitive skills, managing stress, using and knowing one's community
Seeking Safety	Substance abuse, coping with trauma, PTSD
Women Offender Case Management Model	Case management and reentry, family and social support, health and well-being

Source: Van Voorhis (2013).

in order to reduce their risks of prison misconduct and recidivism once released. Prior to designing and delivering a treatment program, however, the prison staff need to assess the individual's risks and needs, and this is carried out in the first weeks of a woman's prison placement.

Assessment and Classification

Assessment and classification systems are central to daily jail and prison operations, a fact underscored in Chapter 6. What should the assessment and classification systems for a women's prison look like? How should they differ from the ones employed in a men's facility, or should they? There are about a half-dozen assessment and classification instruments commonly used for both males and females. With respect to assessing risk, for example, the Level of Service Inventory for adults and the Youth Level of Service are considered gender-neutral tools and are used to identify an individual's risk and needs. The question that some policymakers have asked, however, is whether some factors, such as substance abuse, present the same risk for prison misconduct or recidivism for males and females. These gender-neutral instruments are widely used by state correctional systems, parole boards, as well as community corrections agencies, so it is important that they correctly identify an individual's risks and needs.

Gender-neutral assessment tools have been criticized by some researchers because they do not consider the different pathways that women take in their involvement in crime and the lower risks they pose. These considerations have implications for the people being assessed. When the same tool is used for male and female populations there is a possibility that women are being assessed as having higher risks. If testing reveals that a woman receives a higher than warranted score, she might be required to participate in programs that will keep her incarcerated longer or be placed in a higher security living unit than she needs. Olver and Wong (2019) tell us that the research on this issue is mixed, as some studies have supported the need for separate instruments, while other studies have shown that gender-neutral instruments are accurate. Importantly, Scott, Brown, and Wanamaker (2019) examined this issue using large samples of incarcerated males and females; they did not find that women were being overclassified.

Van Voorhis (2013, p. 47) developed a table showing three different types of risk factors: (a) risk factors that are similar for men and women, (b) gender-responsive risk factors, and (c) gender-responsive strengths. Table 11.5 shows that there is a common set of factors that men and women share. Except for criminal history, which is something that cannot be changed, the remaining risk factors are all dynamic, which means that

TABLE 11.5 Risk Factors by Correctional Setting

Predict Serious Prison Misconducts	Predict Arrests/Parole Failures	Predict Arrests/ Probation Failures
Risk Factors that Are Similar for Men and Women		
Criminal history	Criminal history	Criminal history
Antisocial friends	Employment/financial	Employment/financial
Substance abuse	Antisocial friends	Antisocial friends
	Substance abuse	Substance abuse
Gender-Responsive Risk Factors, Predictive for Women		
Anger	Housing safety	Housing safety
Depression	Anger	Anger
Serious mental illness	Depression	Abuse
Abuse	Serious mental illness	Parental stress
Unhealthy relationships	Abuse	
	Unhealthy relationships	
Gender-Responsive Strengths		
Self-efficacy (one's confidence in achieving goals)	Family support	Educational assets
	Self-efficacy	Family support
		Self-efficacy
		Parental involvement

Source: Van Voorhis (2013).

they can be changed. Thus, while we can't change our age at a first arrest, we can replace our antisocial friends (such as gang members) with people who have more conventional values and beliefs. With respect to gender-specific assessment tools, Scott, Brown, and Wanamaker (2019) report that several assessment instruments for women have been developed, including the Women's Risk Needs Assessment and the Service Planning Instrument for Women. However, there is not a lot of evidence showing that these instruments are any better than the gender-neutral Level of Service Inventory. Given those results, this debate over the effectiveness of these assessments will continue. What is clearly needed is more carefully designed and implemented research on the usefulness of these tools.

A CLOSER LOOK

Prisoner Transports

Every prison system transfers inmates between institutions to ensure they are in facilities that best match their security or rehabilitative needs. In large states such as Florida or Texas these trips can take a week or longer (Colon, 2016). Many of these buses or transport vans will stop at local jails to pick up more sentenced inmates and drop them off at various prisons. When these buses are operated by federal or state employees, their inmates might be held overnight in a prison, whereupon the transfer continues the next day. But many prisoner transports are now being carried out by private operators. Some of the services delivered by these private operators, who receive very little oversight from any organization, are problematic.

The private firms transporting inmates have been criticized for hiring poorly trained or unprofessional guards who are paid only slightly more than the minimum wage, and transport these prisoners in unsafe conditions (Colon, 2016). A letter from three members of Congress alluded to their investigation of "unsanitary practices, gross negligence, physical and sexual abuse, and disturbing inattentiveness to the basic and urgent medical needs of incarcerated people" (Santo, 2019, para. 5). Inmates on these trips are often shackled together and sit on benches with no upholstery. With respect to feeding these prisoners, Colon reports that drivers will often go through the drive-through at fast food restaurants and purchase items from the dollar menu for these prisoners as their daily expenditure could not exceed four dollars per inmate.

Some of these transports mix women and men, including pregnant women. Instead of allowing their inmates to stay overnight in a secure facility, some privately owned transports drive through the night. Even something as simple as a bathroom break can become complicated during these trips as some companies only allowed their vans to stop at secure jails or police departments, and not at rest stops. Few police departments or jails, however, were interested in accommodating these inmates given their vulnerability to a lawsuit if one of them became sick or was injured in their facility.

Prisoner transports sometimes end in escapes and there is a long history of assaults and homicides occurring during these trips. Some inmates die from unknown causes. Furthermore, at least 14 women have alleged in court that they were raped by transport staff working for private companies (Hager & Santo, 2016, para. 14). Other prisoner transports have ended in collisions and in 2015, eight Texas prisoners and two state correctional officers were killed in a crash with a freight train (Associated Press, 2015). Altogether, like many of the issues raised in this book, something that sounds simple—moving a prisoner from point A to point B—can become complicated.

INMATE CULTURE IN WOMEN'S JAILS AND PRISONS

In Chapter 9 we looked at prison subcultures and we now turn our attention to how these inmate communities differ by gender. Although many similarities exist in all inmate communities, we know that women experience incarceration differently than men. Those perceptions of jail and prison life are shaped, in part, by their prior life experiences. We find prisonization in both women's and men's facilities and both experience the deprivations of incarceration. Comparisons of the pains of imprisonment of men and women, however, have found that women serving lengthy prison sentences have a more painful experience than men (Crewe, Hulley, & Wright, 2017). One key difference is that women suffer more when separated from their children. Some scholars have also found that women prisoners are more fearful than men (Pogrebin & Dodge, 2001).

Women also may be affected more than men by the shame of their confinement (Pogrebin & Dodge, 2001). Moreover, the everyday operations of a correctional facilities and the security practices including the use of strip searches and similarly embarrassing events, can traumatize some women. A participant in Pogrebin and Dodge's (2001, p. 538) study described her first hours in prison in the following way:

> I try to forget what it was like in prison most of the time. When I just got there they stripped me down and this guard did a full body search. I was shocked. I never had anyone touch me like that, especially with other guards just standing there watching me. Then they threw me these clothes and took me to a cell. While we were walking some girls were yelling names at me. It was the most scary thing I had ever seen.

Women prisoners also have a greater need for emotional supports in prison, and especially the need to bond with other women. This need is consistent with their other relational needs identified by gender-responsive scholars such as Bloom, Owen, and Covington (2003). Female inmates tend to be less criminalized than their male counterparts, that is, they generally have committed less serious crimes and were far less involved in criminal subcultures outside prison.

Cut off from their children and families and friends, some female prisoners appear to experience feelings of helplessness, powerlessness, dependency, and despair far more than their male peers. Conversely, where women maintain better social support networks with those living outside prison, especially their children, they experience fewer conflicts with prison administrators (Jiang & Winfree, 2006).

Like their male counterparts, female prisoners also live by an inmate code and adopt various social roles to cope with incarceration. Those roles, like those male inmates adopt, center on the exercise of power, the delivery of goods and services, and sexual relationships. In one of the first studies of the inmate culture in women's prisons, Heffernan (1972) employed Sykes's (1958) ideas about inmate culture blunting the pains of imprisonment. Heffernan found that about one-half of her participants she called *squares*, primarily women who were situational offenders, "good Christian women" who wanted to correct their mistakes through good deeds and clean living. Some female

inmates, however, were in the life—that is, they were leading the same antisocial lives in prison that they led on the streets. Prison life was not going to change them. Their defiant attitudes and lengthy experiences with the criminal justice system demanded that they adopt an oppositional and anti-institutional perspective. Still others manipulated other inmates to make their own time pass more quickly and easily. These roles, argued Heffernan, were largely extensions of the women's pre-prison identities.

PHOTO 11.5
Minimum security women prisoners are often placed in cells that hold four or more people. Such living situations can serve to retraumatize women already suffering from psychological problems. Credit: Mikael Karlsson/Alamy Stock Photo.

Owen's (1998) study of the Central California Women's Facility, which is the largest women's prison in the United States, is an important addition to our understanding of women's experiences behind bars. The term she used to describe the defiance exhibited by certain inmates was **the mix**. According to Owen (1998, p. 3), the mix "is characterized by a continuation of the behavior that led to imprisonment, a life revolving around drugs, intense, volatile, and often destructive relationships and non-rule abiding behavior." Like Heffernan, Owen also believes that women's lives in prison are closely tied to their lives before and predictive of their post-release lives. Females in prisons, especially the economically or racially marginalized, have much in common with male inmates. However, women also face the challenges generated by pervasive sexual and personal oppression. Surviving the mix, or making it in prison and on the outside, is a constant struggle for some women. For others, whom Owen describes as a small minority of women inmates, the lure and excitement of the life—drugs, fighting, and volatile intimate relationships—are hard to resist.

The functions of the inmate subculture in prisons for men and women are generally viewed as different. The subculture in men's prisons exists largely to protect inmates from one another; it also helps to neutralize the social rejection associated with incarceration and provides a buffer between inmates and staff. In women's prisons, by contrast, the subculture exists for these reasons plus one more: emotional support. In terms of the inmate subculture in women's facilities, one important contrast is that there are fewer gang members in women's jails or prisons.

Inmate codes also provide stability and predictability in women's correctional facilities. McGuire (2011) describes how the code in a women's prison promoted values like those in a men's facility, including the prevention of theft as a way of reducing conflict and the reduction of snitching. In recognition of the different relational priorities of women, McGuire found that inmates were more likely to become involved in violent incidents when they were disrespectful to other prisoners, invaded another person's space, or if they violated the privacy of other prisoners by gossiping or making comments about other prisoners' time. Like in a male prison, the inmates did not want to be seen as a pushover, so they felt compelled to act violently if they believed that others were disrespectful or trying to take advantage of them.

In an important book examining safety in women's facilities, Owen, Wells, and Pollock (2017) point out that women experience prison life differently than men owing to prison pathways defined by their marginalization and lifetime histories of victimization. Once admitted to prison many women confront the same challenges they experienced in the community: the threats of emotional, physical, and sexual abuse as well as having limited choices in their efforts to live in a safe environment. As a result, living in prison for some women is an extension of community life, and they may feel powerless to cope with the challenges. When describing inmate or prison culture, Owen, Wells, and Pollock (2017, p. 2) introduce the concept of **prison capital**, which they define as any "type of resource, or access to a desired resource, that can keep a woman safe while she does her time" and they describe "social capital (who you know)" and "human capital (what you know)." Other forms of prison capital include economic (e.g. access to resources), cultural (e.g. respect and reputation), and emotional capital (e.g. increasing their well-being). Women who accumulate a greater amount of prison capital may find it easier to complete their sentences. Marginalized women with less prison capital, by contrast, will have a tougher time surviving prison.

One way that women have increased their ability to obtain support is by creating **pseudo-families**, also called **play families**, where different inmates assume various familial roles, including spouse, parent, child, sibling, or grandparent. Some of these relationships are very formal. As Owen (1998, p. 8) observes:

> These relationships with other prisoners mediate how women learn to do their time and may also provide some protection from the self-destruction of the mix. Thus, surviving the mix is grounded in a woman's ability to develop a satisfying and productive routine within the prison and the nature of her relationships with other prisoners.

Pollock (2002) says pseudo-families are less important today than in the past, and although they exist today, there seems to be a movement away from sexual relationships in favor of extended social support networks. About this topic, Wulf-Ludden (2016) found that participating in such relationships can provide acceptance, companionship, emotional and economic support, comfort, affection, security, and help these women achieve stability in their relationships while reducing loneliness. Although these relationships can provide positive supports, some inmates repeat the same behaviors that led to dysfunctional relationships on the streets, and this can contribute to conflict. Not unlike a gang, conflicts and violence could also arise when a family member needed to be protected from other inmates (Kolb & Palys, 2018).

SUMMARY

Women in corrections systems must confront issues, setbacks, challenges, and general neglect unlike those faced by men. The following are among the key points presented in this chapter:

- The absolute number of women under correctional supervision has increased dramatically since 1978.
- The number of prison admissions of White women has increased by over one-half since 2000, while the number of African American women admissions has dropped by nearly one-half.

- Women experience the pains of imprisonment that equal or exceed those of men.
- The pathways to women's imprisonment are different than for men, and typically involve exposure to abuse, traumatic events and addictions.
- Incarcerated women are more likely to suffer from addictions as well as physical and mental health problems than male prisoners.
- There is a lack of consensus about the need for gender-specific assessment and classification instruments.
- A number of gender-responsive interventions are being developed to respond to the distinctive needs of women who have committed crimes.
- The culture of women's prisons may also be in a state of flux, as increasing demands are made on a system whose resources are not keeping pace with its changing population.
- There is a growing interest in offering evidence-based gender-responsive programs to women who have been convicted of committing crimes.
- Whereas once women's issues were neglected due to their small numbers—relative to men jail inmates or prisoners—there is now more interest in developing programs and practices that respond to their needs.

Altogether, our review of women's incarceration reveals that their pathways to becoming involved in the justice system are different than what happens with men. As a result, they often require different supports and programs while incarcerated. Although we know that their risks and needs are different, correctional systems have often fallen short when it comes to delivering gender-responsive programs to these women.

KEY TERMS

- Bangkok Rules
- chivalry
- culturally competent
- evil woman hypothesis
- gender-responsive (gender informed)
- Mandela Rules
- pathways to crime
- play families
- prison capital
- pseudo-families
- reformatory
- relational theory
- re-traumatize
- strip search
- survival strategies
- the mix

THINKING ABOUT CORRECTIONAL POLICIES AND PRACTICES: WRITING ASSIGNMENTS

1. In a short essay describe the evolution of women's corrections programs to their current state.
2. Describe why (or why not) women have different pathways to prison than men.
3. What are some factors that differentiate men and women prisoners?
4. Prepare a one-page paper describing the key points of gender-responsive corrections.
5. In a two-page paper compare the inmate culture in male and female prisons.

CRITICAL REVIEW QUESTIONS

1. Describe the key differences in the types of arrests that occur between men and women.
2. What explains the lower rates of involvement of women at all points in the criminal justice system?
3. What does the term malestream criminology mean to you?
4. What are some common factors in the different types of pathways to crime?
5. The standards for women's imprisonment for all countries are laid out in the Bangkok Rules. Should Americans follow these rules? Why or why not?
6. Provide a working definition of gender-responsive strategies.
7. What is the key idea behind the concept of trauma-informed correctional care?
8. What are some potential shortcomings of using the same assessment and prison classification instruments for male and female offenders?
9. What are the similarities between the inmate code in male and female corrections?
10. Why would incarcerated women form pseudo or play families?

REFERENCES

Abrams, L. S., & Curran, L. (2000). Wayward girls and virtuous women: Social workers and female juvenile delinquency in the progressive era. *Affilia, 15*(1), 49–64.

Adler, F. (1975). *Sisters in crime: The rise of the new female criminal.* New York: McGraw-Hill.

Arisco, A. (2014). Trauma-informed correctional care. *ACEs Connection.* Retrieved from https://www.acesconnection.com/blog/trauma-informed-correctional-care-ticc

Associated Press. (2015, January 14). 10 killed in prison bus crash in West Texas. *NBCDFW*. Retrieved from https://www.nbcdfw.com/news/local/Officials-Prison-Bus-Involved-in-Fatal-Wreck-288552971.html

Balaban, E., & Kuhik, L. (2019). No one should be forced to give birth alone in a jail cell. *American Civil Liberties Union*. Received from https://www.aclu.org/blog/prisoners-rights/women-prison/no-one-should-be-forced-give-birth-alone-jail-cell

Barszewski, L. (2019, June 4). Outrage grows over pregnant inmate left alone for hours while giving birth. *South Florida Sun Sentinel*. Retrieved from https://www.sun-sentinel.com/local/broward/fl-ne-broward-pregnant-inmate-ignored-controversy-20190604-ohshqjtww5ee3charq6tr34iv4-story.html

Beck, A. J., Rantala, R. R., & Rexroat, J. (2014). *Sexual victimization reported by adult correctional authorities, 2009–11*. Washington, DC: Bureau of Justice Statistics.

Bloom, B., Owen, B., & Covington, S. (2003). *Gender-responsive strategies: Research, practice, and guiding principles for women offenders*. Washington, DC: National Institute of Corrections.

Branstetter, Z., Herrera, A., Rowan, H., & Sagara, E. (2018). Let down and locked up: Why Oklahoma's female incarceration is so high. *Reveal*. Retrieved from https://www.revealnews.org/article/let-down-and-locked-up-why-oklahomas-female-incarceration-is-so-high/

Brennan, T. (2015). *A women's typology of pathways to serious crime with custody and treatment implications*. Retrieved from http://go.volarisgroup.com/rs/volarisgroup/images/Women-Typology-Descriptions-Gender-Responsive-4-15.pdf

Bronson, J., & Brzofsky, M. (2017). *Indicators of mental health problems reported by prisoners and jail inmates, 2011–12*. Washington, DC: Bureau of Justice Statistics.

Bronson, J., & Carson, E. A. (2019). *Prisoners in 2017*. Washington, DC: Bureau of Justice Statistics.

Bronson, J., Maruschak, L. M., & Berzofsky, M. (2015). *Disabilities among prison and jail inmates, 2011–12*. Washington, DC: Bureau of Justice Statistics.

Bronson, J., Stroop, J., Zimmer, S., & Berzofsky, M. (2017). *Drug use, dependence, and abuse among state prisoners and jail inmates, 2007–2009*. Washington, DC: Bureau of Justice Statistics.

Bronson, J., & Sufrin, C. (2019). Pregnant women in prison and jail don't count: Data gaps on maternal health and incarceration. *Public Health Reports, 134*(1), 57S–62S.

Bureau of Justice Statistics. (2019). *Corrections statistical analysis tool (CSAT) – prisoners*. Retrieved from https://www.bjs.gov/index.cfm?ty=nps

Butler, A. M. (1997). *Gendered justice in the American west: Women prisoners in men's penitentiaries*. Urbana: University of Illinois Press.

Chesney-Lind, M. (1973). Judicial enforcement of the female sex role. *Criminology, 8*(1), 51–69.

Cho, A., & Tasca, M. (2018). Disparities in women's prison sentences: Exploring the nexus between motherhood, drug offense, and sentence length. *Feminist Criminology*. Available online ahead of print at: doi:10.1177/1557085118773434

Colon, F. (2016, July 7). The horrible things I saw driving a van packed with prisoners. *Vice*. Retrieved from https://www.vice.com/en_ca/article/xdm83q/depressing-prison-transport-van-driver-darkness-america

Covington, S. S., & Bloom, B. E. (2007). Gender responsive treatment and services in correctional settings. *Women & Therapy, 29*(3–4), 9–33.

Crewe, B., Hulley, S., & Wright, S. (2017). The gendered pains of life imprisonment. *British Journal of Criminology, 57*(6), 1359–1378.

Daly, K. (1992). Women's pathways to felony court: Feminist theories of lawbreaking and problems of representation. *Southern California Review of Law and Women's Studies, 2*(1), 11–52.

Death Penalty Information Center. (2020). *Facts about the death penalty (March 12, 2020)*. Retrieved from https://files.deathpenaltyinfo.org/documents/pdf/FactSheet.f1562867044.pdf

DeHart, D. D. (2018). Women's pathways to crime: A heuristic typology of offenders. *Criminal Justice and Behavior, 45*(10), 1461–1482.

Derbes, B. J. (2013). "Secret horrors": Enslaved women and children in the Louisiana state penitentiary, 1833–1862. *The Journal of African American History, 98*(2), 277–290.

Doerner, J. K., & Demuth, S. (2014). Gender and sentencing in the federal courts: Are women treated more leniently? *Criminal Justice Policy Review, 25*(2), 242–269.

Duwe, G. (2017). *Rethinking prison: A strategy for evidence-based reform*. Washington, DC: American Enterprise Institute.

Ellison, J. M., Steiner, B., & Wright, E. M. (2018). Examining the sources of violent victimization among jail inmates. *Criminal Justice and Behavior, 45*(11), 1723–1741.

Federal Bureau of Investigation. (2018). *Crime in the United States, 2017 (Table 33)*. Retrieved from https://ucr.fbi.gov/crime-in-the-u.s/2017/crime-in-the-u.s.-2017/topic-pages/tables/table-33/

Franklin, C. A., & Fearn, N. E. (2008). Gender, race, and formal court decision-making outcomes: Chivalry/paternalism, conflict theory or gender conflict? *Journal of Criminal Justice, 36*(3), 279–290.

Freud, S. (1933). *New introductory lectures on psychoanalysis*. New York: Norton.

Garcia, S. E. (2019, May 7). Ordeal of woman who gave birth in Florida jail cell prompts internal investigation. *The New York Times*. Retrieved from https://www.nytimes.com/2019/05/07/us/woman-gives-birth-jail-cell.html

Gleicher, L. (2017). Implementation science in criminal justice: How implementation of evidence-based programs and practices affects outcomes. *Illinois Criminal Justice Information Authority*. Retrieved from http://www.icjia.state.il.us/articles/implementation-science-in-criminal-justice-how-implementation-of-evidence-based-programs-and-practices-affects-outcomes

Gobeil, R., Blanchette, K., & Stewart, L. (2016). A meta-analytic review of correctional interventions for women offenders. Gender-neutral versus gender-informed approaches. *Criminal Justice and Behavior, 43*(3), 301–322.

Green, B. L., Miranda, J., Daroowalla, A., & Siddique, J. (2005). Trauma exposure, mental health functioning, and program needs of women in jail. *Crime & Delinquency, 51*(1), 133–151.

Hager, E. (2017). A mass incarceration mystery. *The Marshall Project*. Retrieved from https://www.themarshallproject.org/2017/12/15/a-mass-incarceration-mystery

Hager, E., & Santo, A. (2016, July 6). Inside the deadly world of private prisoner transport. *The Marshall Project*. Retrieved from https://www.themarshallproject.org/2016/07/06/inside-the-deadly-world-of-private-prisoner-transport

Harris, A. (2018, April 30). Women in prison take home economics, while men take carpentry. *The Atlantic*. Retrieved from https://www.theatlantic.com/education/archive/2018/04/the-continuing-disparity-in-womens-prison-education/559274/

Harris, M. K. (1998). Women's imprisonment in the United States: A historical analysis of female offenders through the early 20th century. *Corrections Today*, December, 74–78, 80.

Heffernan, E. (1972). *Making it in prison: The square, the cool and the life.* New York: Wiley.

Jiang, S., & Winfree, L. T., Jr. (2006). Social support, gender, and inmate adjustment to prison life: Insights from a national sample. *The Prison Journal, 86*(1), 32–55.

Jones, M. (2015). *Women's prison history: The undiscovered country.* Retrieved from https://www. historians.org/publications-and-directories/perspectives-on-history/february-2015/womens-prison-history

Kaba, M., & Russo, A. (2014). *Violence against women and criminalization of women historical timeline.* Retrieved from https://issuu.com/projectnia/docs/vaw-prison-timeline-2

Kaeble, D. (2018). *Probation and parole in the United States, 2016.* Washington, DC: Bureau of Justice Statistics.

Karlsson, M. E., & Zielinski, M. J. (2020). Sexual victimization and mental health prevalence rates among incarcerated women: A literature review. *Trauma, Violence, and Abuse, 21*(2), 326–349.

Kasdan, D. (2009). Abortion access for incarcerated women: Are correctional health practices in conflict with constitutional standards? *Viewpoint, 41*(1), 59–62.

Kim, B., Wang, X., & Cheon, H. (2019). Examining the impact of ecological contexts on gender disparity in federal sentencing. *Justice Quarterly, 36*(3), 466–502.

King, E. A. (2017). Outcomes of trauma-informed interventions for incarcerated women: A review. *International Journal of Offender Therapy and Comparative Criminology, 61*(6), 667–688.

King, E., & Foley, J. E. (2014). *Gender-responsive policy development in corrections: What we know and roadmaps for change.* Washington, DC: National Institute of Corrections.

Kolb, A., & Palys, T. (2018). Playing the part: Pseudo-families, wives, and the politics of relationships in women's prisons in California. *The Prison Journal, 98*(6), 678–699.

Kreis, M. K. F., Gillings, K., Svanberg, J., & Schwannauer, M. (2016). Relational pathways to substance misuse and drug-related offending in women: The role of trauma, insecure attachment, and shame. *International Journal of Forensic Mental Health, 15*(1), 35–47.

Kubiak, S. P., Covington, S. S., & Hillier, C. (2017). Trauma-informed corrections. In D. Springer & A. Roberts (Eds.), *Social work in juvenile and criminal justice system, 4th edition* (pp. 92–104). Springfield, IL: Charles C. Thomas.

Lambert, J. (2019, March 21). Pregnant behind bars: What we do and don't know about pregnancy and incarceration. *National Public Radio.* Retrieved from https://www.npr.org/sections/health-shots/2019/03/21/705587775/pregnant-behind-bars-what-we-do-and-dont-know-about-pregnancy-and-incarceration

Lilly, J. R., Cullen, F. T., & Ball, R. A. (2019). *Criminological theory: Context and consequences, 7th edition.* Los Angeles, CA: Sage.

Lombroso, C. (1876). *L'uomo delinquent [The criminal man].* Milan: Hoepli.

Maruschak, L. M. (2006). *Medical problems of jail inmates.* Washington, DC: Bureau of Justice Statistics.

Maruschak, L. M., Berzofsky, M., & Unangst, J. (2015). *Medical problems of state and federal prisoners and jail inmates, 2011–12.* Washington, DC: Bureau of Justice Statistics.

Mays, G. L., & Ruddell, R. (2019). *Making sense of criminal justice, 3rd edition.* New York: Oxford University Press.

McGuire, M. D. (2011). Doing the life: An exploration of the connection between the inmate code and violence among female inmates. *Journal of the Institute of Justice International Studies, 11*(1), 145–158.

National Resource Center on Justice Involved Women. (2014). *Using trauma-informed practices to enhance safety and security in women's correctional facilities.* Retrieved from http://www.ncdsv. org/images/NRCJIW_Using-Trauma-Informed-Practices-to-enhance-safety-and-security-in-women's-correctional-facilities_4-2014.pdf

Newman, G. (2008). *The punishment response, 2nd edition.* Piscataway, NJ: Transaction publishers.

Nowacki, J. S. (2019). Gender equity and sentencing outcomes: An examination of state courts. *Criminal Justice Policy Review.* Available online ahead of print at: doi:10.1177/0887403419840804.

Oliver, P. (2018). *Education and poverty as factors in white and black rural and urban prison admission rates.* Retrieved from https://osf.io/preprints/socarxiv/xzq7w/

Olver, M. E., & Wong, S. C. P. (2019). Offender risk and need assessment: Theory, research, and application. In D. L. L. Polaschek, A. Day, & C. R. Hollin (Eds.), *The Wiley international handbook of correctional psychology* (pp. 461–474). New York: Wiley.

Owen, B. (1998). *"In the mix": Struggle and survival in a women's prison.* Albany: State University of New York Press.

Owen, B., Wells, J., & Pollock, J. (2017). *In search of safety: Confronting inequality in women's imprisonment.* Oakland: University of California Press.

Penal Reform International. (2013). *UN Bangkok rules on women offenders and prisoners.* London: Author.

Penal Reform International. (2016). *The revised United Nations standard minimum rules for the treatment of prisoners (Nelson Mandela rules).* London, UK.

Pogrebin, M. R., & Dodge, M. (2001). Women's accounts of their prison experiences: A retrospective view of their subjective realities. *Journal of Criminal Justice, 29*(6), 531–541.

Pollock, J. (2002). *Women, prison, and crime, 2nd edition.* Belmont, CA: Wadsworth.

Pupovac, J., & Lydersen, K. (2018, October 14). Women in prison punished more harshly than men around the country. *Chicago Reporter.* Retrieved from https://www.chicagoreporter.com/women-in-prison-punished-more-harshly-than-men-around-the-country/

Rabin, C., & Smiley, D. (2019, May 6). Mentally ill woman gave birth alone in isolated jail cell, Broward public defender says. *Miami Herald.* Retrieved from https://www.miamiherald.com/article230002894.html

Rafter, N. H. (1985). Gender, prisons, and prison history. *Social Science History, 9*(3), 233–247.

Rantala, R. R. (2018). *Sexual victimization reported by adult correctional authorities, 2012–15.* Washington, DC: Bureau of Justice Statistics.

Reaves, B. (2013). *Felony defendants in large urban counties, 2009.* Washington, DC: Bureau of Justice Statistics.

Reid, J., & Loughran, T. A. (2019). Parallel-process trajectories of exposure to violence and psychological distress among justice-involved youth. *Criminal Behavior and Mental Health, 29*(1), 74–84.

Rodda, J., & Beichner, D. (2017). Identifying programmatic needs of women detainees in a jail environment. *Journal of Offender Rehabilitation, 56*(6), 373–393.

Romain, D. M., & Freiburger, T. L. (2016). Chivalry revisited: Gender, race/ethnicity, and offense type on domestic violence charge reduction. *Feminist Criminology, 11*(2), 191–222.

Santo, A. (2019, February 28). Members of congress seek answers from prisoner transport company. *The Marshall Project.* Retrieved from https://www.themarshallproject.org/2019/02/28/congress-seeks-answers-from-prisoner-transport-company

Sawyer, W., & Bertram, W. (2018) Jail will separate 2.3 million mothers from their children this year. *Prison Policy Initiative*. Retrieved from https://www.prisonpolicy.org/blog/2018/05/13/mothers-day-2018/

Scott, T., Brown, S. L., Wanamaker, K. A. (2019). Female offenders: Trends, effective practices, and ongoing debates. In D. L. L. Polaschek, A. Day, & C. R. Hollin (Eds.), *The Wiley international handbook of correctional psychology* (pp. 297–314). New York: Wiley.

Segal, A. F., Winfree, L. T., & Friedman, S. (2019). *Mental health and criminal justice*. Alphen aan den Rijn, The Netherlands: Wolters Kluwer.

Selman, K. J., & Dunn, M. (2018). Western feminist criminologies: Critiquing "malestream" criminology and beyond. In R. A. Triplett (Ed.), *The handbook of the history and philosophy of criminology* (pp. 255–271), New York: John Wiley & Sons.

Simon, R. J. (1975). *Women and crime*. Lexington, MA: Heath.

Stensrud, R. H., Gilbride, D. D., & Bruinekool, R. M. (2019). The childhood to prison pipeline: Early childhood trauma as reported by a prison population. *Rehabilitation Counseling Bulletin, 62*(4), 195–208.

Streib, V. (1990). Death penalty for female offenders. *University of Cincinnati Law Review, 58*(3), 845–880.

Subramanian, R., Henrichson, C., & Kang-Brown, J. (2015). *In our own backyard: Confronting growth and disparities in American jails*. New York: Vera Institute of Justice.

Substance Abuse and Mental Health Services Administration. (2013). *Creating a trauma-informed criminal justice system for women*. Rockville, MD: Author.

Sufrin, C. (2019). When the punishment is pregnancy: Carceral restriction of abortion in the United States. *Cultural Anthropology, 34*(1), 34–40.

Sun Sentinel Editorial Board. (2020, March 13). For pregnant women in jail, a measure of dignity comes far too late. *Sun Sentinel*. Retrieved from https://www.sun-sentinel.com/opinion/editorials/fl-op-edit-dignity-and-respect-for-pregnant-women-in-jail-20200313-wk2yzm6f6fh55g-p5ab7nglxrai-story.html

Swavola, E., Riley, K., & Subramanian, R. (2017). *Overlooked: Women and jails in an era of reform*. New York: Vera Institute of Justice.

Sykes, G. M. (1958). *The society of captives: A study of a maximum security prison*. Princeton, NJ: Princeton University Press.

Tchekmedyian, A. (2019, July 16). Women in jail endured group strip searches. L.A. County to pay $53 million to settle suit. *Los Angeles Times*. Retrieved from https://www.latimes.com/local/lanow/la-me-ln-lasd-womens-jail-settlement-20190716-story.html

The Crime Report. (2019, July 5). NYPD revises rules on shackling pregnant women. *The Crime Report*. Retrieved from https://thecrimereport.org/2019/07/05/nypd-revises-rules-on-shackling-pregnant-women/

Tripodi, S. J., Mennicke, A. M., McCarter, S. A., & Ropes, K. (2019). Evaluating seeking safety for women in prison: A randomized controlled trial. *Research on Social Work Practice, 29*(3), 281–290.

U.S. Department of Justice. (2018). *Review of the federal Bureau of Prisons' management of its female inmate population*. Washington, DC: Office of the Inspector General.

U.S. General Accounting Office. (1980). *Women in prison: Inequitable treatment requires action*. Washington, DC: Author.

Van Voorhis, P. (2013). *Women's risk factors and new treatments/interventions for addressing them: Evidence-based interventions in the United States and Canada.* Retrieved from https://nicic.gov/womens-risk-factors-and-new-treatmentsinterventions-addressing-them-evidence-based-interventions

Walt, L. C., Hunter, B., Salina, D., & Jason, L. (2014). Romance, recovery and community re-entry for criminal justice involved women: Conceptualizing and measuring intimate relationship factors and power. *Journal of Gender Studies, 23*(4), 409–421.

Washington State Institute for Public Policy. (2019). *Benefit-cost results (Dec. 2019).* Retrieved from http://www.wsipp.wa.gov/BenefitCost?topicId=2

Winfree, L. T., & DeJong, C. (2015). Police and the war on women: A gender linked examination behind and in front of the blue curtain. *Women & Criminal Justice, 25*(1), 50–70.

Wulf-Ludden, T. (2016). Pseudofamilies, misconduct, and the utility of general strain theory in a women's prison. *Women & Criminal Justice, 26*(4), 233–259.

Young, V. D. (2001). All the women in the Maryland state penitentiary: 1812–1869. *The Prison Journal, 8*(1), 113–132.

Zeng, Z. (2019). *Jail inmates in 2017.* Washington, DC: Bureau of Justice Statistics.

Chapter 12
Corrections Law and Inmate Litigation

OUTLINE

OBJECTIVES

After reading this chapter you will be able to:

- Explain how inmates' access to the courts has changed

- Describe the range of issues related to inmate lawsuits

- Explain the legal dimensions of the death penalty

- Describe the potential for the future of inmate lawsuits

CASE STUDY

"Cooked to Death" in a Texas Prison

Allen Webb was a 50-year-old with developmental disabilities who was serving a sentence in an East Texas prison for drunk driving when he died on 4 August 2011. Correctional officers (COs) found him lying on the concrete floor in his underwear when they were doing rounds in the middle of the night. His death was attributed to excessive heat, and Ward (2013) explains that ten Texas inmates died during a six-week period in July and August 2011 from heat-related illnesses. Only a small proportion of Texas prisons have units with air conditioning, and Webb's cell was not one of them. How bad were the conditions? Chammah (2017) reports that when his brother and mother visited Webb several months before his death, he was complaining about the excessive heat in his cell. While his family visited they bought him several cans of soda, which he quickly drank. When asked why he didn't buy soda from the commissary, Webb told his brother that the cans would explode in his cell due to the excessive heat.

Providing air conditioning to prisoners is controversial. Politicians do not want to provide inmates with comforts, such as air conditioning, that some taxpayers can't afford. While the public does not have much sympathy for these prisoners, people living in the free world can take steps to escape the heat by getting "cold water, to go to a mall, to go to a movie theater…to take action to mitigate the effect of heat on them" says a lawyer who has sued prison systems for their failure to provide adequate living conditions (Roth, 2014, para. 10). By contrast, prisoners can be locked in their cells for 23 or more hours a day and if there is no air circulation in the cell—or windows or fans—the conditions can be stifling. When it is 100 degrees outside, it is even hotter inside and some inmates report their cellblocks are like ovens and they have no way of escaping the heat. Although prison administrators promise to make fans, cool showers, and cold drinking water available to the prisoners, these promises are sometimes broken (Clarke & Zoukis, 2018).

The problem of overheated jails and prisons is not limited to Texas. Holt (2015) points out that extreme heat is the most common weather-related cause of death for the public throughout the nation. When he took a closer look at jail inmates and state prisoners, he found that many were living in overcrowded conditions in poorly maintained and outdated facilities which makes them difficult to cool. If prisoners lack air conditioning, the facility administrators sometimes use fans for cooling, but some prisoner advocates say that these fans are placed in the areas where the COs work, and inmates receive little benefit from them. Some prisons lacking air conditioning in the prisoner's living units provide air conditioning to the workers in the administrative areas (Clarke & Zoukis, 2018).

As noted in previous chapters, prisoners have access to the courts to challenge their living conditions when they constitute cruel and unusual punishment. In a federal lawsuit that addressed the issue of prison air conditioning, a federal court recognized that three types of people are vulnerable to injury or death from excessive heat including (a) people suffering from diabetes, heart problems, high blood pressure, high cholesterol, some mental health disorders, and obesity; (b) individuals taking prescription medications that dehydrate them such as anticonvulsants, antidepressants, medications for heart disease, and diuretics (which reduce water retention); and (c) people over 65 years of age (*Yates v. Collier*, 2017). The medications that Allen Webb took for his health problems placed him at higher risk for injury.

Prisoners are not the only people who suffer behind bars: COs in Texas have filed lawsuits to force their employer to provide air conditioning as many suffer from the same physical health conditions as the inmates they supervise. In addition to advocating for healthier working conditions, the officers say that prisoners are harder to manage when they are uncomfortably hot as there are more acts of misconduct.

So, what about Allen Webb? In 2013 his family filed a lawsuit and the Texas Department of Criminal Justice ultimately paid them $600,000. Another eight families were also awarded damages because their relatives died due to heat-related causes in Texas prisons (Clarke & Zoukis, 2018). Despite these payouts, the Texas prison system has been slow to improve the living conditions in their facilities. An editorial in the *Dallas Morning News* (2019) points out that the state spent $7 million defending a lawsuit from inmates in one prison, but lost the case and was required to spend $4 million in legal fees, and it still was required to install air conditioning. The editors questioned the wisdom of spending almost twice as much to defend a lawsuit compared with the cost of improving prisoners' living conditions. If our climate continues to become warmer, it is likely that lawsuits arguing that a lack of air conditioning amounts to cruel and unusual punishment will continue to be filed.

Critical Questions

1. What does our indifference to prisoner welfare tell us about our society?
2. How would you argue that a prisoner is more deserving of air conditioning than an elderly person in the community who cannot afford that comfort?
3. As a family member of a prisoner who is living in dangerous conditions, what steps would you take to improve his or her life?

INTRODUCTION

"Prisons have traditionally been closed organizations, and it has been difficult for citizens in the outside world to learn about conditions inside them" (Rhodes, 1992, p. 215). In the past we built most correctional facilities in out-of-the-way rural locations where they were out-of-sight and out-of-mind. As we noted in Chapter 2, until the mid-1900s most of these

PHOTO 12.1

National Guard troops are guarding New Mexico prisoners who participated in the 1980 riot that claimed 33 lives. Prisons were rocked by riots and other uprisings throughout the 1970s and the early 1980s. Many believe that giving prisoners better access to the courts reduces riots as they have a legitimate way to raise their concerns. Credit: Buddy Mays/ Alamy Stock Photo.

places were almost self-sufficient and prisoners built and maintained many of these facilities, they grew the food and raised the animals that they would eat, and produced their own power. Thus, the organizational isolation was reinforced by geographic isolation. Moreover, the truth was that the public did not really want to know what was going on behind prison walls.

Our interest in corrections increased as prison riots erupted throughout the country starting in the late 1960s. Chase (2015, p. 74) describes how there were five prison riots in 1967; 15 in 1968, and between 1970 and 1972 there were 112 prison riots, including the deadly 1971 riot at New York's Attica Correctional Facility that claimed 39 lives, including 10 correctional personnel. By the time rioting broke out at the New Mexico State Penitentiary in 1980, policymakers and the general public understood that something was very wrong in the nation's prisons. The people wanted to know what was going on in these places and what could be done to solve the unrest and violence that was occurring. Rhodes (1992) observes that a number of problems were endemic to all corrections systems in the country: rising inmate populations, aging prison facilities, and restrictive state budgets. The public was also disillusioned after the release of a widely circulated report that questioned the effectiveness of prison rehabilitation (Martinson, 1974).

One way that positive changes could be made in correctional systems was through litigation. Beginning with cases like *Holt v. Sarver* (1970) and *Pugh v. Locke* (1976) courts in Arkansas, Alabama, and many other states challenged a broad range of prison conditions. Conditions in prisons gradually improved throughout the 1980s, and then seem to have stalled, showing that there were limits to the public's acceptance of how comfortable prisoners should be. Although the courts have placed lower limits on the amenities that prisoners ought to have, between 1980 and the end of 2019 inmates have filed about 950,000 lawsuits alleging violations of their civil rights (U.S. Courts, 2019).

In this chapter we trace the history of corrections litigation in the United States, especially the large body of cases relating to prisons and jails. Of particular interest is the concept of inmates' access to the courts and the issues addressed in inmate lawsuits. Finally we examine what may be the most important issue in contemporary corrections, the impact of 50 years of prisoner lawsuits.

THE HISTORY OF INMATE LITIGATION

Legislation, particularly at the federal level, has been an important instrument of social change for women and minority groups in the United States as they sought access to such issues as voting and equal pay for equal work. However, that method has not been as effective for jail and prison inmates. Instead, they have turned to the appellate courts since the 1970s to challenge the legitimacy of their convictions or their conditions of confinement. Corrections law has gone through four distinct periods of development. Call (1995, pp. 36–38) identified these eras as the hands-off period, before 1964; the rights period, from 1964 to 1978; and the deference period, from 1979 to 1996. We add a fourth period—the post Prison Litigation Reform Act era, from 1996 to the present—to account for legislation making it more difficult for inmates to initiate lawsuits.

The Hands-Off Period: 1871–1963

Any discussion of corrections law must begin with *Ruffin v. Commonwealth* (1871). In this Virginia case the court held that prisoners are slaves of the state and so have no more rights than slaves (Pereira, 2018). According to this ruling, people who have been imprisoned suffer a **civil death** in the wake of their conviction and imprisonment. In practical terms, this status means the courts were largely free to ignore pleas based on alleged deprivations of their rights and inmates were seen as having few, if any, constitutional rights. For almost a century following *Ruffin*, the courts took a hands-off approach toward prison policies and practices.

The courts justified their inaction on three grounds (Coles, 1987; Thomas, 1988). First, federal courts expressed some reluctance to intervene in corrections departments' affairs because those departments are state executive agencies (Collins, 2010). The U.S. Constitution established a federal system of government that gave the national and state governments distinct powers and authority. The judiciary cited the "division of responsibility between federal and state courts" (Mays, 1983, p. 29) to explain its failure to act. Others brought the separation of powers into the argument. They reasoned that the Constitution had divided authority among the three branches of government (executive, legislative, and judicial). It was improper, then, for a court—particularly a federal court—to tell a state corrections system how it should run its prisons. These interpretations may have been convenient, but they were not necessarily correct. Even in a federal system of government, jurisdictions overlap. In addition, the separation of powers served as a system of checks and balances on the conduct of each branch of government, restricting each branch's ability to operate without constraint.

Second, many judges were hesitant to get involved in prison litigation cases because they lacked corrections expertise. This gave prison administrators broad discretion, effectively shielding them from public scrutiny and judicial review. The third defense had to do with prison security. Corrections administrators maintained that court intervention would interfere with their authority and would reduce the ability of institutional personnel to operate safe prisons and the judiciary believed them.

The Rights Period: 1964–1978

By the early 1960s, attitudes were changing as groups that had been marginalized, such as racial minorities, women, resident aliens, and people with disabilities were laying claim to civil rights protections. In a sense, state prison inmates became another minority group wanting to expand their civil rights. In addition, by the 1960s, the effectiveness of public interest law was clear: in a number of landmark cases, activist groups, among them the National Association for the Advancement of Colored People (NAACP) and the American Civil Liberties Union (ACLU), had successfully used litigation to improve the conditions for some marginalized groups. Finally, both publicity and an increased sensitivity to **civil rights claims** made federal district and appellate courts more receptive to lawsuits from state prison inmates (Call, 1995).

The Supreme Court seemed particularly attentive to state prisoners' due process claims during this era. Call (1995, p. 38) takes issue with the assertion by some that during this period the Court was engaged in a "prisoners' rights revolution." Instead, he says that the Court recognized that prisoners had constitutional rights, and that those rights were equal to the rights of unconfined persons. Perhaps Chase (2015) is more accurate when he says that prisoners went from being slaves of the state to imprisoned citizens. Two Supreme Court cases in the early 1960s opened the door to prisoner litigation. The first, *Monroe v. Pape* (1961), simplified the procedures for suing state officials in federal court for alleged violations of constitutional rights. The other—*Cooper v. Pate* (1964)—raised the issue of the free exercise of religion by African American Muslim prisoners. In both of these cases, the Court held that the *Civil Rights Act of 1871* (known in the statutes as 42 USC 1983) provided an appropriate mechanism by which to challenge state actions.

With its decisions in *Monroe* and *Cooper*, the Supreme Court signaled its willingness to take a hands-on approach to state prison litigation. State prisoners now had two options for filing federal lawsuits. They could follow the traditional path, petitioning for a writ of habeas corpus, or they could travel a new path, filing a civil rights claim, or what lawyers and others call a **Section 1983 suit**. Inmates can also file tort claims, in which they allege negligence on the part of corrections personnel, but these claims typically are filed in state courts (Collins, 2010).

The Deference Period: 1979–1996

The deference period began with the Supreme Court's decision in *Bell v. Wolfish* (1979). In *Bell*, the prisoners argued that overcrowded conditions were unconstitutional, and the Court decided just one issue—cell size—in favor of the inmates; on four other issues the justices ruled for the corrections department. According to Call (1995, p. 39):

> In ruling against the inmates, the Court set the tone for the Deference Period. During this period, inmates would lose on most prisoners' rights issues before the Court, which would stress the need to give deference to the expertise of corrections officials.

Since the *Bell* decision, inmates have had few significant victories in court, and those have come only in case of the most blatant violations of prisoners' rights. In most cases, corrections agencies have been given wide latitude to exercise their authority.

The Post Prison Litigation Reform Act Era

Although there were few significant improvements in prison life due to lawsuits after 1979 prisoners continued to file lawsuits and the volume was increasing every year (U.S. Courts, 2019). Policymakers who wanted to be seen as "tough on crime" had little tolerance for jail and prison inmates who were challenging their living conditions. In the early 1990s the media began to report examples of frivolous prisoner lawsuits such as inmates who sued because they received broken cookies or were given crunchy rather smooth peanut butter. Missouri's Attorney General published a top ten list of frivolous prison lawsuits in 1995, including examples of prisoners who had filed lawsuits because they did not receive refills of Kool-Aid or were served margarine rather than butter (see Burnett, 1998, p. 199). In response to the growing number of lawsuits that were filed, Congress passed the *Prison Litigation Reform Act* (PLRA) in 1996, making it difficult for prisoners to file lawsuits. Schlanger (2017, p. 69) reports that "It increased filing fees, decreased attorneys' fees, and limited damages." As a result, the number of petitions for every 1,000 state inmates filed in federal district courts decreased sharply and this trend is shown in Figure 12.1.

PHOTO 12.2
Since the introduction of the Prison Litigation Reform Act in 1996 prisoners have had very few successful cases in the U.S. Supreme Court. Despite that lack of success, thousands of them file petitions and lawsuits in the federal courts in order to secure their release, and some reach the Supreme Court. Credit: Ian Dagnall/Alamy Stock Photo.

INMATE LITIGATION AND POSTCONVICTION RELIEF

We should note that inmates could choose the legal mechanism for bringing suit, the forum (type of court) for the suit, and the targets of litigation. For instance, a prisoner can challenge the actions of individual COs or officials—a superintendent, a warden, or the commissioner of corrections. Alternatively, a lawsuit can be broader, challenging the totality of institutional conditions under which the inmate is confined (Collins, 2010).

Access to the Courts

In habeas corpus appeals, inmates allege that their confinement is unjust and that the state must demonstrate why their incarceration should continue. Writs of habeas corpus challenge the legality of incarceration, and if a court substantiates a prisoner's allegations, he or she may be released. In its 1962–1963 term, the U.S. Supreme Court decided three cases—*Townsend v. Sain*, *Fay v. Noia*, and *Sanders v. United States*—that expanded habeas corpus relief for state prisoners. As a result, they became the primary legal mechanism for most prisoner's appeals.

As Figure 12.1 illustrates, habeas corpus petitions for every 1,000 state prisoners have decreased from 23 in 1980 to 11 in 2018 (a 52% drop). Most prisoners allege that there were deficiencies in one of eight areas: ineffective assistance of counsel, due process concerns, trial court error, Fifth Amendment protections, detention and punishment concerns, prosecutor misconduct, police misconduct, and charges to the jury. In order to qualify for habeas corpus review, the prisoner must be held in custody and exhaust all state remedies, including reviews by state appellate courts.

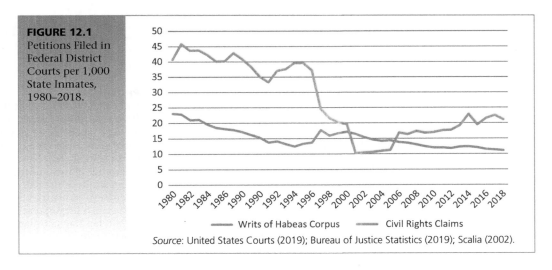

FIGURE 12.1 Petitions Filed in Federal District Courts per 1,000 State Inmates, 1980–2018.

Writs of Habeas Corpus   Civil Rights Claims

Source: United States Courts (2019); Bureau of Justice Statistics (2019); Scalia (2002).

Beginning in 1966, the U.S. Department of Justice began tracking civil rights actions as a separate category of prisoner claims. Figure 12.1 shows the number of these actions has been decreasing since peaking in 1982, with a high of 46 for every 1,000 prisoners to 21 in 2018, a drop of more than one-half (54%). At the lowest point in 2001, there were only 10 civil rights actions for every 1,000 prisoners, a drop of more than three-quarters from the peak. Before the courts will hear a Section 1983 action, there are a number of requirements that the prisoner must fulfill and are described by Collins (2010) as:

- The defendant must be a person—the courts have held that states and state agencies, including corrections departments, are not persons and so are immune from civil rights claims. However, cities and counties, if they are incorporated, are considered persons.
- The defendant must be acting under color of state law—the alleged violation must have occurred in the course of the defendant's employment with the government agency.
- The injury to the inmate-plaintiff must involve a violation of a protected right—the U.S. Constitution or a federal statute may protect the right. Often, allegations of injury or abuse are based on broad constitutional language—for example, the Eighth Amendment's prohibition against cruel and unusual punishment.
- The defendant (or defendants) must have been personally involved in the alleged injury. The exception to this item is **vicarious liability** (or supervisory liability, where employers are alleged to be responsible for the actions of their staff).

Supervisors are not automatically liable for the actions of their subordinates (Collins, 2010). Under two sets of circumstances—failure to train and failure to supervise—supervisors can become parties to Section 1983 suits. In these suits, the inmate-plaintiff must make a direct connection between the supervisor's action or failure to act and the resulting injury.

Decreasing Prisoner Litigation

As is readily apparent from Figure 12.1 prisoner litigation has decreased substantially since the 1980s and this drop can be attributed to three pieces of federal legislation that were intended to restrict prisoner access to the courts. In 1980, Congress passed the **Civil Rights of Institutionalized Persons Act (CRIPA)**. The intent of this law (in Section e) was to reduce the number of Section 1983 claims filed by state inmates by requiring prisoners to exhaust all state administrative remedies before filing a federal suit. As Figure 12.1 demonstrates, while the rate of these suits increased from 1980 to 1982, they decreased afterward, until they hit bottom in 2001.

CRIPA is also intended to protect the constitutional rights of people living in residential facilities (e.g. places caring for persons with developmental disabilities or mental illnesses), as well as juvenile facilities, jails, and prisons operated by local or state governments. The U.S. Department of Justice takes complaints about the living conditions in these places and the care these residents receive. They can act on these complaints by carrying out an investigation and they often attempt to resolve issues informally. In 2018 they received almost 4,000 letters, 128 emails, and about 500 phone calls (U.S. Department of Justice, 2019a, p. 9). The U.S. Department of Justice (2019a, p. 3) reports they were monitoring the operations of 106 facilities in 17 states as well as in Puerto Rico and the Virgin Islands.

Filing civil rights petitions, instead of writs of habeas corpus, came about because state inmates were not interested in using the federal courts to secure their release—as would be the case with habeas corpus petitions. Instead they were more interested in challenging their conditions of confinement. An equally plausible explanation is that the federal courts were demonstrating a lack of receptivity toward state prisoners' habeas corpus writs.

Second, in 1996 Congress passed the PLRA together with the **Antiterrorism and Effective Death Penalty Act (AEDPA)**. Both Acts were designed to reduce appeals in federal courts by prison inmates. The PRLA affirmed that state prisoners must exhaust all of their administrative remedies before filing a claim in a federal court and required inmates to pay appropriate appellate fees. The law did not take away inmates' rights to file *in forma pauperis* (as an indigent, or one who is destitute), but they could no longer claim indigence if two previous petitions had been dismissed as frivolous or malicious. The PLRA also required that there must be a showing of physical injury if the petitioner was claiming mental or emotional injury. The AEDPA set strict time limits for filing habeas corpus writs in federal courts and required that a federal appeals court panel approve habeas corpus petitions for filing in federal district courts.

After these acts became law the number of civil rights claims dropped almost immediately, but the number of habeas corpus claims was more stable. Three Supreme Court decisions—*Williams v. Taylor* (2000), *Lockyer v. Andrade* (2003), and *Harrington v. Richter* (2011)—placed further restrictions on habeas corpus claims (Astrada, 2019). Some scholars are critical of the efforts reducing the access of state prisoners to the federal courts. Adelman (2018, p. 97) says that:

> Once known as the Great Writ of Liberty, habeas corpus has become so extensively diminished that it is no longer a protection against unlawful imprisonment but rather an empty procedure that enables and may actually encourage state courts to disregard constitutional rights.

Astrada (2019) argues that habeas corpus can be liberty-enhancing or liberty-restricting, and the enactment of the AEDPA and the actions of the federal courts have supported the later approach. He contends that a liberty-enhancing approach is more desirable as it supports due process and fairness.

Inmate Grievances

One practice intended to minimize lawsuits was requiring prisoners to exhaust all administrative remedies prior to filing lawsuits. Schlanger (2003, p. 1628) says that "the exhaustion requirement has teeth because many courts have held that an inmate's failure to comply with the grievance system's rules (time limits, form, and so on) usually justifies disqualification of the inmate's lawsuit." Larger jails and all prison systems have grievance systems enabling inmates to make verbal or written complaints about shortcomings in the facility operations (most often related to their living conditions) or because of a prisoner's mistreatment, such as receiving inadequate health care, or claims of excessive force used by correctional personnel. According to the National Institute of Corrections grievance tools can play an important role in facility operations, if they have the following characteristics:

- Readily available to inmates to use
- Taken seriously by staff
- Honestly answered in a timely fashion

(Hoke & Demory, 2014, p. 17)

In most jails and prisons the inmate has to file a grievance with the correctional administrators, who then decide whether the claim is legitimate and if the claim is legitimate, to determine the remedy, essentially making the corrections department the "defendant, judge, and jury of complaints against it" (Jenness & Calavita, 2017, p. 213). These arrangements make it hard for inmates to take these processes very seriously. Other inmates are fearful to file a grievance as they believe the staff will take revenge on them (Adler, 2019).

While some inmate grievances are for minor matters, potentially life-threatening issues are also raised. Jenness and Calavita (2017, p. 212) describe how a prisoner filed a grievance because his cell, located in a California desert prison, reached temperatures of 114 degrees. He argued that his living conditions were cruel and unusual treatment, especially considering the prison dogs lived in air-conditioned kennels. His grievance was denied.

Kaul et al. (2015, p. 11) found that the U.S. Bureau of Prisons (BOP) and several state prison systems—including Missouri, Pennsylvania, Rhode Island, and South Dakota—have informal grievance procedures where prisoners can request to speak with prison officials to informally resolve problems. If these dispute resolutions are unsuccessful, the inmate is free to file a written grievance. These states seem to be the exception and most jurisdictions require inmates to file written grievances. Given that many jail and prison inmates have poor literacy skills, there are significant barriers to filing grievances in some jurisdictions. Grievances are also rejected because the prisoner missed filing deadlines. Kaul and colleagues (2015, p. 22) found that Michigan requires prisoners to file their grievances within two business days of an incident, and nine other states require that grievances be submitted within one week. Most jurisdictions, however, give inmates 30 days to file their grievances. Filing written grievances does not guarantee their acceptance and some states automatically reject grievances failing to meet administrative requirements, such as using a correctly sized piece of paper or envelope, or if the prisoner raises more than one issue in a single grievance (Kaul et al., 2015). Poser (2016) points out that grievances have been rejected because they were submitted in the wrong color ink, when inmates wrote in the wrong part of the grievance form, or if they submitted the wrong form.

Few inmate grievances are successful. For instance, Kaul and colleagues (2015, p. 31) got information about grievances filed in 27 states, and reported outcomes (whether the inmate was successful) for nine states: they found that about 6% were successful and this is shown in Figure 12.2. The nature of successful outcomes varies. Some inmates receive financial compensation (e.g. for lost items), while other grievances result in corrective measures, policy or procedural changes, or apologies. When grievances are rejected, inmates in some jurisdictions can appeal those decisions, although few states have independent bodies to review those appeals. As a result, the corrections department decides whether the appeal has merit.

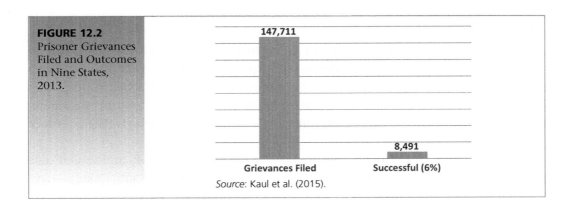

FIGURE 12.2 Prisoner Grievances Filed and Outcomes in Nine States, 2013.

147,711

8,491

Grievances Filed   Successful (6%)

Source: Kaul et al. (2015).

Conviction Integrity Units

Since 2007, when the first **conviction integrity unit** (CIU) was established in Dallas, 60 of these units have been established throughout the country by March 2020 (National Registry of Exonerations, 2020a). CIU, which are also called Conviction Review Units are housed in district attorney's offices—mostly in big cities so far—and are intended to review cases where people were suspected of being wrongfully convicted. Although the process varies across the county, the person claiming their innocence must apply for a review of their case. Applicants who are imprisoned are prioritized for these reviews, but people who have already served their sentence may also apply in some places. Even people who plead guilty to an offense, which is not uncommon for some people who were wrongfully convicted (see Innocence Project, 2020a), are considered for these reviews in some jurisdictions.

Ware (2011/2012, p. 1034) describes the activities of the Dallas CIU as "investigating post-conviction claims of actual innocence, identify the valid claims, and take appropriate corrective action. The CIU would then follow up with an investigation to determine, if possible, what went wrong." Some CIU partner with Innocence Projects based in law schools and review claims of innocence for persons who have been convicted of crimes. These units are intended to be non-adversarial and search for the truth (Is the applicant innocent?), which differs from appeals of convictions that are adversarial. The second goal of these units is prevention: How can [we] prevent this from happening again?

The numbers of exonerations based on the efforts of CIU have been relatively small, and Sheck (2017, p. 705) says there were only 60 cases in 2015, and 70 in 2016, and many of these were drug cases, although ten people convicted of homicide were exonerated. The National Registry of Exonerations (2020a) says that of the 60 CIU in 2020, one-half had not recorded any exonerations. There are mixed feelings about CIU. On the one hand, lawyers such as Barry Sheck, one of the founders of the Innocence Project, applauds the district attorneys who are establishing these units and their efforts to free wrongfully convicted prisoners. On the other hand, some defense attorneys are skeptical that district attorneys may have a conflict of interest if the cause of the wrongful conviction relates to prosecutorial misconduct. Moreover, some of the causes of wrongful convictions include police officers engaging in misconduct or misguided crime laboratory employees (Mays & Ruddell, 2019). Overturning convictions based on misconduct and publicizing those outcomes may be threatening to the legitimacy of the justice system.

This raises the question of how many people are wrongfully convicted. The National Registry of Exonerations (2020b) found that from 1989 to March 2020, there had been 2,570 individuals who were exonerated, and altogether they had served over 23,000 years behind bars. CIUs had accounted for 58 of those exonerations in 2018. So, while the total number of persons who are exonerated through the efforts of CIU is not a large number, compared with the nearly two million jail and prison inmates, it is very important to the person who has been wrongfully convicted.

LEGAL ASSISTANCE AND LEGAL ACCESS

Does the state have to provide inmates with legal aid? And if the state is so obligated, when and how must it provide this aid? Two Supreme Court rulings addressed the issue of legal assistance for inmates. *Johnson v. Avery* (1969) centered on a Tennessee prison regulation prohibiting inmates from giving one another legal help and the rule stated:

> No inmate will advise, assist, or otherwise contract to aid another, either with or without a fee, to prepare Writs or other legal matters. It is not intended that an innocent man be punished. When a man believes he is unlawfully held or illegally convicted, he should prepare a brief or state his complaint in letter form and address it to his lawyer or a judge. A formal Writ is not necessary to receive a hearing. False charges or untrue complaints may be punished. Inmates are forbidden to set themselves up as practitioners for promoting a business of writing writs.

Although *Johnson* involved a Tennessee prison by the mid-1960s a number of prison systems had banned jailhouse lawyers or writ writers. The concern was not the quality of the legal help. Rather the power such knowledge and skills gave the writ writers over other inmates concerned prison administrators. In its decision the Supreme Court ruled that states could only prohibit inmates from helping others file appeals if the states provide legal assistance to inmates who need it.

Eight years later, in *Bounds v. Smith*, the Court extended the states' responsibility to provide legal aid to inmates. In its ruling, the Court noted that inmates must have meaningful legal access. This meant an adequately stocked law library within the institution for the use of inmates and jailhouse lawyers, or the legal assistance of paralegals or attorneys. The standards developed in *Johnson* and *Bounds* strengthened the foundation of contemporary prison litigation. In a long line of right-to-counsel cases—among the most famous of those are *Powell v. Alabama* (1932), *Gideon v. Wainwright* (1963), *Miranda v. Arizona* (1966), and *Argersinger v. Hamilin* (1972)—the Supreme Court has made clear that effective assistance of counsel could well be one of the Constitution's most fundamental due process rights. Most states have fulfilled the Court's mandates by establishing law libraries and allowing jailhouse lawyers to work in them. Although some states discourage jailhouse lawyers from "practicing," to our knowledge none actually prohibit inmates from helping other inmates prepare appeals. Moreover, some jurisdictions hire attorneys for inmates or allow public defenders to handle appeals. In addition, advocacy organizations may take inmates' suits, typically with no charge.

Can jailhouse lawyers be helpful? Shon Hopwood, a federal inmate who was serving a 12-year prison term for committing bank robberies, learned about the law after his sentencing, and he managed to help several other prisoners reduce their sentences or obtain some type of relief. In one case an Illinois inmate with a ninth grade education asked Hopwood to review his sentencing (Hopwood, 2011). It turns out that the inmate had mistakenly been sentenced as a career offender, but he didn't meet the criteria for that designation. The court realized its mistake after Hopwood filed a motion for the other prisoner, and that prisoner's sentence was reduced by ten years. How successful was Hopwood? While serving his prison sentence he filed two cases that were heard by the Supreme Court, and after his release from prison he attended law school, becoming a law professor at Georgetown University.

Some paralegals operating community-based companies exploit the optimism of prisoners and their families who believe they have a chance of being released. Thompson (2019) describes how these businesses advertise to prisoners and charge them to carry out legal research and file motions that are seldom successful. As noted earlier, those failed motions could make the prisoner ineligible for lower filing fees in the future. The people running these businesses exploit the optimism of families and their activities often increase after the Supreme Court hears cases related to prisoners, or there is a change in the law such as the enactment of the *First Step Act*. Thompson (2019, para. 6) describes how these business owners have run afoul of the law and the operators of one Texas outfit were imprisoned after stealing millions of dollars from 22 families.

PHOTO 12.3
Shon Hopwood was a jailhouse lawyer who brought two cases before the Supreme Court. After his release from prison he became a lawyer and he is now a law professor at Georgetown University Credit: Shon Hopwood.

We do not have any information about the relative costs of having inmates versus lawyers prepare appeals. Some contend that hiring attorneys to represent inmate-plaintiffs could well save the state money in the end (Martin, 2011). The use of licensed attorneys could reduce the number of frivolous pro se actions, suits in which inmates represent themselves, and the costs of those suits (see Self-Represented Litigants in the Courts below). Attorneys are in a better position to understand the merits of cases and are more objective in trying to reach negotiated settlements with corrections officials. Fewer frivolous suits also translate into real monetary savings for facilities in the costs of security and transportation, as well as time savings.

Self-Represented Litigants in the Courts

There are financial barriers when the poor appear before the courts. Lawtrades (2019) reports that legal fees throughout the country average about $260 per hour and a civil rights or habeas corpus case could take a week or more of an attorney's time. Those costs are overwhelming for inmates earning between 14 and 63 cents per hour working in prisons (Sawyer, 2017). As few sentenced prisoners are eligible for help from public defenders once sentenced they have few options other than representing themselves in court or relying on jailhouse lawyers. Not only does it cost a lot to hire an attorney, but the courts also require plaintiffs to pay filing fees. It costs $400 to file a case with the federal courts, and if the prisoner loses the lawsuit it will cost them another $500 to appeal that decision.

A portion of the filing fees are waived for prisoners, but the PLRA enacted a three-strike rule where once the prisoner has launched three lawsuits that end in dismissals the courts no longer waive those fees. In 2015, a Michigan inmate challenged the three-strike rule, arguing that he should not be required to pay the filing fees (as one of his dismissed cases was on appeal) but the Supreme Court rejected that argument (see *Coleman v. Tollefson*, 2015).

Prisoners file their lawsuits by mailing a package to the federal courts and even today some are handwritten, although more prisoners have access to computers—without Internet access. Once received, these claims are scanned by court personnel and a record for each case is created. They are then assigned to a federal judge who screens the case and complaints are dismissed if they are not stated correctly. We know from our review of prisoner characteristics that few have been very successful in their formal educations, and they are at a disadvantage compared to attorneys in their attempts to abide by the rules of the federal courts, which require the prisoner to follow a number of complicated procedures. Several guidelines have been published to help prisoners access the courts, including:

• The U.S. District Court, District of Minnesota (2015) has prepared a guidebook for federal litigation that can be accessed online.

- Columbia University (2017) publishes *A Jailhouse Lawyer's Manual*, which is available free of charge (online): it has been published since 1978.
- The Office of the Clerk, Supreme Court of the United States (2018) publishes a guide for petitioners who do not have the assistance of counsel.

Individuals appearing in court without an attorney are called pro se litigants and they are at a considerable disadvantage when arguing points of law against lawyers. As a result, few are successful in obtaining any relief. Schlanger (2015, p. 165) found that about 7% of habeas corpus cases and 11% of prisoner civil rights resulted in some type of success, and she notes that "in cases brought by prisoners, the government defendants are winning more cases pretrial, settling fewer matters, and going to trial less often" (p. 163). With respect to damages awarded to these inmates, Schlanger (2015, p. 167) found that the average was $18,800 and the median was $1,000: in other words, one-half of the prisoners received $1,000 or less and half got more than that amount.

Prisoners who launch numerous lawsuits are called "frequent filers" and Dale Maisano has filed more lawsuits than any other prisoner. Maisano, an Arizona inmate in his late 60s, is serving a 15-year sentence for aggravated assault. He has filed over 9,400 lawsuits since his first admission to prison in the 1980s and his handwritten lawsuits have sought relief because he received inadequate food, got too much exposure to the sun, and received inadequate health care services. Hass (2014, para. 14) reports that Maisano filed 249 lawsuits in a single day in 2014—the year he initiated more than 3,600 lawsuits—and he "filed more federal lawsuits than all the federal cases lodged in the states of Maine, New Hampshire, and Wyoming combined." Few of Maisano's cases have ever been heard in court, and we can't find any record of him winning a case.

Under the PLRA prisoners are required to pay the full amount of a filing fee, or 20% of their prison income. An inmate challenged this rule and the Supreme Court, in a rare unanimous decision, upheld the existing practice (*Bruce v. Samuels*, 2016), thus keeping the existing barriers to prisoners who file frequent lawsuits.

INMATE ADVOCATES, ADVOCACY GROUPS, AND OMBUDSMEN

Inmates are a relatively powerless social group and few of their families are wealthy or influential. What mechanisms, then, do they have to make their concerns heard by the public, politicians, and corrections administrators? Two answers come to mind: riots and lawsuits.

Prison riots throughout the 1970s and early 1980s brought national attention to the plight of inmates (Chase, 2015). However, it has been through litigation that some of the most far-reaching and long-lasting changes have come about in prison policies and practices. Litigation has given prisoners a forum in which they can air their grievances against state authorities. Thomas, Wheeler, and Harris (1986, p. 764) contend that litigation is one of the final "nonviolent and legitimate" mechanisms at prison inmates' disposal.

Few inmates have the economic resources to launch a wide-ranging and protracted **class action lawsuit**—a suit brought on behalf of prisoners as a group. Instead, prisoners' rights groups have acted as their advocates. The practice of inmate litigation since the introduction of the PLRA has reduced the involvement of lawyers because the legislation capped the fees a lawyer can be awarded. Hall (2012) observes that attorneys' fees are capped at 150% of a jury's award to a successful plaintiff, and he describes an example of a lawyer who won a lawsuit where the inmate was awarded $1, and so he received $1.50 for his efforts. Umphres (2019, p. 262) says that this provision in the PLRA is a disincentive for lawyers and discourages them from participating in cases with merit. He observes that "prisoners with vital civil rights claims cannot find lawyers to help them bring suit, and the courts remained clogged with prisoners soldiering on pro se" (without representation).

There are a number of organizations that advocate on behalf of jail inmates and prisoners. The ACLU is perhaps that most obvious, although the American Bar Association (ABA), FAMM (formerly Families Against Mandatory Minimum sentences), the John Howard Association, Marshall Project, Pew Charitable Trusts, the Prison Policy Initiative, Southern Poverty Law Center, Vera Institute of Justice, and the Urban Institute all have played a role in inmate advocacy. These organizations carry out research on corrections-related issues and publicize their findings, and sometimes report cases of correctional wrongdoing to the public. The work of these national organizations is supported by local and state organizations and the ACLU has offices in most states. A small number of university-based innocence projects, usually housed in law schools, also provide support to inmates claiming they were wrongfully convicted. The most famous of these organizations, the Innocence Project (2020b), founded in 1992, has investigated hundreds of cases, and their work has led to the exoneration and release of 367 prisoners, including 21 on death row.

Inmates in several states have access to independent government bodies whose staff will provide assistance to them in resolving conflicts or complaints with the jail or prison system. Some of these advocacy organizations are called **ombudsmen** and they have been around since the 1970s in some jurisdictions. These organizations act with differing degrees of independence. In California they are an organization within the California Department of Corrections and Rehabilitation ([CDCR] 2019, para. 1), and their duties include providing:

> Answers your questions, analyzes your situation, explains CDCR policies and procedures, advocates for fairness of a process as opposed to advocating for an individual party, provides information and at times advice and develops options, suggests appropriate referrals, apprises administration of significant trends and may recommend changes in policies and procedures.

Ombudsmen often can help correctional agencies and inmates work toward a "win-win" solution to a problem without involving the time and expense of the courts. One of the problems, however, is that inmates might be reluctant to trust the ombudsmen staff if they are employees of the correctional system.

In Hawaii, Iowa, and Nebraska (where the agency is known as the Office of Public Counsel), these ombudsmen operate independent of the prison system and an examination of their annual reports reveals that issues related to public safety (including corrections) can occupy up to one-half of their workloads. A review of the issues raised by inmates in these states shows that many of them are related to inappropriate staff conduct, conditions of confinement, applications of correctional policies, and medical care. As these bodies act independently of the correctional system they may be seen more favorably by inmates, especially when they can broker "win-win" solutions to the prisoner's grievances.

LAWS AND LITIGATION DEALING WITH PROBATION AND PAROLE

Until the late 1960s, probation officers enjoyed a great deal of freedom in discharging their duties. For some, that meant cooperating with the police to revoke a term of probation based on information that would not stand up to legal scrutiny. The probation officer would simply take the probationer into custody, claiming some violation, and would request resentencing, which normally resulted in a quick trip to jail for the probationer. Rarely were either the formalities of due process or a hearing on the alleged charges part of the process.

That practice ended in 1967, when the Supreme Court ruled in *Mempa v. Rhay* that the right of an accused to be represented by an attorney is not confined to trials alone and that counsel is required at every stage where substantial rights of the accused may be affected. Sentencing, particularly on probation revocation, qualifies as a critical stage. The Court's ruling in *Morrissey v. Brewer* (1972) expanded legal protections to parolees. At the heart of

Morrissey was the contention of state authorities that parolees do not enjoy a basic right to conditional release from prison and that parole is a privilege extended by the executive branch of government. The Court rejected that position and in its ruling observed that parole had emerged as an integral part of correctional practices and occurred too regularly to be considered a privilege. The Court also noted that by whatever means freedom is obtained, "it must be seen within the protection of the Fourteenth Amendment. Its termination calls for some orderly process, however informal." Finally, citing the fact that parole revocations occur as often as 35–40% of the time, the Court maintained that the protection of parolees' rights is essential.

In *Morrissey*, the Court addressed the nature of due process for parolees. The parole revocation hearing, they ruled, should be a two-stage process: (a) the arrest and preliminary hearing, and (b) the revocation hearing. For those hearings, the Court extended to parolees the following due process rights:

- Written notice of the alleged parole violation
- Disclosure of the evidence against the parolee
- The opportunity to be heard in person and to present witnesses and documentary evidence
- The right to confront and cross-examine adverse witnesses (unless the hearing officer finds good cause for not allowing a confrontation)
- A "neutral and detached" hearing body—like a traditional parole board, for example—whose members need not be judicial officers or lawyers
- A written statement by the fact finders concerning the evidence relied on and the reasons for revoking parole

As it did with probation, the Court left unanswered the question of the right to counsel. In practice, parolees may have attorneys present, but the government need not provide them. The Court emphasized that the hearings should be informal and the justices noted, "It is a narrow inquiry; the process should be flexible enough to consider evidence, including letters, affidavits, and other material that would not be admissible in an adversary criminal trial." In short, like a discretionary-parole hearing, the standards of evidence and of proof required are lower than those required in a trial court for conviction.

In *Gagnon v. Scarpelli* (1973), the Supreme Court formally defined the due process rights of probationers. At a minimum, a probationer is entitled to the following:

- Notice of alleged violations concerning the probation violation
- A preliminary hearing to decide if probable cause exists
- A revocation hearing which, in the words of the Court, is "a somewhat more comprehensive hearing prior to the making of the final revocation decision." The revocation

hearing should allow the accused the opportunity to appear, to present witnesses and evidence

* An opportunity to confront any accusatory witnesses or evidence

Again, the Court failed to clarify the right to counsel at these hearings. The justices suggested that the need for counsel should be determined on a case-by-case basis. In practice, most jurisdictions provide the accused with counsel or allow private counsel at the preliminary hearings.

In June 2019 the Supreme Court added due process protections to individuals convicted of sex offenses in the federal courts and supervised in the community in *U.S. v. Haymond*. This case involved an individual who allegedly violated the conditions of his ten-year supervised release and was sentenced to a five-year prison sentence on the new offense by a federal judge based on the preponderance of the evidence. The prisoner argued that he was entitled to a jury trial to determine his guilt given there was a new criminal charge, and the Court agreed with him. As this ruling relates to a fairly rare type of sentencing (federal offenders serving a supervised release) it may have little impact on state probation or parole operations.

Inmate Litigation and Prisoner Rights

In this chapter we have described how American jail and prison inmates are often subject to conditions that closely approximate cruel and unusual treatment, and that jail and prison administrators work to provide care just above that threshold. When prisoners believe their living conditions are unconstitutional they have access to the courts to challenge those conditions, although we have described the barriers to accessing the courts. Moreover, American prisoners can challenge the basis for their imprisonment and can file habeas corpus petitions claiming they are being held wrongfully. While a relatively small percentage of these claims are ever affirmed by the courts, they do have access to the courts. In some nations, decisions to detain, imprison, or punish an individual are not subject to due process and people who are detained or thrown in prison have few rights. Amnesty International (2019) has identified six areas of concern affecting penal institutions around the world:

* *Prisoners of conscience*: someone who is imprisoned because of who they are (sexual orientation, ethnic, national or social origin, language, birth, color, sex, or economic status) or what they believe (religious, political, or other conscientiously held beliefs).

COMPARATIVE ISSUES IN CORRECTIONS

- *Arbitrary detention*: being detained for no legitimate reason or without legal process.
- *Incommunicado*: being detained without access to family or lawyers.
- *Secret detention*: being detained in a secret location.
- *Inadequate prison conditions*: trials conducted without ensuring minimum legal process.
- *Torture and other forms of ill-treatment.*

While American courts have been somewhat reluctant to get involved in corrections, they have addressed egregious or extreme cases of unconstitutional treatment or government wrongdoing. Moreover, since 2000 the media have become increasingly involved in reporting accounts of correctional life and those accounts have sometimes shamed correctional administrators into improving inmates' living conditions.

But what happens when prisoners have no access to the courts, advocates such as ombudsmen, or the media? Correctional facilities in Saudi Arabia, for example, have been criticized as there are allegations of torturing inmates and conditions have been described as abysmal (Chehayeb, 2019), although Sullivan (2015) reports that conditions for terrorists are much better than those convicted of non-terrorist crimes. Incarceration in the kingdom has been described as highly secretive and there are no official reports describing the number of people held in their correctional facilities. The Consular Section, British Embassy, Riyadh (2018, p. 7) says that inmates can complain to prison authorities about ill-treatment but they are seldom taken seriously, although foreign prisoners contacting their embassy might have more positive outcomes than local prisoners. Saudi prisoners do not have the ability to lodge complaints to an independent body (Nasr, 2013). Instead, appeals go to the Saudi royal family through the Ministry of the Interior. The Ministry might not be receptive to such complaints. Jordan (2019, para. 9) says that the Interior Ministry "has been condemned for years as one of the most brutal human rights violators in the world."

ISSUES RAISED IN CORRECTIONS LAWSUITS

Although somewhat dated, Schlanger's (2003) survey of prison systems and jails is an important work in understanding inmate litigation. Schlanger asked correctional officials if they had been sued, and the issue that led to the lawsuit. Table 12.1 shows the ten top topics of litigation, and there are some differences between lawsuits in jails and prsons. Some of these differences are the result of the longer time prison inmates serve.

TABLE 12.1 Top Ten Issues in Large Jail and Prison Litigation

	Large Jail (%)	Prison (%)
Medical Care	91	89
Use of Force	80	89
Personal Injury	70	81
Loss or Damage to Property	66	81
Inmate-on-Inmate Violence	64	63
Law Library Services	41	78
Crowding	36	52
Suicide Prevention	36	33
Sanitation/Living Conditions	32	59
Food Services/Nutrition/Diet	30	78

Source: Schlanger (2003).

Zeng (2019) reports that the average stay in jail is about a month, whereas the median prison sentence is about three years (Bronson & Carson, 2019). As a result, issues such as food quality become more important for prisoners serving long sentences and over three-quarters of prisons had been sued for food-related issues including diet and nutrition, whereas less than one-third of jails had been sued for the same reason.

The leading cause of lawsuits in either jails or prisons is health care. One of the most important Supreme Court decisions for prisoners was that adequate health care was a right and not a privilege (*Estelle v. Gamble*, 1976). The standard for health care is **deliberate indifference**—that corrections officials knew but did nothing about inmates' physical or medical conditions, and that their failure to act had long-term effects on inmates' condition.

The importance of inmate health care is not surprising given that these people are far more likely to suffer from physical disabilities and chronic health conditions than are members of the public (see Chapters 5 and 6). Moreover, prisoners are powerless when it comes to health care decisions, and have no choice about who will be their doctor, or the type of care they receive. Furthermore, a growing number of jail inmates and prisoners live in facilities where medical care is provided by private contractors. Tucker (2016) describes how these contractors focus on controlling costs—to increase their profits—rather than focusing on inmate care, which has resulted in unnecessary suffering and deaths.

Medical care standards, including dental care and mental health therapies, have been points of legal contention since the 1990s. Health care costs can account for from 20% to 30% of all inmate costs (see Legislative Analyst's Office, 2019). Historically, corrections officials felt they could save money by rationing health care services, and creating barriers for prisoners seeking medical care. Many jails and prisons may require a co-pay. For example, Illinois state prisoners were required to submit a written request to see a doctor and their requests were screened by a nurse. Regardless of whether they saw the doctor, they were charged $5.00, which is a lot of money for them as the lowest paid prisoners are given $10 a month. In January 2020 Illinois eliminated their prisoner copay system although the practice still exists in other state prison systems (Nowicki, 2019).

There is no shortage of reports of needless suffering and deaths due to poor correctional health care. Correctional officials try to save money at every point in the system, including hiring doctors without medical licenses. The Associated Press (2018) reports that Kansas prisons routinely hire physicians, including four of nine doctors specializing in psychiatry, who have "institutional licenses" and could not practice in the community. This practice is not isolated to Kansas, nor is it new as unlicensed physicians and other health care providers have worked in other state prison systems for decades. A lack of resources and unlicensed health care providers sometimes result in negative outcomes. When Dabney and Vaughn (2000, p. 161) looked at 202 cases of prison medical care lawsuits, they found the following outcomes:

Over one-third of the doctors named in these lawsuits denied responsibility for these outcomes, and one-quarter denied there was any injury, while one-sixth blamed the prisoners.

Outcomes	Percentage
Death	9%
Permanent physical disability (e.g. amputation of limbs)	15%
Permanent loss in quality of life such as noticeable scarring or chronic illness	17%
Temporary loss in quality of life (e.g. pain and discomfort)	58%

Schlanger (2003) reports that the inappropriate use of force was a leading cause of prisoner litigation. Prisoners have always alleged that they are at the mercy of correctional personnel and they were seldom believed if they complained of ill-treatment. The increased use of closed circuit television throughout jails and prisons since 2000 was intended to deter inmate-on-officer assaults. The images captured by cameras, however, have led to the prosecution of COs who were using force inappropriately, including assaulting inmates who posed no threat because they were restrained (Cooke, 2019; Golgowski, 2019). Inmates are also filming the activities of the correctional personnel. In July 2019 the Florida Department of Corrections fired a captain and two officers for assaulting a prisoner; the images of the assault were captured by a prisoner using a contraband cellular phone, and then posted on YouTube (Conarck, 2019a). All three of those officers were charged with assault and falsifying reports as the incident reports written by the staff did not describe how the prisoner was "stomped and kicked," or punched "at least 12 times on the ribs" or "struck in the face" (Conarck, 2019a). Their actions are, however, available on YouTube.

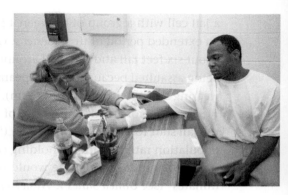

PHOTO 12.4
This state prisoner is getting blood drawn. Health care is the number one cause of inmate litigation in jails and prisons and this is no surprise as these people suffer from rates of disabilities and chronic health conditions several times higher than the general population (see Chapters 5 and 6). Credit: Mikael Karlsson/Alamy Stock Photo.

Food quality and quantity is an ongoing point of inmate dissatisfaction and the courts have ruled that inmates must be provided nutritious, well-balanced meals. Some inmates may have special dietary needs and this is particularly true for followers of some religions. For example, Muslim inmates do not eat pork, which is one of the most common meat items in prison diets. In *Cooper v. Pate* (1964), the Supreme Court ruled that the states must consider inmates' special dietary needs, including religious or medical (e.g. diets for prisoners with diabetes or high blood pressure). Again, like the prison health care system, inmates have little choice about what they will eat. As a result, some prisoners with food sensitivities, such as persons suffering from celiac disease and who cannot eat food with gluten, can get sick eating prison food (Inserra, 2019).

Inmates in the Oregon state prison system filed a lawsuit alleging that some of the food they were given was marked "not for human consumption" or was unhealthy due to mold, was prepared in unsanitary conditions or had passed its expiration date, and other food was undercooked. In their lawsuit the inmates argued that their food made them sick, which violated the Eighth Amendment because it was cruel and unusual punishment. A federal judge who heard the case dismissed the complaint, and referred to examples of previous inmate litigation where "Neither isolated instances of food poisoning, temporary lapses in sanitary food service, nor service of meals contaminated with maggots are sufficiently serious to constitute an Eighth Amendment violation" (*Lyons et al. v. Peters*, p. 18).

About two-thirds of jails and prisons had been sued due to cases of inmate-on-inmate violence. While correctional officials have very little control over when an inmate attacks another prisoner, there are cases when the officers had a reasonable expectation that an assault would occur; this is an example of deliberate indifference. For example, an 18 year-old Kentucky man had been arrested for traffic violations and was placed in a jail cell with a group of between 12 and 14 inmates who beat and gang raped him for an extended period of time (*Sester v. Grant County Detention Center*). The victim, who was about six feet tall and weighed around 125 pounds, might have been more vulnerable to being assaulted because of his appearance (he had blond streaks dyed in his hair and was wearing shorts with hearts on them).

Several factors made this a case of deliberate indifference, including the intention of the jail staff to scare the young man ("teach him a lesson") by placing him in the general population rather than in a holding cell by himself, which was the policy. One of the jail staff apparently said that he would be "pretty and cute" and a "good girlfriend for the inmates" (see *United States v. Wesley Lanham*). After the assault was carried out, the victim was denied medical care and the jail officers tried to minimize their role in the crime in a cover-up. The outcome of the case was that the victim was awarded $1.4 million in damages, two of the jail staff received sentences of 180 and 168 months, respectively, and three of the inmates involved in the assault received sentences of five to fifteen years in prison.

This is not a unique example and Ross (2012, p. 418) describes how "Some COs may instigate violence among prisoners—for example, by putting two cons who hate each other together in the same cell or tier, and sitting back to watch the fireworks during an otherwise monotonous shift." In 2016, for example, a Utah inmate named Jeffrey Vigil was moved to a living unit that housed rival gang members, despite the fact that the officers knew this would be dangerous for him. Vigil was beaten and stabbed to death shortly after his transfer to the new unit. The prisoner convicted of killing Vigil apparently told him that, "You either leave or you're going to die" (as reported by Miller, 2018). But how does a prisoner leave when all the doors are locked? The State of Utah paid Vigil's widow $450,000 to drop the lawsuit she initiated without taking any responsibility or admitting wrongdoing (Miller, 2018).

Education, recreation, and general library services fall into the area of inmate programs and services. Much of the prison and jail time inmates serve is unproductive. Therefore, educational and recreation programs can benefit the inmates and assist in the facility's smooth operations by keeping them occupied. Library services provide inmates with books, which gives them another constructive activity to occupy their time. Access to law libraries is an important issue in both jails and prisons, but since all prisoners have been sentenced to more than one year in custody, having access to these materials can be critical to their ability to file a lawsuit.

Many of the issues reported earlier are related to jail and prison overcrowding and under-funding, and the impacts of correctional crowding are far-reaching. Crowding and limited resources have been linked to increased prison violence, including sexual assaults (U.S. Department of Justice, 2019b). Writing about conditions in California in 2009, the *Sacramento Bee* (2019) reports that:

> The sprawling system had reached a breaking point. Prisoners were sleeping in gyms, hallways and dayrooms. Mentally ill prisoners were jammed into tiny holding cells. There were dozens of riots and hundreds of attacks on guards every year. Suicide rates were 80 percent higher than in the rest of the nation's prisons.

Jail and prison crowding has been addressed by the Supreme Court in three decisions. Newman and Scott (2012) observe that the issue of double-bunking (where two inmates share a cell designed for one person) was reviewed by the Supreme Court in the *Bell v. Wolfish* (1979), and in *Rhodes v. Chapman* (1981). The Court upheld the decisions of the lower courts saying that the practice was constitutional in jails and prisons.

The issue of overcrowding in California's prison system was also addressed in the *Brown v. Plata* (2011) decision, and that ruling had a far-reaching impact on correctional operations. California's prison system—designed to house about 85,000 prisoners—was holding about twice that many. The Court decided that overcrowding resulted in a serious violation of the prisoners' constitutional rights, especially in terms of poor health care that resulted in unnecessary suffering and deaths. They gave the California Department of Corrections and Rehabilitation two years to reduce the size of their prison population by almost 40,000 prisoners. The state engaged in a number of strategies to reduce their prison population including sending state prisoners to serve their sentences in county jails and placing more individuals on probation rather than incarcerating them. While reducing the number of prisoners in state-operated facilities, the number of sentenced prisoners in local jails increased. Some say that the problem simply moved from the prisons to local jails. The *Sacramento Bee* (2019) reports that the jail homicide rate has doubled since this change and that many of the sheriffs running these jails have little interest in providing adequate health care or accommodating the needs of the state prisoners with mental illnesses.

The final issue of concern is a broad area called institutional governance. This encompasses a large number of policies and practices, including visitation, correspondence, administrative segregation, classification, as well as disciplinary and grievance procedures. Concerns about institutional governance, especially discipline and inmate grievances, seem to be a constant source of inmate litigation. It is important to remember that prisons have the authority to discipline inmates for infractions of institutional rules. However, there must also be an orderly process of reviewing complaints, especially those that might result in administrative segregation, loss of privileges, or the loss of good-time credits.

EMERGING ISSUES IN INMATE LITIGATION

In the previous sections we described the history of corrections litigation and the leading sources of prisoner lawsuits. Conditions of confinement, staff use of force, challenging administrative decisions, and medical care will continue to be the key causes of prisoner litigation, but the nature of prisoner litigation is also changing. For example, technology and other social and scientific factors are affecting prison operations. Advancements of medical technology might also affect correctional operations, as there are more trans-gendered people in jails and prisons today and an ongoing question is how we provide safe conditions for them. Moreover, should the correctional system pay for the medications, surgery, and treatments for an individual who is transitioning from one gender to the other? Another possibly contentious issue is access to addictions treatment. In 2019 the First Circuit federal court of appeals decided that jail inmates must have access to treatment for opioid addictions, which might prove to be very costly in some prison systems (Arnold, 2019). Science is also influencing our ideas of crime and criminality, and research about brain science might influence the culpability of young adults (those under 25 years) whose brains are not fully developed. Research is also changing the way we look at risk assessment and classification. Here we examine four of these issues: segregation, risk assessment and classification, work requirements, and issues related to transgendered prisoners.

PHOTO 12.5
This 3D picture shows a prisoner's cell in the Bureau of Prison's ADX Supermax prison in Florence, Colorado. Inmates in some jurisdictions are held in segregation for years and have had no access to the outdoors for years. U.S. Supreme Court Justice Sotomayor called the practice as coming close to being placed in a penal tomb. Credit: Naeblyes/Alamy Stock Photo.

Segregation

In Chapter 6 we discussed that many scholars are increasingly critical of placing inmates in long-term segregation due to the psychological harms attributed to the practice (Haney, 2018). Estimates of the number of state prisoners in segregation range from 39,000 (Frost & Monteiro, 2016) to 61,000 (Association of State Correctional Administrators, 2018, p. 4). There are about another 20,000 jail inmates in segregation on any given day (Beck, 2015). Regardless of the number, placement in segregation touches the lives of tens of thousands of inmates, and some live in these conditions for decades.

The opposition to segregation has been increasing since 2010. The practice is being discontinued in a number of juvenile correctional systems and the federal government has banned the practice for youths held on federal charges. Clark (2017) calls the practice a form of child abuse, and there is growing evidence that finds that segregating youths is harmful. Valentine, Restivo, and Wright (2019), for example, found that the longer juveniles—who were being imprisoned as adults—were held in segregation, the greater the diagnoses for mental illnesses. The periods of confinement can be lengthy and in their study the average juvenile had been in segregation for 199.9 days.

Do these examples from juvenile justice suggest that the practice might be falling out of favor in adult corrections? A review of Supreme Court decisions sheds some light on the issue. The Court, in *Bruscino v. Carlson* (1988), found that placement in the Bureau of Prison's administrative segregation, including the austere conditions of confinement and periods of extended solitary confinement, was not cruel and unusual punishment. Much has changed in the past three decades. The National Institute of Justice (2015, p. 11) says that:

> we are moving toward a general consensus (which can be found across the various court decisions, **consent decrees**, and settlement agreements reached) that these environments are not appropriate for the mentally ill and might constitute cruel and unusual punishment for this subset of the inmate population.

Association of State Correctional Administrators (2018) had a similar observation about the growing involvement of the state appellate courts on issues related to segregation. When two Colorado prisoners who were in long-term segregation placement asked the Supreme Court to review the constitutionality of their access to the outdoors (neither had been outside for several years) the Court declined to hear the case (*Apodaca v. Raemisch*, 2018). Writing about this case, Justice Sotomayor said that courts and corrections officials need to be aware of the constitutional problems of keeping prisoners in near isolation in conditions she says are akin to a penal tomb. If research continues to reveal the harmful effects of long-term segregation, it is likely that this issue will be challenged before the courts.

Risk Assessment and Classification

Risk assessment instruments (RAI) have been used to assess an individual's risk of recidivism for decades, and they are also routinely used to classify the most appropriate security classification in jails and prisons. A growing number of jurisdictions are also using RAI to determine if pre-trial inmates should be released or incarcerated until their court dates. These tools are also used for sex offenders and for perpetrators of domestic violence. Schwartzapfel (2019, para. 1) observes that RAI "plumb your history, demographics, and other details to spit out a score quantifying how likely you are to commit another crime or show up at your next hearing."

There are some very convincing arguments for using RAI because they are seen as removing bias from the decisions made by community corrections, jail, and prison officials. Decisions about releasing pretrial detainees, determining their risk to the community at sentencing, or their release to the community on parole have been informed by the results of these instruments.

But a growing number of advocates and researchers are critical that the results of these tools are flawed. The factors used to assess risk are often based on static factors, which are things that cannot be changed such as the age at first arrest or criminal history (Heffernan, Wegerhoff, & Ward, 2019). Research generally has shown that RAI can accurately predict future risks, but they can also be adjusted to increase their usefulness of assessing risks in local populations (Lovins, Latessa, May, & Lux, 2018). When it comes to pretrial risk assessments, however, there is criticism that they over predict the risk of failing to show for court or engaging in violent crimes if placed on bail. Corey (2019) reports that 99% of defendants in Chicago courts who were thought to be at high risk showed up for their court dates and had not been arrested for committing new crimes.

Another controversial factor about RAI is that the companies developing these instruments have not revealed how they came into being. As a result researchers cannot validate that some populations, such as members of minority groups, are accurately assessed. If, for example, the accuracy of these risk assessments was based on the recidivism of White parolees in New York State, would the results accurately predict the risk posed by African American parolees in Louisiana or American Indians in Nevada? In Chapter 11 we also raised the question of whether RAI developed for men can work equally well for women.

One example of a RAI that is being scrutinized by the courts is the Abel Assessment for Sexual Interest which is an instrument that assesses sexual interest in children and other groups. This risk assessment tool has been used by agencies that supervise adult and juvenile populations in the community and behind bars. The Abel Screening (2019) website indicates that the instrument has been used over 170,000 times in 50 states. Chammah (2015) says that the use of the instrument has been challenged before the courts at least 40 times, and sometimes the courts have found that the instrument was inaccurate, and he notes that:

> The stakes are high; a poorly designed test, coupled with overzealous clinicians and trusting judges, would be a recipe for railroading innocent people into being judged as high-risk pedophiles.

Given that observation, what if only 1% of the 170,000 cases ended in an inaccurate decision made by a judge? That would represent 1,700 ruined lives. Given the high stakes of an inaccurate decision, should we depend on these tools, or rely on a psychologist's gut feelings about the risk to re-offend, which may be more inaccurate? Goel, Shroff,

Skeem, and Slobogin (2019) describe how several cases challenging the accuracy or appropriateness of RAIs have been heard by appellate courts in Iowa and Wisconsin. As research is conducted on these instruments, it is likely that more cases will appear before the courts challenging the accuracy of these tools with different populations.

Transgender Inmates

We noted in Chapter 6 that transgendered individuals pose special challenges for correctional systems, especially related to ensuring their safety and medical needs (Carlino & Franklin, 2018). Transgendered prisoners have launched lawsuits saying that they were treated with deliberate indifference by the staff members or the conditions of their confinement were cruel and unusual, and it is likely that these people will file more lawsuits.

One strategy to ensure their physical safety and to reduce acts of harassment is to place all transgendered inmates on a single living unit. But that strategy is dependent on the number of these inmates in a jail or prison population. This issue can become more complicated if these prisoners have not completed gender reassignment surgery, or are in the process of that change. Some individuals might identify as a member of the opposite sex, but have not taken any steps, such as taking hormones or having surgery, to physically change their gender. In that case should they be placed with the group with which they self-identify?

Transgendered inmates are often placed on living units with persons of the same gender, and a transgendered inmate whose identification at birth identifies him as a male is placed with male prisoners. This may place these individuals at high risk of victimization. Examining data from the National Inmate Surveys carried out between 2007 and 2012, Beck (2014) found that between 33% and 40% of transgendered federal or state prisoners had been sexually victimized, while 27–40% of jail inmates had been sexually victimized. Victimization can take a number of forms, including harassment, beatings, sexual violence, and various forms of harassment including name-calling. Given these greater risks of victimization, some transgendered inmates have won court cases finding that correctional officials have acted with deliberate indifference by placing them with male prisoners. As a result, a growing number of transgendered prisoners are filing lawsuits in order to get the courts to place them on women's units.

The care of transgendered prisoners can become a controversial issue and in 2018 President Trump rolled back some protections granted to these inmates in the BOP that were introduced during the Obama administration. The basis for living unit placement is again back to the inmates' biological sex recorded at birth rather than their self-identified gender. Moreover, the Bureau policies have made it more difficult for transgendered prisoners to receive hormone therapy and other medical treatments (Leventis Lourgos, 2019).

In December 2018 a federal court ordered Idaho to pay for an inmate's gender confirmation surgery. Peacher (2019, para. 10) observes that the inmate argues that "gender confirmation surgery is vital, life-saving treatment and denying her that care constitutes cruel and unusual punishment." Lawyers for Idaho's prison system, by contrast, say that the surgery is not medically necessary. Given this prisoner's success in court, it is likely that more transgendered inmates will use this as a precedent when filing suits to receive these medical procedures. As a result, it is likely that the courts will hear more of these cases in the future.

Prison Work

Is prison work modern day slavery? Correctional systems have always used inmate labor to maintain the buildings and grounds and to ensure that the inmate's basic needs such as meals were being met. Moreover, most prisons built in the 1800s and early 1900s were constructed by prisoners. As noted in Chapter 6, many prisoners are also engaged in some type of prison industry: building furniture for government offices or sewing the uniforms worn by state COs. Others are working in prison industries where the facility partners with a corporation to produce goods or provide services including engaging in data entry, filling prescriptions for eyeglasses, or telemarketing. Some prisons also contract with local or county governments as well as hospitals, nursing homes, and schools to provide inmate labor for various projects. Prisoners and jail inmates have also played an important role in fighting wilderness fires for decades in California.

Wages for prisoners' efforts range from 14 to 63 cents per hour (Sawyer, 2017) and five prison systems in the South do not pay inmates any salary. The thousands of California inmate firefighters who volunteer to risk their lives—three died fighting fires or in training in 2018—are paid $1 per hour (Goldberg, 2018). Prisoners in some systems have very little choice in their work assignments and prisoners who refuse work in Florida or Georgia can receive a disciplinary report on their file; thus reducing their likelihood of earning parole (Conarck, 2019b; Drepaul, 2019). Conarck (2019b) describes how Florida prisoners are sometimes working in unsafe conditions and he says that African American inmates are disproportionately used in these work programs.

Inmate opposition to unpaid work and low salaries has resulted in a series of prisoner strikes throughout the country. These strikes, which were organized by several activist organizations, affected prison operations in 12 states in 2016 and 17 states in 2018. While these strikes may have drawn attention to the issue of unpaid and underpaid work in correctional facilities, it is unlikely there will be any sweeping changes in the near future. That is because the Thirteenth Amendment which was ratified in 1865 allows prisoners to work without pay. In 2010 some federal prisoners argued that their low wages, approximately 31 cents per hour, violated their rights under the Eighth Amendment (cruel and unusual punishment), but their case was dismissed (*Serra v. Lappin*, 2010).

So, what does the future hold for prisoners who contend that unpaid and low-paid work are cruel and unusual punishments? While advocacy groups will continue to make this a contentious issue, it is unlikely that the general public will pay much attention. As Taylor (2011) observes "the experience of prison labor is largely contained within the prison walls" (p. 389). Therefore, this issue may receive more attention from prisoner advocacy groups than from the courts.

SUMMARY

Litigation has been one of the major influences in changing correctional practices since 1970 (Collins, 2010). The number of writs of habeas corpus and civil rights actions filed by state prisoners and jail inmates between 1980 and 2018—almost 1.5 million petitions—indicates that prisoner litigation is a major enterprise. The areas of prisoners' rights and inmate litigation are complex. However, from this chapter you should especially note the following:

- For a long period in our nation's history, the courts took a "hands off" approach to prisoners and prisoners' rights.
- During the 1960s, prison inmates, along with other groups in society, frequently turned to the courts seeking redress for their grievances.
- Although they still hear appeals from prison inmates, courts have largely been deferential to prison authorities and prison policies since the PLRA was introduced in 1996.
- Inmates have a variety of legal mechanisms for their appeals, and two of the most common have been writs of habeas corpus and civil rights actions (Section 1983 suits).
- Before the courts will hear inmate lawsuits they require the individual to have exhausted other avenues of complaint such as launching grievances or making complaints to advocates such as ombudsmen in some states.
- Prison and jail inmates have challenged a wide range of conditions of confinement—such as crowding and medical care—and litigation has also been used by probationers and parolees to challenge the conditions of their supervision.
- Some state and privately-operated prison systems have had to make significant operational changes because of inmate lawsuits and oversight by the federal courts.
- Between 1980 and 2018, jail and prison inmates launched over 925,000 lawsuits to improve the living conditions in their facilities, and nearly 600,000 habeas corpus petitions were filed. Only a very small percentage of these lawsuits or petitions result in a favorable outcome for the inmate.

In some ways our coverage of inmate litigation and correctional law raises additional questions. Is all that legal action working? Is there any evidence that lawsuits lead to real long-term change or reforms? These are important issues for the future of corrections, a topic we address in the next chapter.

KEY TERMS

- Antiterrorism and Effective Death Penalty Act (AEDPA)
- civil death
- civil rights claims Civil Rights of Institutionalized Persons Act (CRIPA)
- class action lawsuit
- consent decree
- deliberate indifference
- habeas corpus appeals
- inmate grievances
- ombudsmen
- Prison Litigation Reform Act (PLRA)
- risk assessment
- Section 1983 suit
- self-represented litigants
- vicarious liability

THINKING ABOUT CORRECTIONAL POLICIES AND PRACTICES: WRITING ASSIGNMENTS

1. Develop a one page summary of the some of the reasons why inmate lawsuits increased so dramatically in the 1970s. Which of those reasons do you think had the greatest impact? Why?
2. Prepare an opinion-editorial (op-ed) for the local newspaper on the issue of whether and to what extent inmates have a right to privacy. What would this mean in terms of COs of one gender monitoring prisoners of the other?
3. In what area of litigation have inmates been most effective in getting basic rights? In what area have they been least effective in getting these same rights? Support your answer with reference to the cases involved.
4. The Prison Litigation Reform Act (PLRA) was successful in reducing inmate lawsuits. Argue why this is a positive or negative development for American corrections.
5. Dale Maisano filed more than 9,400 lawsuits arguing that the conditions of his imprisonment are cruel and unusual. Argue that (a) frequent filers are important for raising issues that might be common to all prisoners, or (b) that the time and resources used to respond to these prisoners make it difficult for the courts to address more serious issues.

CRITICAL REVIEW QUESTIONS

1. What is your reaction to the Supreme Court's ruling requiring California's prison system to reduce its population by almost 40,000 prisoners because the conditions were cruel and unusual? Would you feel different if a family member was a California prisoner?
2. Jailhouse lawyers increase the number of lawsuits filed by prisoners. Give at least two other reasons why prison administrators would want to limit or prohibit the practice of inmates helping other inmates file appeals.
3. After examining the number of petitions and lawsuits filed, list some of the ways the Prison Litigation Reform Act and the Antiterrorism and Effective Death Penalty Act have changed the nature of prison inmate litigation.
4. Compare and contrast inmate habeas corpus petitions with civil rights actions. Are the goals of each the same or different? Explain.
5. Should advocates for inmates' rights, such as the ACLU or Southern Poverty Law Center, be filing lawsuits on behalf of inmates? Why do inmates need advocacy groups?
6. How do the legal status and constitutional protections of probationers and parolees differ?
7. Should attorneys represent offenders when their federal lawsuits are being heard? If these prisoners cannot afford an attorney, should the state appoint counsel?
8. Do you think jails and prisons should be air conditioned for inmates and the correctional staff? Why or why not?
9. What evidence do we have that litigation is improving the lives of jail and prison inmates? Describe the areas where you see the greatest improvement.
10. Could independent advocates that identify problems in correctional facilities, such as ombudsmen, reduce the amount of inmate litigation? Why or why not?

CASES

Apodaca v. Raemisch 586 U.S. ____ (2018)
Argesinger v. Hamlin, 407 U.S. 25 (1972)
Atkins v. Virginia, 536 U.S. 304 (2002)
Batson v. Kentucky, 476 U.S. 79 (1986)
Baze v. Rees, 553 U.S. 35 (2008)
Bell v. Wolfish, 441 U.S. 520 (1979)

Bounds v. Smith, 430 U.S. 817 (1977)

Bruce v. Samuels, 136 S. Ct. 627 (2016)

Bruscino v. Carlson, 654 F. Supp. 609 (SD Ill. 1987)

Clement v. California Department of Corrections, 364 F. 3d 1148 (9th Cir., 2004)

Coleman v. Tollefson, 575 U.S. _____ (2015)

Cooper v. Pate, 378 U.S. 546 (1964)

Estelle v. Gamble, 429 U.S. 97 (1976)

Fay v. Noia, 372 U.S. 391 (1963)

Furman v. Georgia, 408 U.S. 238 (1972).

Gagnon v. Scarpelli, 411 U.S. 778 (1973)

Gideon v. Wainwright, 372 U.S. 355 (1963)

Gregg v. Georgia, 428 U.S. 153 (1976)

Harrington v. Richter, 562 U.S., 86

Helling v. McKinney, 509 U.S. 25 (1993)

Holt v. Sarver, 309 F. Supp. 362 (E.D. Ark. 1970)

Johnson v. Avery, 393 U.S. 483 (1969)

Kennedy v. Louisiana, 554 U.S. 407 (2008)

Lee v. Downs, 641 F2d 1117 (4th Cir., 1981)

Lockyer v. Andrade, 538 U.S. 63

Lyons v. Peters – 3:17-cv-00730-SI (2019)

Mempa v. Rhay, 389 U.S. 128 (1967)

Miranda v. Arizona, 384 U.S. 436 (1966)

Monroe v. Pape, 365 U.S. 167

Morrissey v. Brewer, 408 U.S. 471 (1972)

Panetti v. Quarterman, 551 U.S. 930 (2007)

Penry v. Johnson, 532 U.S. 782 (2001)

Powell v. Alabama, 287 U.S. 45 (1932)

Pugh v. Locke, 406 F. Supp. 318 (MD Ala., 1976)

Ramirez v. Pugh, 379 F3d 122 (3rd Cir. 8-12-04, 2004)

Rhodes v. Chapman, 452 U.S. 337 (1981)

Ring v. Arizona, 536 U.S. 586 (2002)

Roper v. Simmons, 543 U.S. 551 (2005)

Ruffin v. Commonwealth, 62 Va. 790 (1871)

Ruiz v. Estelle, 503 F. Supp. 1265 (S. D. Tex., 1980)

Sanders v. United States, 373 U.S. 1 (1963)

Serra v. Lappin, 600 F.3d 1190 (2010)

Sester v. Grant County Detention Center (2005) USDC ED YK, Case No. 03-33-DLB

Stanford v. Kentucky, 492 U.S. 361 (1989)

Timm v. Gunter, 917F2d 1093 (8th Cir., 1990)

Townsend v. Sain, 372 U.S. 293 (1963)

Turner v. Safley, 482 U.S. 78 (1987)

United States v. Haymond, 588 U.S. _____ (2019)

United States v. Wesley Lanham, 09-5094 (6th Cir. 2010).

Williams v. Taylor, 529 U.S. 362 (2000)

Yates v. Collier 868 F.3d 354 (2017)

REFERENCES

Abel Screening. (2019). *Use and acceptance*. Retrieved from https://abelscreening.com/use-acceptance/

Adelman, L. (2018). Who killed habeas corpus? *Dissent, 65*(1), 97–105.

Adler, J. L. (2019, November 15). Why incarcerated people must be able to speak out about abuse. *The Washington Post*. Retrieved from https://www.washingtonpost.com/outlook/2019/11/15/why-incarcerated-people-must-be-able-speak-out-t-abuse/

Amnesty International. (2019). *Detention and imprisonment*. Retrieved from https://www.amnesty.org/en/what-we-do/detention/

Arnold, W. R. (2019, May 4). Setting precedent, a federal court rules jail must give inmate addiction treatment. *National Public Radio*. Retrieved from https://www.npr.org/sections/health-shots/2019/05/04/719805278/setting-precedent-a-federal-court-rules-jail-must-give-inmate-addiction-treatmen

Associated Press. (2018, May 5). Many state hospital, prison doctors without medical licenses. *Associated Press*. Retrieved from https://www.washingtontimes.com/news/2018/may/5/many-state-hospital-prison-doctors-without-medical/

Association of State Correctional Administrators. (2018). *Reforming restrictive housing: The 2018 ASCA-Liman nationwide survey of time in cell*. Yale University: Arthur Liman Center for Public Interest Law.

Astrada, M. L. (2019). Death, law & politics: The effects of embracing liberty-restrictive vs. liberty-enhancing interpretation of habeas corpus. *University of Baltimore Law Review, 48*(2), 147–202.

Beck, A. J. (2014). *Sexual victimization in prisons and jails reported by inmates, 2011–2012*. Washington, DC: Bureau of Justice Statistics.

Beck, A. J. (2015). *Use of restrictive housing in U.S. prisons and jails, 2011–12*. Washington, DC: Bureau of Justice Statistics.

Bronson, J., & Carson, E. A. (2019). *Prisoners in 2017*. Washington, DC: Bureau of Justice Statistics.

Bureau of Justice Statistics. (2019). *Corrections statistical analysis tool (CSAT) – prisoners*. Retrieved from https://www.bjs.gov/index.cfm?ty=nps

Burnett, C. (1998). "Frivolous" claims by the attorney general. *Social Justice, 25*(2), 184–204.

California Department of Corrections and Rehabilitation. (2019). *Office of the ombudsman*. Retrieved from https://www.cdcr.ca.gov/ombuds/

Call, J. C. (1995). The Supreme Court and prisoner's rights. *Federal Probation, 59*(1), 36–46.

Carlino, R. M., & Franklin, A. (2018). *Out of sight: LGBTQ youth and adults in Texas' justice systems.* Austin: Texas Criminal Justice Coalition.

Chammah, M. (2015). The sex-offender test. *The Atlantic.* Retrieved from https://www.theatlantic.com/politics/archive/2015/07/the-sex-offender-test/397850/

Chammah, M. (2017). "Cooking them to death": The lethal toll of hot prisons. *The Marshall Project.* Retrieved from https://www.themarshallproject.org

Chase, R. T. (2015). We are not slaves: Rethinking the rise of carceral states through the lens of the prisoners' rights movement. *The Journal of American History, 102*(1), 73–86.

Chehayeb, K. (2019, June 7). Torture in Saudi prisons: 'Most oppressive era we have witnessed.' *Al Jazeera.* Retrieved from https://www.aljazeera.com/indepth/features/torture-saudi-prisons-oppressive-era-witnessed-190606091245089.html

Clark, A. B. (2017). Juvenile solitary confinement as a form of child abuse. *Journal of the American Academy of Psychiatry and the Law Online, 45*(3), 350–357.

Clarke, M., & Zoukis, C. (2018). Litigation heats up over extreme temperatures in prisons, jails. *Prison Legal News.* Retrieved from https://www.prisonlegalnews.org/news/2018/jun/29/litigation-heats-over-extreme-temperatures-prisons-jails/

Coles, F. S. (1987). The impact of Bell v. Wolfish upon prisoners' rights. *Journal of Crime and Justice, 10*(1), 47–69.

Collins, W. C. (2010). *Correctional law for the correctional officer.* Laurel, MD: American Correctional Association.

Columbia University. (2017). *A jailhouse lawyer's manual.* Retrieved from http://jlm.law.columbia.edu/current-edition/

Conarck, B. (2019a, May 24). Work forced: A century later, unpaid prison labor continues to power Florida. *Florida Times-Union.* Retrieved from http://gatehousenews.com/workforced/home/site/jacksonville.com?utm_source=The+Marshall+Project+Newsletter&utm_campaign=0af0460c26-EMAIL_CAMPAIGN_2019_05_24_11_47&utm_medium=email&utm_term=0_5e02cdad9d-0af0460c26-174432429

Conarck, B. (2019b, July 24). Florida prison YouTube beating leads to arrests of 3 officers. *The Florida Times-Union.* Retrieved from https://www.jacksonville.com/news/

Consular Section, British Embassy, Riyadh (2018). *Information pack for British prisoners in Saudi Arabia.* Retrieved from https://assets.publishing.service.gov.uk/government/uploads/system/uploads/attachment_data/file/707877/Saudi_Arabia_Prisoner_Pack_for_2018.pdf

Cooke, P. (2019, June 8). Horrifying video shows a prison guard turning off his body camera and beating a mentally-ill inmate strapped to a chair before his colleague joins in. *The Sun.* Retrieved from https://www.thesun.co.uk/news/9248991/video-prison-guard-colleague-body-camera/

Corey, E. (2019, August 8). How a tool to help judges may be leading them astray. *The Appeal.* Retrieved from https://theappeal.org/

Dabney, D. A., & Vaughn, M. S. (2000). Incompetent jail and prison doctors. *The Prison Journal, 80*(2), 151–183.

Dallas Morning News Editorial. (2019, July 15). The debate over heat in state prisons has raged for years. Now Texas is paying the price. *Dallas Morning News.* Retrieved from https://www.dallasnews.com/opinion/editorials/2019/07/15/debate-heat-state-prisons-raged-years-now-texas-paying-price

Drepaul, A. (2019). I had a shitty job in prison. *The Marshall Project*. Retrieved from https://www.themarshallproject.org

Frost, N. A., & Monteiro, C. E. (2016). *Administrative segregation in U.S. prisons*. Washington, DC: National Institute of Justice.

Goel, S., Shroff, R., Skeem, J., & Slobogin, C. (2019). *The accuracy, equity, and jurisprudence of criminal risk assessment*. Retrieved from https://papers.ssrn.com/sol3/papers.cfm?abstract_id=3306723

Goldberg, T. (2018, October 6). Rare honors this weekend for inmate firefighters killed on the job. *KQED news*. Retrieved from https://www.kqed.org/news/11686212/rare-honors-this-weekend-for-inmate-firefighters-killed-on-the-job

Golgowski, N. (2019, May 9). Former corrections officers charged in beating of handcuffed inmate. *Huffington Post*. Retrieved from https://www.huffingtonpost.ca

Hall, G. A. (2012). *Limit on attorney fees barrier to representation for prisoners*. Retrieved from https://adenverlawyer.com/2012/03/22/attorney_plra/

Haney, C. (2018). The psychological effects of solitary confinement: A systematic critique. *Crime and Justice, 47*, 365–416.

Hass, B. (2014, August 15). Man with tummy ache has filed 5,800 lawsuits—and counting. *Tennessean*. Retrieved from https://www.tennessean.com/story/news/crime/2014/08/15/man-tummy-ache-filed-lawsuits-counting/14067811/

Heffernan, R., Wegerhoff, D., & Ward, T. (2019). Dynamic risk factors: Conceptualization, measurement, and evidence. *Aggression and Violent Behavior, 48*(1), 6–16.

Hoke, S., & Demory, R. (2014). *Inmate behavior management: Guide to meeting basic needs*. Washington, DC: National Institute of Corrections.

Holt, D. W. E. (2015). *Heat in US prisons and jails*. New York: Columbia Law School, Sabin Center for Climate Change Law.

Hopwood, S. R. (2011). Slicing through the great legal Gordian knot: Ways to assist pro se litigants in their quest for justice. *Fordham Law Review, 80*(3), 1229–1240.

Innocence Project. (2020). *Exonerate the innocent*. Retrieved from https://www.innocenceproject.org/exonerate/

Innocence Project. (2020b). *DNA exonerations in the United States*. Retrieved from https://www.innocenceproject.org/dna-exonerations-in-the-united-states/

Inserra, P. (2019). I lost 25 pounds in 4 months eating prison food. *The Marshall Project*. Retrieved from https://www.themarshallproject.org/2019/05/16/i-lost-25-pounds-in-4-months-eating-prison-food

Jenness, V., & Calavita, K. (2017). Prisoner grievances, rights, and the culture of control. *Ohio State Journal of Criminal Law, 15*(1), 211–228.

Jordan, J. P. (2019, January 17). Saudi Arabia's jails and U.S. prison imperialism. *Liberation*. Retrieved from https://www.liberationnews.org/saudi-arabias-jails-and-u-s-prison-imperialism/

Kaul, P., Donley, G., Cavataro, B., Benavides, A., Kincaid, J., & Chatham, J. (2015). *Prison and jail grievance policies: Lessons from a fifty-state survey*. Retrieved from https://www.law.umich.edu/special/policyclearinghouse/Site%20Documents/FOIAReport10.18.15.2.pdf

Lawtrades. (2019). What are average lawyer fees per hour in the US? *Lawtrades*. Retrieved from https://www.lawtrades.com/answers/what-are-average-lawyer-fees-per-hour-in-the-us/

Legislative Analyst's Office. (2019). *How much does it cost to incarcerate an inmate? (January 2019)*. Retrieved from https://lao.ca.gov/policyareas/cj/6_cj_inmatecost

Leventis Lourgos, A. (2019). 'I'm safe here': Transgender inmate describes life at Illinois women's prison after rare transfer based on gender identity. *Chicago Tribune*. Retrieved from https://www.chicagotribune.com/news/ct-met-transgender-prisoner-illinois-strawberry-hampton-20190124-story.html

Lovins, B. K., Latessa, E. J., May, T., & Lux, J. (2018). Validating the Ohio risk assessment system community supervision tool with a diverse sample from Texas. *Corrections, 3*(3), 186–202.

Martin, M. W. (2011). Foreword: Root causes of the pro se prisoner litigation crisis, *Fordham Law Review, 80*(3), 1219–1228.

Martinson, R. (1974). What works? Questions and answers about prison reform. *The Public Interest, 35*(1), 22–54.

Mateus, E., & Levy, D. (2019, Oct. 21). Fighting fire while doing time. *San Quentin News*. Retrieved from https://sanquentinnews.com/wall-city-volume-2-issue-2-burned/

Mays, G. L. (1983). Stone v. Powell: The impact on state supreme court judges' perceptions. *Journal of Criminal Justice, 11*(1), 27–34.

Mays, G. L., & Ruddell, R. (2019). *Making sense of criminal justice, 3rd edition*. New York: Oxford University Press.

Miller, J. (2018, June 21). Utah to pay $450K to the widow of an inmate killed in prison, settling a lawsuit. *The Salt Lake Tribune*. Retrieved from https://www.sltrib.com/news/2018/06/21/utah-to-pay-450k-to-the-widow-of-an-inmate-killed-in-prison-settling-a-lawsuit/

Nasr, W. (2013, December 17). Video: The brutal life inside Saudi prisons. *The Observers*. Retrieved from https://observers.france24.com/en/20131217-saudi-prison-beatings-sytem-video

National Institute of Justice. (2015). *Topical working group on the use of administrative segregation in the U.S.* Washington, DC: U.S. Department of Justice.

National Registry of Exonerations. (2020a). *Conviction integrity units*. Retrieved from http://www.law.umich.edu/special/exoneration/Pages/Conviction-Integrity-Units.aspx

National Registry of Exonerations. (2020b). *Exonerations in the United States*. Retrieved from http://www.law.umich.edu/special/exoneration/Pages/Exonerations-in-the-United-States-Map.aspx

Newman, W. J., & Scott, C. L. (2012). Brown v. Plata: Prison overcrowding in California. *The Journal of the American Academy of Psychiatry and the Law, 40*(4), 547–552.

Nowicki, J. (2019, July 22). Pritzker passes 100 mark in bill-signing—with new laws on texting while driving, food stamps, term limits. *Chicago Sun Times*. Retrieved from https://chicago.suntimes.com/2019/7/22/20706477/pritzker-passes-100-mark-laws-texting-driving-food-stamps-term-limits

Office of the Clerk, Supreme Court of the United States. (2018). *Guide for prospective indigent petitioners for writs of certiorari*. Retrieved from https://www.supremecourt.gov/casehand/guide-forifpcases2018.pdf

Peacher, A. (2019, May 16). Court to rule on sex reassignment surgery for Idaho inmate. *National Public Radio*. Retrieved from https://www.npr.org/2019/05/16/723583909/court-to-rule-on-sex-reassignment-surgery-for-idaho-inmate

Pereira, S. (2018). Mass incarceration: Slavery renamed. *Themis: Research Journal of Justice Studies and Forensic Science, 6*(3), 42–54.

Poser, R. (2016). Why it's nearly impossible for prisoners to sue prisons. *The New Yorker*. Retrieved from https://www.newyorker.com/news/news-desk/why-its-nearly-impossible-for-prisoners-to-sue-prisons

Rhodes, S. L. (1992). Prison reform and prison life: Four books on the process of court-ordered change. *Law & Society Review, 26*(1), 189–218.

Ross, J. I. (2012). Debunking the myths of American corrections: An exploratory analysis. *Critical Criminology, 20*(4), 409–427.

Roth, A. (2014, July 24). Do heat-sensitive inmates have a right to air conditioning? *National Public Radio*. Retrieved from https://www.npr.org/2014/07/24/334049647/do-heat-sensitive-inmates-have-a-right-to-air-conditioning

Sacramento Bee. (2019, June 13). Cruel and usual: A guide to California's broken prisons and the fight to fix them. *Sacramento Bee*. Retrieved from https://www.sacbee.com/news/investigations/california-prisons/article230957473.html

Sawyer, W. (2017). How much do incarcerated people earn in each state? *Prison Policy Initiative*. Retrieved from https://www.prisonpolicy.org/blog/2017/04/10/wages/

Scalia, J. (2002). *Prisoner petitions filed in U.S. district courts, 2000, with trends, 1980–2000.* Washington, DC: Bureau of Justice Statistics.

Schlanger, M. (2003). Inmate litigation. *Harvard Law Review, 116*(6), 1555–1706.

Schlanger, M. (2015). Trends in prisoner litigation, as the PLRA enters adulthood. *University of California Irvine Law Review, 5*(1), 153–178.

Schlanger, M. (2017). Trends in prisoner litigation, as the PLRA approaches 20. *Correctional Law Reporter, 28*(5), 69–88.

Schwartzapfel, B. (2019, July 1). Can racist algorithms be fixed? *The Marshall Project*. Retrieved from www.themarshallproject.com

Sheck, B. C. (2017). Conviction integrity units revisited. *Ohio State Journal of Criminal Law, 14*(2), 705–752.

Sullivan, K. (2015, March 1). A rare look inside a Saudi prison that showers terrorists with perks. *Washington Post*. Retrieved from https://www.washingtonpost.com/world/middle_east/a-rare-look-inside-a-saudi-prison-that-showers-terrorists-with-perks/2015/03/01/2da9dfb4-a64e-11e4-a162-121d06ca77f1_story.html?utm_term=.fc5dfe929728

Taylor, J. R. (2011). Constitutionally unprotected: Prison slavery, felon disenfranchisement, and the criminal exception to citizenship rights. *Gonzaga Law Review, 47*(2), 365–392.

Thomas, J. (1988). *Prison litigation: The paradox of the jailhouse lawyer.* Totawa, NJ: Rowman and Littlefield.

Thomas, J., Wheeler, D., & Harris, K. (1986). Issues and misconceptions in prisoner litigation: A crucial view. *Criminology, 24*(4), 775–797.

Thompson, C. (2019). Money-making schemes that ensnare prisoners and their families. *The Marshall Project*. Retrieved from https://www.themarshallproject.org/

Tucker, W. (2016). Profits v. prisoners: How the largest U.S. prison care provider puts lives in danger. *Southern Poverty Law Center*. Retrieved from https://www.splcenter.org/20161027/profits-vs-prisoners-how-largest-us-prison-health-care-provider-puts-lives-danger

Umphres, E. (2019). 150% wrong: The prison litigation reform act and attorney's fees. *American Criminal Law Review, 56*(1), 261–293.

U.S. Courts. (2019). *Caseload statistics data tables.* Retrieved from https://www.uscourts.gov/statistics-reports/caseload-statistics-data-tables?tn=C-3&pn=All&t=All&m%5Bvalue%5D%5Bmonth%5D=&y%5Bvalue%5D%5Byear%5D=&=Apply

U.S. Department of Justice. (2019a). *Department of Justice activities under the Civil Rights of Institutionalized Persons Act. Fiscal year 2018.* Washington, DC: Author.

U.S. Department of Justice. (2019b). *Investigation of Alabama's state prisons for men.* Washington, DC: Author.

U.S. District Court, District of Minnesota. (2015). *Prisoner civil rights federal litigation guidebook.* Retrieved from https://www.mnd.uscourts.gov/Pro-Se/PrisonerCivilRightsLitigGuide.pdf

Valentine, C. L., Restivo, E., & Wright, K. (2019). Prolonged isolation as a predictor of mental health for waived juveniles. *Journal of Offender Rehabilitation, 58*(4), 352–369.

Ward, M. (2013). Lawsuits: At least 13 men overheated, died in un-air-conditioned Texas prisons. *Statesman.* Retrieved from https://www.statesman.com/article/20130614/NEWS/306149720

Ware, M. (2011/2012). Dallas county conviction integrity unit and the importance of getting it right the first time. *New York Law School Law Review, 56*(3), 1033–1050.

Zeng, Z. (2019). *Jail inmates in 2017.* Washington, DC: Bureau of Justice Statistics.

Chapter 13
The Future of Corrections

OUTLINE

- Introduction
- Future Correctional Philosophies
- Forecasting Future Correctional Trends
- External Factors Influencing Correctional Operations
- Internal Factors Influencing Correctional Operations
- Future Correctional Research
- The Challenges Ahead for Corrections
- Vested Interests and the Prison-Industrial Complex
- Summary

OBJECTIVES

After reading this chapter you will be able to:

- Explain the struggles over competing correctional philosophies

- Describe the importance of forecasting for correctional organizations

- Describe the internal and external factors affecting the field of corrections

- Explain why correctional reforms are so difficult to make when we consider the vested interests of stakeholders

CASE STUDY

The Challenge of Detaining Children in Immigration Detention Facilities

A crackdown on people illegally entering the United States in 2017–2019 created a significant challenge for U.S. Customs and Border Protection as it led to overcrowding in detention facilities along the southern border. Although these facilities have been overcrowded in the past, there was considerable media coverage about the treatment of the children of these detainees as they were separated from their parent(s) or other family members and held in separate facilities. The practice of separating children and adult detainees—even though they were family members—had been going on for years. Linton, Griffin, and Shapiro (2017, p. 2) report that over 135,000 unaccompanied youths and children who had been apprehended at the border were detained in 2014. By 2019, however, there was growing attention paid to these children with accompanying outrage that these separations were taking place.

The media accounts of the confinement of these youngsters attracted visits from representatives from the United Nations, US legislators, and various groups of doctors, activists, and scholars. None were complimentary about the conditions of confinement, which were widely considered unsafe and unsanitary. Chotiner (2019, para. 1) writes about a group of lawyers who toured a Texas detention facility and said that:

> flu and lice outbreaks were going untreated, and children were filthy, sleeping on cold floors, and taking care of one another because of the lack of attention from the guards. Some of them had been in the facility for weeks.

Lind (2019, para. 1) says that detained children are only supposed to be held for 72 hours and then transferred to the Department of Health and Human Services, who are responsible for finding relatives in the United States who can care for them until their cases are resolved. Few of these youngsters, however, were discharged within three days and some were held for weeks or longer. Lind notes that the Border Patrol wasn't set up to detain children, but ended up holding over 2,000 in their facilities on any given day. The cramped and sometimes chaotic conditions lead to reports of mistreatment of these youths, including sexual assaults. Beyond their physical well-being, the Department of Health and Human Services' own Office of Inspector General found that these children received insufficient mental health and speculated that the results of their detention could be long lasting (Chiedi, 2019).

Children's advocates were concerned that seven minors died in these facilities, but none had died in the previous ten years (Holpuch, 2019). The U.S. House of Representatives

Committee on Oversight and Reform (2019, p. 1) reports that at least 18 children under two years of age were separated from their parents from 20 to 120 days. Hundreds of these separated children were kept in Border Patrol facilities longer than the 72 hours allowed by law or were transferred between facilities and could not be reunited with their families even after their parents or family members were released from detention. The Committee reported that some youngsters had not been reunited with their families for over a year, and reuniting them could be difficult because their parents had been deported and were now living in other countries.

PHOTO 13.1
A Border Patrol agent is supervising immigration detainees in an Arizona facility. The number of non US citizens held in these facilities reached record numbers in 2019, which has had implications for holding these people. Credit: Jim West/Alamy Stock Photo.

The uproar over detaining these young people in such poor conditions was magnified when it was reported that some facilities were charging up to $775 a day for each child they held, although the average cost of holding these children was one-third that amount (Burnett, 2019). Regardless of the costs or the labels we attach to these young people, or how long this practice was happening prior to 2019, their poor treatment suggests that we can do better.

Critical Questions

1. Some politicians have called immigration detention facilities concentration camps. Do you agree with their assessment? Why or why not?
2. Provide some possible reasons why there was a lack of publicity about the detention of these children and young people prior to 2017.
3. How can one correctional officer working in a detention facility ensure that the people in their care receive just and fair treatment?

INTRODUCTION

One of the exciting things about studying or being involved in corrections is that there always seem to be more questions than answers. This condition is a challenge to those responding to society's long-term crime and punishment dilemmas. For example, how do we increase public safety while treating people convicted of crimes in a fair and just manner? As noted in Chapter 1, these contentious issues have plagued humankind for hundreds of years, and there are no easy answers. These issues are both persistent and critical; moreover, those working in the criminal justice system will no doubt face them well into the future.

In this chapter we examine several issues that have troubled those interested in the field of corrections for some time. After reading the previous 12 chapters, you should have a better appreciation of the challenges posed for the corrections system in managing an accused person's detention in a local jail, their involvement with community corrections (e.g. when presentencing reports are prepared if they are found guilty), and then ensuring their punishments are carried out, whether that sanction is a probationary or a death sentence. In the pages that follow, we identify several challenges correctional systems will confront well into the future. Our list is by no means exhaustive. Indeed, your instructor may add others, while you may feel there are problems that we do not address here. This chapter's case study on immigration detention, for example, was an issue that emerged during the preparation of this book.

We are in good company in our exploration of the future of corrections, as many practitioners, scholars, and other correctional researchers have attempted this same task. For example, a special issue of *The Prison Journal*, published in 1987, drew upon the expertise of 15 contributors who predicted the future of corrections. Looking back at these forecasts three decades later, we find that these contributors were optimistic about the future. Indeed, they predicted a decrease in prison populations, an increased reliance on correctional rehabilitation, and the application of more community-based programs. These contributors did not, however, predict the widespread embracing by policymakers of the "get tough on offenders" philosophy and practices, the increased number of life-sentenced inmates, and the growth in prison populations. Nor did they foresee the move away from correctional rehabilitation and giving incarcerated people only the bare minimum they need to survive, or the political reluctance to get smart on crime rather than getting tough.

We do not have to look back three decades to find efforts at understanding the future of corrections. For instance, the National Institute of Corrections (NIC) conducts a broad assessment of the factors that can influence correctional practices. These **environmental scans** focus primarily on external factors, including changes in the population, economy, workforce, technology, health care, and crime rates (NIC, 2019). RAND has also assembled panels of correctional experts to envision the future of community and institutional corrections (Russo, Drake, Shaffer, & Jackson, 2017). Their efforts help jail and prison administrators predict some future possibilities and thereby reduce the negative impacts of unexpected trends on correctional operations.

As you read this final chapter, you will no doubt recognize material we have discussed elsewhere. We also present new content, statistics, observations, and speculations. Our goal is to suggest that future answers are firmly rooted in the past and in the present. We start our review where we began this book; with the philosophies of corrections.

FUTURE CORRECTIONAL PHILOSOPHIES

An ongoing issue in contemporary corrections is which correctional philosophy or group of philosophies do we choose to follow? Simply put: What underlying social values will guide our approach to correcting criminal behavior as we approach the midpoint of the twenty-first century? For the most part in the United States today, the guiding principle is punishment. The interrelated philosophies of retribution, deterrence, and incapacitation continue to shape our corrections policies as they have since the 1970s. It seems that the public has a desire for more severe criminal sanctions, and policymakers, but especially politicians at all levels, were eager to pander to that penchant. There is some debate about whether the public actually leads the discussion on being tough on crime, or whether they are just repeating the messages that are sent by politicians. Regardless of where these messages originated, they have resulted in America's imprisonment and probation rates being the highest in the world.

In the previous chapters we described the tough on crime strategies that led to mass imprisonment and mass probation. These strategies included three-strikes sentencing, truth-in-sentencing, mandatory minimum sentences, eliminating parole in some jurisdictions, and sentencing guidelines that removed the discretion from judges. Pfaff (2017) says that in a get tough environment city and county prosecutors had almost unchecked power to maximize sanctions on local offenders, but they saw no downside to the resulting harsh sentences, as state taxpayers paid the bill for imposing these harsh sanctions. Pfaff's work is attracting the attention of many reformers who want to end or at least moderate mass imprisonment policies. The problem is that in order to downsize prisons we have to reduce the number of persons incarcerated for committing all types of offenses, including violent crimes. In the sections that follow we question whether there is a political willingness to take that risk.

Our punishments seem to be softening somewhat since correctional populations peaked in 2007. In the previous chapters we described how the number of executions has been dropping since 1998 and prison populations decreased 13% between 2007 and 2017 (Bronson & Carson, 2019). In addition, some tough on crime punishments have been modified to reduce their severity. Californians, for instance, voted for changes in law that rolled back the use of three-strike sentences, and the harsh punishments for violating some drug laws have been lessened in some states. Moreover, laws such as *First Step Act* were introduced to give some federal prisoners pathways to early releases from prison. These changes were also taking place in the juvenile courts and youth incarceration rates for males decreased by 59% between 1997 and 2017 and 53% for females (Sickmund, Sladky, Kang, & Puzzanchera, 2019).

Challenging Mass Imprisonment Policies

In an influential paper, Listwan and colleagues (2008) identified four cracks in the get tough on crime movement. They argued that the public might not be as punitive as many politicians believe and are receptive to ideas about correctional rehabilitation and giving young people second chances. Second, they said that the public was having misgivings about get tough on crime practices, including three-strikes sentencing and mandatory minimum sentences. Third, many members of the public support legislative changes that ease punishments for some offenders. Last, there was a movement to introduce evidence-based correctional interventions, themselves derived from cost-benefit analyses that research shows decreases recidivism (Washington State Institute for Public Policy, 2019).

The movement to moderate mass imprisonment policies that Listwan and colleagues (2008) identified has contributed to lower prison populations, but reforms to the justice system are often gradual, irregular, and slow; what some call a piecemeal approach to policy making. Moreover, Listwan and colleagues (2008) did not anticipate the impacts of the financial crisis that happened after their analysis was published. Karstedt, Bergin, and Koch (2019) say that the financial crisis helped to reduce correctional populations, and even conservative political organizations started to oppose high imprisonment practices. The public began to realize that every taxpayer dollar spent on imprisonment takes funds from schools, roads, health care, and parks that benefit all citizens.

Karstedt and associates (2019) could not find a single cause for putting the brakes on high imprisonment policies. They contend that economic, political, and legal factors all contributed to create this decrease. Are correctional policies and practices based on retribution dead? The short answer is no, and that is not a bad response, as the criminal justice system requires some tough sanctions to respond to those people who pose a high risk to public safety. While all of us would agree there are dangerous people who need to be imprisoned for very long periods of time there is less consensus on who should be considered a serious or dangerous offender, or how long they should remain incarcerated.

Justice Reinvestment

While not a distinct correctional philosophy, justice reinvestment (JR) is most closely related to rehabilitative philosophies. JR was introduced by the Council of State Governments and is based on the notion of reducing the reliance on imprisonment and using those dollars to develop programs that tackle the underlying problems that lead to criminal behavior (Fox, Albertson, & Warburton, 2011). A foundation of the JR model is that local governments use the crime data they collect to better understand the nature of the crime problem, including what crimes are increasing or decreasing, and who is committing these offenses. This information is then used to develop crime-prevention strategies.

JR, as proposed by the Council of State Governments (2018, Part 1), promotes crime reduction by strengthening communities and breaking the cycle of offending by using the following strategies:

- Reducing crime and strengthening communities by improving responses to people who have behavioral health needs, such as persons with mental illnesses, in the local criminal justice systems. Governments should ensure these people have access to supports and interventions that reduce recidivism.
- Local governments must use jail spaces more cost-effectively, including cutting the number of low-risk, pretrial detainees. Communities are encouraged to develop crime-reduction strategies that prevent violent crime and strengthen trust in law enforcement.
- Breaking the cycle of reoffending by using assessments to determine risk and needs and ensuring that interventions are prioritized for high-risk individuals. Moreover, the effectiveness of probation and parole supervision should be improved to reduce recidivism, including giving these individuals the resources they need to succeed.

One of the strengths of the JR approach is that it acknowledges the importance of providing community support to help people who have committed crimes overcome their problems or respond to their unmet needs. The challenge, however, is the reluctance to fund those programs properly. Moreover, reducing the number of jail and prison inmates necessarily diverts those individuals into the community, and some will inevitably commit new crimes, including serious and violent ones. Because the public might be less willing to accept those risks than the developers of these programs, politicians may be reluctant to support those changes.

Abolishing Prisons

The ultimate rejection of tough on crime policies is abolishing prisons altogether. This notion, which is very loosely associated with the restorative justice approach, emerges every decade or so and then seems to disappear. Holloway (1974) and Mathiesen (1986) wrote about prison abolishment decades ago. While this concept never disappears entirely from debates about corrections, the issue resurfaced in 2016–2017 and has become more mainstream since then. Opinion pieces about prison abolishment have appeared in the *New York Times*, and the *Harvard Law Review* published a special issue on abolition in April 2019. The abolitionist movement is not limited to corrections, as various social and political activists, along with academic scholars, have also called for an end to policing as we know it (Meares, 2017; Vitale, 2017). People endorsing the abolition of the police or prisons do not believe these institutions can be reformed and argue that it will take too long before incremental or piecemeal reforms can make any meaningful changes in these institutions. They might have a point, as the Sentencing Project predicts that it would take 75 years to cut America's prison population by one-half (Ghandnoosh, 2018).

Radical abolitionists tend to see criminal justice systems as oppressive and rooted in a capitalist system that profits from the use of punishment. As a result, they argue that the entire system needs to be transformed. A comment by a prison abolitionist describes his feelings toward the justice system:

> Regarding the **prison industrial complex**—a term many abolitionists use to refer to the collective of prisons, jails and detention centers, and the structures that support them, like bail, police and more—Schenwar says, "Once we understand that basically its roots are rotten, then we understand that we can't replace certain aspects of it or improve it or make prison kinder and gentler; we actually have to uproot it."
>
> (Arrieta-Kenna, 2018, para. 22)

Keller (2019) says that while the notion of abolishing prisons is radical, the idea has been gaining momentum and talking about abolition has become mainstream. In March 2020, for example, Rutgers University held an event on prison abolition where a keynote speaker urged the audience "to imagine a world without prisons" (Boccher, 2020, para. 4). While few activists believe that jails or prisons could be completely eliminated, most say that America's reliance on incarceration could be reduced. Like the supporters of JR, these abolitionists believe that crimes would be prevented if the money used for imprisonment was instead invested in housing, education, jobs, and health care. That position is less controversial, and many correctional officials would agree that a strong network of community supports would divert some individuals from the criminal justice system, reduce the need to incarcerate some people, and reduce the recidivism of former prisoners.

Correctional Reforms

History tells us that society's responses to crime and punishment shift from periods of rehabilitation to times when harsh punishments are imposed. Bernard and Kurlychek (2010), in describing this idea, point to the experience of the juvenile justice system in the United States since the 1800s. When the public perceives that leniency is not working and that it seems to promote delinquency, there is a cry for much harsher penalties for youthful offenders, in the belief that more severe punishment will solve the delinquency problem. When those punishments subsequently fail, reformers advocate for new responses that are more lenient, and the cycle continues. Society expects juvenile justice policy to solve the problem of delinquency, but the reality is that juveniles are a high-offending group: no policy, no matter how well intended or conceived, can change this basic fact. On this point, Bernard and Kurlychek observe that the only hope we have for lowering juvenile crime is if we discover a previously undiscovered policy that will somehow convert juveniles into a low-offending group. They argue that this is the best rationale for making the juvenile justice system as lenient as possible.

We would argue that the cycle Bernard and Kurlychek identify in the juvenile justice system also exists for the entire criminal justice system. At some point it becomes apparent—at least to many criminal justice practitioners—that getting tougher does not seem to be working. What happens next? Often, they adapt the harsher penalties to make these practices less severe. Walker (2015) calls this response the **law of criminal justice thermodynamics**. By this phrase, Walker means that the more severe criminal penalties become, the less likely practitioners are willing to apply those sanctions. Examples include punishments that seem out of proportion with their seriousness such as permanently seizing a person's vehicle if they were speeding. While that option might exist in the law, most officials would be reluctant to impose such a punishment. In essence, the crime is made to fit the punishment, and the result is often a more lenient approach to dealing with offenders than the policymakers had intended.

There are other ways of interpreting changes in criminal justice policies. A popular view of criminal justice reform is based on the notion of a pendulum that swings or shifts back and forth from eras of harsh punishments to times when rehabilitation becomes popular. This metaphor has been used for decades. Goodman, Page, and Phelps (2017) challenge that view of reform. They argue that it oversimplifies the nature of correctional changes. Instead, they say that changes are the end result of the long-term struggles of reformers. These changes also occur within the context of larger trends such as changing economic, political, and legal factors. Increases and decreases in crime also contribute to changing correctional priorities.

The arguments posed by Goodman, Page, and Phelps are appealing because they acknowledge the impact of reformers and public interest groups. Some of these individuals and groups are well-organized and they have access to significant economic and political clout. They hire lobbyists who attempt to influence politicians, making financial contributions to their campaigns. Other reformist groups and organizations have fewer resources, but they can successfully communicate their messages to the public. For example, FAMM (once called Families Against Mandatory Minimums) is a non-profit organization that fights to reduce the severity of correctional punishments through their advocacy and public education. FAMM was formed in 1991, after the founder's brother, a first-time offender, was sentenced to a mandatory five-year federal prison sentence for growing marijuana. The judge was critical of the sentence length he imposed, but said that his hands were tied because it was a mandatory sentence. Since that time FAMM has grown to 70,000 members and has become a voice for the people who are affected by what they call a broken criminal justice system (FAMM, 2019).

Regardless whether one supports tougher sanctions on people who have committed crimes, or someone advocates for diverting monies spent on corrections to more rehabilitative efforts, they are not alone. There are advocacy organizations, groups of union workers, academics, researchers, family members (of both offenders and victims), and other stakeholders who have a similar position. And as you read this section, there are people who are working tirelessly to abolish prisons and an equally committed group of people who are working toward putting more people in jails or prisons, and having them serve longer sentences. Taken together, their efforts will shape the future of American corrections.

FORECASTING FUTURE CORRECTIONAL TRENDS

The previous 12 chapters described the current trends and issues in American corrections, including the management of special populations (such as persons with mental illnesses), the relationships between community-based and institutional corrections, moving toward more rehabilitative-oriented corrections, how litigation shapes the roles and activities of correctional officers, and how economic factors have influenced correctional operations. All of these factors, and more, will play a significant role in determining the futures of American corrections. But, which of these factors will likely have the greatest influence and why is learning about these factors important?

The administrators in almost every privately or publicly operated organization attempt to identify the factors that will impact future operations. These attempts at predicting or forecasting can be relatively simple undertakings and may only involve informal conversations with agency stakeholders. That agency could be a ten-person county probation office or a ten-resident jail or it could be something much bigger. The outcomes of these discussions for smaller entities, and how these stakeholders propose to manage the future of their organizations may never be written down. Larger organizations, such as state or federal prison systems with tens of thousands of staff members and many times that number in "clients," invest more time and resources in these efforts to predict the different factors that will influence their future operations. All of these agencies, though, necessarily employ many strategies to conduct these assessments, and their efforts are used to develop **strategic plans**, which provide a roadmap for the agency's operations for the future; typically the next five to ten years.

As part of assessing the factors that will influence their operations in the future, some agencies will carry out environmental scans. Such scans involve an examination of the forces that will influence their agency operations. **External factors** include the impact of political, legal, economic, and demographic conditions and changes. Those external forces may be global, national, or local in nature, and correctional agencies have very little control over them. The NIC (2019) conducts an environmental scan every year in order to increase our understanding about these external trends. **Internal factors**, by contrast, are the activities carried out by the correctional administrators and personnel, partners, and stakeholders. These internal policies and procedures are intended to make the community-based or institutional correctional programs more effective or efficient. An example of an internal factor is the composition of the workforce, and how many women or persons with college degrees are hired as correctional officers.

Officials can use their insights about the future to engage in planning for organizational changes. An example of this future planning happened at the Lexington-Fayette Detention Center. This 1,200 bed-jail, which opened in Lexington, Kentucky in 2000, was designed so it could be expanded to 2,000 beds by adding additional pre-planned housing units. The security, heating, communications, plumbing, and electrical systems in this jail were all constructed to facilitate this expansion, which would reduce the building costs. This expansion may be needed, given the population growth in this region, which may translate into more jail admissions a decade or two into the future. While no new beds may ever be added to this jail, correctional administrators in the future have this capacity; moreover, the costs of adding these beds should be lower given the advance planning.

Although planning for the future is an important strategy, there are no guarantees that our predictions will be correct. Trying to predict the future of corrections is much like attempting to forecast the weather as we tend to be more accurate in predicting tomorrow's conditions than what will happen a month from now. Nevertheless, larger correctional agencies try to minimize the threats to their organizations by identifying the factors that will influence their operations. In the two sections that follow we briefly introduce examples of the internal and external factors that will shape correctional operations in the next two decades.

EXTERNAL FACTORS INFLUENCING CORRECTIONAL OPERATIONS

In this section we briefly describe nine external factors that have the potential to shape the operations of community and institutional corrections.

Economics and Corrections

The global recession in 2008 was a reminder to all correctional personnel about how economic factors can influence correctional operations. Economic downturns, or recessions, occur every five to ten years, and these events can last from months to years. Most correctional agencies are able to endure short-term recessions with little impact on their operations. Longer term and severe recessions, however, often have lasting effects on the organization. Turner and colleagues (2015, p. 402) report that governments in an economic downturn will often attempt to cut correctional costs by "closing prisons, reducing staff, and curtailing services and programming." Correctional agencies can also reduce demand by diverting more individuals from the formal justice system and creating community-based alternatives to incarceration that are cheaper than placing people in jails or prisons (Turner et al., 2015). It is likely that the economic downturn that started in 2020 will force policymakers and correctional administrators to make tough decisions about how scarce taxpayer dollars are spent.

Changing Public Attitudes

From the 1970s to the present, the nation has been engaging in various so-called wars on crime and drugs that led to the introduction of tough on crime policies such as three-strikes and truth-in-sentencing. In addition to increasing the number of persons behind bars, these people were held for longer periods. There are indications that politicians and the public have been softening their views of people who have committed crimes since the crime drop has continued. Beginning around 2010, calls for correctional reforms and support for correctional rehabilitation have increased. These calls for change started with reformers and advocacy organizations, such as FAMM, but have become more popular with the general public. Surveys carried out in tough on crime jurisdictions such as Texas, for example, have found overwhelming support for rehabilitation and alternatives to imprisonment for non-violent offenders (Thielo, Cullen, Cohen, & Chouhy, 2016, p. 137). Public support for relaxing tough on crime policies may play an important role in influencing the views of legislators. Pickett (2019), however, says that in the case of the criminal justice system, we lack a clear understanding of the exact nature of the ties between public opinion and political priorities. One warning, however, is that a few well-publicized tragedies—such as a parolee who commits a series of violent crimes—can change public perceptions.

Political Willingness for Correctional Reforms

The enactment of the *First Step Act* in December 2018 was a sign that federal politicians were willing to take steps to reduce the harsh sanctions imposed on some federal offenders as part of the war on drugs. While this legislation will have no impact on state prison populations, it sends a message to state legislators that tough on crime practices can be softened. As we note later, the reform, including this one, of any long-term practice is difficult, time consuming, and often frustrating. Even when changes appear to happen—a new policy or procedure is introduced, for example—the net result may be something less than that intended by those promoting change. Thus, it takes political courage to enact changes and public and stakeholder support to make those changes actually occur as envisioned. Beckett, Reosti, and Knaphus (2016) observe that while many politicians support relaxing punishments on drug offenders, they are reluctant to tackle the issue of easing sanctions, including release on parole, for people who have committed violent crimes. Until this reluctance to release violent offenders is resolved, Beckett and associates observe, there will be a limit to the impact of reformers on mass incarceration.

PHOTO 13.2
President Trump speaks with officials after signing the *First Step Act* and the *Juvenile Justice Reform Act* in December 2018. Although these were small steps, they did signal the federal government's willingness to engage in criminal and juvenile justice reform. Credit: UPI/Alamy Stock Photo.

Supreme Court Decisions

In Chapter 12 we described how correctional officials are at the mercy of decisions made by the U.S. Supreme Court and other appellate courts. Although the Supreme Court has returned to a hands-off orientation in respect to imprisonment since the 1980s, some of their decisions have had long-term and significant impacts on correctional operations. In May 2011, for example, the Court held in *Brown v. Plata* that overcrowding in the California Department of Corrections and Rehabilitation resulted in cruel and unusual conditions of incarceration, which was a violation of the Eighth Amendment. The Court gave the state two years to reduce their prison population by about 33,000 inmates (Kubrin & Seron, 2016). In order to reduce the state prison population, thousands of long-term inmates were placed in county jails, and rates of misconduct and violence increased in those facilities, including a doubling of the number of murdered jail inmates (Pohl & Gabrielson, 2019). Although few recent Supreme Court decisions have had the impact of *Brown v. Plata*, predicting the impact of future court decisions is a risky business.

Technological Changes

New technological innovations have aided both correctional systems and the people they supervise or hold. Contraband smart phones, for example, have made it easier for jail and prison inmates to carry out their criminal enterprises even while incarcerated. Drones drop drugs, weapons, and smart phones into prison yards. Correctional systems have countered these threats by introducing cell phone detectors and attempting to disable drones flying over the correctional facilities. Correctional facilities have long used surveillance cameras. More recently, however, these cameras are linked to artificial intelligence (AI) programs that detect high intensity motions consistent with assaults. These monitoring systems are then able to alert staff that these actions occurred. Some jails and prisons are also introducing body worn cameras, as well as body and package scanners (to detect contraband without requiring strip searches or opening packages). Bala and Trautman (2019) describe how some technological applications can be interconnected to track inmate behaviors continuously using combinations of AI, voice prints, wristbands that track inmate movements, and facial recognition software. Every technological innovation that is introduced for surveillance, however, decreases inmate and staff privacy. And every such innovation is viewed by inmates as a challenge to defeat.

New and Emerging Forms of Crime and Drug Use

Whereas managing inmates with crack cocaine addiction was a problem for correctional facilities in the 1980s and 1990s, jails and prison systems are now admitting inmates suffering from opioid addictions. These people often require some medically supervised detox after their admissions to jail, and also require treatment if detained for long periods of time or are sentenced. Taylor (2018) reports that a federal judge held that jails could not deny these people treatment for their opioid addiction. That decision could have significant and costly implications in states where rates of opioid addictions are high such as Kentucky, Massachusetts, Ohio, Rhode Island, and West Virginia. The presence of opioids in correctional facilities also poses some threats to the correctional staff as it only takes 3 milligrams of fentanyl (which takes the same space as a few grains of salt) to cause a lethal overdose. Trying to control the inflow of drugs into correctional facilities has been an ongoing challenge. Reyes-Velarde (2019) reports that in a seven month period the Orange County, California jail staff intercepted 147 greeting cards that had been soaked in methamphetamine and mailed to jail inmates.

Legislative Changes

Since the 1980s, most legislative changes affecting sentencing and corrections were intended to get tougher on people convicted of committing crimes. Some states have softened their more punitive sentencing practices. For example, California voters supported a legislative change that made it more difficult to be sentenced on a third strike, as well as giving individuals serving three-strike sentences the ability to petition the courts to shorten their sentences. One legislative change that may have a significant impact on corrections in the future is increasing the age of adult responsibility to beyond 18 years of age. The Campaign for Youth Justice (2019) observes that Vermont passed legislation that will raise the age of juvenile court jurisdiction from 18 to 20 years by 2022, and that Connecticut, Massachusetts, Illinois, and Arizona have introduced similar legislation, and other states are considering these changes. These legal changes may create the need for new correctional facilities that are designed to hold older adolescents and young adults together.

Demographic Changes

Changes in the composition of the general population have an impact on correctional populations. The population of males 15–24 years-of-age in the general population, for instance, has historically been a good predictor of admissions to juvenile and adult facilities. As the size of that population grew, so did the number of admissions, which led to correctional overcrowding. Similarly, the size of different religious groups in the national population can also influence correctional programs. The increased number of Muslims in the US population, for example, has created the need for more Muslim chaplains and accommodating the dietary requirements of these prisoners.

Unforeseen (Black Swan) Events

When we look toward the future we often believe that tomorrow will be much like today. The problem with that belief is that every few decades we are confronted with an unforeseen catastrophic event that can lead to dramatic changes in the way criminal justice systems operate. The 9/11 attacks were one such event, and the movement of resources by all levels of government from crime prevention to thwarting terrorist attacks has shifted resources and spending from street law enforcement to counterterrorism (Davis et al., 2010). One of the challenges in the post-9/11 world for corrections is the managing offenders who promote terrorism while incarcerated. As prisoners are often isolated, depressed, and vulnerable they are good candidates to be converted into terrorists through the process of radicalization. For example, in order to prevent Islamic radicalization, some prison systems have hired Muslim chaplains to provide spiritual guidance. Because such unforeseen or **black swan events** are, by their nature, unpredictable, we won't know the source of the next massive impact on corrections and the criminal justice system until after it happens.

The spread of the COVID-19 virus, which swept through US juvenile facilities, jails, and prisons starting in March 2020 could be considered a black swan event. Although public health officials had long predicted that a pandemic would happen within our lifetimes the spread of this virus was a once-in-a-generation event. Not only did this virus lead to loss of life and changes in correctional practices, but it is likely to have a significant impact on the global economy, and as this book goes to press in May 2020, we are unable to foresee the long-term economic implications of the pandemic on American corrections.

Penal Tourism

Most jurisdictions have replaced their antiquated courthouses, police lockups, and correctional facilities with new institutions to improve staff and inmate safety as these newly designed facilities are more energy efficient, safer for staff and inmates, and cheaper to operate than their older counterparts. As a result, cities, counties, and states are sometimes left with abandoned jail and prison facilities that cannot safely hold inmates and can become eyesores. This problem is not isolated to the United States and officials across the globe are questioning what to do with these abandoned facilities. One answer is to renovate them so they can serve other roles such as penal museums. How popular are these places? McCorkel and DalCortivo (2018) describe how Spike Island, which is a former fortress and prison in Ireland, was named Europe's leading tourist attraction. The most famous American prison museums are Alcatraz—a former federal prison located on an island in the San Francisco bay—and Eastern State Penitentiary in Philadelphia. There are about two million visitors to these prisons every year.

Torture and executions occurred in many ancient jails and prisons. Welch (2015), a visitor to many prison museums, describes them as places of **dark tourism**, where "people gravitate to sites associated with war, genocide, and other tragic events for purposes of remembrance, education, or even entertainment" (p. 1). In Chapter 2 we said that penal tourism has existed for centuries because the public has been always fascinated by what happens in these places. When the federal penitentiary in Leavenworth was being built in the late 1800s, for instance, thousands of people traveled by train from Kansas City to witness its construction. Public tours were a part of Leavenworth's operations, although the warden had to temporarily suspend these visits in 1910 after several hundred people showed up in one day to visit the facility.

PHOTO 13.3
Many people are fascinated by jails and prisons and will pay to stay in places such as the Jail House Inn, which was originally built in the 1770s and has been transformed into a hotel in Rhode Island. Credit: Rob Francis/Alamy Stock Photo.

In order to take advantage of the public's fascination with corrections some business owners have bought smaller jails and converted them to bed and break-fast operations. Some real estate developers have also turned former prisons into hotels. Delahaye (2019) describes how correctional facilities in Australia, Canada, England, Germany, England, the Netherlands, Turkey, and the United States have been converted into hotels. Some of these facilities, such as Clink78 (a former courthouse in England), have been left in their original condition, and provide an austere living experience, while Langholmen prison in Stockholm, Sweden (which was closed as a prison in 1974) offers rooms that look similar to single-occupant college dorm rooms for their guests.

Like almost every topic raised in the previous chapters, the practice of turning jails and prisons into museums can become controversial. Some scholars are critical of places that feature examples of cruelty and death that exploits the pains expe-rienced by these people (see examples in Stone, Hartmann, Seaton, Sharpley, & White, 2018). Some scholars say this exploitation is worsened when photographs of their suffering are displayed. Others question whether professors should take their corrections classes to a local jail or prison on tours as some inmates may feel they were on display like a zoo animal. Regardless of the arguments for or against these tours, Stacer, Moll, and Solinas-Saunders (2019) found that students learned a lot about corrections during these tours.

INTERNAL FACTORS INFLUENCING CORRECTIONAL OPERATIONS

In this section we briefly describe seven internal factors that will shape the operations of community and institutional corrections.

Correctional Security

Safety and security provide the foundation upon which all correctional programs are de-livered. Ensuring that facilities are safe and secure is the end result of continually renew-ing a facility's security strategies, managing jail and prison gangs, accurately classifying and housing inmates, and providing activities that keep them constructively occupied. Some correctional administrators are more successful in achieving these goals, although there has been an uptick in media reports of prison violence in 2018–2019 (Ford, 2019). As only jail and prison murders are tracked by the Bureau of Justice Statistics (BJS)—and not assaults or riots, we don't know whether correctional violence is getting better or worse when it comes to the entire country. Correctional violence is often related to overcrowding, under-staffing, and a lack of resources. Unless these conditions improve, there will be few meaningful changes in facilities or prison systems that have high rates of violence. However, there may be some incentives to devote more time and resources to overcoming violence given our growing recognition of the long-term harms of being victimized in prison. Daquin, Daigle, and Johnson Listwan (2017) found that parolees who had witnessed more violence in prison had higher rates of parole violations and arrests than parolees who saw less correctional violence. The question remains unanswered, however, whether the results of such studies will influence correctional administrators to focus on violence reduction.

Correctional Staff

Although corrections officers are better trained and more professional than in the past, they are often poorly paid and overworked; many are stressed out. Given those factors Ujiyediin (2019) describes how rates of job turnover are high in Kansas prisons, where hundreds of officer positions are vacant. This condition can reduce staff morale, especially given the high rates of physical and psychological injuries associated with these careers. As a result, some jails and prisons are staffed primarily with officers with less than a year or two of experience. This lack of experience can contribute to higher rates of inmate misconduct, which can increase officer stress. Consequently, prison administrators must strive to recruit and retain professional and well-motivated officers who will make positive contributions throughout their careers. This undertaking is not easy, as correctional work is considered one of the worst jobs in America (Suneson, 2019). Russo, Drake, Shaffer, and Jackson (2017) say that the field of corrections has to move the perception of corrections work from that of an occupation to a profession; however, as with policing, such change is difficult to achieve (Winfree, Mays, & Alarid, 2019, pp. 143–152). Any such changes must be initiated within the field of corrections itself.

Women in Corrections

Collica-Cox and Schulz (2019) report that there are a growing number of women in executive corrections positions, including wardens and women leading entire prison systems. Moreover, the proportion of women corrections officers has been increasing. Over a decade ago, Nink (2008, p. 21) found that over half of Mississippi's prison officers were women, and 12 states report that women represent 40% or more of their correctional workforce. Despite those trends, these women have to overcome a number of barriers, including workplace harassment (see Chapter 7). In the future, women will play a greater role in the corrections workforce as front-line workers and administrators. For corrections agencies to meet their staffing needs, they are going to have to employ women in more roles. Once hired, these agencies will also have to take steps to improve the retention of these women, including confronting their harassment, and introducing family-friendly policies such as reducing mandatory overtime.

Evidence-Based Correctional Treatments

Although less than 5% of all correctional spending is devoted to rehabilitative programs, there will be a growing movement to funnel these scarce resources to the inmates with the highest risks and needs. These interventions will increasingly be delivered in programs that have been demonstrated by cost-benefit analysis and outcomes-based evaluation research to have the highest potential to reduce recidivism (Washington State Institute for Public Policy, 2019). In order to achieve this goal, correctional systems will have to overcome programs that are based on commonly held stereotypes about people who have committed crimes or the gut feelings of officers or administrators, and politicians (Latessa, Cullen, & Gendreau 2002).

Green Prisons

The increased interest in environmental sustainability has also raised awareness about the relationship between correctional facilities and the environment with a goal of making the impacts of prisons less harmful. This awareness is important as Corwin and colleagues (2020, p. 2) found that prisons were often built on undesirable or polluted land that exposed staff and inmates to environmental hazards. Prison administrators are increasingly aware of these environmental conditions and are introducing practices to mitigate these harms. Jewkes and Moran (2015, p. 451) describe how these practices are related to "building new prisons to 'green' industry standards; making existing prison buildings less environmentally harmful; incorporating processes such as renewable energy initiatives; offering 'green-collar' work and training to prisoners." Many of these practices are politically popular, save taxpayer dollars, and are supported by the public, and we foresee that a focus on sustainability will continue.

The Relationships between Community and Institutional Corrections

There has been growing attention given to the high proportion of probationers and parolees returning to custody for technical violations (Schwartzapfel, 2019). One important issue is the level of support given to the reentry of jail inmates and prisoners into the community, and the subsequent prevention of their return to custody. Russo, Drake, Shaffer, and Jackson (2017) say that our efforts at reducing recidivism could be supported by using risk and needs assessments and rewarding good behavior (e.g. by shortening probationary terms if the individual is successful). Those experts also advocate for creating jobs and improving access to housing and treatment for probationers and parolees. Their recommendations are not surprising, as these needs were identified decades ago.

There is a lack of political willingness, however, to provide funding for these community resources. Inadequate support for community corrections can be a costly mistake when these parolees and probationers are returned to custody as the costs of supervising a parolee are one-tenth as much as imprisoning them.

Correctional Data

In the previous chapters we highlighted numerous examples of politicians or scholars being unable to plan our correctional interventions because we don't have enough information about various correctional practices. We have no idea of the true number of people on pay-only probation, probationers paying fees for their supervision, state prisoners held past their release dates because they are civilly committed (for committing sexual offenses), or because they cannot arrange a safe place to live. Perhaps more importantly, we do not have the entire national-level picture of what happens to parolees or probationers, and whether their outcomes are successful. In some cases this information is not collected by the BJS. Other organizations seem to be intentionally misleading the BJS when it comes to reporting the true number of inmates involved in their programs and their outcomes. One example is the manipulation of statistics on deaths in custody described in Chapter 10. As few correctional scholars seem interested in these topics, newspaper reporters are exposing many of these issues. We predict that more researchers and organizations will advocate for collecting better data about these issues, but are pessimistic about the likelihood of expanding the information we currently collect.

RACE, CLASS, AND GENDER

Cycles of Arrest, Release, and Repeat: The Future of Jail Imprisonment

There are roughly 10.6 million jail admissions per year, and the average jail stay is less than a month (Zeng, 2019). Some of these people are caught in cycles of being arrested, spending short periods of time in jail, and then being released, whereupon they repeat the cycle. Anecdotally, jail officers label them frequent flyers, although Choi and associates (2019) call them **frequent utilizers**. Some are arrested dozens of times per year. For example, in a study of 800 of these individuals in New York City, MacDonald and colleagues (2015, p. 2263) found the average frequent flyer had 23 jail admissions in a six-year period and one person had 66 admissions. High volume users of local corrections are the exception; however, the Prison Policy Initiative found that there was a group of about 428,000 persons who had three or more arrests of the roughly 10.6 million people admitted to American jails in 2017 (Jones & Sawyer, 2019).

This issue relates to both class and race. African Americans are overrepresented in this cycle; moreover, when it comes to people with three or more jail admissions, they are drawn disproportionately from the economically and socially disadvantaged. About 17% of these frequent flyers are unemployed; over one-third (38%) do not have a high school diploma, and one-half earn less than $10,000 a year. Of the people with two or more arrests, 28% are African Americans, a group that accounts for only 13% of the national population (Jones & Sawyer, 2019). Like the profile of jail inmates presented in Chapter 5, many of them experienced various forms of addiction, as well as physical and mental health problems. Figure 13.1 provides a summary of the characteristics of people arrested two or more times in the previous year.

PHOTO 13.4
Some people with mental health problems can become caught in a cycle of being arrested, taken to jail, and then released, only to repeat the cycle. These people were arrested in California after a search of a homeless encampment was completed. Credit: Marmaduke St. John/Alamy Stock Photo.

One could ask about the level of danger posed by frequent flyers. Only 12% of them had arrests for serious violent offenses. Instead, most were arrested on drug charges, driving under the influence, theft, and drunkenness, common or simple assault, the latter not considered a violent offense (Jones & Sawyer, 2019). This characterization is consistent with prior research showing that most frequent flyers engage in relatively minor crimes, and many of their arrests are related to addictions and mental health problems. MacDonald and colleagues (2015, p. 2265) found that over half of New York City's frequent flyers had been charged with either petit larceny and possession of controlled substances, but less than 3% had been arrested for any type of assault.

When it comes to the future, there is growing interest in developing community-based alternatives to jail incarceration, and especially for the typical suspect caught up in the cycle of arrest, release, and re-arrests. The expansion of diversionary programs may reduce the total number of jail admissions. Furthermore, as described in Chapter 5, some cities are developing sobering centers to provide the police with an alternative

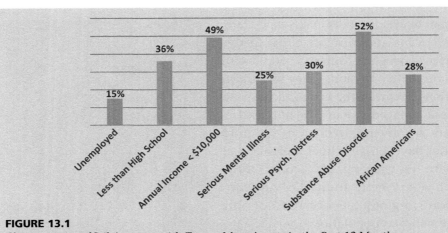

FIGURE 13.1
Characteristics of Jail Arrestees with Two or More Arrests in the Past 12 Months.
Source: Jones and Sawyer (2019).

to admitting intoxicated persons to jails. Other solutions to reducing the number of jail admissions requires a movement away from using the police and jails to manage persons with addictions and mental health problems and responding to them using health and social service programs.

FUTURE CORRECTIONAL RESEARCH

We acknowledge that many components of the corrections system in the United States are among the world's best. What prevents us from doing even better, however, is a lack of information and resources, both of which suggest that local and state governments, in concert with the federal government, need to invest more in expanding these efforts. For example, although even carefully crafted studies cannot rescue us from many of the dilemmas we are confronting, researchers can play an important role in telling us what we are doing right and what we are doing wrong, and possibly how to fix it. Some would argue, however, that we already know how to fix the problem, but lack the political willingness to reduce our reliance on mass imprisonment and mass probation policies (Clear & Frost, 2015).

In the previous chapters we described the growing interest in cost-benefit studies that identify interventions that provide taxpayers with the best return on investment (or maximize the "bang for our buck"). There is a similar interest in increasing our reliance on evidence-based correctional (EBC) interventions. Evidence-based practices were first introduced in medicine in the 1990s, although some practitioners have been slow to embrace this approach, and especially when the research findings run counter to their experiences. How does a researcher, for example, tell the deputy warden of a prison that his or her practice is not the most effective way of dealing with a problem? While some people are very receptive to new ideas, others are not. As a result, although almost everybody agrees that basing interventions on the best available information about their effectiveness is a good idea, there are some hurdles to overcome.

The Center for Effective Public Policy (2017, pp. 32–36) has worked with the NIC to develop strategies to maximize the use of EBC, and their approach is based on four principles summarized as follows:

1. The professional judgment of criminal justice system decision makers is enhanced when informed by evidence-based knowledge. In order for EBC to work, however, this knowledge must be readily available by practitioners and the content must be written in a way that is understandable and clearly highlights how to implement these strategies. One limitation of many academic articles is that they are written in a language that is difficult for practitioners (and even many academics) to understand and this reduces their likelihood of adopting these strategies.

2. Every interaction within the criminal justice system offers an opportunity to contribute to harm reduction. The people working within the justice system can play a powerful role in positively influencing offenders in their interactions with them. People who have been convicted of a crime, like anybody else, want to be treated in a just and fair manner, and sometimes the personnel working within the system need to be reminded of their desire for **procedural justice**.

3. Systems achieve better outcomes when they operate collaboratively. Collaboration can increase the likelihood of success. As a result implementing EBC may be easier to achieve when the activities of the police, courts, and corrections are integrated and their policies and practices are aligned or consistent with each other.

4. The criminal justice system will continually learn and improve when professionals make decisions based on the collection, analysis, and use of data and information. Although the police, courts, and correctional agencies collect a lot of information about crimes, offenders, and the interventions used to prevent crime (including reducing recidivism), very little of that information is ever analyzed or shared with other agencies or researchers. As a result, these agencies lose opportunities to better understand the crime problem in their jurisdiction, and whether their crime reduction strategies are effective.

One challenge of working with offenders is that some will go on to commit awful crimes, even though risk assessments said they were at low risk of re-offending, and they had adequate supports in the community and well-thought-out reentry plans. After all, human behavior is, at some levels, quite unpredictable. This observation again raises the question of whether our politicians have the political will to take risks and the courage to weather the storms when probationers or parolees commit high-profile crimes.

Felony Murders and Life Sentences

Felony murder laws are distinctively American. These laws have been around for over a half-century and allow individuals involved in a felony to be charged with homicide if a death occurs in the commission of that crime, even if the individual took no action that resulted in another person's death. People have been sentenced on felony murder charges when they were operating the getaway cars during robberies where somebody was murdered, and when a civilian or police officer kills a person who is committing a felony offense. Once convicted of a felony, that person is in jeopardy of very long sentences, whether they were an adult or juvenile when the crime occurred (Burton, 2017).

Pilkington (2015) describes how a 16-year-old Indiana youth named Blake Layman was involved with another four youth in a home burglary in 2012. These 16- and 17-year olds thought that the home they were entering was vacant, but the home owner was at home and opened fire, killing one of the burglars and wounding Layman.

Although Layman was not armed he was charged with felony murder as his friend died in the incident. In his trial a year later he was convicted of felony murder and sentenced—at age 17—to a 55-year prison term. The other two youths who were involved in this crime were also sentenced to 50 or more years. Layman and the other two youths appealed their sentences and their convictions were overturned, and shorter sentences imposed for burglary (Brown, Effron, & Hawkins, 2016). While Layman and the other three youths successfully overturned their convictions after the appeal many adults and youths convicted of felony murder remain imprisoned.

Some people convicted of felony murder had very little involvement in the actual offense. In Chapter 9, for example, we described that over one-half of the women in Lempert's (2016) study were charged with being a party to a crime, such as felony murder, that was carried out by their partner. Many of those women claim that they were being abused by their partners and felt they had no choice but to participate in those crimes. When researchers looked at their criminal records they found that few of these women had ever been involved in the justice system before being charged with being a party to a crime such as felony murder (Dye & Aday, 2019; Lempert, 2016). A California survey of women charged with felony murder found that almost three-quarters (72%) did not commit the actual homicide, and their average age when the murders occurred was 20 (Ulloa, 2018, para. 9).

These laws are becoming controversial and some question their fairness. In 2018 California enacted legislation making it harder to prosecute people on felony murder charges, and while the law came into effect in 2019, there was broad opposition to this change from police and prosecutors, and the law has been challenged in court. Although we do not know the outcome of these cases, they show us that court decisions will play an important role in the future of corrections.

THE CHALLENGES AHEAD FOR CORRECTIONS

At this point in the chapter, we think it is important to make a point that we have not thoroughly addressed. Although the corrections system in the United States is something of a loose confederation of agencies, organizations, and institutions, all of these entities are interconnected. Given this high level of interrelatedness, one cannot tinker with one aspect of the system without affecting the other parts. For example, if parole officers within a jurisdiction decide to get tough on the technical violations of parolees, the number of violations will increase. These failed parolees will be temporarily held in jails, and if the violations are proven, they will once again be prison inmates. Thus, the act of cracking down on technical violations must inevitably impact local jails and the state prison system. Lippman and Schiraldi (2019) report that 30% of the parolees returned to prison did not commit a new crime; and, on any given day, 20% of jail inmates in New York were parolees awaiting their court dates.

In this regard, we provide a list 15 changes in policies or practices or both that could have a positive impact on the nation's corrections system, particularly the number of people under its control. Some are unlikely to be implemented, whereas others already have support in state and federal legislatures and among corrections professionals. All have been addressed to some extent in this text. As you consider each, in turn, assess the likelihood of its full implementation.

1. *Change the current correctional philosophy*: Currently, the state and federal governments are operating their corrections systems under what can best be described as a retributionist philosophy. Many corrections experts believe that promoting this

philosophy has led to huge increases in jail, prison, and probation populations, and they describe it as the penal harm movement. This has many scholars, politicians, and activists advocating for a change to a more rehabilitative orientation. Some supporters of the JR perspective advocate for reducing correctional populations and diverting those cost savings into community-based programs that support the community reentry of former prisoners.

2. *Putting the brakes on prosecutorial discretion*: Pfaff (2017) argues that high imprisonment practices will not be reduced as long as local prosecutors are able to advocate for harsh sanctions while state taxpayers pay the bill for those sentences.

3. *Implement diversion and restorative justice practices for juveniles and young adults*: Increasing the use of diversion and promoting RJ interventions will reduce the number of people entering the criminal justice system.

4. *Depoliticize the corrections system*: Bad politics can interfere with good correctional practices. Without politicians, however, corrections programs would have a hard time getting funded or, in the case of introducing new programs, seeing the light of day. The question is one of balance: How do we juggle the needs of politicians to appear tough on crime and the programmatic needs of the correctional system? Perhaps if politicians understood that good programs have the potential to make them look good, they could be persuaded to support alternatives to penal harm.

5. *End pay-only probation and probation supervision fees*: Probationers should not have to pay for their supervision, drug tests, and rehabilitation. While these practices are intended to reduce costs for local probation services they harm the poor and many of these probationers end up in jail when they cannot pay these fees.

6. *Reform probation*: The United States has the highest probation rates in the world (Corda & Phelps, 2017). Shortening the average length of probationary sentences to one year is the practice in many nations around the globe. This would reduce the number of probationers and, logically, their time at-risk in the community, which by itself would reduce the number of technical violations. The number of conditions probationers are expected to follow should also be limited and no probationers should have more than ten conditions.

7. *Transform the bail system*. The United States and the Philippines are the only nations that rely upon cash bail, and this leads to high numbers of pretrial jail inmates who may serve a year or more behind bars because they cannot afford a few hundred dollars to secure their release. These jail populations cost taxpayers billions of dollars every year, and one of the biggest beneficiaries is the bail bond industry (Brennan Center for Justice, 2018).

8. *Abandon three-strikes and truth-in-sentence laws*: The introduction of these laws has only served to increase the nation's prison populations and has led to some people convicted of non-violent offenses serving long sentences. These practices have proven costly, especially considering that public's financial liability increases as these people age. Perhaps more importantly, these practices may provide little crime control benefit as these prisoners are often aging out of crime when sentenced. Existing habitual-offender laws will protect the public even in the absence of three-strike provisions.

9. *Release more violent offenders*: Over one-half of state prisoners have been convicted of violent offenses and there will not be meaningful prison-population reduction until more of them are released (Pfaff, 2017). Many practitioners believe that about 75% of the prison population could be released with no ill effects on society. The key is to determine who should remain imprisoned. Risk assessments can help determine those who represent a higher risk to society. Many prisoners who are assessed as having a low risk to re-offend could be released if they had proper supports in the community.

10. *Encourage the treatment (not criminalization) of mental illness*: Over one-half of jail inmates are suffering from serious psychological problems and many of them also have histories of substance abuse. Because there are so few community-based treatment alternatives, the mentally challenged are jailed in disproportionate numbers; some are admitted dozens of times throughout their lives. This is an expensive and short-sighted approach to mental illness and has few positive outcomes, other than **social sanitation**; the temporary removal of a problematic group from society.

11. *Full implementation of evidence-based correctional programs*: Rather than creating feel-good programs and laws, politicians should turn to the research generated by partnerships between social scientists and practitioners for guidance in developing programs and laws that work. Consistent with the risk, needs, and responsivity approach, medium- and high-risk offenders in community-based and institutional programs should receive correctional treatments that target their criminal thinking. Those interventions should be supplemented with educational and vocational programs.

12. *Return to the full use of parole*: The conditional release of individuals from prisons means that the corrections system has some measure of control over them. Parole is useful for prison operations, that is, the use of good time as an inmate control mechanism is viewed by some as essential. Furthermore, inmates returned to the community without supervision are a greater threat to themselves and to the community

than those supervised by parole officers. Like probation, however, the terms of parole should be shortened, as long periods of parole simply increase the likelihood of a return to prison for a technical violation.

13. *Support an ex-prisoner's community reentry*: Prerelease correctional programs should be developed to ease an individual's return to the free society. These programs should be supported by community-based resources and treatment, including transitional housing, community-based mental- and physical-health programming where needed, work, or educational placements.

14. *Moderate collateral consequences*: Although intended to increase public safety, some collateral consequences of a criminal conviction may push the individual into criminality such as policies making it almost impossible for a sex offender to live in some neighborhoods or even entire cities given restrictions on their living arrangements. As a result, they end up homeless and associating with other sex offenders living under bridges, in tent cities, or other unstable and makeshift arrangements (Kornfield, 2019). Other collateral consequences can place restrictions to limit where some former prisoners can find work or access public housing.

15. *Treat most violations of immigration laws as civil rather than criminal matters*: Changing federal policies could result in a significant decrease in the nation's jails and prison populations. In March 2020 over 38,000 immigration detainees were being housed in local, country or state, privately operated and federal detention facilities (U.S. Immigration and Customs Enforcement, 2020). Changing federal policies on immigration law violations could result in a significant decrease in the nation's jail and prison populations.

There are two final factors that will drive all such attempts to change the nation's corrections system. First, in any society, people are going to violate laws or other rules. Second, when violations occur, some attempt is going to be made to punish or correct those who ignore the society's laws or sense of decency or order. Society will always need some mechanism to deal with people who have committed crimes, a mechanism called corrections.

VESTED INTERESTS AND THE PRISON-INDUSTRIAL COMPLEX

Throughout this book we have said that some people win, while others lose in the quest to punish people our society has defined as offenders. One of the problems of reforming our corrections system is that every stakeholder will resist these reforms, if they see their interests as being harmed. Prisons, jails, and community corrections have become part of an enterprise that Schlosser (1998) calls the **prison-industrial complex** (PIC), which he defines as:

> A set of bureaucratic, political, and economic interests that encourage increased spending on imprisonment, regardless of the actual need. The prison-industrial complex is not a conspiracy, guiding the nation's criminal-justice policy behind closed doors. It is a confluence of special interests that has given prison construction in the United States a seemingly unstoppable momentum. It is comprised of politicians, both liberal and conservative, who have used the fear of crime to gain votes; impoverished rural areas where prisons have become a cornerstone of economic development; private companies that regard the roughly $35 billion spent each year on corrections not as a burden on American taxpayers but as a lucrative market; and government officials whose fiefdoms have expanded along with the inmate population.

Schlosser calls inmates the raw material of the PIC. As we have described throughout this book inmates are often marginalized people such as the homeless, the drug- and alcohol-addicted, and persons with mental illnesses. They are disproportionately drawn from the poor and minority groups; moreover, the public tends to have little empathy toward them. Most are confined in rural prisons that are out-of-sight and out-of-mind, and, consequently, the public is generally unaware or apathetic of most correctional issues.

So, who wins and who loses when it comes to high-imprisonment policies? It turns out that the winners are a pretty big group, including, but not limited to, all correctional employees who earn a living supervising or incarcerating offenders. But there are even bigger winners and losers than just corrections employees. Wagner and Rabuy (2017) say that we should follow the money. When Schlosser (1998) wrote about the PIC, the cost of corrections to society was $35 billion; however, that total has more than doubled to $81 billion in 2017 (Wagner & Rabuy, 2017). Those are just the direct government costs. They do not include family spending on their relatives and lost opportunities for these people and their families, which effectively multiplies those costs.

There are over 750,000 employees of local, state, and federal government agencies that hold inmates in jails or prisons, or supervise these people in the community (Bronson, 2019). There are likely another 100,000 workers employed by either correctional corporations and local and state juvenile corrections. Few of them would actively support reducing correctional populations and some correctional officers are represented by powerful unions such as the California Correctional Peace Officers Association (CCPOA). Page (2011) says corrections-based unions actively lobby to maintain the status quo. For example, Lennard (2018, para. 8) observes that the CCPOA spends about $8 million a year lobbying state officials to thwart reforms; the union maintains that "when prisons close, prison guards lose jobs." This opposition to reform is not isolated to correctional officers. Everyone with a mortgage and a family to feed would resist reforms that threaten their livelihoods, even if those reforms are in the best interests of society.

Businesses also become addicted to the profits generated by supplying goods and services to corrections. Worth Rises (2019), an advocacy group, found over 3,900 corporations that provide goods and services to corrections. The size of these businesses runs from firms such as CoreCivic, a corporation listed on the New York Stock Exchange that contracts directly with the federal and state governments to hold tens of thousands of their prisoners, to small businesses supplying local jails with a few hundred dollars in first-aid supplies. Like correctional officer unions, these businesses also lobby federal and state legislators to maintain the status quo. Some of these efforts are very successful. Richards and Griffin (2019, para. 11) describe how the bail industry "has derailed, stalled or killed reform efforts in at least nine states, which combined cover more than one-third of the country's population." Most bail bond companies are long-term family businesses that will close if the national wave of bail reforms is successful. The people who own these businesses are lobbying and funding political candidates in a fight for their economic survival.

The issue of vested interests extends even beyond correctional employees and the firms supplying goods and services to jails and prisons. Hundreds of county governments benefit from the jobs created in the prisons operating in their backyards. Eason (2017) describes how local governments also lobby their state and federal politicians to build prisons in their jurisdictions. Once built, these towns work hard to keep the facility doors open. The correctional staff living in the community have the loudest voices in opposition to closing an adult or youth correctional facility although many county residents realize their homes will lose value and they will pay more taxes if the institution closes. County taxpayers will also be saddled with a costly "white elephant," often built with public funds that they cannot use. Thus, the opposition to reform is broad and these towns will lobby their state legislators to keep their facilities operating.

While our discussion of who wins or loses has focused on economic interests, some stakeholders in the justice system are also motivated by holding on to their political power and influence. Few elected prosecutors, for example, would willingly surrender any of their discretion to file charges or seek harsh sanctions. As a result, many of them resist even minor reforms, such as continuing to file criminal charges for persons possessing small amounts of marijuana, when many states are legalizing that drug. By the same token, few county sheriffs are willing to support regional jails, or support the introduction of state-run jail systems because they would lose political power and influence, including the ability to hire their supporters to work in their jails.

Given that both sheriffs and district attorneys are elected officials in most counties, the voters can reject their policies by electing reform-minded candidates. Revolts of this kind happened in 2018 and 2019, when reformist prosecutors were elected in cities and counties throughout the country. Pfaff (2019, para. 3) observes that U.S. Attorney General William Barr opposes the efforts of these reformers, as "he argued that anything that scaled back mass incarceration would inevitably lead to more crime." Mangual (2019), a researcher for the Manhattan Institute, a New York-based think tank, says that the only way to make meaningful reductions in prison populations is to release people who have been convicted of committing violent crimes. Releasing more violent offenders, he says, will lead to an increase in violent crime. Although Attorney General Barr and Mangual (2019) are pessimistic about releasing these prisoners, are there lessons we learned throughout this book such as using evidence-based interventions and providing supports to these former prisoners when they are reentering the community that would reduce their risks of recidivism?

Taken together, we find that correctional officer associations and unions, businesses, politicians, and communities are actively opposing reforms to reduce mass imprisonment policies largely because these reforms threaten their livelihoods or status. State and federal politicians have been slow to support legislation that would lessen the use of incarceration: not only would they be perceived as being soft on crime but also unresponsive to the economic well-being of businesses and entire communities. By contrast, the dismantling of mass imprisonment benefits inmates and their families; people who have very little political power or public sympathy. Given those choices, how do you think most politicians would act if they want to be re-elected?

SUMMARY

Much remains to be accomplished in corrections, and much is attainable. The agenda is full; all that is required is a cohort of policymakers and practitioners at all levels who are willing to engage the challenges ahead. The following are among the key findings contained in this chapter:

- We know a great deal about the issues that confront the nation's corrections system. The key is to bring public opinion into line with a corrections philosophy that imprisons fewer people while maintaining public safety.

- The policies and practices that have their roots in the current retributive justice philosophy do not produce just and fair outcomes for some offenders, and this increases their likelihood of recidivism.
- There is growing dissatisfaction with the economic and human costs of mass imprisonment policies and this is reflected in the slowly decreasing jail and prison populations.
- The future of prisoner reentry may lie with an invigorated parole system that includes reentry philosophies and programs that do more than just dump inmates back to the community.
- Correctional programs that address an individual's risks and needs will aid in their community reentry.
- The nation must find some way to remove the institutional racism that plagues its criminal justice system, particularly as the United States moves toward becoming a country where people of color are in the majority.
- Stakeholders with financial interests in the corrections system will oppose reforms that reduce our reliance on mass probation and imprisonment policies.
- Researchers should fill the gaps in our knowledge of corrections process, from the time a person is taken into police custody to the time they are released or die in custody. This will help local, state and federal legislatures make informed decisions about current or projected corrections practices.
- Many challenges remain unaddressed; most will call for rethinking how we view people who commit crime and what we do to and for them.

Despite a slow decrease in correctional populations since those numbers peaked in 2007, there has been some optimism about the future in reducing America's reliance on mass probation and imprisonment. There are hundreds of thousands of dedicated correctional staff, researchers, and other reformers who are working toward that goal. You might consider joining these groups to work toward a brighter future with less crime and fewer people behind bars.

KEY TERMS

- black swan events
- dark tourism
- environmental scans
- external factors
- internal factors
- law of criminal justice thermodynamics
- prison industrial complex
- procedural justice
- strategic plans

THINKING ABOUT CORRECTIONAL POLICIES AND PRACTICES: WRITING ASSIGNMENTS

1. Explain why the vested interests of stakeholders make it so difficult to reform corrections.
2. In one page, explain why administrators in large prison systems engage in forecasting the future.
3. In two pages, explain why one of the 15 policy/practice changes would have the greatest impact on corrections in the United States today. Justify your selection. Which one has the highest chance of success in today's political climate? Which one has the lowest chance of success? Do any of these three questions have the same answer?
4. What factor external to corrections will have the most impact upon the futures of American jails and prisons in the next ten years?
5. What internal factor will have the most influence on the future of community corrections in the next ten years?

CRITICAL REVIEW QUESTIONS

1. What are some of the problems facing women personnel in the corrections workplace? Are these the same kinds of problems they encounter throughout the criminal justice system, or are they distinct to corrections? Explain your answer.
2. Provide some possible reasons why the detention of children in immigration detention facilities has become such a high-profile issue.
3. How are mass imprisonment policies being challenged?
4. What are the strengths (or weaknesses) of justice reinvestment policies?
5. Why do you think the notion of prison abolition has been gaining attention in recent years?
6. Do you think that a class tour of a correctional facility is akin to visiting a zoo, and would the inmates of that facility share your view?
7. Of the issues we listed, what do you think is the most important challenge ahead for corrections? And the least important?
8. Do you agree with the statement that American politicians lack the willingness to tackle the problem of mass probation and imprisonment? Why or why not?
9. Name some possible factors that might lead to an increased use of community and institutional corrections.
10. Given your knowledge of corrections, do you foresee (a) a continued slow reduction in jail and prison populations, (b) a move toward stability where there are no significant changes, or (c) rapid increases or decreases?

CASE

Brown v. Plata, 563 U.S. 493 (2011)

REFERENCES

Arrieta-Kenna, R. (2018). 'Abolish prisons' is the new 'abolish ICE.' *Politico Magazine.* Retrieved from https://www.politico.com/magazine/story/2018/08/15/abolish-prisons-is-the-new-abolish-ice-219361

Bala, N., & Trautman, L. (2019, April 30). "Smart" technology is coming for prisons, too. *Slate.* Retrieved from https://slate.com/technology/2019/04/smart-ai-prisons-surveillance-monitoring-inmates.html

Beckett, K., Reosti, A., & Knaphus, E. (2016). The end of an era? Understanding the contradictions of criminal justice reform. *The ANNALS of the American Academy of Political and Social Science, 664*(1), 238–259.

Bernard, T. J., & Kurlychek, M. C. (2010). *The cycle of juvenile justice, 2nd edition.* New York: Oxford University Press.

Boccher, M. (2020, March 6). Rutgers hosts event on prison abolition. *The Daily Targum.* Retrieved from https://www.dailytargum.com/article/2020/03/rutgers-hosts-event-on-prison-abolition

Brennan Center for Justice. (2018). *21 principles for the 21st century prosecutor.* New York: Author.

Bronson, J. (2019) *Justice expenditure and employment extracts, 2015 – preliminary.* Washington, DC: Bureau of Justice Statistics.

Bronson, J., & Carson, E. A. (2019). *Prisoners in 2017.* Washington, DC: Bureau of Justice Statistics.

Brown, J., Effron, L., & Hawkins, S. (2016, Feb. 17). Indiana man, 21, who was sentenced to 50 years in prison in 'Elkhart 4' controversial felony murder case, enjoys freedom. *ABC News.* Retrieved from https://abcnews.go.com/US/indiana-man-21-sentenced-50-years-prison-elkhart/story?id=33919381

Burnett, J. (2019, Feb. 13). Inside the largest and most controversial shelter for migrant children in the U.S. *National Public Radio.* Retrieved from https://www.npr.org/2019/02/13/694138106/inside-the-largest-and-most-controversial-shelter-for-migrant-children-in-the-u-

Burton, A. (2017). A common sense conclusion: Creating a juvenile carve out of the Massachusetts felony murder rule. *Harvard Civil Rights-Civil Liberties Law Review, 52*(1), 169–192.

Campaign for Youth Justice. (2019). *2019 legislation on youth prosecuted as adults in the states.* Retrieved from http://www.campaignforyouthjustice.org/2019/item/2019-legislation-on-youth-prosecuted-as-adults-in-the-states

Center for Effective Public Policy. (2017). *A framework for evidence-based decision making in state and local criminal justice systems.* Retrieved from https://nicic.gov/sites/default/files/EBDM_Framework_With_Logic_Models_Final.pdf

Chiedi, J. M. (2019). *Care provider facilities described challenges addressing mental health needs of children in HHS custody.* Washington, DC: U.S. Department of Health and Human Services.

Choi, J. J., Gualtieri, B., Travis, J., & Goldberg, A. (2019). *Frequent utilizers: How can prosecutors better address the needs of people who frequently interact with the criminal justice and other social systems?* New York: John Jay College.

Chotiner, I. (2019, June 22). Inside a Texas building where the government is holding immigrant children. *The New Yorker*. Retrieved from https://www.newyorker.com/news/q-and-a/inside-a-texas-building-where-the-government-is-holding-immigrant-children

Clear, T. R., & Frost, N. A. (2015). *The punishment imperative: The rise and failure of mass incarceration in America*. New York: New York University Press.

Collica-Cox, K., & Schulz, D. M. (2019). Women wardens and correction executives: Paths to leadership. *Corrections, 4*(2), 89–111.

Corda, A., & Phelps, M. S. (2017). American exceptionalism in community supervision. *American Probation and Parole Association Perspectives*, Spring, 20–27.

Corwin, M. L., McElroy, J. R., Estes, M. L., Lewis, J., & Long, M. A. (2020). Polluting our prisons? An examination of Oklahoma prison locations and toxic releases, 2011–2017. *Punishment & Society*. Published online ahead of print at: https://journals.sagepub.com/doi/pdf/doi:10.1177/1462474519899949

Council of State Governments. (2018). *50-state report on public safety*. Retrieved from https://50states-publicsafety.us/

Daquin, J. C., Daigle, L. E., & Johnson Listwan, S. (2017). Vicarious victimization in prison: Examining the effects of witnessing victimization while incarcerated on offender reentry. *Criminal Justice and Behavior, 43*(8), 1018–1033.

Davis, L. M., Pollard, M., Ward, K., Wilson, J. M., Varda, D. M., Hansell, L., & Steinberg, P. (2010). *Long-term effects of law enforcement's post-9/11 focus on counterterrorism and homeland security*. Santa Monica, CA: RAND.

Delahaye, J. (2019, February 12). 10 former prisons turned hotels where guests pay to sleep in inmate's cells. *Mirror*. Retrieved from https://www.mirror.co.uk/travel/news/10-former-prisons-turned-hotels-13985252

Dye, M. H., & Aday, R. H. (2019). *Women lifers: Lives before, behind, and beyond bars*. Lanham, MD: Rowman & Littlefield.

Eason, J. M. (2017). *Big house on the prairie: Rise of the rural ghetto and prison proliferation*. Chicago, IL: University of Chicago Press.

FAMM. (2019). *Families are mobilizing for criminal justice reform*. Retrieved from https://famm.org/

Ford, M. (2019, April 5). The everyday brutality of America's prisons. *The New Republic*. Retrieved from https://newrepublic.com/article/153473/everyday-brutality-americas-prisons

Fox, C., Albertson, K., & Warburton, F. (2011). Justice reinvestment: Can it deliver more for less? *Howard Journal of Criminal Justice, 50*(2), 119–136.

Ghandnoosh, N. (2018). Can we wait 75 years to cut the prison population by half? *Sentencing Project*. Retrieved from https://www.sentencingproject.org/publications/can-wait-75-years-cut-prison-population-half/

Goodman, P., Page, J., & Phelps, M. (2017). *Breaking the pendulum: The long struggle over criminal justice*. New York: Oxford University Press.

Holloway, L. X. (1974). Prison abolition or destruction is a must. *Mississippi Law Journal, 45*(3), 757–762.

Holpuch, A. (2019, July 8). Migrant children held in Texas facility need access to doctors, says attorney. *The Guardian*. Retrieved from https://www.theguardian.com/us-news/2019/jul/08/migrant-children-detention-center-texas-attorney-health-crisis

Jewkes, Y., & Moran, D. (2015). The paradox of the 'green' prison: Sustaining the environment or sustaining the penal complex? *Theoretical Criminology, 19*(4), 451–469.

Jones, A., & Sawyer, W. (2019). Arrest, release, repeat: How police and jails are misused to respond to social problems. *Prison Policy Initiative.* Retrieved from https://www.prisonpolicy.org/reports/repeatarrests.html

Karstedt, S., Bergin, T., & Koch, M. (2019). Critical junctures and conditions of change: Exploring the fall of prison populations in US states. *Social & Legal Studies, 28*(1), 58–80.

Keller, B. (2019, June 12). Is 'abolish prisons' the next frontier in criminal justice? *Bloomberg.* Retrieved from https://www.bloomberg.com/opinion/articles/2019-06-12/-abolish-prisons-the-next-frontier-in-criminal-justice-reform

Kornfield, M. (2019, June 20). Florida's sex offender population is aging. Where can they live out their silver years? *Miami Herald.* Retrieved from https://www.miamiherald.com/news/state/florida/article231296693.html

Kubrin, C., & Seron, C. (2016). The prospects and perils of ending mass incarceration in the United States. *The ANNALS of the American Academy of Political and Social Science, 664*(1), 16–24.

Latessa, E. J., Cullen, F., & Gendreau, P. (2002). Beyond correctional quackery: Professionalism and the possibility of effective treatment. *Federal Probation, 66*(1), 43–49.

Lempert, L. B. (2016). *Women doing life: Gender, punishment and the struggle for identity.* New York: New York University Press.

Lennard, N. (2018, August 18). Police unions' opposition to prison reform is about more than jobs—it's about racism. *The Intercept.* Retrieved from https://theintercept.com/2018/08/14/police-unions-prison-reform/

Lind, D. (2019, June 25). The horrifying conditions facing kids in border detention, explained. *Vox.* Retrieved from https://www.vox.com/policy-and-politics/2019/6/25/18715725/children-border-detention-kids-cages-immigration

Linton, J. M., Griffin, M., & Shapiro, A. J. (2017). Detention of immigrant children. *Pediatrics, 139*(5), e20170483.

Lippman, J., & Schiraldi, V. (2019, Feb. 10). Lock the parole-prison revolving door: Rethink a system that's sending far too many people away for minor violations. *New York Daily News.* Retrieved from https://www.nydailynews.com/opinion/ny-oped-lock-the-parole-prison-revolving-door-20190208-story.html

Listwan, S. J., Jonson, C. L., Cullen, F. T., & Latessa, E. J. (2008). Cracks in the penal harm movement: Evidence from the field. *Criminology & Public Policy, 7*(3), 423–465.

MacDonald, R., Kaba, F., Rosner, Z., Vise, A., Weiss, D., Brittner, M.,…, Venters, H. (2015). The Rikers Island hot spotters: Defining the needs of the most frequently incarcerated. *American Journal of Public Health, 105*(11), 2262–2268.

Mangual, R. A. (2019). Issues 2020: Mass decarceration will increase violent crime. *Manhattan Institute.* Retrieved from https://www.manhattan-institute.org/issues2020-mass-decarceration-will-increase-violent-crime

Mathiesen, T. (1986). The politics of abolition. *Contemporary Crises, 10*(1), 81–94.

McCorkel, J., & DalCortivo, A. (2018). Prison tourism in the era of mass incarceration. *Contexts, 17*(3), 63–65.

Meares, T. L. (2017). Abolish the police? *Boston Review.* Retrieved from http://bostonreview.net/podcast-law-justice/tracey-l-meares-vesla-m-weaver-abolish-police

National Institute of Corrections. (2019). *2018 corrections environmental scan*. Washington, DC: Author.

Nink, C. (2008). *Women professionals in corrections: A growing asset*. Centerville, UT: MTC Institute.

Page, J. (2011). Prison officer unions and the perpetuation of the penal status quo. *Criminology & Public Policy, 10*(3), 735–770.

Pfaff, J. F. (2017). *Locked in: the true causes of mass incarceration and how to achieve real reform*. New York: Basic Books.

Pfaff, J. F. (2019, August 13). A no-holds-barred assault on prosecutors. *The Appeal*. Retrieved from https://theappeal.org/bill-barr-prosecutors/

Pickett, J. T. (2019). Public opinion and criminal justice policy: Theory and research. *Annual Review of Criminology, 2*, 405–428.

Pilkington, E. (2015, February 25). Felony murder: why a teenager who didn't kill anyone faces 55 years in jail. *The Guardian*. Retrieved from https://www.theguardian.com/us-news/2015/feb/26/felony-murder-teenager-55-years-jail-indiana

Pohl, J., & Gabrielson, R. (2019, May 28). Cruel and unusual: A guide to California's broken prisons and the fight to fix them. *ProPubica and Sacramento Bee*. Retrieved from https://www.propublica.org/article/guide-to-california-prisons

Reyes-Velarde, A. (2019, July 23). After flood of meth-soaked letters hits O.C. jails, sheriff announces crackdown. *Los Angeles Times*. Retrieved from https://www.latimes.com/california/story/2019-07-23/meth-soaked-letters-at-o-c-jails-leads-to-crackdown

Richards, C., & Griffin, D. (2019, August 30). States are trying to change a system that keeps poor people in jail. The bail industry is blocking them. *CNN*. Retrieved from https://www.cnn.com/2019/08/30/us/bail-reform-bonds-lobbying-invs/index.html

Russo, J., Drake, G. B., Shaffer, J. S., & Jackson, B. A. (2017). *Envisioning an alternative future for the corrections sector within the U.S. criminal justice system*. Santa Monica, CA: RAND.

Schlosser, E. (1998). The prison-industrial complex. *The Atlantic*. Retrieved from https://www.theatlantic.com/magazine/archive/1998/12/the-prison-industrial-complex/304669/

Schwartzapfel, B. (2019) Want to shrink the prison population? Look at parole. *The Marshall Project*. Retrieved from https://www.themarshallproject.org/2019/02/11/want-to-shrink-the-prison-population-look-at-parole

Sickmund, M., Sladky, A., Kang, W., & Puzzanchera, C. (2019). Easy access to the census of juveniles in residential placement. *Office of Juvenile Justice and Delinquency Prevention*. Retrieved from https://www.ojjdp.gov/ojstatbb/ezacjrp/asp/display.asp

Stacer, M. J., Moll, L. M., Solinas-Saunders, M. (2019). New opportunities or closing doors? How correctional facility tours impact students' thoughts about correctional careers. *Journal of Criminal Justice Education, 30*(1), 114–135.

Stone, P. R., Hartmann, R., Seaton, T., Sharpley, R., & White, L. (2018). *The Palgrave handbook of dark tourism studies*. New York: Palgrave Macmillan.

Suneson, G. (2019, April 20). What are the worst jobs in America? These have stress, low pay and lack of job security. *USA Today*. Retrieved from https://www.usatoday.com/story/money/2019/04/20/the-worst-jobs-in-america/39364439/

Taylor, K. (2018, November 28). Jail ordered to give inmate methadone for opioid addiction in far reaching ruling. *The New York Times*. Retrieved from https://www.nytimes.com/2018/11/28/us/inmate-methadone-opioid-addiction-ruling.html

Thielo, A. J., Cullen, F. T., Cohen, D. M., & Chouhy, C. (2016). Rehabilitation in a red state: Public support for correctional reform in Texas. *Criminology & Public Policy, 15*(1), 137–170.

Turner, S. F., Davis, L. M., Fain, T., Briathwaite, H., Lavery, T., Choinski, W., & Camp, G. (2015). A national picture of prison downsizing strategies. *Victims & Offenders, 10*(4), 401–419.

Ujiyediin, N. (2019, Feb. 11). 'I don't want to be poor all my life': Kansas prison staff face low pay and long hours. *KCUR*. Retrieved from https://www.kcur.org/post/i-don-t-want-be-poor-all-my-life-kansas-prison-staff-face-low-pay-and-long-hours#stream/0

Ulloa, J. (2018, Sept. 30). California sets new limits on who can be charged with felony murder. *Los Angeles Times*. Retrieved from https://www.latimes.com/politics/la-pol-ca-felony-murder-signed-jerry-brown-20180930-story.html

U.S. House of Representatives Committee on Oversight and Reform. (2019). *Child separations by the Trump administration*. Retrieved from lhttps://oversight.house.gov/sites/democrats.oversight.house.gov/files/2019-07-2019.%20Immigrant%20Child%20Separations-%20Staff%20Report.pdf

U.S. Immigration and Customs Enforcement. (2020). *Detention management (March 21, 2020)*. Retrieved from https://www.ice.gov/detention-management

Vitale, A. S. (2017). *The end of policing*. New York: Verso books.

Wagner, P., & Rabuy, B. (2017). Following the money of mass incarceration. *Prison Policy Initiative*. Retrieved from https://www.prisonpolicy.org/reports/money.html

Walker, S. (2015). *Sense and nonsense about crime, drugs, and communities, 8th edition*. New York: Cengage.

Washington State Institute for Public Policy. (2019). *Benefit-cost results (adult criminal justice)*. Retrieved from https://www.wsipp.wa.gov/BenefitCost?topicId=2

Welch, M. (2015). *Escape to prison: Penal tourism and the pull of punishment*. Oakland, CA: University of California Press.

Winfree, L. T., Mays, G. L., & Alarid, L. F. (2019). *Introduction to criminal justice: The essentials*. Frederick, MD: Wolters Kluwer.

Worth Rises. (2019). *The prison industrial complex: Mapping private sector players*. New York: Author.

Zeng, Z. (2019). *Jail inmates in 2017*. Washington, DC: Bureau of Justice Statistics.

Glossary / Index

Note: **Bold** page numbers refer to tables; *italic* page numbers refer to figures and page numbers followed by "n" denote endnotes.